Raspberries

MODERNIST CUISINE *at Home*

The Cooking Lab
3150 139th Ave SE
Bellevue, WA 98005
www.modernistcuisine.com

ISBN: 978-0-9827610-1-4
First edition, 2012

Library of Congress Cataloging-in-Publication Data available upon request

Printed in China

MODERNIST CUISINE
at Home

Nathan Myhrvold
with Maxime Bilet

Photography by
Nathan Myhrvold
Melissa Lehuta
and The Cooking Lab
Photography Team

The Cooking Lab

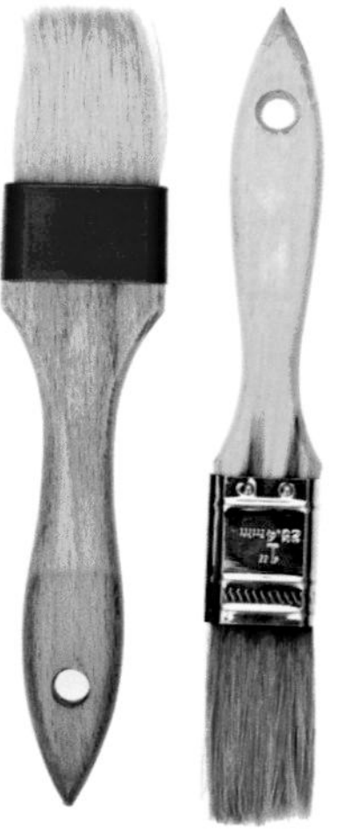

PART TWO: THE RECIPES

Osterizer

Foreword

When Nathan asked me to write the foreword to his newest tome, I was flattered, of course, but also apprehensive that I would not have time to try enough of the recipes, or leisure enough to read this impressive, large volume of recipes, techniques, and suggestions for a new way to cook at home. I had already looked through *Modernist Cuisine: The Art and Science of Cooking*—an amazing, encyclopedic cookbook in six volumes that was published in 2011, and I had also cooked with Nathan and his impressive staff in his laboratory, outside Seattle, where the books are created.

Upon further investigation and after a lot more studying, I became completely hooked on the contents of that book, and also happy that Nathan had decided to distill the very essence of the big book into a smaller volume for the home-cooking enthusiast. It is a pleasure to introduce a wider set of readers to Nathan and *Modernist Cuisine at Home*.

When I first met Nathan, he was still working as the chief technology officer at Microsoft. Having already earned his fortune, he was then building an incredibly eclectic home on Lake Washington, designing much of it and its contents himself. As I toured his fabulous kitchen one day, I discovered that Nathan, a very well-educated scientist proficient in several highly technical fields, was at heart a true foodie—one whom any other foodie could relate to on many different levels.

The kitchen that Nathan had created in his home was hardly an ordinary home kitchen. It contained a machine that freezes food in 20 seconds, another machine that thaws food in 30 seconds, a computer-controlled smoker that can barbecue a whole hog perfectly, as well as convection ovens, induction burners, walk-in refrigerators, and a machine that makes perfect ice cream in the blink of an eye.

It was the kitchen of a scientist, the laboratory of an insatiably curious man who is on a mission to reinvent the way we cook food and think about food. It was in this kitchen that Nathan began his journey to develop an entirely new way to consider ingredients, technology, and artistry in the preparation of the food we all eat and love, from tomato sauce to carrot soup, from hamburgers to roast chicken.

In the Middle Ages, Nathan Myhrvold would have been called "Nathan the Curious." Today he is being hailed as the man who became a chef via science, whose eyes were opened to the infinite possibilities of cuisine and flavors by other food pioneers like Marc Veyrat, Ferran Adrià, and Heston Blumenthal.

Nathan was so inspired, in fact, that he built The Cooking Lab and hired an impressive team of like-minded, highly qualified chefs who mastered a whole new *batterie de cuisine*: from sous vide vacuum sealers, water baths, and combi ovens to centrifuges, ultrasonic homogenizers, and rotary evaporators. Equally impressive, they have now found ways to realize the power of many of those precision cooking techniques in home kitchens that don't have a lot of fancy equipment. Items our mothers or grandmothers used regularly, like the pressure cooker, have been dusted off and put back to use as thoroughly modern tools.

Nathan and his team also applied their curiosity and willingness to experiment to the pantry. He looked beyond the familiar offerings of traditional grocery stores and added agar, xanthan gum, sodium citrate, and liquid lecithin to his shelves. These new ingredients can solve problems that home cooks face every day.

Modernist Cuisine at Home is destined to change the way we cook—and the way we use recipes. I do believe that we will become more questioning of the way we prepare foods. We will wonder: Is this the best way to make mac and cheese? Will the béchamel, thickened with flour, yield the most delicious macaroni, or should I pick up that emulsifier called sodium citrate, and use that instead? And why shouldn't I be cooking all grains under pressure in a fraction of the time?

For all of us who cook regularly, this book opens up a whole new world of possibilities. It is full of insights that encourage us to try something new, and that teach us something on every single page.

Martha Stewart
Martha Stewart Living Omnimedia
May 2012

Foreword

For many of us, our love of cooking is born in an early memory that never leaves us and spurs a desire to establish a culinary path for ourselves from a young age. Nathan Myhrvold's culinary trek has been more direct and distinct in recent years, but that same seed was planted long ago, well before his successes in business. Even though he is one of those rare and gifted intellectuals in the world of mathematics and technology—and his achievements in these fields are extraordinary—Nathan's childhood dream never wavered, and his love for the culinary arts has led him back to carve his own course toward his vision and version of it.

Throughout the process of his research on *Modernist Cuisine*, Nathan and I were engaged in numerous dialogues to discuss my work as a chef. Our conversations culminated with a more-than-gracious invitation to dinner at his test kitchen just outside Seattle after the book was published. It was an extremely memorable evening spent with his coauthors and chefs Chris Young and Maxime Bilet, and I left inspired as I familiarized myself with his viewpoints on food and cooking techniques.

After that dinner and further reading of his work, it became obvious that our entire profession would be forever indebted to Nathan's contributions and dedication to the *Modernist Cuisine* project. He has pushed the envelope in his research and recipe development, and he has put his ever-inquisitive mind to great use for our benefit. His formulas, documentation of procedures, and techniques have resulted in the most extensive coverage on progressive cuisine today, using tools and equipment that we would not have ever thought to marry with cooking in the past.

More important, the set of reference books that he produced has allowed our profession to evolve in a more uniform way. Those who have read his books have witnessed a major step in the world of cooking—something that rarely occurs in a single generation. He didn't just raise the bar when his highly anticipated book set finally came to print in 2011, he brought it to a new plateau. He and his team had set a new standard.

It seems natural, and nearly philanthropic, that Nathan's next step has been to write a version that is accessible for the home cook. It is often the case that scientific advances made for industrial operations make their way slowly but surely to the home kitchen: one need look no further for an example than the ubiquitous microwave oven. In its incipient form, the commercially available oven weighed in at over 700 pounds and stood as tall as a full-grown man. Through the years, not only did the dimensions of microwave ovens become significantly smaller, but they also became more efficient. Today, this appliance is a staple in nearly every home.

Nathan's work has followed the same process. Here he has been successful in distilling the original *Modernist Cuisine* into something that is more user-friendly and practical for daily use—not to mention that it comes in a form that no longer challenges the weight of the first microwave ovens. *Modernist Cuisine at Home* offers useful techniques and solutions that expand our abilities, and it provides us with a practiced and thorough understanding of why things happen the way they do. Most importantly, it ignites a curiosity within and compels us to ask ourselves not "What should we make for dinner?" but rather, "What can we make for dinner?" Not since Harold McGee wrote *On Food and Cooking* have we been offered such a clear and concise scientific approach to guide us. Nathan's sense of fun and wonderment in discovery are ever present, and they call for us to leave our comfort zones and try something new. While his points of view are novel to most for now, I have no doubt whatsoever that these will be embraced as common practice in home kitchens in the very near future. I can readily and happily see that *Modernist Cuisine at Home* will provide another quantum leap in our understanding and in our relationship with the food we like to cook.

Thomas Keller
The French Laundry
May 2012

Our Culinary Journeys

I have always loved food, and when I was nine years old, I discovered cookbooks on a visit to the library. I promptly announced to my mother that I was going to cook Thanksgiving dinner. Amazingly, she let me do the cooking, including nearly setting the dining table on fire. I was hooked.

I got more books from the library and started to learn about cooking. I soon discovered Escoffier's *Le Guide Culinaire* and pored over it, along with books by Julia Child, James Beard, Richard Olney, and other authors of classic cookbooks about French cuisine.

My interest in cooking was so strong that I might have become a chef, had my interest in other things—particularly math and science—not intervened. I was very good at school and often skipped grades, to the point that I started college at age 14. Every topic related to math and science fascinated me, so by the time I was finished with school, I had quite a collection of degrees: a Ph.D. in mathematical physics, a master's degree in economics, another master's degree in geophysics and space physics, and a bachelor's degree in mathematics. By that point I was 23 years old. My next step was to become a postdoctoral fellow at Cambridge University, where I worked with Dr. Stephen Hawking on the quantum theory of gravitation. My career in science was off to a roaring start.

Life takes unexpected twists and turns, however. Partway through my fellowship with Stephen, I decided to take a summer off to work on a software project with some friends from graduate school. By the end of the summer, venture capitalists had expressed interest in our project, so I extended my leave of absence. We incorporated the project as a start-up company, and I became the CEO. Two years later, the start-up was acquired by another software company: Microsoft. Within a couple years, I was working directly for Bill Gates, and in time I became Microsoft's first chief technology officer. The job was demanding, and I had less time for cooking than ever. I did manage to take short leaves from Microsoft to cook as an apprentice at Rover's, a great French restaurant in Seattle run by chef Thierry Rautureau, and then attend La Varenne, a professional culinary school in France. After retiring from Microsoft in 1999 at age 40, I was determined to spend more time in the kitchen.

I began learning about a new trend in experimental cooking techniques, which led to my first cookbook, *Modernist Cuisine: The Art and Science of Cooking.* My coauthors Chris Young, Maxime Bilet, and I, along with the rest of our team, created a six-volume, 2,438-page cookbook that aimed to be the definitive resource on the history, techniques, and ideas behind this culinary revolution.

Now we've turned our attention to writing this book, which explores using the techniques from *Modernist Cuisine* in a home kitchen. Our goal is to broaden the number of people who can use these ideas and to encourage making Modernist cooking part of their daily lives.

If circumstances had been different, I might be a chef today. But I am not unhappy with the way things turned out. I have derived enormous enjoyment from cooking and eating over the years. Ultimately, my strange culinary journey has given rise to both *Modernist Cuisine* and *Modernist Cuisine at Home*—a way to make a contribution of my own to the world of cooking.

Nathan Myhrvold

When I was two years old, I put my family in peril in the name of *chocolat chaud*. I escaped from my room in the middle of the night, found a pot, milk, some Nesquik, and a stool to climb on, but alas could find no matches. And so the gas began filling the apartment as I pondered my next culinary venture. Fortunately, tragedy was averted that night, but my sense for culinary exploration was left uncompromised. Our family had a great passion for sharing good food, and they inspired me to communicate through creative cooking.

My grandfather was a gourmand par excellence who regaled us with stories of his experiences of great restaurants, secret wine cellars, and obscure chocolatiers. To him, food was a philosophy: "the essence of existence," he would exclaim before a feast of Gillardeau No. 2 and cold Chablis. He demonstrated the joys to be found in living with an open mind and an adventurous palate.

I began to cook seriously while studying art and literature in college. My friends and parents were patient guinea pigs as I experimented with recipes selected from my ever-growing collection of cookbooks. Looking back at those early days, I cringe at some of my interpretations of gastronomy. But the creative freedom was alluring, and soon I was catering dinners and small parties.

Having just graduated from Skidmore College, I spent a few months at The Institute of Culinary Education, which led to a two-month externship with Allison Vines-Rushing and Slade Rushing at Jack's Luxury Oyster Bar, where they were serving very refined Southern food. The Rushings returned to Louisiana shortly after I began to work there, so Jack Lamb, one of the great restaurateurs of New York, introduced me to the wild world of running a professional restaurant. Who knows what he was thinking—I was only 22—but I embraced the challenges of being a head chef.

After a year at Jack's, I moved to London to further hone my skills. For a few months, I staged at The Fat Duck with Heston Blumenthal and the development team in his lab to create new dishes for the restaurant and to work on his last *Perfection* series book. Heston's exploration of clever flavor combinations and new ways of presenting and refining food had a profound influence on me.

Through a series of events, I ended up in a nondescript laboratory in Bellevue, Washington, full of fascinating inventors and a level of technology that leant itself to a huge realm of possibilities. This led to my becoming head chef of the *Modernist Cuisine* project and ultimately a coauthor of both that book and *Modernist Cuisine at Home*, as well as an inventor on 10 patents. I spent three years building our culinary team, managing research, and working to define the unique visual style of the book. It was an extraordinary and insightful journey.

Since *Modernist Cuisine* was published in 2011, I have traveled the world sharing and demonstrating the insights of Modernist cooking at many schools and at culinary symposiums at New York University, McGill University, Paris des Chefs, and Madrid Fusión. We and our hugely talented culinary team have cooked for culinary leaders, television audiences, and journalists to show that our food is as delicious as it is fascinating and beautiful.

With the critical and public success of *Modernist Cuisine*, it was time to think about The Cooking Lab's next big project. Having made such tremendous culinary progress during our work on *Modernist Cuisine*, we now wanted to adapt those techniques to make them accessible to passionate cooks of all levels. *Modernist Cuisine at Home* offered us the wonderful opportunity to update classic home dishes and to experiment with improvised methods that enable anyone to produce terrific results.

I want to share my gratitude with everyone who has been deeply connected to making *Modernist Cuisine* and *Modernist Cuisine at Home* possible. Thank you so much Kathryn Suerth Holmes, Gary Holmes, Mom, Dad, Sis, Albane, Marcus, Mamie, Papie, John, Alina, Noelle, Jonathan, Katy, and the entire *MC* and *MCAH* teams (see page XXIV).

I hope this book will be approachable, useful, and inspiring to home cooks and chefs everywhere in expanding the possibilities of healthy, flavorful, and creative cooking.

Maxime Bilet

THE STORY OF THIS BOOK

When it comes to cooking techniques, the classics are well covered. But the latest and greatest techniques, developed by the most innovative chefs in the world, were largely undocumented until we and Chris Young, along with the rest of our team, published *Modernist Cuisine: The Art and Science of Cooking* in 2011. At six volumes and 2,438 pages, it wasn't an ordinary cookbook. Many people were skeptical that it would interest a wide audience.

As it turned out, *Modernist Cuisine* sold out of its first printing within weeks; it is now in its fourth printing. The book has been translated into French, German, and Spanish. It has been reviewed in thousands of news articles. Long discussion threads about the book on the eGullet Internet forum have been viewed more than 300,000 times.

We often get the question "Isn't this book only for professionals?" The answer is no; we wrote and designed *Modernist Cuisine* for anybody who is passionate and curious about cooking. As hundreds of blogs and forum postings show, many amateurs have embraced the book. Of the 1,500 or so recipes in it, probably half could be made in any home kitchen. That number rises to perhaps two-thirds or three-quarters for those willing to buy some new equipment (for cooking sous vide, for example).

The remaining recipes are indeed challenging—even for professionals. We felt that many food enthusiasts would like to be on the front lines of culinary innovation and get a chance to understand the state of the art, even if they couldn't execute every recipe.

At the same time, we realized that we had the right team and resources to bring the Modernist cuisine revolution to an even wider audience of home cooks by developing less complex recipes that require less expensive equipment. The result is this book, *Modernist Cuisine at Home*.

Although we kept *Modernist Cuisine* in the title, this new book is not a condensed version of its predecessor. If you want to learn about food safety, microbiology, the history of foie gras cultivation, or hundreds of other topics, *Modernist Cuisine* is still the book to turn to.

This book focuses on cooking equipment, techniques, and recipes. Part One details tools, ingredients, and cooking gear that we think are worth having. Equipment once available only to professional chefs or scientists is now being manufactured for the home kitchen; we encourage you to try it. But we also show you how to get by without fancy appliances, such as how to cook fish sous vide in your kitchen sink and how to cook steak in a picnic cooler.

Part Two contains 406 recipes, all of which are new. In some cases, we took popular *Modernist Cuisine* recipes—Caramelized Carrot Soup (see page 178), Mac and Cheese (see page 310), and Striped Mushroom Omelet (see page 148)—and developed simpler versions. In general, the food is less formal; you'll find recipes for Crispy Skinless Chicken Wings (see page 254) and Grilled Cheese Sandwiches (see page 318).

What's the same as *Modernist Cuisine* is our focus on quality in both the information in the book and in the way it is presented. You'll find stunning cutaways of equipment, step-by-step photos for most recipes, and ingredients measured in grams (because every serious cook should have a scale). We use the same high-quality paper, printing, and binding that we did for *Modernist Cuisine*. The kitchen manual is again printed on washable, waterproof paper.

We hope that in following the vision we set out to accomplish with our first book, we have created a great experience for home chefs who want an introduction to Modernist cuisine.

WHAT IS MODERNIST CUISINE?

What is Modernist cuisine? This is the single most common question we are asked. When writing our previous book, *Modernist Cuisine: The Art and Science of Cooking*, we arrived at the term because it most completely captured the impetus and the cultural significance of the revolution that was underway in the culinary arts, a revolution that our book chronicled and is now helping to propel. Much like the Modernist movements that transformed fine art, architecture, dance, music, and other cultural disciplines throughout the 20th century, Modernism in cuisine first emerged from groundbreaking work by top professional chefs, but it is quickly becoming a strong influence on popular culture as well.

In cooking, "Modernist" means basically what it does when it is applied to other areas of the arts. Modernists replace the style and tradition of the preindustrial era with a new aesthetic that embraces abstraction and modern technologies or ideas in order to create genuinely new experiences.

This deliberate rejection of the rules and realism of the past can be seen in the paintings of Monet, Picasso, and other giants of Impressionism, whose work was initially very controversial. (The very label "Impressionism" was originally meant as an insult.) Similarly, James Joyce and Ernest Hemingway broke all the rules of narrative in their novels, the Bauhaus school of architecture rejected classical principles for the conceptual creations of Walter Gropius and Le Corbusier, Igor Stravinsky explored discordance in his symphonies, and Martha Graham broke with the conventions of classical ballet to help create modern dance.

Yet while these revolutions were transforming so many areas of art and popular culture in the last century, people were mostly still eating the same old-fashioned, traditional food. The first glimmers of a transformation in the kitchen did not begin to appear until Nouvelle cuisine gained traction as a named movement in the 1970s. Nouvelle cooking was a reaction against the rigidity of classical French cuisine, as codified in the works of La Varenne, Carême, and Escoffier. Although not a fully Modernist approach, Nouvelle cuisine was nevertheless very controversial at first in its emphasis on lightness, simplicity, and new ingredients, and in its introduction of the concept of plated dishes, which granted chefs control over almost every aspect of the presentation of their food.

With Nouvelle and other precursor movements as a springboard, pioneering chefs such as Ferran Adrià and Heston Blumenthal began to think in more systematic ways about how to create new experiences for diners. That desire led them to

explore cooking techniques, such as sous vide, and ingredients, such as modern thickening and gelling agents, that in many cases were developed for either institutional use or mass-produced foods, not for three-Michelin-star restaurants. These chefs had the vision to realize that because these tools let them control food and cooking in ways never before possible, the doors were open to exploring a whole new landscape of culinary surprise and delight.

Through Modernism, cuisine became a kind of conversation between the chef and the diner, with food as the medium, and the goal to be thought-provoking and memorable as well as extraordinarily delicious. Although this foundation has been interpreted and applied in different ways as Modernist cuisine has evolved in recent decades, Modernist chefs all share the quality of being avant-garde—always at the forefront, pushing the boundaries of food and cooking.

The Modernist influence is now global; it extends far beyond high-end restaurants in big cities. And it seems certain to expand further, because this revolution is still in its infancy. Young chefs are now entering cooking schools with a burning desire to make their own mark by demonstrating their inventiveness and expressing their ideas through food. The rapidly falling cost of precision cooking equipment and the increasing availability of Modernist ingredients have brought this revolutionary approach to food within reach of home cooks. All that has been missing is a comprehensive guidebook with recipes that span all skill levels; our hope is that *Modernist Cuisine at Home* will help to fill that need.

In this book, we focus on technologies such as the sous vide water bath, the pressure cooker, and the whipping siphon in our illustration of how home cooking can evolve in a more actively Modernist direction. We chose these technologies because they offer not only new ways to prepare food but also huge benefits in convenience, speed, or reproducibility in cooking. In the spirit of Modernism, we encourage you to use the recipes in this book as a starting point for your own experiments and creative exploration.

TEN PRINCIPLES OF

Modernist Cuisine

In 1972, the Gault-Millau restaurant guide published "The Ten Commandments of Nouvelle Cuisine" to both champion and explain the new style of cooking. We've come up with a variation on the theme in an attempt to explain the Modernist principles we cook by.

1. Cuisine is a creative art in which the chef and diner are in dialogue. Food is the primary medium for this dialogue, but all sensory aspects of the dining experience contribute to it.
2. Culinary rules, conventions, and traditions must be understood, but they should not be allowed to hinder the development of creative new dishes.
3. Creatively breaking culinary rules and traditions is a powerful way to engage diners and make them think about the dining experience.
4. Diners have expectations—some explicit, some implicit—of what sort of food is possible. Surprising them with food that defies their expectations is another way to engage them intellectually. This includes putting familiar flavors in unfamiliar forms or the converse.
5. In addition to surprise, many other emotions, reactions, feelings, and thoughts can be elicited by cuisine. These include humor, whimsy, satire, and nostalgia, among others. The repertoire of the Modernist chef isn't just flavor and texture; it is also the range of emotional and intellectual reactions that food can inspire in the diner.
6. Creativity, novelty, and invention are intrinsic to the chef's role. When one borrows techniques and ideas or gains inspiration from other chefs or other sources, it should be acknowledged.
7. Science and technology are sources that can be tapped to enable new culinary inventions, but they are a means to an end rather than the final goal.
8. First-rate ingredients are the foundation on which cuisine is built. Expensive ingredients such as caviar or truffles are part of the repertoire but have no greater intrinsic value than other high-quality ingredients.
9. Ingredients originating in food science and technology, such as hydrocolloids, enzymes, and emulsifiers, are powerful tools in helping to produce dishes that would otherwise be impossible.
10. Diners and chefs should be sensitive to the conditions under which food is harvested and grown. Whenever possible, they should support humane methods of slaughter and sustainable harvesting of wild foods such as fish.

These points boil down to two key principles: always strive to produce the most delicious, technically exquisite food, and always apply analytical thinking and creativity to constantly advance the face of cuisine.

ABOUT THE RECIPES

Unless you own a copy of our earlier book, *Modernist Cuisine*, the recipes in this book probably look different from those you are used to seeing in cookbooks. There is a good reason for that: our recipes reflect the larger Modernist revolution underway in cooking (see page xviii).

The chefs at the forefront of Modernist cooking are some of the most creative cooks in history, but that creativity builds on a solid understanding of how cooking works and a set of new tools and techniques that allow them to cook with precision and remarkable consistency. With this book and the essential gear and ingredients now widely available, home cooks can achieve equally stunning results with confidence. We deliberately selected our recipes to illustrate how Modernist approaches can transform familiar dishes into extraordinary ones. The recipes span a wide range of techniques to give you many examples of how you can apply these methods and ingredients throughout the cooking you do at home.

Before you jump in and start cooking from our recipes, we encourage you to read through the chapters in Part One that explain what you need to know about any unfamiliar equipment and ingredients. Notes and introductions that accompany many of the recipes also direct you to helpful discussions elsewhere in the book.

The format of our recipes is designed to be clear and easy to follow while reflecting the Modernist approach of precision in cooking. Read the guide on the next page and the scaling instructions at left so that you understand how each element in a recipe functions.

Each of the 406 recipes and variations in this book was developed and tested at The Cooking Lab by our team of seven chefs and a separate recipe tester. Although some of the recipes were adapted for home cooks from *Modernist Cuisine*, the great majority of them are brand-new.

To get the most out of the recipes, weigh all of your ingredients on a high-quality digital scale (see page 7), use an accurate digital thermometer (see page 8), and invest in a sous vide setup of some kind (see pages 62–64). You can share photos of your results and discuss successes and challenges with our growing community of readers at our website, modernistcuisine.com.

The recipes in *Modernist Cuisine at Home* draw inspiration from many of the world's greatest chefs, both living and long past, to whom we are grateful. We hope this book will help you to bring that expertise into your home kitchen.

HOW TO Scale a Recipe

The recipe makes four servings, but you're throwing a dinner party for nine people. You are in luck: we've made it easy to scale the recipes in this book up to greater yields (or down if you have fewer mouths to feed). Just follow these simple steps.

1 Look in the scaling column of the recipe, and find the ingredient having a scaling value of 100%. Note the weight given. The 100% ingredient is usually the one that has the biggest effect on the yield of the recipe.
Example: The 100% ingredient in the Lobster Roll recipe shown on the next page is cooked lobster meat (not the live lobsters, because lobsters vary in their meat content).

2 Calculate the scaling factor by dividing the number of servings (or grams) you want to make by the recipe yield.
Example: This recipe yields four servings. If you are making nine servings, the scaling factor is 9 ÷ 4 = 2.25. (You can use the weight of the yield rather than the servings to calculate the scaling factor: if you want to make 1.3 kg of lobster salad from a recipe that yields 750 g of lobster salad as written, the scaling factor is 1,300 ÷ 750 = 1.73.)

3 Calculate the scaled 100% value for the recipe by multiplying the weight of the 100% ingredient by the scaling factor from step 2.
Example: This four-serving recipe calls for 500 g / 1.1 lb of cooked lobster meat, which is the 100% ingredient. To make nine servings, you will thus need 500 g × 2.25 = 1,125 g (1.1 kg / 2.5 lb) of cooked lobster meat. The scaled 100% value for the recipe is 1,125 g.

4 Calculate the scaled weight for every other ingredient in the recipe by multiplying its scaling percentage by the scaled 100% value from step 3. You can ignore the weights and volumes given in the recipe—just use the scaling percentages.
Example: The scaling percentage given for live lobsters is 300%. Multiplying this by the scaled 100% value from step 3, you find that 300% × 1,125 g = 3,375 g (3.4 kg / 7.4 lb). That's the weight of live lobsters you need to buy to feed nine people. Similarly, you need 8% × 1,125 g = 90 g of diced Granny Smith apple and 4% × 1,125 g = 45 g of vacuum-infused celery (which you can make by following the recipe on page 131).

5 If no scaling percentage is given for an ingredient, multiply the volume or number of pieces listed by the scaling factor from step 2.
Example: Instead of the four buns listed in the recipe, you need 4 × 2.25 = 9 buns. The recipe calls for 16 strips of tomato leather, so you should make 16 × 2.25 = 36 strips.

Because volume measurements given in the recipes are often rounded to the nearest convenient spoon or cup measure, you should not multiply or divide volumes when scaling a recipe up or down. Instead, scale the weights as described above, and then weigh the ingredients.

(1) The yield is the amount of food the recipe makes. With the exception of recipes (such as those in chapter 5 on Basics) that are intended to be used as ingredients in, or accompaniments to, other recipes, recipe yields are given both as a typical number of servings and as the approximate weight of the final dish.

(2) The overall time to make the recipe is given here. When that time includes a substantial amount of unattended preparation or cooking, such as long cooling, marinating, or baking, the unattended time required is listed as well.

(3) Many of the recipes can be made in advance. The refrigerated and frozen storage times given—supplemented in some recipes by "to make ahead" instructions—offer general guidance. But safe storage times depend on the temperatures inside your refrigerator or freezer. For more details on food safety, see page xxiv.

(4) We rate recipes as easy, moderate, or advanced in difficulty for an experienced amateur cook. Advanced recipes also indicate which aspect of the recipe may be particularly challenging.

(5) Unusual equipment or ingredients used in the recipe (even if they are optional) are noted here. We don't list ingredients usually found in city supermarkets. We also don't list equipment, such as a fine sieve, an accurate digital thermometer, a precise scale, an immersion blender, and a silicone baking mat, that we expect most readers already own. For more on equipment, see chapter 1.

(6) Ingredient weights are given in grams only, except for meats and seafood, for which weights are also given in pounds because that is how these products are typically sold in U.S. supermarkets. All recipes in this book were developed and tested by weight, not by volume. To get the same results that we did in our test kitchens, every ingredient should be weighed wherever a weight is given.

(7) Scaling percentages make it easy to make more or less of a recipe: see How to Scale a Recipe on the previous page.

(8) Approximate volume equivalents are listed for convenience only. We give common spoon and cup measures (or unit measures) for all ingredients except those, such as thickeners and emulsifiers, that must be weighed for the recipe to work. We also give volumes in milliters (mL) for thin liquids. We used both the reference table on page XVI and also measurements in our research kitchen to convert ingredient weights to volumes, which we then rounded to the nearest convenient division (see page XVI for details). Volume measurements are difficult to make accurately, and they vary greatly depending on how an ingredient is prepared and how tightly it is packed. We strongly urge you to weigh ingredients instead.

(9) Many recipes involve sealing food and cooking it sous vide in a water bath, either for a specified time at a given temperature or to a given core food temperature. For instructions on equipment and techniques for cooking sous vide, see chapter 3 on page 48.

(10) Recipe tables are divided by colored lines that group ingredients into blocks. Procedure steps apply only to ingredients that are in the same block as the step. In step 7, for example, "combine, and mix thoroughly" means to combine and mix the cooked lobster meat, mayonnaise, apple, chives, tarragon, and pepper—not to combine all the ingredients in the recipe.

(11) Some ingredients (four of those in this recipe) may be made by using other recipes in this book. In such cases, we give a page reference below the ingredient or recipe name. To save time, you can substitute store-bought ingredients, as we indicate by putting the ingredient name in lowercase.

LOBSTER ROLL

YIELD: (1) *four servings (750 g / 3 cups of lobster salad)*
TIME ESTIMATE: (2) *2 hours overall, including 1½ hours of preparation and 30 minutes unattended*
STORAGE NOTES: (3) *cooked lobster and dressed lobster salad keep for up to 1 day when refrigerated*
LEVEL OF DIFFICULTY: (4) *moderate*
SPECIAL REQUIREMENTS: (5) *sous vide setup, Vacuum-Infused Celery (see page 131), Tomato Leather (optional, see page 129)*

You might think it's hard to improve on an old-fashioned lobster roll—until you taste one made with lobster cooked with precision to attain ideal sweetness and tenderness. Butter infused with lobster shells (see page 122) adds extra flavor and color to the toasted bun.

Green apples and herbs freshen the lobster salad, and infused celery and tomato leather add a Modernist twist. Don't bother messing with a boutique hot dog bun in this New England classic—go with the usual supermarket variety. Fancier rolls detract from the lobster.

INGREDIENT	WEIGHT	VOLUME	SCALING	PROCEDURE
Live lobsters	(6) 1.5 kg / 3.3 lb	2 large lobsters	300% (7)	① Preheat a water bath to 50 °C / 122 °F, and arrange an ice bath alongside. ② Kill, blanch, and clean the lobsters; see page 284 for instructions.
Neutral-tasting oil	10 g	(8) 10 mL / 2 tsp	2%	③ Place the tail meat pieces and half of the oil in a zip-top bag. Place the claw and knuckle meat with the rest of the oil in a separate zip-top bag. Remove as much air as possible from the bags, and seal them. (9) ④ Cook the tail meat sous vide to a core temperature of 49 °C / 120 °F, about 15 minutes, and then plunge the bag in ice water. ⑤ Increase the water bath temperature to 55 °C / 131 °F. Cook the claw and knuckle meat sous vide to a core temperature of 54 °C / 129 °F, about 15 minutes, and then plunge the bag in ice water. ⑥ Cut all of the lobster meat into chunks no larger than 1 cm / ⅜ in.
Cooked lobster meat, from above	500 g / 1.1 lb	1½ cups	100%	(10) ⑦ Combine, and mix thoroughly.
Mayonnaise see page 108	200 g	1 cup	40%	
(12) Granny Smith apple, finely diced	40 g	⅜ cup	8%	
Chives, thinly sliced	4 g	2 Tbsp	0.8%	
Tarragon, minced	4 g	1 Tbsp	0.8%	
Black pepper, ground	to taste			
Salt	to taste			⑧ Season the dressed lobster meat.
Hot dog buns (store-bought)		4 buns		⑨ Warm the crustacean butter to room temperature, and spread it generously on the inside of the buns. Place the buns facedown in a dry frying pan, and toast them over medium heat until golden brown, about 2 minutes.
Pressure-Cooked Crustacean Butter or clarified, unsalted butter (11) see pages 122 or 119	30 g	2 Tbsp	6%	
Vacuum-Infused Celery see page 131	20 g	2½ Tbsp	4%	⑩ Divide the dressed lobster meat evenly among the toasted buns. Garnish with celery and tomato leather, and serve immediately.
Tomato Leather, strips (optional) see page 129	16 strips			

(13) *Safety tips for lightly cooked food: see page xxv*

(14) You can substitute cooked shrimp or store-bought cooked crab for the lobster.

(15) VARIATION: **Sous Vide Lobster Tail**
To make a main course of lobster, preheat a water bath to 55 °C / 131 °F. Seal the shelled lobster tail meat with 20 g of butter in a zip-top bag, remove the air, and seal. Cook sous vide to a core temperature of 54 °C / 129 °F, about 12 minutes. Serve with melted butter and fresh herbs, or with Caramelized Carrot Puree (see page 178) and a dusting of Chaat Masala (see page 136).

288 MODERNIST CUISINE AT HOME

(12) Initial ingredient preparation steps, such as cutting and grinding, are indicated following the ingredient name and should be performed before you begin cooking. In some recipes, the mise en place is pictured.

(13) Safety tips that are relevant for the recipe are referenced here; read the tips before making the dish.

(14) Notes provide additional information on simple substitutions, history, or related topics.

(15) Variation recipes change some of the steps or ingredients in the main recipe to make a different dish. Follow all of the steps in the main recipe except as directed in the variation instructions.

(16) In most recipes, the steps are given in concise form in the recipe table, and then in more descriptive form with selected photographs. Usually the picture appears above the step that describes it; when a number appears in the picture, it indicates the corresponding step in the recipe.

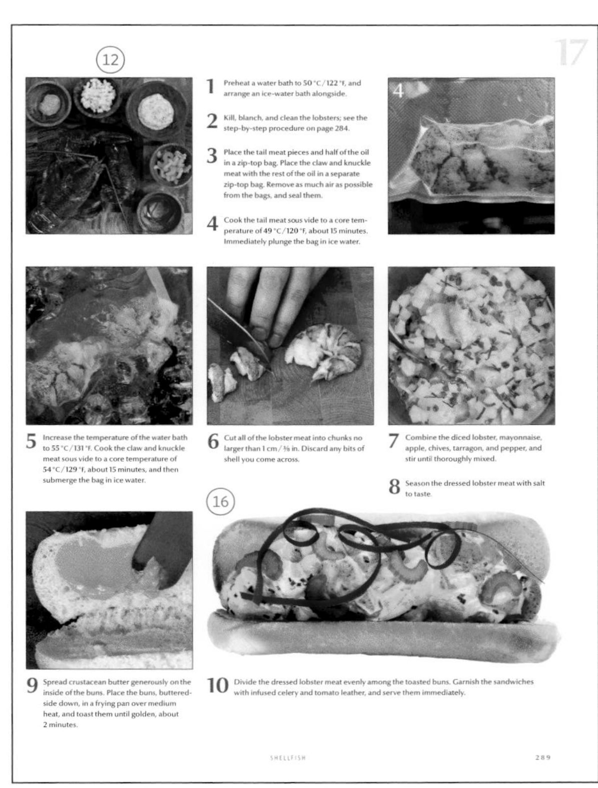
17

(12)

1 Preheat a water bath to 50 °C / 122 °F, and arrange an ice-water bath alongside.

2 Kill, blanch, and clean the lobsters; see the step-by-step procedure on page 284.

3 Place the tail meat pieces and half of the oil in a zip-top bag. Place the claw and knuckle meat with the rest of the oil in a separate zip-top bag. Remove as much air as possible from the bags, and seal them.

4 Cook the tail meat sous vide to a core temperature of 49 °C / 120 °F, about 15 minutes. Immediately plunge the bag in ice water.

5 Increase the temperature of the water bath to 55 °C / 131 °F. Cook the claw and knuckle meat sous vide to a core temperature of 54 °C / 129 °F, about 15 minutes, and then submerge the bag in ice water.

6 Cut all of the lobster meat into chunks no larger than 1 cm / ⅜ in. Discard any bits of shell you come across.

7 Combine the diced lobster, mayonnaise, apple, chives, tarragon, and pepper, and stir until thoroughly mixed.

8 Season the dressed lobster meat with salt to taste.

(16)

9 Spread crustacean butter generously on the inside of the buns. Place the buns, buttered-side down, in a frying pan over medium heat, and toast them until golden, about 2 minutes.

10 Divide the dressed lobster meat evenly among the toasted buns. Garnish the sandwiches with infused celery and tomato leather, and serve them immediately.

SHELLFISH 289

Refined and Unrefined Oils

Fundamentally, all oils are composed of various kinds of fats. The flavor of an oil comes from small amounts of other compounds that are suspended in the fats. These additional compounds affect both the smoke point of the oil and how it reacts to oxidation.

Some oils are flavorful and have a creamy mouthfeel because they are only filtered, not refined. These oils are useful in making emulsions and doughs, as well as to flavor foods. But unrefined oils should never be used at high heat because they quickly break down, begin to smoke, and start to taste bad.

Refined oils have had the majority of their "impurities" removed, including nearly all of the compounds that impart aroma and flavor. As a result, refined oils are much more stable for storage and high-temperature cooking.

Animal fats and clarified butter share many of the properties of refined oils. These fats tend to solidify at room temperature, a characteristic particularly valuable for making pastry dough.

Neutral Oils

In this book, we typically refer to refined oils as "neutral oils" because they can be used for their properties as oils without adding flavor. The neutral oils listed in the table below have varied characteristics, but several may be suitable for a particular application. Use what you have on hand.

When deep-frying or sautéing over high heat, choose an oil that has a high smoke point. Conversely, when making pastry dough, you'll get the best results from oils that are solid near room temperature.

Flavorful Oils

The flavorful oils listed in the table on the next page are best used either for cooking at low temperatures or for finishing a dish. Flavorful oils that are pressed from nuts or seeds are usually available in both virgin and roasted forms; roasting adds depth to the flavor. You can also add flavor to oils by infusing them with herbs, citrus peels, spices, chili peppers, or garlic. Never cook with infused oils, however: as soon as they are heated, they lose their aroma and begin to develop off-flavors.

Neutral Oils

Oils are products of nature and are pressed and refined by using a wide range of techniques. As a result, the temperature at which an oil starts to smoke (the smoke point) or catches fire (the flash point) can vary considerably for a particular oil from one supplier (or even one bottle) to another. The temperatures given in this table and the one on the next page provide a general guide, but your oils may perform differently.

	Smoke point		Flash point		
Fat	(°C)	(°F)	(°C)	(°F)	Notes
beef tallow	205	400	265	510	distinct aroma; melting point: 54 °C / 129 °F
canola (rapeseed) oil	225	435	275	525	prone to off-flavors; readily absorbed by food
chicken fat	190	375	255	490	melting point: 54 °C / 129 °F
clarified butter	252	485			also called "ghee"; flavor depends on production
coconut oil, refined	195	385	290	555	melting point: 25 °C / 77 °F
corn oil	230	445	335	635	drains well
duck fat	190	375	255	490	melting point: 54 °C / 129 °F
grapeseed oil	200	390	250	480	rich in fatty acids; oxidizes easily
peanut oil, refined	230	445	330	625	good for deep-frying; may be allergenic
pork lard	200	390	240	465	melting point: 33 °C / 91 °F
safflower oil	240	465	260	500	
soybean oil	235	455	330	625	prone to off-flavors from oxidation and heating
sunflower oil	235	455	275	525	poor-quality oil; tends to foam

Flavorful Oils

Fat	Smoke point (°C)	Smoke point (°F)	Notes
almond oil	216	420	very mild, light, and slightly sweet
avocado oil, unrefined	271	520	the only oil here that should be used for sautéing above low heat
butter, whole	135	275	sweet and creamy
coconut oil, virgin	177	350	
hazelnut oil	221	430	toasted variety especially reminiscent of hazelnuts
macadamia nut oil	210	410	very light flavor
olive oil, extra-virgin	210	410	flavors vary widely with olive variety, provenance, and processing
peanut oil, unrefined	160	320	dense and heavy, with distinct flavor
pistachio oil	177	350	bright green, with grassy notes
pumpkin seed oil	105	220	very low smoke point; do not heat
toasted-sesame oil	210	410	high-quality oil; available toasted and untoasted; high in antioxidants
walnut oil	160	320	slightly tart and grassy

Sources: *Journal of American Oil Chemists' Society,* vol. 19, no. 11, 193–198; *Vegetable Oils in Food Technology,* Blackwell, 2002; *Ullmann's Encyclopedia of Industrial Chemistry,* Wiley, 2000; *Modernist Cuisine: The Art and Science of Cooking,* The Cooking Lab, 2011

Argan oil is popular among chefs and foodies because of its unique provenance and its occasionally intense feral flavor. Traditionally, the Berbers in Morocco harvested the fruits of the Argan tree by feeding them to herds of goats. After passing through the goats' digestive systems, the seeds were collected, cleaned, and pressed. (Less interesting methods of producing this rare oil are now more common.)

Cutting boards pose a big risk of cross-contamination among different foods if they aren't properly sanitized between uses. Food on the cutting board can contaminate whatever food next comes in contact with the board's surface or the cutting knife. To prevent this, wash cutting boards and other tools between every use.

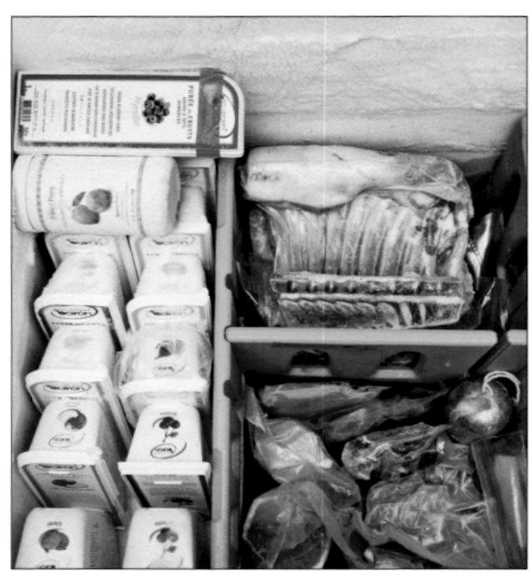

Properly organized freezers make it easier to manage frozen food and to identify and remove packages that have been in the freezer for too long.

Vegetables generally keep best at 3–4 °C / 37–39 °F, whereas fish and meats do best at 0–1 °C / 32–34 °F. If you can consistently keep your refrigerator at 1 °C / 34 °F or lower, you can store most food cooked sous vide for 30 days, according to FDA standards. At a refrigerator temperature of 3 °C / 37 °F, however, the recommended length of storage drops to three days.

Food Safety

Correctly following the steps of a recipe is only part of the cooking process; you also need to keep food safety in mind so that the people you feed don't become ill. Few cookbooks tackle this subject. First, it can be quite complicated; *Modernist Cuisine* has two lengthy chapters devoted to this topic, and that's only a beginning. Second, people tend to get squeamish when you talk about pathogens, sickness, and fecal contamination. We believe it is important for every cook (whether at home or in a restaurant) to understand the basics of food safety. Following a few simple rules makes cooking at home a lot safer.

The first thing to understand about food safety is that the overwhelming majority of food poisoning cases occur because the food is contaminated—and at least 80% of the time, the contaminant is fecal matter (either animal or human). As you might imagine, eating feces is a bad idea for lots of reasons, but for food safety the point is that gastrointestinal illnesses are transmitted by germs (pathogens) in the feces.

Nobody wants to eat feces; it happens accidentally through lapses in hygiene. The single most important thing you can do to eliminate food-borne illness is to practice better hygiene.

Hygiene

Good hygiene is critical wherever food is prepared or eaten, and the most important thing you need to keep clean is your hands. Proper hand washing is not just passing your hands quickly under a faucet—it means carefully scrubbing your hands with soap and water for a full 30 seconds and using a nailbrush to clean under your nails. That's what surgeons do before an operation, and it is what a cook should do before cooking.

Nearly everything in a kitchen is covered in bacteria, even if it looks clean. Even food that arrives to the kitchen clean can become contaminated by pathogens that have been carried into the kitchen on other food, the bottom of a shoe, or other sources. According to New York University microbiologist and immunologist Philip Tierno, the two dirtiest items in a typical house are both found in the kitchen: the sink and the sponge.

To keep things as clean as possible and reduce the risk of cross-contamination, wash small kitchen tools, containers, utensils, dishes, and pans in a hot, sanitizing dishwasher. Or you can mix 1 Tbsp of Clorox bleach per gallon of water (about 4 mL of bleach per liter of water) in a bucket, and submerge your tools in it for at least two minutes. After you drain the bleach solution, do not rinse or wipe dry the implements or the container; doing so might recontaminate them. Let everything drip-dry. Any residue of bleach that remains will be so faint that it will not affect the taste or the safety of the food.

Once a week, heat your sponge in the microwave on high for 1 minute, or toss it in the dishwasher with the drying cycle turned on. You should also stop using your dish towel to wipe down counters, hands, and equipment; it soon accumulates food, bacteria, and yes, feces. Dish towels should be used as nothing more than potholders. For wiping hands and other surfaces, switch to disposable paper towels.

Ingredients

You should always start with high-quality ingredients, and then handle them properly. Many people have a vague idea that meat and seafood are inherently more likely to be contaminated than plant foods are, but this is a myth. Produce is just as likely to carry fecal contaminants as meat and seafood are. Berries, green vegetables, and nuts actually carry an additional risk because they are much more frequently consumed raw than are meat and seafood.

Wash produce thoroughly, especially if you plan to serve it raw. We rinse our produce in a solution of water with 10% cider vinegar (100 g of vinegar for every one liter of water) to reduce surface pathogens. Some stores sell an organic solution made for that purpose.

When handling meat, use a separate cutting board from the one you use for produce. Keep in mind that whole muscles generally are sterile on the inside (thanks to the immune system of the animal); any contamination is much more likely to be on the surface of the meat.

For that reason, puncturing meat—whether with a Jaccard tenderizer, a thermometer, or even a fork—can push germs into the meat from the exterior. You can greatly reduce the risk by adhering to safe cooking times and temperatures.

If you are really concerned, dip the meat into hot water to blanch it before you puncture it. Water at 76 °C / 170 °F pasteurizes the surface in one second. A quick sear of the surface with a blowtorch sanitizes it even more thoroughly (see page 15). It's also a good idea to puncture meat as little as is necessary. Wait to check the temperature, for example, until the cooking is nearly done.

Because fish is cooked optimally at very low temperatures (at least in our opinion), you can't pasteurize fish without overcooking it. So when you eat fish that is properly cooked to the temperatures we call for in our recipes, you must accept that it isn't pasteurized. This is a small risk that most people consider acceptable.

To store food safely, make sure that no part of your refrigerator is above 5 °C / 40 °F; the optimum is a few degrees colder than that. The best way to check this is to put a glass of water in the refrigerator, let it sit for two hours, and then stick a thermometer in it. If the only way to get your top-shelf temperature down to 3 °C / 37 °F is to have the bottom shelf at a freezing temperature, so be it. Minimize the number of times you open the door, and close it again as quickly as possible.

Never put hot food in a refrigerator because it will warm everything else inside: a hot casserole can warm the interior by as much as 15 °C / 60 °F. Counterintuitive though it may seem, it's generally safest overall to cool hot food outside of your refrigerator. Just cover the food to avoid contamination, and don't leave it out for more than four hours. Even better, cool foods quickly in their covered containers using an ice bath or, in a pinch, cold tap water.

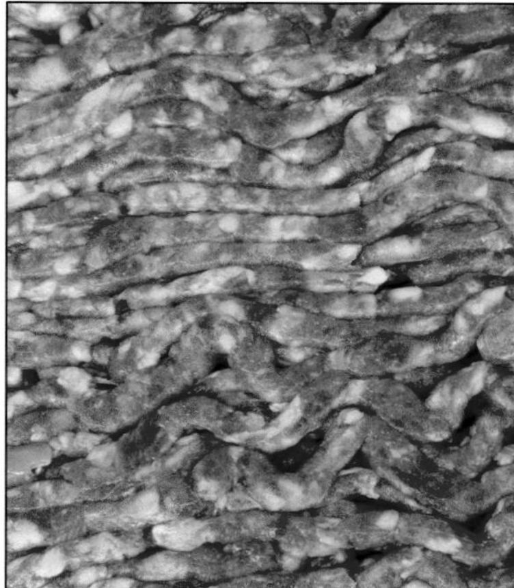

Ground beef, in which interior and exterior parts are thoroughly mixed, is particularly susceptible to contamination. During grinding, pathogens on the food surface can end up in the food interior, which doesn't get as hot as the surface does during cooking.

Just as using a sharp knife requires careful handling, so does other equipment in this book. See our safety guidelines for working with blowtorches (page 15), hot oil for deep-frying (page 26), and pressure cookers (page 33).

THE SCIENCE OF
"Lightly Cooked" Food

In a handful of our recipes, the cooking temperatures we recommend fall below those listed in guidelines published by the U.S. Food and Drug Administration or the U.S. Department of Agriculture (USDA). We've marked these recipes "lightly cooked." You should not serve these foods (or raw foods) to immune-compromised people.

Why don't we always follow government guidelines? Once upon a time, some well-meaning officials decided that food safety recommendations should include only temperatures rather than time-and-temperature combinations. This decision, perhaps the worst oversimplification in all of food safety, has led to years of confusion and mountains of ruined food.

Scientifically speaking, you need the right combination of both time and temperature to kill pathogens. Why give temperature-only rules when the science says otherwise? One can only guess at the reasoning of regulators, but they most likely thought that providing both temperatures and times would be too complicated. If you don't understand the meaning of time, however, you've got bigger problems in the kitchen than food safety.

Once you eliminate time from the standards, the strong tendency is to choose a temperature so hot that it can produce the required level of pathogen reduction nearly instantaneously. This impractically high temperature invariably leads to overcooked meat, seafood, and vegetables.

As we did extensive research for *Modernist Cuisine* (where we cover this topic in greater detail), we found numerous puzzles, inconsistencies, and mistakes in food safety regulations. Some have since been corrected; for example, the USDA's recommended cooking temperature for pork is now 63 °C / 145 °F instead of 71 °C / 160 °F. But most have not.

SAFETY TIPS FOR LIGHTLY COOKED FOOD

Lightly cooked food should be prepared in much the same way that we recommend preparing all food. Seek out the best ingredients, handle and prepare them hygienically, and cook them precisely. The one major difference is that lightly cooked food should be served immediately; leftovers should be discarded. The reason is that pathogens much more quickly colonize and propagate in foods below 50 °C / 120 °F. So if you eat lightly cooked food immediately, you're fine, but if you first let it sit around for a bit, you're taking an unnecessary risk. Raw and lightly cooked food should not be served to anyone who has a compromised immune system.

SousVide
PolyScience

SPER SCIENTIFIC
49.1
TYPE
HOLD
REL
OFFSET

COUNTERTOP TOOLS

Blowtorches, whipping siphons, and syringes? They're not the first things you'd think of to stock your home kitchen. But the tools that we've selected for this chapter we use every day because they are so versatile and produce such creative and delicious results. A whipping siphon, for example, is good for far more than whipped cream: we use it to carbonate soda, to add fizz or infused flavors to fruit, and to marinate meat in a fraction of the normal time. Pair a siphon with a good blender or juicer and a fine sieve, and you can make a delicately flavored foam to top a dish. Just a powerful blender and a fine sieve are sufficient to create almost any puree imaginable.

Two inexpensive pieces of equipment are absolutely essential to all Modernist cooking techniques: a reliable digital scale and an accurate digital probe thermometer. People tend to screw up their recipes or get frustratingly inconsistent results because the ingredient proportions or the temperatures are vague or mysterious. Modernist cooking uses precision instruments and techniques to remove the mystery—and greatly increase the success rate. You might be surprised how empowering it feels to weigh out a precise amount of each ingredient, cook the food to a precise temperature, and then be able to replicate the results of that exact combination every single time. With those basics handled, you can devote more thought and energy to the creative aspects of cooking.

Next to high-quality scales and thermometers, our favorite tools are the Microplane—Max travels with one in his suitcase—and the whipping siphon, both of which are just fun to use. Whenever you feel inventive, these are terrific tools to experiment with.

And they aren't hard to find. Not so long ago, buying a whipping siphon meant opening an account at a restaurant-supply store. Blowtorches were sold only by machine shops and hardware stores. Hypodermic syringes had to be ordered from medical supply houses. But now these gadgets, and all of the other countertop tools we suggest in this chapter, are readily available in most kitchen-supply stores or home improvement centers.

Their cost has come down as well, further lowering the barrier to home use. Although a professional chef may use a $400 digital scale, a $25 model will work just fine for most purposes. You don't need a $2,000 setup to experience the amazing results of cooking sous vide; you can achieve similar results with a $10 digital thermometer, a zip-top bag, and some vigilance.

So we encourage you to pick up some of the tools shown here. They will pay for themselves many times over in the form of greater control, confidence, and creativity—and thus higher-quality cooking.

Compare the new gadgets you see in your local kitchen-supply store to those for sale at the home improvement center. It's fascinating how many tools have made the leap from the garage or workshop to the kitchen. But there's still plenty for cooks to borrow from the realm of the hardware store, so we challenge you to find new culinary uses for tools that aren't yet familiar to most cooks.

FURTHER READING IN *MODERNIST CUISINE*

More must-have and handy special-purpose tools for Modernist cooks: see pages 2·284–287
Guides to juicers, filters, centrifuges, and rotary evaporators: see pages 2·334, 355–357, 361–364, and 384–393
All about food mills and homogenizers: see pages 2·415–423
Details on dehydrators and freeze dryers: see pages 2·434–453
How to get the most out of your coffeemaker or espresso machine: see pages 4·364–397

Invaluable Modernist Tools

Gadgets? Not exactly. These are items that we have come to rely on for efficiency and consistent results. Scales, digital thermometers, whipping siphons, blowtorches, and immersion blenders: we can't imagine cooking without them. Not all brands are listed in the table below; those given are the ones we happen to use in our research kitchen, but others may be just as good.

Rank	Tool	Kind	Brand	2012 Price	Note
1	digital scale	5 kg maximum, 1 g increments	Escali, My Weigh, Salter	$25–$50	both kinds are must-haves for accurate weighing
		200 g maximum, 0.01 g increments	AWS, Polder	$15–$50	
2	thermometer	instant-read digital probe, oven-safe digital probe with wire lead	ThermoWorks	$10–$100	must-haves; precise temperature control is crucial in Modernist cooking
		infrared	Fluke	$75–$200	
3	pressure cooker		Kuhn Rikon, Fagor	$75–$200	essential for making stocks and quickly cooking grains, seeds, and tough meats
4	water bath	heated water bath	SousVide Supreme, PolyScience	$250–$800	essential for precise cooking
		slow cooker with PID controller	SousVideMagic	$120–$180	
		improvised setup	any	$20–$50	
5	vacuum sealer	edge sealer	FoodSaver, Sous-Vide Supreme	$50–$140	convenient—and sometimes essential—for cooking sous vide and freezer storage
6	blowtorch	MAPP or propylene fuel	TurboTorch	$65	propylene-based fuels burn cleanly and avoid tainting food with combustion products
7	whipping siphons	500 mL or 1 L size	iSi, SFG	$30–$130	for making instant foams, and infusing or carbonating solid and liquid foods
8	blender	professional	Vitamix	$400	less expensive models work in most cases
9	immersion blender	stick type	Cuisinart, Bamix, KitchenAid	$30–$100	whisk attachments are handy for making quick foams
10	silicone mats	half-sheet and full-sheet sizes	Silpat, Wilton	$10–$25	useful for baking, spreading, or dehydrating food that tends to stick
11	silicone molds	assorted sizes	any	$20	excellent for casting gels and setting shapes
12	meat tenderizer	15–45 blades, microblades	Jaccard	$25–$40	useful for tenderizing tough meat as well as for quickly perforating pastry or skin
13	dehydrator	with Para-Flexx sheets	Excalibur	$200	for preserving seasonal fruits and salted meats, making fruit and vegetable leathers and chips, dehydrating pork skin for frying
14	long tweezers		any	$5–$20	useful for creative plating and handling delicate ingredients
15	paintbrush		any	$2–$10	useful for applying even layers of oil for baking, sauces for glazing, and for creative plating
16	coffee cold-brewing kit		Toddy	$40	makes full-flavored extracts for use in cooking

Chefs are not limited to equipment made solely for culinary purposes. Plenty of tools can be adapted for use in the kitchen. For example, long tweezers make handling food less cumbersome, and a paintbrush is useful for applying even layers of sauce or oil.

DIGITAL SCALES

If you have been measuring ingredients only by the cup and teaspoon, now is a great time to buy a good scale and to begin applying more precision to your recipe measurements. Digital gram scales are easy to find at cooking stores, and basic models are not expensive. There's just no excuse not to own one—and you really should have two: a general-purpose scale that accurately measures weights from one gram or less all the way to 1,000 grams or more, and an even more precise scale that is accurate to a tenth or hundredth of a gram.

Some higher-capacity scales now display bakers' percentages as well as grams. That is especially useful for our recipes because we list scaling percentages for most of them. So you could place one ingredient on the scale, set it to 100%, and then weigh the remaining ingredients according to the percentages—no math required (see page xx for an example).

A fine-weights scale is a crucial tool when measuring hydrocolloid thickening and gelling agents. These compounds are so powerful that a fraction of a gram can mean the difference between a sauce that is velvety and one that is gummy or slimy. A quality digital pocket scale does the job well and at a fraction of the price of a lab scale.

Be sure to keep your scales clean, calibrate them regularly (check the manufacturer's instructions), take care not to drop or jolt them, and always use them on a level surface.

Pocket scale
Accurate to: 0.01–0.1 g / 0.0004–0.004 oz
Typical max. capacity: 100–200 g
Pros: ultraprecise for delicate, fussy ingredients; very portable
Cons: sufficient only for hydrocolloids and spices
Where to buy: online
Cost: $15–$40

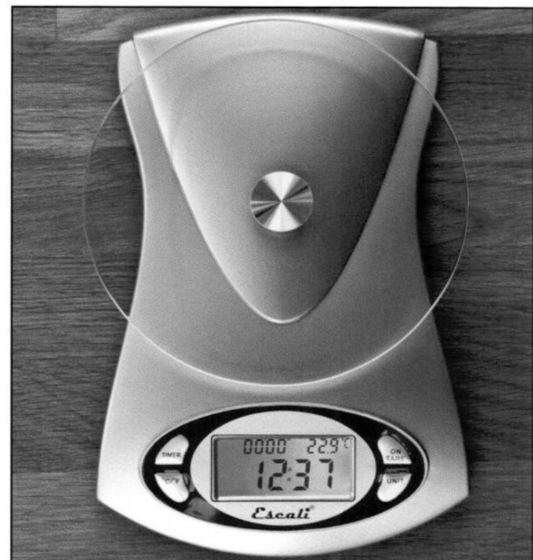

Standard kitchen scale
Accurate to: 1 g / 0.04 oz
Typical max. capacity: 2–5 kg
Pros: good for a wide range of common ingredients
Cons: not ideal for hydrocolloids
Where to buy: kitchen-supply stores
Cost: $25–$40

HOW TO Tare a Digital Scale

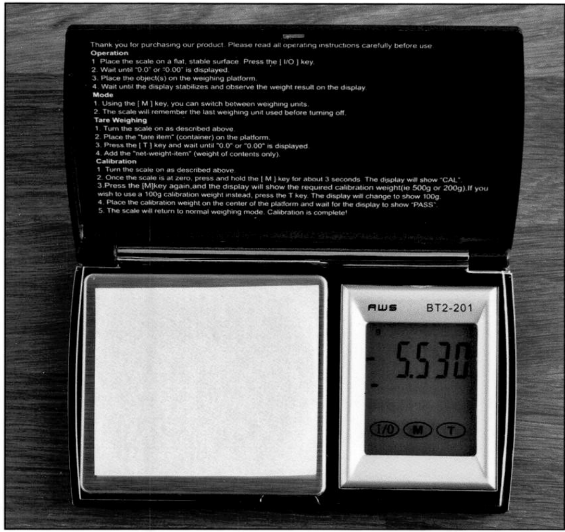

1 Place a piece of parchment or waxed paper on the scale to ensure that you don't leave traces of the ingredient on the weighing platform. You can use a bowl on larger scales.

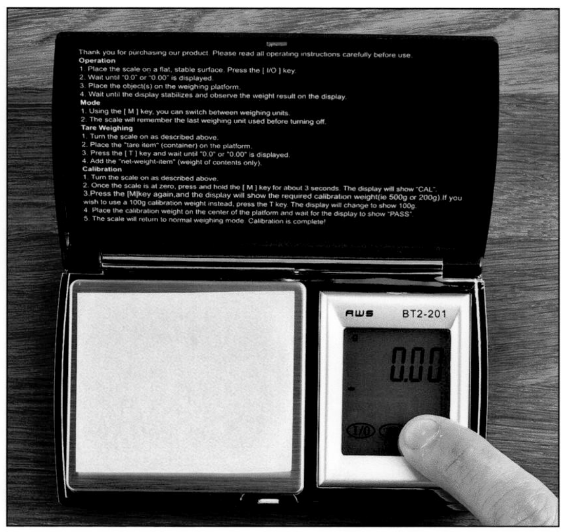

2 Tare (zero) the scale by pressing the tare button to reset the scale to zero. Now the scale will weigh only the ingredient, not the container.

3 Add the appropriate measure of the ingredient. If adding a second ingredient, repeat step 2 to reset the scale to zero.

When writing your own recipes, you can use the tare button in two handy ways to record the weights of the ingredients you use. If you can combine the ingredients in a bowl on the scale, tare before you add each ingredient to taste. Write down the amount added before you tare again.

If you are instead combining ingredients in another container (such as in a pot or blender), place more of the ingredient than you will need on the scale, tare it, and then add to taste from the scale. The amount that you removed from the scale will show up on the display as a negative weight.

DIGITAL THERMOMETERS

Small changes in temperature can make all the difference in cooking, so thermometers are a must. Unfortunately, they are not as accurate as you might think.

First, get rid of your old analog thermometer; it cannot be trusted. Analog thermometers are all but useless at low temperatures, like those used when cooking sous vide. (Sugar thermometers perform fine at high temperatures, but delicate glass is a disaster if it breaks.) Equally worthless are the classic metal spike-and-dial meat thermometers. Their accuracy is rarely better than ±2.5 °C / ±4.5 °F, and they take too long to display the temperature.

A digital thermometer is the best choice. If need be, a good thermometer can serve in place of a fancy sous vide cooker (see page 63). Our all-around favorite is the thermocouple thermometer, but a $10 instant-read thermometer is also fast, accurate, and easy to place just where you want it. That's important because the accuracy of the thermometer depends in part on how skillfully you use it (see page 66).

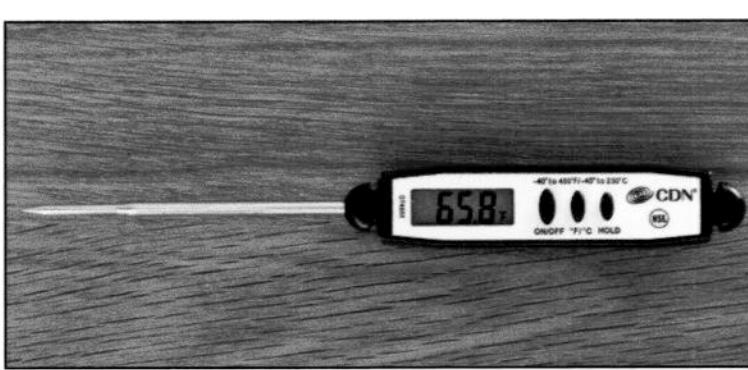

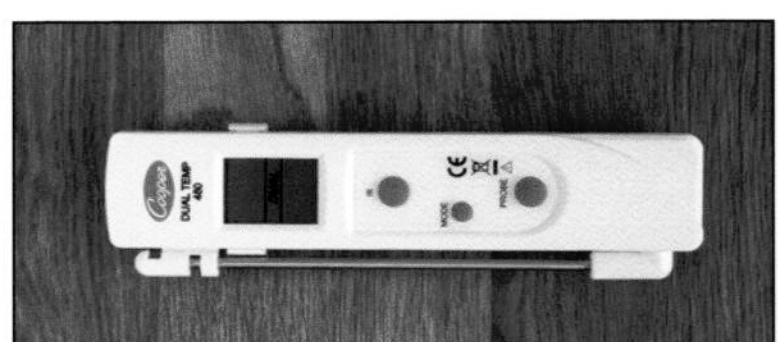

Instant-read
Accuracy: ±2.0 °C / ±3.6 °F
Pros: excellent range and speed, with needle-thin tip; useful for almost any application
Cons: can't remain in oven during cooking; cheaper models not appropriate for deep-frying temperatures
Where to buy: kitchen-supply stores, upscale supermarkets
Cost: $10–$20

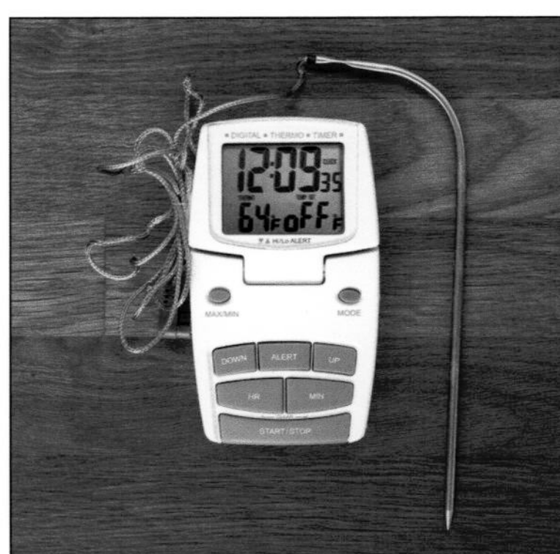

Oven probe
Accuracy: ±1.5 °C / ±2.7 °F
Pros: ideal for cooking sous vide and for low-temperature baking; heat-resistant wire allows probe to be placed in an oven or water bath
Cons: probe is bulky, leaving a visible indentation in the food; sometimes too heavy to stay in place
Where to buy: kitchen-supply stores
Cost: $20–$50

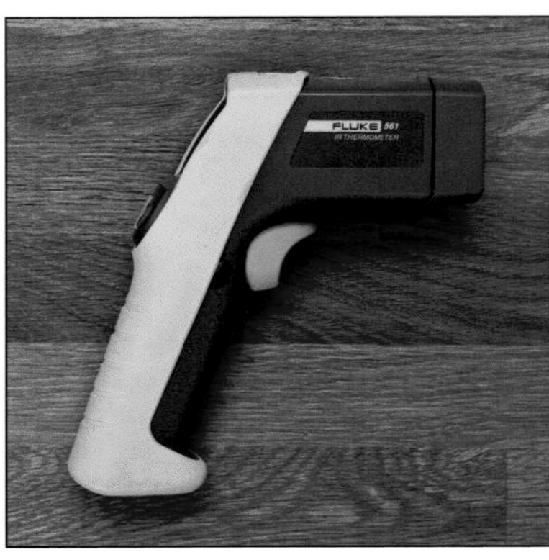

Infrared
Accuracy: ±2.0 °C / ±3.6 °F
Pros: useful for measuring temperatures of cooking surfaces (grills, griddles, pans, pizza stones), oven interiors, and sauces
Cons: won't read the interior temperature of food
Where to buy: online, electronics stores
Cost: $30–$75

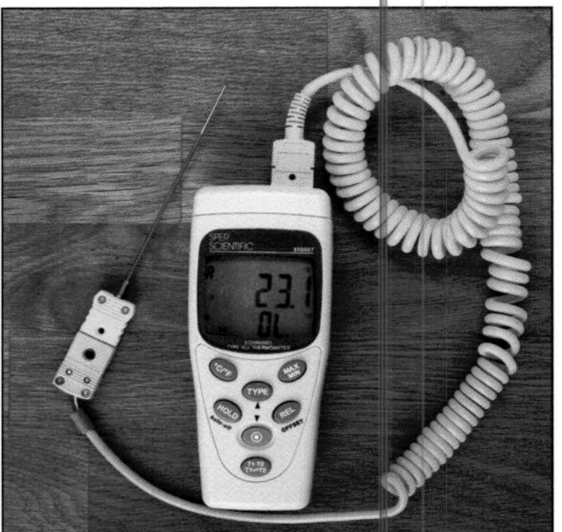

Thermocouple
Accuracy: ±0.5 °C / ±0.9 °F
Pros: extremely accurate; extendable wire allows probe to be placed in the food during cooking in a water bath or oven
Cons: more expensive
Where to buy: online, professional culinary stores
Cost: $60–$150

If you plan to deep-fry, you will need a high-temperature thermometer—any of the four we list here, with the exception of cheaper instant-read thermometers (which we do not recommend), is up to the task.

HOW TO Test the Accuracy of a Thermometer

1. Test the range and accuracy of your thermometer as soon as you buy it by using a pot of boiling water or a glass of crushed ice and water. Stir the crushed ice with the water for 1 minute to make sure the temperature is evenly distributed.

2. Insert the probe into the water. Take care to keep the probe from touching the container.

3. The display should read 0 °C / 32 °F in ice water at any elevation or about 100 °C / 212 °F in boiling water at sea level. (You can easily look up the variation of boiling point by elevation or air pressure at websites such as www.csgnetwork.com/h2oboilcalc.html.)

4. Digital thermometers that are off by more than 2 °C / 4 °F should be adjusted by a professional.

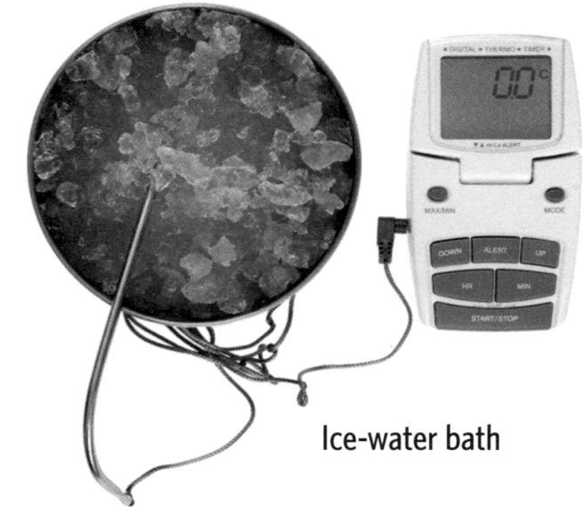

Ice-water bath

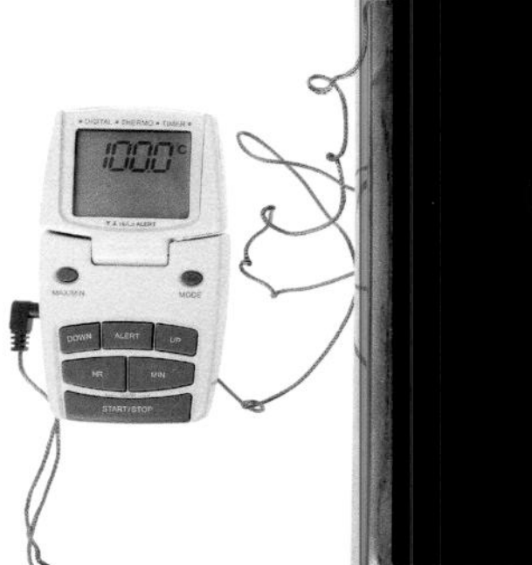

Pot of boiling water

SILICONE MATS AND MOLDS

We love silicone mats: baking sheet liners that are flexible, durable, heatproof, and nonstick. They come in three varieties: Silpat-style mats made of heavy-weave fiberglass mesh coated with food-grade silicone, silicone-coated parchment paper, and pure silicone mats. All three are useful for lining oven trays, setting into pans on the stove, and making thin sheets of food, such as crackers, crisps, and fruit leather. We often cut pure silicone sheets such as Wilton mats, into custom shapes and sizes, as for our Striped Mushroom Omelet recipe on page 148. (Don't cut Silpats, or you will expose the fiberglass core.) Silicone mats replace waxed paper, aluminum, and parchment paper with one reusable item. And, unlike nonstick coatings, the silicone can't be scratched off.

Soft, wobbly pure silicone molds are best for setting and easily turning out shapes, especially those made of semisoft gels. We don't recommend using them for baking when you want to create a golden crust; otherwise, they are fine. We use silicone molds for custards, panna cotta, chocolates and other delicate foods. You don't have to heat or scrape at the food to get it out—you just push.

MICROPLANES

Ask chefs how they feel about their Microplanes, and they'll likely say they can't live without them. We find that Microplanes are more versatile than zesters and much sharper than box graters. You can shave hard cheeses and chocolates into fluffy, snow-like mounds, or make a fine citrus zest. Finely grate frozen meat for a delicate carbonara or potatoes for a crispy, deep-fried garnish. Turn ginger, onions, and garlic into pastes without mincing. Microplane and other brands have created graters in a range of coarseness to suit every application.

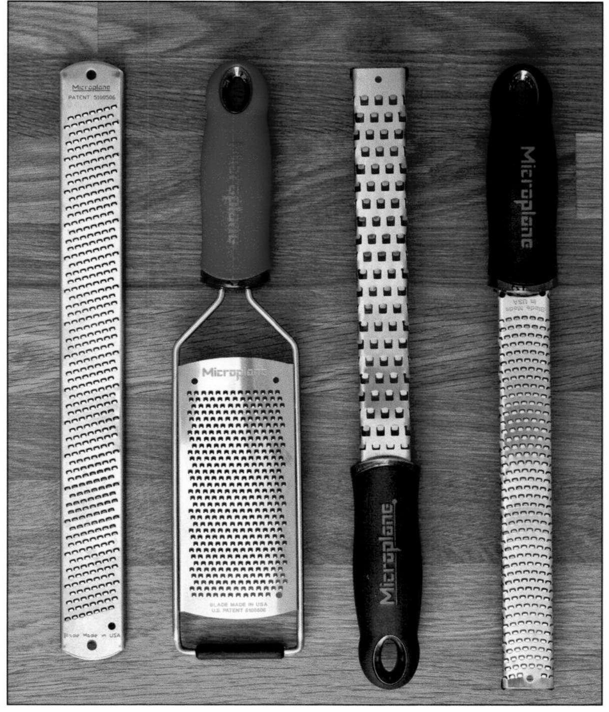

Microplanes cost about $15 at any kitchen-supply store. Maxime travels with his everywhere he goes.

BLENDERS AND FOOD PROCESSORS

Blenders and food processors cut, chop, and pulverize food from rough cubes of about an inch or two into smaller bits, or even fine purees. The smallest particle size a blender can achieve depends on the speed of its motor and how long you process the food. Particles smaller than about 10 microns / 0.0004 in are individually imperceptible to your tongue, so the food feels completely smooth and silky.

Blenders work well on fluid mixtures, but not on large chunks of food or very thick purees. The wide blade of a food processor is a better match for thick, chunky foods, and attachments can allow this tool to slice and dice dry ingredients. Coffee grinders are ideal tools for releasing the flavor and aroma from seeds and other hard spices. We keep one of each of these tools on hand in our kitchens.

Countertop blender

Pros: good for grinding soft foods, pureeing, and making emulsions such as mayonnaise and vinaigrettes

Cons: narrow blade area can't produce the finest purees; soups are noticeably gritty if you don't sieve them after blending. Very thick liquids may not receive adequate turnover. Large chunks of food can get stuck or wedge themselves out of reach of the blade

Features to look for: power (we prefer Vitamix models that can transform chunky food into silk in minutes), a wider bottom for better circulation of food around the blade

Where to buy: kitchen-supply stores

Cost: \$50–\$400

Coffee grinder

Pros: makes quick work of spices compared with a mortar and pestle

Cons: difficult to clean (grinding a bit of rice and wiping it out with a paper towel is the best you can do)

Features to look for: power, design that allows the grinding bowl to be removed for cleaning

Where to buy: kitchen-supply stores

Cost: \$20–\$50

Food processor

Pros: the most versatile of grinding tools; handles dry, soft food better than a blender does. Food has nowhere to hide from the wide blade sweeping close to the broad, flat bottom.

Cons: blades spin at lower speeds than those in a blender, so purees aren't as smooth; best suited for chunky sauces, doughs, and pastes

Features to look for: a bevy of attachments can save time on food preparation such as shredding, chopping, and grinding

Where to buy: kitchen-supply stores

Cost: \$125–\$500

MIXERS AND FROTHERS

The whisk was probably a mind-blowing invention when it first became available to household kitchens. Imagine what an improvement it offered over wooden paddles and spoons. The eggbeater was another technological step up, and then stand mixers revolutionized cooking again. Interestingly, none of these tools completely replaced its predecessors. They can all mix, froth, and emulsify. But they aren't equally efficient; each excels at different tasks.

Stand mixer

Pros: much faster than a whisk or spoon; attachments and speed control make it versatile enough to whip egg whites, knead bread dough, grind meat, and extrude pasta
Cons: food processors often now include a dough hook, grinding plate, and whipping attachment, making them more versatile than stand mixers
Where to buy: kitchen-supply stores
Cost: $200

Milk frother

Pros: good for dispersing a hydrocolloid or other powder; froths milk for coffee, a creamy soup, or a shake (see page 213)
Cons: works only in thin liquids; too little power to blend ingredients fully
Where to buy: kitchen-supply stores
Cost: $5–$20

Handheld whisk

Pros: inexpensive and readily available; makes the large, uneven bubbles characteristic of sabayon; good for quickly mixing liquid ingredients before cooking and for mixing a batter without overworking the gluten and starch
Cons: produces large droplets, so emulsions are not very stable
Where to buy: kitchen-supply stores
Cost: $5–$10

Immersion or handheld blender

Pros: inexpensive (midrange models work just as well as the expensive professional versions); useful for many small blending tasks; can blend directly into a bowl or a pot while it is heating; very good for foaming fatty or starchy liquids and for making basic emulsions such as mayonnaise and vinaigrette (see pages 108 and 117)
Cons: limited motor power and small blades make them inferior to upright blenders for heavy-duty chopping or pureeing
Where to buy: kitchen-supply stores
Cost: $20–$50

ICE-CREAM MAKERS

Making quality ice cream, gelato, granitas, and other frozen desserts at home is challenging, but modern appliances make it much more feasible than the old-fashioned approach of hand-stirring the ingredients in a vessel immersed in salty ice brine. The fanciest new ice-cream makers do the churning for you and self-regulate the temperature of their freezing chambers. In between are semiautomatic methods such as paddles and vessels for stand mixers that can be prechilled enough to produce small quantities of frozen treats.

No matter how you make ice cream, the finer the crystals in it, the silkier the ice cream feels on your tongue. If you freeze the mixture too slowly or with too little churning, the crystals will grow. You can use this to good effect when making snow cones or granitas, but for ice cream, smoother is always better.

Churning thus performs two crucial functions. First, it blends the fat, sugar, and other solids evenly with the water into an emulsion that freezes at a colder temperature than pure water does. Second, it disrupts crystal formation soon after it starts, so the ice particles remain microscopic in size.

Commercial-style ice-cream makers (top left, above) like those made by Gaggia Gelatiera, Cuisinart, DeLonghi, and Lello are now available for the home, albeit at relatively high prices, ranging from $200 to $700. They can make gelato (above, see recipe on page 370) that rivals what you'll get at a gelateria. Semiautomatic appliances (bottom right) from Cuisinart, Hamilton Beach, and others, as well as ice-cream attachments for stand mixers, (bottom left) are less expensive ($30-$70) but require several hours to prefreeze a vessel. They also generally produce ice cream having coarser textures. Old-fashioned barrel-style ice-cream makers (not shown) are similarly affordable and still widely available; these work reasonably well for preparing high-fat ice creams and frozen custards.

ICE CREAM IN A FLASH

The Pacojet is a very expensive ($2,000–$4,000) but remarkably effective tool designed to make instant, silky-smooth ice cream or sorbet. Thanks to its unrivaled versatility, it is now relatively common in restaurants and hotel kitchens worldwide. Ingredients must be frozen solid in special steel canisters at about −22 °C / −8 °F. The frozen mixture then drops into the machine to meet a powerful, tough blade. As the blade spins at high speed, it progressively grinds the icy block into an exceptionally smooth but still frozen paste.

No churning is required, and the grinding process works for many applications beyond producing exquisite desserts. We use ours to puree savory items (for example, to make pea soup, as shown below). Pacojets are handy tools for grinding tough ingredients such as fatty tissues and nuts into fine pastes. You can even produce powders to dust over dishes in their frozen state or to thaw and use as liquid ingredients.

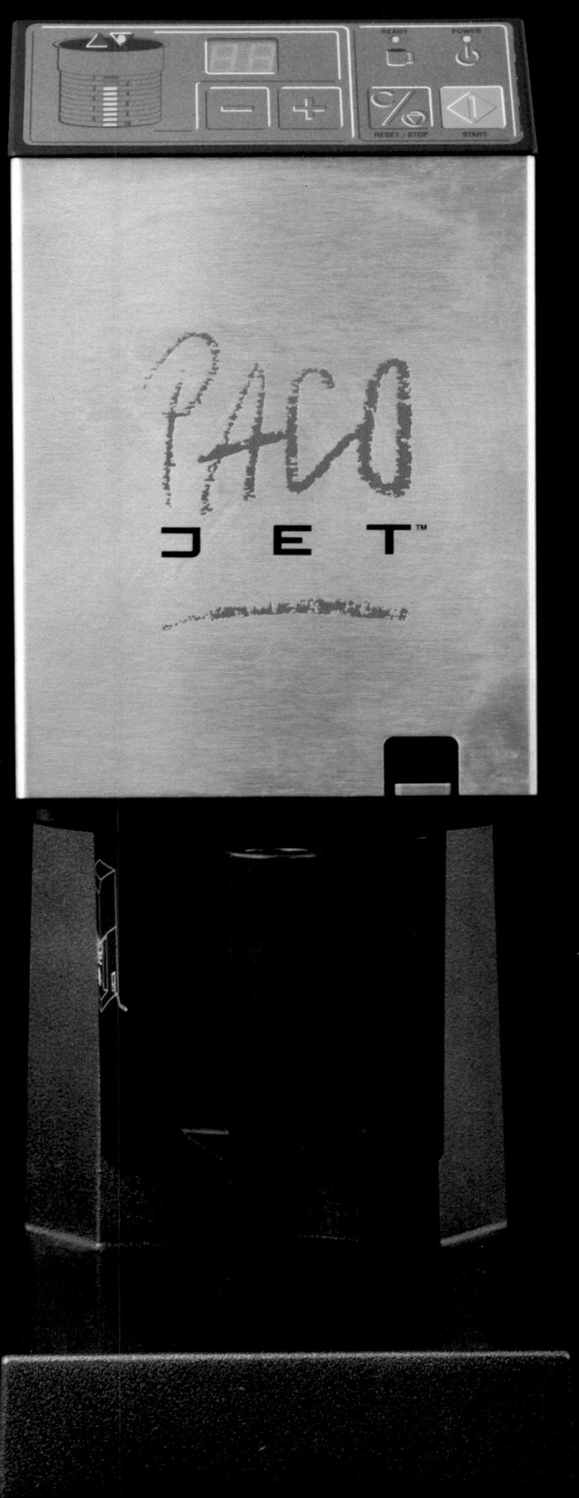

BLOWTORCHES

Blowtorches make for handy portable broilers. We use ours all the time—and not just for crème brûlée. We might flash-sear sushi, add a nice crust to steak cooked sous vide (see page 194), or quickly brown garlic cloves (see page 266). Rather than cooking with radiant heat, as an oven broiler does, blowtorches blast the food directly with a flame at about 1,900 °C / 3,400 °F. The "blow" part of the blowtorch is a powerful jet of hot gas that transfers heat to the food extremely fast.

Used properly, a blowtorch offers one of the quickest ways to sear food. Used carelessly, a blowtorch can leave your food tasting like fuel. Fuel can squirt from the tip when the torch is first lit; a yellow flame is a telltale sign that the fuel is not burning completely. Never point the end of a blowtorch at your food before the flame is lit and burning blue.

Be sure to read the safety tips on the next page before using a torch for the first time.

BLOWTORCHING TECHNIQUE

The intense heat of a torch can quickly sear food to an appetizing brown or caramelize sugars to a golden crust. In most situations, the best blowtorching technique is to sweep the tip of the flame back and forth across the surface of the food in quick and even passes. If you dwell too long in one place, brown spots will appear. Those brown spots are not themselves a problem, but they quickly burn to black if you are not careful. As when painting, you get better-looking results if you apply the browning in two or three "coats" rather than trying to do the whole job in a single pass.

Black edges are a bad sign; this piece of meat is a goner. Don't dwell too long on any spot. Move the flame evenly and quickly to avoid scorching or further cooking the food.

Use the tip of the inner cone of flame, not the base. Closer isn't hotter. To prove this to yourself, bring your hand close to the base of the flame from the side (carefully!). Note that you can nearly touch that part of the flame from the side before your hand really feels the heat. You can't put your hand nearly that close to the tip of the bright blue cone in the flame without burning yourself.

A baking rack placed in a baking tray allows hot air to circulate below the food so that you can torch both sides at once.

A crisp, amber layer will appear on a custard as you lightly sweep a flame over its surface. For a recipe, see Coffee Crème Brûlée on page 362.

Searing

Caramelizing

Melt all of the sugar evenly before it begins to brown, otherwise you'll end up with burnt areas and spots of barely caramelized sugar.

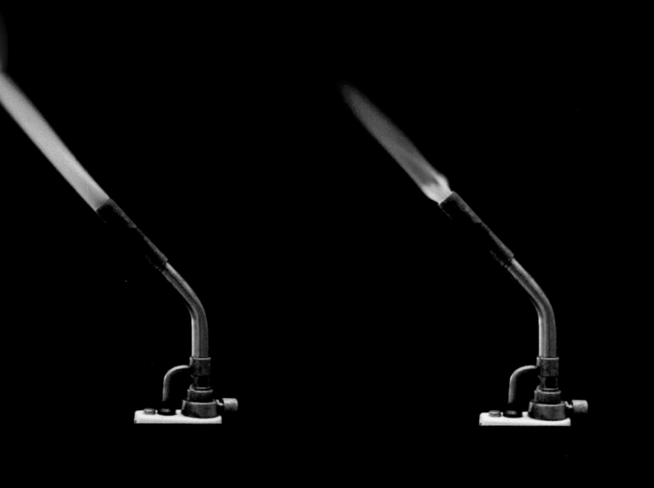

SAFETY TIPS FOR BLOWTORCHING

The risk of getting burned while blowtorching food is similar to that of oil splattering while deep-frying. Keep alcohol and cigarettes away from a blowtorch, and read and follow all manufacturer's instructions. If the food has a lot of fat in it, consider wearing safety goggles. Before you light the torch, set your food on a thick roasting tray placed on the stove top. All surfaces should be heat-safe. Don't use thin baking sheets, and remember that the tray is hot after torching, so don't touch it with bare hands.

Butane or propane

These torches are found in typical crème brûlée kits. They often leave slight traces of odor or the off-flavors of butane because the low-power flame can't burn off the gas fast enough. But they are hot enough to do the job if you have no better tool available.
Where to buy: kitchen-supply stores
Cost: $30

MAPP or propylene gas

We strongly prefer torches fueled by MAPP or propylene gas, which burn at extremely high temperatures. They contribute no flavor or odor to the food, and they sear it quickly. Look for a self-igniting torch.
Where to buy: hardware stores
Cost: $50–$65

Certain foods carbonize before they achieve a texture you recognize as crispy, golden, or caramelized. These include foods with high sugar content, such as fruits; foods with a lot of starch, such as potatoes; and foods with uneven surfaces, such as cauliflower.

HANDY USES FOR BLOWTORCHES

Brown meat

Torching is a faster way to put that familiar brown crust on a steak or a chop than pan-frying, deep-frying, or grilling. The tool is particularly handy for finishing meat after it has been cooked sous vide. Before searing the meat, brush on a thin layer of oil or butter so that the flame doesn't hit a dry surface. A tiny bit of fat is enough; too much creates

Burst bubbles on a foamy liquid

Superheating tiny air bubbles causes them to collapse. Quickly swipe the torch across the top of the foam—just enough to pop the bubbles without heating the food. Use this technique to smooth the surface of crème anglaise (see page 368), scrambled eggs and omelets (see pages 144 and 146), or fresh fruit juices.

Peel an egg

Torching an eggshell makes it easier to peel without damaging the firm egg white. Soft-boil or hard-boil an egg (see page 142), and rest it at room temperature for two minutes. Then flash the egg with the torch while rotating it constantly. The shell should become dry and brittle within about two minutes, and will fall away easily when peeled.

JACCARD TENDERIZERS

Pounding meat may be a satisfying way to tenderize it. But using a Jaccard tool is more discreet and just as effective: it doesn't change the look or shape of the meat, but can have a big effect on the texture. The Jaccard tenderizer contains a set of slender blades (usually 15–45 of them) that are poked through meat in a regular pattern. The blades cut through the meat fibers but leave the basic structure of the meat intact.

A Jaccard can be used on nearly any piece of red meat or poultry; just take care that bones don't break the fine blades. After cooking the meat, you will find that its punctures are virtually impossible to detect—until you take a bite. By cutting some but not all of the muscle fibers, the Jaccard makes the meat seem more tender, while preserving its basic mouthfeel.

Won't poking your meat full of holes let the juices leak out? Actually, Jaccarded meat is juicier, for two reasons: the weakened collagen fibers shrink less during cooking, and the cuts free up myosin protein that thickens juices. Together, these effects reduce the moisture lost during cooking by 5%–15%. Jaccarding also accelerates the absorption of brines or marinades. Jaccarding can be used in combination with injection, below.

Jaccards cost $25-$40 at any kitchen-supply store.

THE HAZARDS OF PUNCTURING

Poking, perforating, or otherwise puncturing pieces of meat can contaminate it. If you are inserting a temperature probe, injecting brines or marinades, or tenderizing meat with a Jaccard, you will push any pathogens on the surface of the meat into the interior. This slightly increases the risk of foodborne illness.

Adhering to safe cooking times and temperatures, however, will mitigate the risk. If you are really concerned, then you can dip the meat in hot water to blanch it before puncturing it. Water at 76 °C / 170 °F sanitizes the surface in one second. Or quickly sear the surface with a blowtorch (see page 14). Contamination occurs only on the surface; you don't have to cook food all the way through to pasteurize it.

INJECTORS

Brining makes meat juicier and enhances its flavor, but salt diffuses through flesh very slowly. You can double or triple the rate of diffusion by injecting the brine deep into muscle tissue. You might give a whole chicken, for example, a couple dozen individual injections, evenly distributed. This is easy to do quickly by using a butcher's syringe.

Next, immerse the meat in the same brine that was injected—called a covering brine—and let it rest so that the brine diffuses fully and evenly. A whole chicken is brined within two days rather than five. Skip the covering brine if the meat has skin on, which acts as a shield and can become rubbery when brined, or if you intend to heavily sear the outside. In our Roast Chicken recipe on page 238, for example, brined skin would be too salty and would not crisp enough during cooking. We inject the meat from the neck and back cavities, without piercing or brining the skin.

Injection works with thin marinades, too. Barbecue sauce is too viscous (we tried). But when we diluted the sauce until it was more like a brine, the flavor infused nicely.

Meat injectors usually include two large needles: one having a slanted tip for marinades with spices; and one that is perforated so as to diffuse liquids. Gun-style injectors cost $50-$60; good stainless-steel syringes cost $20 online. Syringes less expensive than that, and those with plastic parts, are easily clogged.

People tend to make brines with too much salt, which results in meat with a dense and hammy texture. See page 132 for brine recipes having salt levels that won't compromise the texture of the food.

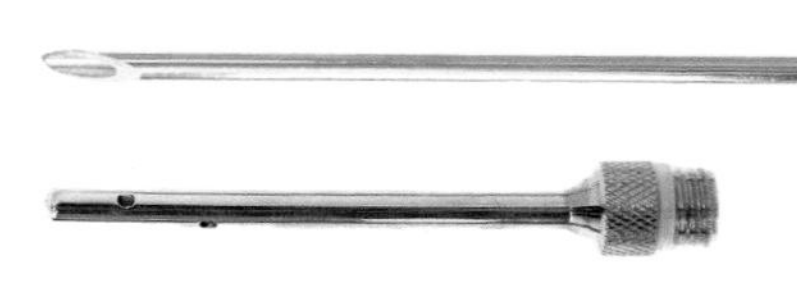

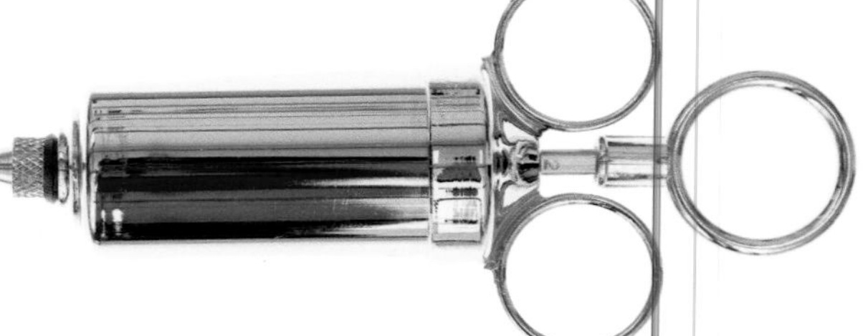

SIEVES AND STRAINERS

Sieving allows you to separate liquids from solids, and vice versa. Think of the colander that you use to drain water from pasta or ball-shaped tea strainers (which we use to infuse broths with herbs). Strainers also allow you to make tender, cooked solids finer by passing the food through the fine mesh with the back of a spatula, scraper, or ladle. In this way, sieving is the ultimate refinement. This simple bit of extra effort is how restaurant chefs create either a potato puree of pure silk or a completely clear broth. It is easy for you to do at home with the right equipment.

Sieves come in varying shapes and degrees of fineness. Pros tend to use a fine mesh or conical sieve and a tamis (or drum sieve). A cone shape maximizes the force as you press the solids of a stock or sauce into the bottom with a ladle. The drum-shaped tamis refines the texture of soft foods, such as riced potatoes or butter, as you push them through its fine mesh.

Our favorite tamis are lab sieves. We recommend owning three: 75 microns (for sieving fat to make consommé or to clarify butter), 300 microns (for velvety purees), and 850 microns (for sifting powders such as flour and nut meal).

Lab sieves come in many degrees of fineness. Some are so fine that you can't tell they're perforated—but wait a moment, and they even sieve out fat. They are well worth the $35–$75. It doesn't matter if they're made of stainless steel or brass.

The great French chef Joël Robuchon passes his potato puree through a tamis three times. That's why its texture is so silky (that, and the fact that it's half butter).

WHIPPING SIPHONS

Siphons are useful for making so much more than whipped cream. We use ours all the time—for making fresh soda, greatly speeding up marinating, infusing fruit with a flavorful juice, or topping a dish with foam for flavor and textural contrast.

Whether you're carbonating, infusing, or foaming, there are a few basics you should know.

The siphon requires cartridges of gas, also called chargers, to pressurize the chamber holding the liquid. Carbon dioxide is best used for carbonation only. We use nitrous oxide for foams, marinating, and infusing. A cartridge holds eight grams of gas, can be used only once, and costs about 50 cents.

Two cartridges are typically sufficient to charge a one-liter siphon. Use about 2% gas, or 8 g of gas for every 400 g of liquid—more if the liquid is low in fat.

HOW TO Use a Siphon

CARBONATING

Create a sparkling drink or give porous food a surprising fizz. We slice carbonated grapes over chilled oysters and pair rich pâtés with sweet, tart, fizzy raisins. You need three cartridges of carbon dioxide to get really good carbonation in a one-liter whipping siphon or soda siphon.

1 Chill both the liquid and the siphon. Carbon dioxide is most soluble in cold liquids.

2 Pour in a cold liquid or add a chilled fruit. Do not overfill. Tighten the lid.

3 Insert the first carbon dioxide cartridge, while holding the siphon upright. Hold down the nozzle to blow out the gas. The venting step is important because it replaces the air sitting above the liquid with carbon dioxide.

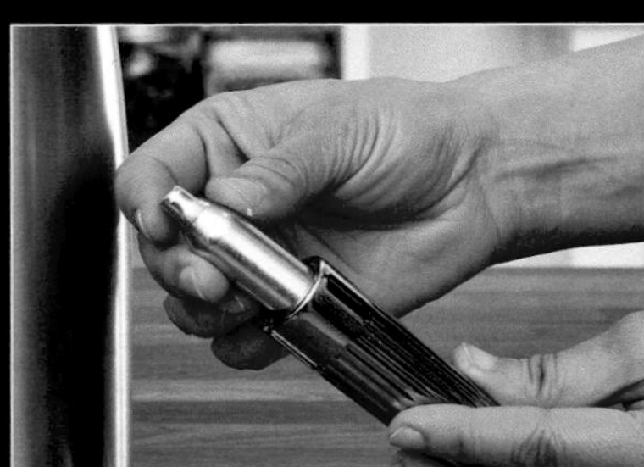

4 Insert one or two more cartridges of carbon dioxide; do not dispense any of the gas. Shake the siphon vigorously for 5–10 seconds.

5 Refrigerate this siphon to allow the gas to fully dissolve into the liquid. Let liquids sit for 2–4 hours. Let fruit sit for at least 4 hours, but preferably for 8–10 hours. Don't open the siphon until you serve the fruit.

6 Open the siphon by holding it upright, pressing a cloth against the nozzle to contain any liquid, and slowly releasing the gas. Then remove the siphon lid, and pour out the soda or fruit. Dispensing soda through the nozzle results in a tingly and foamy drink, not a fizzy one, because the gas exits the liquid too quickly.

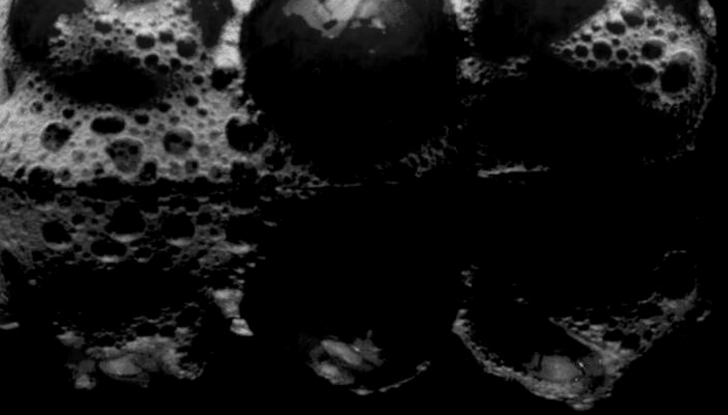

PRESSURE-INFUSING AND PRESSURE-MARINATING

You can use the high gas pressure in a siphon to force liquid into a solid, thus speeding up the processes of infusing, brining, or marinating (see page 132). Meat cut into cubes for kebabs, for example, takes 20 minutes to marinate instead of 1–12 hours. Infusing porous fruit with liquid is a fun twist—think strawberries and lemonade, apple slices bursting with apple juice, or watermelon with hints of green tea.

1 Add cubes of meat to the siphon, and cover them with marinade or brine. To infuse fruit with a liquid, add the fruit and enough liquid to cover it. Tighten the lid.

2 Charge the siphon with nitrous oxide. Use two cartridges in a 1 L siphon. Shake vigorously for 5–10 seconds.

3 Refrigerate the siphon for 20 minutes to let the flavors infuse.

4 Open the siphon by holding it upright, presssing a cloth against the nozzle to contain any liquid, and slowly releasing the gas. Then unscrew the siphon lid, and pour out the contents.

FOAMING

Whipping siphons were designed for aerating cream that is high in fat. (Nitrous oxide dissolves much better in fat than in water.) But you can foam any liquid thick enough to hold bubbles. Add starch, gelatin, eggs, or agar to thin liquids to give them enough body for foaming. A fine, creamy foam comforts and provides contrasting texture, like mashed potatoes, or whipped cream atop a dense dessert. Light, acidic, and airy foams can contribute an additional layer of flavor. The more air in the foam, the less concentrated its flavor, so use a very strong liquid when making a foam to serve as a garnish or sauce. A foam used to top some other flavorful food may not need to be as intense. It's a matter of finding the right balance.

1 Add the liquid to the siphon, and tighten the lid. Do not overfill it.

2 Charge the siphon with only one cartridge of nitrous oxide. Shake vigorously for 5–10 seconds. Resting is unnecessary; the gas dissolves quickly.

3 Turn the siphon upside down, and press the lever to dispense a bit of foam. Check the texture. One cartridge is usually sufficient for high-fat liquids. Add more cartridges to create progressively thicker foams. The foam will release any gas it can't hold, so an extra charge won't ruin it. Shake the siphon each time before you dispense the foam.

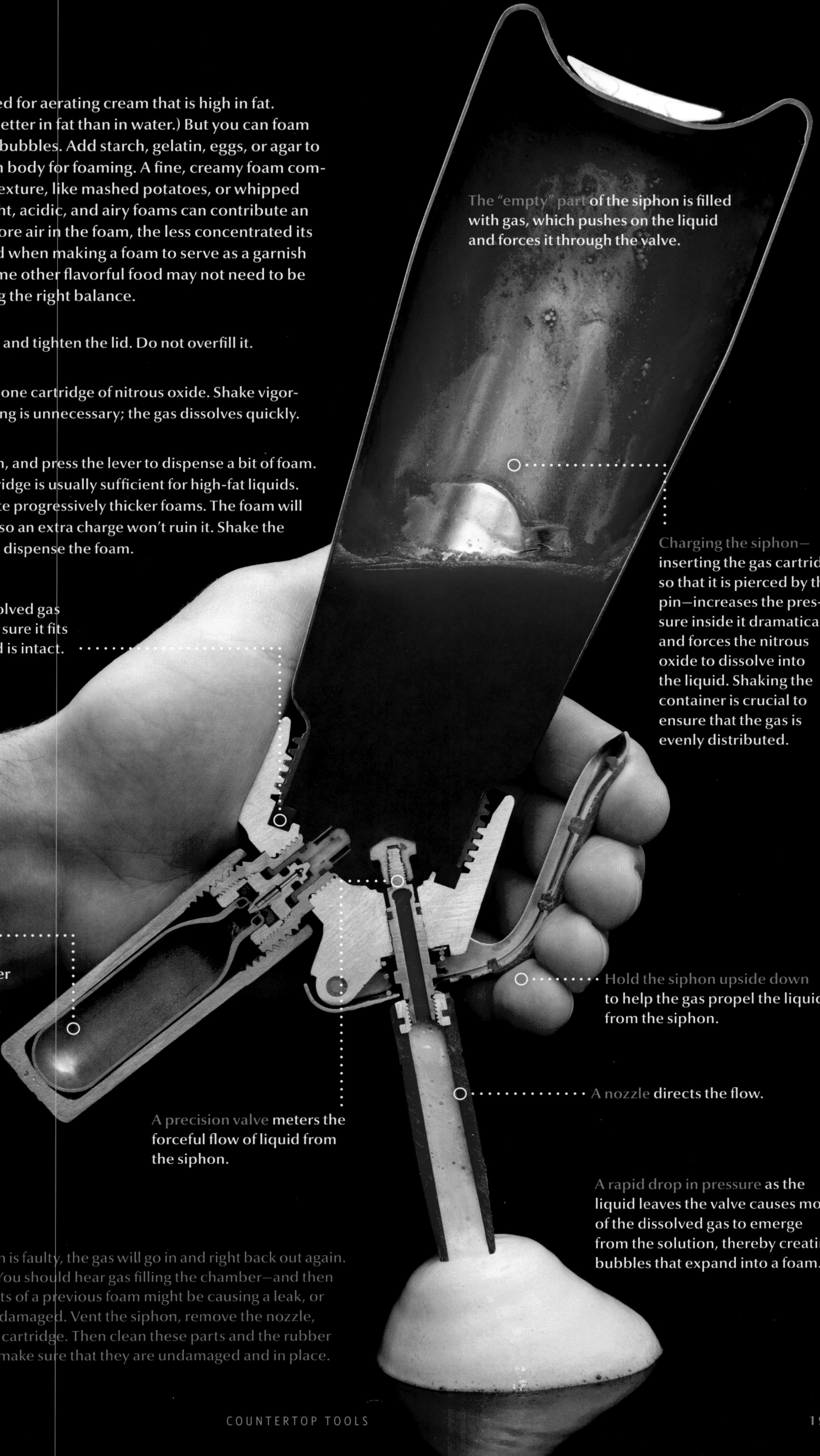

The "empty" part of the siphon is filled with gas, which pushes on the liquid and forces it through the valve.

Charging the siphon—inserting the gas cartridge so that it is pierced by the pin—increases the pressure inside it dramatically and forces the nitrous oxide to dissolve into the liquid. Shaking the container is crucial to ensure that the gas is evenly distributed.

The rubber gasket keeps the dissolved gas from escaping from the lid. Make sure it fits snugly along the top of the lid and is intact.

A disposable cartridge holds 8 g of nitrous oxide, the gas used to pressurize the siphon. The number of cartridges you need depends on the volume of the siphon, how full the siphon is, the fat content of the liquid to be whipped, and the temperature of that liquid. Generally, two cartridges are enough for a one-liter siphon.

Hold the siphon upside down to help the gas propel the liquid from the siphon.

A nozzle directs the flow.

A precision valve meters the forceful flow of liquid from the siphon.

A rapid drop in pressure as the liquid leaves the valve causes most of the dissolved gas to emerge from the solution, thereby creating bubbles that expand into a foam.

Listen to your siphon

If the seal on your whipping siphon is faulty, the gas will go in and right back out again. So listen closely as you charge it. You should hear gas filling the chamber—and then silence. Still hear hissing? Remnants of a previous foam might be causing a leak, or some part of the siphon could be damaged. Vent the siphon, remove the nozzle, unscrew the top, and take out the cartridge. Then clean these parts and the rubber gaskets thoroughly, and check to make sure that they are undamaged and in place.

JUICERS

Until recently, juicing tended to be relegated to late-night infomercials, health-food stores, and trendy juice bars. But now chefs, following the examples that Jean-Georges Vongerichten set in the 1980s with his juice vinaigrettes, are using juices to replace stocks and alcohols in recipes for sauces and broths.

Juice is a natural concentrate. It is loaded with sugars, soluble proteins, emulsified lipids and fat compounds, and volatile aroma molecules—in other words, the essence of flavor. We love to play with its possibilities. A carrot soup made with a broth of carrot juice rather than water or stock, for example, is much more flavorful. (See page 178 for a recipe.) Or try using fresh apple cider in a sauce for pork chops.

Cooking with juice is easy to do at home, whether you use one of the tools below or buy pure, flash-pasteurized juice from raw fruits and vegetables.

Centrifugal juicer

How it works: A broad, flat blade at the bottom of a spinning basket both pulverizes the food and flings it against the mesh basket. Centrifugal force then expels most of the juice from the pulp, through the mesh, and into a waiting container.
Pros: handles both soft fruits and fibrous vegetables, with an attachment for citrus; machines designed to eject pulp are easy to clean
Cons: if not designed to automatically clear pulp, the basket clogs quickly. The friction of centrifugal force oxidizes the juice faster, damaging flavor and color. Yield is smaller than its Champion-style counterpart. Many parts to clean
Where to buy: kitchen-supply stores
Cost: $100–$300

Food press

How it works: A food press forces juice out mechanically by squeezing food between two hard, unyielding surfaces, one of which is perforated. Presses work best for softer foods; hard foods can be softened with slight heating or adding sugar or enzymes. Citrus fruit presses generally pair convex and concave pressing surfaces to accommodate the shapes of orange, grapefruit, lemon, and lime halves. We find a potato ricer to be the most versatile type of food press. It can puree soft fruits and can juice firm ones.
Pros: can quickly apply high crushing forces; little mess to clean up; little setup needed
Cons: juice contains fewer particles because the juicer compresses food rather than tearing it; yield depends in part on your personal force
Where to buy: kitchen-supply stores
Cost: $10–$20

Champion-style juicer

How it works: You push food down a chute onto a serrated, spinning blade. The ruptured cell walls release their contents, and the juice collects in a bowl. The spindle assembly shunts pulp into another receptacle.
Pros: processes food extremely efficiently; good at separating out solids; can juice relatively dry foods like wheatgrass and leafy vegetables
Cons: slower than the centrifugal juicer; smaller feed tube means juicing is more hands-on; many parts to clean
Where to buy: kitchen-supply stores
Cost: $150–$300

Keeping juice fresh

It's one thing to extract an intensely flavored juice, but it's quite another to keep that juice fresh and appetizing until it reaches the table. True freshness is fleeting because the essential oils that give fruits their bright colors and flavors oxidize quickly after juicing.

To delay oxidation, add 0.1%–1% of ascorbic acid (vitamin C), citric acid, malic acid, or tartaric acid. You can enhance the flavor of the juice by adding just a drop of essential oil from the same fruit, such as orange oil for orange juice or lemon oil for lemon juice, right before serving.

Chemical changes also cause juice to brown quickly. To preserve the color, strain out the pulp immediately after juicing, and then chill the juice in an ice bath or the refrigerator.

DEHYDRATORS

Simple dehydration is one of the oldest forms of food preservation, but innovative cooks continue to dream up novel ways to use dehydrated food, from vegetable leathers to edible paper. Perhaps the most versatile, inexpensive tool for drying foods is the cabinet-style dehydrator.

The appliance is simple: just a ventilated chamber, a fan, and a small heater that warms and dries the circulating air. Fresh air blown by the fan carries humid air away from the surface of the food, while warm air speeds drying.

Dehydrating food takes hours or days, so it's tempting to use higher temperatures to get the job done sooner. But lower drying temperatures almost always yield better texture and flavor. That's because water isn't the only thing that vaporizes during drying: aromas do, too, and the higher the drying temperature, the more pronounced the loss.

The simplest way to speed drying is to slice food (or spread purees) thinly: less than 1 cm / ⅜ in thick. The rule to remember is that food sliced half as thick will dry in a quarter of the original time required. Food that is too thick can rot inside before it dries through.

To minimize bacterial growth, cure meats and seafood before drying. Intact pieces of raw fruits and vegetables are likely to have only surface contamination, so you can briefly blanch them in boiling water or steam. Then, dehydrate at temperatures above 50 °C / 120 °F; that is usually hot enough to minimize the proliferation of bacteria.

Place your dehydrator in the least humid part of the kitchen, usually a well-ventilated area.

Fruit leather that won't stick

Beef jerky stays so flexible in part because of its high fat content. Here's a trick for tender fruit leather: add 3%–4.5% of a neutral-tasting oil to the fruit puree. The fat keeps the leather from becoming too brittle or so chewy that it sticks to your teeth. The trade-off is that the leather is no longer fat-free.

See page 129 for a recipe for Tomato Leather, which adds bite to our Lobster Roll on page 288.

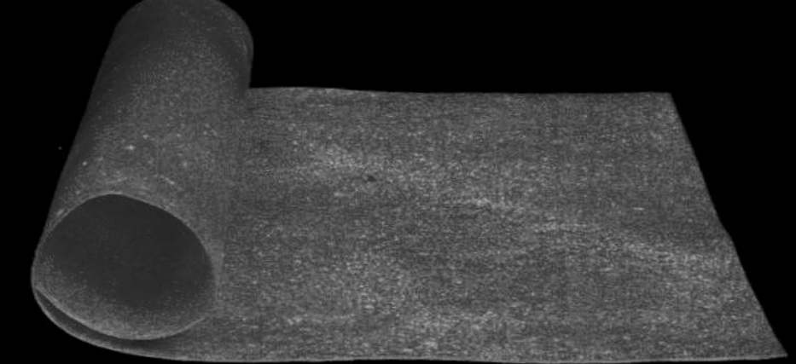

Drying Correctly

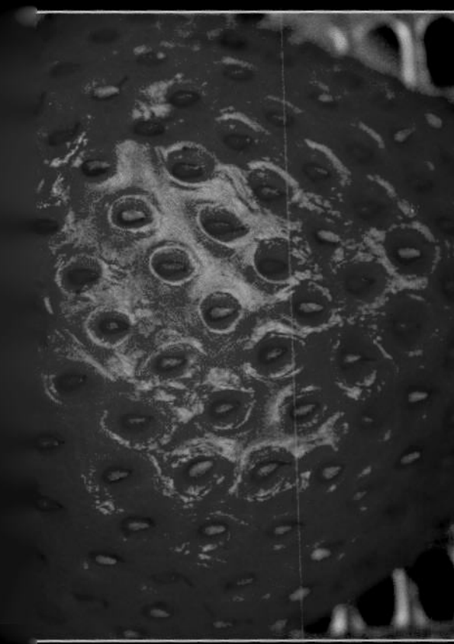

If drying is going too fast, the food surface will become increasingly dry and crusty, while the center of the food remains wet and leathery. Lower the temperature: the food is on the verge of baking rather than dehydrating.

If the surface remains visibly wet, the food is drying too slowly or needs more time. Increase the air temperature (and decrease the humidity, if possible).

Once the bulk of the water has been evaporated, the food is usually tacky, even sticky, and has a leathery texture. This is exactly what you want for fruit leather or beef jerky.

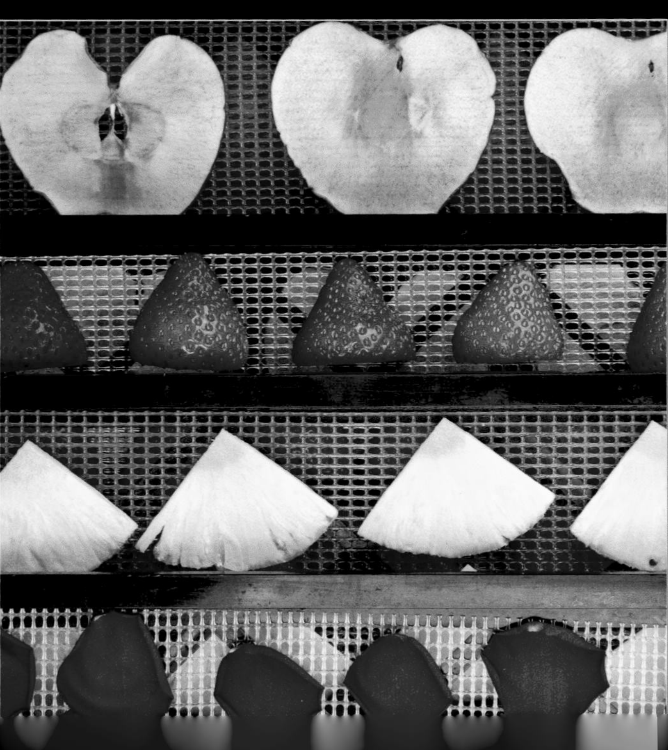

CONVENTIONAL

FURTHER READING IN *MODERNIST CUISINE*

How to find the sweet spot of a grill: see pages 2·14–17

The history of baking: see page 2·101

Cooking with moist air: see pages 2·176–177, 180–181

Microwave myths: see page 2·190

Cooking is as old as humanity itself—it may even have shaped our evolution. The anthropologist Richard Wrangham, in his intriguing book *Catching Fire: How Cooking Made Us Human*, traces the development of our large brains, small mouths, dull teeth, and narrow pelvises to *Homo sapiens*'s taming of fire as a tool to convert raw food to cooked, which has more usable energy. When you bake a loaf of bread, roast a leg of lamb, or even flip a burger on the grill, you're invoking time-honored techniques passed down not just from generation to generation but from the dawn of our species. These traditional methods of cooking have become as familiar and comfortable as our own kitchens.

So it may come as a surprise to learn how traditional cooking techniques actually work (and, too often, don't). Stoves are a vast improvement over our ancestors' open fires, but they still leave a lot to be desired in both efficiency and accuracy. It's the norm for a conventional oven to be off by 14 °C / 25 °F or more from the temperature to which it is set. And most ovens offer no control over one of the most important elements in baking: humidity.

On the other hand, some kinds of conventional cooking gear are more useful than commonly appreciated. People generally think of microwave ovens as unworthy of more than reheating leftovers and popping popcorn, but as our recipes

COOKING GEAR

in chapter 22 on Dishes for the Microwave illustrate, this technology is actually superb for steaming vegetables, drying beef into jerky, and frying herbs. Pressure cookers, which are ubiquitous in India and other countries, suffer in the United States from an outdated perception of their safety. We use them nearly every day to extract amazingly intense flavors and to slash the amount of time it takes to cook the components of a meal.

Understanding how your conventional cooking gear works will help you to make the best use of it. In this chapter, we peer inside some of the appliances we've cut in half to get a closer look at the science and technology that make them tick, and we examine the features that are most useful to have. We also cover many of the innovative new cooking tools available today, such as induction cooktops and home combi ovens. And illustrated instructions guide you step-by-step through the cooking techniques that you'll find in some of our recipes.

With this little bit of knowledge, you can save a lot of money and effort. You'll learn, for example, that fancy copper pans can't compensate for an underpowered burner, and that a pressure cooker can easily transform a cheap cut of meat into something amazing. So keep an open mind; some of our most cherished notions about cooking deserve a closer look.

Even cooks who have modern gear such as water baths and high-tech thermometers often find that stoves, ovens, pots, and pans are at the center of the action in the kitchen. This chapter explains what you need to know about these essential cooking tools.

STOVES

How efficient is your cooking method?

We ran tests in our laboratory to calculate the energy each device required to heat a measured amount of water. The results:

Electric coil: 42% efficient
Induction burner: 56% efficient
Water bath, unstirred and covered: 85% efficient
Water bath, stirred and covered: 87% efficient

Induction cooktops typically generate magnetic fields that oscillate 25,000 times a second. That can produce some vibration in the pan. Most of the vibration is above the range of human hearing, but you may hear a slight humming noise. At partial power, the cooktop turns the field on and off several times a second, which can cause the pan to make an intermittent buzzing sound.

The stove is the modern version of the ancient cooking fire. It is more convenient and easier to control, but the stove still suffers from some intrinsic limitations. It heats food mainly by the slow process of conduction: the heat diffuses from the burner through a metal pan and into the food.

That is an inefficient process. Heat streams from below, beside, and above the food being heated. It is diverted from the burner to the frame. It wafts from the sides of the pot. It radiates from the lid. If the food is uncovered, heat escapes into the air in the form of evaporating water vapor. Heat loss aside, these various forms of inefficiency make cooking more variable.

Cooking in a pot or pan is thus quite imprecise. A batch of food cooks differently in a tall pot than it does in a shallow pan, or even in two pans made of different metals. Cooking with or without a lid, or on different stoves, or even on different burners in the same stove can alter your results. Much of what separates an advanced cook from a novice is experience in coping with these variables. Hence the appeal of newer cooking methods, like sous vide, that are far more precise (see page 48).

If you're in the market for a new stove top, you'll find several options to choose from: electric, gas, and induction. Each has its advantages and disadvantages. Electric stoves are relatively safe, clean, and affordable. They aren't prone to oil flare-ups and can't leak gas. On the downside, electric coils are slow to heat and slow to cool. To take a pot of water from a rapid boil to a low simmer, for example, you have to remove the pot from the burner, wait for the coil to reach the right temperature, and then put the pot back on.

Gas stoves provide much better control over the cooking temperature because the flame responds quickly to a twist of the dial. Gas stoves are excellent for quick cooking techniques that use high heat, such as stir-frying, sautéing, and searing. Experienced cooks enjoy the tricks they can play with gas, like adding a dash of alcohol to a gravy, tilting the sauce to the edge of the pan, and letting the flame burn off the alcohol.

For precise, reproducible results, though, it's hard to beat induction cooktops. Although induction stoves may lack the sexiness of fire, they are far more efficient. That is because the induction element doesn't actually generate heat: it produces an oscillating magnetic field that heats up any nearby ferrous metal. The pan itself becomes the heat source, so the food comes up to temperature much faster than it would on a coil or gas burner. Because an induction element doesn't directly heat the surrounding air or intervening surfaces, more than half of the energy it draws reaches the food, compared to about a third of the energy for a gas burner.

Faster response and higher efficiency translates into less time spent waiting by the stove. A pot full of two liters of water boils in less than five minutes on an induction cooktop, compared with 8–10 minutes on gas or electric stoves. If the pan is no larger than the heating element, then that heat is also distributed very evenly.

Induction cooktops are powerful for their size: built-in elements typically deliver 2,400 watts, about as much firepower as the largest burners on high-end gas stoves for the home. The main drawback of induction ranges has been their cost, but that has been falling rapidly. You may need to buy new pots and pans, however, because pure copper and aluminum pans will not work.

You don't have to replace your range to give induction cooking a try. A countertop unit with one element sells for $75–$250, depending on its features. These are limited by the capacity of wall sockets to 1,800 watts, but that is about as powerful as a typical gas stove.

Gas
Gas stoves are woefully inefficient at directing heat. But natural gas is a cheaper source of power than electricity, and it's delivered without substantial losses en route, so cooking with gas is still a bargain.

Electric
Although it is slow to react to adjustments in temperature, the electric stove is the most affordable option.

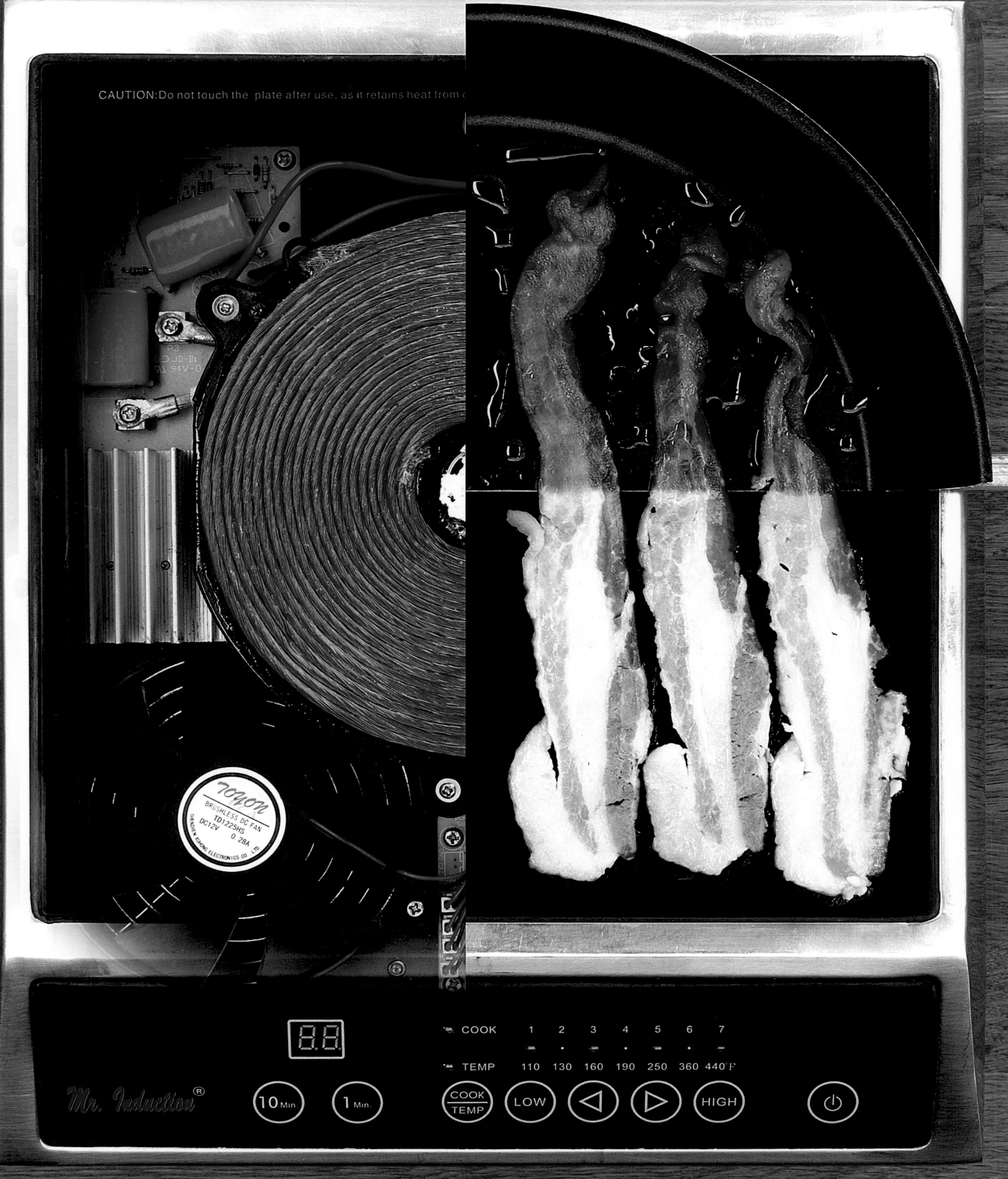

An induction cooktop transmits power through a magnetic field, generated by copper coils below its surface, that turns the pan itself into the heat source. The magnetic field has no effect on nonmetal objects, which is why the bacon touching the cooktop is still raw even as the bacon in the pan cooks. Steel and cast-iron pans work with induction elements, but aluminum, copper, glass, and ceramic cookware do not. If a magnet sticks well to your pan, it will work. Induction is so efficient that we use $10 pans from Ikea and get results as good as the priciest copper cookware on a gas stove.

POTS AND PANS

A pan that is too thin allows heat to flow directly from the burner through the pan and into the food before it spreads much to the sides. In other words, the pan transmits the unevenness of the electric coils or the ring of gas flames right to the food. To compensate for the unevenness of the burner, use a pan having a thick bottom. It will come to full temperature less quickly, but the extra heating time allows the heat to diffuse horizontally as it rises vertically.

Hanging in a restaurant kitchen like trophies, gleaming copper pans are gorgeous to look at. But do they really perform better than much cheaper aluminum or steel pans? Well, that depends on what you mean by "better."

Will a copper frying pan heat fast? Yes.

Will it respond quickly when you adjust the burner? Yes.

Will it diffuse heat evenly across its surface? Not so much.

Let's start with the basics. All of the heat flowing upward from beneath a pan must go somewhere. At first, most of it goes into raising the temperature of the pan. As that occurs, conduction spreads the heat throughout the pan, from hot spots to cool spots.

You might think that eventually the temperature across the bottom of the pan evens out, but it doesn't because the pan is much wider than it is thick. So fluctuations in heat from the burner reach the cooking surface before they have time to average out across the pan. Thicker pans and thick *planchas* (built-in griddles) cook more evenly, but they are heavier—and still not perfect. A pan that diffuses heat perfectly from one edge to the other would have to be so thick that you couldn't lift it.

When it comes to heating food evenly, the metal the pan is made from is the least important factor. What matters more are the thickness of the metal, the size of the pan, and the size of the burner heating the pan.

The thicker a pan is, the more uniform the temperature across its surface. But this evenness comes at a price: the extra mass of metal makes a thicker pan less agile. It is slower to react when the burner is turned up high or down low.

So the question is: how thick is thick enough? The answer to that does depend to some extent on the heat conductivity of the metal. In a typical copper pan, the temperature across the bottom will vary by no more than 22 °C / 40 °F. But if the pan were made of stainless steel, then it would need to be more than 7 cm / 2¾ in thick to perform similarly—and never mind that the weight of such a pan would make it impossible to lift! Fortunately, bonding a lightweight, 6 mm / ¼ in plate of inexpensive aluminum to the bottom of the thinnest, cheapest stainless steel pan produces a pan with nearly the same performance as that of the copper pan.

Now put either pan on a tiny gas burner. Performance drops. Not even copper is conductive enough to spread the heat evenly to the far edges of the pan—it is just too far away compared to the thickness of the pan.

The bottom line: with a properly sized burner—ideally one that is about as wide as the pan itself—any pan, even a cheap and thin one, can be heated fairly evenly.

In Modernist cooking, pots and pans are best suited for preparing ingredients, such as sweating vegetables, and for finishing food cooked sous vide by panfrying or deep-frying it. The main cooking tasks are often better left to more precise, modern tools, such as those covered in the next chapter.

SAFETY TIPS FOR DEEP-FRYING

Our recipes call for frying at temperatures between 190 °C / 375 °F and 225 °C / 440 °F. That's hot! Frying in oil can be more dangerous than other high-heat cooking methods, so you must follow some simple rules.

Make sure your thermometer can display temperatures up to 260 °C / 500 °F. Frying, candy, and thermocouple thermometers usually have this much range. You don't want to be fooled by the wrong temperature.

Deep-fry food in enough oil that the food floats and does not touch the pan. The related technique of shallow frying uses enough oil to cover at least part of the food.

Use a deep pot. Generally the walls of the pot should rise at least 10 cm / 4 in above the oil so that there are no spillovers. This also helps contain splattering and makes cleanup easier.

Pat the food dry before you place it in the oil. Use paper towels to soak up excess moisture, which can cause violent splattering when it hits the oil.

Don't get too close to the oil. Use long tongs, a slotted deep-fry spoon, or a frying basket to place the food gently into the oil and to remove it.

Choose a frying oil that has a smoke point higher than the desired cooking temperature. The smoke points of common oils are listed on page xxii. At these temperatures, oils break down and produce off-flavors.

If the oil gets too hot, remove it from the heat. Turn off the burner. You may also need to move the pot carefully off of an electric burner. If you see the oil smoking, it is too hot.

Never use water, flour, or sugar to put out a grease fire. And do not try to carry a flaming pot outdoors. Use baking soda, a damp towel, or a fire extinguisher specifically designed for grease fires to suffocate a fire.

Sweating

Sweating vegetables (such as onions, garlic, shallots, carrots, or celery) is the technique of cooking the evenly cut pieces over medium-low heat until they soften but do not brown. Sweating gets its name from the moisture that flows out of the vegetables as their cell walls weaken and start to release their liquids. You'll see this technique used in many of our pressure cooker recipes, such as the Pressure-Cooked Paella del Bosco recipe on page 326.

Panfrying

A quick sear over high heat, as we use in the recipe for Low-Temp Oven Steak on page 196, lends an appealing appearance, temperature contrast, and an extra layer of flavor to food cooked sous vide. Preheat the pan, then add the oil, and finally add the food to be seared.

Deep-Frying

Giving cooked food a quick dip in hot oil is a great way to develop a crispy crust. See our Modernist Hamburger Patty recipe on page 208 for an example. Shallow frying in a deep-sided pan works as well, as long as you're generous with the oil; we use that approach when making the Sous Vide Buffalo Wings described on page 250.

Shallow frying is done using a pan, but it cooks the food more like deep-frying does than like panfrying. Use plenty of oil, and don't worry about the food becoming greasy. Counterintuitively, more oil yields less grease because it keeps the temperature high and the crust thin and less absorbent.

HOW TO Deep-Fry Without a Deep Fryer

We're big fans of deep-frying as a finishing technique after cooking sous vide. You don't need to own a dedicated fryer. You just need a deep pot and the proper tools to insert and retrieve the food from a safe distance: long tongs, a slotted deep-fry spoon, or a frying basket.

1 Choose an appropriate frying oil (see page xxii). Peanut, soybean, and sunflower oils are our favorites for frying at high temperatures.

2 Add the oil to a deep pot, but fill it no more than half full. Use enough oil so that you can submerge a small batch of food completely.

3 Preheat the oil to the cooking temperature. For consistent results, cook small batches to minimize the cooling that occurs when you add the food, and warm food to room temperature before frying it.

4 Pat the food dry with paper towels. External moisture causes the oil to splatter.

5 Deep-fry the cooked food. Just 30 seconds may be enough when you don't want to further cook the interior of the food. Allow the oil temperature to recover between batches.

6 Drain the food on paper towels. Absorbing excess oil removes much of the fat.

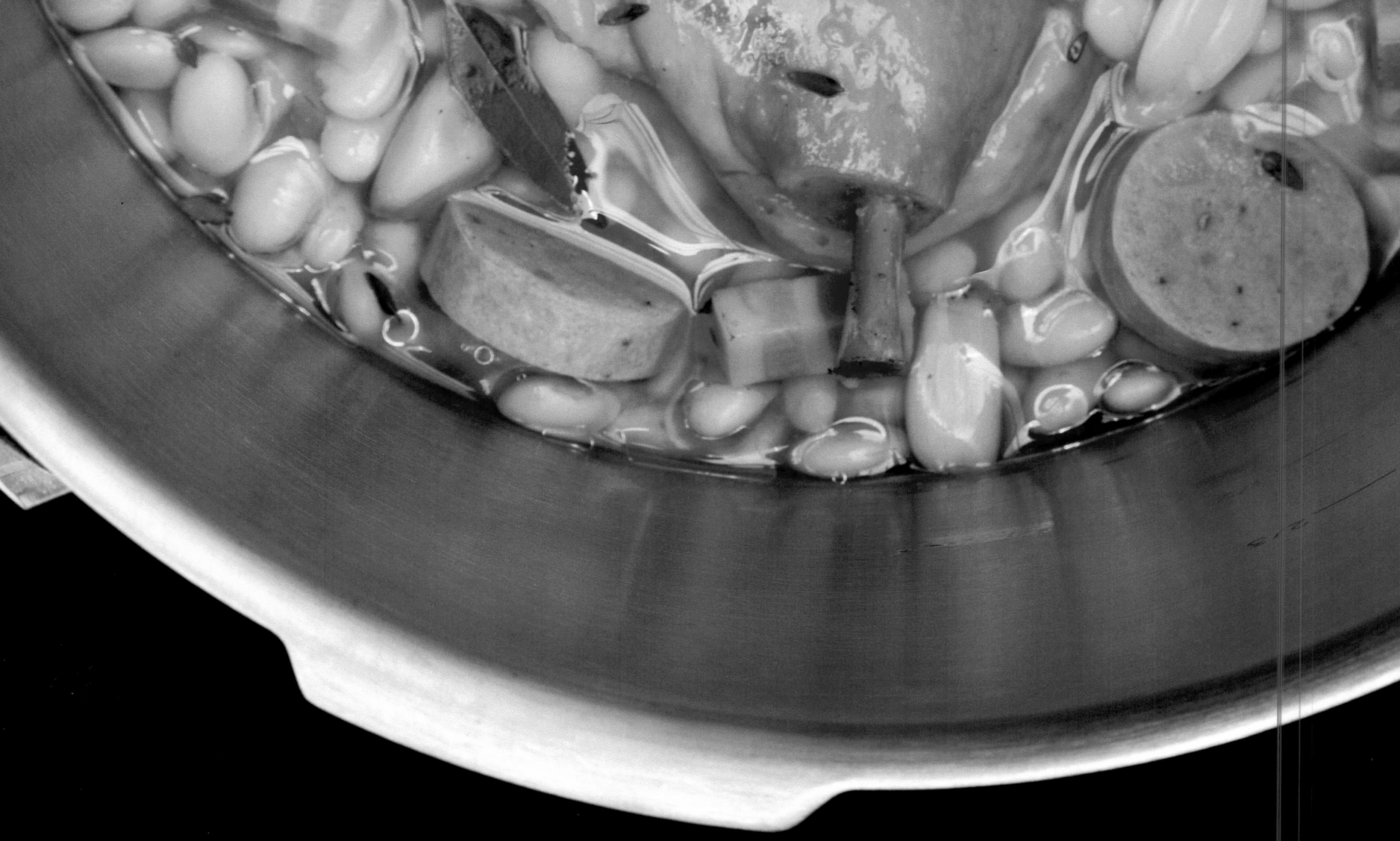

Pressure-cooking isn't how Escoffier made stock early in the last century, but we're sure it is how he would do it now.

PRESSURE COOKERS

Pressure cookers are fantastic tools. They develop the characteristic flavors and textures of foods so quickly that what is conventionally a long, labor-intensive process becomes one hardly more time-consuming than a casual sauté. Risotto takes seven minutes instead of 25 (for a recipe, see page 328). An intense chicken stock takes 90 minutes instead of two or three hours (see page 84). You can even pressure-cook food in canning jars or in oven bags or FoodSaver bags rated for high temperatures (see page 53)—which means grits and polenta, for example, no longer require constant stirring to avoid sticking (see page 336). The high temperatures inside the cooker also promote browning and caramelization, reactions that create flavors you can't get otherwise in a moist cooking environment. If you're not a believer yet, try the Caramelized Carrot Soup recipe on page 178.

A pressure cooker is essentially just a pot with a semi-sealed, lockable lid and a valve that controls the pressure inside. It works by capturing steam that, as it builds up, increases the pressure in the vessel. The pressure increase in turn raises the boiling point of water, which normally limits the cooking temperature of wet foods to 100 °C / 212 °F (at sea level; the boiling point is slightly lower at higher elevations). Because the effective cooking temperature is higher in the pressure cooker—as high as 120 °C / 250 °F—the cooking time can drop substantially.

Fast, even, energy-efficient cooking is all very nice, but it's the higher quality of the food that really clinches the deal. Wonderful culinary aromas wafting through the kitchen while you cook may warm the heart, but those are some of the most crucial components of the flavor of the food, and they are now forever lost to the air. The sealed environment of the pressure cooker locks in more of these volatile aromatic compounds. They condense onto the lid and drip back into the pot, so more of the nuances of the food are there when you put fork to mouth.

Too many people shy away from pressure cookers because they are skittish about safety. Rest easy: today's devices are designed and manufactured with safety as the primary concern. We recommend pressure cookers with built-in spring-loaded pressure valves such as those made by Kuhn Rikon or Fagor, or jiggling-weight pressure cookers. An electric pressure cooker is even simpler—you set the time, and it does the rest. The older pressure cookers and pressure canners will also work, although they are a bit noisy and tend to lose steam and aroma.

Consumer-grade pressure cookers range in size from 4–10 L / 4–10 qt. Look for a stainless-steel cooker having a three-ply base (aluminum sandwiched by stainless steel), which helps avoid hot spots. Also make sure the cooker indicates when it has reached a gauge pressure of 1 bar / 15 psi, as commonly used in recipes.

2

A BUYER'S GUIDE TO PRESSURE COOKERS

The indicator shows two red lines when 1 bar / 15 psi of gauge pressure has been reached.

Spring-Valve Pressure Cooker

Pressure cookers that have spring-loaded valves are the best choice for stock- and sauce-making because the valve seals the cooker before it is vented. This feature traps most aromatic volatiles before they can escape in the vented air. Fagor brand cookers do release some steam when needed to regulate the pressure, but they lose fewer volatile aromas than open pots do.
Where to buy: kitchen-supply stores
Cost: about $80 for Fagor; about $200 for Kuhn Rikon

Electric Pressure Cooker

An electric pressure cooker could hardly be easier to use: just plug it in, press the "high pressure" button, and set the digital timer. The downsides are that you have to make room for another single-use appliance, and you can't use it to finish up a dish on the stove top.
Where to buy: kitchen-supply stores, warehouse stores
Cost: $100–$135

Jiggling-Weight Pressure Cooker

This is the kind of pressure cooker that Grandma had: loud, spewing steam, with no easy way to tell when it reaches full pressure, and with few of the safety features of their modern counterparts. But when used according to their manufacturers' instructions, jiggling-weight pressure cookers are safe and do the job.
Where to buy: kitchen-supply stores, garage sales
Cost: $35–$50

Pressure Canner

These more robust cousins of pressure cookers are intended for canning. They also work for cooking, although multiple locks on the lid make them less convenient, and they are often made of thin aluminum, so any food touching the bottom burns easily. You may be used to venting the cooker before canning, but doing so before cooking releases beneficial aromas, so avoid that temptation. Pressure canners often include jiggling-weight valves so that it will be obvious if the valve fails.
Where to buy: kitchen-supply stores
Cost: $80–$200

COOKING UNDER PRESSURE

Why does a pressure cooker work so well? Because it gets so hot inside—about 121 °C / 250 °F when the pressure gauge shows 1 bar / 15 psi. Whether you're cooking a stock, braising a stew, or fixing a pot of beans, the temperature of these water-laden foods ordinarily won't exceed the boiling point of water, 100 °C / 212 °F, until they dry out—which you usually want to avoid. But that just isn't hot enough to get some of the crucial flavor-forming reactions going quickly or to rapidly break down the cell walls of many plant foods. Raising the pressure gets around this roadblock.

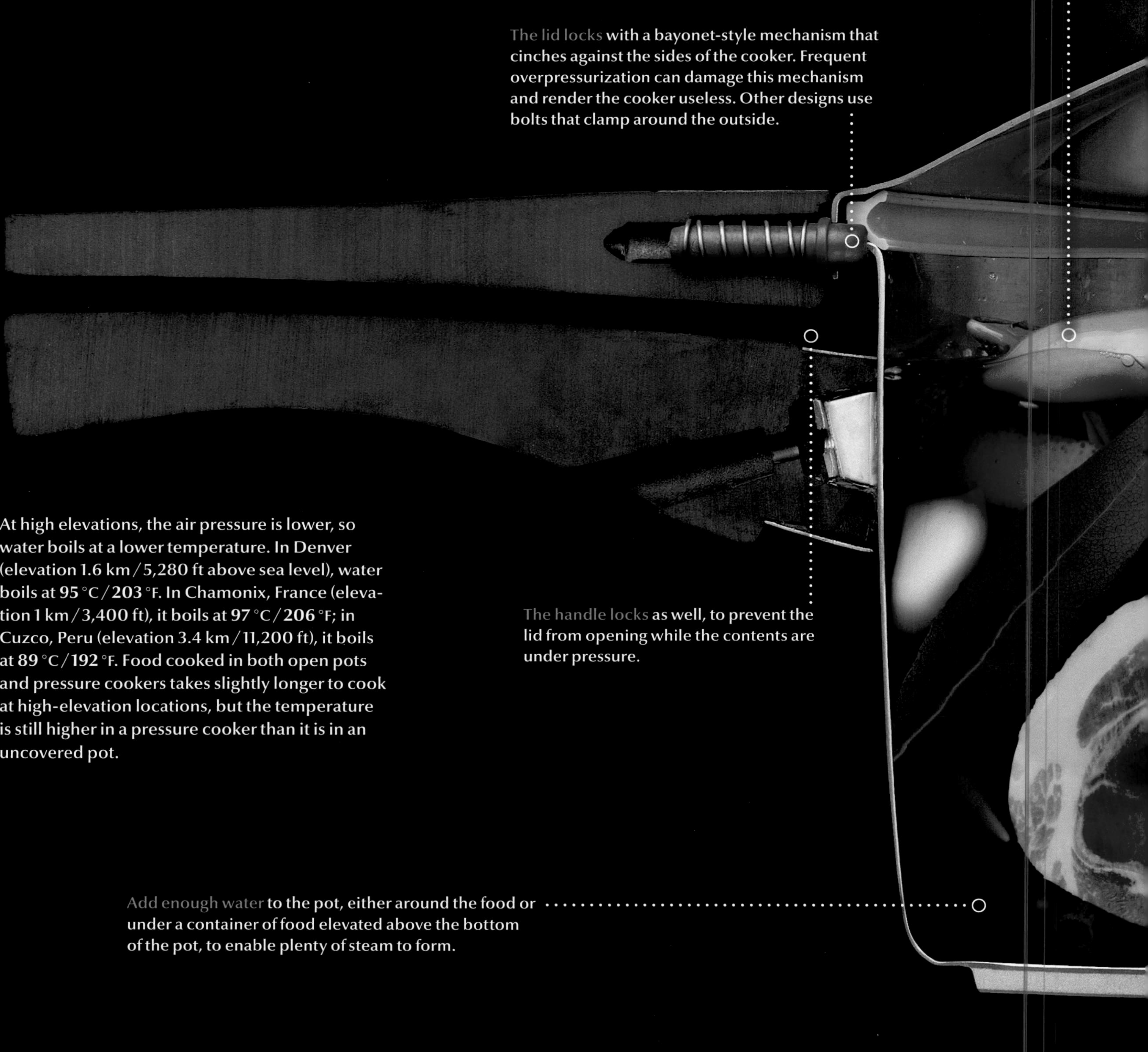

High-pressure steam rapidly transfer heat to the surface of any food not submerged in liquid.

The lid locks with a bayonet-style mechanism that cinches against the sides of the cooker. Frequent overpressurization can damage this mechanism and render the cooker useless. Other designs use bolts that clamp around the outside.

At high elevations, the air pressure is lower, so water boils at a lower temperature. In Denver (elevation 1.6 km / 5,280 ft above sea level), water boils at **95** °C / **203** °F. In Chamonix, France (elevation 1 km / 3,400 ft), it boils at **97** °C / **206** °F; in Cuzco, Peru (elevation 3.4 km / 11,200 ft), it boils at **89** °C / **192** °F. Food cooked in both open pots and pressure cookers takes slightly longer to cook at high-elevation locations, but the temperature is still higher in a pressure cooker than it is in an uncovered pot.

The handle locks as well, to prevent the lid from opening while the contents are under pressure.

Add enough water to the pot, either around the food or under a container of food elevated above the bottom of the pot, to enable plenty of steam to form.

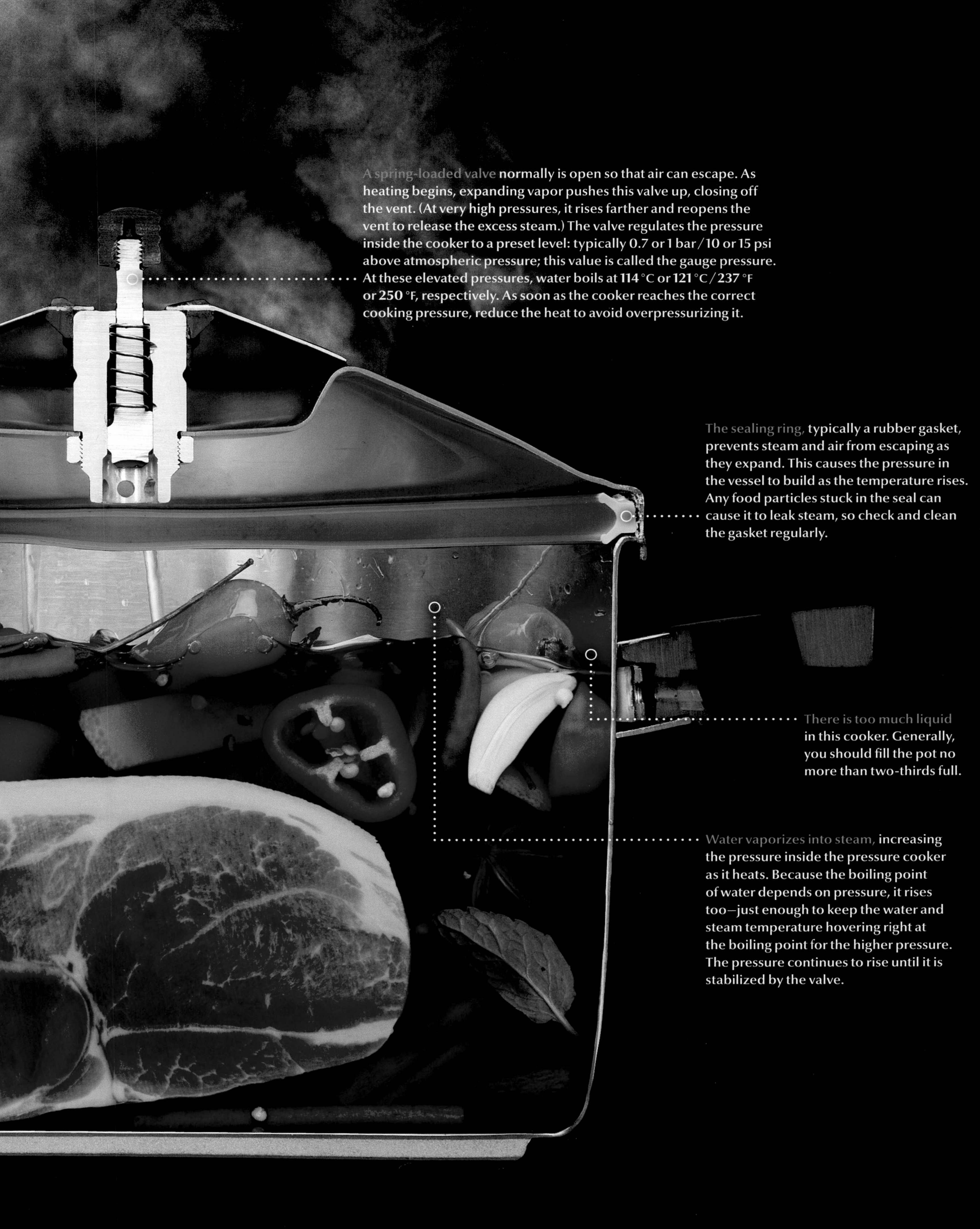
A spring-loaded valve normally is open so that air can escape. As heating begins, expanding vapor pushes this valve up, closing off the vent. (At very high pressures, it rises farther and reopens the vent to release the excess steam.) The valve regulates the pressure inside the cooker to a preset level: typically 0.7 or 1 bar / 10 or 15 psi above atmospheric pressure; this value is called the gauge pressure. At these elevated pressures, water boils at 114 °C or 121 °C / 237 °F or 250 °F, respectively. As soon as the cooker reaches the correct cooking pressure, reduce the heat to avoid overpressurizing it.
The sealing ring, typically a rubber gasket, prevents steam and air from escaping as they expand. This causes the pressure in the vessel to build as the temperature rises. Any food particles stuck in the seal can cause it to leak steam, so check and clean the gasket regularly.
There is too much liquid in this cooker. Generally, you should fill the pot no more than two-thirds full.
Water vaporizes into steam, increasing the pressure inside the pressure cooker as it heats. Because the boiling point of water depends on pressure, it rises too—just enough to keep the water and steam temperature hovering right at the boiling point for the higher pressure. The pressure continues to rise until it is stabilized by the valve.

HOW TO Use a Pressure Cooker

Cooks who are new to pressure-cooking often use too much heat and overpressurize the cooker. It's important to realize that overpressurizing the cooker doesn't make the temperature inside it any higher—it merely causes the safety valve to release steam, which allows the water inside to resume boiling. Repeated overpressurization can ruin both the flanges and the seal around the lid. Familiarize yourself with the manufacturer's instructions for understanding when your cooker is fully pressurized, overpressurized, and depressurized.

1 Prepare the ingredients. If you will be browning onions or other aromatics before pressure-cooking them, save a pan by sautéing the food directly in the base of the pressure cooker before covering it with the lid.

2 Add all of the ingredients, stir, and lock the lid. Stirring to evenly distribute the liquid or fat is important to keep bits from burning on the bottom of the cooker. Once you lock the lid, you won't be able to stir again.

Most spring-loaded pressure valves are ringed with two lines or colors to indicate low pressure and high pressure. We always cook at gauge pressure of 1 bar / 15 psi.

3 Warm the cooker on the stove top over medium-high heat. Watch or listen for the cues that the cooker has reached full pressure, and then turn the heat down to low. Adjust the heat as needed to keep the cooker fully pressurized.

4 Start timing the cooking as soon as the cooker reaches the target gauge pressure given in the recipe. If your cooker has a spring-loaded pressure valve, the valve should pop up just to the line, not beyond it. The cooker should not hiss loudly. If you have a jiggling-weight pressure valve, the weight should move three to five times a minute; it shouldn't dance around wildly.

A jet of steam or fog from an overextended pressure valve means that the pressure cooker is overpressurized, and for safety's sake the valve is relieving the excess pressure. Overpressurizing can bend the flanges that hold the lid tightly on the pot; they won't seal properly, and the pressure cooker will then be useless.

5 After cooking, remove the pressure cooker from the heat, and let it cool. You can simply let the cooker sit for several minutes to cool down if the food can tolerate some additional cooking (as stocks can, for example). For foods that are more time-sensitive, such as risottos, run lukewarm water over the rim of the lid to depressurize the cooker quickly. (Don't let water run into the pressure valve.) Some cookers have a manual quick-release knob or dial; be sure to read the manufacturer's instructions on how to use this feature safely. Never attempt to open a pressurized cooker. Not only will it spray hot liquid, but you'll also lose a lot of the flavorful vapors.

6 Set the cooker in the kitchen sink, and unlock the lid. If the lid is difficult to open, don't force it; let the cooker cool longer until it opens with little resistance.

7 If the food isn't done, simply finish it on the stove top without sealing the lid. Alternatively, return the pressure cooker to full pressure, and continue cooking.

SAFETY TIPS FOR PRESSURE-COOKING

Read and follow the safety instructions in the manual that came with the cooker.

Releasing a pressure cooker lid while its contents are still hot can splatter boiling water or food all over the kitchen—or you. Before opening the cooker, use the pressure-release button, let the cooker sit, or cool the pot under running water. The pressure valve will sink down fully when the cooker is depressurized and is safe to open.

Before cooking, check that the ring of rubber lining around the lid isn't dried out or cracked. These gaskets don't last forever; replace them as recommended by the manufacturer.

Make sure the rim of the pot and the gasket are clean; any food particles stuck there could break the seal.

Don't fill the cooker more than two-thirds full. For beans and grains, which tend to swell as they cook, fill the cooker only half full.

Avoid cooking foods that froth, like oatmeal and pasta. The foam can block the steam valves and pressure-release vents.

Tip the opening away from you as you lift the lid off the cooker to protect yourself from the steam that is released.

Use canning tongs to remove hot canning jars from the cooker, and let the contents cool slightly before opening the jars.

Pressure-Cooking in Canning Jars

Several recipes in this book take advantage of cooking in canning jars (also known as Mason jars). We use them for ingredients that would otherwise need an intensive amount of stirring, such as polenta, and for making small batches of rendered fat, garlic confit, or extracted juices. Always leave at least 1.3 cm / ½ in of headspace when filling the jars. The jars should also never touch the bottom of the cooker. Set them on a metal rack or trivet—or, in a pinch, on crumpled sheets of aluminum foil. Add enough water to cover the rack so that the pressure cooker can build up steam. After fully tightening the lids of the jars, loosen them a quarter turn; otherwise, the pressure may crack the jars or blow their lids off inside the cooker. After using a jar for pressure-cooking, inspect the glass for cracks before cooking with it again.

CONVENTIONAL OVENS

When you dial a temperature into your oven, it matches that thermostat setting by monitoring a dry thermometer, which senses the "dry-bulb temperature." The real baking temperature of your food is the "wet-bulb temperature"—what a thermometer would read if it could sweat. That wet-bulb temperature starts out low, and it rises dramatically as relative humidity increases. Yet there's no way to control it on a conventional oven.

Anyone who has ever overcooked (or undercooked) anything in an oven knows that baking is capricious. It can take years of experience to fully master the idiosyncrasies and quirks of a home oven. Several common limitations of these appliances conspire to make it difficult to get even, consistent results.

First, most home ovens have only crude temperature controls. They tend to be poorly calibrated and often vary by 14 °C / 25 °F or more from their set points as the heat element switches on and off or from high to low. Their performance at very low temperatures—those most useful for Modernist recipes—is typically even less predictable and consistent.

Second, some parts of the oven are hotter than others. The door, especially if it has a glass window, emits the least radiant heat of all the oven walls. The back corners of the oven tend to be quite a bit hotter than the average temperature. Even the cleanliness of the oven walls matters because dark spots emit more radiant heat than light spots do.

The third and biggest problem with ovens is that they don't take humidity into account, so they give you no control over the *real* baking temperature of your food. Compare a hot steam room to a dry sauna at the same air temperature, and you'll immediately see why humidity matters. The steam room feels much hotter to your skin because your sweat barely evaporates when the air already contains so much water vapor (enough that the room actually fogs up). When water (or sweat) evaporates, it absorbs a very large amount of heat energy from the surface it is leaving; that's why it cools your skin. And that's why you can stay in a hot but dry sauna longer than you can in a steam room at the same temperature.

Food "sweats," too, after a fashion; as the oven heats up, the food loses moisture to the air through evaporation. Until the outside of the food dries or the humidity of the air in the oven rises, evaporation from the surface of the food keeps it cooler than the air around it. But the degree and duration of that effect depend on the size of the food, its water content, the weather, and other factors. Humidity inside a conventional oven, unfortunately, is largely under the control of the food, not the cook. It depends on how full the oven is. A small test batch may bake very differently than a full oven-load of the same food.

Newer kinds of ovens, known as combi ovens and water-vapor ovens, do offer some control over humidity. Like sous vide water baths, they produce much more consistent results than traditional ovens do. This extra control commands a premium price, but more affordable options appear every year.

A convection oven, such as this Viking model, uses a powerful fan to circulate the air. Evenly heated air can transfer heat more rapidly, but it doesn't address inconsistencies in radiant heat that lead to inconsistent baking. The conventional wisdom—that a forced-convection oven "cooks 25% faster" or "10 degrees hotter" than a conventional oven—is oversimplified. Convection makes a bigger difference when heating thinner foods than it does thicker foods, but there is no simple rule that applies in all cases.

HOW TO Calibrate Your Oven

Each oven has its own personality. The one in your home is no exception. You don't necessarily understand why it does what it does. You have only a vague idea what the temperature in your oven actually is. But by trial and error you have figured out what you have to do to achieve the result you're trying to achieve. Wouldn't it be nice to add some predictability to the situation? We have a remedy for this relationship: calibrate your oven.

To do that, you need a good digital thermometer that includes an oven-safe probe and wire lead, as well as some patience. If you have graph paper or a spreadsheet program, you can make a quick chart to get a handle on how the temperature in your oven fluctuates as heat leaks out the door and the thermostat turns the burner up and down. You can also map the hot and cold spots inside.

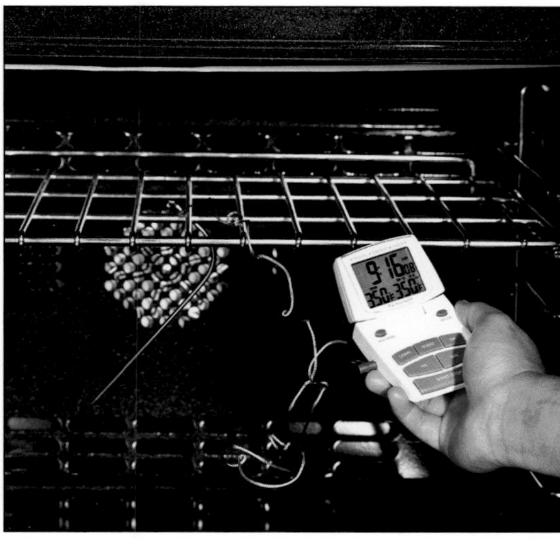

1 Preheat the oven. Then clip the probe of a digital oven thermometer (see page 8) to the rack. The end of the probe should hang in the air and point toward the center of the oven. Close the oven door, and wait a few minutes for the temperature to recover. Write down both the temperature you set and the true temperature shown on the thermometer.

2 Move the probe to various spots in your oven, if you're curious. Oven walls always radiate heat unevenly. The walls are thicker or darker in some spots than in others, and some parts of the wall are closer to the burners or heating elements than others. So the temperature can fluctuate by tens of degrees from one spot to another. Be sure to give the oven time to recover its temperature after you close the door.

3 Repeat these measurements at various temperature settings—say, every 50 degrees. The thermostat is often much less accurate at the low end of the scale than it is at higher temperatures. You might also record how long it takes your oven to preheat from room temperature to various set points; you can then more accurately estimate the total time that baking recipes will require.

TIPS FOR

Better Baking

Given the many factors that influence baking, it seems a small wonder that any cook ever achieves consistent results. Here are a few simple suggestions to minimize the variability of your oven.

Measure the performance of your oven. At a minimum, use a reliable thermometer and the step-by-step procedure above to check the temperature of the oven in the center, where the food will bake.

Preheat the oven. Preheating takes longer than most people would like because the goal is to heat the walls of the oven, not the air. But once the oven is preheated, it holds a large reservoir of heat energy, so it can quickly restore the temperature after you open the door to insert or check on the food.

Pay attention to browned spots. Move the food around and rotate it as often as necessary to keep hot spots of radiant heat from scorching some parts of the food while other parts undercook.

Look into modern ovens. New models of combi ovens that can control both the dry-bulb and wet-bulb temperatures are starting to appear at prices that home cooks can afford. For details, see Combi Ovens, page 38.

THE HOUSEHOLD STOVE

The cooking appliance at the center of most home kitchens—functionally, and often physically as well—is the conventional oven and range. The basic design has not changed in generations. But modern, professional-style stoves like the gas unit shown here (generously provided by the Viking company for us to cut in half) have refined the details in ways that both improve energy efficiency and make it easier to get consistent results.

The stove is a marriage of convenience of two distinct appliances: a range of burners above that push heat into food mainly by direct contact (conduction), and a vented oven below that heats food indirectly by a combination of hot, relatively dry air (convection) and infrared energy (radiation). Except for a few details, gas and electric stoves are very similar in construction and operation.

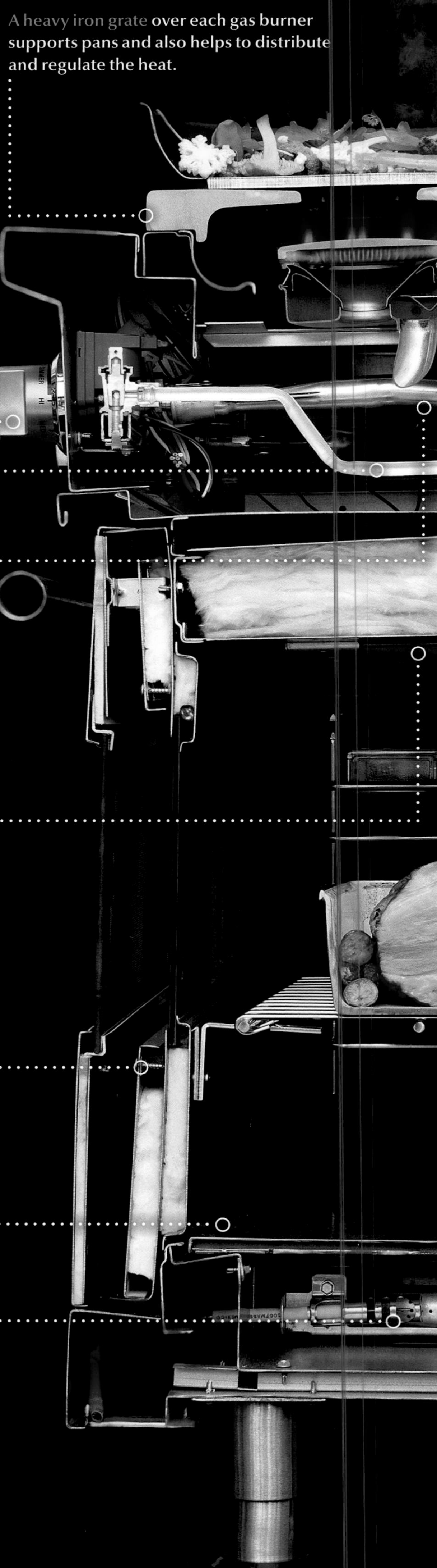

A heavy iron grate over each gas burner supports pans and also helps to distribute and regulate the heat.

Gas for the oven and broiler travels through this small pipe.

The controls for the burners and the oven are both mechanical and electronic on a gas oven. When you turn on a burner, the control sends electric current to make a spark, and at the same time it adjusts a screw valve to regulate the flow of gas and thus the power of the burner. The operation of the oven is controlled electronically in response to the internal temperature sensor and the setting on the control dial. When you turn the oven off, the flow of gas to the heating element is completely shut off for safety.

Gas for each burner is supplied through one of these large pipes. The gas is mixed with air at the beginning of the pipe to ensure complete combustion.

The broiler unit in this oven is a screen that diffuses burning gas across a wide area of the oven ceiling for even cooking. It is similar in design to an outdoor propane heater. In an electric oven, the broiler element is made of resistive wire inside a metal tube that glows red hot as current passes through it.

The oven door contains multiple layers of glass and overlapping panels of insulation to prevent as much heat loss as possible. But the seal is never perfect, so the front of the oven is always cooler than the back—not only due to heat loss but also because the oven window does not absorb and reradiate heat as efficiently as the metal walls do.

The coolest parts of the oven are the bottom corners next to the door.

The main heating element of the oven is at the bottom. As with the burners on the range, a spark of electricity gets the flame going. In gas ovens, the oven burner sits beneath a protective shield that diffuses the heat of the flame evenly, much as the artificial rocks or metal plates of a gas grill do. In electric ovens, the oven element often sits directly on the oven floor.

An electric spark ignites the flow of gas when you turn the burner on the flow of gas.

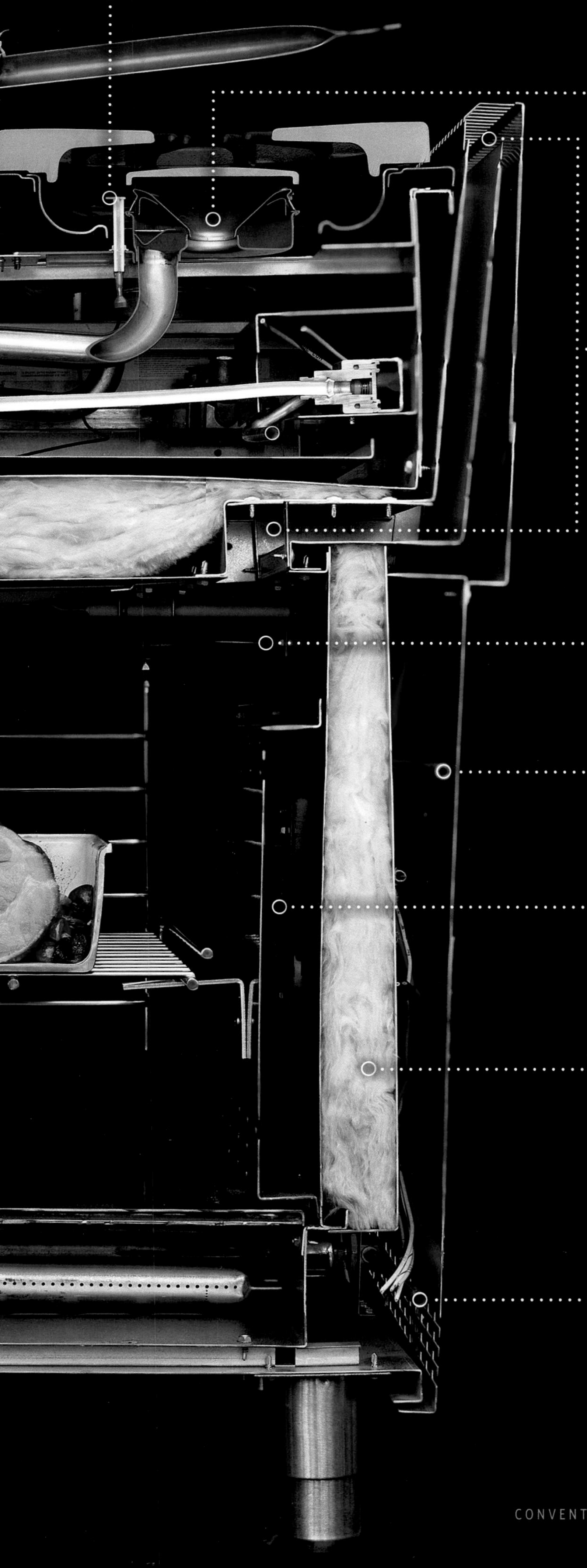

The burners on this professional-style range are more powerful than those on a typical home stove top. This model sends 15,000 BTU per hour / 4.4 kW to each burner, throwing off nearly as much power as the burners on restaurant ranges do (20,000–40,000 BTU per hour). Typical home ranges have much weaker burners that draw 5,000–7,000 BTU an hour.

Exhaust leaves the oven through this duct to a vent behind the range. On all stoves, this vent provides an outlet for steam and smoke that otherwise would build up inside the oven. On gas stoves, this vent also exhausts combusted gas. It's best to also run an external exhaust fan when cooking, especially if using gas, which produces carbon monoxide when it burns.

The temperature sensor is usually located in the hottest part of the oven: at the back, near the top. The opposite corners, at the bottom by the door, are where the oven is the coolest.

Broiler gas is supplied through this small pipe.

A convection fan, increasingly common on home ovens, circulates the hot air inside. That improves the consistency of cooking by making the temperature throughout the oven more even. It also increases cooking efficiency by accelerating heat transfer from the air to the food.

Oven insulation is thickest at the top to retain as much heat as possible. The sides of the oven are also well insulated so that they radiate much of the heat that they absorb inward toward the food, rather than outward to the room. The bottom of a gas oven requires less insulation because the heat rises from the flames.

Oven gas is supplied through this small pipe.

COMBI OVENS

The combi oven is the most versatile kitchen tool we know. It can do just about anything a conventional oven, convection oven, steamer, or sous vide water bath can do: steaming, proofing, incubating, dehydrating, and baking.

Combi ovens can supply moisture directly, by injecting water in its vapor form—steam—into the oven chamber. A setting for humidity lets cooks set the wet-bulb temperature we mentioned on page 34 by controlling how much steam gets mixed in with hot, dry air. That ability makes combi ovens the ideal tool for steaming poultry, meats, and all manner of plant foods. Just set the oven to steam mode with humidity at 100%, and set the temperature anywhere from 30–100 °C / 85–212 °F.

In their convection mode, combi ovens can dehydrate, brown, and bake food with more precision than conventional tools offer. Set the humidity to 0% and the temperature to 30–90 °C / 85–195 °F to quickly dehydrate food without cooking it. For browning, increase the temperature to 175–225 °C / 350–440 °F. The higher the temperature, the faster the surface of the food desiccates and browns.

Combi ovens are not as adept as we'd like, however, at holding temperatures below 60 °C / 140 °F. We have used them to cook fish, which we most often prefer steamed to about 45 °C / 113 °F, and to prepare steaks, which we like rare to medium rare (50–55 °C / 122–131 °F). But the temperature in a combi oven varies by 2–5 °C / 4–9 °F at temperatures this low, whereas a water bath can hold low temperatures within 1–2 °C / 2–3 °F. As when using a water bath to cook sous vide (see page 60), the usual approach to combi oven cooking is to set the oven temperature 1 °C / 2 °F above the target core temperature you want the food to reach. Some combi ovens are self-cleaning, and certain models are programmable as well. You can, for example, program one of these ovens to first sear a roast, and then cook it for many hours at low temperature, and finally to hold it warm until serving time. The result easily matches or even exceeds the quality obtained by slow-cooking sous vide. Roast chicken comes out with extremely crispy skin and a succulent interior; fried eggs come out with both the yolk and white cooked perfectly.

For decades, combi ovens were available only as extremely expensive commercial appliances. But now manufacturers have started making versions for the home kitchen. Consumer-grade combi ovens differ from their professional counterparts in a few ways: they are less precise and powerful, and they have narrower temperature ranges, so they can't do high-temperature roasting or oven frying. But these modern ovens still vastly outperform conventional ovens in both accuracy and versatility. We predict that they will eventually become quite common as they become increasingly affordable.

Combi ovens were once only accessible to professional chefs, but manufacturers such as Electrolux, Gaggenau, and others now make home models that are a fraction of the size and cost.

Steaming

Best for: fish (40–55 °C / 105–131 °F); eggs such as steamed omelets, fried eggs, and custards (65–82 °C / 150–180 °F); vegetables (85–100 °C / 185–212 °F).
For egg recipes, see pages 146 and 152.

WAYS TO USE A COMBI OVEN

Combi ovens excel at a wider range of cooking techniques than any other appliance. But a water bath produces better results when cooking sous vide for long periods of time at temperatures below about 60 °C/140 °F.

Baking
Best for: breads, pizza; can inject steam as desired to keep dough moist until you want a crust to form

Roasting
Best for: meats, poultry, root vegetables

Two-Step Cooking
Best for: creating contrasting textures and cooking each component of a whole at its best temperature

Dehydrating
Best for: jerky, fruit and vegetable leathers (for a recipe, see page 129)

Cooking Sous Vide
Best for: cooking larger volumes of food than a water bath allows

MICROWAVE OVENS

The microwave oven was invented by Percy Spencer in 1945, when he was working as an engineer at Raytheon on a radar system. Spencer got the idea for the oven when he noticed that a chocolate bar in his pocket began to melt shortly after the radar was turned on.

Inexpensive microwave ovens achieve their power levels by turning the microwave generator on and off several times a second. A power level of 50% (or level five on a 10-level oven), for example, generates microwaves during only half of the cooking time. Newer microwave ovens use inverter technology to control the strength of the microwaves directly. In most cooking situations, it's hard to detect a difference between the two kinds of power control.

The microwave has a poor reputation as a second-class appliance not appropriate for "real" cooking. That criticism is undeserved: microwave ovens do an excellent job for many cooking tasks. Black cod turns out beautifully, for example, as does steamed bok choy. If you seal vegetables with a little liquid in a plastic bag or in a container covered by taut plastic wrap, the microwave creates enough steam to counteract its tendency to cook unevenly. And, perhaps surprisingly, microwave ovens are the best tools we know for making beef jerky or fried herbs for garnishes.

The secret to successful microwaving is the Goldilocks principle: choose food that is not too small and not too big. Because of the physics of microwaves (see page 42), they heat small objects less quickly than larger ones—just the opposite of what happens in a conventional oven. The microwaves deposit energy a couple of centimeters deep into the food, not just at the surface. So volume matters more than surface area, at least up to a point. In fact, pieces of food that are much smaller than the 12 cm / 5 in wavelength of microwave radiation may sit on the turntable for quite a while, all but unaffected by the rays bouncing everywhere around them.

Put a single kernel of popcorn in a microwave oven set on high, for example, and it may take minutes to pop. But when a bagful of kernels are all crowded together into one mass, the microwave heats up that larger target rapidly, and the first kernels pop in less than a minute. This phenomenon explains, incidentally, why the last few kernels in the bag are so recalcitrant to pop—they are small and isolated, so they absorb the energy slowly.

Like conventional ovens, each microwave oven has its own idiosyncrasies. Through experimentation, you can determine the best cooking settings for various dishes.

Hybrid devices incorporate a broiler element for browning; some include a convection oven as well. Whichever type of microwave oven you have, experiment with its many applications.

Popcorn was one of the first foods cooked in a microwave oven and remains one of the most popular.

WAYS TO USE A MICROWAVE OVEN

There's more to microwaving than just making popcorn and reheating leftovers. Chapter 22 on Dishes for the Microwave (see page 342) presents a variety of recipes that illustrate the strengths of this tool.

Cooking

High power best for: steaming vegetables (see Sichuan Bok Choy, page 346, and Microwaved Eggplant Parmesan, page 344); quickly softening dense vegetables that are high in water content, such as artichokes, potatoes, and onions
Low and moderate power best for: seafood (see Microwaved Black Cod with Scallions and Ginger, page 348); tender meats

Defrosting or Melting

Low power best for: thawing frozen food; melting butter and other fat-rich foods, such as chocolate

Dehydrating

Moderate power best for: drying fruit and vegetable leathers; making jerky (see Microwaved Beef Jerky, page 350, and Crispy Beef Strands, page 352)

Frying

Moderate power best for: crisping herbs (see Microwave-Fried Parsley, page 354) and tender greens, such as carrot tops

Warming

Low and moderate power best for: reheating previously cooked foods to serving temperature

Puffing

High power best for: puffing snacks, such as tapioca puffs or Indian *papadum*; puffing grains, such as barley or popcorn

MAKING WAVES

The microwave oven is an offshoot of military radar technology that British engineers developed during the Second World War to detect enemy planes and ships. The device uses a magnetron to produce electromagnetic waves at around 2.45 gigahertz, a frequency that causes water and oil molecules to vibrate and heat up. It works best on thin foods that are neither too small nor too large. Put the food in the center of the oven, and master the power level button. You might be surprised by the excellent dishes it can turn out: see chapter 22 on page 342 for examples.

A fan "stirs" the microwaves, bouncing them around to better distribute them. Without it, the waves would travel in a single beam, blazing a hot trail straight through any food in their way and leaving the surrounding food raw.

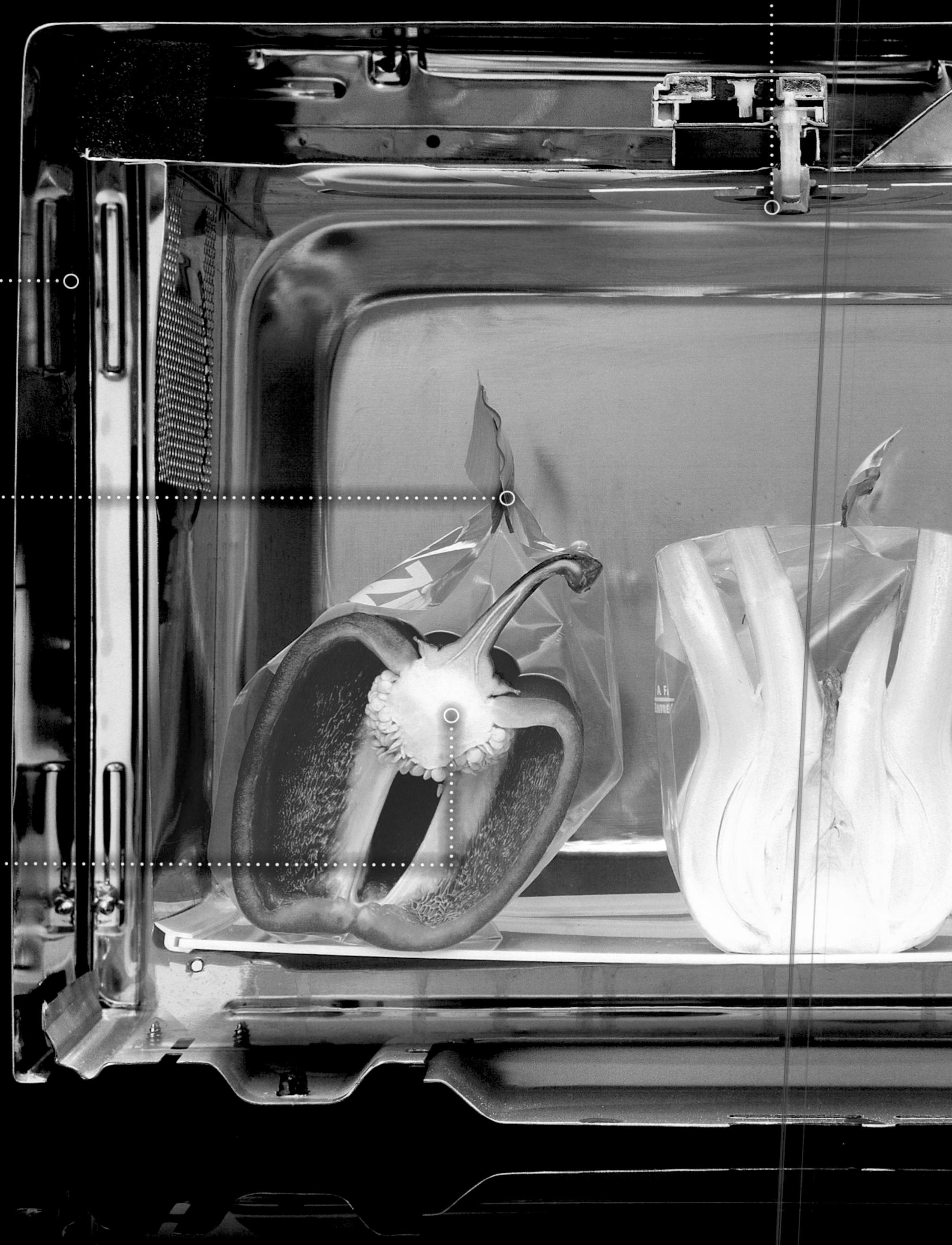

Radiation isn't reaching you. The glass door has a perforated metal shield that allows you to see inside but prevents microwaves from leaving the oven.

Dishes and containers can stay cool because microwaves heat mainly water and oil. So when you microwave vegetables in plastic bags, the water-laden food heats up, but the dry plastic doesn't. If you use a ceramic dish containing metal, however, it will get hot—perhaps hot enough to break. Use microwave-safe browning dishes instead.

Microwaves penetrate only a couple of centimeters into food. That's why frozen food becomes piping hot in some places while remaining frozen in others. As cooking progresses, diffusion of heat within the food helps to even out such temperature differences. When food is sealed, however, steam accumulates in the bag and cooks the food evenly and efficiently. As with popcorn, steam emerges when you open the bag, so take care.

Larger foods absorb microwaves best. Small items may hardly cook at all. The microwaves themselves have a wavelength of 122 mm / 4.8 in.

The secret trick to successful microwaving: use the power level button. If you're used to "nuked" leftovers, oatmeal that overflows with a moment's inattention, splattered soups, and liquefied butter, experiment with lowering the power.

The magnetron generates the microwaves used to cook the food.

Thick items won't cook quickly. Whole chickens, roasts, and other very thick items won't heat any faster than they would in a conventional oven or on a stove top. For the heat to reach the center of the food, it must move by the slow process of thermal conduction.

You can crisp food in a microwave oven with little fear of burning it. Dry foods that are naturally high in fat will brown because fat will not evaporate the way water does, so it keeps on heating the food after the water is gone. In some cases, you can brown food in a microwave by first rubbing oil on its surface.

GRILLS

As old as humanity itself, grilling was the cooking technique that set our primate ancestors on the evolutionary path to becoming civilized humans. The ability to control fire distinguished *Homo erectus* from other animals and allowed the most basic level of nutritional and culinary refinement. Little wonder, then, that our craving for the flavor of food charred over an open flame is practically universal.

The secret to the flavor of grilled food is the dribbles of juice, laden with natural sugars, proteins, and oils, that fall onto the hot coals and burst into smoke and flame. By catalyzing myriad chemical reactions, the intense heat forges these charred juices into molecules that convey the aromas of grilling food. These new molecules literally go up in smoke, coating the food with the unmistakable flavor of grilled food. This is the reason that meats have a pronounced grilled flavor, and vegetables, devoid of natural fat, don't.

As much as people love grilling, grills are hard to control. Hot coals cool slowly, so you must adjust the draft well before you want the temperature to drop. The imprecise temperatures and uneven heat distribution make it difficult to grill food to the right level of doneness. The approach we prefer is to cook our food sous vide or by some other method that is easy to control, and to then use the grill only for a final searing that imparts a great flavor and crust.

We have an unusual way of creating the intense heat that we want for a 30-second sear. Watch a master griller stoke a fire, and you'll see him rake coals around or perhaps adjust a vent under the grill. Rarely will you see him add more coals. Instead, he's making the fire hotter by increasing the amount of oxygen. We accomplish the same goal by aiming a hair dryer or fan at our coals.

A hair dryer can help get the fire going, too. Regardless of how you start the fire—kindling, a little chimney, a blowtorch—the coals are not ready for grilling until they are uniformly covered by gray ash. The entire surface of the coals should be burning, and once the corners are hot, the added airflow of a blower will cause the rest of the coals to burn much more quickly.

Now you're grilling with gas

Gas grills are a great substitute for charcoal grills. They tend to heat more evenly. You get the same grilled flavor because drips of fat still hit a hot surface (typically artificial rocks or metal plates) and flare up in puffs of flavorful smoke. Gas grills offer more control over the intensity of heat than coals do—but because we use the grill only for fast searing, our grill is always turned to high.

WHICH IS BETTER

Briquettes or Hardwood?

Two distinct groups of people swear by charcoal grills: briquette devotees and those who favor hardwood or lump charcoal. Advocates of briquettes cite their ease of use and consistent, steady heat. Grilling purists, on the other hand, point out that honest-to-goodness chunks of hardwood charcoal burn hotter, faster, and cleaner. These are all fair points.

Some evangelists for hardwood fuels also claim that charcoal made from mesquite, or other fragrant-burning woods, imparts flavor that is the secret to grilling nirvana.

But once the flames of ignition have died and the coals are glowing hot, neither briquettes nor hardwood charcoals have any flavor left to impart. Carbon is carbon. Any aromatic compounds the fuel once harbored were vaporized and destroyed long before the food was laid on the grill. The fact is that the conditions of combustion—how much air gets to the coals and how they are distributed—make a much larger difference than the source of the charcoal.

BAKING ON THE BARBECUE

If you're grilling large or thick foods, consider turning your grill into an oven. After a quick sear over the coals, shift the food to one side, push the coals to the other side, and cover the grill with a lid. This technique is called indirect grilling or banked grilling. But really it is not grilling at all—it's baking. Banking the coals prevents the intense heat of direct grilling from burning the surface of the food before the interior is fully cooked. Instead, the food bakes at a lower temperature.

A grill-turned-oven can't compete with a good gas or electric oven, let alone a combi oven or water bath. But this approach has its place when grilling is your only option. (But there is a tailgate version of the water bath, too: cooking in a cooler—see page 198. For recipes using such techniques, see pages 200–202).

Food cooked indirectly on a banked grill can lack that mouth-watering grilled flavor because drippings don't fall on the hot coals. To compensate, leave a few meat trimmings above the coals to drizzle juices onto the embers. The flavorful smoke then permeates the food baking on the other side of the grill. Alternatively, toss a few dry wood chips onto the coals to add a very slight smoke flavor to the food. (But note that the effect is a far cry from what you get by smoking meat in a smoker for hours.)

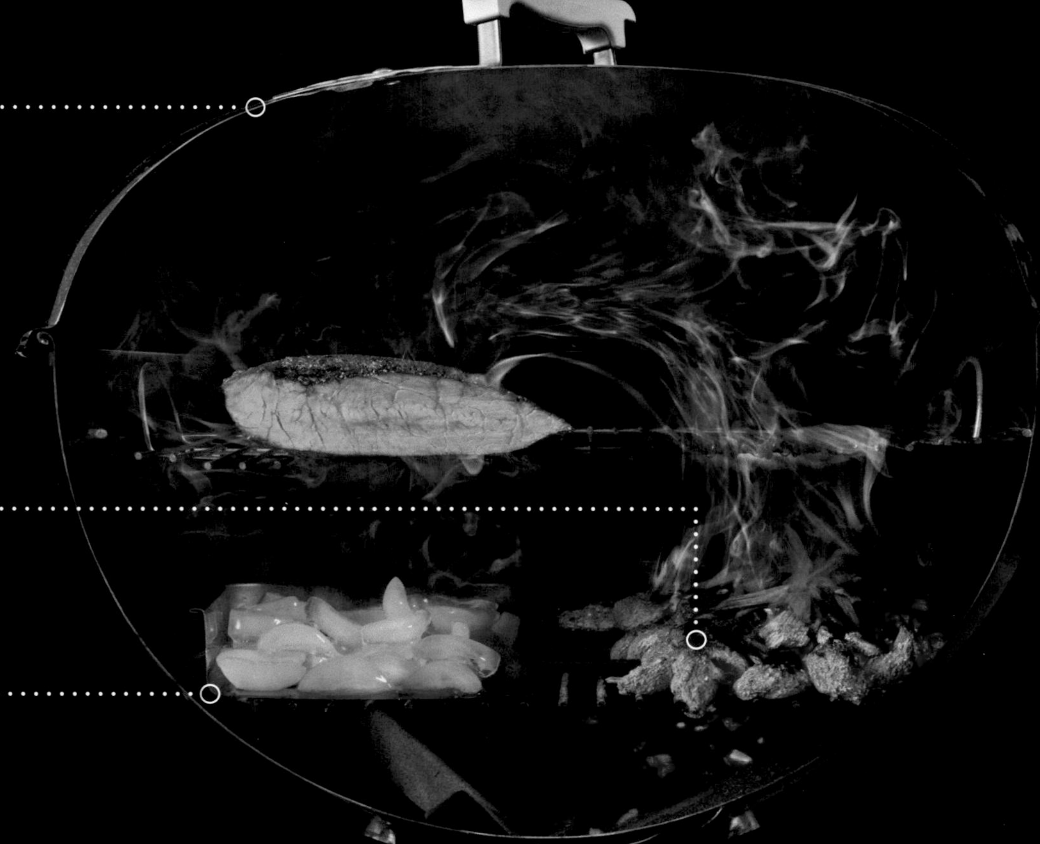

A tight-fitting lid traps hot air that bakes the food. The lid also cuts off the supply of fresh air, starves the fire, and thus lowers the cooking temperature.

Sear the food first, and set it on a bed of onions, aluminum foil, or some other buffer against the intense radiant heat of the coals. Place the food on the far side of the grill from the coals so that the heat doesn't burn the exterior before the interior cooks.

Bank the coals to one side. Use a small pile that is just larger than the food; you want low heat.

A tray of ice under the food humidifies the circulating hot air, which both accelerates heat transfer and slows the evaporation of juices from the food. The food both cooks faster and retains more of its succulence.

TIPS FOR

Grilling

Get that grilled flavor

Classic grilled foods—steaks, hamburgers, sausage, chicken—contain plenty of fat to drip onto the coals, which is what gives food a grilled flavor. Leaner meats, such as flank and skirt steak, and foods without fat, such as vegetables, benefit from being basted with rendered fat (see page 123); melted, clarified butter (see page 119); or neutral frying oil (see page xxii). We just squirt some onto the food or coals with a spray bottle. There's a fine line, however, between the flare-ups that impart grilled flavor and licking flames that burn your food. Flare-ups are short bursts of flame from drips of fat burning. If the flames rise so high that they touch the food, tamp down the pile of coals, close the vent, or remove some coals.

Keep food from sticking

Brush a thin layer of oil on the food, unless it has a ready source of fat that will be rendered by the heat, as do steaks, hamburgers, and sausages. Cure fish before grilling it by soaking it in a solution that's 3.5% salt (3.5 g of salt for every 100 g of fish), 2.5% sugar, and 0.2% lemon zest. Refrigerate the cured fish for 45 minutes, rinse it, and then grill it.

Cook more evenly

Reflective walls bounce the heat back toward the food, a trick that can extend the sweet spot of your grill to cover about 90% of the grill. It is unfortunate that many grills are painted black on the inside and are thus almost completely nonreflective. But the solution is easy: surround the periphery of the grill with a tall ring of reflective aluminum.

A squirt bottle filled with rendered fat, clarified butter, or neutral frying oil lets you baste the food on the grill from a safe distance. The sprayed fat droplets change when they hit the coals into aromatic smoke that intensifies the grilled flavor of the food.

Pat the food dry before you grill it so that the heat goes right into the food and not into the work of boiling surface moisture.

Searing cooks only the exterior of the food, so you'll need to cook the interior some other way. If you're cooking the food in a water bath or combi oven, sear it afterward so that the crust doesn't get soggy.

HOT AS HELL

We set out to create a grill so hot that it sears within seconds. The goal is to add a great crust to the surface of food that we have already fully cooked sous vide, while overcooking as little of the interior as possible. Our first thought was that more oxygen equals more heat. So what would happen if we set up a hair dryer or fan beneath the coals?

We experimented on a basic, kettle-style Weber grill. The technique should also work for most other grills, as long as they use charcoal or hardwood fires. In charcoal grills, the rate at which the fuel burns is limited by the flow of oxygen. Gas grills are already designed to allow the optimum amount of oxygen to mix with the gas. So you won't make a gas grill any hotter by blowing on it.

Aim the hair dryer up at the coals through the open vent on the bottom of the grill. Some of the ash will blow into the air at first, so allow the ash to settle, and clean the grill surface before you put the food on it. A fan works as well as a hair dryer.

A fanned fire is amazingly hot, so watch the food like a hawk. Watch yourself, too—a blower that is too strong can throw sparks or unburned coal.

COOKING SOUS VIDE

Years ago, when we first started cooking sous vide, it felt like a revelation. The taste and texture of the food was perfect—every time. The practical benefits, like being able to store and later reheat our creations without sacrificing any of their subtleties, were also huge. After cooking just a few dishes this way, we were hooked.

Cooking sous vide is easier than its fancy name might suggest. You simply seal the ingredients in a plastic bag (you can also use a canning jar), and then place them in a water bath, a combi oven, or any other cooker that can hit the target temperature you set and hold it there to within a degree or two. When the food reaches the target temperature or time, you take it out, give it a quick sear or other finish, and serve it. That's it.

The method yields results that are nearly impossible to achieve by traditional means. A venison tenderloin cooked sous vide at 52 °C / 126 °F has an unmatched juiciness and is perfectly cooked edge to edge without the ring of gray, overcooked meat you often get from conventional

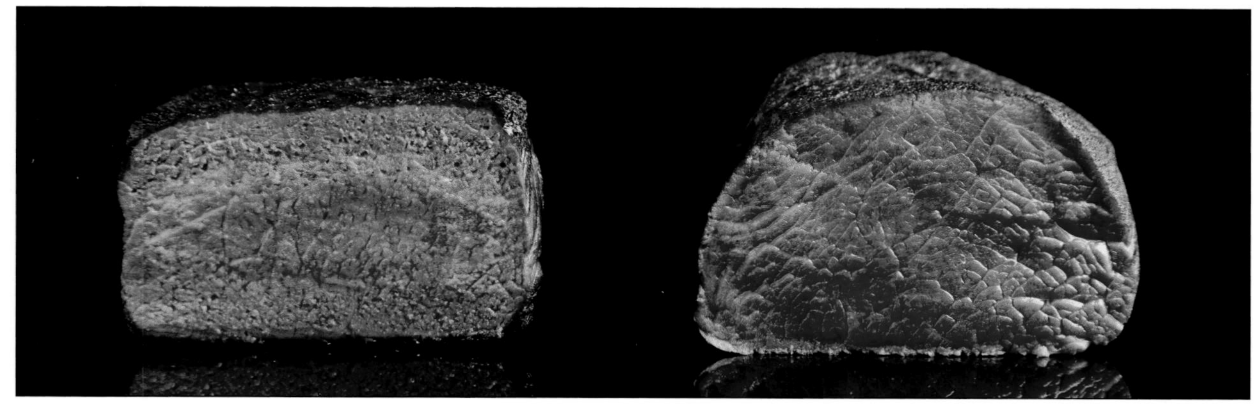

Both of these tenderloins started at the same weight. One steak (left) was cooked in a pan to a core temperature of 52 °C / 126 °F—but more than 40% of the meat was overcooked. The other steak was cooked sous vide to the same temperature, and then seared with a blowtorch to yield a juicier steak that is done to perfection from edge to edge.

methods. Beef short ribs braised at 58 °C / 136 °F for 72 hours are melt-in-your-mouth tender, yet pink and juicy. The delicate, custard-like texture of an egg poached at precisely 65 °C / 149 °F is amazing.

The idea of preserving and cooking food in sealed packages is ancient. Throughout culinary history, food has been wrapped in leaves, potted in fat, packed in salt, or sealed inside animal bladders before being cooked. People have long known that isolating food from air—accomplished more completely by vacuum sealing—can arrest the decay of food. Packaging food also prevents it from drying out.

Although *sous vide* literally means "under vacuum" in French, the defining feature of the sous vide method is not packaging or vacuum sealing; it is accurate temperature control. A computer-controlled heater can warm a water bath to any low temperature you set, and it can keep it there for hours—or even days, if needed. Combi ovens are not quite as accurate, but like water baths they bathe the food with uniform heat on every side.

Such mastery over the heat pays off in several important ways. It frees the cook from the tyranny of the clock, for example. Traditional cooking with a range, oven, or grill uses high and fluctuating temperatures, so you must time the cooking exactly; there is little margin for error. With just a moment's inattention, conventional cooking can quickly overshoot perfection.

When cooking sous vide, in contrast, most foods will taste just as good even if they spend a few extra minutes at the target temperature. So you can relax and devote your attention to the more interesting and creative aspects of cooking.

Precise control and uniformity of temperature has two other big advantages. First, it allows you to cook food to an even doneness all the way through—no more dry edges and rare centers. Second, you get highly repeatable results. The steak emerges from the bag just as juicy and pink every time.

A final important benefit is that the closed bag creates a fully humid environment that effectively braises the food, so ingredients cooked this way are often noticeably juicier and more tender. Food cooked sous vide doesn't brown, but a simple sear adds that traditional flavor where needed so that you can have the best of both worlds.

Cooking sous vide isn't complicated or expensive. In this chapter, we guide you through the various kinds of sous vide equipment and supplies available for home cooks. We also explain the basics of how to use them and how to chill, freeze, and reheat food you've cooked sous vide.

Getting started with cooking sous vide doesn't require a big investment in new gear. A good slow cooker, when connected to a digital temperature controller, does just fine for simple dishes, and costs less than $200. For other options, see pages 62–65.

FURTHER READING IN *MODERNIST CUISINE*

The history of sous vide at home: see page 1·73

FDA rules on cooking and storing food sous vide: see pages 1·182, 186, 189

Simplified standards for cooking sous vide: see page 1·193

How vacuum packing works: see page 2·212

A guide to chamber sealers: see pages 2·214–221

How to use rigid vacuum containers for storage: see page 2·226

Cooking in multiple water baths: see pages 2·248–249

Cooking fruits and vegetables sous vide: see pages 3·286–293

FOUR SIMPLE STEPS

The four basic steps in cooking sous vide are preparation, packaging, cooking, and finishing. Most of our recipes call for cooking to a specific core temperature, meaning you remove the food from the bath as soon as the temperature at the center of its thickest part hits the target value. If you set the temperature of the water bath or oven to just a degree or two higher than the target temperature, you won't have to worry about overcooking. This approach works well for tender red meats, poultry, fish and other seafood, and certain fruits and vegetables. Tough meats, however, often take time to tenderize. So our recipes for tougher foods typically indicate how long to hold the food at the target temperature.

Step 1: Preparation

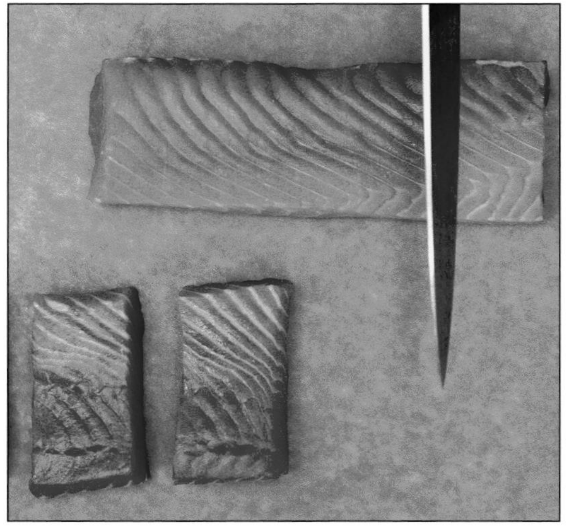

Cut individual portions so that they are equal in thickness.

Prepare and organize the ingredients for cooking sous vide much as you would for any other cooking technique. Usually, you want to cut the food into individual portions because smaller pieces take less time to cook. Make the portions as similar in thickness as possible so that when cooked together they are all done at the same time.

You can add flavors by seasoning, marinating, brining, or curing the food before cooking it. You can also change the color or firm the texture of certain ingredients by searing or blanching them before cooking.

Step 2: Packaging

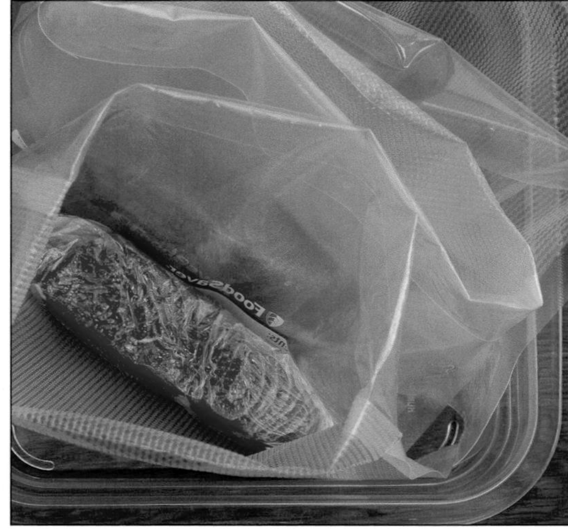

To vacuum seal the food, place portions in separate sous vide bags, optionally add oil, and seal. For details, see page 56.

Food is usually packaged before cooking it sous vide in a water bath (the most common method); if you just put the food directly in the water, some of the flavor and juices could wash away.

Restaurants and caterers who cook sous vide vacuum seal the food in special plastic bags. Vacuum-sealed bags are less likely to float, and they allow cooked food to keep longer in the refrigerator after cooking, which is handy for commercial operations that make many of their dishes in advance.

Home vacuum sealers are now widely available and easy to use (see page 54), but you don't need to vacuum pack food to cook it sous vide. Except when cooking for very long periods of time or when you want to store food after cooking it, zip-top bags work fine. Canning jars offer another convenient alternative in many situations.

If you use a combi oven rather than a water bath to cook sous vide, you don't need any package at all—just put the food in an open pan, and stick it in the oven.

See page 58 for tips on removing the air from zip-top bags.

You can use canning jars instead of bags for some foods.

Step 3: Cooking

You can cook many foods sous vide in a combi oven without packaging them.

A kitchen sink or cooler can maintain water temperature long enough to cook salmon or steak (see page 198).

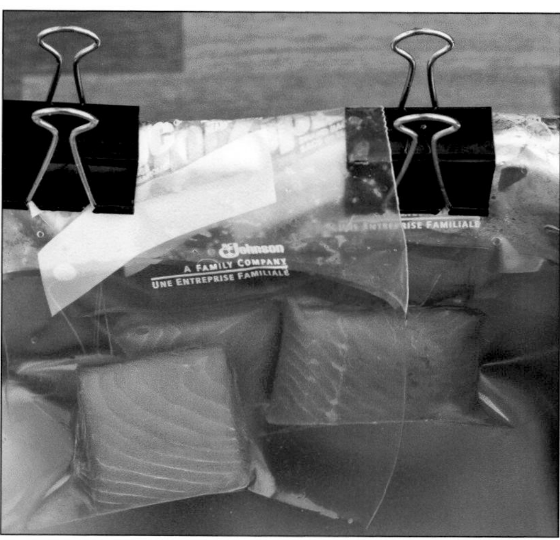

If bags float, use binder clips or a wire rack to hold them underwater; the food should be fully submerged.

Both water baths and combi ovens require preheating, which usually takes 15–30 minutes, before the food goes in. (You can minimize the preheating time of your bath by filling it with hot water from the tap.) The bath or oven temperature you select will vary depending on the kind of food and the degree of doneness you prefer. The recipes and tables we include in Part Two are a good starting point, and experience will guide you to the temperatures that produce the results that you like best.

When cooking to a target core temperature given in a recipe or table, set the water bath or oven 1–2 °C / 2–3 °F hotter than the target temperature. (Although setting the bath much hotter does accelerate cooking, it makes timing trickier, so we don't recommend it.) Use a probe thermometer to keep tabs on the food temperature (see How to Check the Core Temperature, page 66) until you gain confidence in knowing how long particular foods of a given thickness take to cook this way.

The cooking time required varies as a function of both the kind of food and its thickness. As a rough rule, doubling the thickness of the food quadruples the cooking time. So adjust the cooking time if your food is thicker or thinner than what we specify in the recipe. Note, however, that you don't need to adjust holding times; once the core has hit the target temperature, the holding time doesn't vary with thickness. You can experiment with longer or shorter holding times, however, to achieve different textures. Each kind of food responds differently as cooking continues.

Step 4: Finishing

Sear food in a pan, on a grill, in a deep fryer, or with a blowtorch (our favorite method).

Add sauces and garnishes to complete the dish.

Food cooked sous vide takes on a texture and appearance similar to that of food that has been poached or steamed. If that's acceptable, simply open the bag, and transfer the food to a serving plate. Some foods, however—such as a medium-rare steak—look and taste much better if you give them a seared crust. Searing not only browns the food but also generates flavorful compounds that form only at high temperatures. These taste and aroma components give roast beef, grilled chicken, and panfried salmon their unmistakable, irreplaceable flavors. Because the interior of the food is cooked to perfection, you want to use very high heat to quickly sear only the exterior of the food. Pansearing is perhaps the easiest method, but you can instead use a blowtorch, a deep fryer, or a grill (see pages 14, 27, and 44).

GETTING THE AIR OUT

Will plastic containers leach harmful chemicals into my food?

Since writing *Modernist Cuisine*, we've been asked many times to comment on the safety of cooking in plastic bags. The bottom line is that bags made expressly for cooking sous vide are perfectly safe—as are oven bags, popular brands of zip-top bags, and stretchy plastic wraps such as Saran Wrap.

The plastic that comes into contact with the food is called polyethylene. It is widely used in containers for biology and chemistry labs, and it has been studied extensively. It is safe. Do avoid very cheap plastic wraps when cooking, however. These are made of polyvinyl chloride (PVC), and heating them presents some risk of chemicals leaching into the food.

The chief reasons to package food without air before cooking sous vide are simple: most unpackaged foods get messy in a water bath, and air-filled bags float, so the food in them cooks unevenly. But there are other good reasons as well. Air is a poor conductor of heat, so the food heats faster and more uniformly without air around it. Even more important, water needs air to evaporate into; exclude the air, and you squelch evaporation, which both cools the food and dries it out. Consistent temperature control is critical for Modernist cooking, and cooking without air helps provide this consistency.

Packaging food without air can be as easy as dipping a plastic bag of food in a bowl of water and allowing the weight of the water to squeeze out the majority of the air. Or it can be as quick and convenient as inserting the edge of a textured bag into a machine, called an edge sealer, that sucks the air out and then uses heat to seal the bag closed (see page 56). Edge sealers work best with solid foods; liquids tend to get sucked into the vacuum pump as the bag collapses.

Vacuum sealing and canning are the only safe approaches when storing food for long periods, but sealing isn't necessary when food will be served shortly after cooking. You can remove air from a bag by lowering it into water or running it over the edge of your countertop. Then either press it closed (for zip-top bags) or seal it with a $50 impulse sealer (for sous vide or oven bags). Alternatively, you can buy a variety of zip-top bag that includes a port and handheld pump.

Any of these methods work for our sous vide recipes, except for the few that specifically call for vacuum sealing.

Bags for cooking sous vide come in a wide range of dimensions and prices. An edge sealer requires special bags that have a waffle-like texture on one side that creates channels through which the sealer can suck out the air. If you own a chamber sealer, use the bags recommended for it. Premade bags are the most convenient, but you can also buy long rolls of bag material.

Bags must keep juices in and water out. They also must maintain their strength at high cooking temperatures, remain flexible when very cold, and prevent gases from moving in and out. No single plastic has all of these characteristics, which is why the better bags combine multiple layers of different plastics laminated together. The more layers the bag has, the higher its quality—and its price. These thicker bags also are suitable for storing frozen food, as they're more puncture-resistant than cheaper bags. Bags made for cooking food are perfectly safe (see note on the previous page).

For foods that are liquid or surrounded by liquids, canning jars offer a handy packaging option for cooking sous vide. If you are sealing food only to marinate or store it, not to cook it, you can use a rigid container that attaches to your vacuum sealer.

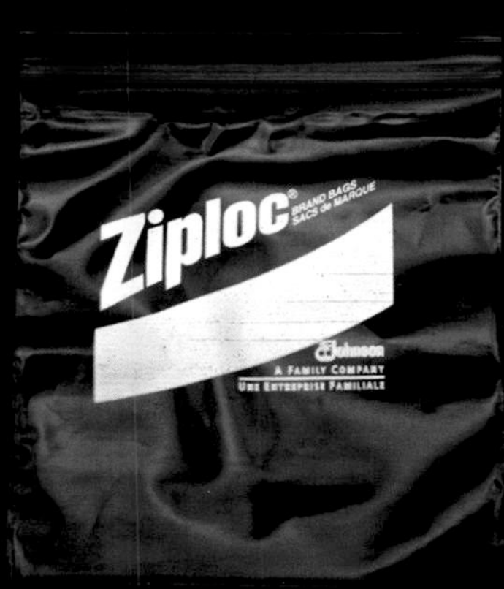

Zip-top freezer bags

Zip-top bags allow you to seal liquids, which is hard to do with edge-sealer bags. They soften at higher temperatures, so do not use them in the oven or on the stove.
Suitable for freezing: yes, if sealed by using the water-displacement method
Where to buy: grocery and convenience stores
Cost: less than 15 cents each

Edge-sealer vacuum bags

A waffled texture makes these bags more expensive, but they are quite durable and can be used in a pressure cooker or to store food cooked sous vide.
Suitable for freezing: yes
Where to buy: grocery and kitchen-supply stores
Cost: 50 cents–$1 each; less for rolls

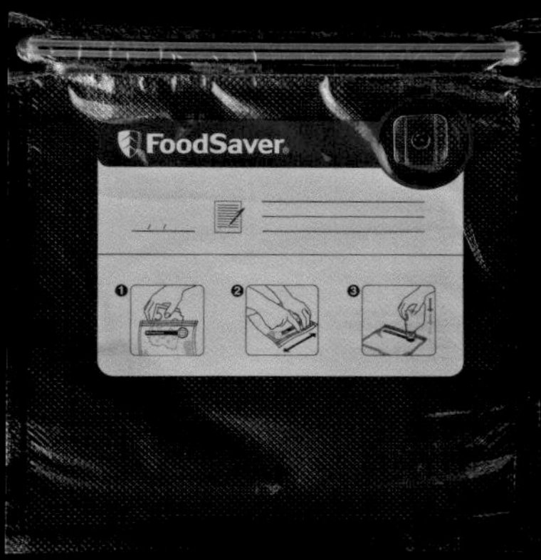

Ported zip-top bags

These bags are sold with a handheld pump that sucks air through the one-way valve in a port. Like ordinary zip-top bags, they soften at higher temperatures.
Suitable for freezing: yes
Where to buy: grocery and kitchen-supply stores
Cost: 45 cents each

Oven bags

Oven bags are large and well suited for high heat. Use an impulse sealer or the water-displacement method to seal the bag; clip it to the bath so that water does not leak into it.
Suitable for freezing: no
Where to buy: grocery and kitchen-supply

Rigid containers

A hard-sided container with a port is useful for longer-term, oxygen-free refrigeration of fruits, vegetables, and delicate foods. They are not suitable for cooking, however, and freezing may break the seal.
Suitable for freezing: no

Canning jars

Glass jars with airtight lids, most often used in canning, can be used to cook food in a water bath or pressure cooker. Food in the jar must be surrounded by liquid. Cooking takes longer than it does in a bag.
Suitable for freezing: yes, but leave headroom

VACUUM SEALERS

The easiest way to get started with vacuum sealing is to buy an edge sealer, which costs about $100 and is well suited for home use. In the United States, FoodSaver is the most common brand. The edge sealer works by sucking the air out of a specially textured bag. Restaurants use chamber vacuum sealers (shown at right), which cost $1,500–$3,500. They offer the most reliable seal. And, unlike edge sealers, they expertly seal liquids, which allows for some neat tricks—like impregnating watermelon with strawberry juice (see page 59).

SAFETY TIP FOR VACUUM SEALING

Vacuum-sealed food is not the same as canned food. Even in the absence of oxygen, any anaerobic bacteria on or in the food will continue to grow. So you should store food in vacuum-sealed bags only in a refrigerator or freezer. In general, U.S. Food and Drug Administration guidelines state that you can keep vacuum-sealed food in the refrigerator for five days or in the freezer indefinitely.

Five layers of material are laminated together to make an edge-sealer bag. Four inner layers made of polyethylene are capped by an outer layer of tough, gas-impermeable nylon. This structure makes the bags quite durable and particularly good for storing frozen food.

Special bags for edge sealers have a waffled texture on one side that creates small channels through which the air can be removed. Smooth bags won't work in edge sealers, but are suitable for use in chamber vacuum sealers.

Vacuum sealing is a great way to store food. Oxygen causes chemical damage, so sealing the food without air keeps fish smelling fresh, meat from discoloring, and produce from turning brown for far longer than refrigeration alone can. It also helps to prevent chemical reactions that can give reheated foods a warmed-over flavor.

Solid foods work best in edge sealers; liquids tend to get sucked into the vacuum pump as the bag collapses. If that happens, the pump may fail to remove all of the air in the bag or to seal it properly—not to mention that the flavorful liquid you wanted to cook in winds up in the machine, rather than in the bag.

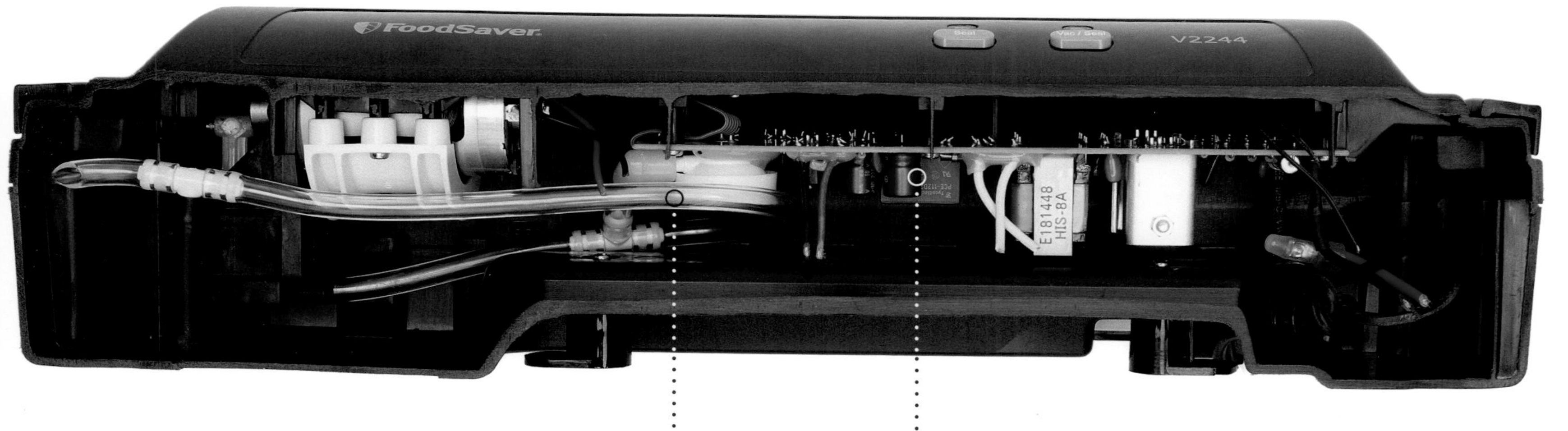

Electronic controls automatically switch off the pump and activate the sealing bar when nearly all the air has been removed from the bag.

A vacuum pump pulls air out of the bag through the reservoir.

Rubber seals close off the vacuum reservoir. Were it not for the waffle-like texture of the bag, these seals would clamp the sous vide bag so tightly that no air could get through. The ridges in the bag act like straws, but they can also allow liquid to get sucked in.

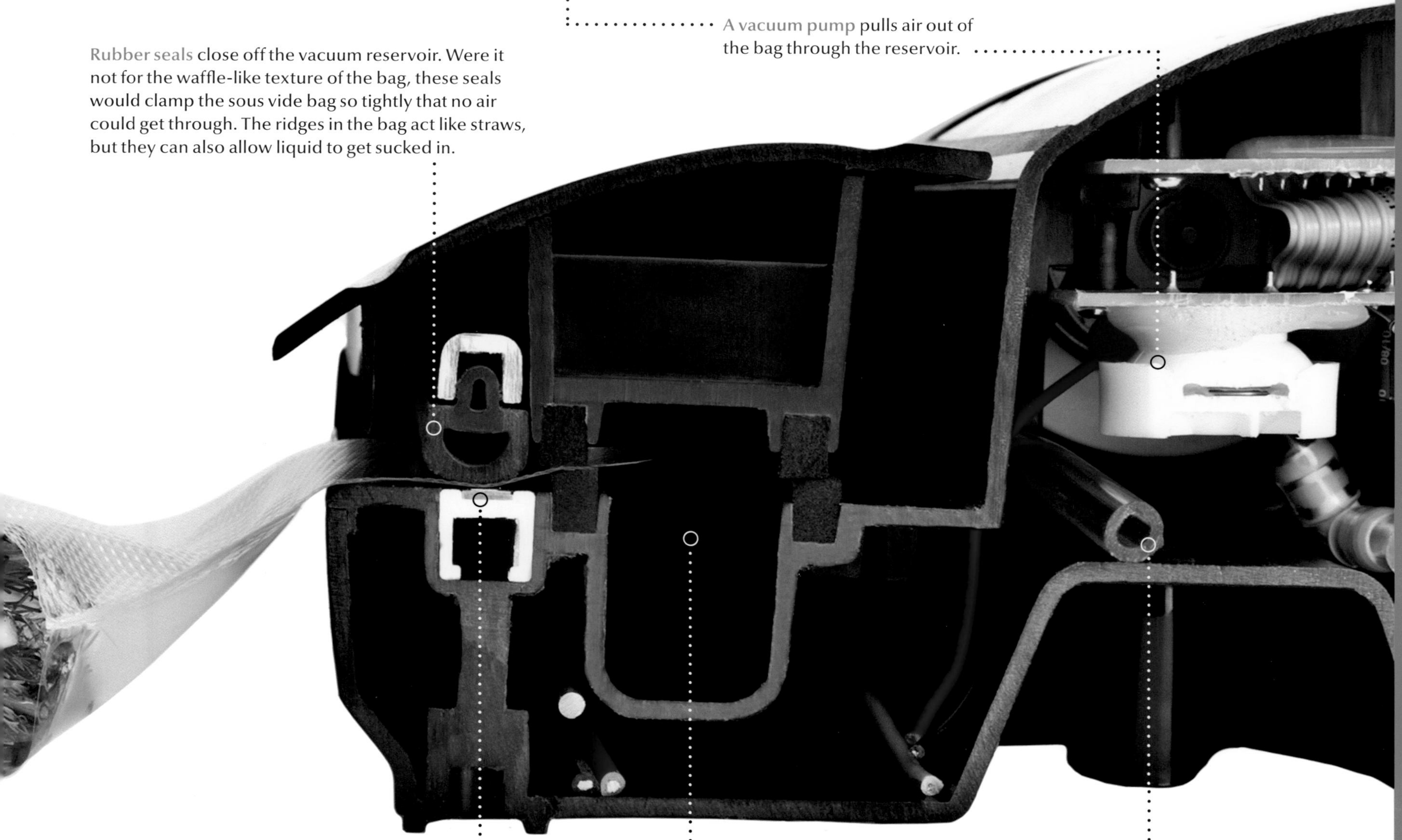

The sealing bar is heated electrically. It gets just hot enough to fuse the two sides together so that the bag seals completely.

The vacuum reservoir is where air gets sucked out of the bag.

Hoses connected to the reservoir, the vacuum pump, and an external vacuum port carry the air out.

HOW TO Use an Edge Sealer

Edge sealers bring vacuum sealing within reach of most home cooks. An edge sealer requires specially textured bags. It doesn't handle liquids well, but you can freeze or otherwise solidify liquids before sealing them (see the next page). Seal food only when it is cold.

1 Use a premade textured bag, or make your own by cutting a suitable length of waffle-textured plastic from a roll and using the seal-only option to close one end. Flip the top 4 cm / 1¼ in of the bag inside out to keep it clean and prevent a faulty seal.

2 Fill the bag with food, and unfold the lip of the bag. Delicate foods, such as salmon, will keep their shape better if you first wrap them in cling film.

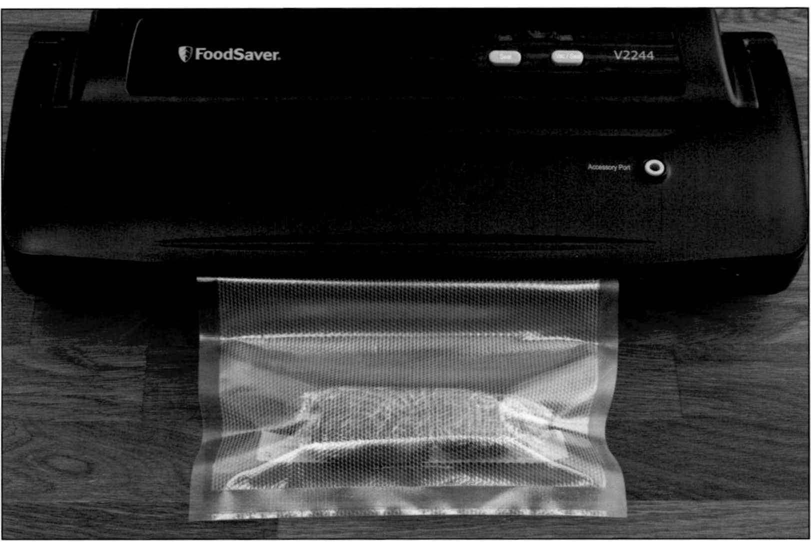

3 Place the open end of the bag in the vacuum sealer so that it rests on the sealing strip and extends into the vacuum reservoir (on some models, this happens automatically when you insert the bag into the sealer). Stretch the bag flat across the sealing strip as you place it to prevent any wrinkles, which cause a poor seal.

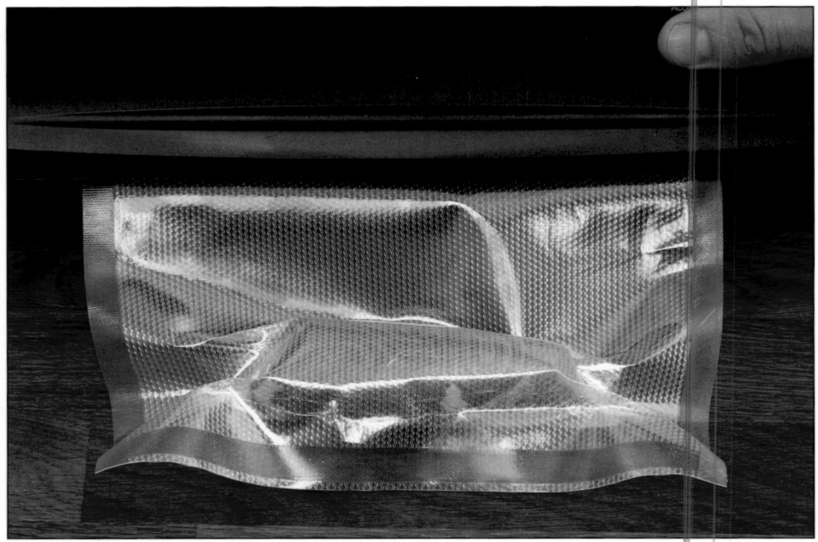

4 Close the lid, and engage the vacuum pump (on a FoodSaver, for example, press the Seal button). The pump will stop on its own. Although it is possible to seal liquids by pressing the Seal button to stop the vacuum just before the liquid gets sucked in, it makes quite a mess if your timing is off. For extra security, you can place a second seal about 5 mm / ¼ in above the first seal.

Using an impulse sealer

An impulse sealer only seals; it doesn't remove air. But this stapler-looking tool has its advantages. Impulse sealers cost about half as much as edge sealers. And they are handy tools for sealing oven bags and making custom-sized sous vide bags from a bulk roll of plastic: two options that work better for storage and high-temperature cooking than zip-top bags do. An impulse sealer can also seal liquids without risking the mess that usually occurs when using an edge sealer.

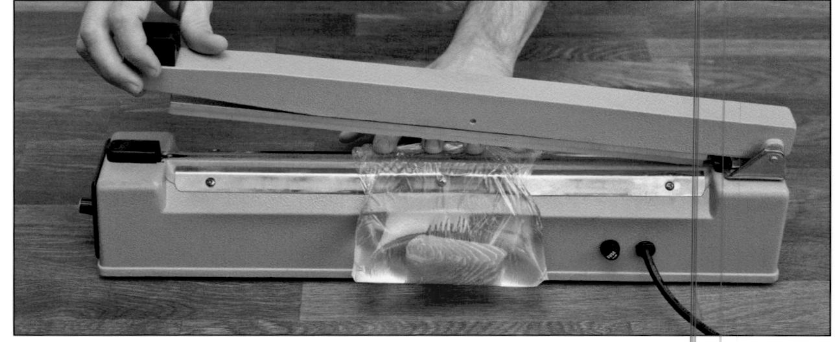

SOLUTIONS FOR COMMON SEALING PROBLEMS

Problem: Liquid was sucked into the vacuum-pump reservoir, preventing a good seal and making a giant mess.

Solution: Freeze the liquid first, and then add it to the bag as cubes of ice or frozen broth.

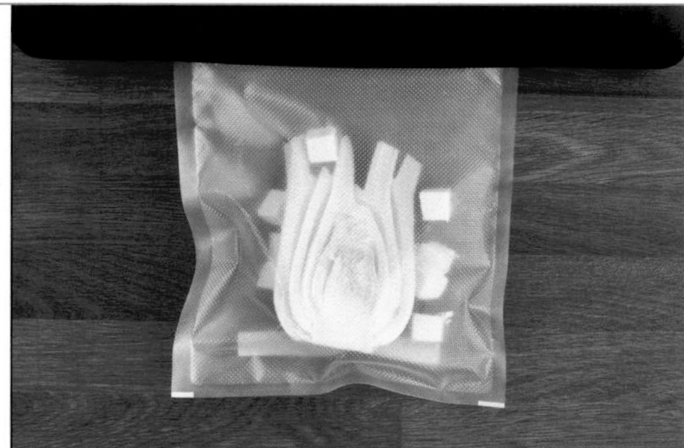

Solution: Use a semisolid form of the liquid. Add fat in the form of butter instead of oil, for example, or solidify a stock by freezing it or using gelatin (see page 98).

Problem: The food was not sealed tightly enough.
Solution: Check the bag and the seal for leaks; repackage the food, if necessary. Cool warm foods before sealing; hot food gives off vapor.

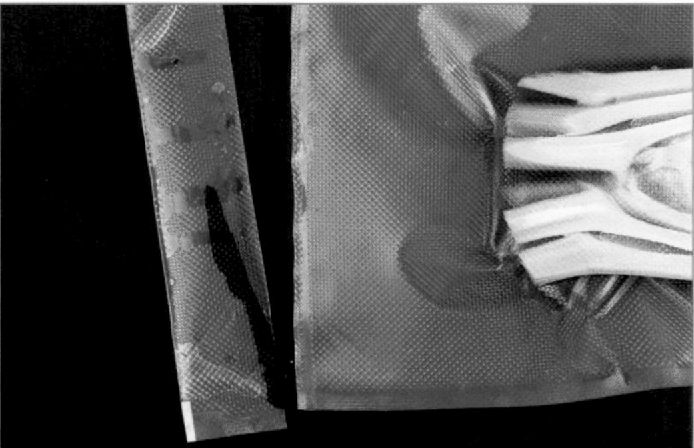

Problem: The bag sealed tightly, but now air has gotten back in.
Solution: Wrinkled or dirty seals often fail eventually. Cut off the top of the bag and reseal it, or repackage the food in a new bag.

Problem: The shape of the food was distorted and ruined.
Solution: Use a weaker vacuum setting, if available, for delicate items. Or wrap the food with a thin, high-quality plastic film to help it hold its shape. Use a rigid container if you are sealing the food only to store it.

Problem: The bag was punctured.

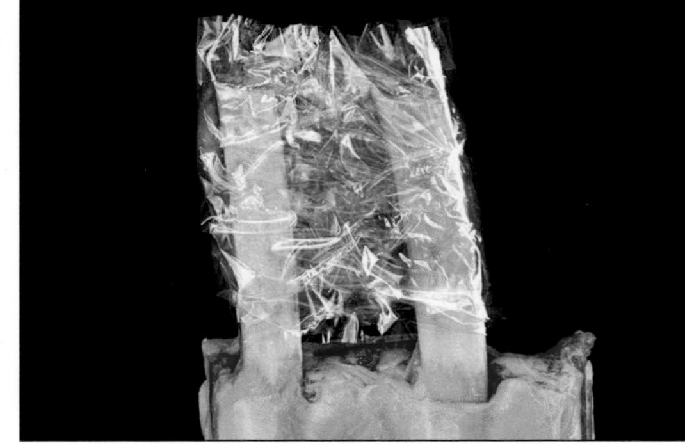

Solution: Wrap any bones or sharp edges in protective padding, such as plastic wrap. Alternatively, use a heavier bag.

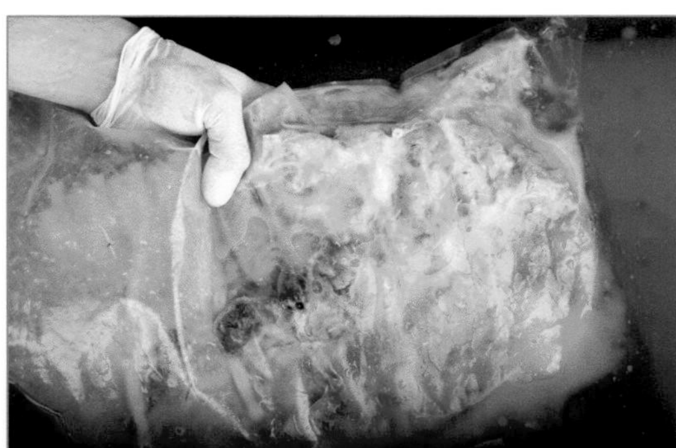

Problem: The bag burst or the seal failed during cooking.

Solution: Use bags rated for high temperatures; some plastics weaken when heated to 70 °C / 158 °F and fail at temperatures above 80 °C / 176 °F.

HOW TO **Seal Food in a Zip-Top Bag**

If you need to seal food along with a liquid, or if you don't have a vacuum sealer, ordinary zip-top bags offer a handy alternative to vacuum sealing. The two methods below allow you to quickly remove much of the air from the bag. The water-displacement method is the more effective technique, and it doesn't require as much liquid in the bag to remove nearly all of the air.

BY WATER DISPLACEMENT

1 Fill a bowl or sink with water, and place the food along with some oil or water in a zip-top bag. The liquid is needed to remove as much air as possible and to prevent the bag from floating. If you'll be cooking the food immediately, there's no need for an extra bowl: just use the warm water bath itself to seal the bag.

2 Slowly lower the open bag into the water. The water squeezes the air out of the bag and presses the plastic tightly around the food.

3 Seal the bag when the water level is 1–2 mm / 1⁄16 in below the zip seal.

ON THE EDGE OF A COUNTERTOP

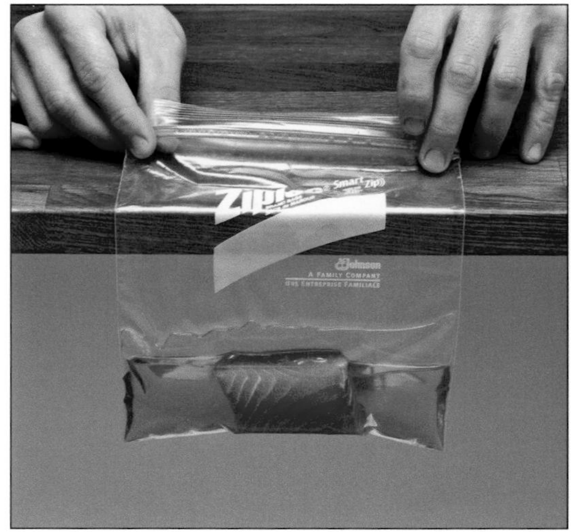

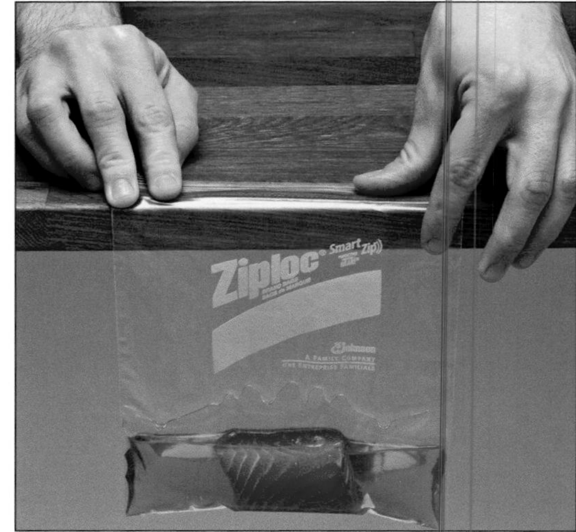

1 Place the food and enough liquid to cover it in a zip-top bag, grasp the top of the bag, and hang the filled part of the bag over the counter so that the top of the liquid is just below the edge of the countertop. This method requires enough liquid in the bag to completely surround the food; otherwise, air pockets form around the food.

2 Hold the bag taut, and lower it slowly. The edge of the counter should squeeze the air out of the bag.

3 When the seal reaches the edge of the counter, zip it closed.

HOW TO Use a Handheld Pump

If you don't have the countertop or cupboard space for an edge sealer, a more compact alternative is a special kind of zip-top bag that includes a built-in port for a handheld pump. The pump costs about $20; the bags are relatively expensive, but some are reusable after washing.

Like an edge sealer, a handheld pump doesn't work well with liquids.

Ported bags tend to lose vacuum over time, so they are best suited for immediate cooking and short-term storage of foods that you use regularly, such as cheese and fresh produce.

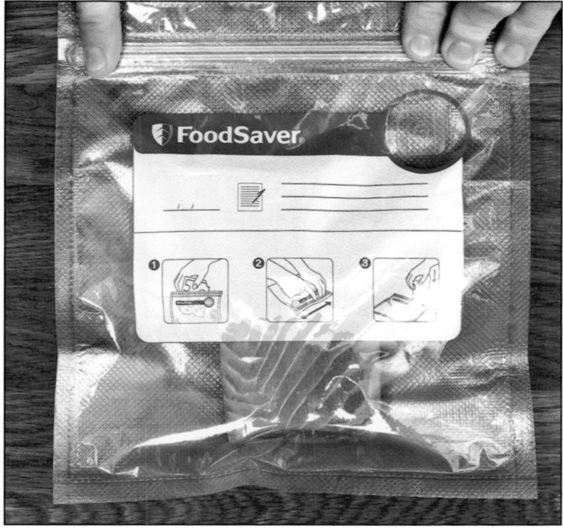

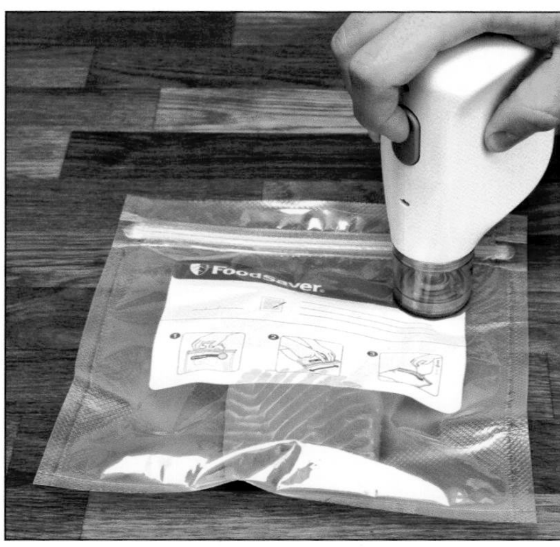

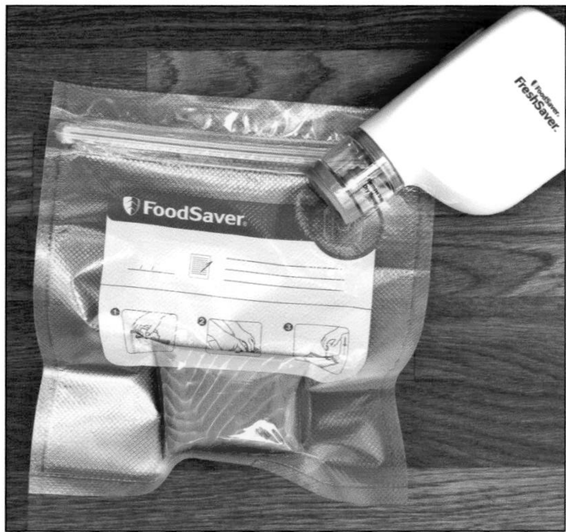

1 Place the food in the bag in a single layer, leaving the top third of the bag free. Zip the seal closed.

2 Press the handheld pump over the port on the bag, and push the start button.

3 Let the pump run until it has sucked out the air and sealed the bag around the food.

HOW TO Compress Fruits and Vegetables

Vacuum sealing delicate fruits and vegetables is tricky: they are too porous to hold their structure under pressure, so the process often crushes them. But there are creative ways to turn this drawback to an advantage as a way to manipulate texture and color. Pineapple, for example, becomes pleasantly dense when it is vacuum sealed. Compressed peaches and watermelon seem juicier and denser. After compressing produce, keep it sealed until you're ready to use it.

1 Peel the fruit or vegetable if necessary, and cut it into evenly sized pieces. In the case of strawberries, shown here, we like to combine them with a bit of sugar.

2 Arrange the food in a single layer in a sous vide bag, and begin vacuum sealing it. The vacuum causes air pockets, called vacuoles, in the plant cells to burst.

3 As more vacuoles collapse, the food darkens.

4 Let the produce rest in the bag for at least 10 minutes after the vacuum sealing is complete before using it.

COOKING AND REHEATING

A pot, a good thermometer, and patience are tools enough to cook sous vide. A slow cooker outfitted with an external temperature controller is more convenient and reliable. Better still is a commercially made water bath that combines the heater, temperature control, and insulated container all in one unit—and adds wire racks to boot. In basic sous vide cookers, the water sits still; professional-grade baths typically include pumps that keep the water circulating. On the following pages, we walk through your options for each type of water bath.

Once you have a water bath set up, how do you cook in it? All of the recipes in this book use one of two basic techniques: either cooking the food to a target core temperature, or bringing the food to the target temperature and holding it there for a specified time.

In the first technique, a recipe or reference table provides the temperature to which the deepest part of the food should cook. You set the bath temperature 1–2 °C / 2–3 °F higher. Most bath controllers and kitchen thermometers are accurate only to within a degree or two (see page 8), so the slightly hotter bath helps ensure that the food cooks as fully as you want it to. Then you wait for the food temperature to come into equilibrium with the bath temperature.

This approach, called equilibrium cooking, is more forgiving than traditional cooking methods. Timing does matter, but the food can sit in the bath a little longer than the recommended time (within a 10% margin or so) without dramatic consequences. Even irregularly shaped pieces of food cook properly. The cooking time must be long enough that the thickest parts get done, but it doesn't harm the thin parts to spend extra time at the target temperature. If you are making a complex dish, you can often let various components of the recipe sit in the bath until it is time to assemble them—just set the bath temperature lower than the cooking temperature of the components.

Equilibrium cooking can take a very long time. The slow pace is a result of the basic physics of heating: heat flows quickly into the food at the start, when the food is much cooler than the bath, but slows dramatically during the last part of the cooking process as the temperature difference between the two narrows. Fortunately,

Tender meats are usually cooked to a particular core temperature; for example, filet mignon should be cooked to 50 °C / 122 °F for rare, 53 °C / 127 °F for medium rare (see page 192). The steak is done as soon as the deepest part of the meat hits that target temperature. The time it takes to reach this depends on the thickness of the steak.

Tougher cuts, in contrast, must be held at the target temperature for a long time to tenderize. We often cook short ribs, for example, for 72 hours at 58 °C / 136 °F. You can get good but different results with higher temperatures and shorter cooking times.

Chicken breasts and other poultry cuts are often held at the target temperature for a different reason: to kill potential pathogens and improve the safety of the food.

This bath is overcrowded. An overcrowded bath obstructs convection currents in the water that are needed to equalize temperatures, so hot and cold spots develop, and the food cooks unevenly. Noncirculating baths are particularly susceptible to overcrowding. Put only as much food into the bath as will fit with ample circulation space in between. You may need to work in batches or use a larger water container.

it's unattended cooking that leaves you free to do other things. The results are worth it.

Cooking time depends more on the thickness of the food than you might expect, so if your food is thicker or thinner than a recipe calls for, timing can be tricky to estimate. As a rough rule, cooking time is proportional not to the thickness of the food but to the thickness squared. A steak that is 5 cm / 2 in thick, for example, must sit in a water bath for about four times as long as a steak that is half as thick before it reaches medium rare. For this reason, we generally cut large pieces into individual portions for cooking sous vide.

The second technique, called hold-at-temperature cooking, keeps the food at the target temperature for a certain amount of time. This technique is sometimes required to pasteurize the food for safety; more often, however, the goal is tenderizing tough cuts of meat. Short ribs cooked at 58 °C / 136 °F for 72 hours, for example, end up utterly unlike the same ribs cooked at 82 °C / 180 °F for 10 hours.

Once we got the hang of cooking sous vide, we found ourselves using it as much for its convenience as for the terrific results it produces. If you have a vacuum sealer and a good-size bath, you can prepare many single-portion bags and cook them all at once. Any you don't use right away will keep much better in the refrigerator or freezer than leftovers typically do. And reheating is a cinch.

When it comes to chilling, thawing, and reheating food, most people are careless. They set hot food in the refrigerator, or they leave food out on the counter for too long, letting bacteria grow.

Cooked food should be cooled quickly, for two reasons. First, bacteria thrive in the "danger zone" from 10–50 °C / 50–122 °F. The longer that food remains in the danger zone while cooling, the more likely that the few bacteria remaining in it after cooking will multiply and dangerously repopulate the food. The warmer end of the zone poses the greatest risk because bacteria multiply faster in warm environments.

Second, rapid cooling maintains juiciness and a fresh-cooked flavor better than slow cooling can. A quick chill thickens and gels juices before they can leak out.

The best way to quickly cool food to refrigeration temperatures is to dunk your sealed sous vide bags in ice water, which can be as simple as a sink or bowl of cold water with lots of ice cubes. Once the food is chilled, it can then be stored, still sealed, in a freezer or in the enclosed drawers at the bottom of the fridge, which maintain the most stable temperatures. Avoid the shelves in the door, which are the warmest part of a refrigerator.

You can put frozen bags of food straight into a water bath, and do the thawing and cooking in one step. Cooking from frozen obviously takes longer (often considerably longer) than cooking the same food from refrigerator temperature does. How much longer is hard to estimate, so it's imperative to use the technique of equilibrium cooking that we described above. When cooking from frozen, make sure you set the bath temperature to at least 55 °C / 131 °F, high enough to prevent bacterial growth while the food sits in the bath for an extended period of time. Foods best cooked at temperatures below that shouldn't be cooked from frozen; thaw them first in the refrigerator.

Perhaps surprisingly, it takes exactly as much time to reheat foods cooked sous vide as it does to cook them from raw by using the equilibrium method. For that reason, it doesn't make sense to cook fish, tender meats, or vegetables in advance. Tough meats are a different matter because they require long holding times at the target temperature. Reheating only requires that you bring them back up to the original target core temperature; you don't have to hold them there again. Short ribs cooked for 72 hours and then frozen, for example, may take just one hour to defrost and reheat.

A water bath is an excellent tool for reheating leftovers. The best approach is to chill the leftovers after the meal, and then vacuum seal them and put them in the refrigerator. Red meats should be heated to their original cooking temperature; for other foods, try 60 °C / 140 °F. Avoid reheating at temperatures above 65 °C / 149 °F.

Some chefs cook with the bath temperature much hotter than the desired final core temperature. This approach reduces the margin of error, however, and also introduces more of a temperature gradient within the food, thus undermining two of the biggest benefits for home cooks of cooking sous vide. We cover this technique, called hotter-than-core cooking, in *Modernist Cuisine*, but we don't recommend it.

WATER BATHS

Water baths come in two major varieties: those that circulate the water, and those that don't. Noncirculating baths are more affordable. The SousVide Supreme, a model specifically designed for home use, costs \$250–\$400. These baths rely on convection—the natural tendency of hotter fluids to rise and colder fluids to sink—to even out any temperature differences within the bath. A noncirculating bath is sufficient for most home uses because home cooks typically don't add and remove food from the cooker frequently. When using a bath of this kind, keep bags of food small and well separated so that convective currents can flow around them easily.

Professional chefs prefer circulating baths, which distribute heat uniformly by pumping the water around. The stronger the circulation, the better it prevents hot and cold spots, and the more food you can safely pack into the bath. Laboratory-quality baths integrate the pump, heater, and temperature controller within an insulated tank, but cost upward of \$2,500. Immersion circulators designed for kitchen use, such as the PolyScience unit shown on the next page, cost less than \$800 and attach to any water tank or container.

Noncirculating Water Baths

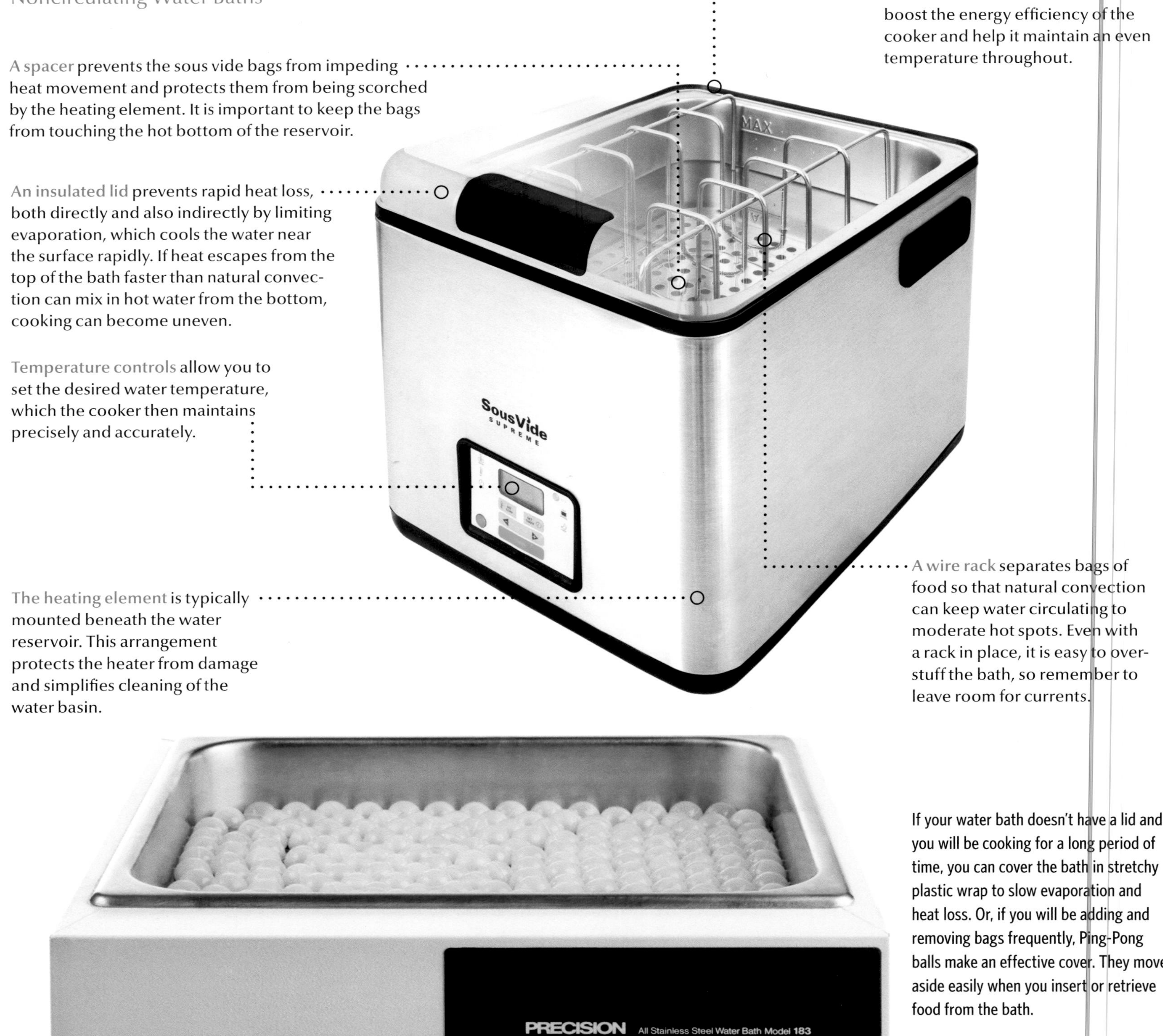

If your water bath doesn't have a lid and you will be cooking for a long period of time, you can cover the bath in stretchy plastic wrap to slow evaporation and heat loss. Or, if you will be adding and removing bags frequently, Ping-Pong balls make an effective cover. They move aside easily when you insert or retrieve food from the bath.

Circulating Water Baths

A pump built into this immersion heater circulates the water and helps maintain a more consistent temperature throughout the bath.

Your oven thermostat probably allows the air temperature to vary by at least 10 °C / 18 °F, whereas a sous vide cooker can maintain temperature to within about 2 °C / 4 °F—and very good units stray less than 0.5 °C / 1 °F.

A heavy-duty polycarbonate container provides insulation while letting you see the food you're cooking. Containers like this cost about $20 at specialty kitchen-supply stores and come in a range of sizes. You can also use a picnic cooler, which retains heat better than polycarbonate does.

The temperature readout can be changed at the flick of a switch to display either degrees Celsius or degrees Fahrenheit.

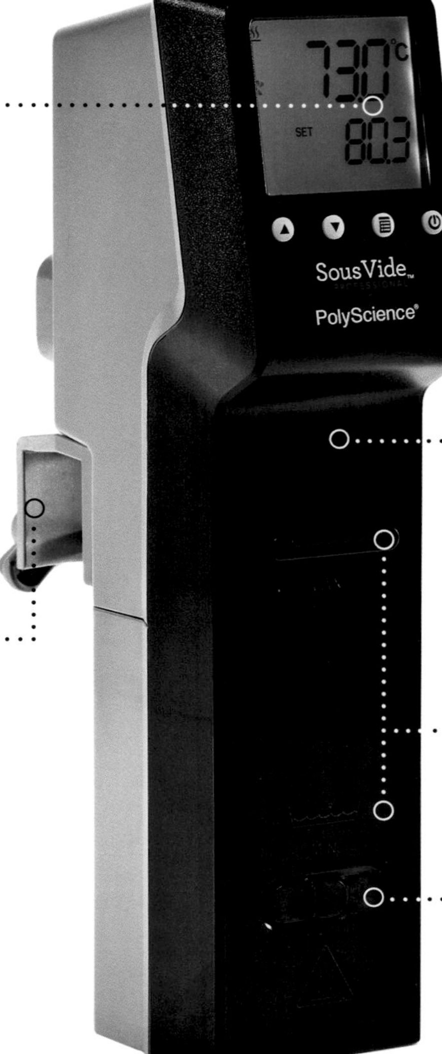

The casing of the immersion circulator protects its heating element and pump. It also prevents the heating element from scorching the sous vide bags.

The screw mount can be attached to containers of many sizes, shapes, and materials. This feature makes the unit very versatile.

"Min" and "max" lines indicate the acceptable range for the water level. The water inlet and outlet are just below the "min" level.

Flow adjustment slider allows you to tailor the pump output.

IMPROVISED WATER BATHS

You can cook sous vide with any setup that heats food accurately at low temperatures. It doesn't have to be fancy. Clip a digital thermometer onto the side of a large pot full of water, fill your kitchen sink, or put hot water in a cooler, and you've got a serviceable water bath. These improvised approaches can't maintain a steady temperature for more than a few hours, but for shorter cooking times they can cook food just as well as any commercial sous vide cooker.

An improvised setup replaces the sophisticated computerized thermostat of a special-purpose cooker with an even more sophisticated biological controller: you. You must use a digital thermometer to measure the water temperature accurately. You'll find it easier to keep the temperature steady if you use a much greater volume of water than of food (in other words, don't crowd the bath). Start with water that is 2–5 °C / 4–9 °F higher than the target core temperature of the food, and with food that is at room temperature; chilled or frozen food will cool the water too much. Always cover the container between temperature checks, and always clean the container thoroughly before filling it with water.

Kitchen Sink or Bathtub

For cooking fish or cooking beef to medium rare, the hot water from your tap may be hot enough. Choose a target core temperature (see the tables on pages 192 and 281), adjust the water to be 2–5 °C / 4–9 °F hotter, fill a clean sink or tub, and add your bagged food. If the bags float, use silverware to hold them down. Refresh with hot water as needed.

Cooler

An insulated ice chest makes a particularly efficient improvised bath. Fill a cooler at home with hot water that is 2–5 °C / 4–9 °F above the target temperature of the food you'll be cooking, and take it with you on a picnic. The insulated walls should hold the temperature for several hours, but check it occasionally. See Sous Vide Steak in a Cooler, page 198.

Pot on the Stove

Perhaps the simplest way to cook sous vide is in a pot on the stove top. Clip bags of food and a thermometer to a wire cooling rack, and hang it on the rim of the pot. Heat the water to the target temperature, adjust the burner to a setting that maintains that temperature, and start cooking. A heavy, high-quality pot will retain heat better than a thin-walled one, although metal is not a great insulator. Cover the pot between temperature checks.

Rice Cooker or Slow Cooker

You can make a do-it-yourself version of a noncirculating water bath for \$100–\$150. Start with a budget slow cooker or rice cooker that has a simple mechanical on–off or low–medium–high switch; avoid any that is programmable or has digital controls. Fill the cooker with water, and plug it into a digital temperature controller. At least two companies—Fresh Meals Solutions and Auber Instruments—make controllers for just this purpose. A temperature sensor attached to the controller hangs in the water. You set a desired temperature on the controller, and it then switches the power to the cooker on and off to maintain that temperature.

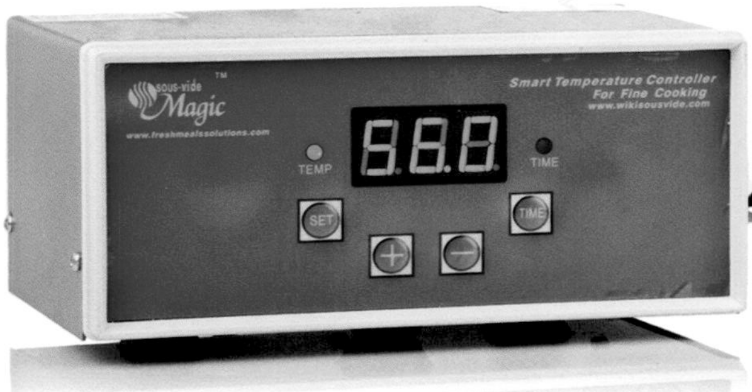

Pan in the Oven

Heat your tap water to the target temperature of the food, and then fill a deep baking dish. Set your oven to its lowest setting, typically around 100 °C or 200 °F, and place bags of food in the water. The oven will maintain the temperature of the water reasonably well, but experiment first by placing an oven probe in the water and checking it after an hour to see how much it has heated or cooled. If the temperature remains stable enough, you can use this method to cook longer than with other improvised setups, especially if you cover the pan.

Hot Tub

Believe it or not, if you like your fish lightly cooked (as we do), then a hot tub can do the trick. The water in most hot tubs is set to 38–40 °C / 100–104 °F. Try it at your next party!

HOW TO Check the Core Temperature (Without Obsessing About It)

One of the benefits of cooking sous vide is that it greatly reduces anxiety about time and temperature. If you leave the food in for a little more time than the recipe suggests, the consequences aren't nearly as perceptible as they are when you cook on a stove top or in a hot oven. That said, doing a quick temperature check every once in a while will help you learn how long it takes to heat various foods to particular temperatures.

Use either of the two methods below to insert a digital thermometer into the food without interrupting the cooking. But do this in moderation: there is no need to check the temperature frequently.

Many of our recipes call for cooking food to a specific core temperature. What we mean by "core temperature" is the temperature at the center of the thickest part of the food—the part that heat reaches last as it diffuses through the food.

ZIP-TOP BAG IN A BATH

Using an Instant-Read Thermometer

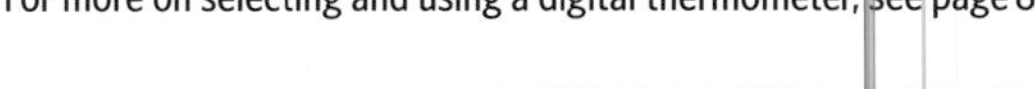
For more on selecting and using a digital thermometer, see page 8.

1 While the food is cooking, lift out just the top of the bag, and open it. Keep the bag submerged in the water so that the food doesn't cool, which would change the cooking time, and so that the bag doesn't fill with air.

2 Insert the tip of the probe into the middle of the thickest part of the food. Hold the thermometer in place until the reading stabilizes at the core temperature; the first reading it gives may be the higher temperature near the surface of the food.

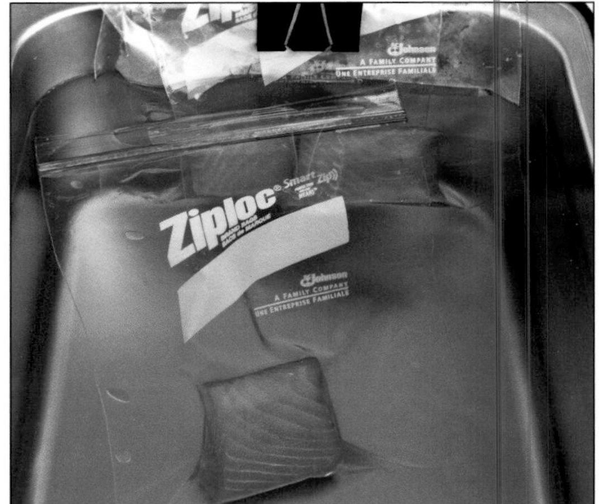

3 Remove the thermometer, wash it well with soapy water or sanitize it with an antibacterial hand wipe, and then rinse it well.

4 Lower the bag into the water until just the top edge is above the surface (see How to Seal Food in a Zip-Top Bag by Water Displacement, page 58), and then press the top closed again.

Using an Oven Probe Thermometer

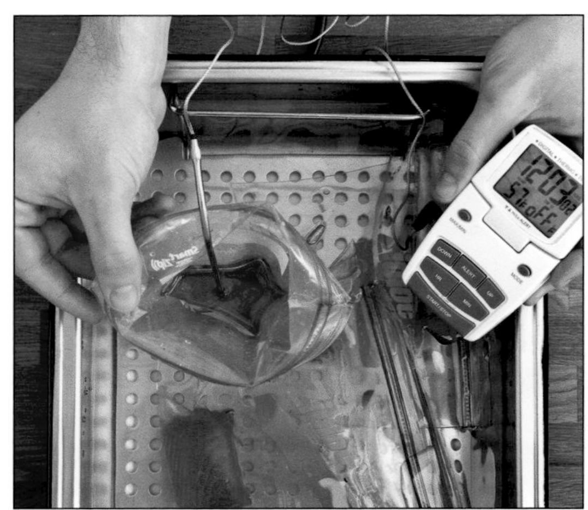

1 Before cooking, insert the tip of the probe into the middle of the thickest part of the food. Push the probe in at an angle so that it remains in place during cooking. Check that the probe hasn't penetrated all the way to the other side.

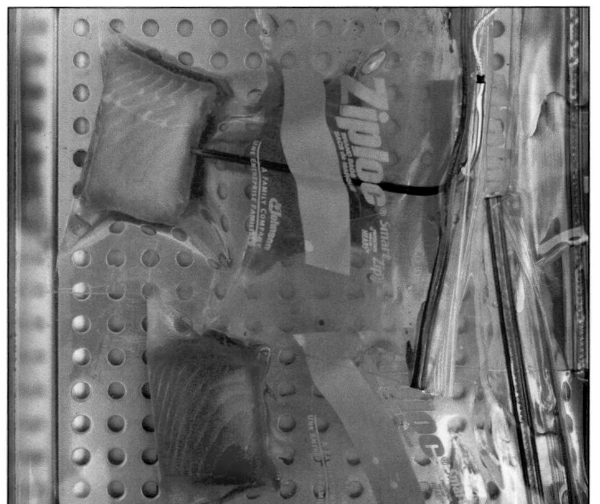

2 Lower the bag into the water until just the top edge is above the surface (see How to Seal Food in a Zip-Top Bag by Water Displacement, page 58), and then press the top closed around the probe. The seal should hold the probe in place, but it will not be watertight.

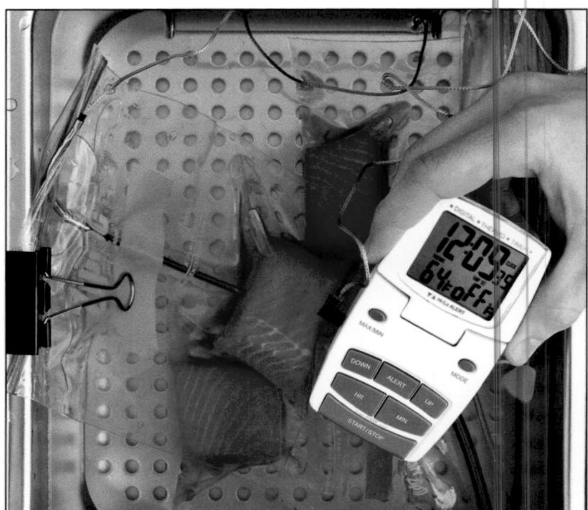

3 Clip the bag to the side of the bath so that the top is above the water line. Make sure the food in the bag is completely submerged. Run the lead wire from the probe between the lid and the rim of the cooker so that the lid covers the bath as tightly as possible.

VACUUM-SEALED BAG IN A BATH

1 Fill the bag with food, and then seal it. When cooking multiple bags of food in one bath, place portions of the same size in each of the bags. That way, you can leave the thermometer in one of the bags during the entire cooking process; the temperature of all the others will be approximately the same. Place the probe in the largest piece to ensure that all of the pieces cook fully.

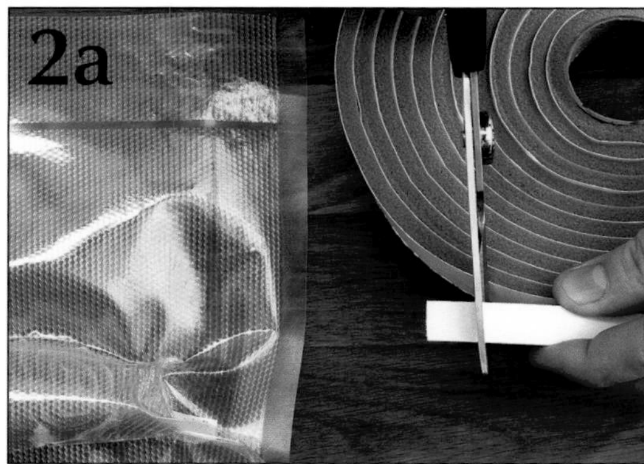
2a

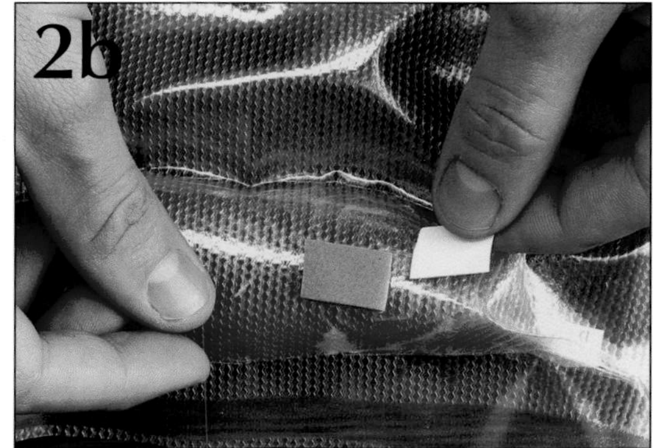
2b

2c

2 Before dunking the bag in water, press a small square of weather-stripping tape or other thick foam tape (available from hardware and home improvement stores) onto the outside of the sealed bag. Place the tape a bit off center from the part of the food you want to check so that you can insert the thermometer probe at an angle. Needle-tipped probes are preferable because FoodSaver bags are tough and not easily pierced by larger probes unless the food inside is dense, such as steak. Insert the thermometer probe through the tape and bag at an angle into the center of the food at its thickest part. It may help to place the bagged food on a cutting board first. The foam tape forms a seal around the probe that keeps water out of the bag. The probe must remain in place to preserve the seal.

3 Carefully place the bag with the probe into the bath, and thread the lead wire between the lid and the rim of the cooker so that the lid covers the bath as tightly as possible.

3

SAFETY TIPS FOR USING THERMOMETERS

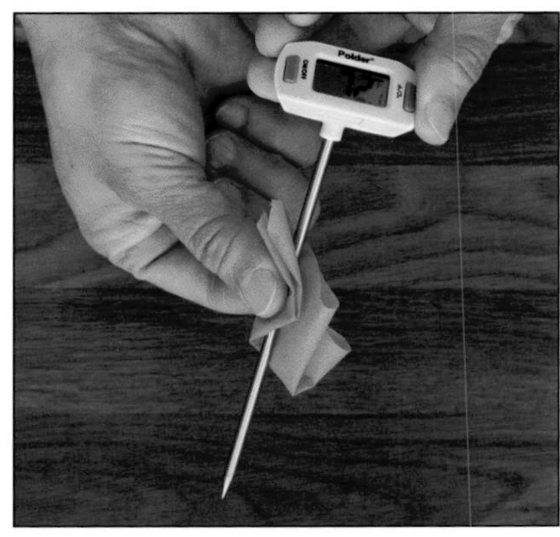

Keep in mind that piercing food with a thermometer effectively pushes into your food whatever is outside the bag, including any bacteria or viruses in the water or on the surface of the food or the thermometer probe. That's one reason we don't recommend checking the temperature too frequently.

To prevent contamination, sterilize your thermometer each time it comes out of a piece of food. We find that sanitizing hand wipes are more convenient for this purpose than washing with soap and water, but both work. Rinse the probe well with clean water after washing or wiping it. Also change the bathwater after every meal you cook. Just because the food is in a bag doesn't mean the water stays clean.

INGREDIENTS

Good food comes from great ingredients. There was a time when only the best cooks appreciated that fact. Now the entire food world, it seems, is putting a major emphasis on ingredients. Several distinct movements are going strong. The organic movement focuses on growing food without using chemicals. In the farm-to-table movement, restaurants operate their own gardens or farms to supply their kitchens. The local food movement emphasizes eating food grown nearby as a way to support local economies.

Excellent goals, all of them. But they come with caveats. Some large companies have cheapened "organic" into a marketing buzzword by lobbying for loopholes in government regulations. Cooks must actively seek out small, artisanal producers growing heirloom varieties to benefit from the original intent. The local movement suggests that food grown nearby, not shipped across the country, is better for the planet. Sometimes that's true. But in other cases, local production of certain crops is actually more energy-intensive than efficient production in another region, even when you add in the effects of transportation. Fortunately, we have access to enough information these days to be able to make well-informed choices. What you do with it is a personal decision.

We're strong believers in using every available tool and ingredient to make eating a richer, more diverse, and more stimulating experience. So we love that a cook in the Midwest can now easily find chocolates from Ecuador, bananas from Brazil, or rice candies from China. That's amazing. At the same time, it's wonderful to see people embracing local ingredients.

There's a whole other category of ingredients that we think chefs could add to their pantry. Modern ingredients, such as xanthan gum (a thickener) and N-Zorbit (which turns fats into powders), allow the creative cook to achieve certain results that were previously unobtainable.

Take, for example, our Mac and Cheese recipe on page 310. Normally when you melt cheese, it separates into greasy clumps. Cooks typically add a lot of flour or cornstarch to keep the cheese smooth as it melts, but that just creates a gluey texture and dulls the flavor. We use sodium citrate instead. With that small change, the dish takes on the cleanest, brightest cheese flavor of any mac and cheese we've ever had. It has proved to be one of the most popular recipes from *Modernist Cuisine*.

There's nothing alien about sodium citrate: it is simply a salt made with citric acid from citrus fruit. Most Modernist ingredients have natural origins, as illustrated on the next page. They are produced in much the same way as traditional refined ingredients, such as flour, yeast, sugar, and baking soda.

If some ingredients in this book seem weird, it's just because you're not used to them—yet. The goal of this chapter is to make you more familiar and comfortable with a wider set of ingredients. That includes fresh produce from your local farmers' market, unfamiliar ingredients from international markets, specialty items available for order online, and Modernist ingredients that allow you to prepare dishes you couldn't make any other way.

Regional authenticity

Another movement in food gravitates toward "authentic" foods that come only from a specific region. The Copenhagen restaurant Noma, for example, is famous for using ingredients only from Scandinavia (which requires great creativity in the middle of winter). The concept is admirable—except that, broadly speaking, few foods are truly authentic to just one location. Case in point: the best wheat in the world for making pasta thrives in places that have cold winters. Most Italian pasta is thus made from Canadian wheat. Does that mean it's not authentic Italian food? And in any regional cuisine, many of the ingredients and dishes were borrowed long ago from somewhere else. The Chinese ate noodles at least 3,000 years before the Italians did. Today you can find geoduck on the menus of many fine restaurants in Asia, but this unusually large variety of clam has been harvested for centuries by Native Americans in the Pacific Northwest.

FURTHER READING IN *MODERNIST CUISINE*

The origin and history of Modernist ingredients: see pages 1·250–258

How to handle food safely like a pro: see pages 1·165–195

Guides to using flavor enhancers, acidifiers, alcohols, essences, and extracts: see pages 2·312, 314, 317, 324–326

The properties and uses of thickening and gelling agents: see pages 4·28–30, 42–47

odernist chefs have added a growing number of foods to their ntries, and these new ingredients are enabling amazing creativity he kitchen. But some people feel suspicious of ingredients with familiar names, such as agar and xanthan gum. We are frequently ked, "Aren't your dishes chock-full of chemicals?" Well, yes—*all* ods, including the most natural and organic, are composed of emicals.

But nearly all of these chemicals are derived from natural ingredi- ts or processes, and many have been used for decades. They are more harmful than table salt (also known as sodium chloride). Agar, for example, is a white powder much like gelatin, but agar s a higher melting point and is extracted from seaweed rather n from pig hides or fish bones. Which is the weirder one?

Although dozens of Modernist ingredients like those shown re are now available, we selected only a handful for the recipes this book. A few of these ingredients are available at supermar- ts, health-food stores, or brewing-supply stores. Others are most sily purchased online: see Scientific Ingredients, page XXII, for election of vendors.

What it is: tapioca maltodextrin
Derived from: tapioca
Used to: turn fats into powders
Where to buy: online
Cost: $7 for 50 g
Try it in: Fish Spice Mix (see page 137), other spice blends

What it is: milk protein
Derived from: cow's milk
Used to: add texture when foaming liquids
Where to buy: grocery and health-food stores
Cost: $6 for 50 g
Try it in: Clams in Chowder Sauce (see page 292), Ultra-frothy Milk Shake (see page 213)

al Wheat Gluten
at it is: powdered wheat protein
rived from: wheat
d to: add structure to yeast bread
ere to buy: online or in grocery stores
t: $7 for 624 g
it in: Neapolitan Pizza Dough e page 296), Fresh Egg Noodles e page 268)

Xanthan Gum
What it is: a naturally occurring carbohydrate
Derived from: fermentation of sugars
Used to: thicken liquids and stabilize emulsions
Where to buy: grocery stores
Cost: $15 for 450 g
Try it in: Pistachio Pesto (see page 102), Pistachio Gelato (see page 370), Tomato Leather (see page 129)

Wondra
What it is: a precooked flour
Derived from: wheat
Used to: thicken without adding flavor
Where to buy: grocery stores
Cost: $2 for 397 g
Try it in: Creamed Spinach (see page 199), Stilton Cheese Slice (see variation on page 319), Crispy Chicken Wings, Korean-

Monosodium Glutamate

What it is: a salt of an amino acid
Derived from: fermentation of beets, sugar cane, or other sugar-rich foods
Used to: add umami flavoring
Where to buy: grocery stores
Cost: $2 for 57 g
Try it in: Aromatic Chicken Broth (see page 266)

Some people strongly believe that they react badly to MSG, but so far no scientific study has ever linked MSG consumption to health problems.

Insta Cure #1

What it is: a blend of salt and sodium nitrite, plus safety coloring
Derived from: salt, soda ash, or other sources of nitrogen
Used to: cure meats, add pink color
Where to buy: butcher or sausage-making supply stores
Cost: $6 for 450 g
Try it in: Pork Belly B.L.T. (see page 232)

Diastatic Malt Powder (not shown)

What it is: malted grain containing active enzymes
Derived from: grains
Used to: convert starches to sugars; rising agent for doughs
Where to buy: online
Cost: $2 for 450 g
Try it in: Modernist Vichyssoise (see page 162)

Albumin Powder

What it is: powdered egg white
Derived from: eggs
Used to: make flavorful gels and foams
Where to buy: grocery and kitchen-supply stores
Cost: $7 for 142 g
Try it in: Striped Mushroom Omelet (see page 148), Ultrafrothy Milk Shake (see page 213)

Agar

What it is: a naturally occurring polysaccharide
Derived from: red seaweed
Used to: thicken and gel liquids
Where to buy: online and in grocery stores
Cost: $15 for 450 g
Try it in: Onion Fluid Gel (see page 100), Vegetarian Panna Cotta (see variation on page 366)

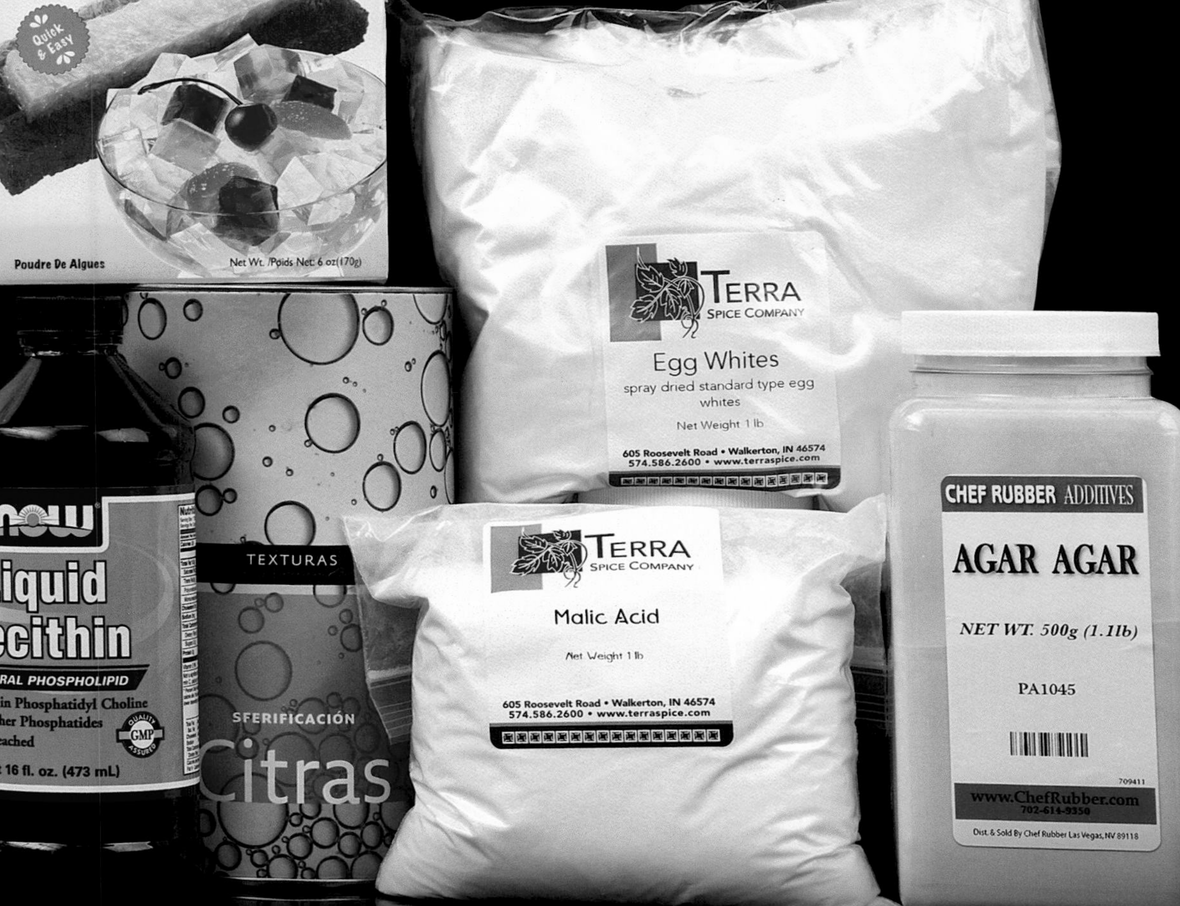

Malic Acid

What it is: a naturally occurring acid
Derived from: fruits
Used to: add extreme tartness; often used with, or in place of, citric acid
Where to buy: brewing-supply stores
Cost: $3 for 57 g
Try it in: Fruit Minestrone (see page 158), Vacuum-Infused Celery (see page 131), Pressure-Caramelized Ketchup (see page 110)

Liquid Soy Lecithin

What it is: a naturally occurring phospholipid
Derived from: soybeans
Used to: emulsify liquids
Where to buy: health-food stores
Cost: $15 for 567 g
Try it in: Home Jus Gras (see page 93), Modernist Vinaigrette (see page 117)

Sodium Citrate

What it is: a salt of citric acid
Derived from: citrus fruits
Used to: keep cheese from separating
Where to buy: online or in health-food stores
Cost: $6 for 50 g
Try it in: Mac and Cheese (see pages 310–313)

Some health-food stores and pharmacies sell malic acid nutritional supplements; these are not the same as malic acid powder and will not work in recipes.

NOT YOUR PARENTS' SUPERMARKET

Since the invention of the self-service grocery store in 1916 by a small shop in Memphis that grew to become the Piggly Wiggly chain, most people have bought their groceries at supermarkets. But if you're interested in adding diversity to your cooking and your palate, venture outside that aisle shopping and wander into other kinds of food purveyors.

Farmers' Markets

Nearly every community now has a farmers' market. In the Seattle area, where we live, the Pike Place Market has been going strong for generations. But we go less frequently than we used to because small farmers now also gather for a weekly market closer to us in Bellevue, Washington, a city of less than 125,000 people. If you're not aware of a market in your area, ask around—there probably is one.

Warehouse Stores

Surprisingly, shopping clubs such as Costco, Sam's Club, and PriceSmart often offer unique seasonal ingredients in bulk quantities at a fraction of the usual cost. We've seen green chickpeas and wild salmon here in Seattle; New Yorkers might find beautiful scallops.

Sustainable Aquaculture Farms

Marine wildlife is dwindling at an alarming pace, and conventional fish farms have developed a reputation for causing ecological harm. But sustainable forms of aquaculture are now in operation. You can buy sustainably farmed fish and shellfish online and at specialty retailers (see page XIX for sources).

Internet Vendors

Sometimes the cheapest—or only—way to buy specialty items is to get them online. Shipping is a small percentage of the cost for small, light items such as spices (see page XIX for sources). Websites for professional chefs, such as chefrubber.com and le-sanctuaire.com, are good sources of modern gelling agents and thickeners, as well as exotic baking ingredients. Check the reviews on food forums, such as egullet.org, to find out which products work the best.

Specialty Markets

Shop owners who specialize offer higher-quality products, hard-to-find ingredients, and more knowledgeable service. At specialty shops, you can find intriguing imports, such as complex olive oils from Liguria, Italy, potent fruit vinegars from the southwest of France, aged cheeses from all over the world, and artisan-cured meats, such as the Ibérico ham shown above. The shops are often an outlet for boutique food producers from the local area.

Local Butchers

Food scientists, chefs, and ethicists all agree that the best-quality meat comes from animals that are raised healthy and slaughtered humanely. The scientific reason is that stress causes animals to release hormones that negatively affect the texture and taste of the resulting meat. Local and artisanal butchers make an effort to find the best suppliers. Some online sources allow you to buy directly from the farmer (see page XIX).

Growing Your Own Food

Millions of people are rediscovering something we've known for a long time: if you grow your own food, you can eat it at the peak of its perfection. That is why there are probably more chefs running farms now than at any point in history. You can start small—all you really need is a burlap sack, soil, and seeds.

Where can you find the best ingredients? Good local restaurants are an excellent source of knowledge. The Internet can also help you find things in your own community as well as on the other side of the world.

TAKE A WALK ON THE WILD SIDE

Globalization has caused an explosion of culinary diversity in cities and towns of all sizes. Taco stands and sushi bars are now ubiquitous, and people are also increasingly aware of regional culinary nuances, such as the differences among Thai, Vietnamese, and Malaysian foods.

Immigrants who carried their culinary traditions with them have created a demand for specialty markets that serve the needs of particular ethnic communities. But these markets also provide wonderful opportunities for locals to experience new foods and taste other cultures. We encourage you to step outside of your comfort zone and try ingredients that are unfamiliar. No matter what your food tradition, there are plenty of others to sample.

Accept at the outset that you won't like everything you try. That's okay. Learning to enjoy strong tastes, strong odors, or unfamiliar textures takes a certain amount of practice. If you are open to experimentation, and you taste without expectation, you will discover new flavors you love, but never knew existed. We use some of the ingredients listed below in the recipes in this book; the others are simply among our favorites.

Japanese Markets

A good source for: white soy sauce, *matcha* (powdered green tea), *genmaicha* (green tea with toasted brown rice), aged rice vinegar, sake, miso, *natto* (fermented soybeans), preserved cherry blossoms, black sesame paste, Kewpie brand mayonnaise, *shichimi* (chili spice mix), dried baby sardines and crabs, bonito flakes, *kombu* and *nori* (dried seaweed), fresh wasabi, *kinome* (prickly ash) leaves, *myoga* (ginger bud), *maitake* and *enoki* mushrooms, *satsuma-imo* and Okinawan sweet potatoes, *kabocha* squash, *fuyu* and *hachiya* persimmons, *yuzu* (Japanese citrus), short-grain rice varieties, quail eggs, sea urchin, sashimi-quality seafood

Indian Markets

A good source for: mustard oil; ghee; whole spices such as Ceylon cinnamon, nutmeg, ajowan, cardamom, coriander, cumin, mace, and mustard seeds; black salt; saffron; orange blossom water and rose water; fresh and dried chilies; *amchoor* (dried sour mango); *anardana* (dried pomegranate); *alubukhara* (dried sour plums); preserved black lime; raw cashews; fresh turmeric, chickpeas, and coconut; curry and fenugreek leaves; snake beans; Indian eggplants; red bananas; tamarind; various pickles; long-grain rice varieties; black and yellow lentils; breads such as *papadums* and *paratha*; flours and mixes for *dosa,* chapati, and *idli*

Chinese Markets

A good source for: dried fermented black beans, toasted-sesame oil, Shaoxing and *michiu* wines, dried lily buds and orange peel, Sichuan pepper and chilies, black fungus, cassia, licorice root, chrysanthemum leaves, lotus root, taro root, peavines, lychees, longan fruit, red dates, bitter and winter melons, daikon radishes, Chinese eggplant, freshwater chestnuts, river potatoes, garlic chives, fresh bamboo shoots, salt-preserved duck eggs, *lup cheong* (Chinese sausage), fresh duck, offal, tofu

Southeast Asian Markets

A good source for: fish sauce, shrimp paste, dried shrimp, chili sauces and spice pastes, preserved turnips, palm sugar, coconut cream, star anise, galangal root, mangosteen and durian fruit, lemongrass, Thai eggplant, betel and Makrud lime leaves, straw mushrooms, baby corn, *ngo om* (rice paddy herb), fresh coconut, roasted rice flour, tapioca starch

Latin American Markets

A good source for: fresh *masa harina*; *crema*; Cotija cheese and *queso fresco*; fresh banana leaves; tomatillos; nopales (cactus paddles); epazote (herb); avocado leaves; Mexican oregano; fresh and dried chilies such as poblano, *puja*, and *guajillo*; dried corn husks and chamomile; hot sauces; *chicharrones*; fresh lard; pork skin; beef tongue

Korean Markets

A good source for: *ssam jang* (spice condiment), *gochujang* (fermented chili paste), kimchi and other fermented vegetables, black garlic, preserved seaweed, dried ferns and seafood, *duk* (soft rice cakes), chili threads, bean sprouts, *negi* (giant scallions), fragrant pears, taro, mung bean flour, monosodium glutamate (MSG), oxtails, fresh pork belly

Middle Eastern and African Markets

A good source for: palm oil; *harissa* (chili sauce); grains such as teff, fonio, millet, bulgur, and sorghum; *egusi* (gourd), baobab, and *ogbono* (bush mango) seeds; kola, cashew, and palm nuts; dates; green bananas; cassava; taro; okra; guava; *injera* flatbread; *ouarka* pastry sheets; couscous; plantain; *mahlab* (cherry stone spice); preserved lemons; dried roses; bush mint; grains of paradise; fresh goat

UNUSUAL FRUITS AND VEGETABLES

At local produce markets in and around Seattle, where we're based, we were able to find a cornucopia of fresh produce from almost every corner of the world. The exotic textures and flavors of unfamiliar fruits and vegetables can add whole new dimensions to your cooking.

1. durian
2. jackfruit
3. papaya
4. chestnut
5. quince
6. pomegranate
7. Haden mango
8. cherimoya
9. African cucumber
10. pineapple quince
11. banana blossom
12. dragon fruit *(pitaya)*
13. Nashi pear
14. passion fruit
15. prickly pear cactus fruit
16. mangosteen
17. star fruit
18. longan
19. Pepino melon
20. fragrant pear
21. kiwi
22. red bananas
23. soursop
24. Shinko pear
25. Chinese dates

1. kohlrabi
2. snake melon
3. Thai eggplant
4. *gobo* (burdock)
5. yuca
6. *hon shimeji* mushrooms
7. celery root
8. bitter melon
9. Chinese eggplant
10. Okinawan sweet potato
11. lion's mane mushroom
12. galangal
13. lotus root
14. dumpling squash
15. chayote
16. peavine
17. *myoga* (ginger bud)
18. okra
19. taro
20. golden *enoki* mushroom

FORAGED FOODS: AUTUMN AND SPRING

Modernist chefs such as Marc Veyrat, René Redzepi, and David Kinch have helped create a burgeoning movement of cooking with obscure wild ingredients. Now cooks at all levels have been discovering that foraging for wild ingredients presents a whole new realm of possibilities.

Each season brings an array of wild edibles. Here in the Pacific Northwest, autumn is the season of mushrooms: porcinis, black trumpets, matsutake, hedgehogs, lobster mushrooms, and many others (pictured above). Winter is a slow time for foraging, but wild mushrooms are still available in some areas. Oxalis (wood sorrel), morels, stinging nettles, and fiddlehead ferns sprout in

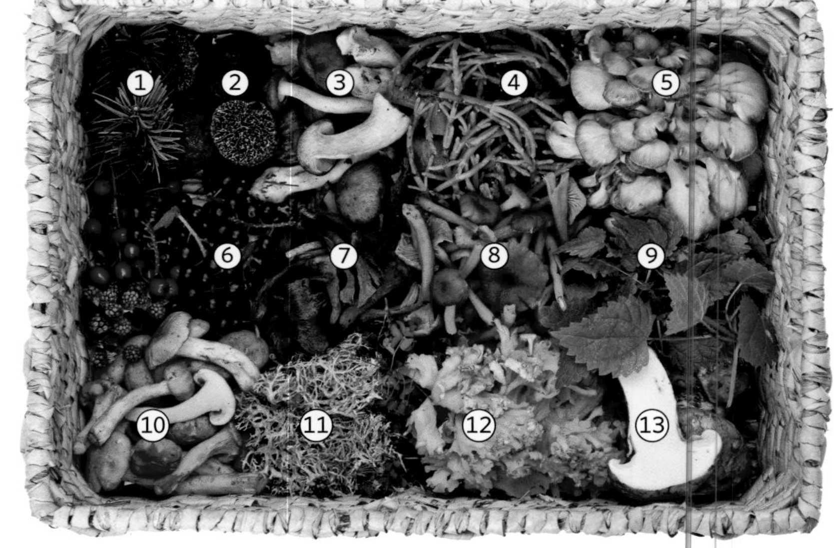

① pine
② black truffle
③ fried chicken mushroom
④ sea bean
⑤ *maitake* mushroom
⑥ wild currants
⑦ black trumpets
⑧ yellow foot chanterelle
⑨ stinging nettles
⑩ golden chanterelles
⑪ lichen
⑫ cauliflower mushroom
⑬ matsutake mushroom (pine mushroom)

the spring (pictured above), as do ramps (wild leeks), garlic, and asparagus. Summer brings chanterelles, purslane, miner's lettuce, and wild berries ripe for the picking.

Each region offers its own menu of native wild foods. Before you go on your own foraging excursions, pick up a good guide, such as Bradford Angier's *Field Guide to Edible Wild Plants*, to steer you toward the delicacies and away from the dangers. Some mushrooms, in particular, can be quite toxic, so be sure to check with a knowledgeable expert before making a mushroom omelet after a hike!

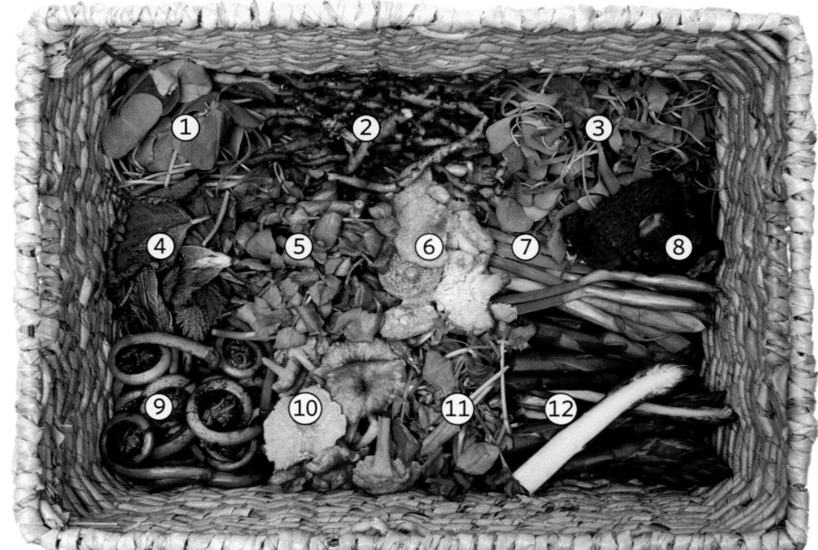

① oxalis (wood sorrel)
② wild licorice
③ miner's lettuce
④ stinging nettles
⑤ chickweed
⑥ hedgehog mushrooms
⑦ garlic shoots
⑧ morels
⑨ fiddlehead Lady ferns
⑩ gray chanterelles
⑪ wild watercress
⑫ purple asparagus

PART TWO:
THE RECIPES

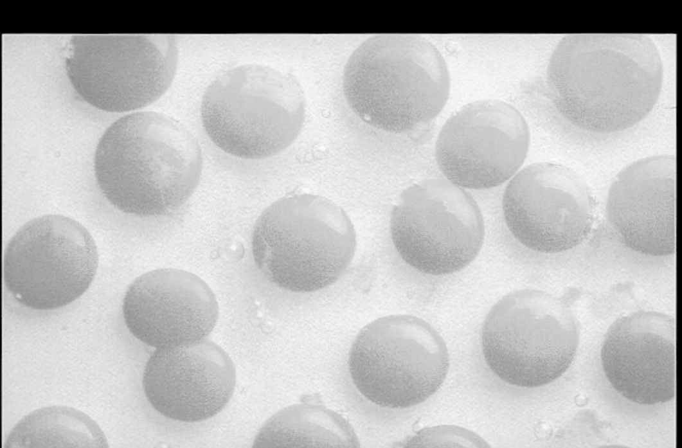

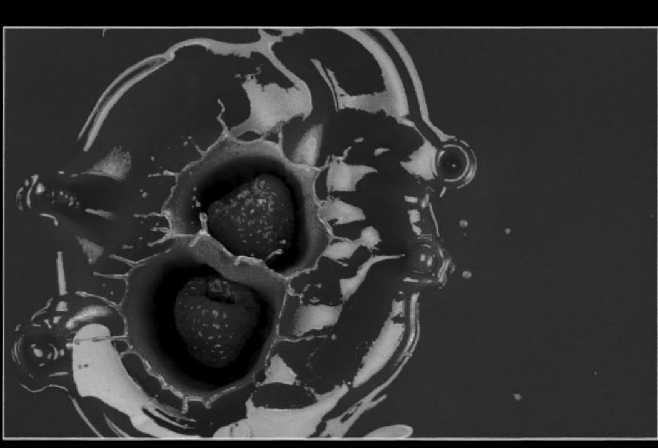

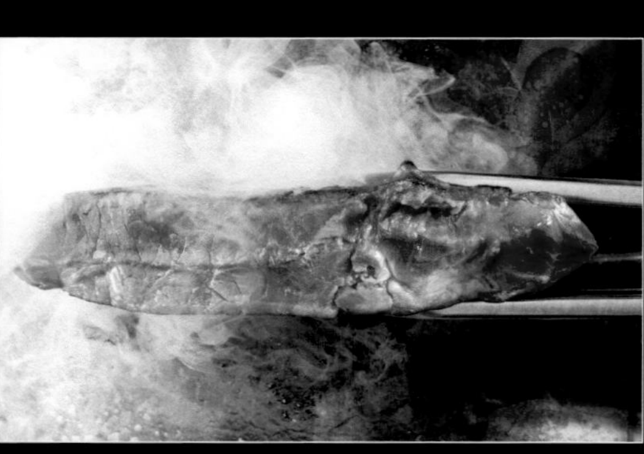

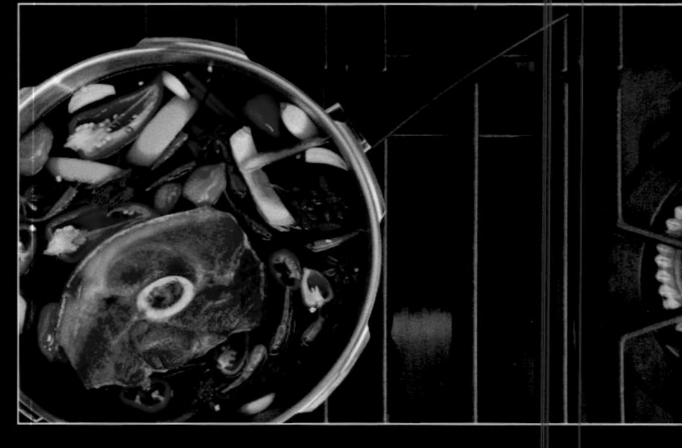

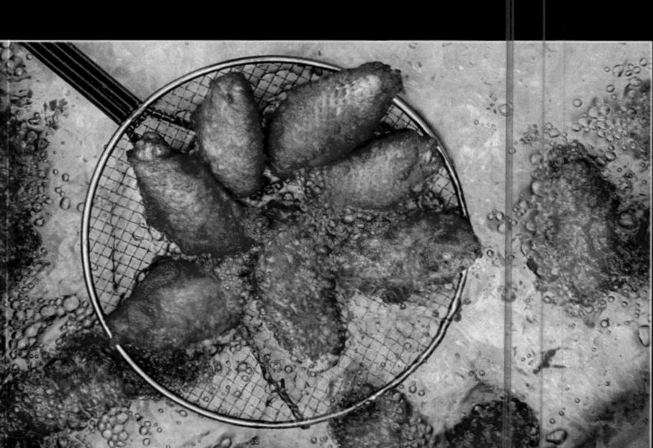

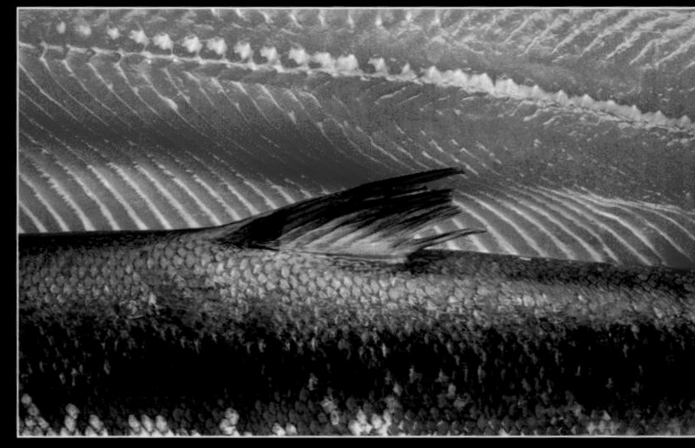

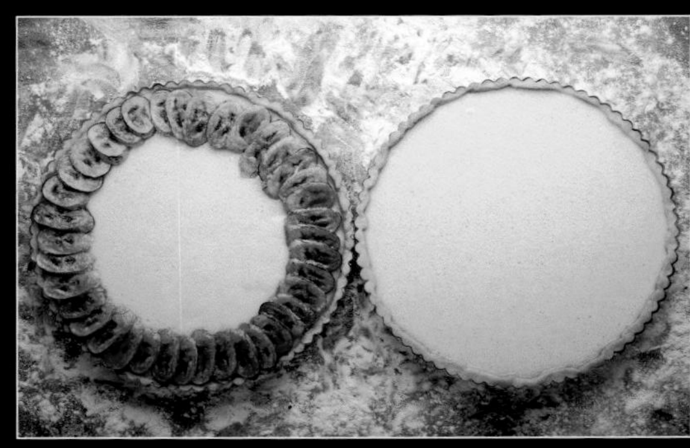

BASICS

Virtually all good cooking rests on a core set of basics—those fundamental prepared ingredients you routinely keep on hand in your pantry and refrigerator. There are, after all, only so many ways to cook meats, vegetables, and grains. It is through the stocks and sauces, the infused oils and emulsions, the gravies and glazes that you express your creativity and make a dish your own. That little extra flavor or a novel aroma can turn an ordinary meal into something special.

As you make recipes in other parts of this book, you'll find that they often incorporate the building blocks collected in this chapter. The recipes steer you back here because we consider these basic elements to be intrinsic parts of the flavor and refinement of those dishes. It is, admittedly, more time-consuming to make a recipe when some of the ingredients involve recipes of their own. When you don't have time, you can always use water instead of stock, or store-bought ketchup in place of homemade. But it is worth the effort to make your own once in a while. We have, wherever possible, suggested methods that are fast, such as pressure-cooking, or that can be left mostly unattended, such as cooking sous vide. You can also make large batches and freeze them so that they are handy when time is short.

The best thing about these basics is their versatility. When you pressure-render chicken fat for Home Jus Gras (see page 93) or make a carotene butter for Caramelized Carrot Soup (see page 178), taste the result by itself and imagine other applications. Also try combining techniques from throughout the book. If you make a cream infused with cinnamon and vanilla, as described in the Custards and Pies chapter (see page 358), you can pop it in a whipping siphon, store it in the fridge, and use it on your morning pancakes.

Each recipe in this chapter may, along the way, also teach you something about cooking. Take pesto, for example. A conventional pesto eventually separates into coarse solids floating on watery liquid, with a big slick of oil on top. But if you add a small amount of xanthan gum, the liquid stays creamy and cohesive. Just one pinch of powder produces a beautifully homogenized pesto (see page 102).

Or consider hollandaise, that unctuous mixture of warm egg yolks and butter. The sauce is so fragile because butter congeals and separates as soon as it cools. But we show you how to avoid that problem by putting the sauce in a whipping siphon; you no longer have to make hollandaise at the last minute while pulling together all the other parts of a meal.

The stock recipes contain useful insights, too. A pressure cooker is the best tool for the job because it concentrates all the aromas released by the delicate ingredients. You don't smell them while you're cooking because they stay in the food instead of vaporizing into the air.

These are just a few examples of the dozens of foundational recipes in this chapter that are not only approachable and versatile but very tasty, too.

Stocks, see page 84

Condiments, see page 124

Sauces, see page 94

Oils and Fats, see page 116

Brines and Marinades, see page 132

Spice Mixes, see page 135

STOCKS

Sauces lie at the foundation of Western cuisine, and stocks form the foundation of most sauces. Unlike jus, the liquid that emerges from meats or vegetables as they cook, stocks include added water. When fully seasoned, stocks become broths and the basis for complete soups.

The goal when making a stock is to wring as much of the flavor as possible out of the meat, fish, or vegetables. Even a two-day simmer is rarely sufficient to pull all the flavorful compounds from the deep interior of food, so the first trick in making great stock is to chop the food into tiny pieces or thin slices. A pressure cooker is also an invaluable tool for accelerating the extraction of flavors while preventing their escape into the air. Stocks made sous vide similarly retain flavors where you want them: in the liquid, not the air.

PRESSURE-COOKED WHITE CHICKEN STOCK

YIELD:	*1.2 kg / 5 cups*
TIME ESTIMATE:	*1¾ hours, including 15 minutes of preparation and 1½ hours unattended*
STORAGE NOTES:	*keeps for 5 days when refrigerated or up to 6 months when frozen*
LEVEL OF DIFFICULTY:	*easy*
SPECIAL REQUIREMENTS:	*meat grinder or food processor, pressure cooker*
USED IN:	*Aromatic Chicken Broth (see page 266)*

This recipe makes a white chicken stock. It can also be made using other fowl by simply replacing the chicken meat and bones with those of duck or game fowl. Carcasses left over from roasted chickens can be substituted for the chicken wings; freeze them until you have enough to make a batch of stock. To make a brown chicken stock, see the variation on the next page.

INGREDIENT	WEIGHT	VOLUME	SCALING	PROCEDURE
Chicken wings, chopped	700 g / 1.5 lb	6–8 wings	70%	① Cover with cold water in a pot, and bring just to a boil. ② Drain the chicken immediately, discarding the water.
Boneless, skinless chicken thigh meat	700 g / 1.5 lb	from 6 thighs	70%	③ Grind coarsely in a food processor or meat grinder.
Water	1 kg	1 L / 4¼ cups	100%	④ Combine with the blanched and ground chicken in a pressure cooker.
Sweet onion, thinly sliced	100 g	1 cup	10%	⑤ Pressure-cook at a gauge pressure of 1 bar / 15 psi for 1½ hours. Start timing when full pressure is reached.
Carrots, thinly sliced	50 g	¾ cup	5%	⑥ Depressurize the cooker.
Leeks, thinly sliced	50 g	⅞ cup	5%	⑦ Strain through a fine sieve.
Garlic, thinly sliced	10 g	1½ Tbsp	1%	⑧ Use the stock in warm or cold dishes.
Italian parsley	2 g	2–3 sprigs	0.2%	
Black peppercorns	1 g	½ tsp	0.1%	

Safety tips for pressure-cooking: see page 33

1 Cover the chopped chicken wings with cold water in a pot, and bring it just to a boil to blanch the chicken and remove the bitter flavor from the bones. Roasting the bones has the same effect.

2 Drain the chicken as soon as the water starts to boil; discard the water. We have found, through extensive blind taste tests, that white stocks have better flavor and clarity when made with blanched meat and bones.

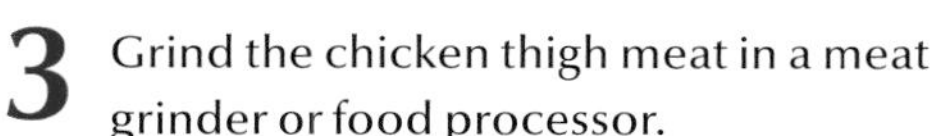

3 Grind the chicken thigh meat in a meat grinder or food processor.

4 Combine the water, onions, carrots, leeks, garlic, Italian parsley, and peppercorns with the blanched wing pieces and ground thigh meat in a pressure cooker.

5 Pressure-cook at a gauge pressure of 1 bar / 15 psi for 1½ hours. Start timing as soon as full pressure has been reached.

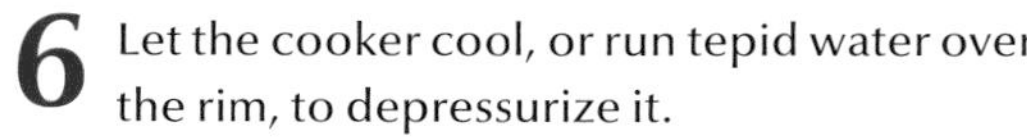

6 Let the cooker cool, or run tepid water over the rim, to depressurize it.

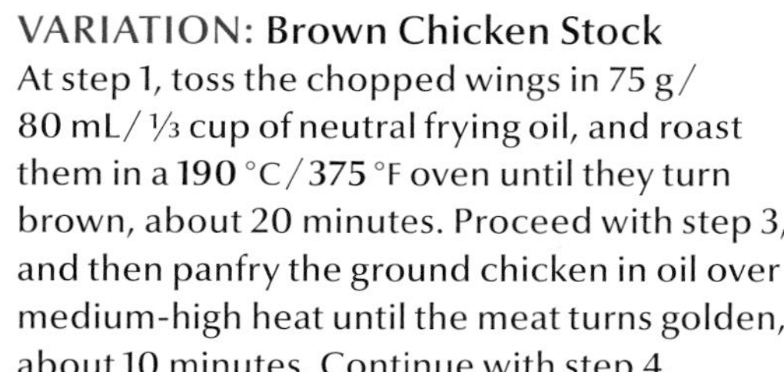

VARIATION: **Brown Chicken Stock**
At step 1, toss the chopped wings in 75 g / 80 mL / ⅓ cup of neutral frying oil, and roast them in a 190 °C / 375 °F oven until they turn brown, about 20 minutes. Proceed with step 3, and then panfry the ground chicken in oil over medium-high heat until the meat turns golden, about 10 minutes. Continue with step 4.

7 Strain the stock through a fine sieve; discard the solids.

8 Use the stock in warm or cold dishes.

PRESSURE-COOKED BROWN BEEF STOCK

YIELD:	*1 kg / 4¼ cups*
TIME ESTIMATE:	*3½ hours overall, including 30 minutes of preparation and 3 hours unattended*
STORAGE NOTES:	*keeps for 5 days when refrigerated or up to 6 months when frozen*
LEVEL OF DIFFICULTY:	*easy*
SPECIAL REQUIREMENTS:	*pressure cooker, oxtail*
USED IN:	*Red Wine Glaze (see page 97); French Onion Soup (see variation on page 127); Thai Sweet, Sour, and Savory Glaze (see page 115); Korean Short Rib Lettuce Wraps (see variation on page 221)*

Our recipe for brown beef stock avoids much of the fuss and ritual typically associated with this classic kitchen staple. You can easily adapt this recipe to make brown pork, lamb, veal, and game stocks. Simply substitute the appropriate ground meat and flavorful, meaty bones. Shanks, knuckles, and other bony cuts of beef can be substituted for the oxtail.

INGREDIENT	WEIGHT	VOLUME	SCALING	PROCEDURE
Oxtail, jointed	500 g / 1.1 lb	6–8 pieces	100%	① Preheat the oven to 190 °C / 375 °F.
Rendered beef fat or neutral frying oil (see pages 123 and xxii)	30 g	30 mL / 2 Tbsp	6%	② Toss together to coat, and roast until dark brown, 40–45 minutes.
Beef chuck, finely ground	200 g / 0.4 lb		40%	③ Sear the meat in the base of a pressure cooker over medium-high heat until dark brown, about 8 minutes.
Rendered beef fat or neutral frying oil	50 g	50 mL / ¼ cup	10%	
Water	750 g	750 mL / 3¼ cups	150%	④ Combine with the browned beef and roasted oxtail in the pressure cooker.
Full-bodied red wine	120 g	120 mL / ½ cup	24%	⑤ Pressure-cook at a gauge pressure of 1 bar / 15 psi for 2½ hours. Start timing as soon as full pressure has been reached.
Carrots, thinly sliced	50 g	¾ cup	10%	⑥ Let the cooker cool, or run tepid water over the rim, to depressurize it.
Yellow onion, thinly sliced	50 g	½ cup	10%	⑦ Strain.
Leeks, white parts only, thinly sliced	20 g	⅜ cup	4%	⑧ Use the stock in warm or cold dishes.
Italian parsley	10 g	4 sprigs	2%	
Thyme	1 g	1–2 sprigs	0.2%	
Fresh bay leaf	0.2 g	1 leaf	0.1%	

Safety tips for pressure-cooking: see page 33

VARIATIONS

Brown Pork Stock

Substitute 500 g of spare ribs or meaty pork bones for the oxtail, 200 g of ground pork for the beef, and white wine or lager beer for the red wine.

White Beef Stock

Skip steps 1–3, and substitute white wine for the red wine.

SOUS VIDE FISH STOCK

YIELD:	*800 g / 3½ cups*
TIME ESTIMATE:	*1½ hours overall, including 15 minutes of preparation and 1¼ hours unattended*
STORAGE NOTES:	*keeps for 3 days when refrigerated or up to 3 months when frozen*
LEVEL OF DIFFICULTY:	*easy*
SPECIAL REQUIREMENTS:	*sous vide setup, fish bones*
USED IN:	*Arborio Rice with Sea Urchin and Cocoa (see variation on page 333), Bell Pepper Soup (see variation on page 181)*

Fish oils oxidize very easily, so to get the most flavor out of fish bones, you need to cook them gently in a sealed environment. Slow-cooking them sous vide produces excellent results. If fish bones are unavailable, any scraps of flesh or chopped fish heads will do. You can also increase the gelatin content and richness of the stock by adding skins from delicate white fish such as halibut, sole, trout, or sea bass. Darker, oilier fishes like mackerel, fresh sardines, tuna, or salmon yield a stock that is too strongly flavored for most uses.

INGREDIENT	WEIGHT	VOLUME	SCALING	PROCEDURE
Dry vermouth	175 g	175 mL / ¾ cup	23%	① Preheat a water bath to 80 °C / 176 °F.
Dry white wine	100 g	100 mL / ½ cup	13%	② Combine the wines in a pot, bring to a boil, and simmer for 5 minutes.
				③ Cool the mixture completely.
Fish bones, cleaned, rinsed, and chopped	1 kg		133%	④ Combine with the cooled wines. Vacuum seal if using ice; alternatively, transfer to a large (4 L / 1 gal) zip-top bag, remove as much air from the bag as possible by using the water-displacement method (see page 58), and seal it.
Crushed ice (if vacuum sealing) or water	750 g	6 cups of ice / 750 mL of water	100%	⑤ Cook sous vide for 1¼ hours.
Carrots, thinly sliced	250 g	2½ cups	33%	⑥ Strain.
Onion, thinly sliced	200 g	2 cups	27%	⑦ Use warm or cold.
Fennel, thinly sliced	100 g	1 cup	13%	
Leeks, thinly sliced	100 g	1½ cups	13%	
Garlic, thinly sliced	15 g	2 Tbsp	2%	

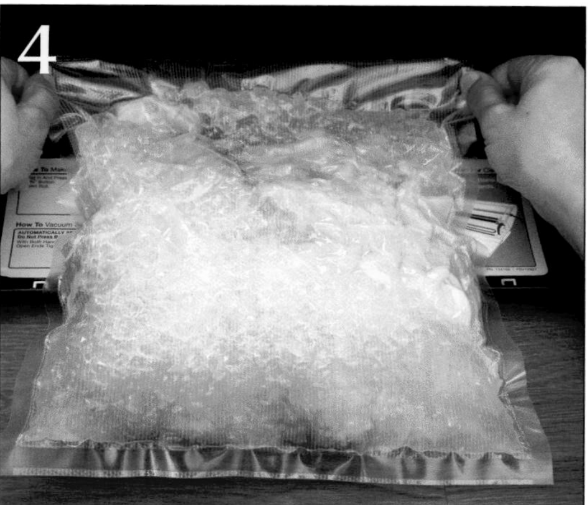

Bottled clam juice, available at most grocery stores, is a good substitute for fish stock if you don't have time to make it yourself.

VARIATION: **Brown Fish Stock**
After step 3, panfry the fish bones in 30 g / 30 mL / 2 Tbsp of neutral frying oil until they brown, 4–6 minutes. Cool the bones completely, and then continue with step 4.

Use only the freshest lean fish for stock.

PRESSURE-COOKED CRUSTACEAN STOCK

YIELD:	*1.1 kg / 4½ cups*
TIME ESTIMATE:	*1½ hours overall, including 30 minutes of preparation and 1 hour unattended*
STORAGE NOTES:	*keeps for 3 days when refrigerated or up to 3 months when frozen*
LEVEL OF DIFFICULTY:	*moderate*
SPECIAL REQUIREMENTS:	*pressure cooker; shells of lobsters, crabs, or shrimp (or whole shrimp with heads on)*
USED IN:	*Forbidden Rice with Squid Ink and Sous Vide Clams (see variation on page 330), Shrimp and Grits (see page 338), Thai Soup (see variation on page 267)*

Anytime you find yourself with crustacean shells left over from a seafood feast, save them! Collect them in the freezer until you have enough to make stock. If you don't have shells, use whole shrimp (with the heads on), which are relatively inexpensive and easy to find.

INGREDIENT	WEIGHT	VOLUME	SCALING	PROCEDURE
Shells of lobsters, crabs, crayfish, shrimp, or prawns	650 g / 1.4 lb of shells or 650 g / 1.4 lb of whole shrimp	from 2 lobsters or 2 large crabs	65%	① Clean by discarding any organs, including the gills and eyes. ② Chop into pieces with a heavy knife or cleaver. Smaller pieces infuse more flavor into the stock. ③ Place the pieces in a large (4 L / 1 gal) zip-top bag. Partially seal the bag, cover it with a towel, and pound it with a mallet to crush the shells.
Clarified, unsalted butter or neutral-tasting oil see page 119	50 g	55 mL / ¼ cup	5%	④ Sauté the shells in the base of a pressure cooker over medium heat, stirring often, until golden brown, 6–8 minutes. ⑤ Remove the shells from the pot, and reserve them for use in step 9.
Carrots, thinly sliced	50 g	¾ cup	5%	⑥ Add to the pot, and panfry until the onions soften and start to brown, 3–4 minutes. Add more butter or oil as needed.
Onion, thinly sliced	50 g	½ cup	5%	
Leeks, thinly sliced	20 g	⅜ cup	2%	
Fennel, thinly sliced	20 g	¼ cup	2%	
Button mushrooms, thinly sliced	20 g	⅜ cup	2%	
Tomato paste (optional)	50 g	3 Tbsp	5%	⑦ Stir in, and continue frying until a rich, cooked tomato aroma develops, about 3 minutes. Take care not to burn the mixture.
Water	1 kg	1 L / 4¼ cups	100%	⑧ Deglaze the pot.
Dry vermouth	150 g	150 mL / ⅝ cup	15%	
Italian parsley	2.5 g	1 sprig	0.3%	⑨ Add, along with the sautéed shells, to the vegetable mixture, and stir. ⑩ Pressure-cook at a gauge pressure of 1 bar / 15 psi for 1 hour. Start timing as soon as full pressure has been reached. ⑪ Let the cooker cool, or run tepid water over the rim, to depressurize it. ⑫ Strain the stock through a sieve lined with cheesecloth. ⑬ Use in warm or cold dishes.
Thyme	1 g	1–2 sprigs	0.1%	
Fresh basil leaves	2 g	3–4 leaves	0.2%	
Fennel seeds	0.1 g	5 seeds	0.01%	
Saffron		2–3 threads		

Safety tips for pressure-cooking: see page 33

VEGETABLE STOCK

YIELD:	*500 g / 2 cups*
TIME ESTIMATE:	*3½ hours overall, including 30 minutes of preparation and 3 hours unattended*
STORAGE NOTES:	*keeps for 5 days when refrigerated or up to 6 months when frozen*
LEVEL OF DIFFICULTY:	*easy*
SPECIAL REQUIREMENTS:	*sous vide setup, vacuum sealer*
USED IN:	*Vegetable Risotto (see page 328), Farro with Chicken, Artichokes, and Black Olives (see variation on page 332), Quinoa with Pistachio Pesto and Asparagus (see variation on page 332)*

Making stock sous vide is the best way to capture the subtle, nuanced flavors of the vegetables—especially if you have time to infuse the liquid overnight in the refrigerator. When time is more pressing, however, we pressure-cook the stock (see the variation below), which produces a stronger flavor.

You can tailor the flavor of this stock by selecting the varieties of vegetables you use. A stock made with sweet onions tastes different from one based on white onions, for example. For a recipe for an all-allium (onion-family) vegetable jus, see page 182.

INGREDIENT	WEIGHT	VOLUME	SCALING
Ice	500 g	2 cups	100%
Onion, thinly sliced	280 g	2¾ cups	56%
Carrots, thinly sliced	200 g	2¾ cups	40%
Celery, thinly sliced	100 g	1½ cups	20%
Leeks, white parts only, thinly sliced	100 g	1½ cups	20%
Button mushrooms, thinly sliced	50 g	⅞ cup	10%
Tomato, chopped	50 g	⅓ cup	10%
Chives, sliced	10 g	¼ cup	2%
Italian parsley, chopped	10 g	3 Tbsp	2%
Coriander seeds	1 g	1 tsp	0.2%
Black peppercorns	1 g	1 tsp	0.2%
Thyme	1 g	1–2 sprigs	0.2%
Fresh bay leaf	0.5 g	2 leaves	0.1%
Star anise, crushed	0.5 g	½ pod	0.1%

PROCEDURE

1. Preheat a water bath to 85 °C / 185 °F.
2. Vacuum seal the ingredients together.
3. Cook sous vide for 3 hours.
4. Plunge the sealed bag into an ice bath until it is fully chilled. Optionally, refrigerate the sealed ingredients for another 12 hours to allow the flavors to infuse more fully into the stock.
5. Strain.
6. Use the stock in warm or cold dishes.

Safety tips for pressure-cooking: see page 33

VARIATIONS

Pressure-Cooked Vegetable Stock

Pressure-cooking the stock reduces the overall time to 1 hour, including 35 minutes of unattended cooking. Combine all of the ingredients in a pressure cooker, and pressure-cook at a gauge pressure of 1 bar / 15 psi for 35 minutes; start timing as soon as full pressure has been reached. Depressurize the cooker. Strain the stock, and use it warm or cold.

Brown Vegetable Stock

Preheat an oven to 220 °C / 425 °F. Toss the vegetables in 40 g / 40 mL / 3 Tbsp of neutral frying oil, and roast them in the preheated oven until they turn dark brown. Combine the roasted vegetables with the water and aromatics, and then continue at step 3 or with the pressure-cooking in the pressure-cooked variation at left.

TOASTED CORN STOCK

YIELD:	*750 g / 3¼ cups*
TIME ESTIMATE:	*1 hour overall, including 15 minutes of preparation and 45 minutes unattended*
STORAGE NOTES:	*keeps for 5 days when refrigerated or up to 6 months when frozen*
LEVEL OF DIFFICULTY:	*easy*
SPECIAL REQUIREMENTS:	*pressure cooker*
USED IN:	*Pressure-Cooked Polenta (see page 336), Pressure-Cooked Fresh-Corn Tamales (see page 340)*

INGREDIENT	WEIGHT	VOLUME	PROCEDURE
Fresh corn with husks	600–700 g	5 large ears	① Preheat the oven to 175 °C / 350 °F. ② Shuck the corn, reserving the husks. ③ Scatter the husks on a baking sheet. Top with an inverted cooling rack. ④ Bake until golden brown, about 15 minutes. ⑤ Cut the kernels from the cobs; reserve them for some other use.
Cold water	1.2 kg	1.2 L / 5 cups	⑥ Place the corncobs and toasted husks, but not the kernels, in a pressure cooker, add the water, and pressure-cook at a gauge pressure of 1 bar / 15 psi for 30 minutes. Start timing when full pressure is reached. ⑦ Depressurize the cooker. ⑧ Strain through a sieve lined with cheesecloth, and use warm or cold.

Safety tips for pressure-cooking: see page 33

1 Preheat the oven to 175 °C / 350 °F.

2 Shuck the corn, reserving the husks.

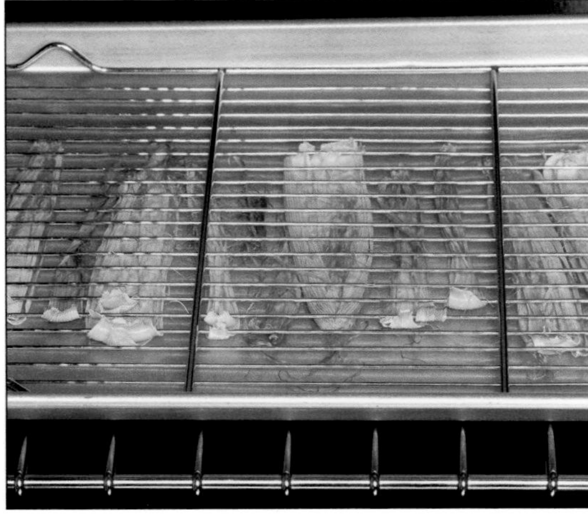

3 Scatter the corn husks on a baking sheet, and place an inverted cooling rack on top of them to hold them in place.

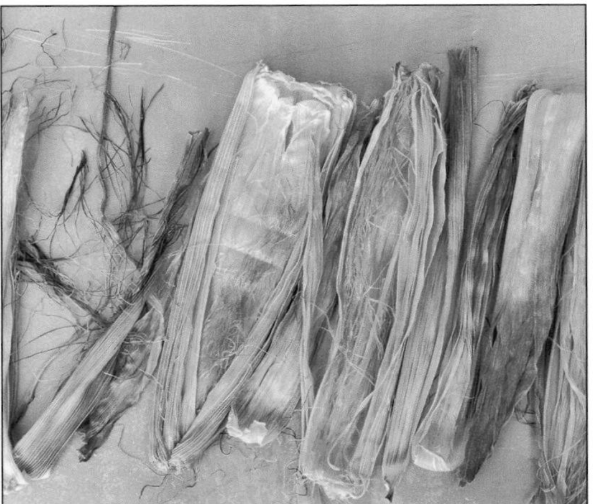

4 Bake the husks, tossing them occasionally until they all turn golden brown, 15–25 minutes.

5 While the husks are baking, cut the kernels from the cobs. Reserve the kernels for another use.

6 Place the corncobs, toasted husks, and water in a pressure cooker, and pressure-cook at a gauge pressure of 1 bar / 15 psi for 30 minutes. Do not add the corn kernels. Start timing as soon as full pressure has been reached.

7 Let the cooker cool, or run tepid water over the rim, to depressurize it.

8 Strain the corn stock through a sieve lined with cheesecloth. Use the stock in warm or cold dishes.

This recipe uses the husks and cobs of the corn, but not the kernels. The kernels are good when cooked sous vide, and you can use them to make Corn Soup (see variation on page 181).

MUSHROOM JUS

YIELD:	*500 g / 2 cups*
TIME ESTIMATE:	*50 minutes overall, including 20 minutes of preparation and 30 minutes unattended*
STORAGE NOTES:	*keeps for 5 days when refrigerated or up to 6 months when frozen*
LEVEL OF DIFFICULTY:	*easy*
SPECIAL REQUIREMENTS:	*pressure cooker, white miso*
USED IN:	*Cream of Mushroom Soup (see variation on page 150), Barley with Wild Mushrooms and Red Wine (see variation on page 331)*

This recipe makes an unseasoned mushroom stock if you follow it just through step 4; continue to step 8 to make a savory yet meatless jus that you can use as you would meat jus. We also serve the jus as a broth and use it to dress risotto (see page 328), poached eggs (see page 142), and steak (see page 200).

For an earthier flavor that goes well with our barley risotto, add 15 g / 2 Tbsp of crumbled dry porcinis in step 1. For a more savory version, add 75 g / ¾ cup of thinly sliced smoked bacon at step 1.

INGREDIENT	WEIGHT	VOLUME	SCALING	PROCEDURE
Crimini mushrooms, thinly sliced	300 g	4 cups	75%	① Sauté in the base of a pressure cooker over high heat until the mushrooms and shallots turn golden, about 12 minutes.
Shallots, thinly sliced	80 g	¾ cup	20%	
Clarified, unsalted butter or neutral-tasting oil see page 119	50 g	55 mL / 3½ Tbsp	13%	
Water	400 g	400 mL / 1⅔ cups	100%	② Combine with the cooked mushroom mixture, and pressure-cook at a gauge pressure of 1 bar / 15 psi for 25 minutes. Start timing as soon as full pressure has been reached.
Fino sherry	80 g	80 mL / ⅓ cup	20%	③ Let the cooker cool, or run tepid water over the rim, to depressurize it.
Dry white port or Chardonnay	80 g	80 mL / ⅓ cup	20%	④ Strain the stock through a fine sieve. Discard the solids. ⑤ Measure 500 g / 500 mL / 2 cups of the mushroom stock.
White miso	28 g	2 Tbsp	7%	⑥ Blend into the measured stock, and allow to infuse for 4 minutes.
Soy sauce	4 g	3 mL / ¾ tsp	1%	⑦ Strain.
Salt	to taste			⑧ Season the jus, and serve it warm.
Sherry vinegar	to taste			

Safety tips for pressure-cooking: see page 33

BROWN CHICKEN JUS

YIELD:	*500 g / 2 cups*
TIME ESTIMATE:	*2½ hours overall, including 30 minutes of preparation and 2 hours unattended*
STORAGE NOTES:	*keeps for 5 days when refrigerated or up to 6 months when frozen*
LEVEL OF DIFFICULTY:	*easy*
SPECIAL REQUIREMENTS:	*pressure cooker, chicken feet (optional)*
USED IN:	*Home Jus Gras (see page 93), Shiitake Marmalade (see page 151)*

This jus further fortifies an already intense stock with roasted chicken wings and feet, which add gelatin to produce a rich mouthfeel. If chicken feet are unavailable, replace them with an equal weight of wings.

INGREDIENT	WEIGHT	VOLUME	SCALING	PROCEDURE
Chicken wings, chopped	450 g / 1 lb	3–4 wings	45%	① Preheat the oven to 190 °C / 375 °F.
Chicken feet (optional)	80 g / 0.2 lb	3–4 feet	8%	② Toss together.
Neutral frying oil see page xxii	as needed			③ Roast the chicken wing pieces and feet until brown, about 40 minutes.
Ground chicken	1 kg / 2.2 lb		100%	④ Panfry over medium heat, stirring constantly, until brown, about 15 minutes.
Neutral frying oil	as needed			
Brown chicken stock see variation on page 85	1 kg	1 L / 4¼ cups	100%	⑤ Combine with the browned chicken parts and ground chicken in a pressure cooker, and pressure-cook at a gauge pressure of 1 bar / 15 psi for 1 hour. Start timing as soon as full pressure has been reached.
Fino sherry or dry white port	200 g	200 mL / ⅞ cup	20%	⑥ Let the cooker cool, or run tepid water over the rim, to depressurize it.
Shallots, thinly sliced	200 g	1¾ cups	20%	⑦ Strain the jus into a pot. Discard the solids.
Thyme	1 g	1–2 small sprigs	0.1%	⑧ Simmer the jus over medium-high heat until it is reduced by half and becomes slightly syrupy, 20–25 minutes.
Salt	to taste			⑨ Season the jus, and serve it warm.
Lemon juice	to taste			

Safety tips for pressure-cooking: see page 33

VARIATIONS

Brown Beef Jus

Substitute ground beef for the ground chicken, oxtail for the wings and feet, red wine for the fino sherry, and beef stock (see page 86) for the chicken stock. In step 5, increase the pressure-cooking time to 2 hours.

Game Bird Jus

Substitute bones and ground meat of game birds, such as pheasant, duck, or grouse, for the chicken. You may want to replace the sherry or white port with a stronger-flavored alcohol, such as whiskey or red port.

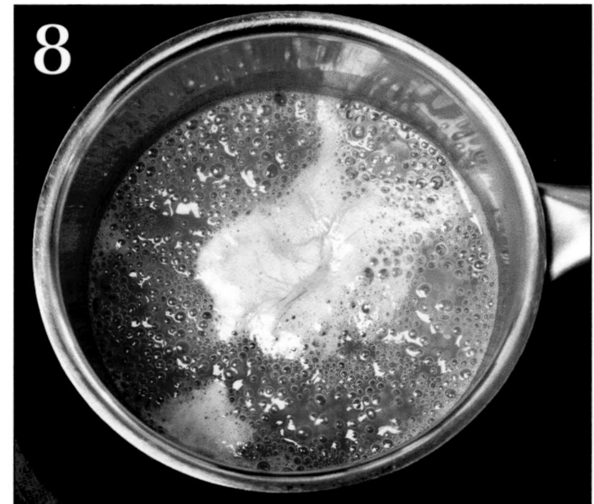

HOME JUS GRAS

YIELD:	*280 g / 1¼ cups*
TIME ESTIMATE:	*20 minutes*
STORAGE NOTES:	*serve the same day*
LEVEL OF DIFFICULTY:	*moderate*
SPECIAL REQUIREMENTS:	*Brown Chicken Jus (see the previous page), Pressure-Rendered Chicken Fat (see page 123), xanthan gum, liquid soy lecithin*
GOES WELL WITH:	*Roast Chicken (see page 238), Turkey Confit (see page 246)*

Many classic sauces are enriched with butter or oil, usually added at the last second in a step called "finishing" or "mounting." The reason for waiting until the last minute to add the fat is that the emulsion you form when you whisk it in is unstable when hot: the fat soon separates out. We solve that problem by adding lecithin, a heat-stable emulsifier found in egg yolks and soybeans. The resulting sauce is so stable that you can even make it in the afternoon, hold it at room temperature, and then just warm it up at dinnertime.

This sauce is also special in its use of rendered chicken fat rather than oil, butter, or cream. Especially if you use pressure-rendered chicken fat, which has a strong roasted-chicken flavor, you'll taste the chicken much more than in traditional versions. For a delicious, smoky bacon taste instead, substitute bacon fat for the chicken fat.

INGREDIENT	WEIGHT	VOLUME	SCALING	PROCEDURE
Brown Chicken Jus see the previous page	200 g	200 mL / ⅞ cup	100%	① Blend in a pot by using an immersion blender until fully incorporated. ② Bring to a simmer.
Xanthan gum	0.8 g		0.4%	
Pressure-Rendered Chicken Fat see page 123	80 g	95 mL / ⅜ cup	40%	③ Warm the fat in a separate small pot over low heat, and stir in the lecithin. ④ Blend the warm fat slowly into the jus mixture until fully homogenized. Use an immersion blender.
Liquid soy lecithin (NOW brand)	1.6 g		0.8%	
Salt	to taste			⑤ Season the jus generously, and serve it warm.
Lemon juice	to taste			

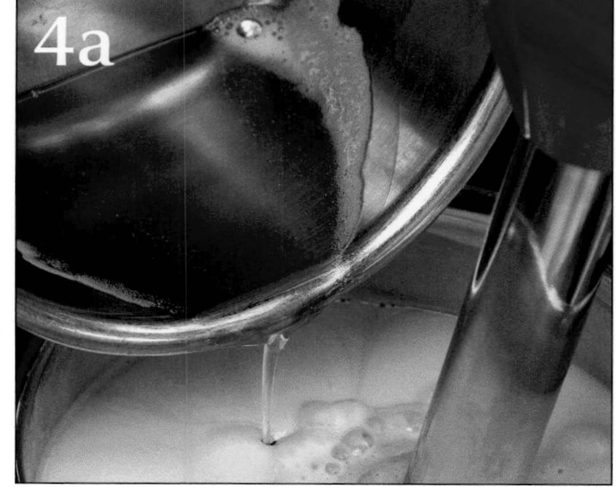

1 Place the brown chicken jus in a small pot, and use an immersion blender to blend in the xanthan gum until it is fully incorporated. Xanthan gum is very potent, so weigh it carefully. If the liquid becomes very sticky, you added too much.

2 Bring the jus to a simmer.

3 Warm the fat in a second small pot over low heat, and then stir in the lecithin.

4 Slowly pour the warm fat into the jus mixture while mixing with an immersion blender. Continue blending until the mixture is fully homogenized.

VARIATION: **Ultrastable Butter Sauce**
Blend 100 g of a wine reduction, stock, juice, or other flavorful liquid with 0.4 g of xanthan gum. Melt 120 g / ½ cup of butter in a separate pot, and stir in 2.4 g of liquid soy lecithin. Blend the butter mixture into the thickened liquid. Season generously with salt and lemon juice.

5 Season the jus generously with salt and lemon juice, and serve it warm.

Liquid soy lecithin is not the same as soy lecithin powder. The powdered lecithin is deoiled and often used by Modernist chefs to make delicate foams. The liquid soy lecithin called for in these recipes is available from health-food stores. It is a powerful emulsifier and is very useful for making vinaigrettes and warm butter sauces. Always dissolve it in an oil or fat before combining it with other ingredients.

SAUCES

A sauce is just a flavorful liquid that has been thickened enough to coat food. Fat, cornstarch, and flour are the thickeners most commonly used in traditional cooking. But each of these adds a lot of bulk to the sauce while muting the flavors of the primary ingredients. Modernist thickeners—such as the agar we use in our Onion Fluid Gel recipe on page 100 and the xanthan gum in our Pressure-Cooked Drippings recipe on page 101—don't have these drawbacks. You use them in such small quantities that they have no perceptible impact on the flavor. Once you get the hang of using them, you can make a terrific sauce from almost any flavorful liquid that complements your dish.

HOW TO Make Full-Flavored Pan Gravy

Chefs often refer to the delicious brown residue that sticks to your pan when you sauté or panfry food as "fond." It makes a wonderful basis for sauce, such as pan gravy. The trick is to deglaze the pan by adding a liquid to remove the fond at just the right time: it must be browned, but not black and bitter. Adding a little xanthan gum thickens the gravy; there is no need to boil off water, and with it many flavorful aromas.

1 Sauté meat or sliced vegetables until they turn brown.

2 While the pan is still hot, add just enough liquid to deglaze it. Use water to obtain a clear, pure flavor. Alternatively, add a flavored liquid such as chicken, meat, or vegetable stock—or even a fruit or vegetable juice—to produce a richer flavor. Don't add too much, or you will dilute the flavor of the gravy.

3 Heat the liquid in the pan while you use a spatula or a clean scrubber brush to loosen the fond and dissolve the scrapings. Keep stirring to dissolve the fond as the liquid comes to a simmer. Simmer for 2–3 minutes. Strain the sauce into a saucepan.

4 Adjust the seasoning of the sauce, which will still be fairly thin. The goal at this point is a potent, balanced flavor; you can thicken it later, if needed. You can reduce the liquid slightly if the flavor is weak, but the flavor molecules evaporate along with the water, so don't overcook it. Once the flavor is correct, serve the gravy as is, or continue with the next steps to refine the texture.

5 To make the gravy smoother, process it in an immersion blender, countertop blender, or food processor.

6 To add body to the sauce, use an immersion blender to thoroughly mix in a little xanthan gum. For a thin sauce, use 0.1–0.15 g of xanthan gum for every 100 g of liquid. Use 0.2–0.3 g per 100 g for a sauce closer in thickness to salad dressing or ketchup.

7 Finish the sauce by whisking in cream, butter, olive oil, flavored oil, or rendered fats (including drippings), if desired. Adjust the seasoning once more by adding salt and acid, such as lemon juice or vinegar, as needed.

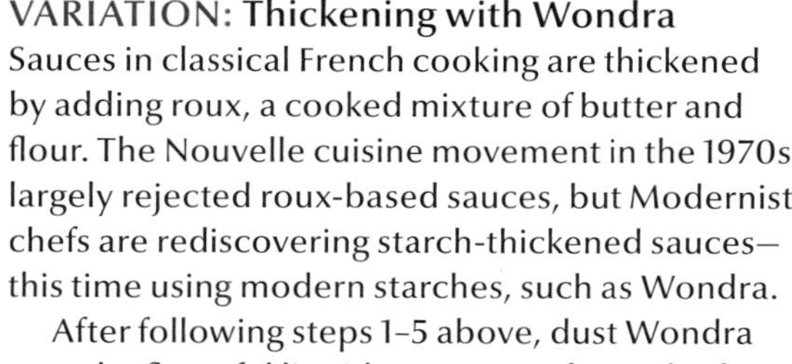

VARIATION: Thickening with Wondra

Sauces in classical French cooking are thickened by adding roux, a cooked mixture of butter and flour. The Nouvelle cuisine movement in the 1970s largely rejected roux-based sauces, but Modernist chefs are rediscovering starch-thickened sauces—this time using modern starches, such as Wondra.

After following steps 1–5 above, dust Wondra over the flavorful liquid; use 4–5 g of Wondra for every 100 g of liquid. Whisk to distribute the starch evenly (do not blend, as that can produce a gummy consistency). Bring the liquid to a simmer, and then remove it from the heat. Continue with step 7.

REDEYE GRAVY

YIELD:	*200 g / 1 cup*
TIME ESTIMATE:	*45 minutes overall*
STORAGE NOTES:	*keeps for 5 days when refrigerated or up to 6 months when frozen after step 6; continue with step 7 when reheating*
LEVEL OF DIFFICULTY:	*easy*
SPECIAL REQUIREMENTS:	*Brown Pork Stock (see variation on page 86), smoked salt*
USED IN:	*Shrimp and Grits (see page 338)*

INGREDIENT	WEIGHT	VOLUME	SCALING	PROCEDURE
Sweet onion, thinly sliced	80 g	¾ cup	16%	① Sauté in a skillet over medium heat until the onions become golden and tender, about 15 minutes.
Rendered pork fat or bacon fat see page 123	30 g	30 mL / 2 Tbsp	6%	
Star anise	0.2 g	1 pod	0.04%	② Add, reduce heat to medium-low, and continue cooking, stirring frequently, until the onions turn dark amber and the star anise is fragrant, 10–12 minutes.
Brown Pork Stock see variation on page 86	500 g	500 mL / 2 cups	100%	③ Deglaze the pan with the stock, add the syrup, and simmer until the liquid thickens and reduces by two-thirds, about 10 minutes.
Maple syrup (grade B preferred)	15 g	1 Tbsp	3%	④ Remove the pan from the heat.
Whole coffee beans (French roast)	25 g	⅓ cup	5%	⑤ Stir in, cover the pan, and allow to infuse for 5 minutes. ⑥ Strain the gravy into a small pot. Discard the solids. ⑦ Warm the gravy over low heat.
Unsalted butter, cubed	35 g	2½ Tbsp	7%	⑧ Whisk into the warm gravy to thicken it. Do not boil.
Smoked salt	to taste			⑨ Season the gravy, and serve it warm.

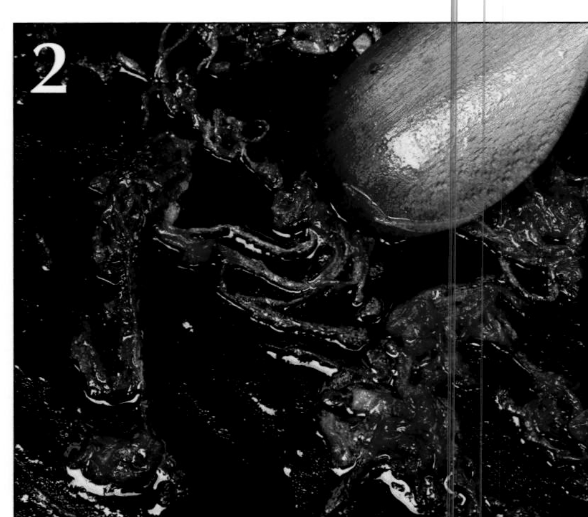

When making a glaze such as this one, choose a syrah, a big zinfandel, or some other strong, fruity red wine that has a low tannin content. It doesn't need to be expensive, just flavorful.

RED WINE GLAZE

YIELD:	*100 g / ⅓ cup*
TIME ESTIMATE:	*4 hours overall, including 2 hours unattended*
STORAGE NOTES:	*keeps for 5 days when refrigerated or up to 6 months when frozen*
LEVEL OF DIFFICULTY:	*moderate*
SPECIAL REQUIREMENTS:	*pressure cooker, beef knucklebones*
USED IN:	*Braised Short Ribs (see page 229)*

INGREDIENT	WEIGHT	VOLUME	SCALING	PROCEDURE
Lean ground beef	1.3 kg / 2.8 lb		100%	① Fry the meat in a large skillet over high heat until it turns dark brown, about 8 minutes. Do not overcrowd the pan; work in batches. ② Drain the browned meat in a colander placed over a bowl. Measure 40 g / 40 mL / ¼ cup of the drained oil. Reserve the beef for use in step 6.
Neutral frying oil see page xxii	75 g	80 mL / ⅓ cup	6%	
Sweet onion, thinly sliced	500 g	5¼ cups	40%	③ Combine with the reserved oil in the base of a pressure cooker, and sauté uncovered over medium heat, stirring often, until the vegetables become completely soft and brown, 30–35 minutes.
Carrots, thinly sliced	500 g	7 cups	40%	
Leeks, thinly sliced	250 g	3¾ cups	20%	
Garlic, thinly sliced	25 g	⅓ cup	2%	
Tomato paste	50 g	3 Tbsp	4%	④ Stir into the vegetable mixture, and cook, stirring often, until brown, about 10 minutes.
Red wine	750 g	750 mL / 1 bottle	60%	⑤ Pour in, and cook over high heat, stirring often, until the wine reduces to a syrup, 10–12 minutes.
Beef knucklebones	1.3 kg / 2.8 lb		100%	⑥ Add to the pressure cooker, and stir in the reserved beef until combined. ⑦ Pressure-cook at a gauge pressure of 1 bar / 15 psi for 2 hours. Start timing as soon as full pressure has been reached. ⑧ Let the cooker cool, or run tepid water over the rim, to depressurize it. ⑨ Strain the broth into a large pot through a fine sieve lined with cheesecloth. Discard the solids. ⑩ Cook the broth over high heat, skimming off the fat frequently, until reduced to a syrupy glaze, 45–60 minutes.
Water	1 kg	1 L / 4¼ cups	80%	
Italian parsley, bruised	5 g	5 medium sprigs	0.4%	
Thyme	3 g	3–4 sprigs	0.2%	
Fresh bay leaves	0.6 g	3 leaves	0.04%	
Black peppercorns	0.5 g	10–12 peppercorns	0.03%	
Balsamic vinegar	to taste			⑪ Season the glaze, and serve it warm.
Dark soy sauce	to taste			

Safety tips for pressure-cooking: see page 33

HOW TO Make Gels and Fluid Gels

Gels are hardly new to cooking: cooked eggs are gels; so are cheeses, custards, and yogurts. But modern gelling agents have opened up a fantastic range of new culinary applications. You can use them to add body to a broth, mold a sauce into an attractive shape, or even solidify a liquid such as onion milk into a block, and then shear it back into a fluid (see page 100).

The basic process is the same in each case. First, you dispense the gelling agent evenly throughout the liquid. Sometimes, you must heat the mixture to activate the gelling agent. The molecules of the agent link up to form a mesh that traps water and other molecules like fish in a net. As the mesh tightens, the liquid sets into a semi-solid gel.

You can puree certain gels after they have set to make a sauce that is thick on a spoon but thins to a pleasant texture as you eat it. Fluid gels, as these sauces are called, often have a creamier mouthfeel than you can get from a comparable sauce thickened with starch or xanthan gum. Agar is the most useful gelling agent for making fluid gels, but it does require heat to activate—not ideal if you are making a raw vegetable sauce or a cold soup such as gazpacho. Agar is derived from seaweed and has been used for centuries in Asian cooking.

1 Use an accurate gram scale (see page 7) to measure the right amount of agar. Use 0.25 g of agar for every 100 g of liquid when making a thin broth; 0.4–0.5 g per 100 g for a moderately thick sauce; or 0.9–1.1 g per 100 g for a thickness like that of a puree.

2 Place the liquid in a saucepan—any cold, flavorful liquid works, including stock, pan juices, or dissolved fond—and sprinkle the agar into the liquid while blending with an immersion blender. Alternatively, mix the powder into the liquid in a countertop blender, and then transfer the mixture to a pan.

3 Bring the mixture to a boil, and stir until the agar dissolves completely.

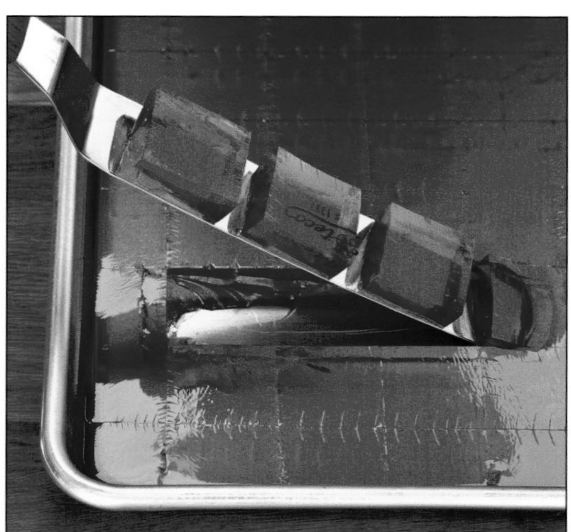

4 To make a semisolid gel, pour the mixture into a mold or bowl, and allow it to cool until it sets. To make a fluid gel, allow the gel to set, and then puree it in a blender until it is smooth.

Quick-set fluid gel: Place the hot mixture in a bowl, set the bowl in an ice-water bath, and then use an immersion blender to blend the mixture as it cools to below 30 °C / 86 °F and sets into a fluid gel.

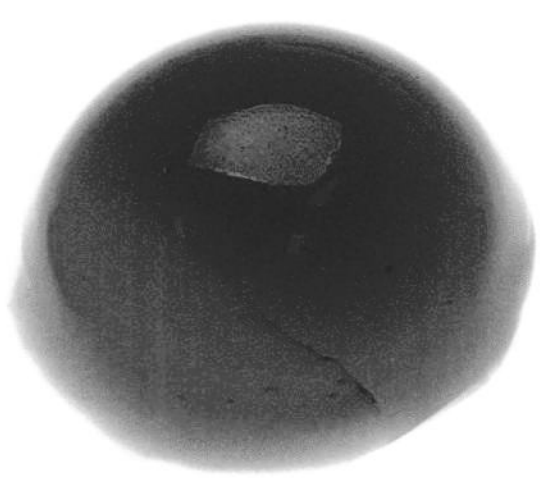
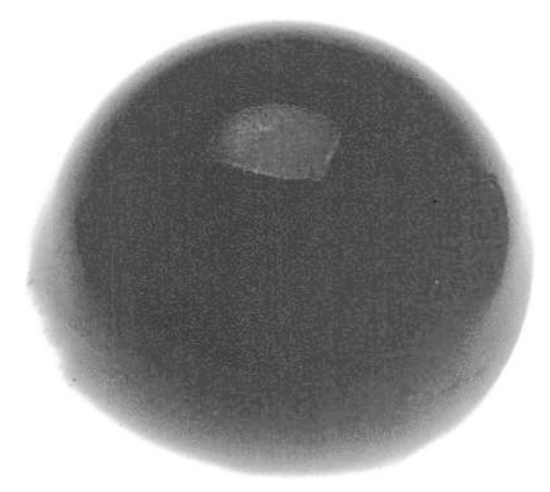

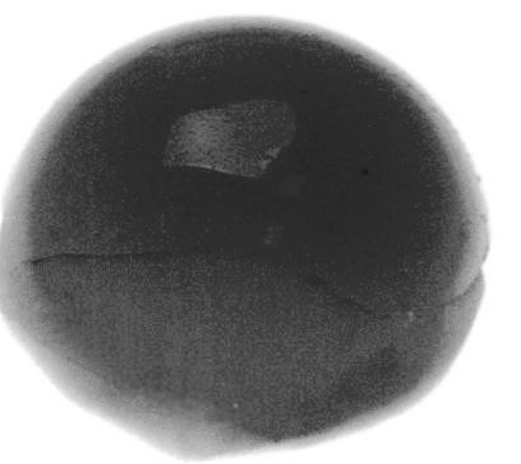

5

Solutions to Common Problems When Thickening and Gelling

Modern gelling agents and thickeners, such as gelatin, agar, xanthan gum, and Wondra, are incredibly versatile and practical. But it does take a bit of practice to build an intuition for how these ingredients work.

The table below lists the telltale signs that something has gone wrong, as well as the most likely causes of these occasional problems.

	Problem	Possible Causes	Solutions
	Clear lumps that look like fish eyes appeared in the liquid.	The thickener or gelling agent was dispersed unevenly.	Dust the agent evenly over the surface of the liquid while blending. Mix the agent with a dry bulking agent, such as sugar, or disperse it in a small amount of oil before adding to the liquid.
		Steam caused the agent to clump together before it was fully distributed, or it was blended into a hot liquid.	Keep the powder away from steam, and keep the liquid to be thickened or gelled cool until the agent is fully dispersed.
	The liquid did not gel or thicken, even though the granules of powder swelled up.	Too little gelling agent or starch was used.	Check the recipe, and weigh the ingredient carefully on an accurate scale. If a greater concentration of gelling agent is needed, increase the quantity very gradually.
		The liquid contains an enzyme that prevents gelation. Fresh kiwi, pineapple, and papaya juices, for example, contain enzymes that inhibit gelatin from setting.	Cook fresh juice, and then cool it before adding the gelling agent, or substitute canned or frozen fruit.
		The gel was frozen and later thawed. The freezing process destroys the protein matrix of gelatin.	Refrigerate a gelatin mixture for at least 4 hours to set it, but do not let it freeze.
	The granules of powder did not swell in size or dissolve, and the liquid did not set.	The gelling agent did not come up to the right temperature.	Monitor the liquid after dispersing the agent to check that it remains at the recommended activation temperature for the amount of time indicated. Most gelling agents activate when simmered for 2–3 minutes.
		The alcohol concentration was too high.	Use an alcohol-tolerant gelling agent, such as agar. Gelatin will gel a liquid containing up to 36% alcohol, but the gels taste best when the concentration is 10% or less.
		Another ingredient interfered with the action of the gelling agent.	Some gelling agents cannot tolerate high levels of salt, acid, or certain minerals.
	The liquid became gummy after thickening it with Wondra.	Wondra was blended rather than whisked into the liquid, it was whisked for too long, or too much was added.	Always sift modified starches before adding them to a liquid to avoid having to overwork them. Use a hand whisk rather than a blender.

ONION FLUID GEL

YIELD:	*500 g / 2 cups*
TIME ESTIMATE:	*2 hours overall, including 30 minutes of preparation and 1½ hours unattended*
STORAGE NOTES:	*keeps for 5 days when refrigerated either before or after pureeing in step 10*
LEVEL OF DIFFICULTY:	*moderate*
SPECIAL REQUIREMENTS:	*sous vide setup, agar powder*

This recipe is adapted from Heston Blumenthal's update of the classic Escoffier *sauce soubise*, a Béchamel sauce flavored with onion puree. Making the sauce as a fluid gel (see page 98) results in a cleaner flavor and much greater stability. The sauce won't separate, even when reheating it after several days in the refrigerator. Unlike gelatin, agar gels can tolerate moderate heat (up to 85 °C / 185 °F).

INGREDIENT	WEIGHT	VOLUME	SCALING	PROCEDURE
Sweet onion, thinly sliced	635 g	6 cups	127%	① Preheat a water bath to 88 °C / 190 °F.
Shallots, thinly sliced	155 g	1⅝ cups	31%	② Sweat the onions and shallots in oil in a large skillet over low heat until translucent and dry, but not brown, 20–30 minutes.
Neutral-tasting oil	100 g	110 mL / ½ cup	20%	
Whole milk	500 g	520 mL / 2⅛ cups	100%	③ Combine with the onions in a large (4 L / 1 gal) zip-top bag, remove as much air as possible from the bag (see page 58), and seal it. ④ Cook sous vide for 1 hour. ⑤ Sieve, pressing the onions firmly to extract as much milk as possible. ⑥ Measure 500 g of the onion milk, and chill it.
Agar powder	3.5 g		0.7%	⑦ Sprinkle over the cold onion milk, and then whisk or use an immersion blender to blend the agar completely. ⑧ Boil until fully dissolved and hydrated, 1–2 minutes. ⑨ Pour into a tray or bowl, and chill until completely set, 15–20 minutes. ⑩ Puree until smooth and fluid.
Salt	to taste			⑪ Season, and serve warm or cold.

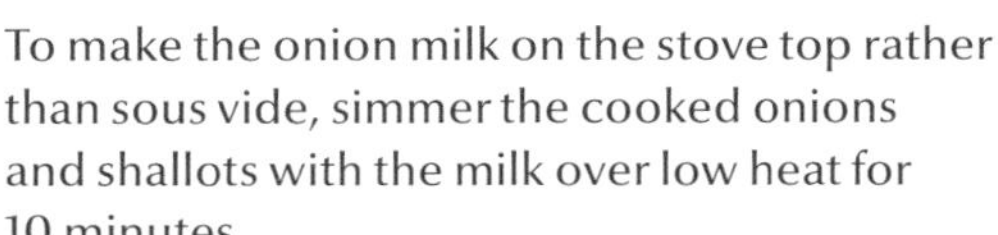

To make the onion milk on the stove top rather than sous vide, simmer the cooked onions and shallots with the milk over low heat for 10 minutes.

You can grind flaked agar in a coffee grinder to make agar powder.

VARIATION: Egg-Yolk Fluid Gel
Vacuum seal 150 g / 10 Tbsp of egg yolks (about 10 yolks), and then cook them sous vide in a 80 °C / 176 °F bath for 35 minutes. Blend the cooked yolks with 150 g / 150 mL / ⅝ cup of flavored cream or stock, and season to taste. Add lemon juice or more liquid if needed to thin the sauce.

Quick-set method: After step 8, place the hot, hydrated mixture in a tall container, and set it in an ice-water bath. Use an immersion blender to puree the gel as it cools. Stop blending when the fluid gel is cold. Season and serve.

PRESSURE-COOKED DRIPPINGS

YIELD:	*200 g / 1 cup*
TIME ESTIMATE:	*1¼ hours overall, including 15 minutes of preparation and 1 hour unattended*
STORAGE NOTES:	*keeps refrigerated for 5 days or up to 6 months when frozen*
LEVEL OF DIFFICULTY:	*moderate*
SPECIAL REQUIREMENTS:	*pressure cooker, three 500 mL / 16 oz canning jars, xanthan gum*

Why scrape the drippings from the pan to make gravy? Just pressure-cook ground chicken to extract the delicious juices without scorching or scraping. If you prefer a brighter or more complex flavor to the gravy, add some good vinegar or citrus juice, ground spices, and fresh herbs. To make a thinner jus, omit the xanthan gum. You can substitute a few cubes of cold butter for the xanthan gum. The emulsion can be further stabilized by adding 1–2 g of liquid soy lecithin (see page 93).

INGREDIENT	WEIGHT	VOLUME	SCALING	PROCEDURE
Chicken wings, chopped	450 g / 1 lb	3–4 wings	100%	① Mix thoroughly.
Boneless, skinless chicken thighs, ground	450 g / 1 lb	from 3 thighs	100%	② Divide evenly into three 500 mL / 16 oz canning jars. Tighten the lids fully, and then unscrew them one-quarter turn.
Soy sauce	9 g	8 mL / 1½ tsp	2%	③ Place the filled jars on a rack or trivet in the base of a pressure cooker, and add 2.5 cm / 1 in of water.
Honey	9 g	1¾ tsp	2%	④ Pressure-cook at a gauge pressure of 1 bar / 15 psi for 1 hour. Start timing as soon as full pressure has been reached.
				⑤ Let the cooker cool, or run tepid water over the rim, to depressurize it. Let the jar contents cool slightly before opening.
				⑥ Strain, reserving the juices and fat. Discard the solids.
Xanthan gum (Bob's Red Mill brand)	as needed			⑦ Weigh the reserved drippings, and measure the xanthan gum equal to 0.15% of the weight. For example, if the drippings weigh 200 g, measure 0.3 g of xanthan gum.
				⑧ Blend the xanthan gum into the warm drippings until thickened.
Salt	as needed			⑨ Season the gravy, and serve it warm.

Safety tips for pressure-cooking: see page 33

VARIATION: Caramelized Onion Gravy
To make a thicker gravy without adding more starch or fat, blend in 30 g / 2 Tbsp of Pressure-Caramelized Onions (see page 127) and 10 g / 2½ tsp of Pressure-Cooked Garlic Confit (see page 126) before step 9.

If you have a potato ricer, you can line it with cheesecloth to strain as much juice as possible from the cooked chicken at step 6. As you blend in the xanthan gum in step 8, adjust the texture to your taste by adding melted butter.

Sauce Verte

Chervil, Thyme, and Scallion Pesto

Green Onion and Sorrel Pesto

PISTACHIO PESTO

YIELD:	*350 g / 1⅝ cups*
TIME ESTIMATE:	*1¼ hours overall, including 15 minutes of preparation and 1 hour unattended*
STORAGE NOTES:	*keeps for 3 days when refrigerated or up to 3 months when frozen*
LEVEL OF DIFFICULTY:	*easy*
SPECIAL REQUIREMENTS:	*roasted pistachio oil, xanthan gum (optional)*
USED IN:	*Quinoa with Pistachio Pesto and Asparagus (see variation on page 332), Genovese Pizza (see variation on page 306), Pesto Chicken Thighs (see variation on page 262), Barley Noodles (see variation on page 271), Pistachio Clam Chowder (see variation on page 292), Goat Cheese on Baguette with Tomato Confit and Basil (see variation on page 318)*

Pesto, which simply means paste in Italian, is most often associated with the Genovese version that combines pine nuts, basil, Parmesan, and olive oil. But this reinterpretation that replaces pine nuts with pistachios has become one of our favorites. You can find recipes on the next page for the variations pictured above.

The function of the xanthan gum, which is optional, is to thicken natural juices that otherwise tend to separate from the greens. Toss the pesto with pasta, mix it into a warm potato salad, slather it over salmon before baking, or serve it as a dip for crusty grilled bread.

INGREDIENT	WEIGHT	VOLUME	SCALING	PROCEDURE
Basil leaves	40 g	2¼ cups	80%	① Bring a pot of water to a boil. Arrange an ice-water bath alongside.
Chives	35 g	1 cup	70%	② Combine, and blanch in the boiling water until just cooked, about 1 minute. Use a skimmer or slotted spoon to lift the greens out, and plunge them immediately into the ice bath.
Cilantro leaves	35 g	2 cups	70%	
Scallion, green parts only, cut into 5 cm / 2 in pieces	35 g	½ cup	70%	③ Drain the greens, wrap them in cheesecloth, and squeeze to remove excess moisture.
Baby spinach	15 g	1 cup	30%	
Garlic cloves	8 g	2–3 cloves	16%	④ Boil until tender, about 2 minutes.
Parmigiano-Reggiano, finely grated	50 g	¾ cup	100%	⑤ Combine with the blanched greens and garlic in a food processor, and puree.
Pistachios, toasted	50 g	⅜ cup	100%	
Extra-virgin olive oil	95 g	110 mL / ½ cup	190%	⑥ Add to the puree gradually while processing to form a paste.
Roasted pistachio oil (or other nut oil)	20 g	20 mL / 1½ Tbsp	40%	
Lemon juice	10 g	10 mL / 2 tsp	20%	
Salt	to taste			⑦ Season the pesto.
Xanthan gum (Bob's Red Mill brand), optional	as needed			⑧ If not using xanthan gum, refrigerate the pesto for 1 hour. Otherwise, weigh the pesto, calculate 0.2% of the weight, and measure that amount of xanthan gum. For example, if the pesto weighs 350 g, measure 0.7 g of xanthan gum.
				⑨ Whisk the xanthan gum into the pesto until fully incorporated.

Cilantro Pesto

Spinach Pesto

Roasted Red Pepper Pesto

When blanching the greens in step 2, plunge them into ice water immediately after taking them out of the pot. They should be barely cooked through.

Wrap all the blanched greens together in cheesecloth when squeezing out their juices.

When the oils and lemon juice are fully incorporated, the pesto takes on the consistency of a paste. For a crunchier pesto, pulse it to a coarse texture.

VARIATIONS

Follow the steps for Pistachio Pesto on the previous page, but substitute the greens indicated below for the greens in steps 1–3, the cheese and nuts indicated for the Parmigiano-Reggiano and pistachios in step 5, and the oils indicated for the olive and pistachio oils in step 6.

Spinach Pesto

Spinach	125 g	6¼ cups
Italian parsley leaves	15 g	1½ cups
Aged Gouda cheese, grated	50 g	1 cup
Roasted almonds	50 g	¼ cup
Almond oil	20 g	25 mL/ 1½ Tbsp
Extra-virgin olive oil	90 g	100 mL/ ½ cup

Roasted Red Pepper Pesto

Roasted piquillo peppers	120 g	½ cup
Mint leaves	10 g	¾ cup
Gorgonzola cheese	50 g	½ cup
Roasted cashew nuts	50 g	⅜ cup
Extra-virgin olive oil	90 g	100 mL/ ½ cup

Cilantro Pesto

Cilantro leaves	120 g	9 cups
Spinach	20 g	1 cup
Parmesan cheese, grated	50 g	1¼ cups
Toasted pumpkin seeds	50 g	⅓ cup
Extra-virgin olive oil	90 g	100 mL/ ½ cup
Lime juice	to taste	

Green Onion and Sorrel Pesto

Scallions, green parts only	60 g	1 cup
Sorrel (do not blanch)	50 g	2½ cups
Piave Vecchio cheese, grated	50 g	1 cup
Macadamia nuts	50 g	⅜ cup
Extra-virgin olive oil	90 g	100 mL/ ½ cup

Chervil, Thyme, and Scallion Pesto

Scallions	60 g	1 cup
Chervil leaves	35 g	3 cups
Thyme (do not blanch)	5 g	2 Tbsp
Aged goat cheese, crumbled	50 g	⅝ cup
Hazelnuts	50 g	⅜ cup
Hazelnut oil	20 g	20 mL/ 1½ Tbsp
Extra-virgin olive oil	90 g	100 mL/ ½ cup

Sauce Verte

Italian parsley leaves	50 g	4 cups
Mint leaves	50 g	3 cups
Chives	20 g	⅝ cup
Basil leaves	20 g	2 cups
Chervil leaves	15 g	1⅛ cups
Dijon mustard	10 g	1 Tbsp
Walnuts, finely chopped	50 g	½ cup
White wine vinegar	10 g	2 tsp
Extra-virgin olive oil	90 g	100 mL/ ½ cup

MUGHAL CURRY SAUCE

YIELD:	*700 g / 2½ cups*
TIME ESTIMATE:	*13 hours overall, including 1 hour of preparation and 12 hours unattended*
STORAGE NOTES:	*keeps for 5 days when refrigerated or up to 6 months when frozen*
LEVEL OF DIFFICULTY:	*moderate*
SPECIAL REQUIREMENTS:	*white poppy seeds, fresh turmeric, ghee (see page 119)*
USED IN:	*Lamb Curry (see page 234)*

The Mughal Empire, which dominated northern India in the 16th and 17th centuries, built lasting monuments such as the Taj Mahal, but it also left a monumental culinary legacy. Mughal cuisine inspired this recipe, which is a versatile template that you can easily extend (see two variations below).

Although this recipe makes more nut paste than you need, the paste keeps well when frozen. Go ahead and make extra sauce; it is excellent with lamb, chicken, or beef, and tastes even better the following day. If fresh turmeric is unavailable, substitute 0.5 g / ½ tsp of powdered turmeric.

INGREDIENT	WEIGHT	VOLUME	SCALING	PROCEDURE
Whole blanched almonds	50 g	½ cup	25%	① Cover with water, and soak for 12 hours in the refrigerator.
Raw cashews	50 g	½ cup	25%	② Strain through a fine sieve, and transfer the nuts and seeds to a blender.
White poppy seeds	5 g	1 tsp	2.5%	
Water	240 g	240 mL / 1 cup	120%	③ Add to the blender, puree to form a smooth paste, and measure 240 g / 1 cup of paste for use in step 8.
Shallots, thinly sliced	200 g	2 cups	100%	④ Sauté in a large pot over medium-low heat until shallots become tender and golden, about 10 minutes.
Ghee (clarified, unsalted butter) see page 119	40 g	3 Tbsp	20%	
Salt	4 g	1 tsp	2%	
Tomato, peeled, seeded, and diced see page 128	120 g	¾ cup	60%	⑤ Add to the shallots, and cook until slightly thickened, about 5 minutes.
MC Curry Powder see page 135	7.5 g	1½ Tbsp	3.8%	⑥ Stir into the shallot-tomato mixture, and sauté over low heat for about 5 minutes.
Garlic, grated	6 g	½ Tbsp	3%	⑦ Remove the bay leaf, and discard it.
Ginger, grated	6 g	½ Tbsp	3%	
Green Thai chili, minced	5 g	½ Tbsp	2.5%	
Fresh turmeric, peeled and grated	4 g	½ Tbsp	2%	
Fresh bay leaf		1 leaf		
Water	240 g	240 mL / 1 cup	120%	⑧ Stir into the mixture.
Blended nut-seed paste, from above	240 g	1 cup	120%	⑨ Blend to a coarse puree.
Raisins, minced	25 g	¼ cup	13%	⑩ Cover, and simmer over low heat for about 25 minutes, stirring occasionally.
Plain yogurt	15 g	1 Tbsp	8%	⑪ Remove the pot from the heat, and stir the yogurt and nutmeg into the sauce.
Nutmeg, grated	0.5 g	½ tsp	0.3%	
Fresh lime juice	to taste			⑫ Season the sauce, and serve it warm.
Salt	to taste			

To soften the nuts and seeds more quickly than an overnight soak, pressure-cook them with enough water to cover at a gauge pressure of 1 bar / 15 psi for 45 minutes.

VARIATIONS

Kerala Curry Sauce

Skip steps 1–3. In step 4, add 3 g / 1 tsp of black mustard seeds and 2 g of curry leaves (about 9 leaves) while sautéing the shallots. In step 9, substitute 240 g / 1 cup of coconut milk for the nut-seed paste.

Muslim Curry Sauce

Skip steps 1–3. In step 9, substitute 240 g / 260 mL / 1⅛ cups of heavy cream for the nut-seed puree. In step 11, add a pinch of saffron threads. Garnish the finished sauce with rose petals and roasted pistachios.

1 Cover the almonds, cashews, and poppy seeds with water, and soak them in the refrigerator for 12 hours. If white poppy seeds are unavailable, omit them.

2 Strain the soaked nuts and seeds through a fine sieve. Discard the soaking water, and place the nuts and seeds in a blender.

3 Add fresh water to the blender, and puree the mixture until a smooth paste forms. If the paste seems grainy, pass it through a fine sieve. Measure 240 g / 1 cup of the paste, and set it aside for use in step 8.

4 Sauté the shallots with the ghee and salt in a large pot over medium-low heat until the shallots turn golden and tender, about 10 minutes.

5 Add the diced tomato to the shallots, and continue cooking until the mixture thickens slightly, about 5 minutes.

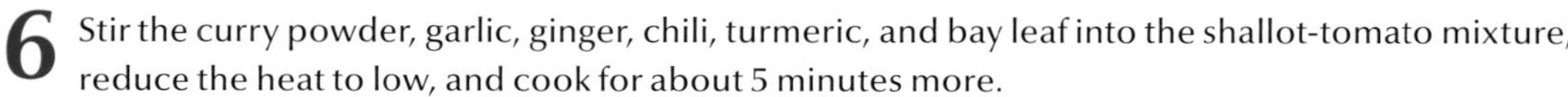

6 Stir the curry powder, garlic, ginger, chili, turmeric, and bay leaf into the shallot-tomato mixture, reduce the heat to low, and cook for about 5 minutes more.

7 Remove and discard the bay leaf.

8 Stir additional water, the reserved nut-seed paste, and the minced raisins into the mixture.

9 Blend the mixture to a coarse puree. An immersion blender works well.

10 Cover the pot, and simmer the sauce over very low heat for about 25 minutes, stirring frequently. The sauce will thicken.

11 Remove the pot from the heat, and stir the yogurt and grated nutmeg into the sauce.

12 Season the sauce with plenty of fresh lime juice and salt, and serve it warm.

SOUS VIDE HOLLANDAISE

YIELD:	*265 g / 5 cups of foam*
TIME ESTIMATE:	*45 minutes overall, including 15 minutes of preparation and 30 minutes unattended*
STORAGE NOTES:	*serve within 2 hours*
LEVEL OF DIFFICULTY:	*moderate*
SPECIAL REQUIREMENTS:	*sous vide setup, 1 L whipping siphon, two cartridges of nitrous oxide, malic acid or citric acid (optional)*

Hollandaise is traditionally a tricky, labor-intensive sauce; it is all too easy to overheat the eggs and curdle the sauce. That risk is removed when you cook it sous vide instead of on the stove. Just this change alone yields a reliably delicious sauce that can be served directly after step 9 of the recipe below. But for an extra-light hollandaise, continue with the last two steps.

INGREDIENT	WEIGHT	VOLUME	SCALING	PROCEDURE
Dry white wine	100 g	100 mL / ⅜ cup	133%	① Preheat a water bath to 65 °C / 149 °F.
Shallots, minced	50 g	⅜ cup	67%	② Combine in a pot.
White wine vinegar	35 g	40 mL / 3 Tbsp	47%	③ Simmer until the liquid becomes syrupy, about 8 minutes. ④ Strain, discarding the solids, and measure 20 g / 20 mL / 4 tsp of the wine reduction for use in the next step.
Egg yolks	75 g	5–6 yolks	100%	⑤ Blend together with the wine reduction.
Stock or water see pages 84–91	20 g	20 mL / 4 tsp	27%	⑥ Place in a zip-top bag, remove as much air as possible from the bag by using the water-displacement method (see page 58), and seal it. ⑦ Cook sous vide for 30 minutes.
Unsalted butter, melted	225 g	240 mL / 1 cup	300%	⑧ Blend into the egg yolk mixture until fully emulsified.
Salt	4 g	1 tsp	5%	⑨ Season the sauce, and serve it warm, or continue through step 11 to aerate it.
Malic acid or citric acid (or fresh lemon juice to taste)	1 g		1%	⑩ Pour the sauce into a 1 L siphon. Charge the siphon with two cartridges of nitrous oxide, and shake it vigorously. ⑪ Dispense to serve immediately, or keep warm in the siphon in a 55 °C / 131 °F water bath for up to 1½ hours.

VARIATIONS

Crustacean Hollandaise
Replace the unsalted butter in step 8 with Pressure-Cooked Crustacean Butter (see page 122), and serve the sauce with poached lobster (see page 288).

Garlic Hollandaise
Blend 40 g of garlic into the yolks after step 7, and at step 8 replace half of the melted butter with oil from Pressure-Cooked Garlic Confit (see page 126).

Spicy Hollandaise
In step 8, replace 20 g / 20 mL / 1½ Tbsp of the melted butter with toasted-sesame oil, and whisk in 50 g / ¼ cup of Korean Wing Sauce (see page 260). Strain the sauce, and serve it with grilled vegetables.

If you choose to use stock rather than water, consider the ingredient for which the hollandaise is being prepared: use fish stock for a sauce that you will serve with fish, poultry stock for poultry, and so on. You can similarly tailor the sauce by using other kinds of vinegars or wines in place of the white wine vinegar. Red wine and sherry vinegar pair well with grilled hanger steak, for example.

To produce a lighter foam, set the water bath to 63 °C / 145 °F in step 1; a 67 °C / 153 °F bath will yield a denser foam.

1 Preheat a water bath to 65 °C / 149 °F.

2 Combine the white wine, shallots, and vinegar in a pot.

3 Simmer until the liquid is almost completely reduced and syrupy, about 8 minutes.

4 Strain the wine reduction, and measure 20 g / 20 mL / 4 tsp of the liquid for use in the next step. Discard the solids.

5 Blend the egg yolks and stock into the wine reduction thoroughly by using an immersion blender.

6 Place the mixture in a zip-top bag. Use the water-displacement method (see page 58) to remove as much air as possible from the bag, and seal it.

7 Cook the mixture sous vide for 30 minutes.

8 Blend the melted butter gradually into the egg yolk mixture until fully emulsified. Use an immersion blender in a bowl, or a countertop blender for larger quantities.

9 Season the sauce with salt and malic acid, citric acid, or lemon juice to taste. The sauce, which should now be similar to a warm mayonnaise, can be served as is.

10 Pour the mixture into a 1 L siphon. Charge the siphon with two cartridges of nitrous oxide, and shake it vigorously.

11 Serve the sauce immediately by dispensing it from the siphon, or keep it warm in the siphon in a 55 °C / 131 °F water bath for up to 1½ hours.

MODERNIST MAYONNAISE

YIELD:	*450 g / 2¼ cups*
TIME ESTIMATE:	*45 minutes overall, including 10 minutes of preparation and 35 minutes unattended*
STORAGE NOTES:	*keeps for 3 days when refrigerated*
LEVEL OF DIFFICULTY:	*easy*
SPECIAL REQUIREMENTS:	*sous vide setup*
USED IN:	*Pork Belly B.L.T. (see page 232), Sweet Onion Slaw (see page 165), Lobster Roll (see page 288)*

Mayonnaise is a classic emulsion of oil, mustard, and a touch of acid held together by egg yolk acting as an emulsifier. It has literally hundreds of uses in the kitchen. This recipe lightly cooks the yolks, which has two benefits. First, it eliminates any food safety concerns about using raw eggs; these yolks are pasteurized. Second, the heat amplifies the emulsifying power of the yolks, so the mayonnaise is much more stable. If you're pressed for time, however, you can use raw egg yolks and skip steps 1–3.

This basic recipe supports a huge range of variations; we've included just a few below. As you add more oil, the mayonnaise will get stiffer; use less oil for a thinner sauce. Try substituting extra-virgin olive oil or other seed or nut oils for some or all of the neutral-tasting oil. You can swap out the lemon juice in favor of other acidic fruit juices (such as lime, blood orange, grapefruit, or passion fruit). Red wine vinegar works in place of white. Even the water can be replaced by stock or various kinds of juice.

INGREDIENT	WEIGHT	VOLUME	SCALING	PROCEDURE
Egg yolks, blended	75 g	5–6 yolks	100%	① Preheat a water bath to **67 °C / 153 °F**. ② Place the blended yolks in a zip-top bag, remove as much air as possible from the bag by using the water-displacement method (see page 58), and seal it. ③ Cook sous vide for 35 minutes.
Water	45 g	45 mL / 3 Tbsp	60%	④ Mix, and then whisk together with the cooked egg yolks until smooth.
Dijon mustard	25 g	1½ Tbsp	33%	
Neutral-tasting oil or any flavorful oil	300 g	320 mL / 1⅓ cups	400%	⑤ Blend gradually into the egg yolk mixture until fully emulsified.
Lemon juice	18 g	20 mL / 1½ Tbsp	24%	⑥ Add as needed to season the sauce.
White wine vinegar	10 g	10 mL / 2½ tsp	13%	⑦ Use cold.
Salt	to taste			

VARIATIONS

Aioli
In step 5, replace 150 g / 160 mL / ⅔ cup of the oil with the oil from Pressure-Cooked Garlic Confit (see page 126), and blend in 50 g / 3 Tbsp of garlic from that recipe.

Bacon Mayonnaise
In step 5, replace the oil with rendered bacon fat (see page 123), and blend in 0.7 g of xanthan gum. In step 6, fold in 65 g / ½ cup of crumbled, crispy bacon as you season the sauce. This mayonnaise solidifies when chilled. Temper it at room temperature for 5–10 minutes before serving.

Rouille
Make the Aioli variation, but at step 6 stir in 59 g / ½ cup of pimentón dulce (smoked, sweet paprika) and 0.5 g / ¼ tsp of cayenne pepper (or more to taste).

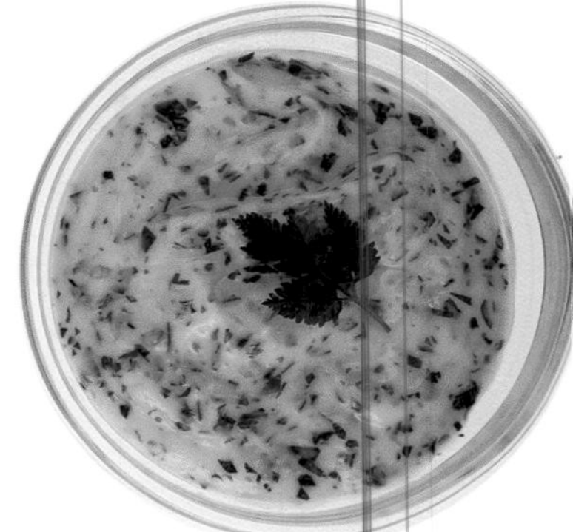

Tartar Sauce
In step 6, stir in 35 g / 3½ Tbsp of minced gherkins and 15 g / 4 Tbsp of chopped Italian parsley.

MC SPECIAL SAUCE

YIELD:	*615 g / 2½ cups*
TIME ESTIMATE:	*30 minutes overall*
STORAGE NOTES:	*keeps for 3 days when refrigerated*
LEVEL OF DIFFICULTY:	*easy*
SPECIAL REQUIREMENTS:	*spicy cucumber pickles*
USED IN:	*Modernist Cheeseburger (see page 212)*

In 1968, McDonald's rolled out a new double cheeseburger with three buns, garnished with a "special sauce." They called it the Big Mac, and it was an instant hit worldwide, attaining such ubiquity that *The Economist* magazine to this day uses the price of a Big Mac as an indicator of what currencies are worth around the globe.

One day when we were working on a pork loin sauce for *Modernist Cuisine*, we tasted the latest batch in the research kitchen, and our eyes lit up with recognition: it was McDonald's special sauce! Not exactly, of course. Ours is fancier and less sweet, although the exact flavor depends on your choice of mustard and pickles.

INGREDIENT	WEIGHT	VOLUME	SCALING	PROCEDURE
Leeks, minced	220 g	4 cups	100%	① Sweat in a pan over medium-low heat, stirring often, until very tender, about 15 minutes.
Shallots, minced	95 g	¾ cup	43%	
Neutral-tasting oil	70 g	75 mL / ⅓ cup	32%	
Heavy cream	220 g	240 mL / 1 cup	100%	② Add, increase heat to medium-high, and simmer, stirring often, until thickened, 8–10 minutes.
Dry vermouth (Noilly Prat brand)	200 g	200 mL / ⅞ cup	91%	
Spicy cucumber pickles, minced (Baumgardner brand)	40 g	4 Tbsp	18%	③ Fold in.
Dijon mustard	20 g	4 tsp	9%	
Pickle juice, from spicy pickles	to taste			④ Season the sauce generously, and serve it cool.
Salt	to taste			

Call it the "Big MC," if you like: a short-rib patty cooked sous vide and then deep-fried (see page 208), topped with MC special sauce, and served between two slices of white toast.

PRESSURE-CARAMELIZED KETCHUP

YIELD:	*330 g / 1 cup*
TIME ESTIMATE:	*35 minutes overall, including 10 minutes of preparation and 25 minutes unattended*
STORAGE NOTES:	*keeps for 5 days when refrigerated*
LEVEL OF DIFFICULTY:	*easy*
SPECIAL REQUIREMENTS:	*pressure cooker, malic acid (optional), agave syrup (optional)*
USED IN:	*Modernist Cheeseburger (see page 212)*

We exploit a little basic chemistry in this recipe to make a ketchup having a deep color and subtle flavor profile that one can get only by caramelizing the sugars in the tomato sauce. That isn't easy to do in an open pan because the sauce never gets much hotter than the boiling point of water. But the addition of a little baking soda neutralizes the natural acidity of the tomatoes and even makes the sauce slightly alkaline, which allows caramelization to occur at temperatures that a pressure cooker can generate. As with our caramelized vegetable soups and purees (see pages 180–181), the resulting ketchup delivers a wonderful combination of fresh and cooked flavors.

INGREDIENT	WEIGHT	VOLUME	SCALING	PROCEDURE
Tomato paste	100 g	⅜ cup	100%	① Whisk together in the base of a pressure cooker.
Water	100 g	100 mL / ⅜ cup	100%	② Pressure-cook at a gauge pressure of 1 bar / 15 psi for 25 minutes. Start timing when full pressure is reached.
Baking soda	3 g	¾ tsp	3%	③ Depressurize the cooker, and stir the sauce.
Red wine vinegar	60 g	70 mL / 5 Tbsp	60%	④ Stir into the tomato sauce.
Agave syrup or sugar	40 g	30 mL / 2 Tbsp	40%	
Maple syrup (grade B preferred)	30 g	25 mL / 1½ Tbsp	30%	
Mustard powder	10 g	3 tsp	10%	⑤ Mix together until evenly combined, sieving if necessary, and then whisk into the sauce.
Sweet paprika	9 g	3 tsp	9%	
Onion powder	6 g	1½ tsp	6%	
Malic acid (optional)	3 g		3%	
Salt	to taste			⑥ Season the ketchup, and serve it cool.
Red wine vinegar	to taste			

Safety tips for pressure-cooking: see page 33

1 Whisk together the tomato paste, water, and baking soda in the base of a pressure cooker. The mixture will become slightly foamy as the baking soda reacts with the acid in the tomato paste.

2 Pressure-cook the tomato paste mixture at a gauge pressure of 1 bar / 15 psi for 25 minutes. Start timing as soon as full pressure has been reached.

3 Let the cooker cool, or run tepid water over the rim, to depressurize it. Stir the tomato paste, which should be a dark, brick-red color.

4 Stir the vinegar and syrups into the tomato sauce.

VARIATION: Barbecue Ketchup
At step 4, substitute 40 g / ¼ cup of brown sugar for the agave syrup, and add 20 g / 25 mL / 5 tsp of bourbon, 1 g / ⅛ tsp of liquid smoke (Lazy Kettle brand), and 0.1 g / pinch of cayenne pepper.

5 Mix the spices and, optionally, the malic acid until they are evenly combined—sieve the mixture, if necessary—and then whisk them into the sauce. To thicken the ketchup slightly and prevent it from "weeping," add 0.5 g of xanthan gum to the spice mixture.

6 Season the ketchup generously with salt and additional vinegar to taste. Rest the ketchup for a few hours before serving to allow the raw taste of the spices to mellow.

SALSA VERDE

YIELD:	*490 g / 2 cups*
TIME ESTIMATE:	*30 minutes overall*
STORAGE NOTES:	*keeps for 3 days when refrigerated*
LEVEL OF DIFFICULTY:	*easy*
SPECIAL REQUIREMENTS:	*open flame (gas stove burner, barbecue grill, or blowtorch)*
GOES WELL WITH:	*Pressure-Cooked Fresh-Corn Tamales (see page 340)*

INGREDIENT	WEIGHT	VOLUME	SCALING	PROCEDURE
Tomatillos, with husks	415 g	5–6 medium	100%	① Char each tomatillo over an open flame, a gas stove burner, or by using a blowtorch until the skin blisters and blackens. ② Rub off the charred husks and skin with a clean, dry dish towel. ③ Stem and quarter the tomatillos.
Yellow onion, diced	215 g	2½ cups	52%	④ Combine with the tomatillos in a pot, and cook over medium heat until tender and sauce-like, about 15 minutes.
Neutral-tasting oil	35 g	40 mL / 2½ Tbsp	8%	
Jalapeño, chopped	25 g	1 large pepper	6%	⑤ Lightly blend by using an immersion blender to break up any large pieces.
Salt	to taste			⑥ Serve warm or cold.

Safety tips for blowtorching: see page 15

PRESSURE-CARAMELIZED PEANUT SAUCE

YIELD:	*760 g / 3¼ cups*
TIME ESTIMATE:	*1 hour overall, including 20 minutes of preparation and 40 minutes unattended*
STORAGE NOTES:	*keeps for 5 days when refrigerated or up to 6 months when frozen*
LEVEL OF DIFFICULTY:	*moderate*
SPECIAL REQUIREMENTS:	*pressure cooker, galangal, palm sugar*
USED IN:	*Chicken Breast Satay (see variation on page 263), Rice Noodles (see variation on page 271)*

For excellent-tasting peanut sauce, start with the freshest, most aromatic roasted peanuts you can find. Fresh galangal is similar to ginger but has a more robust, peppery taste; it is sold at Asian markets (fresh ginger may be substituted).

INGREDIENT	WEIGHT	VOLUME	SCALING	PROCEDURE
Unsweetened coconut cream (canned)	400 g	410 mL / 1¾ cups	333%	① Combine in a pressure cooker. ② Pressure-cook at a gauge pressure of 1 bar / 15 psi for 40 minutes. Start timing as soon as full pressure has been reached.
Skinless, roasted, unsalted peanuts	120 g	⅞ cup	100%	③ Depressurize the cooker quickly by running tepid water over the rim.
Shallots, sliced	70 g	¾ cup	58%	④ Puree the sauce in a blender until smooth.
Water	50 g	50 mL / ¼ cup	42%	
Galangal, peeled and sliced into coins	35 g	3–4 coins	29%	
Peanut oil	20 g	20 mL / 1½ Tbsp	17%	
Baking soda	3.2 g	½ tsp	2.7%	
Asian fish sauce	40 g	35 mL / 2 Tbsp	33%	⑤ Season the sauce, and serve it warm.
Palm sugar, grated	20 g	3 Tbsp	17%	
Salt	5 g	1½ tsp	4%	

Safety tips for pressure-cooking: see page 33

Pizza Sauce
Skip steps 1 and 2 below. Fry 50 g/ ¼ cup of chopped garlic in 100 g/ 110 mL/ ½ cup of olive oil until the garlic turns golden brown, about 5 minutes. Continue with step 3. For pizza recipes, see chapter 18, page 295.

MARINARA

YIELD:	*1 kg / 4 cups*
TIME ESTIMATE:	*1 hour overall, including 15 minutes of preparation and 45 minutes unattended*
STORAGE NOTES:	*keeps for 5 days when refrigerated or up to 6 months when frozen*
LEVEL OF DIFFICULTY:	*easy*
SPECIAL REQUIREMENTS:	*pressure cooker*
USED IN:	*Microwaved Eggplant Parmesan (see page 344), Whole Wheat Noodles (see variation on page 271)*

Marinara is a simple, flavorful tomato sauce. By combining the ingredients in a pressure cooker, there is even less fuss than usual. We like the added sweetness of onions and carrots, but our pizza sauce variation, above, might appease the tomato purists.

We consider marinara a starting point that has endless potential for customization. For classic pasta sauce, stir in fresh basil and chili flakes, or olives and anchovy fillets.

INGREDIENT	WEIGHT	VOLUME	SCALING	PROCEDURE
Yellow onion, large dice	260 g	2 cups	33%	① Mince in a food processor.
Carrots, medium dice	160 g	1 cup	20%	
Garlic	18 g	5–6 cloves	2.3%	
Olive oil	20 g	20 mL / 1½ Tbsp	2.5%	② Add to the base of a pressure cooker, and sauté the minced vegetables over medium heat until the onions turn translucent, about 4 minutes.
Canned, crushed tomatoes (San Marzano or other high-quality variety)	794 g	1 large can	100%	③ Stir into the sautéed vegetables. ④ Pressure-cook at a gauge pressure of 1 bar / 15 psi for 45 minutes. Start timing when full pressure is reached. ⑤ Depressurize the cooker.
Extra-virgin olive oil	to taste			⑥ Season the sauce to taste.
Salt	to taste			⑦ Serve warm.

Safety tips for pressure-cooking: see page 33

VARIATIONS

Tomato Sofrito
In step 1, omit the carrots, reduce the quantity of diced onion to 115 g / 1 cup, and add 63 g / ⅝ cup of chopped piquillo peppers. In step 3, add 0.2 g / ⅛ tsp of saffron threads with the crushed tomatoes.

Bolognese
Brown 450 g / 1 lb of ground pork in the base of a pressure cooker, and then proceed with step 1. In step 2, add 8 g / 1 Tbsp of porcini powder. In step 6, stir in 60 g / 65 mL / 4½ Tbsp of heavy cream before seasoning the sauce.

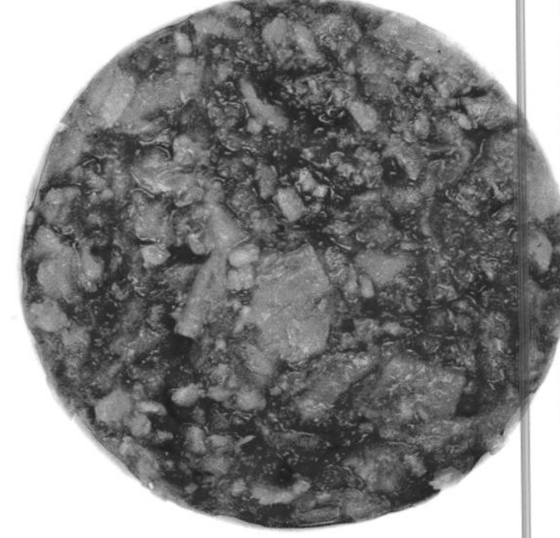

Pineapple Marinara
In step 1, add 400 g / 2⅜ cups of diced, fresh pineapple and 40 g / ½ cup of chopped prosciutto. In step 3, reduce the quantity of crushed tomatoes to 400 g / ½ large can.

1 Mince the onions, carrots, and garlic in a food processor.

2 Add the olive oil to the base of a pressure cooker, and sauté the minced vegetables over medium heat until the onions become translucent, about 4 minutes.

3 Stir the tomatoes into the sautéed vegetables.

4 Pressure-cook the vegetables at a gauge pressure of 1 bar / 15 psi for 45 minutes. Start timing as soon as full pressure has been reached.

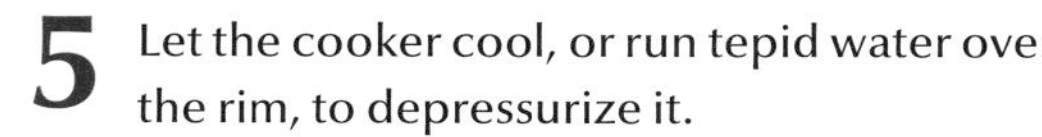

5 Let the cooker cool, or run tepid water over the rim, to depressurize it.

6 Season the sauce to taste with olive oil and plenty of salt.

7 Serve the sauce warm.

STRAWBERRY MARINARA

YIELD:	*400 g / 1½ cups*
TIME ESTIMATE:	*1¼ hours overall*
STORAGE NOTES:	*keeps for 3 days when refrigerated or up to 6 months when frozen*
LEVEL OF DIFFICULTY:	*easy*
SPECIAL REQUIREMENTS:	*juicer*
GOES WELL WITH:	*Pressure-Cooked Polenta (see page 336)*

This bright red sauce looks remarkably like tomato marinara—tomatoes are also acidic, red berry fruits, after all—and you can serve this marinara with polenta or ricotta-stuffed ravioli, or even use it as a pizza sauce. When strawberries are not in season, we use pears and pressure-cooked quince.

INGREDIENT	WEIGHT	VOLUME	SCALING	PROCEDURE
Strawberries, hulled	500 g	4 cups	227%	① Rinse and juice. Measure 185 g / 180 mL / ¾ cup of the juice for use in the next step.
Strawberries, thinly sliced	220 g	1½ cups	100%	② Combine with the measured strawberry juice in a large, heavy-bottomed pot.
Tomatoes, peeled, seeded, and diced	175 g	1 cup	80%	③ Simmer uncovered, stirring often, until the sauce becomes as thick and intensely flavored as a rich marinara, about 35 minutes.
Sweet onion, minced	100 g	¾ cup	45%	
Dry white wine	100 g	100 mL / ½ cup	45%	
Garlic, thinly sliced	3 g	½ Tbsp	1.4%	
Basil leaves, torn	2 g	3–4 leaves	0.9%	
Tarragon leaves, bruised	2 g	7–9 leaves	0.9%	
Salt	to taste			④ Season the sauce, and serve it warm.
Lime juice	to taste			

Flavor boost

For even more flavor, fold in freshly grated lemon zest and julienned basil just before serving.

THAI SWEET, SOUR, AND SAVORY GLAZE

YIELD:	*135 g / ⅔ cup*
TIME ESTIMATE:	*40 minutes overall, including 10 minutes of preparation and 30 minutes unattended*
STORAGE NOTES:	*keeps for 5 days when refrigerated or 6 months when frozen*
LEVEL OF DIFFICULTY:	*easy*
SPECIAL REQUIREMENTS:	*tamarind concentrate, palm sugar*
USED IN:	*Crispy Beef and Shallot Salad (see page 353), Coconut Noodles (see variation on page 271)*

This recipe makes a vibrant, tangy version of a classic concentrated beef glaze. Toss it with noodles, or use it to glaze grilled lamb, chicken, or fish. Add a spoonful to toasted-sesame oil to make a warm dressing for grilled asparagus. Season the glaze generously with acidic lime juice to balance the sweetness of the sugar. And feel free to add more tamarind concentrate as well; you can find the dark, molasses-like concentrate at Asian markets. Use the glaze in a crispy beef salad with braised short ribs (see page 229).

INGREDIENT	WEIGHT	VOLUME	SCALING	PROCEDURE
Brown beef stock see page 86	1 kg	1 L / 4¼ cups	100%	① Reduce over medium-high heat until thick enough to coat the back of a spoon, about 30 minutes.
Cilantro leaves	5 g	½ cup	0.5%	② Add to the hot, reduced stock.
Star anise	5 g	3–5 whole	0.5%	③ Stir, and allow to infuse for about 5 minutes.
Thai basil leaves	5 g	⅜ cup	0.5%	④ Strain, pressing the solids to extract the intense flavors.
Tamarind concentrate (Tamicon brand)	20 g	4 tsp	2%	⑤ Add to the strained glaze.
Palm sugar, grated or Demerara	12 g	1½ Tbsp	1.2%	
Lime juice	to taste			⑥ Season the glaze generously, and serve it warm. The glaze will solidify as it cools.
Salt	to taste			

Porcini, bell pepper, spinach, and carotene butters; for recipes, see page 121

OILS AND FATS

Fats are a fundamental component of food, and they play many important roles in defining the texture of foods and in their preparation. Oils and fats are the source of that unctuous, satiny mouthfeel of rich foods. They transfer heat with amazing efficiency, a property exploited by many cooking techniques, from sauté to sous vide. Fats make layered pastries possible by keeping delicate sheets of dough from adhering. And they are an indispensable part of emulsions and certain kinds of foams.

But some of the most creative applications of fats and oils put them to use as vehicles of color and flavor—particularly savory flavors. You can often extract the essence of an ingredient by using a fat, as in the lemon herb oil below, and then incorporate that flavor into a dressing or garnish. You can even cook in flavor-infused fats, as long as you use low temperatures. Flavor- and color-infused fats add a new and often unexpected dimension to dishes. The fat coats the tongue, and the flavors they carry hang around. A little goes a long way.

SOUS VIDE LEMON HERB OIL

YIELD:	*200 g / 1 cup*
TIME ESTIMATE:	*13¾ hours overall, including 15 minutes of preparation and 13½ hours unattended*
STORAGE NOTES:	*keeps for 2 weeks when refrigerated*
LEVEL OF DIFFICULTY:	*easy*
SPECIAL REQUIREMENTS:	*sous vide setup, lemon thyme leaves, lemon balm leaves, Makrud lime leaves*

Lemon balm and lemon thyme can be found in grocery stores that have a good selection of fresh herbs. Or better yet, you can grow your own—starter plants are often available at plant nurseries.

INGREDIENT	WEIGHT	VOLUME	SCALING	PROCEDURE
Grapeseed oil or unsalted butter	200 g	220 mL / 1 cup	100%	① Preheat a water bath to **60** °C / **140** °F.
Lemongrass, thinly sliced	40 g	½ cup	20%	② Combine in a zip-top bag, remove as much air as possible from the bag by using the water-displacement method (see page 58), and seal it.
Lemon thyme leaves	25 g	⅞ cup	13%	③ Cook sous vide for 1½ hours.
Lemon balm leaves, sliced	10 g	1¼ cups	5%	④ Refrigerate for 12 hours.
Makrud lime leaves, sliced	10 g	20 leaves	5%	⑤ Strain the oil (if using butter, melt it first). Discard the solids.

MODERNIST VINAIGRETTE

YIELD:	*275 g / 1¼ cups*
TIME ESTIMATE:	*10 minutes overall*
STORAGE NOTES:	*keeps for 5 days when refrigerated*
LEVEL OF DIFFICULTY:	*easy*
SPECIAL REQUIREMENTS:	*liquid soy lecithin (optional)*
USED IN:	*Pressure-Cooked Lentil Salad (see page 175)*

This recipe serves as a template for any basic vinaigrette; we list a half-dozen variations below, but you can substitute other oils and acids to create a variety of flavors. The liquid soy lecithin is optional, but adding 1%–2% of this emulsifier to any vinaigrette prevents the oil from separating out. A pasteurized egg yolk (see page 142) also works well as an emulsifier, but it adds flavor, whereas lecithin does not.

INGREDIENT	WEIGHT	VOLUME	SCALING	PROCEDURE
Champagne vinegar	40 g	45 mL / 3 Tbsp	40%	① Mix together.
Dijon mustard	25 g	1½ Tbsp	25%	
White balsamic vinegar	15 g	15 mL / 1 Tbsp	15%	
Apple juice	10 g	10 mL / 2 tsp	10%	
Extra-virgin olive oil	100 g	110 mL / ½ cup	100%	② Whisk together.
Walnut oil (or similar nut oil)	85 g	90 mL / ⅜ cup	85%	③ Blend gradually into the vinegar mixture by using an immersion blender until fully emulsified.
Liquid soy lecithin (NOW brand), optional	2 g		2%	
Salt	to taste			④ Season the dressing generously, and serve it cold or warm.

VARIATIONS

Cilantro Vinaigrette
Blanch, drain, and chop 75 g / 7 cups of cilantro. Puree the cilantro with 25 g / 4 tsp of tahini, 10 g / ½ Tbsp of agave nectar, and the ingredients in step 1. Gradually blend in 100 g / 110 mL / ½ cup of extra-virgin olive oil until fully emulsified. Season with salt.

Sesame Dressing
Mix together 40 g / 45 mL / 3 Tbsp of rice vinegar, 15 g / 15 mL / 2½ tsp of dark soy sauce, and 10 g / 2 tsp of honey. Gradually blend in 80 g / 90 mL / ⅜ cup of toasted-sesame oil, and 100 g / 110 mL / ½ cup of neutral-tasting oil. Add 26 g / ⅜ cup of sliced scallions. Season with salt.

Vietnamese-Style Dressing
Mix together 40 g / 45 mL / 3 Tbsp of rice vinegar, 25 g / 20 mL / 4¼ tsp of fish sauce, 15 g / 15 mL / 1 Tbsp of lime juice, 10 g / 1 Tbsp of palm sugar, and 1.2 g / 1 green Thai chili, minced. Gradually blend in 100 g / 110 mL / ½ cup of neutral-tasting oil. Season with salt.

Spiced Chili Dressing
Mix together 68 g / 55 mL / 3½ Tbsp of fish sauce and 56 g / 2½ Tbsp of agave nectar. Gradually blend in 92 g / 100 mL / ½ cup of Sous Vide Spiced Chili Oil (see next page) and 36 g / 40 mL / 2½ Tbsp of toasted-sesame oil. Season with salt.

Cherry Vinaigrette
At step 1, add 100 g / ½ cup of fresh or frozen cherries, pureed.

Fines Herbes Vinaigrette with Pistachio Butter
Blanch, drain, and chop 50 g / 3 cups of basil, 25 g / ⅞ cup of chives, and 15 g / 2 Tbsp each of scallions and tarragon. Puree the blanched herbs with the ingredients in step 1. Gradually blend in 110 g / 120 mL / ½ cup of extra-virgin olive oil and 50 g / 2½ Tbsp of pistachio butter until emulsified. Season with salt.

SOUS VIDE SPICED CHILI OIL

YIELD:	*500 g / 2 cups*
TIME ESTIMATE:	*8½ hours overall, including 30 minutes of preparation and 8 hours unattended*
STORAGE NOTES:	*keeps for 2 weeks when refrigerated*
LEVEL OF DIFFICULTY:	*easy*
SPECIAL REQUIREMENTS:	*sous vide setup, mace blades (optional)*
USED IN:	*Sichuan Bok Choy (see page 346), Spiced Chili Dressing (see variation on the previous page), Deep-Fried Tsukune (see variation on page 262)*

Many aromatic compounds in spices and herbs are fat-soluble, so oil extracts a lot of flavor from these ingredients. This particular oil is spicy, sweet, and fragrant. Drizzle it over steamed vegetables, crispy tofu, steamed rice, or panfried fish. Do not substitute ground mace for blades of mace, or else the flavor will be overwhelming.

INGREDIENT	WEIGHT	VOLUME	SCALING	PROCEDURE
Dried chipotle chilies, thinly sliced	85 g	1½ cups	17%	① Preheat the oven to 135 °C / 275 °F, and preheat a water bath to 70 °C / 158 °F.
Coriander seeds, cracked	15 g	¼ cup	3%	② Combine.
Dried red chilies	15 g	½ cup	3%	③ Toast in the oven until aromatic, 15–20 minutes.
Star anise	15 g	10 pods	3%	④ Cool completely.
Cinnamon sticks	10 g	2–3 sticks	2%	⑤ Crush with a mortar and pestle, or place in a zip-top bag, cover with a paper towel, and crush with a mallet or rolling pin.
Fennel seeds, cracked	6 g	1 Tbsp	1.2%	
Mace blades (optional)	5 g	1 Tbsp	1%	
Grapeseed oil or similar neutral-tasting oil	500 g	540 mL / 2¼ cups	100%	⑥ Combine with the crushed spices in a new zip-top bag, remove as much air as possible from the bag, and seal it.
				⑦ Cook sous vide for 8 hours.
				⑧ Cool, and then strain. Allow the oil to infuse overnight before straining, if possible.

VARIATIONS

Pressure-Cooked Spiced Chili Oil
Skip steps 6 and 7. Instead, pressure-cook the oil and spices in canning jars at a gauge pressure of 1 bar / 15 psi for 30 minutes, and then continue with step 8.

Basic Chili Oil
Skip steps 1–5. At step 6, seal 15 g / 3 Tbsp of dry chili flakes with the oil, and cook sous vide at 70 °C / 158 °F for 24 hours.

Rosemary Oil
Skip steps 1–5. At step 6, seal 50 g / 1 cup of fresh rosemary with the oil, and cook sous vide at 80 °C / 176 °F for 1 hour.

Garlic Oil
Skip steps 1–5. At step 6, seal 250 g / 2 cups of thinly sliced garlic with the oil, and cook sous vide at 90 °C / 194 °F for 4 hours.

Ginger Oil
Skip steps 1–5. At step 6, puree 225 g / 2 cups of fresh ginger, thinly sliced, with the oil. Cook sous vide at 70 °C / 158 °F for 3 hours. Decant the oil from the bag.

Thyme Oil
Skip steps 1–5. At step 6, seal 100 g / 3 cups of fresh thyme sprigs with the oil, and cook sous vide at 55 °C / 131 °F for 45 minutes.

Lemon Oil
Skip steps 1–5. At step 6, seal 45 g / 5 Tbsp of freshly grated lemon zest with the oil, and cook sous vide at 60 °C / 140 °F for 2 hours.

Vanilla Oil
Skip steps 1–5. At step 6, seal vanilla seeds scraped from two pods and the pod membranes with the oil, and refrigerate for 24 hours.

How To Make Clarified Butter and Brown Butter

High-powered blenders and emulsifiers like egg and soy lecithin allow you to make a fine emulsion and stabilize it. Clarified butter (called ghee in Indian cuisine) is one of those rare cases in which chefs intentionally break an emulsion—in this case, the emulsion of water, fat, and milk solids that we know and love as butter. When fully heated, these components separate, and you can isolate the pure, clarified butterfat.

Once clarified, butter tolerates higher temperatures without burning. And with no milk proteins to go rancid, it keeps longer. If you cook butter thoroughly enough during the clarification process, the milk solids can caramelize and lend their flavors and colors to the clarified butter, yielding the dark, nutty brown or black of *beurre noisette* and *beurre noir*.

1 Melt unsalted butter slowly in a saucepan over gentle heat.

2 Wait for the butter to start to bubble—your sign that the emulsion has broken. Set the pan aside to let the layers settle.

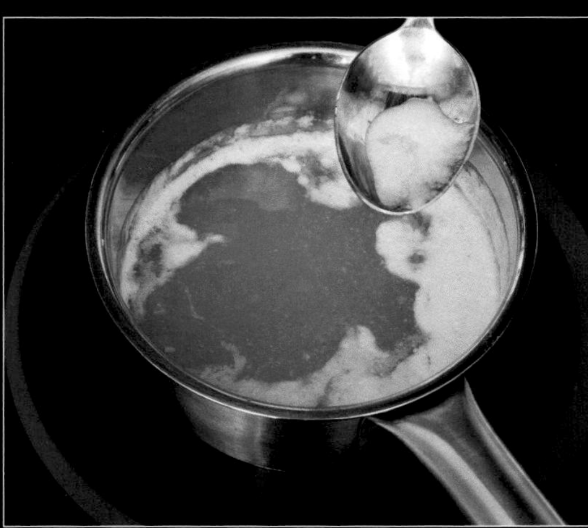

3 To make ghee, skip to step 5. For brown butter, skip to step 6. For black butter, skip to step 7. For clarified butter, spoon off the froth from the top.

4 Clarify the butter by filtering it through a very fine sieve or through cheesecloth.

5 To make ghee, continue to warm the melted butter from step 2 over low heat for 45 minutes. As the milk proteins oxidize and solidify, the flavor will deepen, but the butter will not brown. Sieve the ghee immediately, or let it rest overnight to develop even more flavor.

6 To make brown butter, seal 100 g of melted butter from step 2 with 30 g of nonfat milk powder in a canning jar, place the jar in a pressure cooker filled with 1 cm / ⅜ in of water, and then pressure-cook at a gauge pressure of 1 bar / 15 psi for 30 minutes. Then sieve the butter as in step 4.

7 To make black butter, stir 30 g of nonfat milk powder into 100 g of melted butter from step 2, and heat the mixture until the solids brown and darken but do not scorch. Then sieve the butter as in step 4.

For safety tips on pressure-cooking, see page 33.

Clarified butter

Brown butter

Black butter

Adding nonfat milk powder while you cook brown or black butter effectively increases the amount of milk solids, which in turn creates more flavor and deeper color. We first saw this technique mentioned on the website IdeasInFood.com.

MONTPELLIER BUTTER

YIELD:	*850 g / 3¾ cups*
TIME ESTIMATE:	*45 minutes overall*
STORAGE NOTES:	*keeps for up to 6 months when frozen*
LEVEL OF DIFFICULTY:	*moderate*
SPECIAL REQUIREMENTS:	*sous vide setup*
USED IN:	*Filet Mignon with Montpellier Butter (see variation on page 263)*
GOES WELL WITH:	*Sous Vide Braised Snails (see page 293)*

Classic French cooking features many compound butters that melt onto hot food to create a sauce. One of the most famous is Montpellier butter. Unfortunately, compound butters tend to separate upon melting; the great advantage of this recipe is that the eggs and gelatin help the butter to stay better emulsified when hot.

INGREDIENT	WEIGHT	VOLUME	SCALING	PROCEDURE
Egg yolks, blended	100 g	6½ Tbsp / 7–8 yolks	22%	① Preheat a water bath to **67 °C / 153 °F**. ② Place the yolks in a zip-top bag, remove as much air as possible from the bag by using the water-displacement method (see page 58), and seal it. ③ Cook sous vide for 30 minutes. Continue with steps 4–7 while the egg yolks cook.
Unsalted butter	450 g	2 cups	100%	④ Soften to room temperature, and whisk until very smooth.
Cold water	45 g	45 mL / 3 Tbsp	10%	⑤ Sprinkle the gelatin over the water in a small pan, and allow to soften for 5 minutes. ⑥ Warm over low heat until melted. ⑦ Blend into the soft butter until fully combined. ⑧ Blend the butter mixture into the egg yolks gradually until fully emulsified. Use an immersion blender or a stand mixer.
Unflavored gelatin (Knox brand)	18 g		4%	
Pressure-Cooked Garlic Confit see page 126	90 g	6½ Tbsp	20%	⑨ Combine. ⑩ Fold into the butter mixture until evenly distributed. ⑪ Roll the butter in plastic wrap into logs, or spread it into sheets on a silicone mat, and cut it into pieces. If freezing the butter, wrap it with plastic wrap first. ⑫ Serve the butter finely grated or in thin sheets over hot food.
Anchovy paste or Asian fish sauce	30 g	1½ Tbsp	7%	
Pickled onions, minced see page 130	25 g	4 Tbsp	6%	
Chives, thinly sliced	15 g	½ cup	3%	
Italian parsley, chopped	15 g	4 Tbsp	3%	
Fresh ginger, peeled and grated	10 g	½ Tbsp	2%	
Salt	9 g	2¼ tsp	2%	
Lemon zest	2.5 g	¾ tsp	0.6%	
Cayenne pepper	2 g	1 tsp	0.4%	
Lime juice	2 g	2 mL / ½ tsp	0.4%	
Black pepper	1.2 g	1 tsp	0.3%	
Star anise, finely ground	0.7 g	¼ tsp	0.2%	

STOVE-TOP CAROTENE BUTTER

YIELD:	*250 g / 1 cup*
TIME ESTIMATE:	*14 hours overall, including 30 minutes of preparation and 13½ hours unattended*
STORAGE NOTES:	*keeps for 2 weeks when refrigerated or up to 6 months when frozen*
LEVEL OF DIFFICULTY:	*moderate*
USED IN:	*Caramelized Carrot Soup (see page 178)*

The carotene pigment that makes carrots orange is fat-soluble; that is why your butter turns a beautiful orange when you make glazed carrots. By cooking carrot juice and butter together, you can dissolve the pigment into the butterfat. You can use a similar trick to capture the pigment that makes lobsters turn red when cooked; it, too, makes a flavorful butter (see the next page).

This carotene butter is superb for finishing soups and purees, cooking fish and shellfish, and whisking into warm vinaigrettes. So make plenty, if you can, and pull it out of the freezer when you want to add an elegant twist to simple dishes.

In addition to the variations we suggest below, try making butters from other ingredients having fat-soluble pigments and flavor compounds, such as tomatoes, fresh chilies, fresh turmeric, and greens and herbs of all kinds.

INGREDIENT	WEIGHT	VOLUME	SCALING	PROCEDURE
Fresh carrot juice	700 g	700 mL / 3 cups	100%	① Measure 450 g / 450 mL / 2 cups, and bring the juice to simmer in a pot over medium heat. Reserve the remaining juice for use in step 4.
Unsalted butter, cubed	450 g	2 cups	64%	② Blend gradually into the juice by using an immersion blender.
				③ Simmer for 1½ hours, stirring frequently.
				④ Remove from the heat, and stir or blend in the remaining carrot juice.
				⑤ Cool, and then refrigerate overnight.
				⑥ Scoop the congealed butterfat into a pot, and warm it until melted.
				⑦ Strain the melted butter through a fine sieve lined with cheesecloth.

4

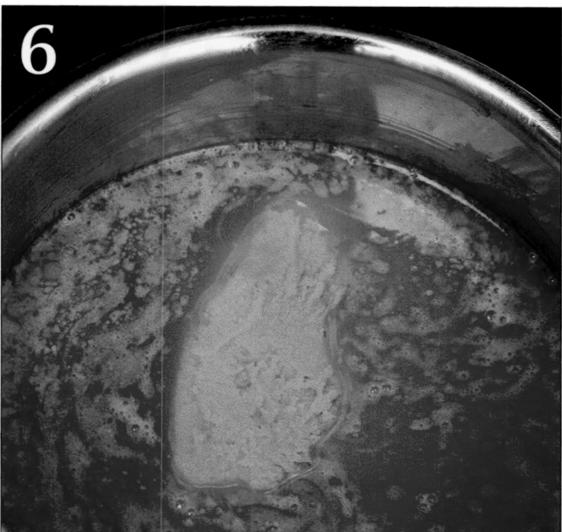

VARIATIONS

Bell Pepper Butter
Substitute fresh red bell pepper juice for the carrot juice.

Spinach Butter
Puree 450 g / 3¼ cups of blanched, drained spinach into 450 g / 490 mL / 2 cups of melted butter, and then continue at step 5.

Coffee Butter
Combine 250 g / 3 cups of whole coffee beans (never ground) with the butter. Vacuum seal, and cook sous vide at **70** °C / **158** °F for 12 hours. Strain.

Porcini Butter
Combine 225 g / 1⅞ cups of crumbled dry porcini with the butter. Vacuum seal, and cook sous vide at **70** °C / **158** °F for 1 hour. Strain.

PRESSURE-COOKED CRUSTACEAN BUTTER

YIELD:	*350 g / 2 cups*
TIME ESTIMATE:	*1½ hours overall, including 30 minutes of preparation and 1 hour unattended*
STORAGE NOTES:	*keeps for 5 days when refrigerated or up to 2 months when frozen*
LEVEL OF DIFFICULTY:	*moderate*
SPECIAL REQUIREMENTS:	*pressure cooker; shells of lobsters, crabs, or shrimp*
USED IN:	*Crustacean Hollandaise (see variation on page 106), Lobster Roll (see page 288)*

The shells of lobster, crab, and shrimp turn pink or red when cooked thanks to carotenes, the same family of molecules that give carrots and tomatoes their color. And you can extract these fat-soluble pigments from crustacean shells, along with lots of flavor, the same way as when making carotene butter from carrots (see previous page): by cooking them in butter, oil, or some other fat. Use this highly flavorful butter in place of ordinary butter to make an amazing hollandaise or beurre blanc sauce, or stir it into soups, sauces, and sautés.

INGREDIENT	WEIGHT	VOLUME	SCALING	PROCEDURE
Shells of lobsters, crabs, crayfish, shrimp, or prawns	600 g	from 2 lobsters or 2 large crabs	100%	① Clean by discarding all organs, including the gills and eyes. ② Chop into pieces by using a heavy knife or a cleaver. ③ Place the pieces into a large (4 L / 1 gal) zip-top bag, and partially seal it. Cover the bag with a towel, and pound it with a mallet to crush the shells into smaller pieces. This step accelerates flavor extraction.
Unsalted butter	450 g	2 cups	75%	④ Melt in the base of a pressure cooker over low heat.
Baking soda	4.5 g	1 tsp	0.75%	⑤ Add, stir to dissolve completely, and stir in the shells. ⑥ Pressure-cook at a gauge pressure of 1 bar / 15 psi for 1 hour. Start timing as soon as full pressure has been reached. ⑦ Let the cooker cool, or run tepid water over the rim, to depressurize it. ⑧ Refrigerate the shells in the butter overnight, if time permits, to further infuse their flavor. Reheat until melted. ⑨ Strain. Discard the shells. ⑩ Let the butter rest until it clearly separates, and then pour the butter off the top. Alternatively, chill the butter until it sets, and then scoop it off the top.

Safety tips for pressure-cooking: see page 33

Save any rendered lobster juices that are beneath the butter when you pour it off in step 10. They are quite sweet and delicious when added to a shellfish bisque or sauce.

VARIATIONS

Sous Vide Crustacean Butter

Preheat a water bath to 88 °C / 190 °F. Follow steps 1–3, vacuum seal the pieces together with the butter and baking soda, and cook sous vide for 5 hours. Plunge the bag in an ice bath, and then refrigerate it for 12 hours to allow the flavors to infuse. Reheat until melted, and then continue at step 9.

Pressure-Cooked Lobster Bisque

Heavy cream	450 g	500 mL / 2 cups
Lobster shells, broken into small pieces	350 g	from 1 lobster
Dry white wine	200 g	200 mL / ⅞ cup
Sweet onion, sliced	150 g	1½ cups
Tomato paste	20 g	1½ Tbsp
Tarragon, leaves	2 g	7–9 leaves
Cayenne pepper	0.1 g	pinch
Salt	to taste	

Combine all the ingredients in a pressure cooker, and cook at a gauge pressure of 1 bar / 15 psi for 45 minutes. Depressurize the cooker. Strain into a pot. Discard the solids. Simmer the liquid over medium-high heat until reduced by half. Season the soup to taste, and serve with minced chives and lobster meat cooked sous vide (see steps 1–5 on page 288).

PRESSURE-RENDERED CHICKEN FAT

YIELD:	*100–200 g / ½–1 cup, depending on the fat content of the chicken skin*
TIME ESTIMATE:	*2 hours overall, including 30 minutes of preparation and 1½ hours unattended*
STORAGE NOTES:	*keeps for 2 weeks when refrigerated and up to 6 months when frozen*
LEVEL OF DIFFICULTY:	*moderate*
SPECIAL REQUIREMENTS:	*meat grinder, pressure cooker, two 500 mL / 16 oz canning jars*
USED IN:	*Home Jus Gras (see page 93), Chicken Noodle Soup (see page 273)*

A recipe for fat may strike some as strange, but fat is one of the key flavor elements in food. French cuisine would be unrecognizable without cream and butter. Indian cuisine relies heavily on ghee (clarified butter). Chefs in Mediterranean countries turn habitually to olive oil, while those in Tibet always have yak butter on hand. The recipe here is for rendered chicken fat, which is widely used in Ashkenazi Jewish cuisine. (The Yiddish word for it—*schmaltz*—has taken on a whole other connotation in American English.)

As much as we love cream, butter, and olive oil, rendered fat is sometimes a better choice for use in a sauce or as a complement to meats because it does not distract from the flavor of the other ingredients. We use our Modernist schmaltz to enrich chicken sauce, salad dressing, and garlic, but it has innumerable applications—you can even use it to fry eggs!

Buy chicken skin from your butcher, or collect scraps of fat and skin from other chicken recipes in the freezer until you have enough to render. Note that the same technique can be used for any animal fat, including turkey, duck, or goose skin, and fatty trimmings from cuts of pork, veal, or beef.

INGREDIENT	WEIGHT	VOLUME	SCALING	PROCEDURE
Chicken skin, ground	500 g / 1.1 lb	2¼ cups	100%	① Combine, and divide equally into two 500 mL / 16 oz canning jars. Tighten the lids fully, and then unscrew them one-quarter turn so that they do not explode.
Baking soda (optional)	2.5 g	½ tsp	0.5%	
				② Place the filled jars on a rack or trivet in the base of a pressure cooker with 2.5 cm / 1 in of water.
				③ Pressure-cook at a gauge pressure of 1 bar / 15 psi for 1½ hours. Start timing as soon as full pressure has been reached.
				④ Let the cooker cool, or run tepid water over the rim, to depressurize it. Let the jar contents cool before opening to avoid splattering.
				⑤ Strain. Discard the solids.
				⑥ Allow the liquid to settle, and then decant the warm fat. Alternatively, refrigerate it until the fat solidifies, at least 4 hours, and then scoop the clear fat off the top.

Safety tips for pressure-cooking: see page 33

OTHER WAYS TO RENDER FAT

We use canning jars inside the pressure cooker because it simplifies cleanup, and we aren't usually rendering more fat than will fit in a couple jars. But you can render a large batch by putting 2.5 cm / 1 in of water in the pressure cooker, and then adding the ground skin. The pressure cooker should be no more than two-thirds full.

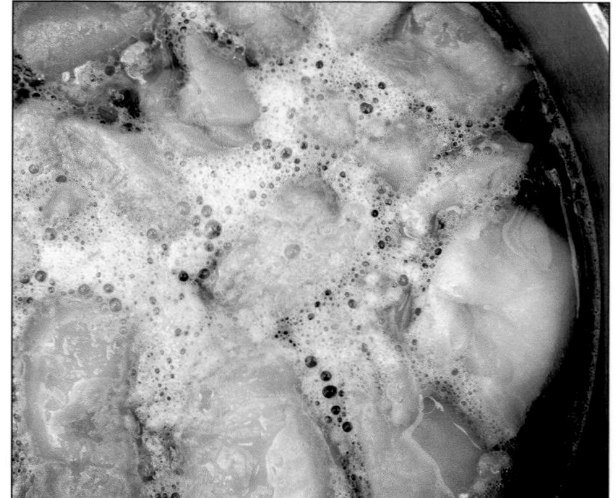

Wet-Rendering
Drop the skin or fat into boiling water, and reduce it until all that is left are pieces of meat and tissue floating in bubbling fat. Strain. Discard the solids. Allow the liquid to separate, and then pour the warm fat off the top.

Dry-Rendering
Sauté the skin or fat over low heat until the fat melts. The cooking causes Maillard reactions that enhance the flavor of the rendered fat. Dry-rendered fat keeps for several weeks in the refrigerator. This method works particularly well with fatty bacon.

CONDIMENTS

Condiments are small, usually intensely flavored additions to a plate that help to round out and highlight the dish. Often, condiments are served in such a way that the eater has some control over how much to add to each bite. Each region has its traditional condiments; in the United States, we're used to ketchup, mustard, pickle relish, and tartar sauce (eaten with foods like hot dogs, French fries, and fried seafood). Elsewhere in the world, bottles of vinegar or hot chili sauce are standard table settings. But the spectrum of condiments is practically infinite and allows for wide creativity.

Use condiments to give a dish more depth by adding layers of complementary flavors. Or devise accompaniments that balance the dominant flavor of the dish: something creamy and cool to accompany a spicy food, or something tart to go with a rich, savory dish. Condiments also allow you to add visual contrast or a final touch of richness to the presentation of a plate. In this section, we present several of our favorite condiments that pair well with other recipes in this book. Together, they illustrate a range of techniques that you can extend with your own ideas.

GRILLED APPLESAUCE

YIELD:	*380 g / 1⅝ cups*
TIME ESTIMATE:	*40 minutes overall, including 20 minutes of preparation and 20 minutes unattended*
STORAGE NOTES:	*keeps for 1 day when refrigerated*
LEVEL OF DIFFICULTY:	*moderate*
SPECIAL REQUIREMENTS:	*sous vide setup, charcoal grill*
GOES WELL WITH:	*Grilled Pork Chop (see page 202), Aged White Cheddar on Sourdough with Apples (see variation on page 318)*

The apples for this sauce are twice-cooked: first sous vide, which establishes just the right texture, and again on the grill, which develops the roasted flavors that make this applesauce distinctive. When the apples emerge from the water bath, they should be firm enough to hold together on the grill but soft enough to puree to a creamy sauce. We call for green apples, but other varieties work well, too.

INGREDIENT	WEIGHT	VOLUME	SCALING	PROCEDURE
Green apples, peeled, quartered, and cored	1 kg	4 large	100%	① Preheat a water bath to 90 °C / 194 °F. ② Vacuum seal the apples in a single layer. ③ Cook sous vide until tender, about 20 minutes. ④ While the apples are cooking, build a fire in a charcoal grill, and prepare an ice-water bath alongside the sous vide water bath. ⑤ Place a clean grill rack over the coals to preheat for at least 10 minutes. When the coals are gray and ashy, bank them to one side. ⑥ Plunge the bag of cooked apples into the ice bath until completely cool.
Cooking spray or neutral frying oil see page xxii	as needed			⑦ Remove the apples from the bag, and spray or brush them with a light coating of oil. ⑧ Sear the apples, on one side only, on the grill over the banked coals until the side facing the grill turns brown, about 3 minutes. ⑨ Puree the seared apples in a blender until smooth. ⑩ Pass the puree through a fine sieve, and measure 250 g / 1⅛ cups for use in the next step.
Dijon mustard	40 g	3 Tbsp	4%	⑪ Combine with the apple puree, and stir together.
Rendered bacon fat, warm see the previous page	40 g	45 mL / 3 Tbsp	4%	
Honey	35 g	2 Tbsp	3.5%	
Cider vinegar	16 g	20 mL / 3¾ tsp	1.6%	
Salt	to taste			⑫ Season the sauce, and serve it cold or warm.

PRESSURE-COOKED PICKLED MUSTARD SEEDS

YIELD:	*350 g / 1 cup*
TIME ESTIMATE:	*13 hours, including 30 minutes of preparation and 12½ hours unattended*
STORAGE NOTES:	*keeps for 5 days in brine when refrigerated*
LEVEL OF DIFFICULTY:	*easy*
SPECIAL REQUIREMENTS:	*pressure cooker*
USED IN:	*Honey Mustard Sauce (see page 259), Microwaved Potato Salad (see page 346)*

Mustard seeds are naturally bitter, but overnight soaking followed by five rounds of blanching removes any trace of bitterness. We then pressure-cook the seeds to give them a pleasant "pop" when eaten.

Serve the pickled seeds as a condiment with braised meat, or stir them into vinaigrettes, mayonnaise, hollandaise, or reduction sauces to add both texture and a sweet-and-sour accent.

INGREDIENT	WEIGHT	VOLUME	SCALING	PROCEDURE
Yellow mustard seeds	50 g	4½ Tbsp	100%	① Cover with cold water, and refrigerate overnight or for 12 hours. ② Strain. ③ Cover with more cold water in a small pot, bring to a boil, and then strain. ④ Repeat step 3 four more times.
Apple cider vinegar	100 g	120 mL / ½ cup	200%	⑤ Combine in the base of a pressure cooker, and stir until dissolved. ⑥ Bring to a simmer, and add the strained seeds to the brine. ⑦ Pressure-cook at a gauge pressure of 1 bar / 15 psi for 25 minutes. Start timing as soon as full pressure has been reached. ⑧ Let the cooker cool, or run tepid water over the rim, to depressurize it. ⑨ Strain the seeds, reserving the brine for storing the seeds, and serve them warm or cold.
Water	70 g	70 mL / ⅓ cup	140%	
Sugar	40 g	3 Tbsp	80%	
Salt	5 g	1¼ tsp	10%	

Safety tips for pressure-cooking: see page 33

PRESSURE-COOKED GARLIC CONFIT

YIELD:	*300 g / 1¼ cups*
TIME ESTIMATE:	*2¼ hours overall, including 15 minutes of preparation and 2 hours unattended*
STORAGE NOTES:	*keeps for 1 month when refrigerated*
LEVEL OF DIFFICULTY:	*moderate*
SPECIAL REQUIREMENTS:	*pressure cooker, 500 mL / 16 oz canning jar*
USED IN:	*Montpellier Butter (see page 120), Aioli (see variation on page 108), Garlic Hollandaise (see variation on page 106), Steel-Cut Oats with Sous Vide Braised Snails (see variation on page 331), Caramelized Onion Gravy (see variation on page 101), Broccoli Raab Pizza (see variation on page 306), Creamed Spinach (see page 199), Garlic Mashed Potatoes (see variation on page 230)*

Garlic confit is a staple condiment. The garlic is soft enough to spread on bread with a sprinkle of salt. Or use it to add depth to broths, sauces, purees, and vinaigrettes. The silky, soft cloves add body to any liquid. The oil, which is just as flavorful, is delicious drizzled over salads or into vegetable stews (see page 185).

INGREDIENT	WEIGHT	VOLUME	SCALING
Olive oil	200 g	220 mL / 1 cup	160%
Garlic cloves, peeled	125 g	about 50 cloves	100%
Rosemary	2 g	1 sprig	1.6%
Thyme	2 g	2–3 sprigs	1.6%

PROCEDURE

1. Place in a 500 mL / 16 oz canning jar, tighten the lid fully, and then unscrew it one-quarter turn so that the jar doesn't explode.
2. Place the filled jar on a rack or trivet in the base of a pressure cooker, and add 2.5 cm / 1 in of water.
3. Pressure-cook at a gauge pressure of 1 bar / 15 psi for 2 hours. Start timing as soon as full pressure has been reached.
4. Let the cooker cool, or run tepid water over the rim, to depressurize it. Let the jar contents cool before opening.
5. Serve the confit warm or cold.

Safety tips for pressure-cooking: see page 33

VARIATIONS

Provençal Garlic Confit

Add other Provençal aromatics such as oregano, fennel seed, bay leaf, lavender, and sage to the rosemary and thyme.

Make a double batch: it keeps well.

Mediterranean Vegetable Confit

Zucchini, sliced into 0.5 cm / 3⁄16 in rounds	225 g	about 18 rounds
Red bell pepper, julienned	125 g	about 1 pepper
Button mushrooms, cut into eighths	100 g	about 8 mushrooms
Extra-virgin olive oil	370 g	410 mL / 1¾ cups
Balsamic vinegar	6 g	7 mL / 1½ tsp
Salt	to taste	

Divide the vegetables into two 500 mL / 16 oz canning jars, and cover with the olive oil. Pressure-cook at a gauge pressure of 1 bar / 15 psi for 45 minutes. Start timing as soon as full pressure has been reached. Depressurize the cooker. Let the jar contents cool before opening. Strain the vegetables from the jars, and season with balsamic vinegar, olive oil from the jar, and salt to taste.

Fingerling Potatoes Confit

Fingerling potatoes, cut into 2.5 cm / 1 in pieces	300 g	2⅜ cups
Thyme		2 sprigs
Pressure-rendered chicken fat, melted	250 g	280 mL / 1⅛ cups
Salt	to taste	

Divide the potatoes and thyme into two 500 mL / 16 oz canning jars, and cover with the fat. Pressure-cook at a gauge pressure of 1 bar / 15 psi for 45 minutes. Start timing as soon as full pressure has been reached. Depressurize the cooker. Let the jar contents cool before opening. Drain the potatoes, season, and serve them warm. They pair very well with roasted chicken (see page 238).

PRESSURE-CARAMELIZED ONIONS

YIELD:	*380 g / 1½ cups*
TIME ESTIMATE:	*1 hour overall, including 20 minutes of preparation and 40 minutes unattended*
STORAGE NOTES:	*keeps for 5 days when refrigerated*
LEVEL OF DIFFICULTY:	*moderate*
SPECIAL REQUIREMENTS:	*pressure cooker, three 500 mL / 16 oz canning jars*
USED IN:	*Caramelized Onion Gravy (see variation on page 101), Alsatian Omelet Filling (see variation on page 145), Savory Cheese Pie (see variation on page 379)*

Caramelized onions are a favorite component of many dishes. They can be used as a topping for a hamburger or pizza, served as a side dish for a steak, or placed center stage as the featured ingredient of a French onion soup or an onion tart.

There are many ways to make caramelized onions. This Modernist method browns the onions perfectly with no hands-on effort, maximizing their flavor while minimizing the risk of burning them. After pressure-cooking, the onions are quite soft; you can dry them on the stove top or in a dehydrator (see variation below).

INGREDIENT	WEIGHT	VOLUME	SCALING	PROCEDURE
Yellow onion, julienned	500 g	4¾ cups	100%	① Combine in a large bowl, and mix thoroughly.
Baking soda	1.5 g	¼ tsp	0.3%	② Divide the onion mixture evenly into three 500 mL / 16 oz canning jars.
Unsalted butter, cubed	35 g	3 Tbsp	7%	③ Divide the butter evenly among the filled jars. Tighten the lids fully, and then unscrew them one-quarter turn so that the jars don't explode.
				④ Place the filled jars on a rack or trivet in the base of a pressure cooker, and add 2.5 cm / 1 in of water.
				⑤ Pressure-cook at a gauge pressure of 1 bar / 15 psi for 40 minutes. Start timing as soon as full pressure has been reached.
				⑥ Let the cooker cool, or run tepid water over the rim, to depressurize it. Let the jar contents cool before opening to avoid splattering.
				⑦ Transfer the cooked onions to a pot.
				⑧ Simmer over medium heat, stirring occasionally, until the liquid has reduced to a syrup, 10–12 minutes.
Salt	to taste			⑨ Season the onions to taste, and serve them warm.
Sugar	to taste			
Black pepper, ground	to taste			

Safety tips for pressure-cooking: see page 33

VARIATIONS

Dried Caramelized Onions

For a drier texture and more concentrated flavor, drain the liquid from the cooked onions after step 6. (You can use this liquid as a flavorful broth or stir it into a meat or poultry jus.) Arrange the onions in a dehydrator, and dehydrate them at 63 °C / 145 °F until slightly leathery, 1½–2 hours. Alternatively, sauté the onions in a pan over very low heat; take care not to burn them.

French Onion Soup

After step 7, add 200 g / 200 mL / ⅞ cup of brown beef stock (see page 86), 15 g / 15 mL / 1 Tbsp of dry sherry, and a sprig of fresh thyme. Bring the soup to a boil, and then divide it into bowls. Top each bowl with toasted crusty bread covered with a Perfectly Melting Cheese Slice (see page 317) or some other variety of constructed cheese.

TOMATO CONFIT

YIELD:	*150 g / 1 cup*
TIME ESTIMATE:	*up to 8½ hours overall, including 20 minutes of preparation and 5–8 hours unattended*
STORAGE NOTES:	*keeps for 5 days when refrigerated or up to 6 months when frozen*
LEVEL OF DIFFICULTY:	*easy*
SPECIAL REQUIREMENTS:	*vacuum sealer*
USED IN:	*Tomato Leather (see the next page), Goat Cheese on Baguette with Tomato Confit and Basil (see variation on page 319), Pork Belly B.L.T. (see page 232)*

INGREDIENT	WEIGHT	VOLUME	SCALING	PROCEDURE
Tomatoes (Roma or on-the-vine)	1 kg	6–8 medium	100%	① Preheat the oven to **110** °C / **230** °F. ② Bring a large pot of water to a boil, and arrange an ice-water bath alongside. ③ Core the tomatoes, and slice a small X in the skin opposite the core. ④ Blanch the tomatoes for 30 seconds, and then plunge them into the ice bath. ⑤ Peel the tomatoes. ⑥ Cut them in half lengthwise, and gently remove and discard the seeds. ⑦ Pat them dry, and place them cut-side down on a baking sheet lined with a silicone mat.
Extra-virgin olive oil	40 g	45 mL / 3 Tbsp	4%	⑧ Brush evenly onto the tomato halves.
Garlic, thinly sliced	15 g	2 Tbsp	1.5%	⑨ Scatter over the tomato halves. Basil or tarragon may be substituted.
Thyme	4 g	4–5 sprigs	0.4%	
Fresh bay leaves, torn	1 g	2 leaves	0.1%	
Salt	2 g	½ tsp	0.2%	⑩ Sprinkle evenly over the tomato halves. ⑪ Place the tomatoes in the oven, and dry them for 1 hour. ⑫ Turn the tomatoes over, lower the oven temperature to **95** °C / **205** °F, and return them to the oven to dry until they become deep red and shriveled, 5–8 hours depending on their size and water content. ⑬ Cool, and then pick off and discard the garlic and herbs.
Sugar	2 g	½ tsp	0.2%	
Extra-virgin olive oil	40 g	45 mL / 3 Tbsp	4%	⑭ Vacuum seal with the tomatoes to infuse the olive oil. ⑮ Serve warm or cold.

(adapted from Heston Blumenthal)

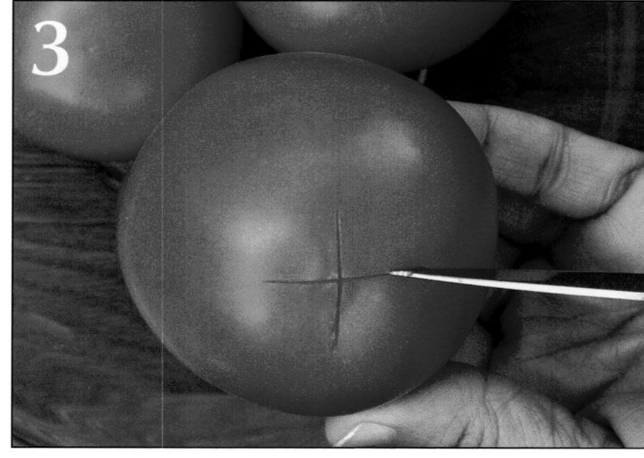

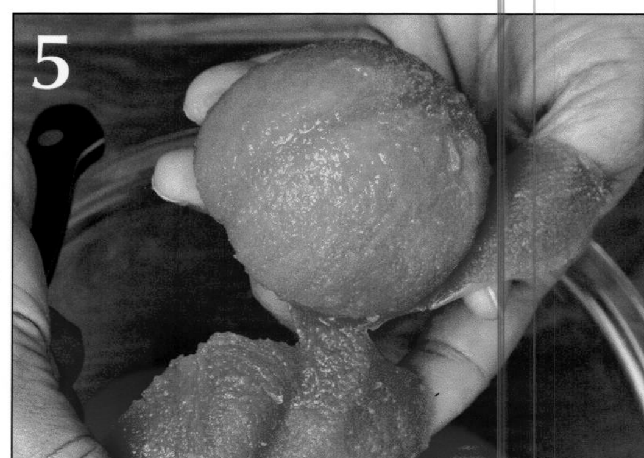

We always have oven-dried tomatoes on hand to add depth of flavor to simple dishes. Roma-style tomatoes give the most consistent results, and they don't have to be perfect: blemishes can't be seen once they shrivel, and drying concentrates the flavors of watery or bland tomatoes.

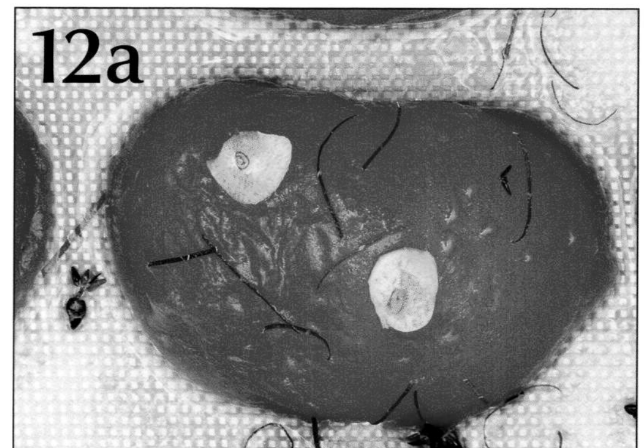

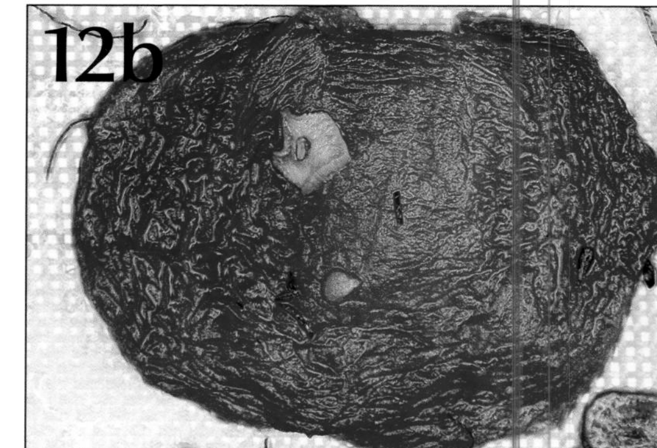

TOMATO LEATHER

YIELD:	*40 g / one 10 cm by 15 cm / 4 in by 6 in sheet*
TIME ESTIMATE:	*up to 2¼ hours overall, including 15 minutes of preparation and 2 hours unattended*
STORAGE NOTES:	*keeps for 1 week when rolled in a single layer in waxed paper and sealed in plastic wrap*
LEVEL OF DIFFICULTY:	*moderate*
SPECIAL REQUIREMENTS:	*food dehydrator, xanthan gum (optional)*
USED IN:	*Lobster Roll (see page 288)*

Leathers make a healthy snack or a fancy garnish (say, a little tangle of apple leather atop squash soup). The variations below show how to extend this recipe to myriad other fruits and even vegetables, such as onion. The oil in the recipe prevents the leather from sticking to your teeth; the more oil you use, the more tender and supple the resulting leather.

INGREDIENT	WEIGHT	VOLUME	SCALING	PROCEDURE
Tomato Confit, pureed, or tomato paste see previous page	100 g	6 Tbsp	100%	① Stir thoroughly to combine. ② Spread onto a nonstick surface in a rectangle 10 cm by 15 cm / 4 in by 6 in, about 2 mm / 1⁄16 in thick.
Extra-virgin olive oil	5 g	6 mL / 1⅛ tsp	5%	③ Dry the mixture in a food dehydrator at 65 °C / 150 °F until it turns leathery, 1½–2 hours. Alternatively, dry until leathery in an oven set to its lowest temperature setting. Drying times vary.
Red wine vinegar	5 g	7 mL / 1⅛ tsp	5%	
Hot sauce (Tabasco brand)	1 g	1 mL / 2 drops	1%	
Xanthan gum (Bob's Red Mill brand), optional	0.2 g		0.2%	④ Peel the leather from the nonstick surface, and cut it into desired shapes. ⑤ Serve at room temperature.

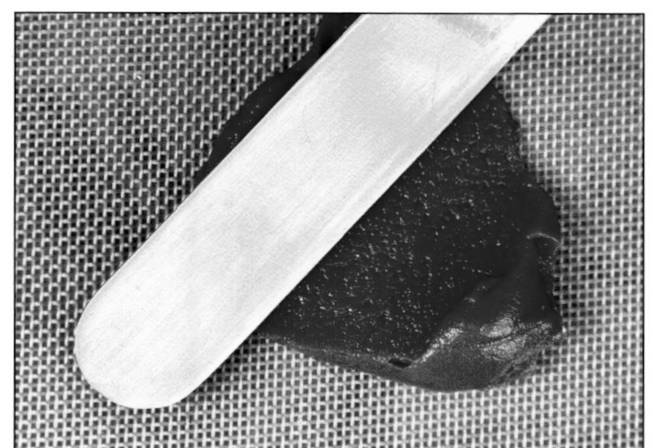

1 Stir the tomato confit or paste, olive oil, vinegar, Tabasco, and xanthan gum (optional) together thoroughly. If you are using the xanthan gum, make sure to stir until it is well distributed.

2 Spread the mixture onto a nonstick surface in a rectangle 10 cm by 15 cm / 4 in by 6 in, about 2 mm / 1⁄16 in thick. An offset spatula is the ideal tool for this.

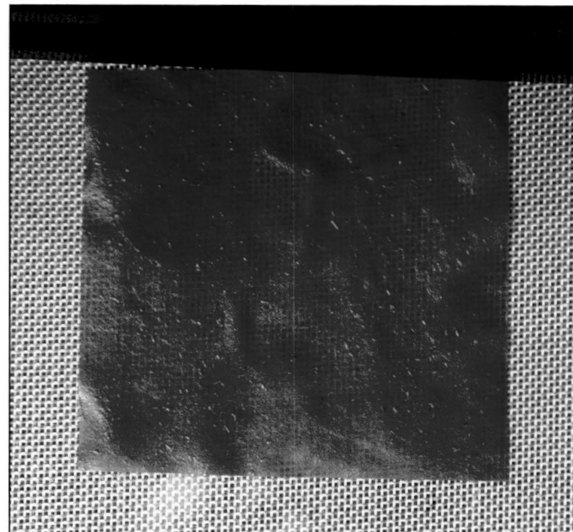

3 Dry the mixture in a food dehydrator at 65 °C / 150 °F until it turns leathery and flexible, and is easy to peel, 1½–2 hours. If a dehydrator is not available, use an oven set to its lowest temperature; the drying time will vary.

4 Peel the tomato leather from the nonstick surface, and cut it into the desired shapes.

5 Serve the leather at room temperature.

VARIATIONS

Mango Chili Leather

Mango, diced and peeled	100 g	⅞ cup
Neutral-tasting oil	4 g	4 mL / ⅞ tsp
Sugar	2 g	½ tsp
Red Thai chili	1 g	½ tsp

Puree together, and continue with step 2.

Fruit Leather

Substitute apple, pear, apricot, raspberry, or persimmon for the mango in the variation at left, and add 0.2 g of xanthan gum and up to 15 g of sugar for every 100 g of puree. You can also use whole mandarin oranges or quince, but these fruits must first be pressure-cooked until tender and then sieved.

Onion Leather

At step 1, substitute cooked onion or shallot puree for the tomato confit, and replace the olive oil with a neutral-tasting vegetable oil. Puree, and then continue with step 2.

VACUUM-PICKLED VEGETABLES

YIELD:	*300 g / 2 cups*
TIME ESTIMATE:	*12¼ hours overall, including 15 minutes of preparation and 12 hours unattended*
STORAGE NOTES:	*keeps for 2 weeks when refrigerated*
LEVEL OF DIFFICULTY:	*easy*
SPECIAL REQUIREMENTS:	*vacuum sealer with marinating attachment, rigid vacuum storage container or canning jars*
USED IN:	*Sweet Onion Slaw (see page 165), Autumn Flavors Bok Choy (see variation on page 346)*

We use pickled vegetables minced and mixed into salads, as condiments for grilled meats, and as a garnish for stews. This recipe uses carrots, but it works just as well with other vegetables—and even with fruits—such as cauliflower florets, thinly sliced lemons, radishes, pearl onions, apples, beets, cucumbers, blanched mushrooms, julienned red onions, and sunchokes (Jerusalem artichokes). Simply substitute them for the carrots at step 2.

The thinner you slice the vegetables, the quicker they pickle. We seal the pickles while the brine is warm to create a mild vacuum and a more tender pickle; if you prefer crisp pickles, chill the brine before adding it at step 4. When the pickles are gone, don't throw the pickling liquid away. Use it as a base for a vinaigrette, or stir it into a dirty martini.

INGREDIENT	WEIGHT	VOLUME	SCALING	PROCEDURE
Water	200 g	200 mL / ⅞ cup	100%	① Combine in a pot to make a brine, and bring it to a simmer.
White wine vinegar	200 g	230 mL / 1 cup	100%	
Sugar	80 g	½ cup	40%	
Salt	12 g	1 Tbsp	6%	
Yellow mustard seeds	3 g	1 tsp	1.5%	
Black peppercorns	2.5 g	1½ tsp	1.3%	
Coriander seeds	1.5 g	1 tsp	0.8%	
Fresh bay leaves	0.5 g	2 leaves	0.3%	
Carrots, sliced 3 mm / ⅛ in thick	300 g	2½ cups	150%	② Pour the warm brine over the carrots, and stir until moistened. ③ Cool slightly. ④ Pour the carrots and liquid into a rigid vacuum storage container or canning jars, and vacuum seal. ⑤ Refrigerate for at least 12 hours.

1 Combine all ingredients except the vegetables in a pot, and bring them to a simmer. This is the brine.

We like our pickles on the sweet side. For a more traditional sour pickle, reduce the amount of sugar to 15 g / 1½ Tbsp.

To preserve the pickled vegetables and give them a fresh, distinct snap, add 2 g of calcium chloride or calcium lactate at step 1.

2 Pour the warm brine over the vegetables, and stir until they are moistened.

3 Cool the mixture slightly.

4 Place the vegetables into a rigid vacuum storage container or canning jars, and pour the warm brine over top. Seal the jars, or vacuum seal the container by using a tube attachment until bubbles no longer rise to the surface. Vacuum sealing accelerates the infusion of the brine into the vegetables.

5 Refrigerate for at least 12 hours for best flavor, agitating several times to ensure that the vegetables are evenly pickled.

The pickled carrots, Romanesco, radishes, and beets above were made in old-fashioned canning jars, but you can infuse brine into vegetables more quickly by using a modern tool: a whipping siphon. Place the vegetables and brine in the siphon, charge it with two cartridges of nitrous oxide, and refrigerate it for 20 minutes.

VACUUM-INFUSED CELERY

YIELD:	*60 g / ½ cup*
TIME ESTIMATE:	*35 minutes overall, including 5 minutes of preparation and 30 minutes unattended*
STORAGE NOTES:	*serve immediately*
LEVEL OF DIFFICULTY:	*moderate*
SPECIAL REQUIREMENTS:	*vacuum sealer with marinating attachment, malic acid or citric acid*
USED IN:	*Lobster Roll (see page 288)*

Any porous fruit or vegetable, such as celery, apple, fennel, or watermelon, can be vacuum-infused with its own juice or with another flavorful thin liquid. The process fills the air pockets, called vacuoles, in the cells of the plant tissue with the liquid of your choice. Malic acid, available from wine-making and brewing suppliers, adds the tartness of green apples. Do not use malic acid dietary supplements.

INGREDIENT	WEIGHT	VOLUME	SCALING	PROCEDURE
Apple juice	200 g	200 mL / ⅞ cup	100%	① Stir together until the malic acid has dissolved.
Celery seeds	20 g	3 Tbsp	10%	② Allow to infuse for 30 minutes, and strain. Discard the seeds.
Malic acid or citric acid	4 g		2%	
Celery, sliced 5 mm / 3⁄16 in thick	60 g	½ cup	30%	③ Combine with the strained apple juice in a small bowl. The liquid should cover the slices. ④ Place the bowl in a canister specifically designed for vacuum sealing or marinating, and vacuum seal. Alternatively, place in a canning jar having a special vacuum-sealing lid, and seal. ⑤ Release the vacuum to infuse the celery. ⑥ Drain the celery, and serve it immediately.

VARIATIONS

Pressure-Infused Celery

If you have a whipping siphon, you can infuse the food by using high pressure rather than a vacuum. After step 3, pour the mixture into a whipping siphon. The liquid should cover the celery slices. Charge the siphon with two cartridges of nitrous oxide, and refrigerate it for 20 minutes. Release the pressure, drain the celery, and serve it immediately.

Waldorf Salad

Apple-infused celery makes a great addition to this classic New York salad. To 40 g / 5 Tbsp of the infused celery slices, add 100 g / 1 cup of chopped butter lettuce, 50 g / ⅜ cup of finely julienned celery root, 50 g / ¾ cup of thinly sliced green apple, and 25 g / 2½ Tbsp of chopped walnuts. Toss with 45 g / 3½ Tbsp of romaine dressing (see steps 1–9 on page 168).

BRINES AND MARINADES

Salt is not just a universal seasoning. It also has a powerful chemical ability to retain juices within fish and meat during cooking, provided you distribute the salt evenly throughout the meat at the proper concentration. That isn't easy, but a few special tools make it manageable.

Slathering salt on the outside of a fish or a piece of meat doesn't work very well, unless you want the distinctive flavor and firm, smooth texture of a cured meat, like corned beef or smoked salmon. At such high concentrations, salt actually causes the proteins in meat to fall apart.

The subtler effect of brining is more widely useful. Brining is the technique of soaking meat in a dilute salt solution until the dissolved salt permeates the muscle tissue. You're shooting for a final concentration of about 0.5% salt throughout the meat—weak compared to curing. The challenge with brining is getting the meat deep in the interior to be just as salty as the meat on the outside. Unless you know what you're doing, it's easy to end up with a steep gradient of saltiness.

This challenge is very similar to cooking—you want the meat done the way you like it, all the way from core to edge—and the solution is analogous, too. In cooking, low temperatures and long cooking times are the sure path to evenly cooked meat. If you just throw food on a roaring hot grill, timing is crucial and easy to misjudge, and some overcooking is inevitable. Likewise when brining, the conventional approach of soaking meat in a strong salt solution requires you to pull it out at just the right moment—hard to do without the equivalent of a thermometer for measuring salinity. Resting the meat does allow the salt gradient to even out somewhat, but there's just no avoiding an oversalted exterior and an undersalted interior.

Modernist brining, akin to cooking sous vide, soaks the meat for long periods (up to 24 hours) in a solution having a salt concentration only slightly higher than that target of 0.5%. The risk of oversalting is eliminated. You can accelerate the process by using a brine injector, syringe, Jaccard tenderizer, or even a whipping siphon.

SWEET BRINE FOR MEATS

YIELD:	*170 g / ⅝ cup of brine for 750 g / 1.7 lb of meat*
TIME ESTIMATE:	*12¼ hours, including 12 hours unattended*
STORAGE NOTES:	*brine keeps for up to 3 days when refrigerated; brined and drained meat keeps for up to 24 hours when refrigerated but must then be cooked*
LEVEL OF DIFFICULTY:	*easy*
SPECIAL REQUIREMENTS:	*brine injector or syringe*

This brine works well with all meats. For a less sweet variation, simply replace the milk and juice with water. Bear in mind, however, that whole milk and apple juice both contain natural phosphates that tenderize the meat as it brines.

If you have a Jaccard meat tenderizer, you can use that instead of an injector; puncture the meat on all sides, and then soak it in the brine for 24 hours.

INGREDIENT	WEIGHT	VOLUME	SCALING	PROCEDURE
Whole milk	75 g	75 mL / 5 Tbsp	10%	① Stir together until the salt and sugar are completely dissolved.
Apple juice	75 g	75 mL / 5 Tbsp	10%	
Salt	10 g	2½ tsp	1.3%	
Sugar	9 g	1 Tbsp	1.2%	
Raw, boneless meat, no thicker than 3.5 cm / 1⅜ in	750 g / 1.7 lb		100%	② Inject the meat with as much brine as it will hold, and then immerse it in any leftover brine. ③ Refrigerate the brined meat for 12 hours before cooking.

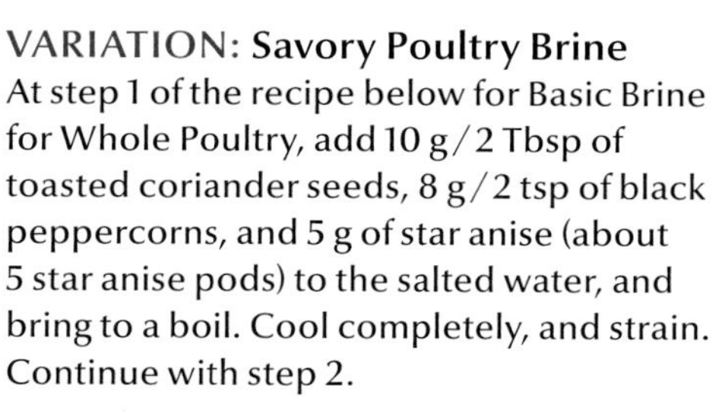

VARIATION: **Savory Poultry Brine**
At step 1 of the recipe below for Basic Brine for Whole Poultry, add 10 g / 2 Tbsp of toasted coriander seeds, 8 g / 2 tsp of black peppercorns, and 5 g of star anise (about 5 star anise pods) to the salted water, and bring to a boil. Cool completely, and strain. Continue with step 2.

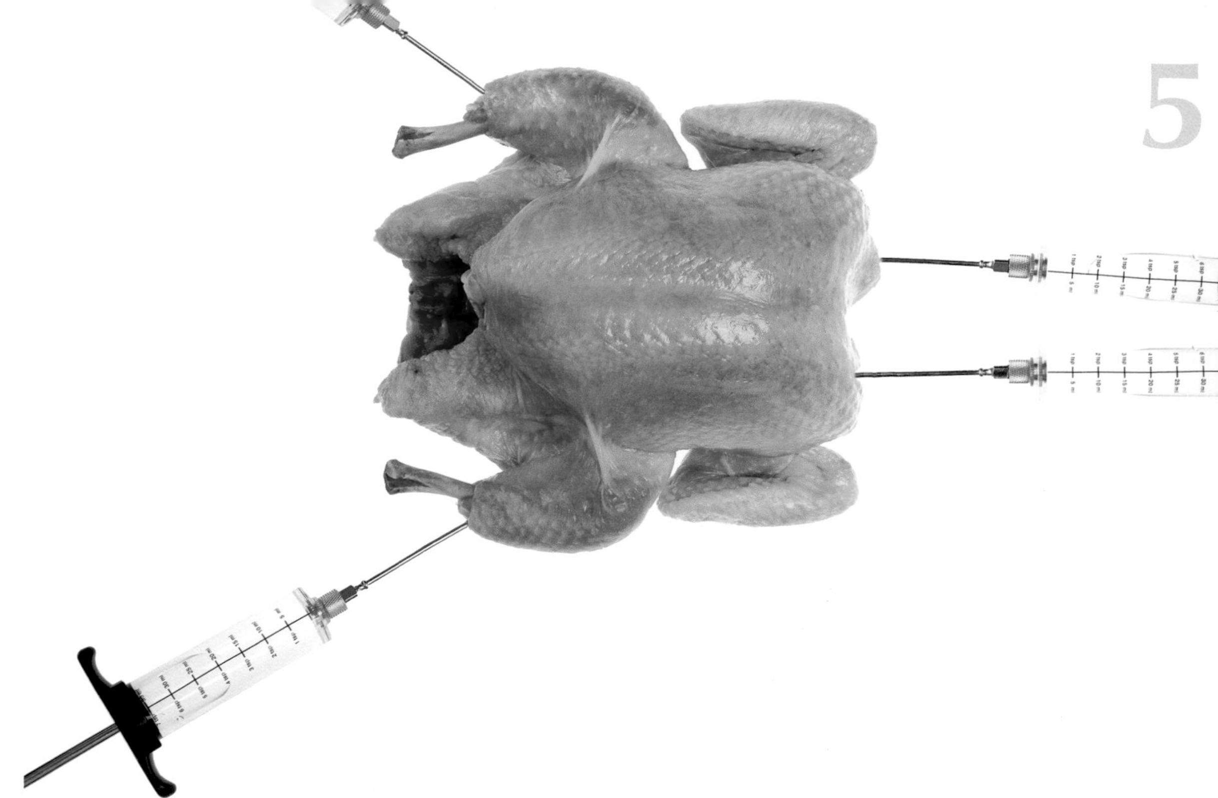

BASIC BRINE FOR WHOLE POULTRY

YIELD: *210 g / ⅞ cup of brine for 2 kg / 4.4 lb of poultry*
TIME ESTIMATE: *24¼ hours, including 24 hours unattended*
STORAGE NOTES: *brine keeps indefinitely before use; brined poultry keeps for up to 24 hours when refrigerated*
LEVEL OF DIFFICULTY: *easy*

INGREDIENT	WEIGHT	VOLUME	SCALING	PROCEDURE
Water	200 g	200 mL / ⅞ cup	10%	① Stir together until the salt is completely dissolved.
Salt	12 g	1 Tbsp	0.6%	
Chicken	2 kg / 4.4 lb	1 whole	100%	② Inject the brine as evenly as possible throughout the meat. Place the needle as shown above and into the neck and back cavities to avoid puncturing the skin. ③ Refrigerate the brined chicken for 24 hours, uncovered, to dry the skin before roasting (see page 238), steaming, or poaching the bird.

FISH BRINE

YIELD: *1.1 kg / 4¼ cups of brine for 600 g / 1.3 lb of fish*
TIME ESTIMATE: *up to 12¼ hours, including 10 minutes of preparation and 5–12 hours unattended*
STORAGE NOTES: *brine keeps indefinitely before use; cook brined fish immediately*
LEVEL OF DIFFICULTY: *easy*

INGREDIENT	WEIGHT	VOLUME	SCALING	PROCEDURE
Water	1 kg	1 L / 4¼ cups	167%	① Stir together until the salt and sugar are completely dissolved.
Salt	50 g	4½ Tbsp	8%	
Sugar	40 g	3½ Tbsp	7%	
Fish, cut into individual portions	600 g / 1.3 lb		100%	② Soak in the brine for 5 hours for a light brine with delicate seasoning, or for up to 12 hours for a firmer, more intensely flavored result. Use the longer brining time when making cold fish dishes.

VARIATIONS

Seaweed Fish Brine
After step 1, add 10 g / 2 Tbsp of toasted coriander seeds, 10 g (about 2 sheets) of kombu seaweed, and 3 g / 3 tsp of grated lemon zest to the brine, and bring it to a boil. Cool the brine completely, and then strain it. Continue with step 2.

Fish Cure
Curing is generally faster than brining because the salt and sugar are not diluted in liquid. To make a quick cure for fish, combine 35 g / 3½ Tbsp of salt with 25 g / 2½ Tbsp of sugar for every 1 kg / 2.2 lb of fish. Cut the fish into about six portions. Coat each portion evenly with the cure. Refrigerate the fish, covered, for 45 minutes, and then rinse it, pat dry, and cook.

MARINADES

By mixing together just a few flavorful items from the pantry, you can create a marinade that adds an evocative regional flavor to meats, poultry, seafood, or vegetables. Each of the variations below is made the same way. Stir all of the ingredients together, and add up to 450 g / 1 lb of the food you want to marinate. Refrigerate for the time indicated, and then cook.

Each of these recipes includes a good bit of salt, either directly or in one of the liquid ingredients. As such, these marinades are actually flavored brines. Although most of the flavor of the marinade penetrates only the surface of the food, the salt sinks in more deeply. It firms the texture and enhances the juiciness of the food as it seasons. Acids in the marinade also can change food texture, and not always for the better, so don't leave them on for longer than suggested.

Kalbi Marinade		
Apple juice	200 g	200 mL / ⅞ cup
Sugar	75 g	⅜ cup
Light soy sauce	50 g	40 mL / 3 Tbsp
Gochujang, Korean fermented chili paste	50 g	3 Tbsp
Garlic, chopped	7 g	1 Tbsp

Mix together, add to food, and marinate for 12 hours.

Vietnamese Marinade		
Asian fish sauce	130 g	100 mL / ⅜ cup
Rice vinegar	95 g	110 mL / ½ cup
Sugar	60 g	5 Tbsp
Water	55 g	55 mL / ¼ cup
Garlic, chopped	5 g	2 tsp
Thai chili, chopped	3 g	1 tsp

Mix together, add to food, and marinate for 6 hours.

Mediterranean Yogurt Marinade		
Plain yogurt	250 g	1 cup
Garlic, chopped	14 g	1½ Tbsp
Mint, thinly sliced	5 g	2 Tbsp
Salt	5 g	1¼ tsp
Cinnamon, ground	1 g	½ tsp
Coriander, ground	1 g	½ tsp

Mix together, add to food, and marinate for 6 hours.

Mexican Marinade		
Orange juice	300 g	300 mL / 1¼ cups
Chipotle chilies in adobo, chopped	60 g	½ cup
Garlic, chopped	25 g	¼ cup
Cilantro, chopped	15 g	5 Tbsp
Salt	6 g	1½ tsp

Mix together, add to food, and marinate for 12 hours.

Barbecue Marinade		
Tomato juice	300 g	300 mL / 1¼ cups
Apple cider vinegar	100 g	120 mL / ½ cup
Dark brown sugar	50 g	5 Tbsp
Pimentón dulce (smoked, sweet paprika)	5 g	2½ tsp
Mustard powder	2 g	1 tsp

Mix together, add to food, and marinate for 12 hours.

SPICE MIXES

Spices are so integral to people's enjoyment of food that the trade in them was, for centuries, one of the driving forces that brought different cultures into contact. Even in the globalized world of the 21st century, certain spice mixes are still emblems of cultural heritage. The set of flavors that are unique to a region or cultural group is usually the product of spice mixtures that evolved along with that community and were passed down by culinary traditions.

The particular blend of a curry powder, for example, can not only differentiate a dish as being Indian rather than Thai but also can identify the part of India in which it originated. The same can be said of dry rubs used in American barbecue, and of adobo spice mixes in Spanish-influenced cuisines.

Spice traders altered traditional patterns of spice use by connecting spice "islands" with the larger world. Cooks everywhere then took the idea of combining tastes and smells, and ran with it. The resulting mélanges include Chinese five-spice powder, American Southern-fried chicken spices, Mexican mole, and the famously complicated *ras el hanout* of the Middle East and North Africa, among innumerable others.

When making spice mixtures, the goal is always to arrive at a balance of tastes and aromas that complement the dish to which it will be added. The six examples we present here illustrate several ways to process spices as you perfect your own "secret" blends.

MC CURRY POWDER

YIELD:	*70 g / ⅔ cup*
TIME ESTIMATE:	*30 minutes overall*
STORAGE NOTES:	*keeps for 2 weeks in an airtight container and up to 2 months when vacuum sealed and refrigerated*
LEVEL OF DIFFICULTY:	*easy*
SPECIAL REQUIREMENTS:	*coffee grinder, mace blades, Kashmiri chilies (optional), green cardamom pods*
USED IN:	*Mughal Curry Sauce (see page 104), Crispy Skinless Chicken Wings (see page 254)*

Toasting spices before you grind them dramatically improves the flavor, but it is very easy to scorch the spices if you toast them in a dry sauté pan over a low burner, so use the oven instead.

A coffee mill works as well as a spice grinder, but dedicate a separate grinder for spices to avoid coffee-flavored spices and vice versa.

If you have a vacuum sealer, consider vacuum sealing all your spice blends, which both protects the aromas and volatile oils and also prevents clumping and absorption of moisture.

INGREDIENT	WEIGHT	VOLUME	SCALING	PROCEDURE
Cumin seeds	30 g	¼ cup	100%	① Preheat the oven to 170 °C / 340 °F.
Coriander seeds	20 g	⅓ cup	67%	② Combine, and toast in the oven on a baking sheet until golden and aromatic, 8–10 minutes.
Black peppercorns	20 g	2½ Tbsp	67%	
Cinnamon stick, broken into small pieces	2.7 g	1 stick	9%	
Cloves	2 g	1 tsp	6.7%	
Kashmiri chilies (optional)	1 g	2 large	3.3%	
Mace blades, broken into small pieces	1 g	½ tsp	3.3%	
Green cardamom seeds	0.5 g	from about 6 pods	1.7%	
				③ Grind to a fine powder in a coffee grinder.

VARIATION: Vindaloo Spice Mix
Double the amount of black peppercorns. This variation is used in the Pork Vindaloo with Naan recipe (see variation on page 221).

If Kashmiri chilies are unavailable, substitute 2 g / 1 tsp of sweet paprika at step 3. Powdered paprika will burn if toasted.

CHAAT MASALA

YIELD:	*60 g / ⅔ cup*
TIME ESTIMATE:	*20 minutes overall*
STORAGE NOTES:	*keeps for 2 weeks in an airtight container and up to 2 months when vacuum sealed and refrigerated*
LEVEL OF DIFFICULTY:	*easy*
SPECIAL REQUIREMENTS:	*coffee grinder, ajowan seeds, amchoor, anardana, kala namak (optional)*
GOES WELL WITH:	*Caramelized Carrot Soup (see page 178), Sous Vide Lobster Tail (see variation on page 288)*

Chaat masala is a quintessential spice blend of India, where it is sometimes referred to as a summer sprinkle or a comforting winter dust. A sprinkle of this pungent combination of dried mango and spices pairs perfectly with steamed potatoes, grilled chicken or vegetables, baked root vegetables, and deep-fried cauliflower. Also, try dusting it over fresh pineapple, mango, or cucumber.

If you can't find Indian black salt (*kala namak*), which has a very strong smell and is actually purplish in color, substitute kosher salt for it.

INGREDIENT	WEIGHT	VOLUME	SCALING	PROCEDURE
Coriander seeds	19 g	⅓ cup	76%	① Preheat the oven to 170 °C / 340 °F.
Cumin seeds	15 g	2 Tbsp	60%	② Combine, and toast in the oven on a baking sheet until golden and aromatic, 8–10 minutes.
Ajowan seeds	3 g	1½ tsp	12%	
Black peppercorns	3 g	1 tsp	12%	
Dried chilies	1 g	½ tsp	4%	
Indian black salt	25 g	2½ Tbsp	100%	③ Combine with the toasted spices.
Dried green mango powder (amchoor)	8 g	1¼ tsp	32%	④ Grind the mixture to a powder in a coffee grinder.
Dried pomegranate seeds (anardana)	4 g	1¼ tsp	16%	⑤ Pass the powder through a fine sieve.

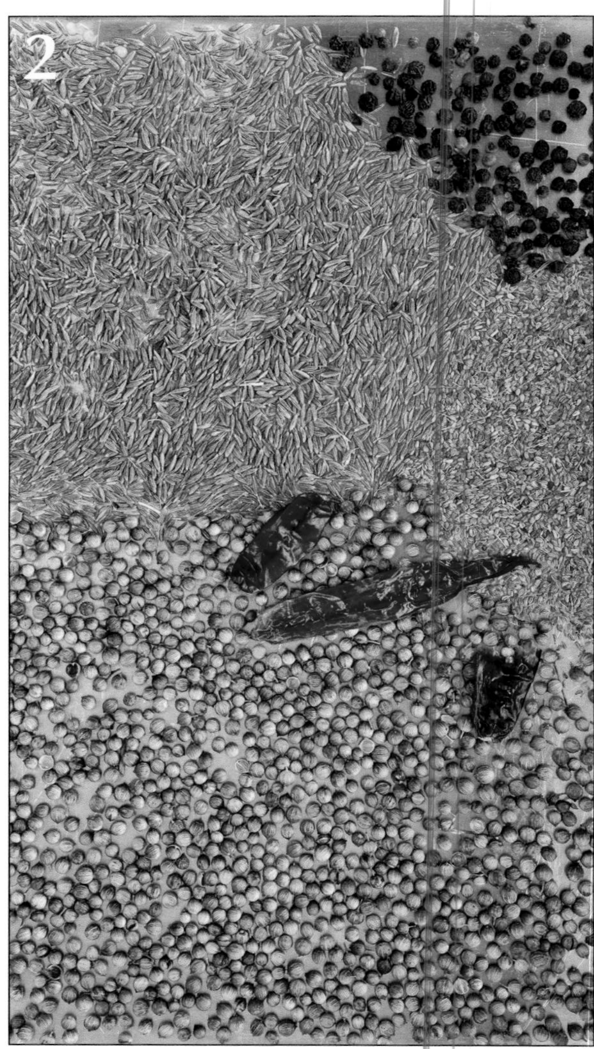

FISH SPICE MIX

YIELD:	*120 g / 1 cup*
TIME ESTIMATE:	*30 minutes overall*
STORAGE NOTES:	*keeps for 2 weeks in an airtight container and up to 2 months when vacuum sealed and refrigerated*
LEVEL OF DIFFICULTY:	*easy*
SPECIAL REQUIREMENTS:	*coffee grinder or mortar and pestle, dried chamomile blossoms, white poppy seeds (optional), tapioca maltodextrin (N-Zorbit brand, optional)*
USED IN:	*Fragrant Sous Vide Salmon (see page 276)*

This tremendously versatile spice mixture is delicious on sole, turbot, or any similar fish simply panfried in butter. It is also wonderful on roasted winter squash, buttered potatoes, steamed asparagus, and any simple chicken preparation. The tapioca maltodextrin absorbs the oils from the nuts and spices and keeps the powder from clumping. You can find whole chamomile blossoms for sale in tea shops.

INGREDIENT	WEIGHT	VOLUME	SCALING	PROCEDURE
Hazelnuts	50 g	½ cup	100%	① Preheat the oven to 175 °C / 350 °F. ② Roast the hazelnuts until the skins turn dark brown, 10–12 minutes. ③ Rub the nuts with a cloth to remove the skins. Discard the skins. ④ Chop the nuts.
Sesame seeds	44 g	⅓ cup	88%	⑤ Toast the sesame seeds in a dry frying pan over medium-high heat, stirring constantly, until they begin to pop, about 3 minutes.
Coriander seeds	12 g	2½ Tbsp	24%	⑥ Toast the coriander seeds in a dry frying pan over medium-high heat, stirring constantly, until they become golden brown and fragrant, about 3 minutes. ⑦ Crush in a coffee grinder or with a mortar and pestle.
Tapioca maltodextrin (N-Zorbit brand), optional	12 g		24%	⑧ Combine with the hazelnuts, sesame seeds, and coriander seeds, and grind to a coarse powder in a coffee grinder or mortar and pestle. Work in batches if necessary.
White poppy seeds (optional)	10 g	1 Tbsp	20%	
Dried, ground ginger	4 g	2 tsp	8%	
Salt	4 g	1 tsp	8%	
Dried chamomile blossoms	2.5 g	2 Tbsp	5%	

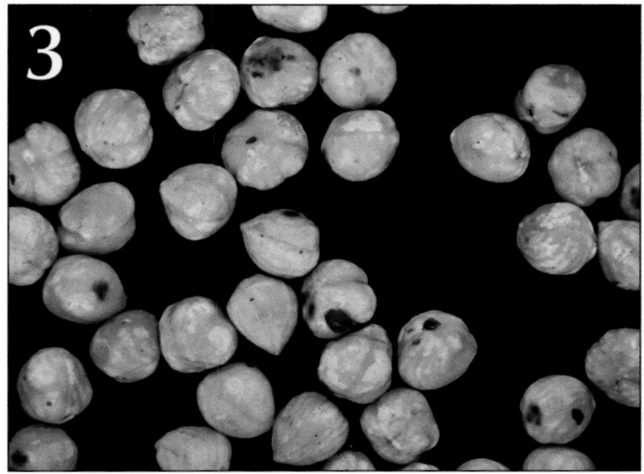

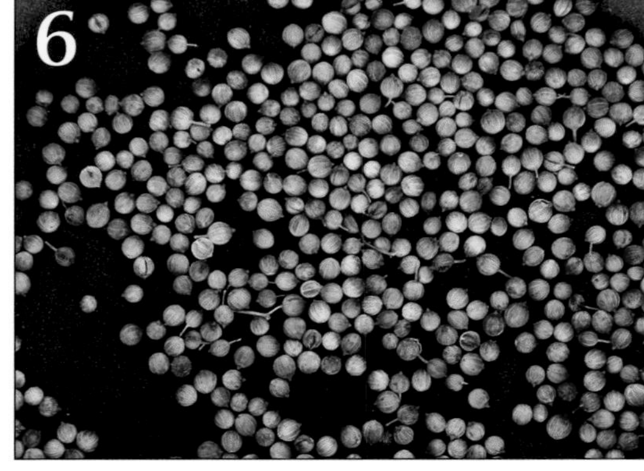

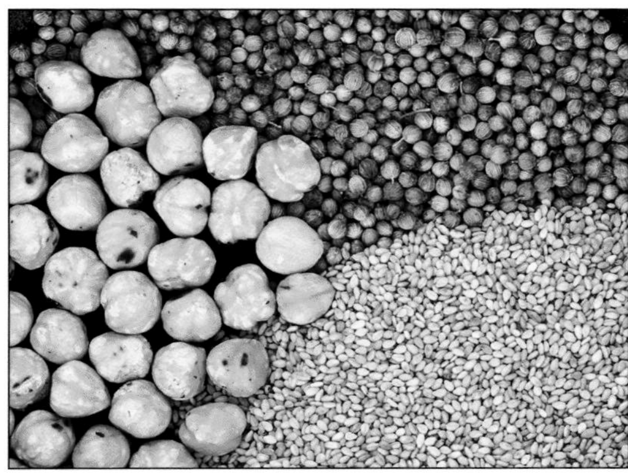

Fragrant Sous Vide Salmon, see page 276

AUTUMN SPICE MIX

YIELD:	*250 g / 1⅝ cups*
TIME ESTIMATE:	*22 minutes overall*
STORAGE NOTES:	*keeps for 2 weeks in an airtight container and up to 2 months when vacuum sealed and refrigerated*
LEVEL OF DIFFICULTY:	*easy*
SPECIAL REQUIREMENTS:	*coffee grinder, honey powder, dried orange peel*
USED IN:	*Gingerbread Crust (see variation on page 372)*

Honey powder is available at health-food stores and some Asian or specialty food markets. A flavorful sugar, such as brown sugar or palm sugar, can be used instead. This spice mixture can be used to make spectacular gingerbread, and makes for a delicious chai when stirred into tea.

INGREDIENT	WEIGHT	VOLUME	SCALING	PROCEDURE
Cinnamon stick, broken	8 g	2 sticks	3.3%	① Preheat the oven to **170 °C / 340 °F**.
Star anise	3.2 g	2–3 pods	1.3%	② Combine, and toast in a dry frying pan, tossing and stirring often, until golden and aromatic, 8–10 minutes.
Cloves	2.5 g	1¼ tsp	1%	③ Cool slightly, and grind to a fine powder in a coffee grinder.
Fennel seeds	2 g	1 tsp	0.8%	④ Pass through a fine sieve.
Coriander seeds	2 g	1½ tsp	0.8%	
Honey powder	240 g	1⅜ cups	100%	⑤ Mix with the toasted spice powder.
Salt	12 g	1 Tbsp	5%	
Dried, ground ginger	3 g	1½ tsp	1.3%	
Nutmeg, grated	3 g	1½ tsp	1.3%	
Ground mace	1.5 g	¼ tsp	0.6%	
Dried orange peel	1.2 g	½ tsp	0.5%	

CHILI SPICE MIX

YIELD:	*260 g / 1 cup*
TIME ESTIMATE:	*10 minutes overall*
STORAGE NOTES:	*keeps for 2 weeks in an airtight container and up to 2 months when vacuum sealed and refrigerated*
LEVEL OF DIFFICULTY:	*easy*
SPECIAL REQUIREMENTS:	*coffee grinder, honey powder (optional)*
USED IN:	*Crispy Skinless Chicken Wings (see page 254)*

This mix is excellent when sprinkled on barbecued chicken. Make it unsweetened, without the honey powder, to spice up chili or to use as a dry rub on grilled meats.

INGREDIENT	WEIGHT	VOLUME	SCALING	PROCEDURE
Garlic powder	50 g	5 Tbsp	100%	① Combine.
Pimentón dulce (smoked, sweet paprika)	50 g	7½ Tbsp	100%	
Cinnamon, ground	12 g	2 Tbsp	24%	
Allspice, ground	8 g	1 Tbsp	16%	
Black pepper, ground	7.5 g	1 Tbsp	15%	
Cumin, ground	7 g	1 Tbsp	14%	
Cayenne	6.5 g	1 Tbsp	13%	
Dark cocoa powder	6 g	1 Tbsp	12%	
Honey powder (optional)	88 g	9 Tbsp	176%	② Mix into the spice powder to adjust the seasoning.
Salt (optional)	29 g	3 Tbsp	58%	

GRILLING SPICE MIX

YIELD:	*40 g / ½ cup*
TIME ESTIMATE:	*10 minutes overall*
STORAGE NOTES:	*keeps for 2 weeks in an airtight container and up to 2 months when vacuum sealed and refrigerated*
LEVEL OF DIFFICULTY:	*easy*
SPECIAL REQUIREMENTS:	*coffee grinder, porcini powder, honey powder, smoked salt*

This spice mix works wonders on grilled steaks. Use store-bought porcini powder, or make your own by grinding dried porcini mushrooms in a coffee grinder. Smoked salt is available at specialty food stores.

INGREDIENT	WEIGHT	VOLUME	SCALING	PROCEDURE
Sweet paprika	10 g	1½ Tbsp	100%	① Combine.
Porcini powder	10 g	1½ Tbsp	100%	② Grind in a coffee grinder.
Honey powder	10 g	1 Tbsp	100%	
Onion powder	5 g	1 Tbsp	50%	
Smoked salt	5 g	1¼ tsp	50%	
Black pepper, ground	1 g	¼ tsp	10%	

BREAKFAST EGGS

Poached, scrambled, shirred, coddled, sunny-side up, over easy, deep-fried, hard-boiled, soft-boiled, baked . . . in omelets and *oeufs à la coque*, quiche and cocottes, flans and frittatas . . . there seems to be no end to the delicious ways one can prepare eggs. We showcase only a few of them, but by applying the principles in this chapter, you can master any egg dish.

We also love eggs because they represent an ideal way to communicate one of the most important ideas of Modernist cooking: the beauty of cooking with precise temperature. The difference in taste and texture between a runny yolk and a rubbery one is a consequence of a remarkably small difference in cooking temperature. The photos on the next pages illustrate the progression of a cooked egg from an almost raw, pasteurized state to a very firm, brittle, hard-cooked state. You can see that egg yolks start to coagulate when the temperature rises above 62 °C / 144 °F, and they become progressively firmer as they warm until they're finally hard-boiled, at about 80 °C / 176 °F.

The traditional way to hard-boil an egg is to boil it for a specified amount of time. That works on average, but it's inconsistent because of the many variables at play, such as the size and starting temperature of the egg, as well as the volume of water in the pot.

A better approach is to use a water bath, a thermometer, and an understanding of the way the viscosity of the egg increases as its temperature rises. Once you become familiar with the temperatures that cause each state, you can deftly create any texture—from creamy to custardy to fudge-like—every time, perfectly.

THE SCIENCE OF EGGS AS GELS

A cooked egg is a gel, in which water is trapped within a mesh of cross-linked proteins. You can transform a fluid, raw egg into a semisolid state either by heating it or by subjecting it to chemical agents, such as acids, alkalis, or minerals like salt and calcium. Cooking and pickling whole eggs, and freezing egg yolks, all cause irreversible gelling—once the gel is set, the egg will never return to a fluid state. That's a fascinating, and useful, property.

The linking ability of the proteins in eggs is so potent that they can bind together even when the egg is in powdered form or is mixed with lots of other ingredients. The gelling power of eggs is what holds together the constituents of a muffin batter, the flour granules in some pasta doughs, and the elements of a sweet dessert custard, a quiche, or a *chawanmushi* (a savory Japanese egg custard). It also helps to bind the ground meat in meatloaf and some sausages. The egg's versatility as a gelling agent is unmatched by other ingredients in conventional cooking, and it provides a fun and flexible component for Modernist cooking as well.

HIGHLIGHTS

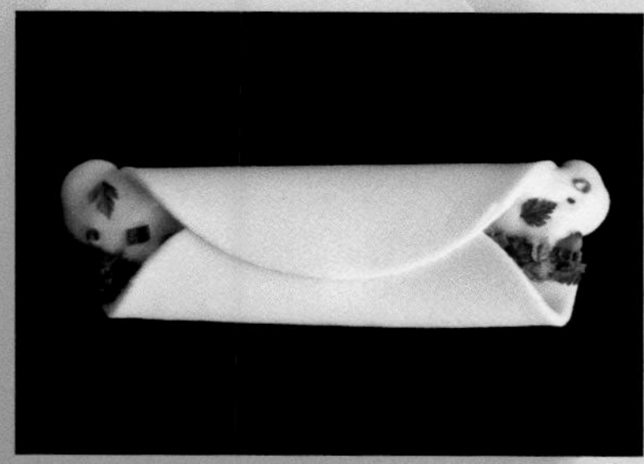

The best omelet we've made yet has a very rich texture, is delicately thin, and serves as a perfect platform for flavorful fillings.

see page 146

Create a beautiful, stable foam by using a whipping siphon. Eggs foam so well because they are rich in proteins that stabilize the bubbles, and the nitrous oxide used to charge the siphon dissolves easily into the fatty mixture of cream, butter, and yolk.

see page 144

Eggs are mostly water, and you can **reconstruct an egg** by replacing that water with any flavorful liquid. In our Striped Mushroom Omelet, we start with albumin powder (egg white without the water), and then we add liquid in the form of a mushroom puree.

see page 148

An egg yolk becomes spherical when cooked at 72 °C / 162 °F. One fun recipe: **serve perfectly round egg yolks** with a sauce made from the egg white. It's a Modernist version of deviled eggs.

see page 152

FURTHER READING IN *MODERNIST CUISINE*

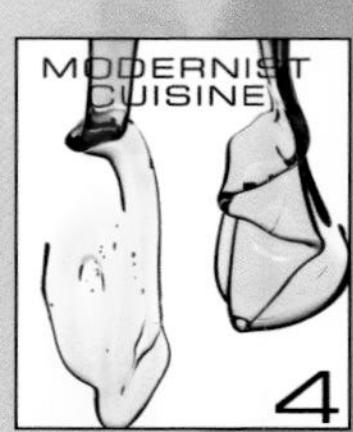

Forming foams with eggs: see pages 4·247, 251, 255
Emulsions of eggs: see pages 4·226–229
How to make omelets in a combi oven: see page 4·95
Recipes for pickled and preserved eggs, including a "century" egg: see pages 4·82–83
Plated-dish recipes for eggs: see pages 5·209–221

EGG TEXTURES

Temperature and time are important factors in precise cooking, and that is equally true for egg cookery. Like meats and vegetables, eggs develop a fairly predictable texture when heated to a particular core temperature, but that texture changes when the food is held at that temperature for an extended time. The visual chart below illustrates the dramatic effects that just a few degrees' increase in temperature has on the white and the yolk.

After 40–45 minutes at around 60 °C / 140 °F, the white begins to become opaque, whereas the yolk is not firmly solid until 74 °C / 165 °F. Each degree of doneness up to 80 °C / 176 °F has its unique virtues. Individual preferences vary, of course, but with modern equipment such as a water bath, you can dial in a core temperature and consistently hit the texture you like best, from pasteurized but raw, to moist and jammy, to brittle and dry.

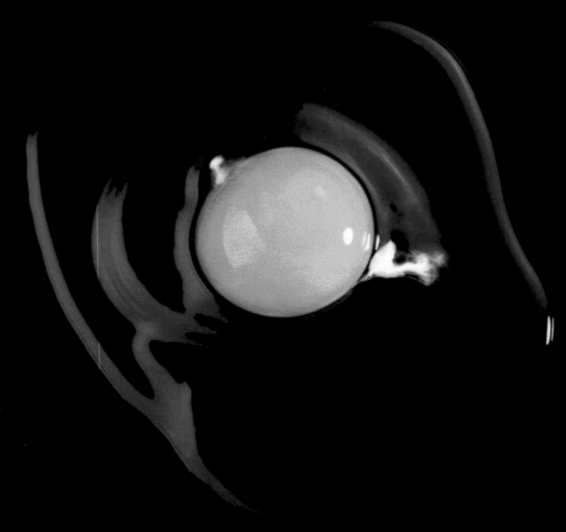

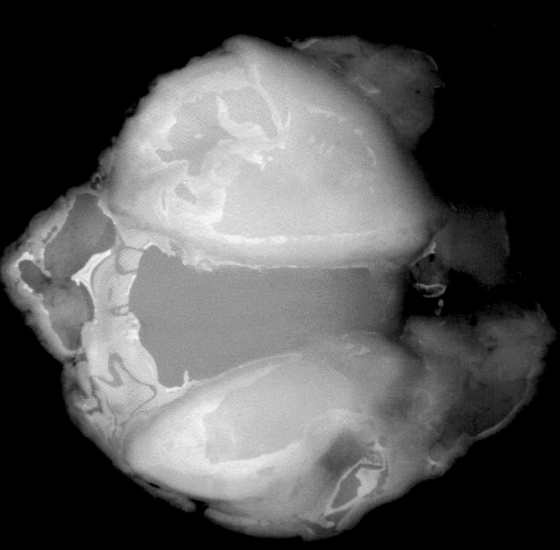

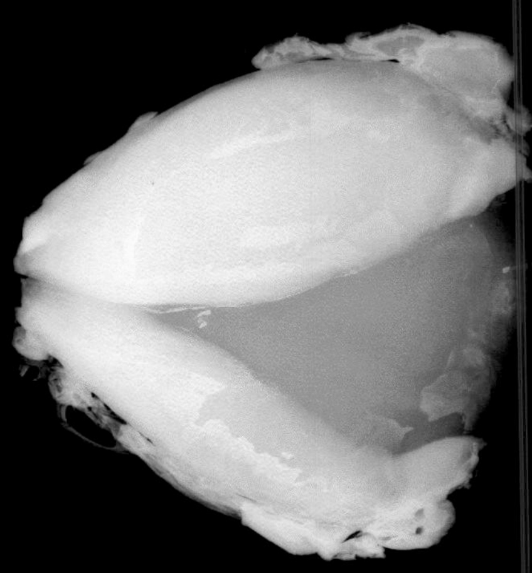

	55 °C / 131 °F	60 °C / 140 °F	62 °C / 144 °F
Whole egg:	pasteurized, 2 h	semiliquid	*onsen* egg
Egg white:	pasteurized, 2 h	starting to gel	runny
Egg yolk:	pasteurized, 2 h	runny	viscous

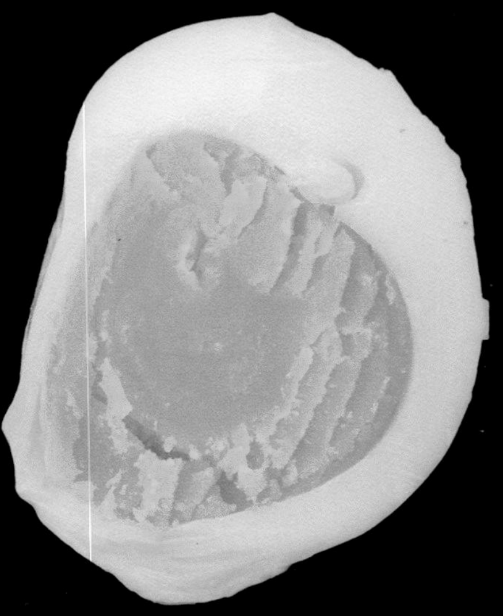

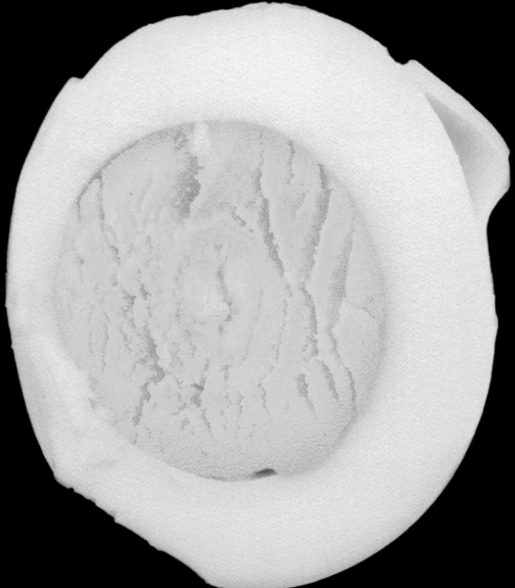

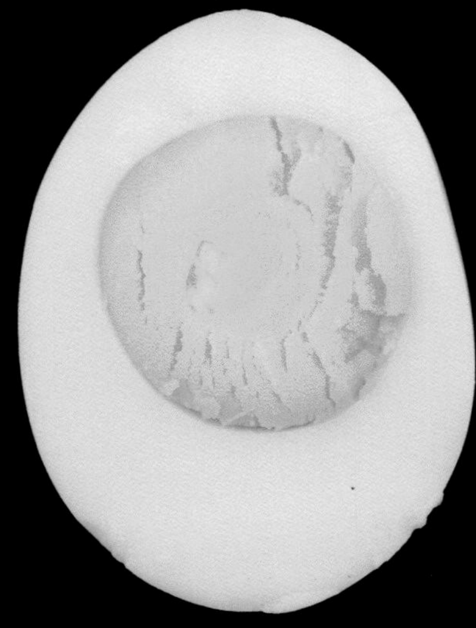

	74 °C / 165 °F	78 °C / 172 °F	80 °C / 176 °F
Whole egg:	white and yolk set, best bet for whole egg	medium-boiled, elastic	hard-boiled
Egg white:	just set	moderately firm	firm
Egg yolk:	just solid	moist	tender

Many kinds of eggs are delicious, including those of duck, turkey, and quail.

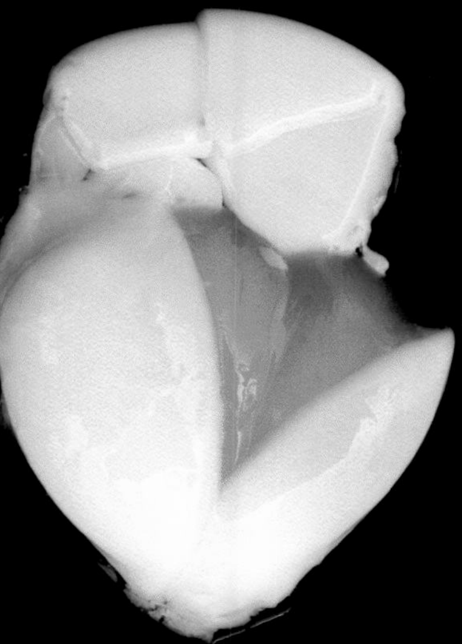

65 °C / 149 °F
firm *onsen* egg
loose
syrupy

68 °C / 154 °F
poached
barely set
jammy

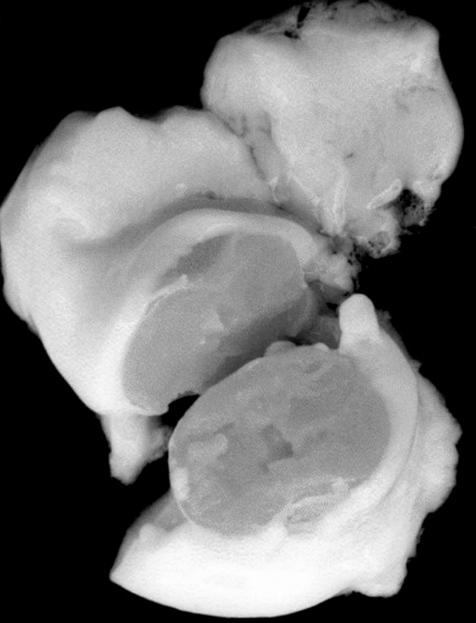

70 °C / 158 °F
soft-boiled
tender
fudge-like

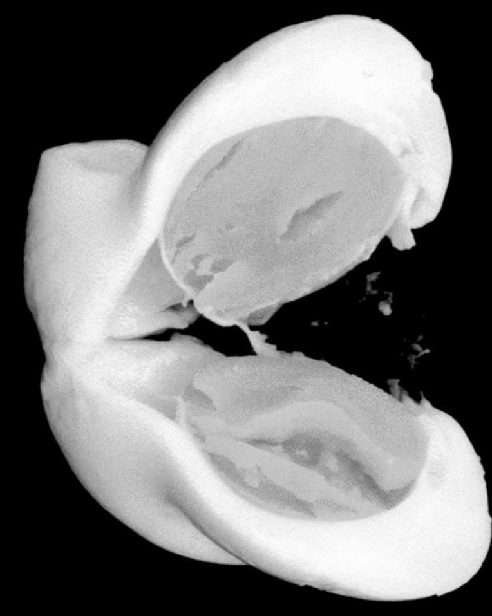

72 °C / 162 °F
peeled yolk is spherical
silky
pasty

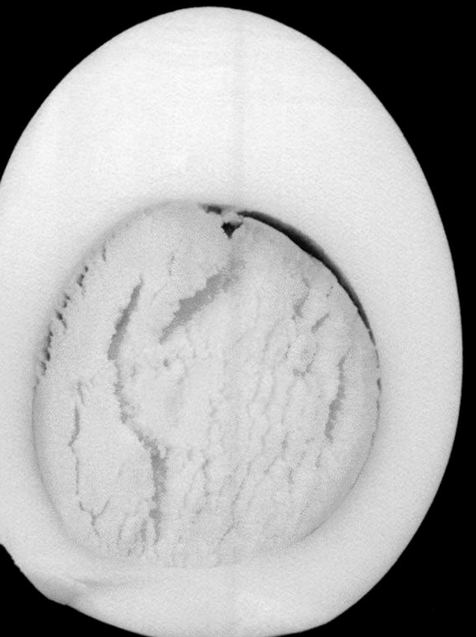

82 °C / 180 °F
rigid
very firm
slightly dry; greening begins

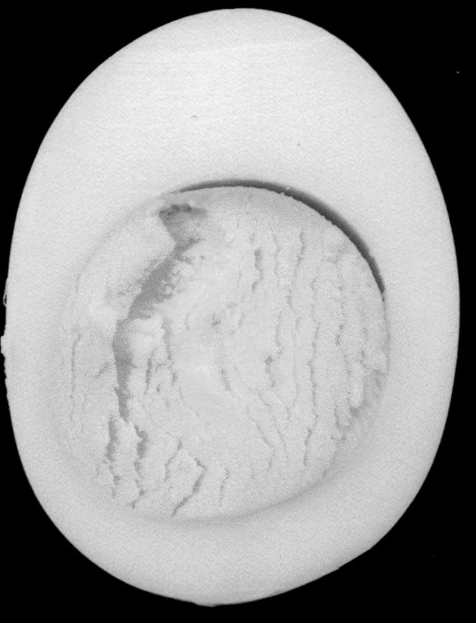

84 °C / 183 °F
rigid
rubbery
dry; greening increases

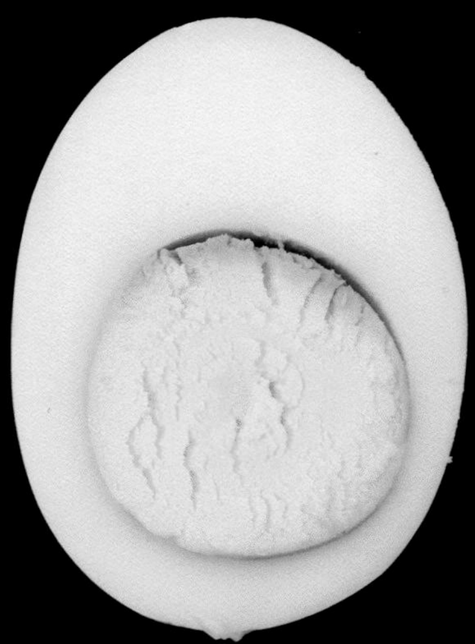

86 °C / 187 °F
solid
brittle and rubbery
powdery; more greening

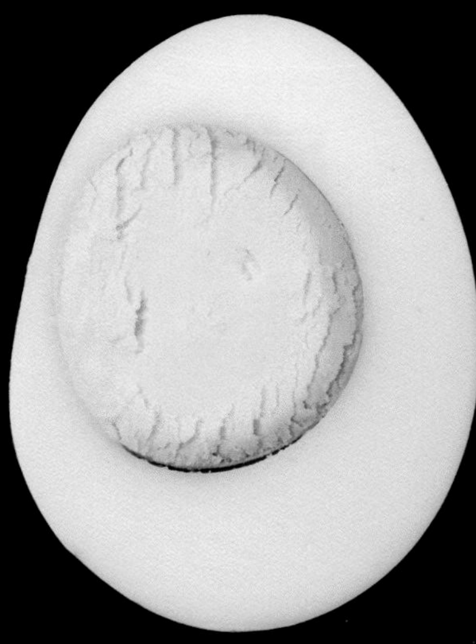

90 °C / 194 °F
solid
very brittle and rubbery
very powdery; a lot of greening

FRENCH SCRAMBLED EGGS

YIELD:	*four to six servings (380 g)*
TIME ESTIMATE:	*45 minutes overall, including 10 minutes of preparation and 35 minutes unattended*
STORAGE NOTES:	*serve immediately after dispensing from the siphon*
LEVEL OF DIFFICULTY:	*easy*
SPECIAL REQUIREMENTS:	*sous vide setup, 500 mL whipping siphon, two cartridges of nitrous oxide*
GOES WELL WITH:	*Steamed Herb Omelet (see page 146), Sous Vide Steak (see page 194)*

This ultrarich dish is one of our favorites. We create a texture as smooth as custard, having no lumps whatsoever, by using an immersion blender. Then we aerate the eggs in a whipping siphon to make them foamy and light. We also love the pudding-like texture of nonaerated eggs; see the variation below. Serve the eggs as a breakfast entree, as a filling for omelets, or as a side dish for the ultimate steak and eggs.

INGREDIENT	WEIGHT	VOLUME	SCALING
Eggs	200 g	4 large	100%
Egg yolks	60 g	3–4 yolks	30%
Unsalted butter, melted	60 g	65 mL / 4½ Tbsp	30%
Whole milk	60 g	60 mL / ¼ cup	30%
Salt	4 g	1 tsp	2%

PROCEDURE

① Preheat a water bath to 72 °C / 162 °F.
② Mix all ingredients, and blend until smooth by using a whisk or immersion blender.
③ Place the mixture in a zip-top bag, remove as much air as possible from the bag by using the water-displacement method (see page 58), and seal it.
④ Cook sous vide until just set, about 35 minutes.
⑤ Transfer to a bowl, and puree until smooth using an immersion blender.
⑥ Pour into a whipping siphon, charge with two cartridges of nitrous oxide, and dispense.

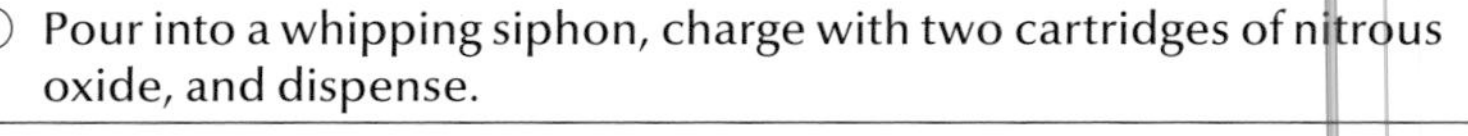

TO MAKE AHEAD

After step 5, place cooked eggs in a bag or siphon, and hold in a 55 °C / 131 °F water bath for up to 1 hour. Continue with step 6 to serve.

VARIATIONS

Scrambled Egg Pudding

Prefer a velvety, pudding-like texture that's not aerated? Increase the temperature in step 1 to 74 °C / 165 °F, and decrease the cooking time in step 4 to about 30 minutes. This yields a firmer texture. After step 5, spoon the pureed eggs from the bowl, and serve immediately.

Olive Oil Scrambled Eggs

Increase the egg yolks to a total of 80 g / 5–6 yolks, and replace the butter with extra-virgin olive oil. We use this as a filling in our Espagnole omelet (see variation on the next page).

Mini Egg Cups

Fill the bottom of warm ramekins with Shiitake Marmalade (see page 151). Top with the scrambled-egg foam. Garnish with grated cheddar or Gruyère. This makes a terrific amuse-bouche or snack for special guests.

Eggs pair well with so many flavors that the variety of tasty filling combinations for omelets is almost infinite. The classic combinations below have stood the test of time. They are still among our favorites. Try these fillings, or others you develop, in place of the French Scrambled Eggs and chives in the Steamed Herb Omelet recipe on the next page. The Raviolo filling can be served open-faced or sandwiched between two omelet sheets. Quantities shown below yield four servings.

Florentine Omelet Filling

Creamed Spinach see page 199	140 g	½ cup
Ricotta cheese	80 g	5 Tbsp
Parmigiano-Reggiano, grated	16 g	4 Tbsp
Lemon zest, grated	1.6 g	½ tsp

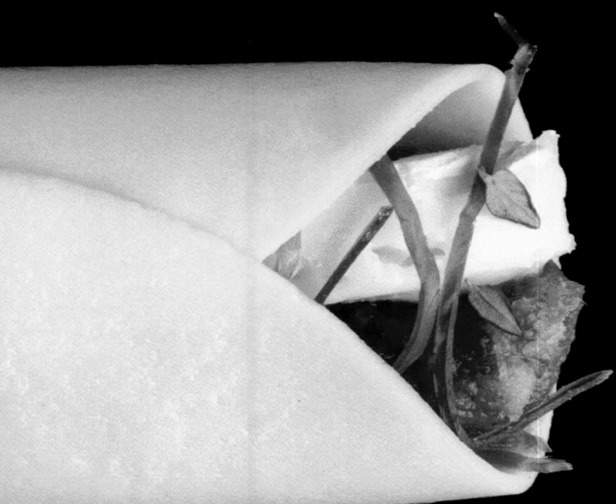

Alsatian Omelet Filling

Pressure-Caramelized Onions see page 127	140 g	½ cup
Muenster or Camembert cheese, rind removed and cut into a long strip	80 g	2 cups
Black Forest ham, julienned	48 g	½ cup
Thyme leaves	1.6 g	½ tsp

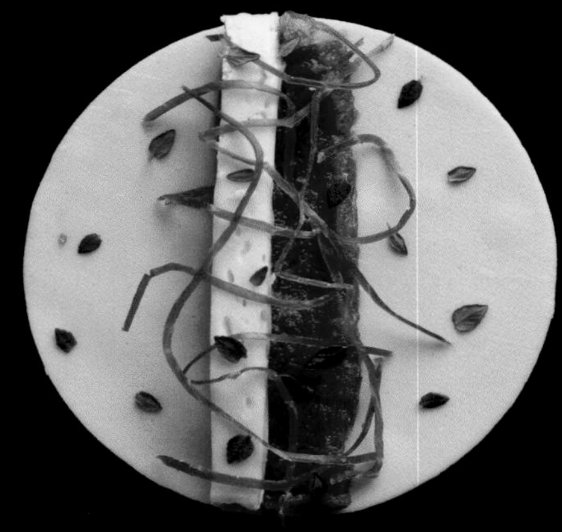

Espagnole Omelet Filling

Tomato Sofrito see variation on page 112	140 g	½ cup
Olive Oil Scrambled Eggs see variation on the previous page	80 g	¾ cup
Chives, minced, or seasoned herbs	8 g	2 Tbsp

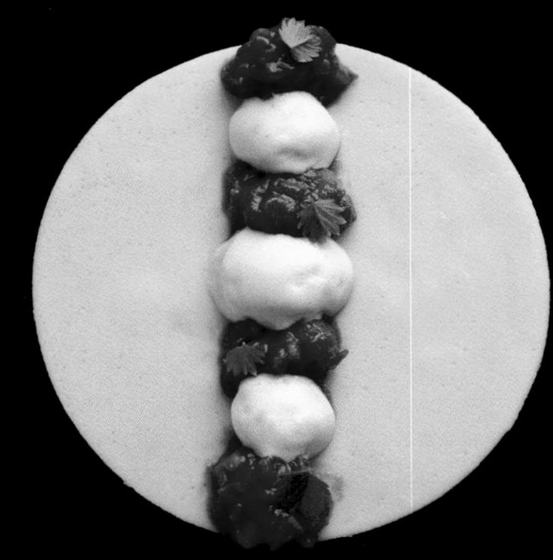

Raviolo Omelet Filling

Eggs, cooked sous vide, whites removed see steps 1–3, page 152		4 eggs
Bacon lardons, crispy	32 g	¼ cup
Chives, minced	5 g	2 Tbsp
Pecorino cheese, grated	16 g	4 Tbsp
Black pepper, coarsely ground	1.6 g	½ tsp

STEAMED HERB OMELET

YIELD:	*four appetizer-size omelets (40 g each plus filling)*
TIME ESTIMATE:	*40 minutes overall*
STORAGE NOTES:	*omelet sheets keep for 2 days when refrigerated; serve assembled omelets immediately*
LEVEL OF DIFFICULTY:	*moderate*
SPECIAL REQUIREMENTS:	*nonstick frying pan (20 cm / 8 in) with metal lid or oven-safe glass lid*

We think this is the perfect omelet: it is tender and delicate, with a pure, fresh egg flavor. Our goal here is to steam the omelet at a precise temperature. A combi oven or water-vapor oven is made to do exactly that, but you can achieve similar results in a home oven. The trick is to heat the omelet evenly while avoiding evaporation and browning. The best way we've found to do that is to cook it in a skillet topped with a hot, metal lid on an oven rack that is perfectly level.

Although this omelet recipe is made only with eggs and cream, modern versions almost always contain a filling of some kind; some of our favorite combinations are listed on the previous page.

INGREDIENT	WEIGHT	VOLUME	SCALING	PROCEDURE
Eggs, blended	150 g	3–4 eggs	100%	① Preheat the oven to 175 °C / 350 °F. Once the oven is hot, place the oven-safe lid to a nonstick, 20 cm / 8 in frying pan in the oven to preheat for about 15 minutes.
Heavy cream	15 g	15 mL / 1 Tbsp	10%	② Blend thoroughly by using a whisk or immersion blender. Allow any foam to dissipate, or use a spoon to skim it from the surface.
Egg yolk	12 g	1 yolk	8%	
Salt	2 g	½ tsp	1.3%	
Cooking spray	as needed			③ Spray the bottom of the frying pan with a thin film of cooking spray.
				④ Pour one quarter of the egg mixture into the frying pan.
				⑤ Place the hot lid on the pan, and put it in the oven. Cook until the eggs set, about 6 minutes.
				⑥ While the eggs cook, line a baking sheet with parchment paper, and spray it with cooking spray.
				⑦ Slide the cooked omelet onto the baking sheet. Leave the lid in the oven while you prepare the next omelet.
				⑧ Repeat steps 3–7 three times with the remaining egg mixture. After the first one, the omelets will cook in the warm pan in about 3 minutes.
				⑨ Cover the omelets on the baking sheet with another sheet of sprayed parchment, and place them in the oven for 1½–2½ minutes to reheat.
Scrambled Egg Pudding, warm (optional) see variation on page 144	200 g	½ cup	133%	⑩ Divide the warm scrambled eggs evenly among the omelet sheets.
				⑪ Fold the edges of each omelet carefully over the filling.
Chives, minced	5 g	2 Tbsp	3%	⑫ Sprinkle with the chives, and serve immediately.

1 Preheat the oven to 175 °C / 350 °F. When the oven reaches its set temperature, put the lid of a nonstick, 20 cm / 8 in frying pan into the oven to preheat for about 15 minutes. Choose a lid that is oven-safe and fits snugly on the pan.

2 Blend the whole eggs, cream, yolks, and salt thoroughly by using a whisk or immersion blender. If a foam rises on the surface, allow it to dissipate, or skim it off with a spoon.

3 Coat the bottom of the pan with a thin film of cooking spray.

4 Pour one quarter of the egg mixture into the frying pan. It will spread into a thin layer.

5 Cover the pan with the hot lid, and put the covered pan into the oven. Cook the eggs until they set, about 6 minutes. The pan should sit level on the oven rack. Use pieces of folded aluminum foil as shims if needed to ensure a flat, evenly cooked omelet.

6 While the eggs are baking, line a baking sheet with parchment paper, and spray the paper with a light coating of cooking spray.

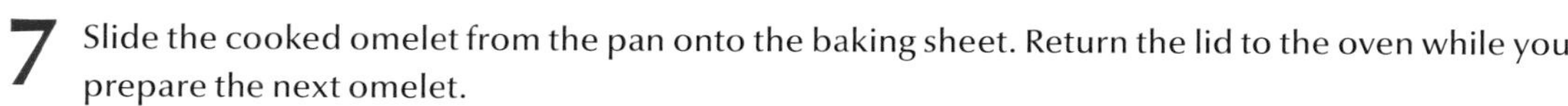

7 Slide the cooked omelet from the pan onto the baking sheet. Return the lid to the oven while you prepare the next omelet.

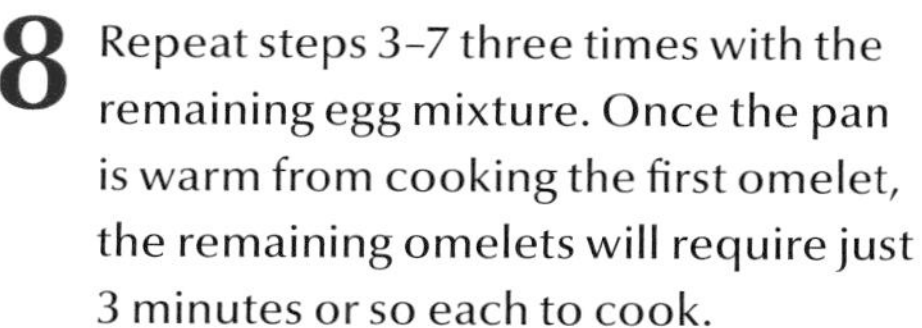

8 Repeat steps 3–7 three times with the remaining egg mixture. Once the pan is warm from cooking the first omelet, the remaining omelets will require just 3 minutes or so each to cook.

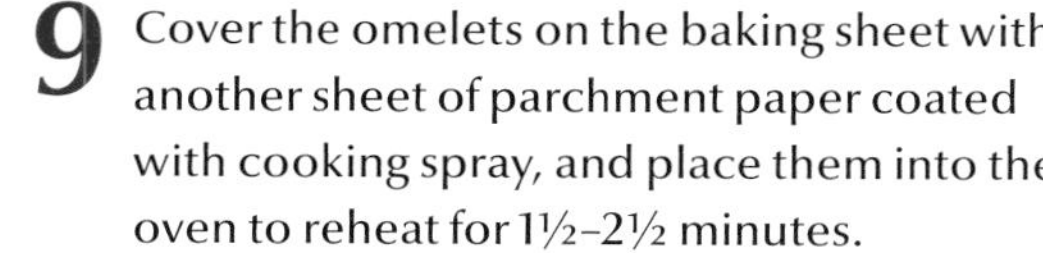

9 Cover the omelets on the baking sheet with another sheet of parchment paper coated with cooking spray, and place them into the oven to reheat for 1½–2½ minutes.

10 Divide the warm scrambled eggs, if using, evenly among the omelet sheets. You can add or substitute any other filling at this point. Sprinkle the filling with the chives.

11 Use a thin-edged spatula to fold the edges of each omelet carefully over its filling.

12 Sprinkle with the chives, and serve the omelets immediately.

TO MAKE AHEAD

After step 8, cover the baking sheet with oil-rubbed plastic wrap, and store it in the refrigerator for up to 2 days. When you're ready to serve the omelets, preheat the oven to 175 °C / 350 °F. Remove the plastic wrap from the baking sheet, and reheat the omelets for 1½–2½ minutes. Continue with step 10.

ENTREE-SIZE OMELET

We serve these omelets as an appetizer, which is how we get away with using so few eggs to feed four people. To make an omelet large enough to serve as an entree, use all of the egg mixture in one 30 cm / 12 in pan. Cook 3–4 minutes longer, until just set.

IF YOU HAVE A COMBI OVEN

If you have access to a professional or home combi oven, set the oven to full steam at 82 °C / 180 °F. Follow steps 2–4, cover the frying pan with plastic wrap, and then cook the omelet for 10 minutes. Continue with step 10.

STRIPED MUSHROOM OMELET

YIELD:	*four appetizer-size omelets (140 g each)*
TIME ESTIMATE:	*1 hour overall*
STORAGE NOTES:	*omelet sheets keep for 2 days when refrigerated; serve assembled omelets immediately*
LEVEL OF DIFFICULTY:	*advanced (level of effort)*
SPECIAL REQUIREMENTS:	*two silicone discs, 15 cm / 6 in across, cut from a larger mat; 20 cm / 8 in nonstick frying pan with metal lid or oven-safe glass lid; pastry comb with 3 mm / ⅛ in teeth; albumin powder (powdered egg whites)*

Once you get the hang of making these omelets, you won't want to serve your special guests anything else. The result is both beautiful and delicious; we promise it is worth the effort. The silicone disc must lie flat and seal tightly in the base of your nonstick frying pan. Make sure the mat is silicone only; do not cut mats that contain fiberglass, such as Silpat brand mats.

INGREDIENT	WEIGHT	VOLUME	SCALING	PROCEDURE
Eggs, blended	150 g	3–4 eggs	100%	① Preheat the oven to 175 °C / 350 °F. Once the oven is hot, place the oven-safe lid of a 20 cm / 8 in nonstick frying pan in the oven to preheat for about 15 minutes.
Heavy cream	15 g	15 mL / 1 Tbsp	10%	② Line a baking sheet with parchment, and spray it with cooking spray.
Egg yolk, blended	12 g	1 yolk	8%	③ Blend thoroughly by using a whisk or immersion blender. Allow any foam that appears to dissipate, or use a spoon to skim it from the surface.
Salt	2 g	½ tsp	1.3%	
Mushroom Puree see page 150	100 g	⅜ cup	67%	④ Whisk together thoroughly to create the mushroom base.
Egg yolks	40 g	3 yolks	27%	⑤ Spread one quarter of the mushroom base onto a round silicone mat in a layer 2 mm / ¹⁄₁₆ in thick.
Heavy cream	10 g	10 mL / 2 tsp	7%	⑥ Pull a pastry comb through the mushroom base to create even lines across the mat.
Albumin powder	8.8 g	5 tsp	5.8%	
Salt	2 g	½ tsp	1.3%	
Neutral-tasting oil or cooking spray	as needed			⑦ Coat the pan with a thin layer of oil, and carefully place the mushroom-striped silicone disc into the pan.
				⑧ Pour one quarter of the omelet base over the back of a spatula or large spoon and onto the lines of mushroom base.
				⑨ Place the hot lid on the pan, and bake the omelet sheet in the oven until the egg sets, about 6 minutes.
				⑩ While one sheet is baking, repeat steps 5 and 6 to prepare strips of mushroom base on a second, cool silicone disc.
				⑪ Remove the pan from the oven, lift out the silicone disc, and cool the cooked omelet sheet slightly.
				⑫ Peel the omelet sheet carefully from the silicone, and transfer it to the prepared baking sheet.
				⑬ Repeat steps 7–12 three times with the remaining ingredients; skip step 10 the last time. After the first omelet sheet, the remaining omelet sheets will cook in the warm pan in about 3 minutes.
French Scrambled Eggs, warmed see page 144	200 g	2 cups	133%	⑭ Top the omelet sheets with a second piece of sprayed parchment. Reheat in a 175 °C / 350 °F oven for 1½–2½ minutes.
Shiitake Marmalade, warmed see page 151	as needed			⑮ Lay the omelet sheets stripe-side down, and divide the French scrambled eggs and shiitake marmalade evenly among them.
Clarified, unsalted butter see page 119	as needed			⑯ Fold the edges of the omelet sheets carefully over their fillings, and brush the omelets with clarified butter. Serve immediately.

1 Preheat the oven to 175 °C / 350 °F. Once the oven reaches its set temperature, place the oven-safe lid of a 20 cm / 8 in nonstick frying pan into the oven to preheat for about 15 minutes.

2 Line a baking sheet with parchment paper, and spray it with cooking spray.

3 Blend the whole eggs, cream, yolks, and salt thoroughly; use a whisk or immersion blender. If foam rises on the surface, allow it to dissipate, or use a spoon to skim it off. This is the omelet base.

4 Whisk together the mushroom puree, yolks, cream, albumin powder, and salt thoroughly to make the mushroom base.

TO MAKE AHEAD

After step 12, cover the baking sheet with plastic wrap, and refrigerate the omelet sheets for up to 2 days. To reheat, remove the plastic, and warm in a 175 °C / 350 °F oven for 1½–2½ minutes.

5 Spread one quarter of the mushroom base onto a round silicone mat to form an even layer 2 mm / 1⁄16 in thick. We use an offset spatula to do this.

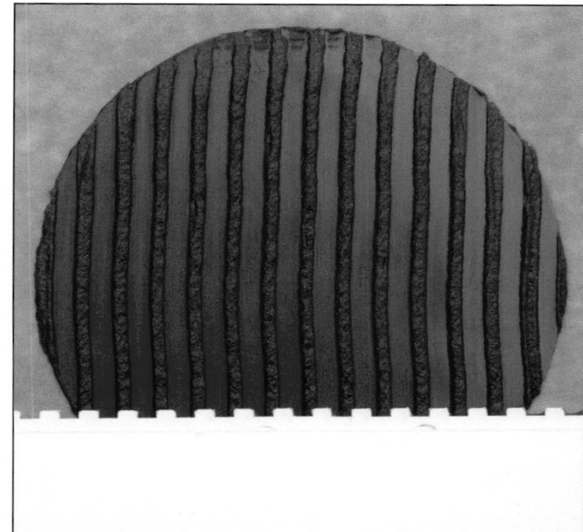

6 Pull a pastry comb having 3 mm / 1⁄8 in teeth through the mushroom mixture to create straight, parallel lines across the mat. You may want to stabilize the silicone mat by using double-sided tape to stick it to the counter—just make sure to remove the tape before cooking. If the lines are not straight, simply scrape off the mushroom mixture, remake the layer, and try again.

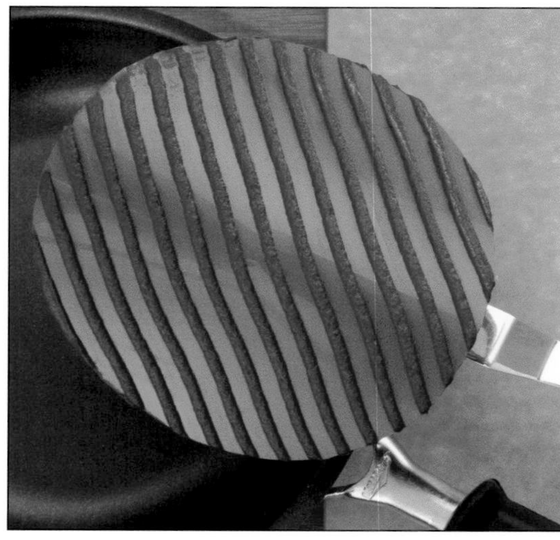

7 Rub or spray a thin layer of oil onto the pan, and carefully place the silicone disc with the stripes of mushroom base into the pan. The oil should create an airtight seal between the silicone mat and the pan, thus preventing any egg from seeping under.

8 Pour one quarter of the omelet base over the back of a spoon to flood gently over the mushroom base. The spoon helps prevent the flow from smearing the lines.

9 Cover the pan with the hot lid, place it in the oven, and bake until the egg sets, about 6 minutes. The pan should sit level on the oven rack; use folded pieces of aluminum foil as shims, if needed, to ensure that the omelet is flat and cooks evenly.

10 While one sheet is baking, repeat steps 5 and 6 to prepare strips of mushroom base on a second, cool silicone disc.

11 Remove the pan from the oven, lift out the silicone disc, and cool the omelet sheet slightly.

12 Peel the omelet sheet from the mat, and transfer it to the prepared baking sheet.

13 Repeat steps 7–12 three times with the remaining ingredients; skip step 10 the last time. Do not stack the omelets. After the first omelet sheet has cooked, the remaining three omelet sheets will cook in the warm pan in about 3 minutes.

14 Top the omelet sheets with another piece of sprayed parchment. Place the baking sheet in the oven for 1½–2½ minutes to reheat all of the omelets at once.

15 Lay the omelet sheets stripe-side down, and divide the French scrambled eggs and shiitake marmalade among them.

16 Fold the edges of the omelet sheets over their fillings, flip them seam-side down, and brush them with clarified butter.

MUSHROOM PUREE

YIELD:	*200 g / ⅞ cup*
TIME ESTIMATE:	*45 minutes overall*
STORAGE NOTES:	*keeps for 3 days when refrigerated or up to 1 month when frozen*
LEVEL OF DIFFICULTY:	*easy*

This puree is versatile, having many uses in addition to making omelets. We like to serve it as a garnish for poached fish or chicken; you can also transform it into a simple, yet intense, cream of mushroom soup (see variation below).

Shiitake and portobello mushrooms are generally easy to find year-round, but we substitute other varieties as they come into season. Criminis, morels, chanterelles, and porcinis make flavorful substitutes for the shiitakes. Black trumpets are preferable to portobellos when you can find them. If you like the flavor of truffle oil, add a few drops at step 4.

INGREDIENT	WEIGHT	VOLUME	SCALING	PROCEDURE
Shiitake mushroom caps, thinly sliced	250 g	4⅓ cups	100%	① Sauté the mushrooms until golden brown, about 10 minutes.
Unsalted butter	30 g	3 Tbsp	12%	
Shallots, minced	50 g	¼ cup / 2 shallots	20%	② Add, and cook over low heat, stirring occasionally, until the shallots are very tender, about 20 minutes. The portobello gills will darken the mixture.
Portobello mushroom gills, spooned from the cap	20 g	from 1 large	8%	
Mushroom Jus or water see page 91	165 g	165 mL / ¾ cup	66%	③ Stir in, increase to medium heat, and simmer for 1 minute. ④ Puree in a blender until smooth. ⑤ Pass through a fine sieve.
Salt	3 g	¾ tsp	1.2%	⑥ Season the puree, and serve it warm.

VARIATION: Cream of Mushroom Soup

Mushroom Puree from recipe above	200 g	⅞ cup
Mushroom Jus see page 91	165 g	165 mL / ⅝ cup
Heavy cream	100 g	110 mL / ½ cup
White miso	5 g	1 tsp
Salt	to taste	
Brioche croutons, cut into small cubes, and fried in bacon fat	as needed	

Stir together the puree, jus, cream, and miso in a pot, and bring to a simmer. Season with salt, and garnish with brioche croutons or sautéed mushrooms.

SHIITAKE MARMALADE

YIELD:	*300 g / 1 cup*
TIME ESTIMATE:	*40 minutes overall*
STORAGE NOTES:	*keeps for 3 days when refrigerated or up to 1 month when frozen*
LEVEL OF DIFFICULTY:	*easy*

This condiment transforms the intense umami flavor of caramelized shiitake mushrooms into an unctuous marmalade. Fold in some grain mustard, and serve it with steak, or spread the marmalade on toast topped with grilled sweet onions. When they are available, substitute seasonal mushrooms such as criminis, morels, chanterelles, and porcinis. For a different flavor, replace the soy sauce with our rich Brown Chicken Jus (see page 92).

INGREDIENT	WEIGHT	VOLUME	SCALING	PROCEDURE
Shiitake mushroom caps	300 g	5⅛ cups	100%	① Pulse the mushrooms in a food processor until they are minced but not pureed.
Unsalted butter	60 g	4 Tbsp	20%	② Melt in a frying pan, and add the mushrooms. ③ Cook over medium-low heat, stirring occasionally, until lightly browned and dry, 15–18 minutes.
Shallots, minced	60 g	⅓ cup	20%	④ Stir into the mushroom mixture, and cook until tender, 8–10 minutes.
Water	100 g	100 mL / ⅜ cup	33%	⑤ Add to the pan, and stir to combine.
Soy sauce	36 g	30 mL / 2 Tbsp	12%	⑥ Simmer until thick but still fluid, about 1 minute.
Honey	4 g	1 tsp	1.3%	
Chives, thinly sliced	10 g	¼ cup	3.3%	⑦ Fold in just before serving.
Tarragon, minced	5 g	½ Tbsp	1.7%	
Salt	to taste			⑧ Season the marmalade, and serve it warm.

The mushrooms should be processed just until they are minced. Use the pulse feature to ensure that the mushrooms do not become a paste or puree.

When the mushrooms are brown and the shallots are tender but not brown, it is time to add the water, soy sauce, and honey.

You can refrigerate the marmalade after step 6. When you are ready to serve it, reheat it in a pan, fold in the chives and tarragon, and season it with salt.

Savory marmalades

The concept of a savory marmalade may seem odd at first, but marmalade is an excellent form for a flavorful warm condiment. Try making one with just minced onions and shallots seasoned generously with thyme and black pepper. You can make a marmalade of minced bacon and apple by adding a bit of reduced apple juice or maple syrup to serve as a binder.

EGGS SUNNY-SIDE UP

YIELD:	*four servings (400 g / 4 eggs)*
TIME ESTIMATE:	*1¼ hours overall, including 15 minutes of preparation and 50 minutes unattended*
STORAGE NOTES:	*egg whites keep for 1 day when refrigerated*
LEVEL OF DIFFICULTY:	*moderate*
SPECIAL REQUIREMENTS:	*sous vide setup, four small nonstick frying pans (10–12 cm / 4–5 in), foil covers cut to fit frying pans*

Cooking an egg sunny-side up to perfection poses an inherent problem: the yolk and the white reach their ideal textures at different temperatures. Our solution is to cook the yolk separately from the white and to then reassemble the two parts just before serving. That way, the yolk is like jam and the white is still buttery.

We love the pudding-like consistency of a yolk cooked at 67 °C / 153 °F. For a more traditional runny yolk, cook it instead at 62 °C / 144 °F, but cook an extra egg or two, because yolks are very fragile at this temperature, and you might lose one. Raise the temperature to 70 °C / 158 °F to make a perfectly spherical yolk having a fudge-like consistency. It's up to you.

INGREDIENT	WEIGHT	VOLUME	SCALING	PROCEDURE
Eggs	200 g	4–5 large	67%	① Preheat a water bath to **67 °C / 153 °F**, and preheat the oven to **160 °C / 320 °F**. Cut four foil lids just slightly larger in diameter than the rims of four 10–12 cm / 4–5 in nonstick frying pans. ② Cook the whole eggs sous vide for 40 minutes. ③ Shell the eggs, and carefully clean off the whites to isolate the yolks.
Neutral-tasting oil or clarified, unsalted butter (optional) see page 119	150 g	160 mL / ⅝ cup	50%	④ Keep the egg yolks warm for up to 1 hour, if needed, by holding them in a rigid container that is filled with oil or butter and then placed in a **60 °C / 140 °F** water bath.
Egg white	300 g	1⅓ cups / 10 whites	100%	⑤ Blend by using a whisk or immersion blender, and then strain. Allow any surface foam to dissipate, or skim it from the surface.
Heavy cream	90 g	100 mL / ⅜ cup	30%	
Salt	3 g	¾ tsp	1%	
Cooking spray	as needed			⑥ Coat the four pans with a thin film of cooking spray. ⑦ Place one quarter of the egg white mixture into each of the pans. ⑧ Cover the pans with the foil lids. ⑨ Place the pans in the oven, and bake until the egg whites are just set, about 12 minutes. ⑩ Slide the cooked egg whites gently onto individual plates. ⑪ Scoop a small divot out of each egg white to hold the yolk.
Brown butter, warm see page 119	30 g	30 mL / 2 Tbsp	10%	⑫ Place an egg yolk in each divot. ⑬ Drizzle the brown butter over the eggs, and serve them immediately.

1 Preheat a water bath to **67 °C / 153 °F**, and preheat the oven to **160 °C / 320 °F**. Cut four foil lids just slightly larger in diameter than the rims of four 10–12 cm / 4–5 in nonstick frying pans.

2 Cook the whole eggs sous vide for 40 minutes.

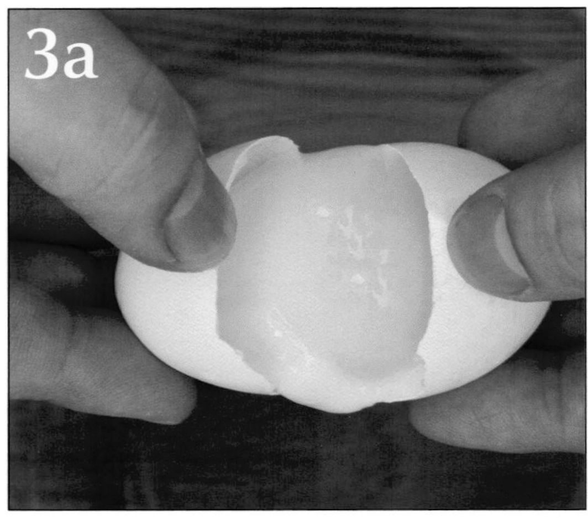

3 Shell each egg, and clean off the whites to isolate the perfectly cooked yolk. Dip or rinse the yolk in water to clean it. Be very gentle with the yolk: if you puncture the membrane, it will burst.

TO MAKE AHEAD

The egg whites can be made up to 24 hours in advance. As the egg whites bake in step 9, lay a piece of parchment paper in a baking sheet, and spray it with cooking oil. Arrange the cooked whites on it, and cover them with another sheet of sprayed parchment paper. Cover the baking sheet with plastic wrap, and refrigerate it. To reheat the egg whites, remove the plastic, and warm them in a 135 °C / 275 °F oven for 5–6 minutes. Time the cooking of the yolks accordingly.

VARIATION: Deviled Eggs

For a modern take on deviled eggs, whip the egg whites with vinegar, oil, mustard, and herbs to make a vinaigrette. Serve it as a dressing for the cooked whole yolks.

4 Keep the egg yolks warm for up to 1 hour, if needed, by holding them in a rigid container that is filled with neutral-tasting oil or clarified butter and then placed in a **60** °C / **140** °F water bath. This technique prevents a skin from forming over the yolk.

5 Blend the egg whites, cream, and salt, and then strain the mixture. Skim off any foam that forms on the surface, or allow it to dissipate on its own.

6 Spray a thin coat of cooking spray over the bottom of the four pans.

7 Pour one quarter of the egg white mixture into each of the pans.

8 Cover the pans with the foil lids. Don't let the foil wrap under the bottom.

9 Place the pans in the oven, and bake until the eggs are just set, about 12 minutes. The pans should be level on the oven rack. Use folded pieces of aluminum foil as shims, if needed, so that the white is even in thickness.

10 Slide the cooked egg whites carefully onto individual plates.

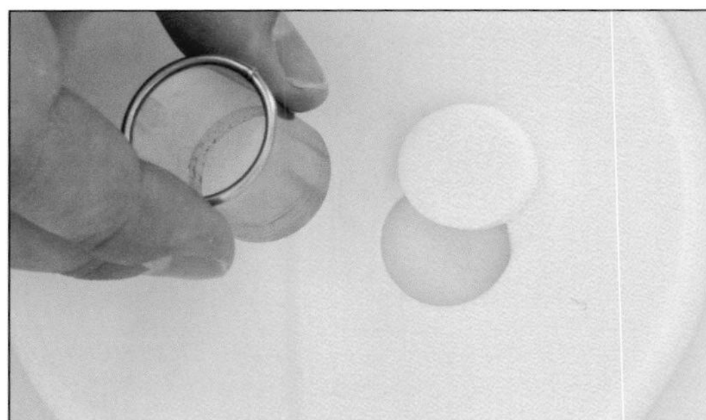

11 Use a ring cutter or a spoon to scoop a small divot from each egg white.

12 Place one drained, warm egg yolk in each divot.

13 Drizzle warm brown butter over the eggs, and serve them immediately.

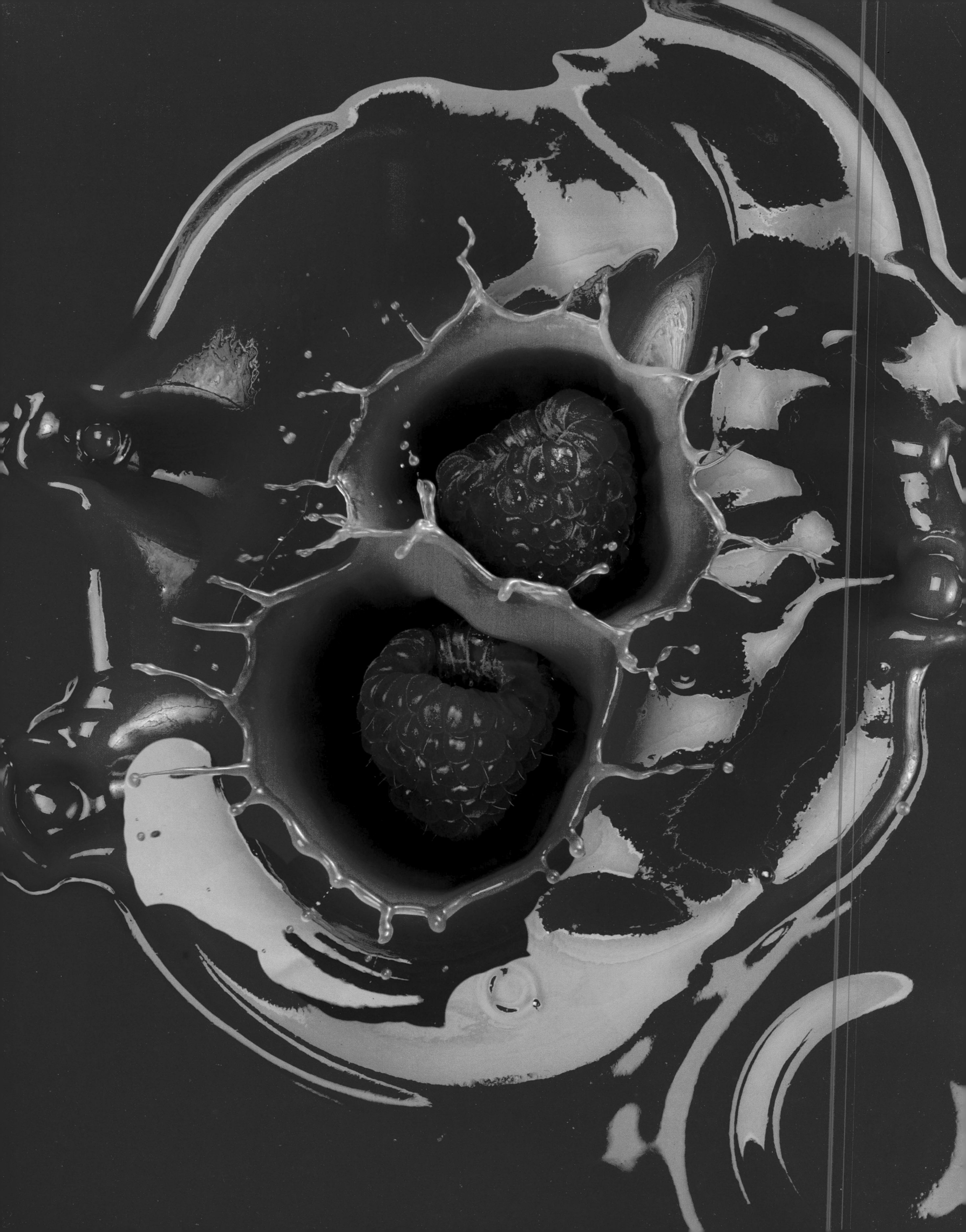

SALADS AND COLD SOUPS

A salad can be so much more than the stereotypical pile of greens that some chefs deride as "rabbit food." Look at a salad as an opportunity to create appealing textural contrasts and flavor combinations. Putting together a balanced salad that avoids soggy homogeneity takes thought and practice. This chapter can help. The salad recipes presented here illustrate a wide range of attractive options: a green salad mixed with a creamy, tart dressing of lettuce puree; a chickpea salad with tuna confit and no greens at all; and the delicate grain quinoa tossed with cauliflower and apple to make a kind of Modernist tabbouleh.

Cold soups often get a bad rap, too. Americans in particular tend to idealize soup as hearty, heartwarming, and piping hot. But soups can be incredibly satisfying without being warm. Cold soups—robust, refreshing, and complex—are popular in Italy, Spain, France, Scandinavia, and Russia.

Gazpacho is probably the best-known example, although few are aware that it wasn't originally made with tomatoes. One of the oldest recipes for gazpacho, which the Moors likely brought to Spain, was based on grapes, almonds, garlic, and bread. We like to reinterpret the dish to include seasonal fruits such as peaches, cherries, strawberries, or (as in the recipe here) raspberries.

Vichyssoise—a simple soup of potatoes, leeks, and cream—is challenging because it's so minimal. The cream is often added too heavily, to mask the graininess of the potato. We wanted more of the potato flavor to shine through, so we borrowed a trick from brewers: we use diastatic malt powder to transform the potato starch into sugars, thus removing the graininess.

THE SCIENCE OF HOW COLD AND FAT AFFECT FLAVOR

No matter how perfectly you cook and puree a potato, it seems grainy on the tongue unless you add butter or cream. The fat coats the natural starch granules of the potato to create that creamy mouthfeel. But, like cold, fat numbs flavor perception. For example, you don't perceive the true saltiness of ham—which has triple the salt content of most foods—because it's both cold and fatty. When making cold, creamy sauces or soups, you have to compensate for this phenomenon by adding more salt, sweetness, or acid than you would for warm foods.

HIGHLIGHTS

To dress a salad, put the dressing in the bottom of the bowl, and then toss in the greens to give them a thin, even coating. Lettuce can become oversaturated quickly if dressing is poured over the top.

see page 166

Add crunch to a quinoa salad by mixing in shaved cauliflower tips, apple, and celery.

see page 170

Try your hand at using Modernist ingredients and techniques to create vacuum-infused rhubarb and a beautifully plated Fruit Minestrone.

see page 158

You don't need tons of cream to create a silky smooth vichyssoise. We extract the essence of leeks, and then use that juice as the main liquid to give it an intense flavor.

see page 162

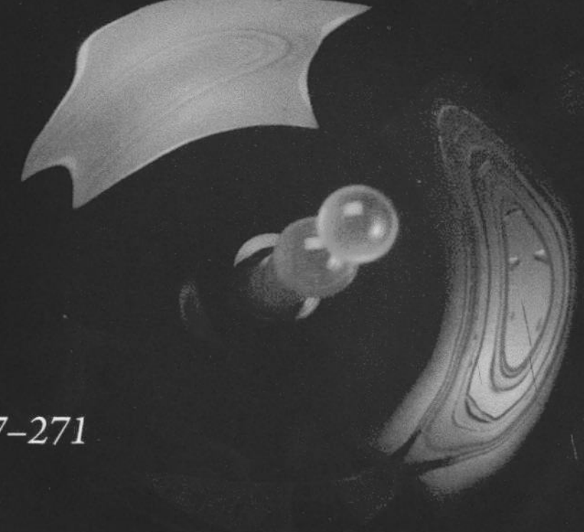

FURTHER READING IN *MODERNIST CUISINE*

Cooking fruits and vegetables sous vide for purees: see page 3·290

A seasonal mélange of cooked and raw fruits: see pages 3·294–295

A plated-dish recipe for Lentil Salad with foie gras cherries: see pages 5·267–271

A plated-dish recipe for Strawberry Gazpacho with sour rhubarb sorbet: see pages 5·277–279

RASPBERRY GAZPACHO

YIELD:	*four servings (450 g / 2 cups)*
TIME ESTIMATE:	*1¼ hours overall, including 15 minutes of preparation and 1 hour unattended (optional)*
STORAGE NOTES:	*keeps for 2 days when refrigerated; raspberry syrup keeps for up to 6 months when frozen*
LEVEL OF DIFFICULTY:	*easy*
SPECIAL REQUIREMENTS:	*sous vide setup, piquillo peppers, xanthan gum (optional)*

Showcase the best fruit of the season with this refreshing twist on gazpacho. *Ajo blanco,* one of the original forms of gazpacho, was made from white bread, garlic, almonds, and grapes, rather than the tomatoes used most frequently today for the base.

David Kinch, chef at Manresa in Los Gatos, California, gave us the idea to use strawberries in place of tomatoes. We have extended this idea to raspberries. Cherries, peaches, nectarines, and apples make equally delicious gazpachos when those fruits are at their peak.

The raspberry syrup made in the first four steps of this recipe is optional; you can use it to adjust the consistency and sweetness of the soup. The technique for extracting raspberry juice sous vide, however, works well with all berries. The resulting brightly colored, clear syrup can also be used to garnish a light dessert or stirred into sparkling white wine for a refreshing cocktail resembling a *kir royale.*

INGREDIENT	WEIGHT	VOLUME	SCALING	PROCEDURE
Raspberries, rinsed (optional)	225 g	2 cups	80%	① If making the optional raspberry syrup, preheat a water bath to **65 °C / 149 °F**. Otherwise, skip to step 5.
Sugar (optional)	25 g	2 Tbsp	9%	② Toss together. Place in a zip-top bag, and use the water-displacement method (see page 58) to remove as much air as possible. Seal the bag.
				③ Cook sous vide for 1 hour.
				④ Strain without pressing to obtain the raspberry syrup. Measure 35 g for use in step 7.
Raspberries, rinsed	280 g	2¼ cups	100%	⑤ Combine in a blender, and puree until smooth.
Cucumber, peeled, seeded, and thinly sliced	70 g	½ cup	25%	⑥ Pass the puree through a sieve.
Piquillo peppers (canned)	57 g	½ cup	20%	
Sweet onion, thinly sliced	57 g	½ cup	20%	
Extra-virgin olive oil	25 g	30 mL / 2 Tbsp	9%	
White balsamic vinegar	10 g	10 mL / 2⅜ tsp	3.6%	
Balsamic vinegar	5 g	6 mL / 1⅛ tsp	1.8%	
Garlic clove, thinly sliced	2 g	½ tsp	0.7%	
Xanthan gum (optional)	0.7 g		0.25%	
Raspberry syrup, from above (optional)	35 g	35 mL / 2 Tbsp	13%	⑦ Add the raspberry syrup (optional), season the soup, and serve it chilled.
Lime juice	to taste			
Salt	to taste			
Black pepper	to taste			

1 If you are making the raspberry syrup (which is optional), preheat a water bath to 65 °C / 149 °F. If omitting the syrup, skip ahead to step 5.

2 Toss the raspberries in sugar, and then use the water-displacement method to seal them together in a zip-top bag while excluding as much air as possible.

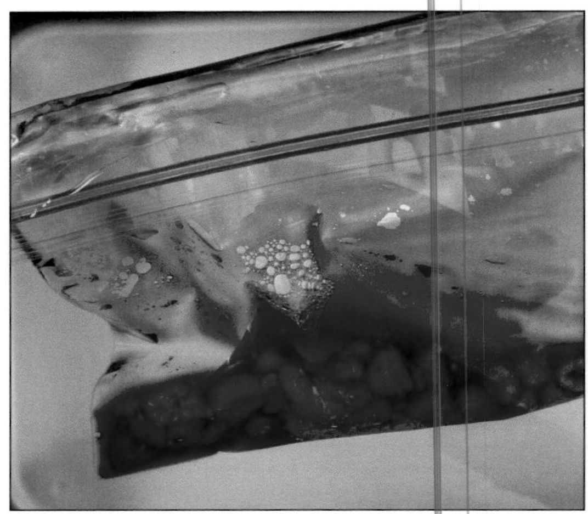

3 Cook the raspberries sous vide for 1 hour.

4 Strain the cooked raspberries, without pressing, to make a clear, thin syrup. Measure 35 g for use in step 7. Use any extra syrup as a topping for yogurt or pancakes, or freeze it for up to 6 months.

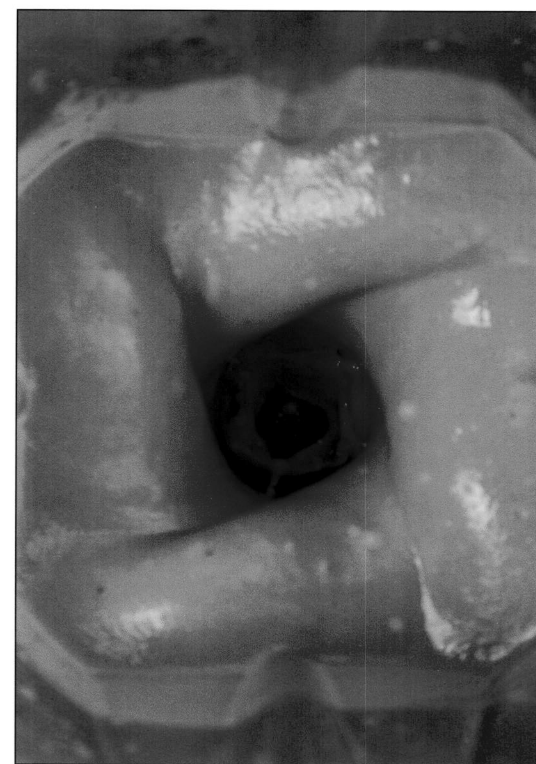

5 Combine the fresh raspberries, cucumber, peppers, onion, olive oil, vinegars, garlic, and xanthan gum (optional) in a blender, and puree until smooth.

6 Pass the puree through a sieve.

7 Season the soup with the raspberry syrup (optional), lime juice, salt, and pepper. Add more syrup to thin the puree or to sweeten a tart soup. Add the lime juice to brighten a sweet soup.

To serve the gazpacho, place several raspberries, a mint leaf, and finely julienned basil in each bowl, and pour the chilled soup at tableside. You can drizzle a little olive oil or almond oil on top.

FRUIT MINESTRONE

YIELD:	*four servings (400 g / 2 cups)*
TIME ESTIMATE:	*4 hours overall, including 1 hour of preparation and 3 hours unattended*
STORAGE NOTES:	*serve immediately*
LEVEL OF DIFFICULTY:	*advanced (complexity of timing and assembly)*
SPECIAL REQUIREMENTS:	*vacuum sealer with marinating attachment, juicer, malic acid*

Like any good minestrone, this fruity dessert soup is best when made with ingredients at their seasonal peak. At our cooking lab, we make a very fancy version from cucumber sorbet, vacuum-infused fruits, and shards of berries that we freeze in liquid nitrogen and then shatter. This recipe is less technically demanding, albeit one of the more complex in this book. Don't be intimidated by the number of steps; it's easier to assemble than it looks, and many of the components can be made in advance and used in other ways.

Serve the soup in chilled bowls, and pour the broth at the table. You can chill the minestrone even more by adding a scoop of a high-quality, store-bought fruit sorbet such as lychee, raspberry, or passion fruit. If you don't have time to make the candied beans, use Chinese red beans cooked in syrup, which you can find at Asian markets or other specialty food stores.

INGREDIENT	WEIGHT	VOLUME	SCALING	PROCEDURE
For the candied beans:				
Water	1.5 kg	1.5 L / 6⅓ cups	300%	① Combine in a large pot, stir to dissolve fully, and then slowly bring to a boil to make a syrup.
Sugar	1 kg	5⅛ cups	200%	
Cannellini beans (canned), drained, rinsed, and cleaned of any skins or broken pieces	200 g	1 cup	40%	② Place in a pot with 500 g of the syrup, and simmer over medium-low heat for 30 minutes. ③ Pour off the syrup, replace with 500 g of fresh syrup, and simmer the beans for another 30 minutes. ④ Repeat step 3 twice more for a total simmering time of about 2 hours. The beans should turn translucent and become fudge-like. ⑤ Cool the beans in the remaining syrup, and refrigerate them.
For the strawberry broth:				
Strawberries, washed and hulled	500 g	3 cups	100%	⑥ Process through a juicer. ⑦ Strain.
Sugar	50 g	¼ cup	10%	⑧ Stir into the strawberry juice until dissolved.
Lime juice	to taste			⑨ Season with the lime juice to make a broth, and refrigerate it.
For the infused rhubarb:				
Fresh red rhubarb	100 g	1 large stalk	20%	⑩ Peel the skin from the rhubarb, and reserve the peelings. ⑪ Slice the peeled rhubarb into 6 mm / ¼ in pieces.
Sugar	100 g	½ cup	20%	⑫ Combine in a small pot, stir to dissolve, and bring to a boil over medium-high heat to make a syrup. ⑬ Pour the warm syrup over the rhubarb slices and reserved rhubarb skins, and vacuum seal together in a rigid container (see page 53). ⑭ Refrigerate until cold, at least 1 hour. Drain and discard the skins. The syrup may be saved for another use.
Water	100 g	100 mL / ⅜ cup	20%	
Malic acid	2 g		0.4%	
For the cucumber rolls:				
English cucumber	150 g	1 large	30%	⑮ Slice lengthwise, as thinly as possible, on a mandoline, to form evenly sized, rectangular sheets of cucumber. Stop when you reach the seeds. ⑯ Roll up the sheets so that the green edges are exposed. Store the rolls, covered, in the refrigerator.
To assemble:				
Cucumber rolls, from above		8–12 rolls		⑰ Arrange two or three cucumber rolls in the center of four chilled bowls.
Candied cannellini beans, from above		24 beans		⑱ Distribute the beans, fruit, rhubarb, and mint leaves evenly among the bowls.
Infused rhubarb slices, from above		8–12 slices		
Kumquats, sliced		8 slices		
Raspberries, halved	24 g	8 berries	4.8%	
Blueberries, halved	16 g	8 berries	3.2%	
Mint leaves	4 g	16 small	0.8%	
Strawberry broth, from above	250 g	260 mL / 1⅛ cups	50%	⑲ Serve immediately by pouring the strawberry broth evenly into the bowls at tableside.

1 Combine the sugar and water for the candied beans in a large pot, and stir to dissolve fully. Then slowly bring the mixture to a boil to form a syrup. Sugar crystals may form in the syrup if the sugar is not fully dissolved before boiling.

2 Pick through the beans to find and discard any broken pieces or skins, and then place them in a pot with 500 g of the syrup. Simmer over medium-low heat for 30 minutes.

3 Pour the syrup off the beans, and replace with 500 g of fresh syrup. Simmer the beans for another 30 minutes.

4 Repeat step 3 two more times, for a total simmering time of about 2 hours. The beans should turn translucent and fudge-like. This is a variation on the technique used to make prized European sweets such as marron glacé (candied chestnuts) and sugared fruits.

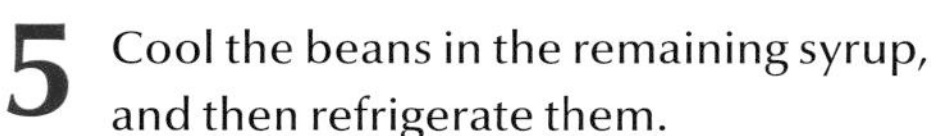

5 Cool the beans in the remaining syrup, and then refrigerate them.

6 Use a juicer to extract juice from the strawberries.

7 Strain the juice with a fine sieve to remove seeds and extra pulp.

8 Stir the sugar into the strained strawberry juice until it has dissolved.

9 Season the sweetened strawberry juice with lime juice to taste, and then refrigerate the broth. You may need a little more or less sugar or lime juice, depending on the sweetness of the berries.

10 Peel the skin from the rhubarb. If your rhubarb is green or muddy-colored, discard the skins; otherwise, save the reddish skin for use in step 13: it adds a more intense color to the infused slices.

continued on the next page

11 Slice the peeled rhubarb into pieces 6 mm / ¼ in long.

12 Combine the sugar, water, and malic acid in a small pot, stir until dissolved, and then bring to a boil over medium-high heat to make a syrup.

13 Place the sliced rhubarb and reserved skins in a rigid vacuum container, pour in the warm syrup, and vacuum seal it.

14 Refrigerate the rhubarb until cold, at least 1 hour. Drain and discard the skins. You can reserve the syrup for another use.

15 Slice the cucumber lengthwise on a mandoline, using the thinnest setting available, to make 8–12 rectangular sheets of cucumber. Try to make the slices even in size, and avoid the seedy part of the cucumber.

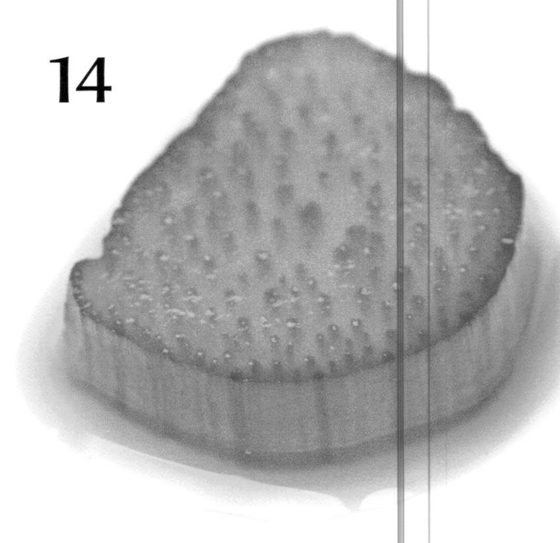

16 Lift the short edge of each cucumber sheet, and roll it up. The green edges should be exposed. Store the sheets, covered, in the refrigerator.

17 When you are ready to assemble the minestrone, chill four bowls, and then arrange two or three cucumber rolls in the center of each bowl.

18 Scatter the beans, fruit, rhubarb, and mint leaves evenly among the bowls in a decorative pattern. Tweezers are a handy tool for this step.

19 Pour the strawberry broth evenly into the bowls at tableside. We use a decorative pitcher for serving the broth.

VARIATIONS

Strawberry Panna Cotta

At step 3 in the recipe for Raspberry Panna Cotta (see page 366), substitute strawberry juice for the raspberry puree. Serve with vacuum-compressed strawberries (see page 59), black peppercorns, and thyme.

Fruit Salad

Combine slices of kumquats, blueberries, and raspberries with vacuum-compressed strawberries (see page 59), vacuum-infused rhubarb from steps 10–14, cucumber rolls from steps 15–16, and mint leaves.

Cheese Course

Serve Stilton or goat cheese with vacuum-compressed strawberries (see page 59) and mint leaves. Optionally, add candied cannellini beans (from steps 2–5).

Strawberry Juice with Green Apple Foam

To make a refreshing summer beverage, top fresh strawberry juice (from steps 6–9) with a foam made from fresh green apple juice. Pour the apple juice into a whipping siphon, charge the siphon with two cartridges of nitrous oxide, shake vigorously for 5–10 seconds, and then dispense the apple foam into cups of juice (see page 19).

MODERNIST VICHYSSOISE

YIELD:	*four servings (950 g / 4 cups)*
TIME ESTIMATE:	*6 hours overall, including 5 hours unattended*
STORAGE NOTES:	*keeps for 3 days when refrigerated*
LEVEL OF DIFFICULTY:	*advanced (special ingredient)*
SPECIAL REQUIREMENTS:	*sous vide setup, vacuum sealer, diastatic malt powder*

The secret to velvety-smooth potatoes is diastatic malt powder, an ingredient available from specialty baking- or brewing-supply stores, that converts potato starches into sugars and leaves no trace of gumminess or graininess. Excessive cream or milk is no longer needed; in fact, you can make this recipe with no cream at all. The main liquid is pure leek jus, squeezed from whole, cooked leeks. Delicate strands of blanched leek and potato make an elegant and flavorful garnish.

If you don't acquire the enzyme-rich malt powder, pass the potatoes through a fine sieve after step 4, and then continue with step 10.

INGREDIENT	WEIGHT	VOLUME	SCALING	PROCEDURE
Water	1 kg	1 L / 4¼ cups	200%	① Preheat a water bath to 52 °C / 126 °F.
Yukon Gold potatoes, peeled and cut into 2.5 cm / 1 in pieces	500 g	3⅔ cups	100%	② Place in a large pot, and bring to a boil. ③ Reduce the heat, and simmer the potatoes until very tender, 30–40 minutes. ④ Drain.
Salt	15 g	5 tsp	3%	
Sugar	10 g	2 tsp	2%	
Diastatic malt powder (King Arthur Flour brand)	5 g		1%	⑤ Stir into the cooked potatoes. ⑥ Blend the warm potato mixture in a blender until smooth and sticky. ⑦ Place in a zip-top bag. Use the water-displacement method (see page 58) to remove as much air as possible from the bag, and seal it. ⑧ Cook sous vide for 30 minutes. ⑨ Transfer the potato puree to a pot, and heat it to at least 75 °C / 167 °F. ⑩ Cool the puree, and chill it over an ice bath or in the refrigerator.
Leeks, white parts only, washed and halved lengthwise	1 kg	4–5 leeks	200%	⑪ Increase the water bath temperature to 90 °C / 194 °F. ⑫ Vacuum seal the leeks. ⑬ Cook sous vide for 2 hours. ⑭ Squeeze in a strainer to collect as much jus as possible; discard the pulp.
Potato puree, from above	400 g	1¾ cups	80%	⑮ Stir together, cool, and refrigerate the soup until fully chilled.
Leek jus, from above	400 g	400 mL / 1⅔ cups	80%	
Heavy cream	100 g	110 mL / ½ cup	20%	
Salt	12 g	1 Tbsp	2.4%	
Leeks, white parts only, finely julienned	25 g	½ leek	5%	⑯ Bring a pot of water to a boil, and arrange an ice-water bath alongside. ⑰ Blanch the leeks in boiling water for 5 seconds, and then plunge them in the ice water, and drain.
Yukon Gold potato, peeled and finely julienned	25 g	1 whole	5%	⑱ Blanch the potatoes in boiling water for 1 minute, and then plunge them in the ice water, and drain.
Chives, thinly sliced	7 g	3 Tbsp	1.4%	⑲ Toss together with the drained strips of leek and potato to make the garnish. Place a small amount of the garnish in four chilled bowls. ⑳ Pour the chilled soup at tableside.
Olive oil	5 g	6 mL / 1¼ tsp	1%	
Salt	to taste			
White wine vinegar	to taste			

1 Preheat a water bath to 52 °C / 126 °F.

2 Bring the water, potatoes, salt, and sugar to a boil in a large pot. Adding 1–2 g of sugar for every 100 g of water helps preserve the natural sweetness of the potatoes.

3 Reduce the heat, and simmer until the potatoes become very tender, 30–40 minutes. It may take longer if your tap water is rich in minerals.

4 Drain the potatoes.

5 Stir the diastatic malt powder into the warm potatoes.

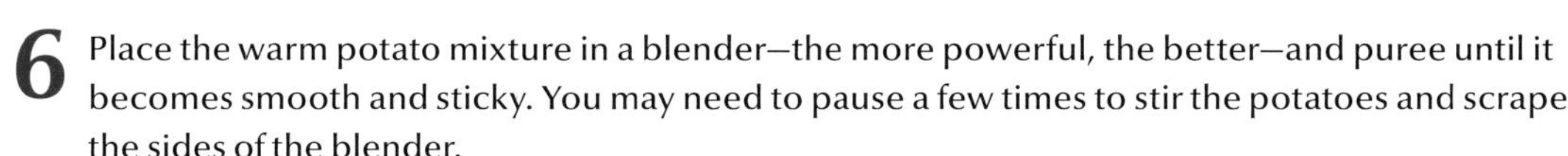

6 Place the warm potato mixture in a blender—the more powerful, the better—and puree until it becomes smooth and sticky. You may need to pause a few times to stir the potatoes and scrape the sides of the blender.

7 Place the potato puree in a zip-top bag, remove as much air as possible from the bag by using the water-displacement method (see page 58), and seal it. Alternatively, vacuum seal the puree.

8 Cook the puree sous vide for 30 minutes.

9 Transfer the puree to a pot, and heat it to at least 75 °C/167 °F. This halts the enzymatic reactions. Use a thermometer, and note that the mixture may boil below this temperature.

10 Cool the puree, and chill it.

11 Increase the temperature of the water bath to 90 °C/194 °F.

12 Vacuum seal the halved leeks.

13 Cook the leeks sous vide for 2 hours. If the leeks float, use an upturned plate to keep them submerged.

Young, fresh leeks yield the most juice.

VARIATIONS

Vichyssoise with Potato Peel Reduction

For a more intense potato flavor, place the peels from the Yukon Gold potatoes in a pressure cooker, add enough water to cover them completely, and pressure-cook at 1 bar/15 psi for 30 minutes. Strain the liquid; discard the peels. Simmer the liquid over medium heat until its volume is reduce by about half. At step 15, add the potato-peel reduction to the puree along with half of the cream, leek jus, and salt.

Roasted-Potato Vichyssoise

To give the soup a roasted-potato flavor, make the Vichyssoise with Potato Peel Reduction variation at left, but add 25 g/2½ Tbsp of butter and 1 g/¼ tsp of baking soda to the potato skins before you pressure-cook them.

continued on the next page

14 Strain the liquid from the bag. Squeeze the leeks by pressing them with a spoon to collect as much jus as possible. Discard the pulp. Wearing gloves makes it easier to handle the hot leeks.

15 Measure 400 g / 400 mL / 1⅔ cups of the leek jus and 400 g / 1¾ cups of the potato puree. Stir the jus, cream, and salt into the potato puree. Then cool the soup in an ice bath, and refrigerate it until it is fully chilled, at least 2 hours.

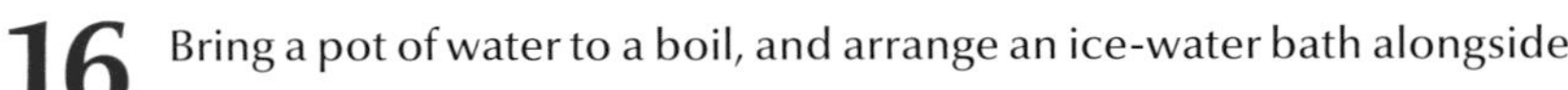

16 Bring a pot of water to a boil, and arrange an ice-water bath alongside.

17 Blanch the julienned leeks in boiling water for 5 seconds, lift them out with a strainer, plunge them into the ice-water bath, and then drain them.

18 Blanch the julienned potatoes for 1 minute, plunge them in the ice water, and then drain them.

19 Toss the blanched leeks and potatoes together with the chives, olive oil, salt, and vinegar in a small bowl. Divide this garnish among four chilled bowls.

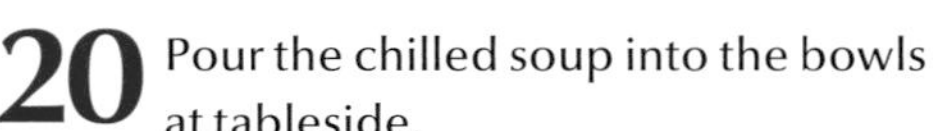

20 Pour the chilled soup into the bowls at tableside.

SWEET ONION SLAW

YIELD:	*four servings (440 g / 4 cups)*
TIME ESTIMATE:	*15 minutes of preparation*
STORAGE NOTES:	*serve immediately*
LEVEL OF DIFFICULTY:	*easy*
SPECIAL REQUIREMENTS:	*pickled red onion (see page 130), Modernist Mayonnaise (see page 108)*

Why does cabbage get to have all the fun? This twist on a classic coleslaw substitutes onions for the traditional red and green cabbage. Use just about any kind of sweet onion—Vidalia, Maui, or Walla Walla work just as well.

Throw in some charred fresh corn kernels, chopped Sous Vide Chicken (see page 244), and slices of peeled cucumber to transform this slaw into a composed salad. Or use it on sandwiches, like our Modernist Meatloaf Sandwich (see page 214).

INGREDIENT	WEIGHT	VOLUME	SCALING	PROCEDURE
Sweet onion, julienned	280 g	3 cups	100%	① Combine, and mix thoroughly.
Sour cream	100 g	⅓ cup	36%	② Serve immediately.
Scallions, sliced	56 g	⅔ cup	20%	
Pickled red onion see page 130	40 g	¼ cup	14%	
Modernist Mayonnaise see page 108	20 g	4 tsp	7%	
Dijon mustard	12 g	1 Tbsp	4%	
Salt	4 g	1 tsp	1.4%	
Cayenne pepper	0.4 g	pinch	0.14%	

1 Combine the sweet onion, sour cream, scallions, pickled red onion, mayonnaise, mustard, salt, and cayenne pepper, and mix thoroughly.

2 Serve immediately.

COMPOSING A GREAT SALAD

A salad is much more than just a bowl of vegetables. A great salad is composed, much in the same way that a classical symphony is composed so that melody, counterpoint, and harmony are balanced in each moment and from beginning to end. A well-composed salad similarly balances diverse textures, flavors, and colors. Like musical compositions, salads come in many styles, shapes, and sizes. Whenever you make a salad, think about some of the major factors listed below.

Season

Generations ago, the season was the biggest determining factor in what ingredients were available for salads. That is less true now that global trade delivers produce from all parts of the planet. But the success of any salad still hinges on using ingredients that are at their peak of freshness, so it pays to stay informed on what is in season when.

Spring: asparagus, fava beans, peavines, new potatoes, rhubarb, radishes, baby carrots, tarragon, borage

Summer: tomatoes, cucumbers, green beans, bell peppers, avocados, zucchini, stone fruit, melons, chervil, lemon verbena, basil, goat cheese

Autumn: sweet onions, arugula, celery root (celeriac), butter lettuce, apples, pears, figs, thyme, parsley, cheddar cheeses

Winter: spinach, young chard, beets, celery root, dried fruits, citrus fruits, watercress, winter savory, chives, legumes, whole grains, aged Parmesan cheese

Texture

Textural contrast is one of the most satisfying components of eating. Crispy, crunchy, creamy, tender, and chewy: a salad can cover a huge range of textures. Mix elements from these categories in various combinations.

Crispy: lettuce, cucumbers, peppers, apple slices, melons

Crunchy: sliced raw vegetables, fresh pickles, sunflower seeds, hazelnuts, croutons

Creamy: thin vegetable purees, egg-based dressings, creamy cheeses

Tender: baby lettuces, avocados, braised beets, cooked potatoes, cooked tender grains

Chewy: dried fruits, cooked whole grains, aged cheeses

Temperature

Salad may seem synonymous with cold, but many delicious salads are served best at room temperature, warm, or even hot. Greens do wilt when warmed, but quickly braised greens can provide an enjoyable contrast in temperature—the classic salad of spinach greens wilted in bacon fat comes to mind. Moreover, there's no law that a salad must contain greens. A warm salad of lentils dressed with mustard vinaigrette makes a hearty meal in winter.

Snip fresh herbs into the salad at the last second so that the aromas are at their most potent. If you chop the herbs in advance, they can lose flavor and start to brown.

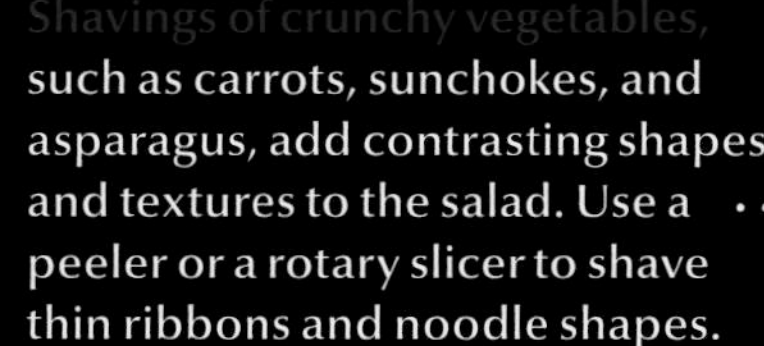

Shavings of crunchy vegetables, such as carrots, sunchokes, and asparagus, add contrasting shapes and textures to the salad. Use a peeler or a rotary slicer to shave thin ribbons and noodle shapes.

HOW TO Dress a Salad

The dressing binds together all of the components that you've assembled. It can be as simple as a light coating of olive oil and lemon juice—see page 117 for several variations on the classic vinaigrette—or much more complex. With any dressing, the goal is to coat the salad ingredients evenly without drowning them.

1 Fill the bottom of the salad bowl with most of the dressing you intend to use.

2 Add the salad ingredients.

3 Toss the salad with large spoons.

4 Drizzle more dressing, as necessary, with a spoon or squeeze bottle until all the components are uniformly dressed but not saturated.

5 Season with additional salt just before serving. Do this at the last second; otherwise, the lettuce will wilt.

6 Garnish with snipped fresh herbs or colorful highlights, and serve.

GREEN SALAD WITH ROMAINE DRESSING

YIELD:	*four to six servings (436 g / 6 cups)*
TIME ESTIMATE:	*1 hour overall, including 20 minutes of preparation and 40 minutes unattended*
STORAGE NOTES:	*dressing keeps for 2 days when refrigerated*
LEVEL OF DIFFICULTY:	*moderate*
SPECIAL REQUIREMENTS:	*sous vide setup*

This refreshing salad uses greens for the dressing as well as for the base. Serve it alongside grilled steak, or toss in shaved seasonal vegetables to make it a main course. You can prepare the dressing (steps 1–9) a day or two in advance.

INGREDIENT	WEIGHT	VOLUME	SCALING	PROCEDURE
Eggs		2 large	100%	① Preheat a water bath to 68 °C / 154 °F. ② Cook sous vide for 40 minutes. ③ Cool, peel, and refrigerate.
Romaine lettuce leaves (green parts only)	40 g	1 cup	40%	④ Bring a pot of water to a boil, and arrange an ice bath alongside. ⑤ Blanch the greens for 1 minute, and then plunge the leaves into the ice water immediately. ⑥ Drain the cooked greens and herbs, and squeeze out the excess water.
Chives, cut into 5 cm / 2 in pieces	15 g	⅓ cup	15%	
Mint leaves	15 g	1½ cups	15%	
Tarragon leaves	5 g	¼ cup	5%	
Basil leaves	5 g	¼ cup	5%	
Soft-cooked egg, from above	50 g		50%	⑦ Combine with the cooked greens in a blender, and puree until smooth.
Buttermilk	50 g	50 mL / ¼ cup	50%	
Parmigiano-Reggiano, finely grated	28 g	⅓ cup	28%	
Anchovy fillets (packed in oil), drained	10 g	3 fillets	10%	
Neutral-tasting oil	40 g	45 mL / 3 Tbsp	40%	⑧ Add to the pureed greens gradually while blending until fully emulsified.
Lemon juice	to taste			⑨ Season the dressing, and store it refrigerated.
Salt	to taste			
Butter lettuce, trimmed, washed, and dried	250 g	2 heads	250%	⑩ Pour half of the dressing into a salad bowl, add the lettuce, and toss. Drizzle the remaining dressing over the top.
Dressing, from above	106 g	⅜ cup	106%	
Red radishes, very thinly sliced	80 g	6 radishes	80%	⑪ Scatter over the salad, and serve it immediately.

VARIATIONS

Herb and Romaine Broth

You can make a beautiful green broth from the cooked greens to serve with fish or poached chicken. After step 6, blend the cooked lettuce and herbs with 300 g / 300 mL / 1¼ cups of water or vegetable stock. Alternatively, make a puree by blending in just 25 g / 25 mL / 5 tsp of liquid.

Beet Salad

Beets and other root vegetables can give a green salad more substance. Seal baby yellow or red beets whole in a zip-top bag, cook them sous vide in an 85 °C / 185 °F water bath until tender, 15–20 minutes, and then cool. Quarter or shave the cooked beets, season them with olive oil, salt, and pepper, and then toss them with the salad.

Blanching the greens for just 1 minute makes them tender enough to puree but preserves their bright green color.

After you have blanched and chilled all of the greens, you can bundle them together in cheesecloth to press out any excess water before blending them with the egg, milk, cheese, and anchovies to form a smooth puree.

Substitute any fresh salad greens and herbs in this dressing. We like arugula leaves as a substitute for the romaine; it makes for a more assertive dressing that pairs well with roasted root vegetables.

WHILE YOU'RE AT IT: **Parmesan Crisp**

Give the salad some crunch by pairing it with a Parmesan crisp. Use a Microplane to finely grate Parmesan cheese over a baking sheet to a depth of about 3 mm / ⅛ in. Bake the cheese in the oven at **175 °C / 350 °F** until the cheese turns golden brown, 10–15 minutes. Let the sheet cool, and then cut it into whatever shapes you like.

PRESSURE-COOKED QUINOA SALAD WITH CAULIFLOWER

YIELD:	*six servings (955 g / 6 cups)*
TIME ESTIMATE:	*45 minutes overall*
STORAGE NOTES:	*keeps for 3 days when refrigerated*
LEVEL OF DIFFICULTY:	*easy*
SPECIAL REQUIREMENTS:	*pressure cooker, macadamia nut oil, honey vinegar (optional)*

Pressure-cooked quinoa is ready to serve in minutes. Slice off just the tender tips of the cauliflower florets so that they fall apart into tiny, grain-like pieces. We add honey vinegar and macadamia oil, but you can use your favorite flavorful, sweet vinegar and any rich nut oil instead. The cauliflower florets and stems left over after trimming can be used to make a soup or puree (see page 180).

INGREDIENT	WEIGHT	VOLUME	SCALING	PROCEDURE
Water	690 g	690 mL / 3 cups	345%	① Place a baking sheet in the freezer to chill for at least 15 minutes.
White quinoa	200 g	1¾ cups	100%	② Combine in a pressure cooker, and pressure-cook at a gauge pressure of 1 bar / 15 psi for 4 minutes. Start timing when full pressure is reached. ③ Depressurize the cooker quickly by running tepid water over the rim. ④ Strain the quinoa, and spread it in an even layer on the frozen baking sheet to cool quickly.
Cauliflower florets	500 g	1 medium head	250%	⑤ Shave off the tips of the cauliflower florets by carefully using a mandoline. ⑥ Measure 160 g / 1¾ cups of the shaved cauliflower tips for use in the next step.
Green apple, peeled and finely diced	72 g	⅝ cup	36%	⑦ Combine, and mix gently with the cooked quinoa and measured cauliflower tips until all ingredients are evenly distributed.
Pine nuts, toasted	40 g	¼ cup	20%	⑧ Serve the salad cold.
Italian parsley, minced	40 g	½ cup	20%	
Celery, peeled and diced	35 g	¼ cup	17.5%	
Honey vinegar or white balsamic vinegar	35 g	40 mL / 2½ Tbsp	17.5%	
Extra-virgin olive oil	35 g	40 mL / 2½ Tbsp	17.5%	
Dried currants	34 g	¼ cup	17%	
Macadamia nut oil	16 g	20 mL / 3½ tsp	8%	
Salt	to taste			
Lemon juice	to taste			

Safety tips for pressure-cooking: see page 33

To avoid overcooking the quinoa, depressurize the cooker quickly after 4 minutes at full pressure by running lukewarm water over the rim, and then immediately strain the quinoa, and spread it onto a prechilled baking tray.

Although you can use a Microplane or other fine grater to shave the tips off cauliflower florets, a mandoline is faster. Use the finest cut available on the tool; the pile of shaved tips should resemble couscous.

Use the leftover stalks to make soup or puree (see page 180), or "Fat-Free" Mac and Cheese (see page 314).

The renowned Modernist chef Ferran Adrià came up with the idea of using cauliflower to make a faux couscous by shaving just the surface with a very sharp knife. Here, the shaved tips of the florets add something unexpected to this quinoa salad.

PRESSURE-COOKED CHICKPEA SALAD

YIELD:	*six servings (575 g / 2½ cups)*
TIME ESTIMATE:	*13 hours overall, including 30 minutes of preparation and 12½ hours unattended*
STORAGE NOTES:	*keeps for 3 days when refrigerated*
LEVEL OF DIFFICULTY:	*easy*
SPECIAL REQUIREMENTS:	*pressure cooker*

We created this recipe to go with our Sous Vide Tuna Confit (see page 174), which produces a flavorful oil that you can use in the dressing for this salad. The salad actually improves with a night in the refrigerator, which gives the flavors more time to blend.

We cook the chickpeas in mineral water because its high calcium content helps keep the chickpeas from breaking down and preserves their integrity. For a more refined presentation, you can also peel the skins from the cooked chickpeas at step 6, before making the salad.

INGREDIENT	WEIGHT	VOLUME	SCALING	PROCEDURE
Water	500 g	500 mL / 2⅛ cups	333%	① Combine, and soak the chickpeas for at least 12 hours in the refrigerator.
Dry chickpeas	150 g	¾ cup	100%	② Drain.
Mineral water	350 g	350 mL / 1½ cups	233%	③ Combine with the drained chickpeas in a pressure cooker, and pressure-cook at a gauge pressure of 1 bar / 15 psi for 20 minutes. Start timing when full pressure is reached.
Salt	5 g	1¼ tsp	3%	④ Depressurize the cooker.
Garlic clove, whole	3 g	1 clove	2%	⑤ Drain, and then remove and discard the garlic and herbs.
Thyme	1 g	1 sprig	0.7%	⑥ Cool the chickpeas completely.
Fresh bay leaf	0.2 g	1 medium leaf	0.1%	
Sherry vinegar	45 g	50 mL / ¼ cup	30%	⑦ Combine in a blender, and blend until smooth.
Anchovy fillets (packed in oil), drained	25 g	6–8 fillets	17%	
Lemon juice	10 g	10 mL / 2 tsp	7%	
Lemon zest, grated	5 g	2 Tbsp	4%	
Extra-virgin olive oil or oil from Sous Vide Tuna Confit see page 174	140 g	160 mL / ⅔ cup	93%	⑧ Add gradually to the vinegar and anchovy mixture while blending, and blend until completely emulsified. Store the dressing in the refrigerator.
Kalamata olives, pitted and chopped	50 g	¼ cup	33%	⑨ Toss gently with the chickpeas and the dressing until mixed.
Capers, chopped	6 g	2 tsp	4%	⑩ Serve cold.
Basil leaves, torn	3 g	5–6 leaves	2%	
Mint leaves, torn	3 g	5–6 leaves	2%	

Safety tips for pressure-cooking: see page 33

1 Soak the chickpeas in water for at least 12 hours in the refrigerator. The dried chickpeas can triple in size as they absorb the water, so use plenty of water.

2 Drain the chickpeas.

3 Combine the mineral water, salt, garlic, thyme, and bay leaf with the drained chickpeas in a pressure cooker, and then pressure-cook at a gauge pressure of 1 bar / 15 psi for 20 minutes. Start timing as soon as full pressure has been reached.

4 Let the cooker cool, or run tepid water over the rim, to depressurize it.

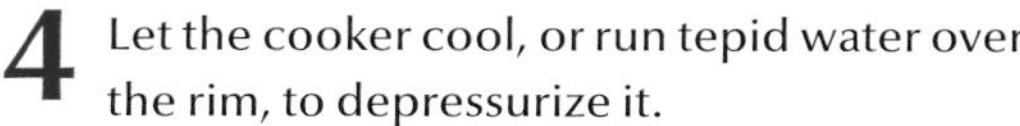

5 Drain the chickpeas, and discard the garlic clove and herbs.

6 Allow the chickpeas to cool completely. You can peel off their skins at this point if you want a cleaner look.

7 Combine the vinegar, drained anchovy fillets, lemon juice, and lemon zest in a blender. Blend until smooth. You can also use an immersion blender.

8 While blending, add the oil gradually to the vinegar and anchovy mixture, and continue blending until the dressing is completely emulsified. Refrigerate the dressing if you will not be using it immediately.

9 Toss the chopped olives and capers with the herbs, chickpeas, and dressing to mix them gently.

10 Serve cold. The salad is delicious when topped with slices of Sous Vide Tuna Confit (see next page).

SOUS VIDE TUNA CONFIT

YIELD:	*six servings (500 g)*
TIME ESTIMATE:	*25½ hours overall, including 30 minutes of preparation and 25 hours unattended*
STORAGE NOTES:	*keeps for 3 days when refrigerated*
LEVEL OF DIFFICULTY:	*moderate*
SPECIAL REQUIREMENTS:	*sous vide setup, three 500 mL / 16 oz canning jars*

The tuna in this recipe is cooked sous vide in jars rather than in bags as an example of how you can cook in a low-temperature water bath without using plastic. Because the tuna is fresh and lightly cooked, it is more fragile and perishable than the preserved, pressure-canned variety. Handle it delicately, store it in the refrigerator, and eat it within 3 days.

INGREDIENT	WEIGHT	VOLUME	SCALING	PROCEDURE
Water	600 g	600 mL / 2½ cups	120%	① Combine, and stir until dissolved to make a brine.
Salt	24 g	2 Tbsp	4.8%	
Sugar	12 g	2 tsp	2.4%	
Ahi tuna, cut into 2.5 cm / 1 in pieces	500 g / 1.1 lb		100%	② Place in the brine, and refrigerate for 24 hours.
Olive oil	500 g	560 mL / 2⅓ cups	100%	③ Preheat a water bath to **51 °C / 124 °F**. ④ Drain the tuna, rinse it in cold water, and then pat it dry. ⑤ Divide the tuna evenly into three 500 mL / 16 oz canning jars, and add enough oil to cover the fish by 1 cm / ⅜ in. Seal the jars tightly. ⑥ Place the sealed jars in the water bath, and cook sous vide to a core temperature of **50 °C / 122 °F**, about 1 hour. ⑦ Serve the tuna warm, or store it, refrigerated, in the canning jars.

Safety tips for lightly cooked food, see page xxv

1 Add the salt and sugar to the water, and stir until they dissolve. This is the brine.

2 Place the tuna in the brine, and refrigerate it for 24 hours to marinate.

3 Preheat a water bath to **51 °C / 124 °F**.

4 Drain the brine from the tuna pieces, rinse them in cold water, and then pat them dry with paper towels.

5 Divide the tuna pieces evenly into three 500 mL / 16 oz canning jars, and add enough olive oil to cover the fish by 1 cm / ⅜ in. Don't leave much headspace, or the jars will float in the water bath. Seal the jars tightly.

6 Place the sealed jars in the water bath, and cook sous vide until the core temperature of the tuna pieces reaches **50 °C / 122 °F**, about 1 hour.

7 Serve the tuna warm, or store it in the sealed canning jars for up to 3 days in the refrigerator.

You can substitute swordfish, black cod, halibut, salmon, or escolar for the tuna in this recipe with excellent results.

We use ordinary cooking-grade olive oil, as extra-virgin olive oil tends to overpower the flavor of the tuna. But other mild oils, such as rice bran, avocado, or macadamia nut oil, will work as well.

WHILE YOU'RE AT IT: **Tuna Confit Salad and Tuna Melt Sandwich**

Make a tuna salad by combining 150 g / 1 cup of flaked or chopped tuna confit with 30 g / 2 Tbsp of mayonnaise or aioli (see page 108) and 15 g / 2 Tbsp chopped pickled onions. To make a tuna melt sandwich, spread the tuna salad on sourdough bread, and top with two Perfectly Melting Cheese Slices (see page 317). See Grilled Cheese Sandwiches on page 318 for finishing instructions.

PRESSURE-COOKED LENTIL SALAD

YIELD:	*six to eight servings (750 g / 4 cups)*
TIME ESTIMATE:	*3½ hours overall, including 30 minutes of preparation and 3 hours unattended*
STORAGE NOTES:	*keeps for 3 days when refrigerated*
LEVEL OF DIFFICULTY:	*easy*
SPECIAL REQUIREMENTS:	*pressure cooker, Modernist Vinaigrette (see page 117)*

INGREDIENT	WEIGHT	VOLUME	SCALING	PROCEDURE
Dry green lentils (common)	200 g	1 cup	100%	① Cover with plenty of cold water, and leave to soak at room temperature for 2 hours. ② Drain.
Carrots, thinly sliced	85 g	1¼ cups	43%	③ Wrap in cheesecloth, and tie closed to create a sachet.
Leeks, thinly sliced	70 g	¾ cup	35%	
Sweet onion, thinly sliced	50 g	¾ cup	25%	
Shallots, thinly sliced	50 g	¾ cup	25%	
Celery, thinly sliced	50 g	½ cup	25%	
Garlic, thinly sliced	8 g	2 cloves	4%	
Black peppercorns	2 g	1 tsp	1%	
Thyme	1 g	1 sprig	0.5%	
Fresh bay leaf	0.2 g	1 leaf	0.1%	
Mineral water	750 g	750 mL / 3¼ cups	375%	④ Combine with the lentils and sachet in a pressure cooker. ⑤ Pressure-cook at a gauge pressure of 1 bar / 15 psi for 7 minutes. Start timing as soon as full pressure has been reached. ⑥ Depressurize the cooker quickly by running tepid water over the rim. ⑦ Check the lentils for tenderness; they should be al dente. If necessary, simmer them uncovered for 1–2 minutes longer. ⑧ Discard the sachet, and allow the lentils to rest in the cooking liquid at room temperature for 30 minutes. ⑨ Drain, and refrigerate until chilled.
Modernist Vinaigrette see page 117	85 g	100 mL / ⅜ cup	43%	⑩ Toss gently with the chilled lentils, and season with salt to taste.
Salt	to taste			
Walnuts, chopped	95 g	⅔ cup	48%	⑪ Stir into the lentils. Serve immediately, or refrigerate for 1 day, which improves the balance of the flavors in the salad.
Fuji apple, peeled and finely diced	80 g	1 cup	40%	
Chives, finely minced	5 g	2 Tbsp	3%	

Safety tips for pressure-cooking: see page 33

Larger lentils and French green lentils take up to 20 minutes to cook in step 5.

FURTHER READING IN *MODERNIST CUISINE*

More recipes for vegetable purees: see pages 2·424–427
A recipe for Autoclaved Onion Soup: see page 3·302
The chemistry of the Maillard reaction and the Allium genus: see pages 3·89–91
The science and technique of pressure-cooking plant foods: see pages 3·298–309

8

PRESSURE-COOKED VEGETABLE SOUPS

HIGHLIGHTS

Throughout most of history, only those wealthy enough to have a personal chef—willing to sieve cooked vegetables—routinely enjoyed **velvety vegetable soups**. Now anyone with a good blender can make them.

see page 178

Pressure-cooking ensures that the **flavors aren't diluted in our allium jus**. Seasonal root vegetables such as carrots, turnips, or parsnips make wonderful variations.

see page 182

Replace the carrots in the Caramelized Carrot Soup recipe with other vegetables to yield **any number of creative soup combinations**.

see page 180

While you're at it, make a **delicate vegetable stew** by using a similar pressure-cooking technique to cook whole vegetables.

see page 185

Something magical happens when you combine chopped carrots, butter, a little water, and a pinch each of baking soda and salt in a pressure cooker for 20 minutes. At a slightly alkaline pH of about 7.5 (because of the baking soda) and a temperature of up to 120 °C / 250 °F (from the pressure), the caramelization reactions flourish. The result is a terra-cotta-colored mixture that is the concentrated essence of caramelized carrots.

Under pressure, many kinds of vegetables and fruits transform into something dramatically new, yet strikingly familiar. Think of Campbell's Tomato Soup: much of its iconic flavor comes from the tomatoes reacting with the high temperature of the canning process. That profile simply can't be reproduced with fresh tomato soup.

When pressure-cooked, sweet corn transforms into popcorn-flavored cream; fresh bananas taste like warm, baked banana bread; and sweet potatoes intensify tenfold in flavor. If there is a way to induce kids to eat their vegetables, this may be it. We exploit a similar technique to re-create a classic vegetable stew.

Pressure-cooked barley is quick to make and perfectly toothsome. The pressure extracts juices undiluted from sweet onions, leeks, and garlic to yield an intense broth. And all of the season's best vegetables take on the texture of fudge in a matter of minutes. You can use whichever vegetables and greens are currently at their peak. The techniques in this chapter are versatile enough to accommodate a wide range of flavors.

THE SCIENCE OF PRESSURING VEGETABLES TO COOK

Vegetables are made up of cells with strong walls that soften at higher temperatures than the cells in meat do. Vegetables are composed mostly of water, however, and their temperature normally won't exceed the boiling point of water, 100 °C / 212 °F, until they are dried out.

Cooking at elevated pressures gives us a way around this roadblock because the boiling point rises in step with the pressure. Even at 120 °C / 250 °F, vegetables in a fully pressurized cooker don't dry out as they quickly become tender. And because the air is sealed in, you don't need to add much water, so juices are extracted without becoming diluted.

CARAMELIZED CARROT SOUP

YIELD:	*six servings (1.3 kg / 6 cups)*
TIME ESTIMATE:	*40 minutes overall, including 20 minutes of preparation and 20 minutes unattended*
STORAGE NOTES:	*keeps for 3 days when refrigerated or up to 2 months when frozen*
LEVEL OF DIFFICULTY:	*moderate*
SPECIAL REQUIREMENTS:	*pressure cooker, Stove-Top Carotene Butter (optional, see page 121)*

The quality of this soup depends entirely on the quality of the carrots that go into it, so use the highest-quality carrots you can find. Carrot cores, rich in calcium, can add a bitter taste and unpleasant texture to this delicate soup, so we always remove them. It's an optional step, however; you can try the soup both ways and compare.

Add a swirl of coconut cream and a few sprigs of tarragon in the final step to enhance the inherent sweetness of the carrots. Shredded young coconut and ajowan seeds are other favorite garnishes of ours.

INGREDIENT	WEIGHT	VOLUME	SCALING	PROCEDURE
Carrots, peeled	500 g	5 cups / 5 medium	100%	① Core the carrots by quartering them lengthwise and slicing away any tough or fibrous cores. Cut the cored carrots into pieces 5 cm / 2 in long.
Unsalted butter	113 g	½ cup	22.6%	② Melt in the base of a pressure cooker over medium heat.
Water	30 g	30 mL / ⅛ cup	6%	③ Stir to combine, and then add with the carrots to the melted butter.
Salt	5 g	1¼ tsp	1%	④ Pressure-cook at a gauge pressure of 1 bar / 15 psi for 20 minutes. Start timing when full pressure is reached.
Baking soda	2.5 g	⅜ tsp	0.5%	⑤ Depressurize the cooker quickly by running tepid water over the rim. ⑥ Blend the mixture to a smooth puree. ⑦ Pass the puree through a fine sieve into a pot.
Fresh carrot juice	635 g	690 mL / 2½ cups	127%	⑧ Bring to a boil in a separate pot, and then strain through a fine sieve. ⑨ Stir into the carrot puree. Add water, if necessary, to thin the soup to the desired consistency.
Stove-Top Carotene Butter (or unsalted butter) see page 121	40 g	3½ Tbsp	8%	⑩ Blend into the soup by using an immersion blender until the butter has just melted.
Salt	to taste			⑪ Season, and serve warm.

Safety tips for pressure-cooking: see page 33

This recipe was one of the most popular in *Modernist Cuisine*. We do not use stock or cream in this recipe because we want to avoid diluting the carrot flavors. The juice from some kinds of carrots is so strongly flavored, however, that it overpowers the more delicate, caramelized carrot flavor. If that happens, substitute water, chicken stock, or vegetable stock for some or all of the carrot juice in step 8.

1 Slice the carrots lengthwise into quarters, and cut out and discard the tough and fibrous core from each quarter. Then cut the cored carrots into pieces 5 cm / 2 in long. Removing the cores improves the texture and sweetness of the soup.

2 Melt the butter in the base of a pressure cooker. The coating of butter helps to prevent the carrots from sticking.

3 Stir the water, salt, and baking soda until combined. Add this mixture and the carrot pieces to the melted butter, and stir well.

4 Pressure-cook the carrot mixture at a gauge pressure of 1 bar / 15 psi for 20 minutes. Start timing as soon as full pressure has been reached. Gas and electric burners tend to cause solids to catch on the bottom of the pressure cooker, so carefully give the pot a few shakes as it heats to prevent sticking. After 20 minutes, the carrots should be fully caramelized.

5 Depressurize the cooker quickly by running tepid water over the rim.

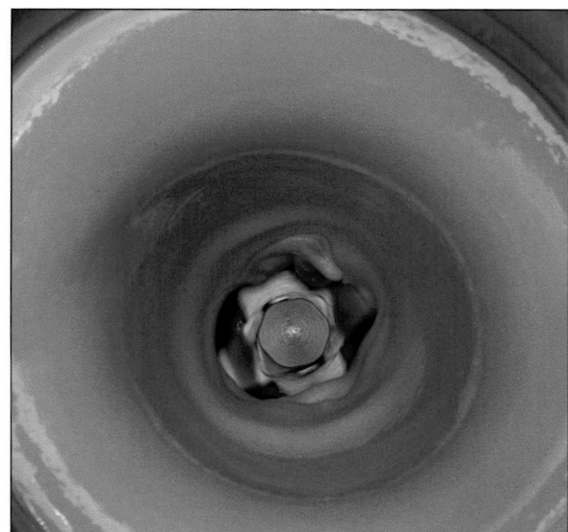

6 Blend the carrot mixture to a smooth puree.

7 Pass the puree through a fine sieve into a pot.

8 Bring the carrot juice to a boil in a separate pot. Then strain the juice through a fine sieve to remove any solids.

9 Stir the strained juice into the carrot puree, and return it to a simmer. Add water as needed to thin the soup to the desired consistency.

10 Blend the butter into the soup until it has just melted. Use an immersion blender; the blending is crucial to achieve a velvety texture.

11 Season the soup with salt to taste, and serve it warm.

VARIATION: Caramelized Carrot Puree
To make a delicious carrot puree that pairs well with Sous Vide Lobster Tail (see variation on page 288), skip steps 8–10. See the next page for additional variations.

OTHER PRESSURE-COOKED VEGETABLE SOUPS AND PUREES

Pressure-cooking works well for making soups and purees from a wide range of vegetables. In each of the variations below, replace the carrots in the Caramelized Carrot Soup recipe on page 178 with the vegetable listed, and then continue with steps 1–7. Replace the carrot juice with the flavorful liquid indicated, and thin to the desired consistency in step 9. Finally, add the garnishes, and serve the soup hot. To make a thick puree from any of these variations, skip steps 8–9. These recipes scale up well, but because they rely on the internal water content of the vegetables to produce steam, quantities should not be scaled down.

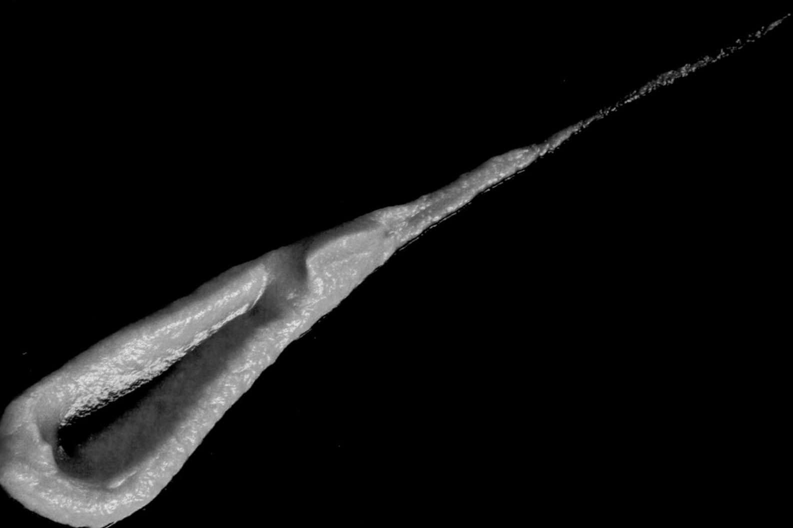

Squash Soup

Delicata or butternut squash, peeled and diced	500 g	5 cups / 1–2 medium
Lemongrass, trimmed and sliced	18 g	⅛ cup / 1 stalk
Coconut milk	as needed	

Garnishes: seared scallops, shredded young coconut, and lime zest

Artichoke Soup

Trimmed artichoke bottoms or peeled and diced sunchokes	500 g	4½ cups / 10–11 medium
Chicken stock see page 84	as needed	

Garnishes: mussels cooked sous vide (see page 290), saffron, and olive oil

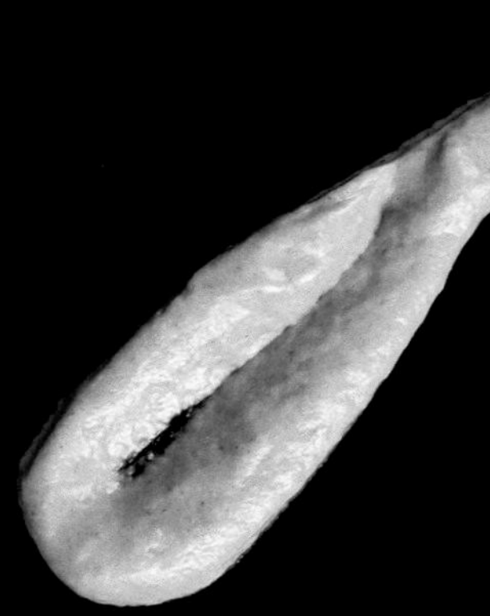

Mushroom Soup

Shiitake mushroom caps, sliced	500 g	8½ cups
Mushroom Jus see page 91	as needed	

Garnishes: chives, cognac, and Pressure-Caramelized Onions (see page 127)

Cauliflower Soup

Cauliflower florets, sliced	500 g	7 cups / 1 large head
Vegetable stock see page 89	as needed	

Garnishes: chopped Marcona almonds, peeled grapes, and Chaat Masala (see page 136)

Leek and Onion Soup (not shown)

Leeks, thinly sliced, white parts only	500 g	8 cups / 10 medium
Yellow onions, thinly sliced	500 g	6 cups / 7 large
Cheese water see page 314	as needed	

Garnishes: rendered bacon fat (see page 123), pressure-cooked leeks (see page 272), and low-temperature poached egg (see page 142)

Apple and Parsnip Soup

Parsnips, peeled and diced	400 g	3½ cups / 6 medium
Honeycrisp apples, peeled and diced	200 g	2 cups / 2–3 medium
Chicken stock see page 84	as needed	

Garnishes: pickled apples (see page 130), speck, and brown butter (see page 119)

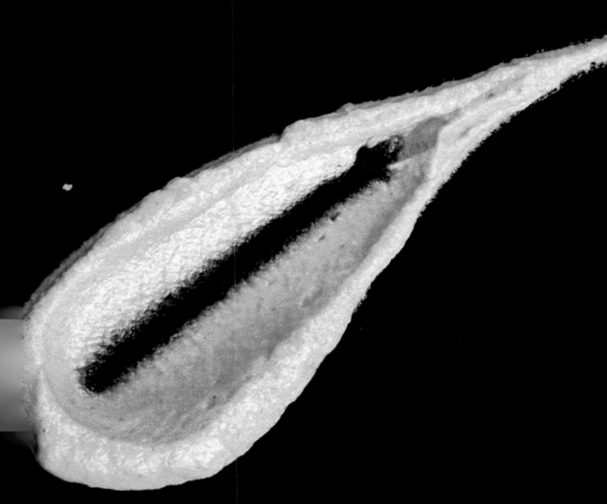

Broccoli-Gruyère Soup

Broccoli florets, sliced	500 g	8 cups / 2 heads
Gruyère cheese, grated	40 g	¾ cup
Chicken stock see page 84	as needed	

Garnishes: fried broccoli florets, toasted hazelnuts, and

Pressure-Caramelized Banana Puree (not shown)

Unsalted butter	80 g	5½ Tbsp
Sugar	10 g	1 Tbsp
Baking soda	2.5 g	½ tsp
Bananas, peeled and sliced	500 g	2 bananas
Salt	to taste	

Melt the butter in the base of a pressure cooker. Add the sugar and baking soda, and stir to combine. Add the bananas, and stir until they are evenly coated with the butter mixture. Pressure-cook at a gauge pressure of 1 bar / 15 psi for 28 minutes. Start timing as soon as full pressure has been reached. Depressurize the cooker by running tepid water over the rim. Puree the banana mixture in a blender until it is smooth. Season the puree with salt to taste, and serve it warm or cold.

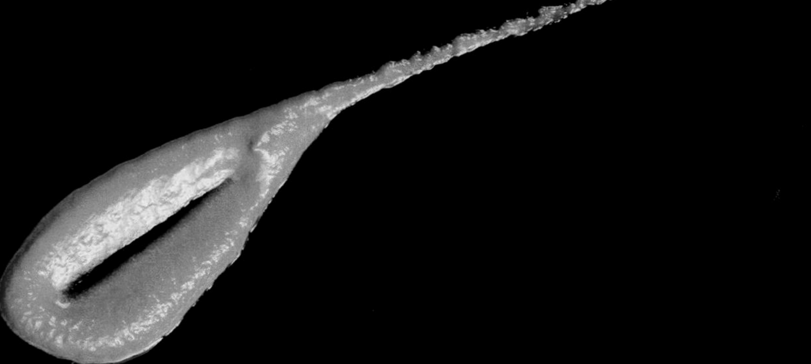

Bell Pepper Soup

Red bell pepper, seeded and sliced	500 g	5 cups / 8 medium
Sous Vide Fish Stock see page 87	as needed	

Garnishes: blue cheese, fresh mint, sliced black olives, and white anchovies

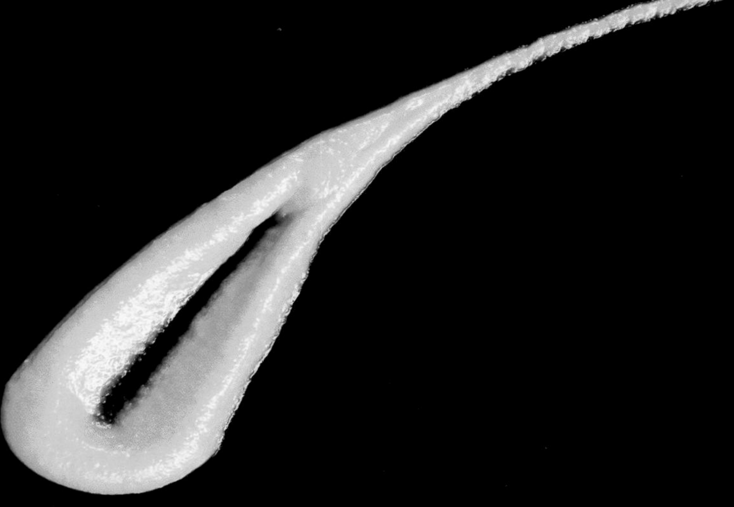

Corn Soup

Fresh corn kernels cut from the cob	500 g	3¾ cups / 4 ears
Toasted Corn Stock see page 90	as needed	

Garnishes: shrimp poached sous vide (see page 286),

PRESSURE-COOKED VEGETABLE JUS

YIELD:	*420 g / 1⅞ cups*
TIME ESTIMATE:	*2 hours overall, including 30 minutes of preparation and 1½ hours unattended*
STORAGE NOTES:	*keeps for 5 days when refrigerated or up to 6 months when frozen*
LEVEL OF DIFFICULTY:	*moderate*
SPECIAL REQUIREMENTS:	*pressure cooker, three 500 mL / 16 oz canning jars*

You can combine this recipe and the two that follow into a Modernist Vegetable Stew—see page 185 for instructions. Pressure-cooking can extract the essence of vegetables using much less water than you typically would when making stock. The concentrated result is so flavorful that it is really a jus, although you can use it much as you would an intense stock, for example to make sauces and broths. The technique here lends itself to wonderful variations, such as jus made from carrots, turnips, parsnips, and other seasonal root vegetables, or from a combination of vegetables and fruits such as cabbage and apple, or bell pepper and tomato.

INGREDIENT	WEIGHT	VOLUME	SCALING	PROCEDURE
Sweet onions, thinly sliced	265 g	3¼ cups	100%	① Toss together, and divide evenly among three 500 mL / 16 oz canning jars.
Garlic cloves, thinly sliced	160 g	1½ cups	60%	
Shallots, thinly sliced	135 g	1⅜ cups	51%	
Leeks, white parts only, thinly sliced	135 g	1½ cups	51%	
Water	120 g	120 mL / ½ cup	45%	② Add 40 g / 40 mL / 8 tsp of water to each jar. Tighten the lids fully, and then unscrew one-quarter turn so that the jars do not explode. ③ Place the filled jars on a metal rack or trivet in the base of a pressure cooker, and add 2.5 cm / 1 in of water. ④ Pressure-cook at a gauge pressure of 1 bar / 15 psi for 1½ hours. Start timing as soon as full pressure has been reached. ⑤ Depressurize the cooker by running tepid water over the rim. Let the jar contents cool slightly before opening to avoid splattering. ⑥ Strain through a fine sieve, reserving the juices. Discard the solids, or reserve for another use (see caption below).
Salt	to taste			⑦ Season the jus, and serve it warm.

Safety tips for pressure-cooking: see page 33

Onions, leeks, shallots, and garlic are all closely related members of the Allium genus. After you put the allium slices and water in the canning jars and tighten the lids, be sure to then unscrew each lid one-quarter turn. Otherwise, the jars may explode.

Pressure-cooking is a remarkably efficient way to extract the intensely flavored juices of alliums. Use the jus as a broth for risotto or other grains.

To obtain a clear jus, strain the juices through a fine sieve. Although you can increase the yield a bit by pressing on the solids, doing so may make the jus cloudy. After straining, you can puree the solids with salt and a little butter or olive oil.

PRESSURE-COOKED VEGETABLES

YIELD:	*300–400 g / 4–6 cups*
TIME ESTIMATE:	*10 minutes overall*
STORAGE NOTES:	*keeps for 1 day when refrigerated*
LEVEL OF DIFFICULTY:	*easy*
SPECIAL REQUIREMENTS:	*pressure cooker*

Pressure-cooking is well suited to any firm vegetable, including root vegetables, onions, shallots, leeks, garlic, hard squashes, and stalks like celery, rhubarb, chard, and cardoon. The vegetables emerge from the cooker very soft and having a delicate, fudge-like texture.

Pressure-cooking also works well with hard fruits, such as apples, Asian pears, and quince. If baby vegetables aren't available, peel and cut larger ones into bite-size pieces. Make sure all the pieces are the same size so that they cook evenly.

INGREDIENT	WEIGHT	VOLUME	SCALING
Baby carrots, trimmed		24 pieces	
Pearl onions, trimmed		24 pieces	
Baby turnips, trimmed		12 pieces	
Baby radishes, trimmed		12 pieces	
Water	120 g	120 mL / ½ cup	100%
Unsalted butter, cubed	14 g	1 Tbsp	12%
Salt	2 g	½ tsp	1.7%

PROCEDURE

① Combine in a pressure cooker.

② Pressure-cook at a gauge pressure of 1 bar / 15 psi for 3 minutes. Start timing as soon as full pressure has been reached.

③ Depressurize the cooker quickly by running tepid water over the rim.

④ Drain the liquid, and serve the vegetables immediately.

Safety tips for pressure-cooking: see page 33

TO MAKE AHEAD

After draining the liquid in step 4, cool the vegetables, and refrigerate them in a covered container. To reheat the vegetables, place them on a microwave-safe plate, cover with plastic wrap, and microwave for 30 seconds at 550 watts.

PRESSURE-COOKED BARLEY

YIELD:	*480 g / 3 cups*
TIME ESTIMATE:	*30 minutes overall, including 10 minutes of preparation and 20 minutes unattended*
STORAGE NOTES:	*keeps for 3 days when refrigerated*
LEVEL OF DIFFICULTY:	*easy*
SPECIAL REQUIREMENTS:	*pressure cooker*

Any whole grain—barley, wheat, spelt, farro, amaranth, quinoa, millet—can be cooked perfectly in a pressure cooker in very little time (for cooking times, see the table on page 324). The hulled barley we call for here includes the intact bran, but pearl barley is fine as a substitute and takes even less time to cook.

INGREDIENT	WEIGHT	VOLUME	SCALING	PROCEDURE
Hulled barley (with bran intact), rinsed and drained	200 g	1 cup	100%	① Combine in a pressure cooker, and bring to a boil. ② Pressure-cook at a gauge pressure of 1 bar / 15 psi for 20 minutes. Start timing as soon as full pressure has been reached.
Water	500 g	500 mL / 2⅛ cups	250%	③ Depressurize the cooker quickly by running tepid water over the rim. ④ Strain the barley, and serve it immediately.

Safety tips for pressure-cooking: see page 33

TO MAKE AHEAD

After straining the barley in step 4, rinse it with cold water, and drain well. Transfer the barley to a baking sheet, and refrigerate it uncovered until completely cool, about 1 hour. Then toss the barley with a bit of oil to keep the grains from sticking together, and store it, covered, in the refrigerator. To reheat the barley, warm it in a pot with a small amount of broth or water.

WHILE YOU'RE AT IT: **Barley Salad**

Combine 480 g / 3 cups of cooked and cooled barley with 175 g / ¾ cup of Spinach Pesto (see page 103), 72 g / ⅝ cup of minced green apple, and 35 g / ¼ cup of peeled and diced celery.

VEGETABLE STEW

YIELD:	*four servings (435 g / 2 cups)*
TIME ESTIMATE:	*20 minutes of preparation*
STORAGE NOTES:	*serve immediately*
LEVEL OF DIFFICULTY:	*easy*
SPECIAL REQUIREMENTS:	*Pressure-Cooked Barley (see the previous page), Pressure-Cooked Vegetables (see page 183), Pressure-Cooked Vegetable Jus (see page 182), Pressure-Cooked Garlic Confit oil (see page 126)*

You can compose pressure-cooked barley, vegetables, and vegetable jus from the three preceding recipes in this chapter to make an impressively elegant vegetable stew. Both the individual preparations and the plate-up are straightforward, and offer a good example of how home cooks can produce restaurant-quality food with confidence and relative ease.

INGREDIENT	WEIGHT	VOLUME	PROCEDURE
Pressure-Cooked Barley, warm see the previous page	100 g	½ cup	① Distribute the barley, turnips, carrots, onions, and radishes evenly among four bowls. Tweezers are a handy tool for this step.
Pressure-Cooked Vegetables, warm see page 183	all pieces		
Seasonal greens and herbs	a few small leaves of each		② Garnish. Use your imagination, and experiment with a variety of colors and arrangements (see variations below).
Pressure-Cooked Vegetable Jus, warm see page 182	250 g	250 mL / 1 cup	③ Divide equally among the four bowls.
Pressure-Cooked Garlic Confit oil see page 126	40 g	45 mL / 3 Tbsp	④ Drizzle into the prepared bowls of soup.
Salt	to taste		⑤ Sprinkle over the bowls, and serve the stew immediately.

1

3

VARIATIONS: Seasonal Herb Garnishes

Many combinations of fresh herbs work as garnishes. Here are some seasonal possibilities.
Winter: amaranth, baby beet greens, and rosemary
Spring: baby chard, chervil, basil, and chive blossoms
Summer: purslane, nasturtiums, and tarragon
Autumn: baby mustard greens, watercress, and thyme

STEAK

Making a great steak takes experience if you follow the traditional route: spending many weekends sweating over a grill or cooktop to develop a fine intuition for timing and doneness. Even grill masters flub a steak occasionally. Even when they do their best, the outside of a grilled steak inevitably is overcooked by the time the center reaches the perfect temperature. That's just the way that high heat works.

Thanks to new methods of precise, low-temperature cooking such as sous vide, it is now much easier to prepare consistently terrific steaks. There are still nuances, to be sure. Each cut of meat, from rib eye to filet and flat iron to flank, differs in its proportions and distribution of fat and muscle fibers, and these factors affect the tenderness, juiciness, and ideal cooking temperature of the meat. But steaks cooked sous vide lose just 3%–5% of their moisture to evaporation—about a tenth as much as is lost during conventional grilling. So in exchange for a somewhat longer cooking process, you reap big dividends in juiciness and consistency.

We ran tests on a range of cooking and finishing strategies, and the following pages cover the best approaches for preparing an evenly cooked, juicy steak having a seared crust.

THE SCIENCE OF AGING MEAT

Dry-aged beef is prized for good reason. It has a pleasantly nutty aroma, with mild cheesy notes, caused by the oxidation of fat and the concentration of sugar and savory protein molecules. The meat becomes more tender as enzymes dismantle the muscle fibers into fragmented proteins that retain more of the natural juices during cooking.

But dry-aging is expensive. It requires both time and storage facilities that can control temperature and humidity. It removes moisture: the volume of the meat visibly shrinks. You have to trim away and discard the outer layer, which has essentially rotted. That leaves you with a pricey, if delicious, cut of meat.

We can't easily replicate the aging process, but we have discovered one shortcut. Brush on Asian fish sauce (3 g of fish sauce for every 100 g of steak), vacuum seal the steak, and then refrigerate it for three days. This both tenderizes the meat and creates the deeper umami flavor that is characteristic of aged meat but with much less effort and waste.

HIGHLIGHTS

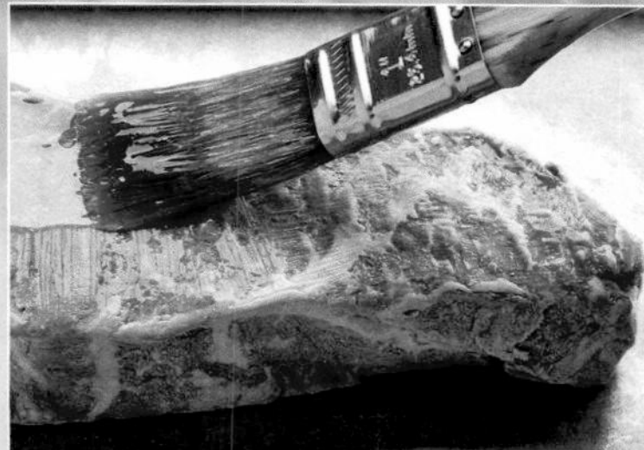

Pressure-rendered fat imparts a **grilled flavor without any of the flame or the fuss.** Make a jar of the fat to have on hand, and panfry your beef in it. It's like liquid grilled steak.

see page 196

Partially freeze your steak before grilling or presearing it to prevent the high temperatures of the grill or griddle from penetrating the surface and overcooking the interior.

see page 196

Serve awesome steak at your next tailgating party or picnic. Just cook the steak sous vide in a cooler of warm water, and then use a blowtorch to brown it just before serving.

see page 198

Creamed spinach is a steakhouse classic. The secret to the success of our recipe is Wondra, a modified flour that soaks up liquid. This addition, plus a finishing dose of cream and cheese, yields **creamed spinach that is unctuous and intensely flavorful.**

see page 199

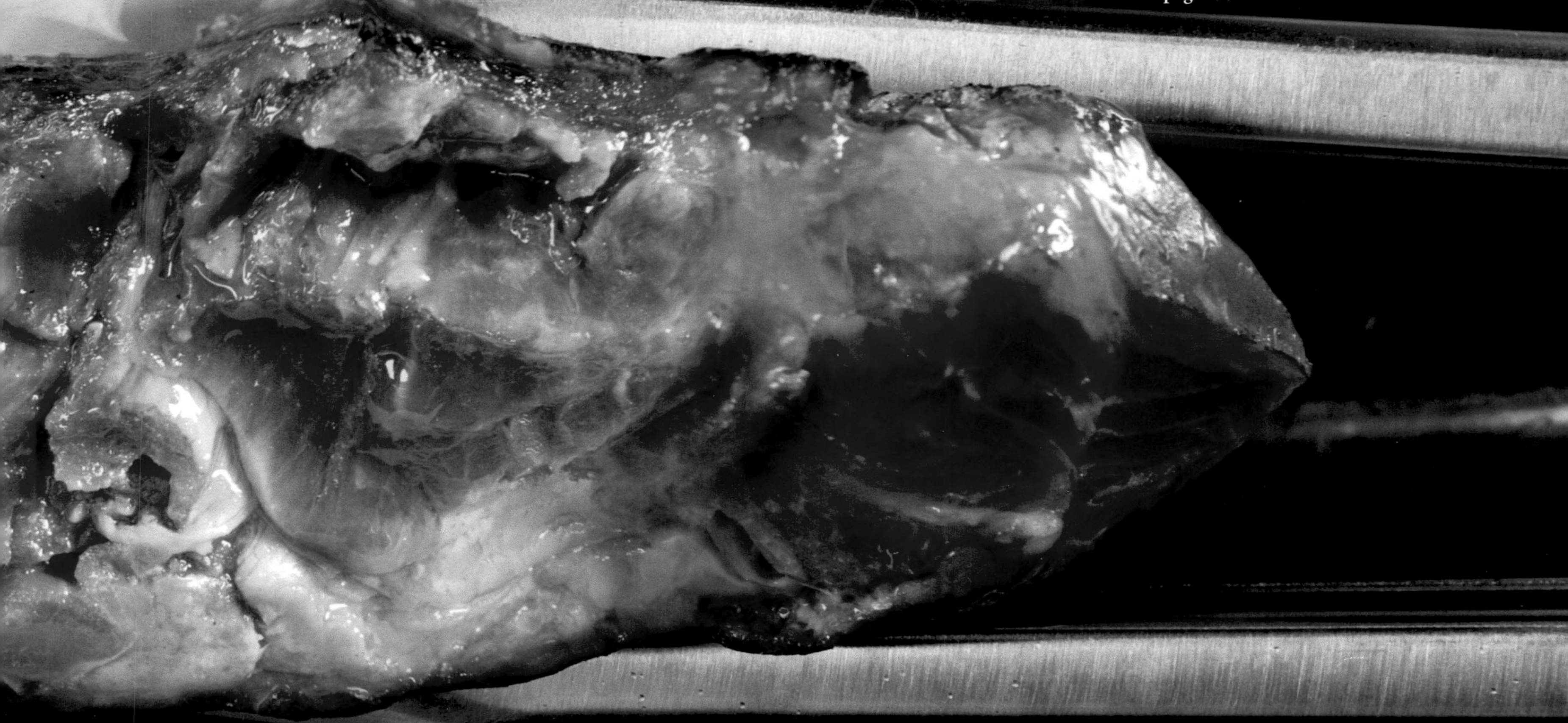

FURTHER READING IN *MODERNIST CUISINE*

Steak is not a "heart attack on a plate." What's in a fat: see page 1·233
How muscle works: see pages 3·6–19
From raw to cooked, how meat transforms with heat: see pages 3·72–79
Why cooking spinach makes it more nutritious, as well as tastier: see page 3·267

CUTS OF STEAK

"Butchering" connotes a certain roughness, an image of chopping with wild abandon. But butchers actually often work with the precision of surgeons—and with a comparable knowledge of anatomy—as they break down primal cuts into portions convenient for cooking and eating. Cuts of meat are divided broadly into the tender cuts, which are best for quick grilling, broiling, frying, or oven-roasting; and the tough cuts, which require lengthy braising, stewing, or pot-roasting. The most tender portions are also the most expensive. But cheaper tough cuts often have more flavor. When cooked gently for a long time or sliced thinly against the grain, a tough cut of meat can become as tender as a filet mignon.

TENDER CUTS

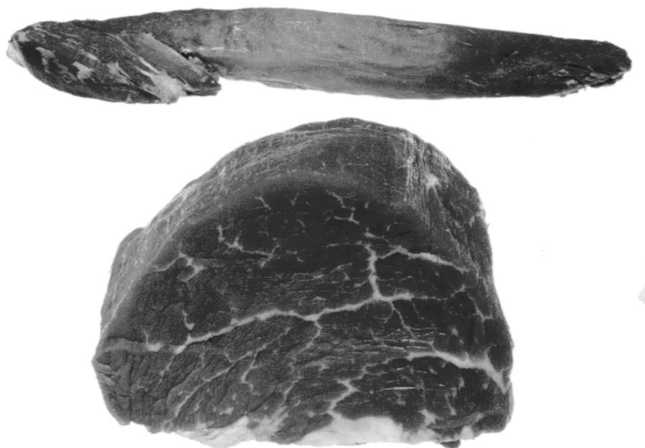

Filet or Tenderloin

The most tender and most expensive per pound, filet is a leaner cut of uniform texture and fat marbling. It is best cooked rare to medium rare. Some beef lovers find the flavor too mild.

Also known as: whole filet, filet mignon roast, tenderloin tip roast, Chateaubriand

New York Strip

The strip provides a good balance of tenderness and flavor. We prefer to trim the layer of fat and silverskin tendon that runs along one side.

Also known as: strip steak, top loin, strip loin, Kansas City steak, ambassador steak, boneless club steak, hotel-style steak, veiny steak

Rib Eye

The steak version of a rib roast or "prime rib," the rib eye takes our prize for best flavor. Sinews do make this cut gristly near the bone, however, where the meat also takes on a denser texture. That portion is removed from boneless and Spencer rib eyes.

Also known as: Delmonico steak, beauty steak, market steak, Spencer steak, *entrecôte*

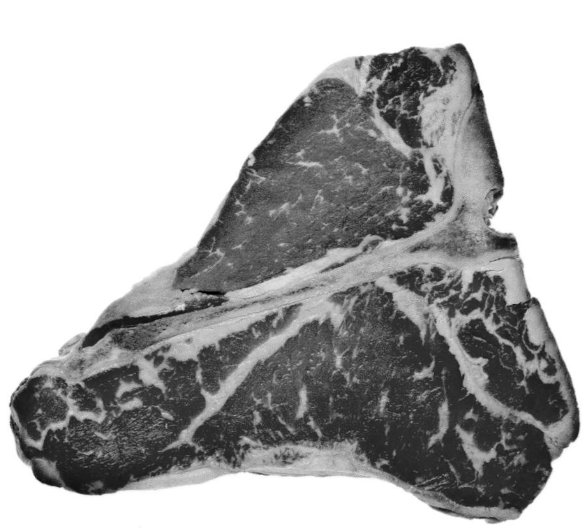

T-Bone or Porterhouse

The T-bone offers the best of both worlds: a New York strip plus a filet, connected by a bone. It is a larger steak that is often too big for a single portion. Cooking the meat on the bone keeps it juicier and more flavorful.

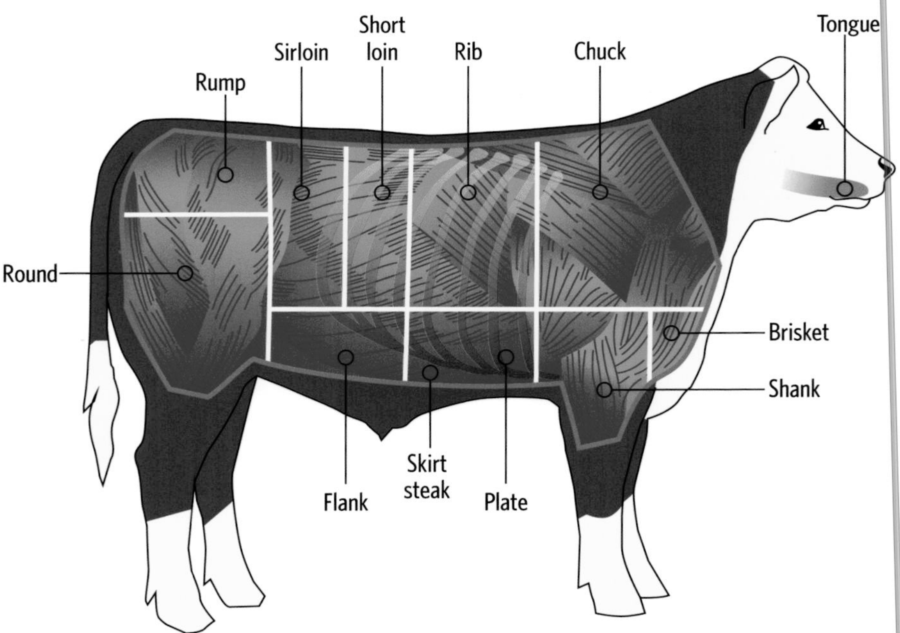

The various muscles of a cow play different roles in its daily life. The more active and load-bearing muscles, such as the shoulders and legs, are tougher and richer in connective tissue and collagen. They are more suitable for grinding, braising, or low-temperature cooking before searing. Less-active muscles, such as the loin, are much more tender and make excellent steaks. The muscles around the belly are more fibrous and much higher in fat because they support and insulate the animal's organs.

TOUGH CUTS

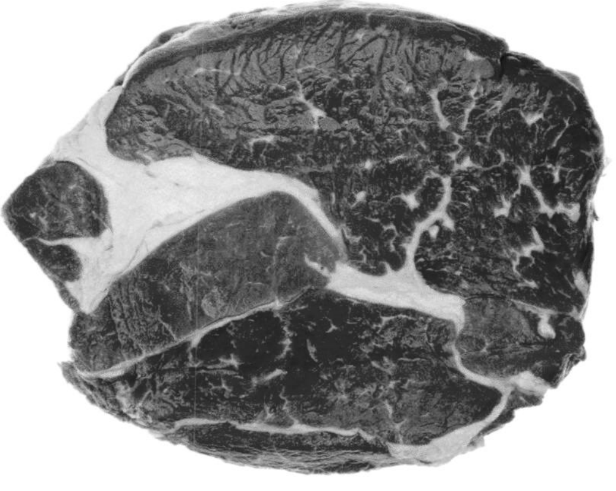

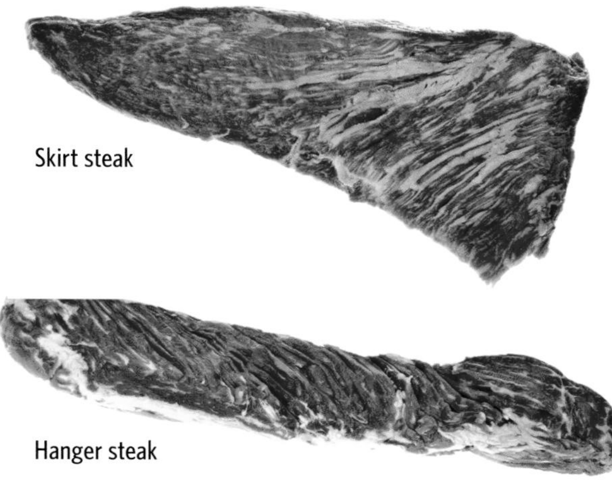

Chuck Top Blade

Chuck steaks are tough, inexpensive cuts usually used for braising, stew meat, or pot roasts, but they are nevertheless very flavorful. As the beef equivalent of pork shoulder, this cut includes parts of many different muscles as well as fat, sinew, and bone. Chuck is best cooked sous vide for 36–48 hours.
Also known as: boneless chuck slices, boneless chuck fillet steak, chuck eye steaks

Hanger and Skirt

The skirt and hanger steak have a pronounced gamey flavor and long grain that makes for a chewier texture. They are best either slow-cooked sous vide or grilled quickly, served rare, and sliced thinly against the grain.
Also known as: Philadelphia steak, butcher's steak, hanging tenderloin, hanging tender, *bavette*

Flat Iron

A chuck steak cut from the shoulder region—often into two thin steaks to remove a tough strap of sinew—the flat iron has an excellent flavor. It is most tender when cooked sous vide.
Also known as: top boneless chuck steak, shoulder tip blade steak, top blade steak, petite steak, lifter steak, book steak, butler steak, *paleron*

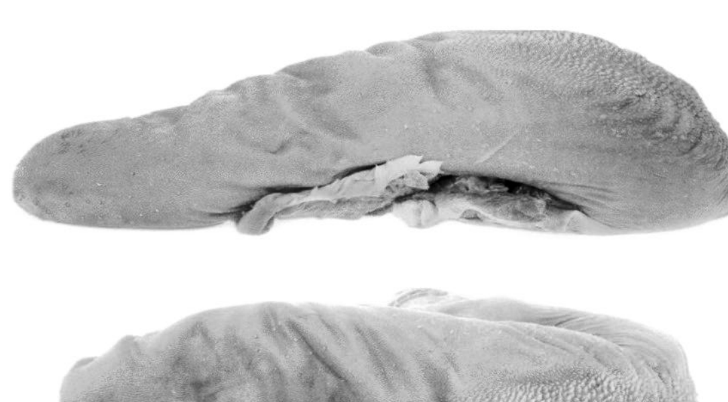

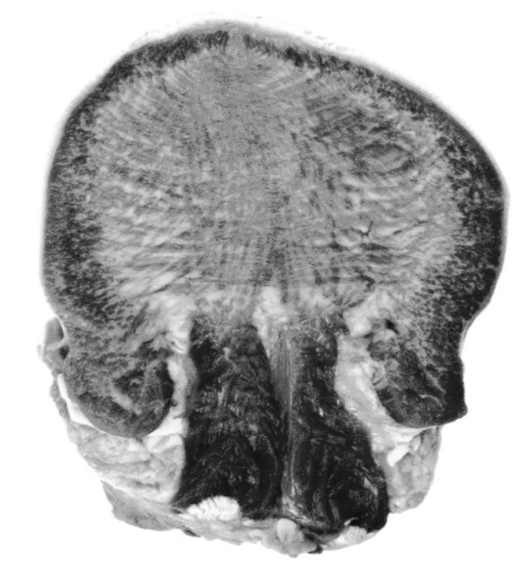

Name that steak

Confused about which cut of meat is which at the grocery store? Naming conventions for cuts of meat—even for the primal cuts shown in the diagram on the previous page—vary widely, not just from one country to another but within a country as well. We've listed some of the more common synonymous names here.

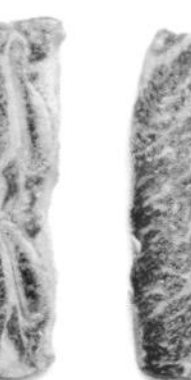

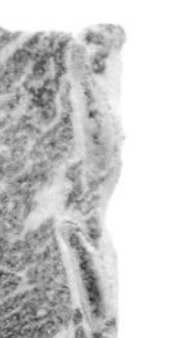

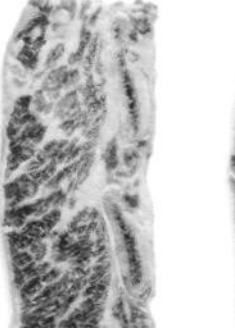

Flank

Lean and flavorful, the flank steak accepts marinades well thanks to its strong grain pattern, which also gives it a coarse texture. A thin cut, it is easy to overcook; when cooked conventionally, it's best served rare to medium rare and sliced thinly against the grain.
Also known as: London broil, *bavette de flanchet, bife de vacio*

Tongue

Although usually classified as an organ meat rather than a steak, beef tongue is actually a muscle and can pass as a tender, delicious steak if you cook it sous vide at 62 °C / 144 °F for 48 hours, long enough to turn the tough collagen into smooth gelatin. The texture can range from rubbery, when cooked too hot or too fast, to so tender that we call it "meat butter."

Short Rib

Our favorite overall cut of beef is the short rib, which is particularly delicious when cooked ultraslow for 24–72 hours (see page 229) to medium rare. You can either cut a thick, steak-like layer of meat off the ribs, or use them in braised dishes and stews.
Also known as: oven-busters, flanken ribs

GRADES OF MEAT

Americans have been using the U.S. Department of Agriculture's meat-grading system since the early years of the 20th century. Consisting of prime, choice, select, standard, utility, cutter, and canner grades, it was the first formalized system in the world for meat inspection and grading. It was spawned in large part by public outrage at the meat industry after the publication in 1906 of Upton Sinclair's exposé *The Jungle*, which described in gruesome detail the deplorable meat-processing practices of the time. That same year, Congress passed the Meat Inspection Act, which set up government oversight of slaughtering and packing operations. That law spurred much-needed reform. But the USDA grading system, as it stands today, still leaves a lot to be desired for judging meat quality. Although some countries have copied the American system, others, such as Japan and Australia, have since surpassed it.

United States

USDA inspectors determine the grade of meat by considering such factors as age and marbling. The emphasis on marbling is based on the presumption that fat content is a good indication of the quality of the meat—in particular, of its tenderness. Although marbling may be a convenient proxy for quality, it's not always reliable, especially for gauging tenderness or flavor. Cuts below the "select" grade are rarely seen intact by consumers; instead, these cuts are used by food manufacturers to make processed meat products.

Prime

Excellent quality and marbling; very tender and juicy; usually found only in fine restaurants and premium meat stores

Choice

Tender and flavorful, with three levels of marbling: small, modest, and moderate; available in supermarkets

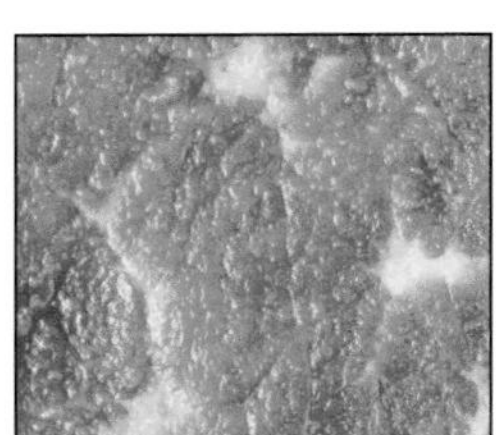

Select

Leaner and thus less tender; lowest grade sold at retail; formerly termed "good"

Japan

Japan's meat-grading system is more nuanced and demanding than that of the United States. Marbling, color, firmness, texture, fat quality, and yield are evaluated to grade meat on a scale of 1 to 5. It has also been adapted to include beef from Wagyu cattle, a specialized Japanese breed renowned for the intense marbling of its muscle tissue. USDA prime is equivalent to Japan's rating of 3 ("average quality"); the top grade in Japan is A5.

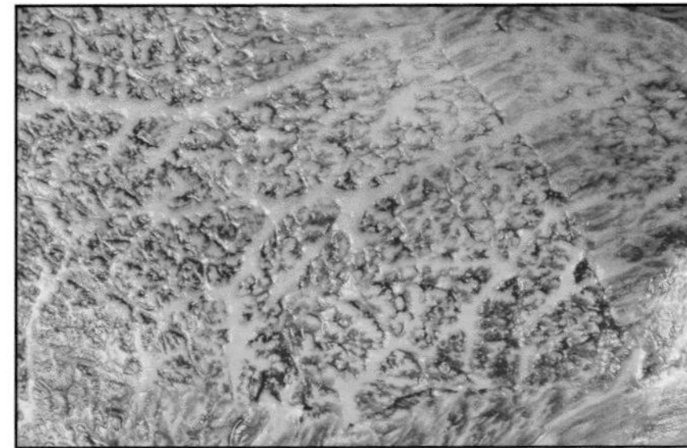

Japanese Wagyu beef

Europe

Europe, surprisingly, has no government-based system at all for grading meat. Large-scale purchasers and suppliers set their own proprietary standards. The economic incentive is for ranchers to concentrate on carcass yield rather than meat quality.

This isn't to say that there isn't excellent meat in Europe. On the contrary, small farmers and ranchers often work to stand out by producing superior meat. But such farmers and ranchers must either remain relatively small and sell directly to the public and to independent restaurants, or they must successfully build a recognizable premium brand.

Canada

The Canadian beef-grading system, with its focusing on marbling, parallels the U.S. government's system and assigns the labels Canada prime, AAA (equivalent to USDA choice), AA (equivalent to USDA select), and A. The A grades represent 90% of graded beef in Canada, while B–E grades are used for cattle that are too young or old. Grading is voluntary; producers must request and pay for the service provided by the Canadian Beef Grading Agency. Thus, lower-quality meat is more likely to be marked "no-roll" or "ungraded" when it is sold. (Inspection is not voluntary.)

Australia

The Australian beef-grading system, known as Eating Quality Assured, uses a sophisticated statistical model to predict the quality of each cut of meat from a given animal. Producers are rewarded for doing the things that ensure the highest quality: careful breed selection, attention to the animals' diet and welfare, and, perhaps most important, carefully managed slaughter—something that no other grading system recognizes. The system is not based on marbling; researchers found that marbling accounts for only 20% of the variation in meat tenderness. We believe that Australia's is the best and most innovative grading system on the planet.

PREMIUM VARIETIES OF BEEF

Wagyu, Kobe, and Kobe-Style

Wagyu is the name for the superlative meat from specific breeds of Japanese cattle. Although it is sometimes called "Kobe beef," after the port city from which much of this meat is shipped, Wagyu comes from high-quality beef cattle that are raised all over Japan.

Wagyu beef is prized worldwide for its rich flavor, tenderness, and juiciness. Its amazingly dense marbling exceeds that of any other beef, and is the product of genetics, diet, and a luxurious upbringing that includes long, slow walks; regular massages; and a diet that includes beer or sake.

The market prices for Wagyu beef are just as extravagant, often exceeding $100 per pound in Japan and even more overseas—if you can find it at all. Although some find the meat too fatty, it can be part of a memorable experience for a special occasion.

In general, the best cuts of Wagyu beef are the rib eye and the strip loin (or New York strip), which have the most extreme marbling. Wagyu tenderloin is also good, but the difference between it and non-Wagyu tenderloin is less pronounced. Waygu beef is often best served medium rare and, because of its richness, in small portions.

Some ranches in the U.S. and Australia sell "Kobe-style beef" that is raised domestically. Japan now prohibits export of live Wagyu cattle, but a few cows were exported before the ban. Although much darker and less marbled than true Japanese Wagyu, this beef can still make for excellent eating.

Angus

Angus cattle originated in the counties of Aberdeen and Angus in Scotland in the mid-19th century. The breed was developed largely by Hugh Watson from hornless cattle that traditionally flourished in the area. Watson's selective breeding created a variety of cattle that became famous for both the quantity and quality of its meat.

Most Angus cattle are black, but some purebred Angus have red hides.

Today, one can buy "Certified Angus Beef" in the United States, but it is mostly an empty marketing slogan. Animals can qualify for "Certified Angus" status by having 51% black hides and meeting some size, marbling, and age tests. Purebred Angus that happen to be red aren't eligible, and some cattle that are genetically not Angus but happen to be black are. The labeling would be more accurate if it read "Certified Half-Black Cattle Beef"—but that wouldn't sell as well.

Feed

Butchers ask premium prices for beef based not only on the breed of the cow or where it was raised but also on what kind of food it ate—particularly when it was in the "finishing" stage shortly before slaughter. But the choices are not as clear as the marketing suggests.

The norm is to finish cattle on a diet of corn, soybeans, barley, alfalfa, and/or other grains. Each has its advocates. Corn contains a good balance of protein and sugars, whereas soybeans contribute fat as well as protein. Alfalfa, a legume distantly related to soybeans, is relatively high in protein and easier to transport (in the form of pellets) than loose hay is.

Some ranches tout their "grass-fed" beef. It is generally true that an all-grass diet makes for more flavorful beef. But the quality of the flavor depends on the quality of the grass. Cattle grazing on poor-quality pasture or bitter grass can make for bad beef—meat that is inferior to even cheap, grain-fed beef. On the other hand, cattle fed on excellent grass can produce amazing meat. Unfortunately, there's no way to tell, just by looking at a label, exactly what went into the animal before it appeared on the butcher's counter.

COOKING STEAK

The secret to making consistently great steak is to cook it in two steps: first the interior, and then the exterior. Traditional techniques try to do both at once, but that requires near-perfect timing. A better approach is to cook the interior slowly at a low temperature—sous vide if you can, although a low-temperature oven or a covered grill with coals shoved to one side (to mimic a low-temperature oven) works nicely, too. Use high heat to sear the exterior and produce the browning Maillard reactions that give steak its attractive look and terrific taste. All of the options we recommend for preparing, cooking, and finishing steak are listed below. As the diagram at right shows, some finishing techniques can be done either before or after cooking. Choose the options that best fit the results you want and the time and equipment you have available.

Strategies for Preparing and Cooking Steak

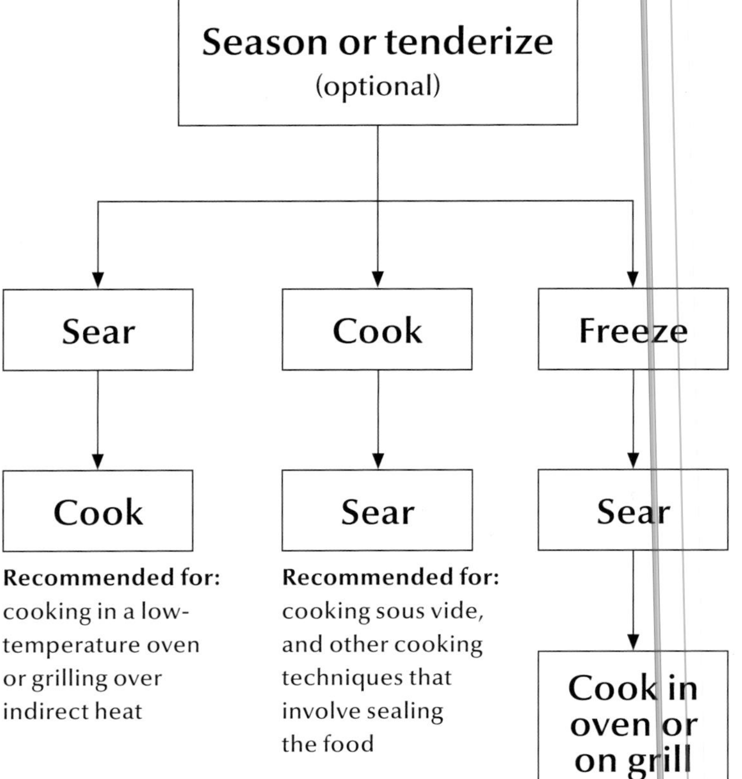

Sous Vide Steak, see page 194

Best Bets for Cooking Tender Meat Sous Vide

To cook steak sous vide, follow the steps on page 194. For more on cooking to a target core temperature and other sous vide techniques, see chapter 3. For suggested times and temperatures for cooking tough cuts sous vide, see the table on page 228. Flank steak can be treated as either a tender or tough cut.

	Target core temperature									
	Rare		Medium rare		Pink		Medium			
Ingredient	(°C)	(°F)	(°C)	(°F)	(°C)	(°F)	(°C)	(°F)	Note	See page
beef, filet	50	122	53	127	56	133	62	144		
beef, flank	54	129	56	133	59	138	62	144	cut thinly against the grain for maximum tenderness, or use a kalbi marinade	134
beef, rib eye	54	129	56	133	58	136	60	140	to tenderize, hold at 56 °C / 133 °F for 3 hours	
beef, strip steak	52	126	55	133	57	135	62	144	dry-aged is ideal; see page 186 for a trick that mimics aging	196
lamb loin, rack	54	129	57	135	59	138	62	144	coat with olive oil to prevent a strong lamb flavor from developing	
pork loin chop	n/a		58	136	60	140	62	144	brine before cooking	202
pork tenderloin	n/a		56	133	59	138	61	142		

(temperatures in red are those that we prefer)

Preparation Before Cooking and Searing

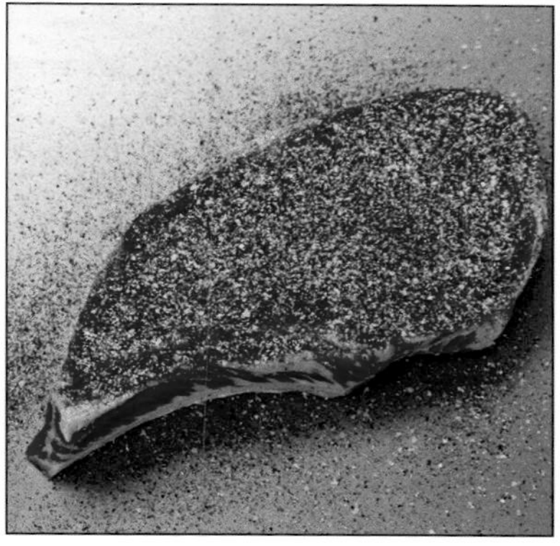

Cure, Marinade, or Spice Rub

These pretreatments add flavor to the meat and can tenderize it as well, if applied well in advance of cooking. Spice rubs and marinades can also be used to season meats after they are cooked or seared.

Freeze

One way to prevent overcooking the interior is to freeze just the outer layer of the meat first. You can then sear it, which thaws the frozen layer, and finally cook it at low temperature until the interior is done.

Cooking Methods

Sous Vide in a Water Bath

A digitally controlled water bath is the most precise instrument for cooking sous vide (see page 63). It is also the only method that lets you cook cheaper but flavorful cuts of meat as you would steak (see page 228).

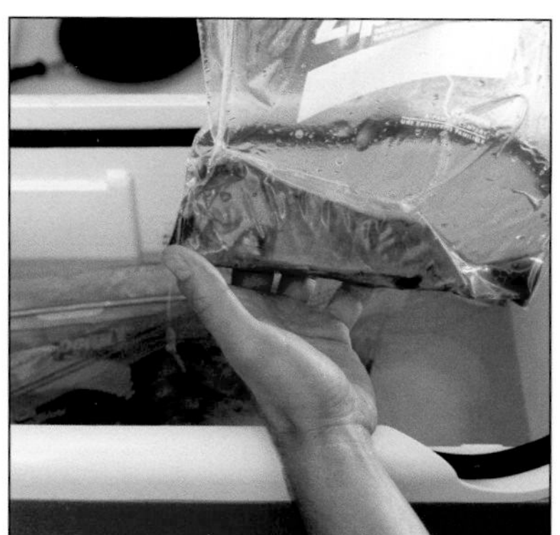

Sous Vide in a Cooler

You can improvise a water bath out of an ice chest. It's the perfect way to cook steak for an outdoor barbecue, tailgate party, or camping trip (see page 198). A large cooler can hold hot water to within a few degrees of a set temperature for up to 5 hours.

Low-Temperature Oven

A conventional oven, when set to its lowest temperature, can gently cook the interior of a steak much like a combi oven would—especially if you freeze the outside layer of the steak first (see page 196).

Grill with Banked Coals

Grilling is probably the most difficult way to cook steak perfectly because your timing must be perfect. But we have devised an indirect grilling technique that greatly improves your chances of success (see page 200).

Searing Strategies

Sear with a Blowtorch

Believe it or not, a blowtorch is the fastest way to sear a steak (see page 14). We recommend using a blowtorch that burns MAPP or propylene gas rather than propane because it produces a hotter flame and leaves no odor residue.

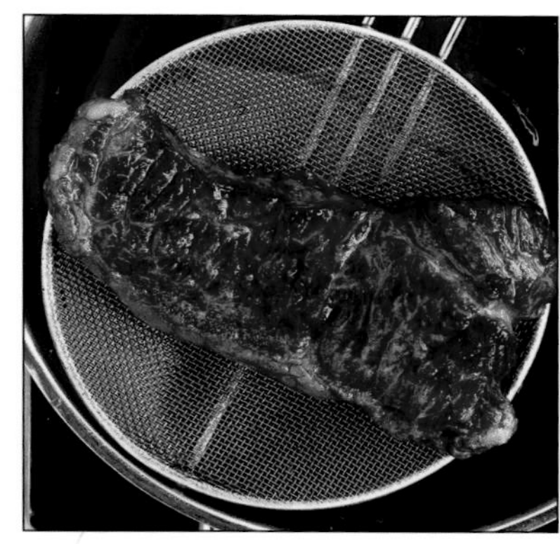

Deep-Fry

Oil conducts heat with amazing efficiency. You can exploit that property to brown the outside of a steak beautifully without overcooking the interior: simply deep-fry the cooked steak very briefly in hot oil.

Sear in a Pan

Perhaps the most familiar way to get a nice seared crust on your steak is to sear it in pan (see page 196). The pan must be very hot to avoid overcooking the interior. A pan or griddle made of heavy cast iron works best.

Sear on a Grill or Broiler

Grills and broilers are better for searing steak than for cooking it all the way through. If you know what you're doing, you can use a hair dryer to superheat the coals in a grill (see page 47).

SOUS VIDE STEAK

YIELD:	*four servings (1 kg / 2 steaks)*
TIME ESTIMATE:	*1 hour overall, including 50 minutes unattended*
STORAGE NOTES:	*serve immediately*
LEVEL OF DIFFICULTY:	*moderate*
SPECIAL REQUIREMENTS:	*sous vide setup, blowtorch or deep-frying setup*

Cook steaks sous vide to perfection, and then quickly sear the outside to a crisp, savory brown. Our two favorite searing methods are deep-frying in very hot oil and searing with a blowtorch. Alternatively, sear the steaks for 30 seconds per side in a large, oiled skillet over very high heat. The temperatures we give here cook strip steaks just the way we like them; see the table on page 192 for recommended cooking temperatures for other kinds of tender steaks or chops.

INGREDIENT	WEIGHT	VOLUME	SCALING	PROCEDURE
Beef strip steaks, at least 2.5 cm / 1 in thick	1 kg / 2.2 lb	2 large	100%	① Preheat a water bath to 55 °C / 131 °F. ② Place each steak in a separate zip-top bag with a small amount of oil. Remove as much air as possible from the bags, and seal them.
Neutral-tasting oil	as needed			③ Cook sous vide to a core temperature of 54 °C / 129 °F, about 50 minutes.
Neutral frying oil see page xxii	as needed			④ Preheat to 225 °C / 437 °F in a large, deep pot no more than half full. ⑤ Remove the cooked steaks from the bags, and pat them dry. ⑥ Deep-fry the steaks until they turn dark brown and crispy, about 30 seconds, and then drain them on a wire rack.
Unsalted butter, melted (optional)	as needed			⑦ Brush over the steaks.
Flaky salt (Maldon brand)	to taste			⑧ Season generously. Slice and serve immediately.

Safety tips for deep-frying: see page 26
Safety tips for blowtorching: see page 15

Creamed Spinach (see page 199) and Spinach Butter (see variation on page 121) make wonderful accompaniments to steak.

1 Preheat a water bath to 55 °C / 131 °F.

2 Place each steak in a separate zip-top bag with just enough oil to coat the meat. Remove as much air as possible, and seal.

3 Cook sous vide to a core temperature of 54 °C / 129 °F for medium rare, about 50 minutes. Cooking time will vary with the thickness of the meat and its starting temperature; it's best to monitor the internal temperature by using a probe. A steak that is 5 cm / 2 in thick may take more than 3 hours to reach the target temperature, for example. If you prefer meat cooked more fully, use the table on page 192 to select the desired core temperature, and set your water bath temperature 1 °C / 2 °F above that.

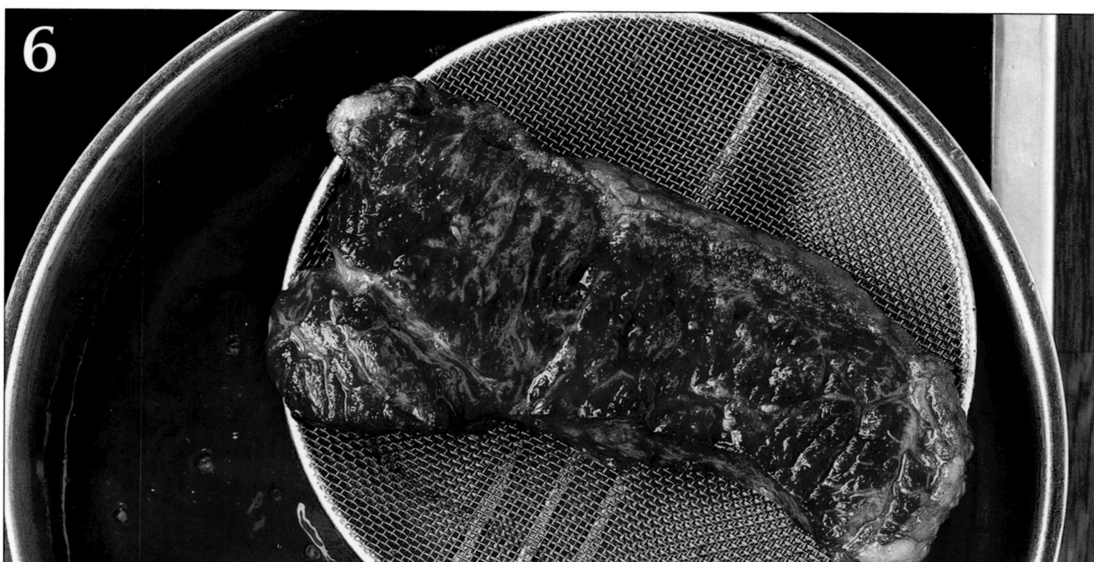

4 Preheat the frying oil to 225 °C / 437 °F in a large, deep pot no more than half full.

5 Remove the cooked steaks from the bags, and pat them dry.

6 Deep-fry the steaks until they turn dark brown and crispy, about 30 seconds, and then drain them on a wire rack.

7 Brush the steaks with melted butter.

8 Season generously with salt to taste. Slice and serve immediately.

LOW-TEMP OVEN STEAK

YIELD:	*four servings (1 kg / 2 steaks)*
TIME ESTIMATE:	*1½ hours overall, including 10 minutes of preparation and 80 minutes unattended*
STORAGE NOTES:	*serve immediately*
LEVEL OF DIFFICULTY:	*easy*
SPECIAL REQUIREMENTS:	*digital thermometer with oven-safe probe*

Some professional chefs use water-vapor ovens to cook with greater precision at very low temperatures. Although home ovens don't yet offer such "set it and forget it" convenience, you can achieve similar results by using a warm conventional oven (even a good toaster oven), a digital probe thermometer, and frequent checking and adjustment to compensate for inevitable drifts in the oven temperature.

We highly recommend that you first freeze the outside of the steaks so that you can sear them without overcooking the interior. The preseared meat then cooks to perfection in the low-temperature oven. This technique takes some patience, but the result is worth it. If your oven cannot hold a low temperature, try a different improvised setup, such as the recipe on page 198 for cooking in a cooler.

INGREDIENT	WEIGHT	VOLUME	SCALING	PROCEDURE
Beef strip steaks, at least 2.5 cm / 1 in thick	1 kg / 2.2 lb	2 large	100%	① Place the steaks on a baking sheet, and freeze them for 30 minutes. ② Preheat the oven to **70** °C / **160** °F or its lowest temperature setting.
Neutral frying oil or pressure-rendered beef fat see pages xxii or 123	25 g	25 mL / 2 Tbsp	2.5%	③ Brush the fat on the partially frozen steaks. ④ Heat a dry skillet over high heat, and sear the steaks until dark brown, about 60 seconds on each side. ⑤ Transfer the seared steaks to a baking sheet. Insert the oven-safe probe of a digital thermometer into the thickest part of one steak. ⑥ Cook in the oven to a core temperature of **55** °C / **133** °F, about 50 minutes.
Unsalted butter, melted (optional)	as needed			⑦ Brush over the steaks.
Flaky salt (Maldon brand)	to taste			⑧ Season generously. Slice and serve immediately.

1 Place the steaks on a baking sheet, and set in the freezer for 30 minutes to freeze the exterior. The interior of the meat should remain unfrozen.

2 Preheat the oven to **70** °C / **160** °F or its lowest temperature setting. If you have a water-vapor oven or home combi oven, set it to **1** °C / **2** °F higher than the desired final core temperature of the steaks (see the table on page 192 for suggested core temperatures).

3 Brush the fat on the partially frozen steaks.

4 Heat a dry skillet over high heat, and sear the steaks until they turn dark brown, about 60 seconds on each side. Press down on the steaks to ensure even browning. You may want to sear the fat as well by holding the steak on its side.

5 Transfer the seared steaks to a rack or a baking sheet. Insert the oven-safe probe of a digital thermometer into the thickest part of one steak.

6 Place the steaks in the oven, and cook them to a core temperature of 55 °C / 133 °F for medium-rare strip steaks, or to another temperature selected from the table on page 192. The cooking time will vary greatly depending on the thickness of the meat; allow about 50 minutes for strip steaks 2.5 cm / 1 in thick. The core temperature rises slowly at first but increases more quickly as time passes. Once the temperature is within about 10 °C / 18 °F of the target temperature, check the steaks every minute or so to avoid overcooking. The core temperature will continue to rise a few degrees after the steaks come out of the oven.

7 Brush the steaks with melted butter.

8 Season the steaks generously with salt to taste. Slice the meat, and serve it immediately.

VARIATION: **Frozen Steak**
This recipe works with a fully frozen steak as well. Preheat a pan with neutral frying oil to its smoke point. Add the steak, and sear on one side until it turns dark brown. Searing one side is usually sufficient to develop the desired appearance and flavor. But you can also flip the steak, and sear the other side. Then continue with step 5. At step 6, add 20–25 minutes to the cooking time.

SOUS VIDE STEAK IN A COOLER

YIELD:	*four servings (1 kg / 2 steaks)*
TIME ESTIMATE:	*1 hour overall, including 50 minutes unattended*
STORAGE NOTES:	*serve immediately*
LEVEL OF DIFFICULTY:	*easy*
SPECIAL REQUIREMENTS:	*cooler, blowtorch or grill*

You can make perfectly cooked steak even when tailgating or at a picnic by simply using your cooler as an improvised water bath. Pour hot water into the cooler, drop in the sealed steaks, and head to the game or the beach. That's it! You need about 8 quarts of water per steak to maintain the water temperature, which will drop when you add the meat. Start with room-temperature steaks and water that is 8 °C / 14 °F hotter than the target core temperature. Eat the steak within 4 hours of putting it in the water; steak held longer than that is not safe to eat. Fish and tender cuts of chicken also can be cooked this way; see the tables on pages 281 and 245 for temperatures.

INGREDIENT	WEIGHT	VOLUME	SCALING	PROCEDURE
Beef strip steaks, at least 2.5 cm / 1 in thick	1 kg / 2.2 lb	2 large	100%	① Bring the steaks and a large cooler to room temperature.
				② Place each steak in a separate zip-top bag with 10 g / 15 mL / 1 Tbsp of oil, and seal by using the water-displacement method (see page 58).
Neutral-tasting oil	20 g	25 mL / 1½ Tbsp	2%	③ Fill the cooler with **60 °C / 140 °F** water, drop in the bags, and close the lid. Make sure there is plenty of space between the steaks.
				④ Cook sous vide to a core temperature of **52 °C / 126 °F**, about 50 minutes, for medium-rare steaks.
				⑤ Transfer the cooked steaks to a rack or a baking sheet.
				⑥ Sear on all sides by using a blowtorch or on a very hot grill.
Unsalted butter, melted (optional)	as needed			⑦ Brush over the steaks.
Flaky salt (Maldon brand)	to taste			⑧ Season generously. Slice, and serve immediately.

Safety tips for blowtorching: see page 15

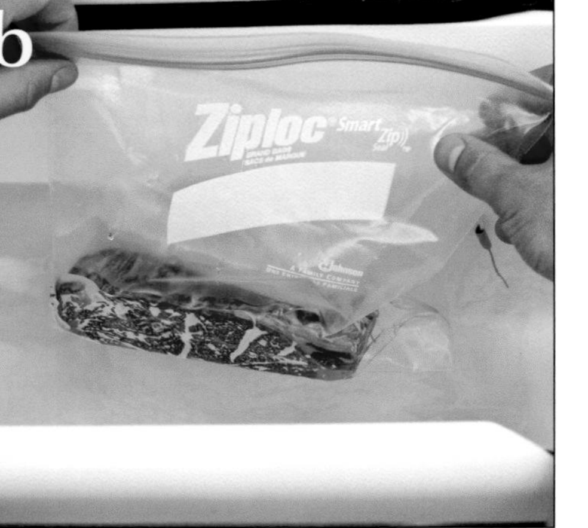

CREAMED SPINACH

YIELD:	*four to eight servings (525 g / 2⅓ cups)*
TIME ESTIMATE:	*30 minutes overall*
STORAGE NOTES:	*serve immediately*
LEVEL OF DIFFICULTY:	*easy*
SPECIAL REQUIREMENTS:	*Wondra, xanthan gum, Comté cheese, Pressure-Cooked Garlic Confit (optional, see page 126)*

Creamed spinach is a classic pairing for grilled steak, and it deserves more attention than the typical side dish does. We add salt at the start of the recipe to help draw excess moisture from the greens. Xanthan gum absorbs residual moisture, thickening the sauce without dulling the flavor. A hint of lemon zest and the savory, nutty Comté cheese make this dish bold enough to stand alone.

INGREDIENT	WEIGHT	VOLUME	SCALING	PROCEDURE
Baby spinach, washed	600 g	10 cups	100%	① Working in batches, sauté over medium-high heat until the spinach is wilted, about 1 minute. Alternatively, steam it until just tender.
Neutral-tasting oil	20 g	25 mL / 1½ Tbsp	3%	② Cool the spinach completely.
Salt	2 g	½ tsp	0.3%	③ Squeeze it in cheesecloth or in the bottom of a sieve to remove excess liquid. ④ Chop it finely.
Pressure-Cooked Garlic Confit, mashed (or Dijon mustard) see page 126	24 g	1½ Tbsp	4%	⑤ Sauté until the shallots become translucent, about 2 minutes. ⑥ Stir in the chopped spinach, and cook for 3 minutes.
Shallots, minced	20 g	2½ Tbsp	3%	
Neutral-tasting oil	20 g	25 mL / 1½ Tbsp	3%	
Mascarpone	100 g	½ cup	17%	⑦ Stir into the mixture until melted, and then remove it from the heat.
Whole milk, cold	80 g	80 mL / ⅓ cup	13%	⑧ Whisk together in a bowl.
Xanthan gum	0.4 g		0.07%	⑨ Mix the milk mixture into the prepared spinach, and bring it to a simmer.
Comté cheese, finely grated	40 g	⅝ cup	7%	⑩ Fold into the warm, creamed spinach just before serving.
Lemon zest, finely grated	0.5 g	½ tsp	0.08%	
Black pepper, ground	to taste			⑪ Season the spinach, and serve it warm.
Salt	to taste			

3

4

9

If xanthan gum isn't available, you can substitute 2 g / ½ tsp of Ultra-Sperse 3 or Wondra for the xanthan gum in step 8. Ultra-Sperse 3 is made from precooked tapioca and has better flavor release than products based on wheat or cornstarch.

VARIATION: **South Indian Watercress**
In steps 1–4, use watercress in place of some or all of the spinach. At step 5, sauté 40 g / 4 Tbsp of minced shallots and 5 g / 2½ tsp of black mustard seed in 25 g / 25 mL / 2 Tbsp of mustard oil. Omit steps 7–10. Instead, stir 30 g / 2½ Tbsp each of coconut milk and coconut cream into the greens, remove the mixture from the heat, and continue with step 11. Garnish the dish with young coconut and finely sliced mint leaves.

GRILLED STEAK

YIELD:	*four servings (1 kg / 2 steaks)*
TIME ESTIMATE:	*2½ hours overall, including 1 hour of preparation and 1½ hours unattended*
STORAGE NOTES:	*serve immediately*
LEVEL OF DIFFICULTY:	*advanced (temperature control)*
SPECIAL REQUIREMENTS:	*charcoal grill*

Cooking steaks on the backyard barbecue is so festive and social that people tend to overlook the quality of the result. Try the Modernist technique described here to capture the aroma and appearance of a grilled steak with the succulent, even results of low-temperature cooking. The trick is to maintain a very low and even temperature on the grill. You can accomplish this by partially freezing the steaks before you give them an initial sear on a hot grill. Then let them thaw off the grill while the coals smolder. The final cooking is done slowly over indirect heat and on a cool, buffering layer of sliced onions (or another root vegetable). The onions won't be fully cooked at this point, but they will have some of the grilled-beef flavor, so you can quickly sear or sauté them, and then serve them as a side dish.

INGREDIENT	WEIGHT	VOLUME	SCALING	PROCEDURE
Beef strip steaks at least 2.5 cm / 1 in thick	1 kg / 2.2 lb	2 large	100%	① Place the steaks on a baking sheet, and freeze for 40 minutes. ② While the steaks freeze, build a large fire in a charcoal grill. When the coals are gray and ashy, bank them to one side of the grill. ③ Place a clean rack over the coals to preheat for at least 10 minutes.
Neutral frying oil see page xxii	as needed			④ Brush generously onto all sides of the partially frozen steaks. ⑤ Grill the steaks over very hot coals until marked and well seared, about 1 minute per side. ⑥ Transfer to a rack placed on a baking sheet, and leave at room temperature until completely thawed, about 1 hour.
Sweet onions	1.2 kg	3–4 medium	120%	⑦ Cut the onions into slices 1 cm / ⅜ in thick. ⑧ Adjust the airflow of the grill so that the coals maintain a low, even smolder. Place a steel pan full of ice opposite the banked coals. ⑨ Arrange a bed of onion slices on the grill rack, above the ice. Place the steaks on the onion slices. ⑩ Cook the steaks covered, flipping and rotating them every 5 minutes, until they reach an internal temperature of **50 °C / 122 °F**, 30–40 minutes. ⑪ Remove the steaks from the grill, and let them rest for 5 minutes.
Flaky salt (Maldon brand)	to taste			⑫ Season the steaks generously. Slice the meat, and serve it immediately.

1 Place the steaks on a baking sheet, and freeze for 40 minutes. The goal is to freeze only the outer 1 cm / ⅜ in, so that the surface can be seared without cooking the interior.

2 While the steaks freeze, build a large fire in a charcoal grill. When most of the coals are completely covered with gray ash, bank them to one side of the grill. This creates a more intense heat source for searing the meat.

3 Place a clean rack over the coals to preheat for at least 10 minutes.

If you prefer a different degree of doneness, use the table on page 192 to select the appropriate target core temperature.

4 Brush all sides of the steaks generously with the oil.

5 Grill the steaks over very hot coals until they are marked and well seared, about 1 minute per side.

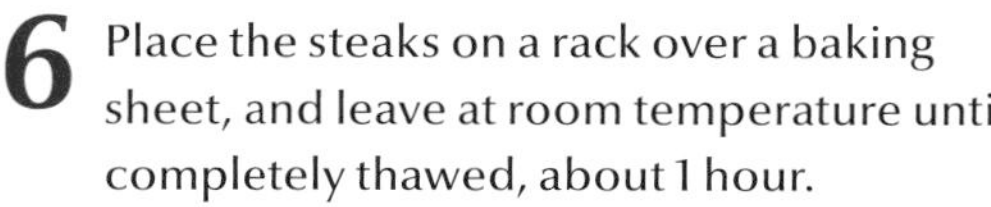

6 Place the steaks on a rack over a baking sheet, and leave at room temperature until completely thawed, about 1 hour.

7 Cut the onions into slices 1 cm / ⅜ in thick.

8 Adjust the airflow of the grill so that the coals maintain a low, even smolder while the steaks are thawing. You will need to add about three coals every 10 minutes to maintain an even temperature. Opening and closing the vent every time you add coals also helps remove the ash and keep the air flowing over the hot coals. Place a steel pan full of ice opposite the banked coals under the grilling surface. The slow melting and evaporation of the ice moderates the temperature for more even cooking.

9 Arrange the onion slices on the cool side of the rack, over the pan of ice. Place the steaks on the onion slices. The onions act as a buffer from the direct heat of the grill rack and the radiant heat of the coals. Use an oven thermometer or infrared thermometer to check the air temperature of the closed grill at the level of the steaks; it should be about 80 °C / 176 °F.

10 Cook the steaks covered. Flip and rotate them every 5 minutes, and remove them from the grill when they reach an internal temperature of 50 °C / 122 °F for medium rare, 30–40 minutes. The core temperature changes slowly at first, but then rises more quickly. When the core reaches 43 °C / 110 °F, check the steaks frequently to avoid overcooking them. The steaks will continue to cook after they are removed from the heat, and should reach a final core temperature of about 54 °C / 129 °F.

11 Remove the steaks from the grill. Let them rest for 5 minutes.

12 Season the steaks generously with salt to taste. Slice the meat, and serve it immediately.

GRILLED PORK CHOP

YIELD:	*four to eight servings (1 kg / four pork chops)*
TIME ESTIMATE:	*1 hour 30 minutes overall, including 1 hour unattended*
STORAGE NOTES:	*serve immediately*
LEVEL OF DIFFICULTY:	*moderate*
SPECIAL REQUIREMENTS:	*sous vide setup, charcoal grill, portable fan or hair dryer*
GOES WELL WITH:	*Grilled Applesauce (see page 124), Shiitake Marmalade (see page 151), Chinese Garlic Chili Condiment (see page 261)*

Poor grilled pork chops! People often feel obligated to cook them into dry pieces of leather for safety reasons—but, as we explained in *Modernist Cuisine*, this concern is outdated. Pork today is as safe as beef, and should be served done to juicy perfection and with a crisp crust—a result you can get every time by combining low-temperature cooking with high-temperature searing. In this recipe, we suggest using a hair dryer to fan the coals so that they become extremely hot just before you sear the meat. Be aware that some ash will blow off the coals at first, and the embers will then burn much faster than usual, so do not leave the grill unattended.

INGREDIENT	WEIGHT	VOLUME	SCALING	PROCEDURE
Pork chops, loin end, bone in, at least 2.5 cm / 1 in thick	1.8 kg / 4 lb	4 large	100%	① Preheat a water bath to 57 °C / 135 °F. ② Place each pork chop in a separate zip-top bag with 10 g / 15 mL / 1 Tbsp of oil. Use the water-displacement method (see page 58) to remove as much air as possible from the bag, and seal it.
Neutral frying oil see page xxii	40 g	45 mL / 3 Tbsp	2%	③ Cook sous vide to a core temperature of 56 °C / 133 °F, about 1 hour.
Rendered bacon fat or neutral frying oil see page 123	200 g	220 mL / 1 cup	11%	④ While the pork chops are cooking, build a large fire in a charcoal grill. ⑤ When the coals are gray and ashy, bank them to one side. ⑥ Place a clean rack over the coals to preheat for at least 10 minutes. ⑦ Warm the bacon fat gently until it is just melted. ⑧ Remove the pork chops from the bags, and pat them dry. ⑨ Brush the bacon fat generously over all sides of the pork chops. ⑩ Hold a hair dryer underneath the grill, with the grill vents open, and aim the airflow at the coals. ⑪ Sear the pork chops over the very hot coals until they are marked by the rack, 30–60 seconds. Flip the chops over, and sear the other sides. ⑫ Turn off the hair dryer, and allow the chops to rest for 3 minutes.
Salt	to taste			⑬ Cut the pork from the bone, and slice it if desired. Season the meat, and serve it hot.

You can turbocharge your grill for fast searing by opening the bottom vents and then holding a hair dryer below it. Aim the airstream through the coals, and watch them glow as the burning accelerates. For more grilling tips, see page 47.

Any of the methods listed in the table on page 192 for cooking steak work for pork chops as well.

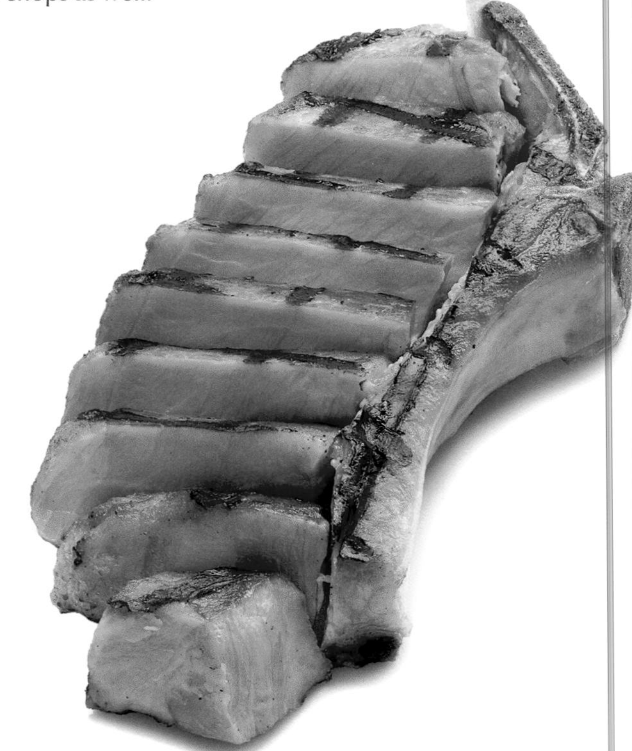

SOUS VIDE LAMB SKEWERS

YIELD:	*four servings (300 g)*
TIME ESTIMATE:	*1½ hours overall, including 30 minutes of preparation and 1 hour unattended*
STORAGE NOTES:	*serve immediately*
LEVEL OF DIFFICULTY:	*moderate*
SPECIAL REQUIREMENTS:	*sous vide setup (optional), 1 L whipping siphon, four cartridges of nitrous oxide, blowtorch, metal or bamboo skewers, sumac*

Pressure-marinating infuses flavor from a liquid into meat, and it can tenderize tough cuts in as little as 20 minutes. If you are in a hurry, you can cook these skewers straight from raw on a hot grill in 3–4 minutes. Although lamb loin, which we call for here, is the most flavorful and tender cut, lamb leg or top round can be used instead. Alternatively, try using beef, pork, chicken, or other meats (see page 192 for cooking temperatures and page 262 for other skewer recipes).

Sumac—a tart, red spice used in Native American and Middle Eastern cuisines—provides a distinctive flavor in this recipe; you can find it at Mediterranean markets.

INGREDIENT	WEIGHT	VOLUME	SCALING	PROCEDURE
Tomato juice	300 g	320 mL/1⅓ cups	100%	① Preheat a water bath to 58 °C/136 °F. ② Combine. ③ Pour into a 1 L siphon, and charge the siphon with two cartridges of nitrous oxide. Alternatively, marinate the meat, covered, for 6–12 hours, and then skip to step 10. ④ Shake the siphon well, and then leave it to infuse for 20 minutes. ⑤ Depressurize the siphon carefully by aiming the nozzle upward and slowly releasing the gas. ⑥ Strain, reserving the marinade. Discard the solids.
Red onion, thinly sliced	75 g	⅞ cup	25%	
Salt	21 g	2 Tbsp	7%	
Extra-virgin olive oil	9 g	10 mL/2 tsp	3%	
Garlic, crushed	6 g	2 cloves	2%	
Oregano sprigs	3 g	2–3 sprigs	1%	
Rosemary sprigs	3 g	1 large sprig	1%	
Lemon juice	3 g	3 mL/½ tsp	1%	
Sumac	0.8 g	¼ tsp	0.27%	
Fresh bay leaves	0.3 g	1–2 leaves	0.1%	
Lamb loin, cut into 2.5 cm/1 in cubes	300 g/0.7 lb		100%	⑦ Combine with the marinade in a 1 L siphon, and charge the siphon with two cartridges of nitrous oxide. ⑧ Shake well, and then refrigerate for 20 minutes to marinate. ⑨ Depressurize the siphon. ⑩ Remove the meat from the marinade, and place it in a zip-top bag. Use the water-displacement method to remove as much air as possible from the bag (see page 58), and seal it. ⑪ Cook the meat sous vide to a core temperature of 57 °C/135 °F, about 25 minutes.
Red pearl onions, peeled and cut in half	80 g	8–10 onions	27%	⑫ Cook in boiling water until just cooked through, about 3 minutes. Cool, and set aside. ⑬ Thread the lamb pieces and onion halves onto skewers. ⑭ Brown the meat by using a blowtorch, or sear it on a grill or in a very hot sauté pan for 15 seconds on each side. Serve the skewers hot.

Safety tips for blowtorching: see page 15

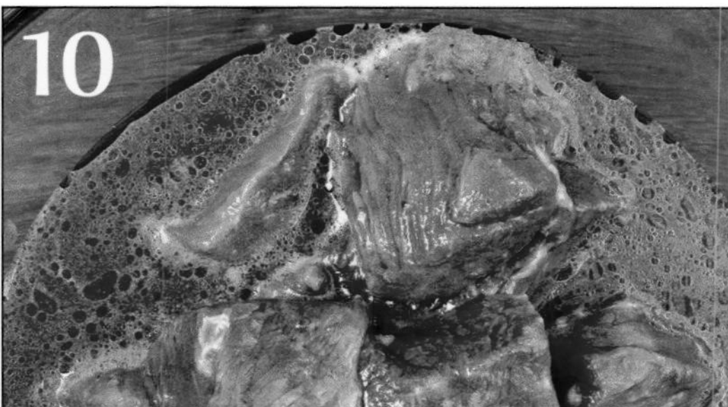

TO MAKE AHEAD

After step 13, seal the skewers in zip-top bags. When ready to serve, heat the skewers in a 58 °C/136 °F bath for 15 minutes. Continue with step 14.

CHEESEBURGER

Is there any American food more iconic than the cheeseburger? Although ground beef patties seem to have originated in Hamburg, Germany, most historians place the creation of the sandwich we know and love as the hamburger firmly in the United States. Louis' Lunch in New Haven, Connecticut, started serving ground beef between two slices of toast at the turn of the 20th century, and still does to this day. A café in Athens, Texas, reportedly started selling burgers as early as the 1880s.

Our cheeseburger stays fairly true to the original, but we've refined each of the elements. The bread is moist and dense; seeds add extra crunch and flavor. The cheese slice is silky. The ketchup is intense. If ketchup isn't your condiment of choice, try our homage to the Big Mac: MC Special Sauce.

As for the patty—the heart of any hamburger—three techniques can elevate what is too often a merely filling piece of meat to a truly extraordinary one. First, use top-quality meat and grind it well: our favorite is a blend of short rib and aged rib eye, mixed with a bit of hanger steak. Plenty of fat in this mix helps keep it tender and juicy. Second, cook the patty carefully so that as much of the interior as possible is done just the way you like it. Low-temperature cooking can't be beat here. Finally, give the meat a quick sear in hot oil to develop a beautiful, uniform crust.

Building a high-end cheeseburger like this one requires planning and coordination to finish the multiple elements simultaneously. It's good practice for making other complex gourmet dishes. But mostly it's just delicious.

THE SCIENCE OF SEASONING THE GROUND BEEF

Unless you like tough, rubbery burgers, you should season beef after you grind it and not long before you put the hamburger patties on the grill. Grinding the beef and forming it into patties releases proteins, particularly myosin, from the meat. These proteins coagulate into a gel when the meat is cooked; this is what holds the cooked patty together. If you add salt or other additives too early, they can accelerate the extraction of myosin and make the meat quite sticky. Certain recipes actually exploit this effect: see Modernist Meatloaf Sandwich on page 214, for example. But for burgers, we've found that it's best to add a little salt to the ground meat exactly one hour before cooking it.

Although many cooks add eggs, starches such as bread crumbs, or protein-laden liquids such as milk to the ground beef, these ingredients gel during cooking and act like edible glue. We believe that they detract from the taste and texture of a knockout burger.

HIGHLIGHTS

Grinding your own meat is easy with an inexpensive attachment for your stand mixer. Small, automated grinders are also available at department stores. You can get great results by mixing different cuts of meat into the grind.

see page 206

Air in the patty keeps the meat crumbly. So don't mash the patties too hard, and use a zip-top bag for cooking the meat sous vide rather than vacuum sealing it. Compression makes the beef denser and less juicy.

see page 208

Brush a little rendered beef fat onto the toast for an extra layer of rich flavor. Pressure-rendered fat (see page 123) is one of the most flavorful and versatile ingredients to keep on hand.

see page 210

The burger is so savory and bold that it's nice to pair it with an **ethereal, creamy milk shake.** Our fresh shake is very simple; it tastes like excellent, sweet milk.

see page 213

FURTHER READING IN *MODERNIST CUISINE*

Grinding meat and fat: see pages 3·228–233

Bernard Mense's strand-aligning trick for forming patties that seem to melt in your mouth: see pages 3·234–235

How to make the ultimate French fries: see pages 3·322–325

A wide range of options for constructed cheeses: see page 4·223

HOW TO Grind Meat Like a Pro

When grinding meat for burgers or sausages, you can achieve a much wider range of flavors and textures by blending two or three different cuts together. Process each kind of meat separately—in fact, it's also best to remove the fat from the meat, and grind it separately, too—and then gently mix the ground components together at the end. The hamburger patty recipe on page 208 calls for grinding through a medium plate to produce a texture somewhat finer than you can get by hand-chopping. For even finer grinds, such as those typically used for filler meats or emulsion-style sausages, pass the meat first through a coarse grinding plate, and then through progressively finer plates.

1 Trim off and discard the sinew, silverskin, and connective tissue. Separate any easily removed fat from the meat, and reserve it.

2 Cut the meat into 2.5 cm / 1 in cubes.

3 Chill the meat to near freezing (as low as -1 °C / 30 °F). Chill the fat to below freezing (as low as -10 °C / 14 °F).

4 Rinse the grinder with ice water.

5 Place a medium (4–6 mm / 3⁄16–1⁄4 in) or large (10 mm / 3⁄8 in) grinding plate in the grinder.

6 Grind in small batches. Check the temperature of the grinding plate with your finger—stop if it gets noticeably hot to the touch.

7 Chill the grinder between batches as necessary by rinsing it with ice water.

8 Replace the grinding plate with one that has a finer aperture, if needed, and repeat steps 4–7 until the food is fully ground.

9 Repeat steps 4–8 to grind the fat and any other kinds of meat that will go into the blend.

Best Bets for Hamburger Patties

Meat blend	Ingredients	(scaling)	Overall leanness	Cook to core temperature (°C)	(°F)
rare beef	filet mignon short-rib meat	100% 45%	80%	52	126
short rib	short-rib meat	100%	70%	54	129
MC favorite	short-rib meat aged rib eye hanger steak	100% 100% 22%	75%	54	129
steak-house blend	chuck sirloin flank	100% 50% 50%	75%	56	131

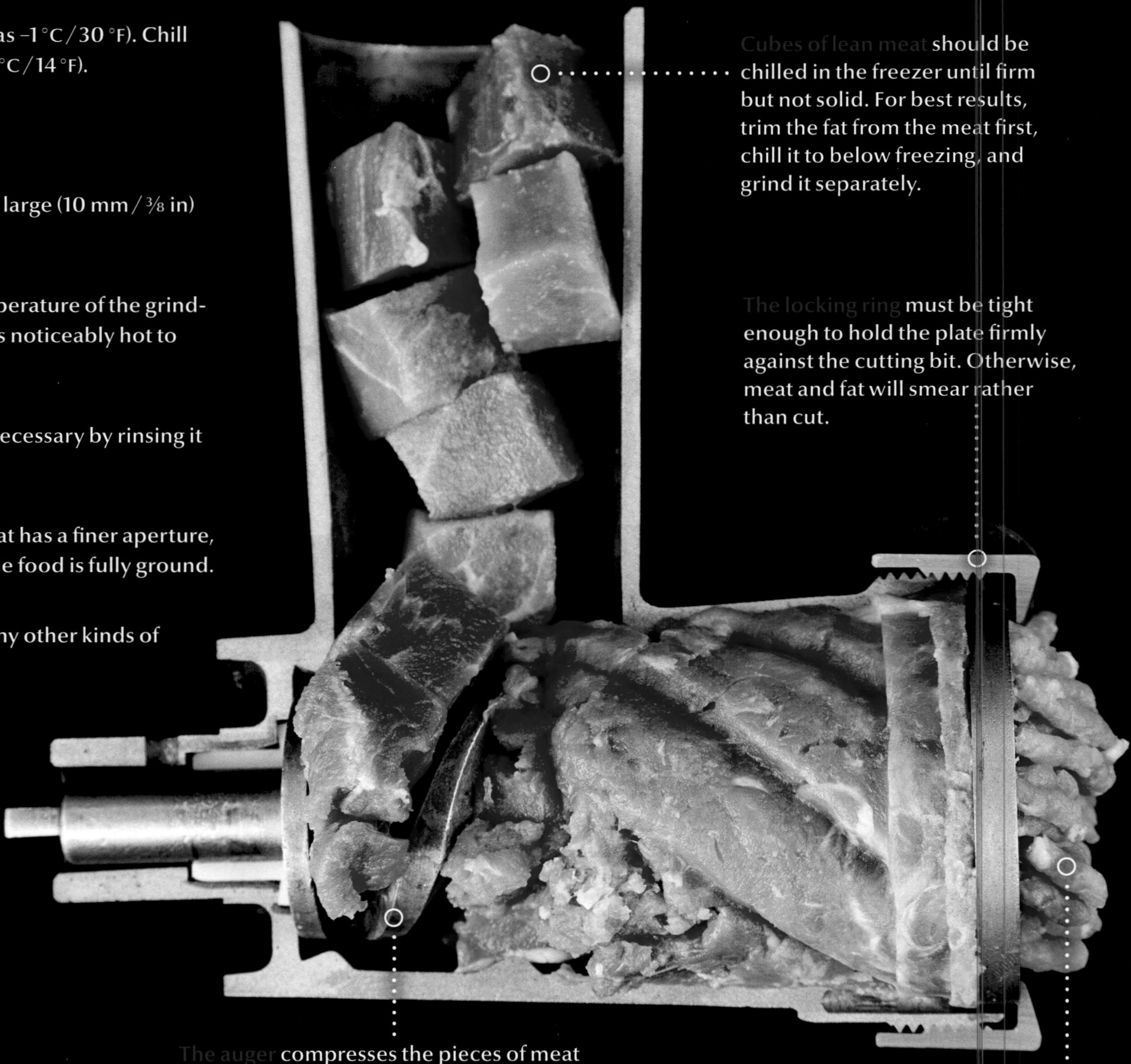

Cubes of lean meat should be chilled in the freezer until firm but not solid. For best results, trim the fat from the meat first, chill it to below freezing, and grind it separately.

The locking ring must be tight enough to hold the plate firmly against the cutting bit. Otherwise, meat and fat will smear rather than cut.

The auger compresses the pieces of meat and fat, heating them in the process. Chill the grinder head and meat between batches to ensure clean cuts.

Meat extruded from the holes in the plate can be ground more finely in subsequent passes. Always grind meat through a large or medium plate first.

HOW TO Form a Square Hamburger Patty

When the hamburger was first invented, it was a square, pressed patty on toasted white bread. The technique shown here re-creates that authentic form. You can, of course, make the patties round if you will be serving them on buns. Whatever the shape, the patty should be neither too dense nor too loose—just tight enough to hold its shape but friable enough to be pleasantly juicy as it crumbles in your mouth.

In a Loaf Pan or Baking Tray

1 Line a loaf pan or baking tray with plastic wrap.

2a

2b

2 Press the ground meat into the pan. Use a rubber spatula to pack the meat evenly. Take care not to mash the meat so much that the patties lose their tenderness. If using a baking tray (2a), pack the meat to a depth of 2.5 cm / 1 in. If using a loaf pan (2b), pack the meat as deep as the pan is wide.

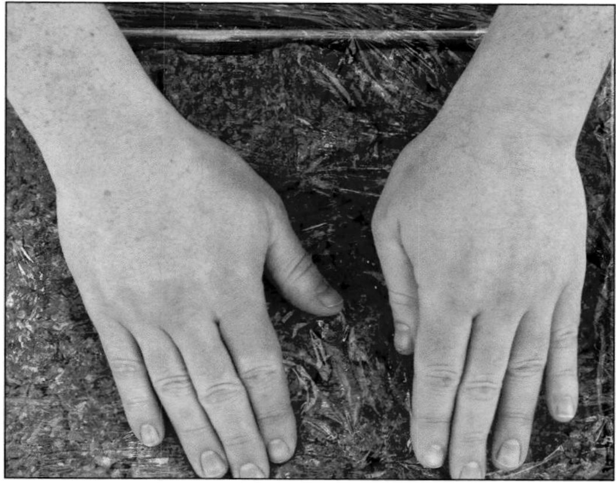

3 Cover the meat with plastic wrap. The covering guards against oxidation and prevents a skin from forming on the meat.

4 Put the meat in a freezer for 25 minutes to firm.

5a

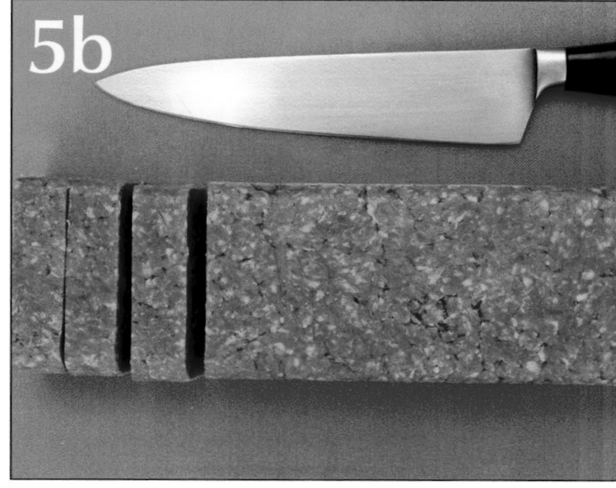

5b

5 Slide the meat out of the baking tray, and cut it into squares (5a), or remove it from the loaf pan, and slice it into patties 2.5 cm / 1 in thick (5b).

By Hand or in a Square Cake Mold

1 Divide the meat into 200 g / 0.4 lb portions. To shape the patty, place one hand edgewise on the counter, thumb up, and use your other hand to press the meat against the raised palm. Rotate four times to form a square patty. If making round patties, cup your upturned hand into an arc.

2 For cleaner edges, insert the meat into a cake mold, and use a spatula to gently work the meat into the corners.

3 Place the patty on a baking tray, and press down gently with your palm or a rubber spatula to flatten the top and bottom.

MODERNIST HAMBURGER PATTY

YIELD:	*four patties, 200 g each*
TIME ESTIMATE:	*2 hours overall, including 1¼ hours of preparation and 45 minutes unattended*
STORAGE NOTES:	*serve immediately*
LEVEL OF DIFFICULTY:	*moderate*
SPECIAL REQUIREMENTS:	*meat grinder or stand mixer with meat-grinding attachment, sous vide setup*

The extra effort to grind your own meat (see page 206) pays off in superior textures and flavors—and it allows you to customize the leanness and the tenderness. We love a combination of short-rib meat, rib eye, and hanger steak, but we know people who prefer 100% short-rib patties. For other options, see the table on page 206.

We performed many trials to figure out both when to salt the meat and how much salt to use. More salt makes for bouncier meat, like a sausage patty, but adding the salt too early can make the burger tough or rubbery.

Although we briefly deep-fry our patties to create a nice crust without overcooking the meat, another approach is to use a blowtorch (see page 14) to sear all the sides of the patty to a dark brown, 1½–2 minutes per patty. Alternatively, sear the patties on a very hot grill for 30 seconds on each side.

INGREDIENT	WEIGHT	VOLUME	SCALING	PROCEDURE
Boneless rib eye	360 g / 0.8 lb		100%	① Trim the fat from the meat, and grind each meat and fat separately through a 4.5 mm / 3⁄16 in plate.
Boneless short-rib meat	360 g / 0.8 lb		100%	② Mix the ground meats and fats together gently, and refrigerate them until 1 hour before cooking.
Hanger steak	80 g / 0.2 lb		22%	
Salt	6.4 g	1½ tsp	1.8%	③ Preheat a water bath to 55 °C / 131 °F. ④ Fold the salt gently into the ground beef mixture exactly 1 hour before cooking. ⑤ Divide the meat into four equal portions, about 200 g / 0.4 lb each. Form into square patties that are 2.5 cm / 1 in thick (see previous page).
Neutral frying oil see page xxii	20 g	20 mL / 1½ tsp	5.6%	⑥ Place each patty in a separate zip-top bag with 5 g / 5 mL / 1 tsp of oil. Remove the air from the bags by using the water-displacement method (see page 58), and seal them. Do not vacuum seal. ⑦ Refrigerate until 1 hour has passed since adding the salt. ⑧ Cook sous vide to a core temperature of 54 °C / 129 °F, about 45 minutes.
Neutral frying oil	as needed			⑨ Fill a large, deep pot no more than half full of frying oil, and preheat the oil to 220 °C / 428 °F. ⑩ Transfer the patties to a tray lined with paper towels, and pat them dry. ⑪ Deep-fry the patties one at a time until they turn dark brown and crispy, about 30 seconds each. ⑫ Drain the patties on paper towels.
Salt	to taste			⑬ Season the patties generously, and serve them hot.

Safety tips for deep-frying: see page 26
Safety tips for lightly cooked food: see page xxv

SPECIAL SCALING FOR SALT
If you're making smaller or larger batches, determine the amount of salt to use for curing by multiplying 0.8% times the weight of the meat. For example, if making 1.6 kg / 3.5 lb of meat, use 12.8 g of salt.

1 Trim the fat from the rib eye, short-rib meat, and hanger steak, and then grind each kind of meat and fat separately through a 4.5 mm / 3⁄16 in plate. For step-by-step instructions, see page 206.

2 Mix the ground meats and fats together, and refrigerate them until 1 hour before cooking.

3 Preheat a water bath to 55 °C / 131 °F.

VARIATION: Firm Burger Patty
If you prefer burgers that are richer in flavor and more cohesive, add 15 g of egg yolk (1 yolk) for every 400 g / 0.9 lb of ground meat at the same time you add the salt in step 4. Continue with step 5.

4 Wait until exactly 1 hour before cooking, note the time, and then fold the salt gently into the ground beef mixture. Salt activates the binding properties of the meat, and folding it in makes the meat more homogeneous in texture. Do not stir the meat aggressively or for long periods; doing so diminishes its tenderness.

5 Weigh and divide the meat into four equal portions of about 200 g / 0.4 lb each. Form each portion into a square patty 2.5 cm / 1 in thick. For step-by-step instructions, see page 207. If serving on buns rather than bread, make the patties round.

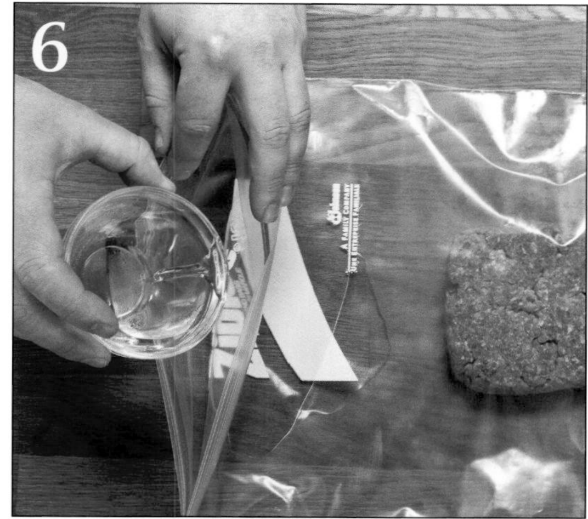

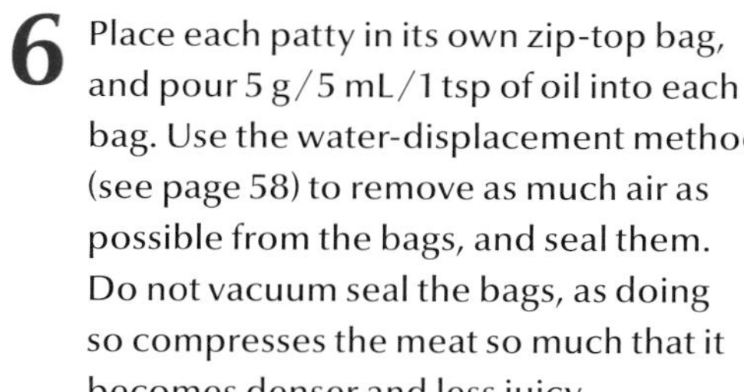

6 Place each patty in its own zip-top bag, and pour 5 g / 5 mL / 1 tsp of oil into each bag. Use the water-displacement method (see page 58) to remove as much air as possible from the bags, and seal them. Do not vacuum seal the bags, as doing so compresses the meat so much that it becomes denser and less juicy.

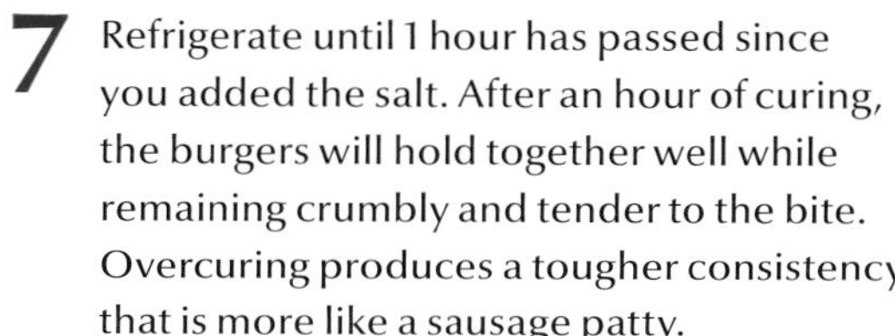

7 Refrigerate until 1 hour has passed since you added the salt. After an hour of curing, the burgers will hold together well while remaining crumbly and tender to the bite. Overcuring produces a tougher consistency that is more like a sausage patty.

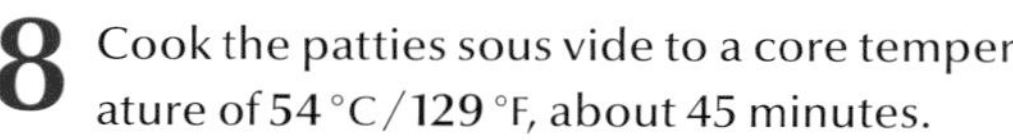

8 Cook the patties sous vide to a core temperature of 54 °C / 129 °F, about 45 minutes.

9 Fill a large, deep pot no more than half full of frying oil, and preheat it to 220 °C / 428 °F.

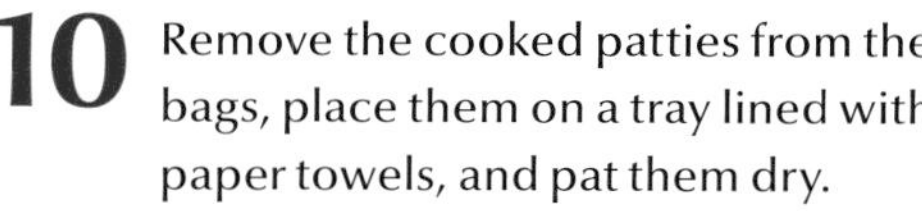

10 Remove the cooked patties from the bags, place them on a tray lined with paper towels, and pat them dry.

11 Deep-fry each patty individually until it becomes dark brown and crispy, about 30 seconds per patty.

12 Drain the fried patties on paper towels.

13 Season the patties generously with salt, and serve them hot. To make cheeseburgers, see page 212.

WHITE SANDWICH BREAD

YIELD:	*one 40 cm by 12 cm / 16 in by 4 in loaf or two 23 cm by 13 cm / 9 in by 5 in loaves (1.5 kg)*
TIME ESTIMATE:	*4 hours overall, including 30 minutes of preparation and 3½ hours unattended*
STORAGE NOTES:	*keeps for 2 days*
LEVEL OF DIFFICULTY:	*moderate*
SPECIAL REQUIREMENTS:	*stand mixer with paddle and dough hook attachments, loaf pan, buttermilk powder*

We included a recipe for the ultimate burger bun in *Modernist Cuisine*, but frankly it requires a lot of work to make. At home, we either buy top-quality buns or rolls from a local bakery or we take the old-school-diner approach of making a white bread that we can broil or panfry. The juices from the burger combine nicely with the crispy texture of the toast.

Try this recipe with different flours and flavors, such as a whole wheat loaf with caramelized onions. Leave the seeds out for a classic dense, chewy white loaf. It is also a fantastic bread to use for Grilled Cheese Sandwiches (see page 318), especially if you use one of our recipes for constructed cheese slices (see page 317).

INGREDIENT	WEIGHT	VOLUME	SCALING	PROCEDURE
Water Unsalted butter Buttermilk powder or nonfat milk powder	460 g 125 g 50 g	460 mL / 2 cups ⅝ cup ¼ cup	54% 15% 6%	① Combine in a pot. Warm over low heat, whisking occasionally, until the butter melts and the buttermilk powder is fully blended. ② Cool to room temperature.
Cooking spray or oil All-purpose flour	as needed as needed			③ Lightly coat the pan with cooking spray or wipe it with oil, and then dust the pan with flour.
All-purpose flour	850 g	5 cups	100%	④ Measure half (425 g / 2½ cups) of the flour into the bowl of a stand mixer having a paddle attachment. Reserve the remaining flour for step 8.
Sugar Salt Active dry yeast Baking soda	50 g 15 g 3 g 1 g	¼ cup 5 tsp 1 tsp ¼ tsp	6% 2% 0.4% 0.1%	⑤ Combine with the flour in the mixing bowl. ⑥ Mix on low speed while gradually pouring in the buttermilk mixture. ⑦ Beat on low speed for 5 minutes.
Reserved flour, from above	425 g	2½ cups	50%	⑧ Switch to the dough hook, and continue to mix at low speed. Gradually mix in the remaining flour until it is fully incorporated. ⑨ Knead on medium speed for 8 minutes.
Black sesame seeds Poppy seeds	15 g 15 g	2 Tbsp 2 Tbsp	2% 2%	⑩ Sprinkle in the seeds, mixing at low speed until they are evenly dispersed. ⑪ Transfer the kneaded dough to a lightly floured work surface. Shape it into a rectangle about the size and shape of the loaf pan. ⑫ Place the dough in the prepared pan, and cover it with plastic wrap or a clean, dry dish towel. ⑬ Let the dough rise in a warm, draft-free environment until it has doubled in size, 2–3 hours. ⑭ Preheat the oven to 190 °C / 375 °F. ⑮ Bake the dough until the top turns evenly golden, 15–20 minutes. ⑯ Remove the loaf from the pan immediately, put it on a rack, and cool it completely before slicing.

1 Combine the water, butter, and buttermilk powder in a pot. Warm the mixture over low heat, whisking occasionally, until the butter melts and the buttermilk powder is fully blended.

2 Remove the mixture from the heat, and allow it to cool to room temperature.

3 Lightly coat the loaf pan with cooking spray or oil, and dust the pan lightly with flour.

4 Measure half of the flour into the bowl of a stand mixer, and reserve the other half for step 8. Affix a paddle attachment to the mixer.

5 Combine the sugar, salt, dry yeast, and baking soda with the flour in the mixing bowl.

6 Mix on low speed while gradually pouring in the room-temperature buttermilk mixture.

7 Continue beating on low speed for 5 minutes more. Gluten, a protein in the flour, develops the structure of the dough as the kneading progresses.

8 Replace the paddle attachment with a dough hook. Start kneading at medium speed, and gradually mix in the remaining flour until fully incorporated. If the dough doesn't pull away from the side of the bowl once all the flour has been mixed in, add small amounts of flour until it does.

9 Knead on medium speed for 8 minutes.

10 Sprinkle in the seeds, and mix at low speed until they are evenly dispersed.

11 Transfer the kneaded dough to a lightly floured work surface. Shape it into a rectangle about the size and shape of the loaf pan. If you are using two loaf pans, divide the dough in half before shaping the pieces.

12 Place the dough in the prepared pan, and cover it with plastic wrap or a clean, dry dish towel.

13 Put the pan in a draft-free place at about 24 °C / 75 °F, and allow the dough to rise until it has doubled in size, 2–3 hours. This is a slow-rising dough; don't rush it.

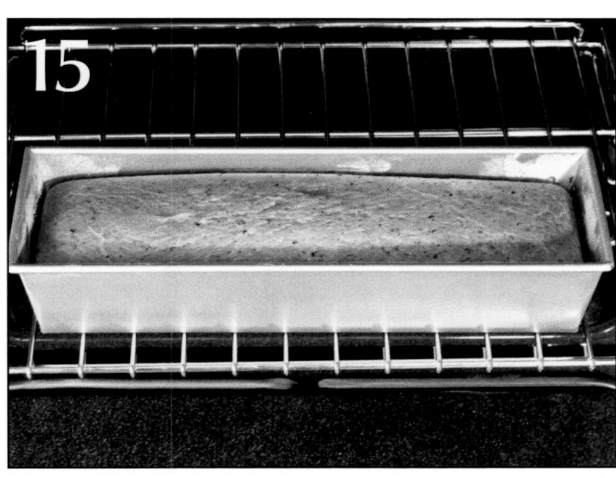

14 Preheat the oven to 190 °C / 375 °F.

15 Bake the bread until the top turns an even golden color, 15–20 minutes.

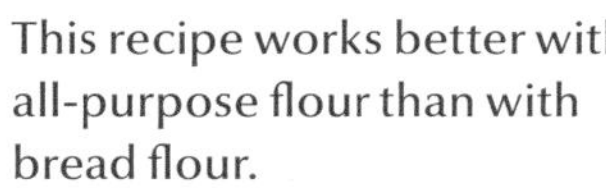

This recipe works better with all-purpose flour than with bread flour.

16 Remove the bread from the pan immediately. Set it on a rack, and let it cool completely before you slice it.

MODERNIST CHEESEBURGER

YIELD:	*four burgers*
TIME ESTIMATE:	*10 minutes for assembly of components*
STORAGE NOTES:	*serve immediately*
LEVEL OF DIFFICULTY:	*easy*
SPECIAL REQUIREMENTS:	*White Sandwich Bread (see page 210), Modernist Hamburger Patty (see page 208), Perfectly Melting Cheese Slice (see page 317), MC Special Sauce (see page 109) or Pressure-Caramelized Ketchup (see page 110)*

The original hamburger was served on toasted white bread with little else. We're paying homage to that tradition, but you can of course use store-bought buns instead. If tomatoes are not in season, replace them with lettuce, grilled mushrooms, thinly sliced raw onions, or thick slices of pickle. Use this guide as a template for your favorite burger combinations.

INGREDIENT	WEIGHT	VOLUME	PROCEDURE
White Sandwich Bread, sliced 1 cm / ⅜ in thick see page 210		8 slices	① Preheat the broiler. ② Brush fat evenly over one side of each slice of bread. ③ Toast the bread, fat-side up, under the broiler until it turns golden brown, about 2 minutes.
Rendered beef fat or unsalted butter, melted see page 123	as needed		
Modernist Hamburger Patty see page 208		4 patties	④ Place the cooked burger patties on a baking sheet, and top each with one or two slices of cheese. ⑤ Broil until the cheese melts, 1–2 minutes.
Perfectly Melting Cheese Slice see page 317		4–8 slices	
MC Special Sauce or Pressure-Caramelized Ketchup see page 109 or 110	80 g	5 Tbsp	⑥ Divide evenly among four slices of the prepared bread, and top with the cheeseburger patties and remaining bread. ⑦ Serve immediately.
Tomato or sweet onion, sliced		4 thick slices	

2

3

4

6a

6b

ULTRAFROTHY MILK SHAKE

YIELD:	*four to eight servings (1 L / 4¼ cups)*
TIME ESTIMATE:	*1½ hours overall, including 10 minutes of preparation and 1 hour and 20 minutes unattended*
STORAGE NOTES:	*serve immediately*
LEVEL OF DIFFICULTY:	*easy*
SPECIAL REQUIREMENTS:	*albumin powder, whey protein isolate, Freeze-Dried Raspberry Powder (see page 377)*

This shake tastes like the milk itself, so we use fresh raw milk from a local dairy. You can use regular supermarket milk instead, but it won't have the same subtle flavors. Use half-and-half, or a mixture of heavy cream and milk, to make a richer shake.

We garnish this shake with Freeze-Dried Raspberry Powder, but good alternatives include cocoa powder, malt powder, and powdered strawberries. You can also add flavors directly to the milk, for example by stirring in 5 g / 5 mL / 1 tsp of vanilla extract to make a rich vanilla shake. But we prefer the pure milk flavor.

To avoid any unpleasant flavor, use only high-quality, deodorized whey protein isolate, available at health-food stores or online.

INGREDIENT	WEIGHT	VOLUME	SCALING	PROCEDURE
Fresh, raw whole milk	1 kg	1 L / 4¼ cups	100%	① Combine in a metal or glass bowl, and blend by using an immersion blender until the sugar and powders are fully incorporated.
Sugar	180 g	1¼ cups	18%	② Refrigerate for 1 hour to hydrate the powders. This step is essential for the shake to foam properly.
Albumin powder	20 g	3 Tbsp	2%	③ Prepare an ice bath, and stir lots of salt into the bath.
Whey protein isolate	10 g	1 Tbsp	1%	④ Place the container of cooled milk into the salted ice bath for 20 minutes.
Salt	as needed			⑤ Blend the chilled milk at high speed in a blender for 3 minutes to aerate it.
Freeze-Dried Raspberry Powder see page 377	10 g	4 tsp	1%	⑥ Pour the milk shake into small, chilled glasses, dust the berry powder over the shakes, and serve them immediately.

Safety tips for lightly cooked food: see page xxv

1

4

MODERNIST MEATLOAF SANDWICH

YIELD:	*four sandwiches (about 200 g each)*
TIME ESTIMATE:	*13½ hours overall, including 1 hour of preparation and 12½ hours unattended*
STORAGE NOTES:	*serve immediately*
LEVEL OF DIFFICULTY:	*moderate*
SPECIAL REQUIREMENTS:	*meat grinder or stand mixer with meat-grinding attachment, sous vide setup, Sweet Onion Slaw (see page 165)*

Leftover meatloaf often ends up in a sandwich. But we think this delicious next-day treat is a worthy dish in its own right. We use several tricks to make it great. First, salt-cure the meat before grinding it to draw out the sticky myosin protein that improves the texture of the meatloaf and reduces the amount of egg needed as a binder. The meatloaf should be denser and springier than a burger. Second, keep the meat juicy by cooking it sous vide. And finally, flash-fry each portion of meat to produce a perfect, just-baked crust. You can substitute a fatty cut of beef, such as short-rib meat, for the pork to make an all-beef meatloaf; just keep the overall fat content about the same.

INGREDIENT	WEIGHT	VOLUME	SCALING	PROCEDURE
Beef chuck, cut into 2.5 cm / 1 in cubes	400 g / 0.9 lb		100%	① Toss together in a shallow container until thoroughly combined, cover with cheesecloth, and cure in the refrigerator overnight (about 12 hours).
Pork shoulder, cut into 2.5 cm / 1 in cubes	120 g / 0.3 lb		30%	② Grind through a 4.5 mm / 3⁄16 in plate.
Salt	5 g	1¼ tsp	1.25%	
Sweet onion, grated	200 g	1 cup	50%	③ Preheat a water bath to **60 °C / 140 °F**.
Neutral frying oil (see page xxii)	10 g	10 mL / 2 tsp	2.5%	④ Sauté the onion over medium heat until it turns dry but not brown, about 12 minutes, and then allow it to cool.
Ketchup (store-bought)	32 g	2 Tbsp	8%	⑤ Combine with the cooled onion.
Egg, beaten	20 g	1 Tbsp	5%	⑥ Add the ground meat, and mix thoroughly.
Dry bread crumbs	10 g	1½ Tbsp	2.5%	⑦ Divide the meat mixture into four equal portions of about 160 g each, and form into patties 2 cm / ¾ in thick.
Asian fish sauce	10 g	8 mL / ½ Tbsp	2.5%	
Dijon mustard	8 g	2 tsp	2%	
Worcestershire sauce	8 g	7 mL / ½ Tbsp	2%	
Parmesan, grated	4 g	1 Tbsp	1%	
Black pepper, ground	2 g	½ tsp	0.5%	
Neutral frying oil	20 g	20 mL / 1½ Tbsp	5%	⑧ Place each patty in a separate zip-top bag with 5 g / 5 mL / 1 tsp of oil. Use the water-displacement method (see page 58) to remove the air from the bags, and seal them. Do not vacuum seal. ⑨ Cook sous vide to a core temperature of **59 °C / 138 °F**, about 35 minutes.
Neutral frying oil	as needed			⑩ Fill a deep pot with about 5 cm / 2 in of frying oil, and preheat the oil to **190 °C / 374 °F**.
Dry bread crumbs	120 g	1 cup	30%	⑪ Transfer the cooked patties to a tray lined with paper towels, and pat dry. ⑫ Coat the warm patties in bread crumbs. ⑬ Deep-fry the breaded patties one at a time until each turns dark brown and crisp, about 30 seconds per patty. ⑭ Drain the patties on paper towels.
Sweet Onion Slaw (see page 165)	110 g	1⅓ cups	28%	⑮ Divide the patties and onion slaw evenly among the bread slices. Serve immediately.
White sandwich bread, toasted (see page 210)		8 slices		

Safety tips for deep-frying: see page 26
Safety tips for lightly cooked food: see page xxv

1 Toss the beef and pork pieces with salt until thoroughly combined. Place the salted meat in a shallow container, cover it with cheesecloth, and cure the meat in the refrigerator overnight (about 12 hours). The cheesecloth keeps the surface of the meat from drying out.

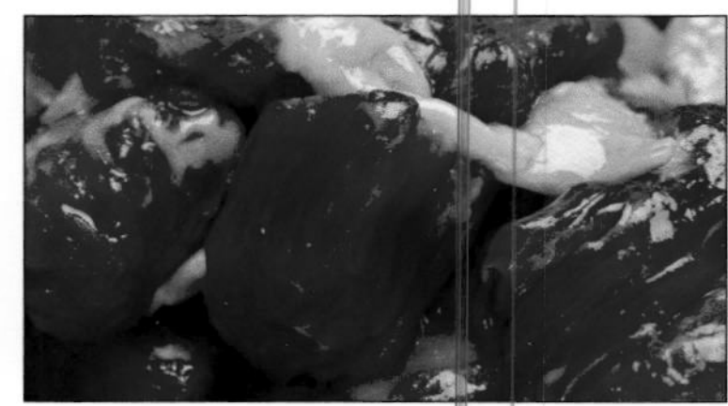

The meat pieces, before (left) and after salting.

2 Grind the cured meat through a 4.5 mm / 3⁄16 in plate.

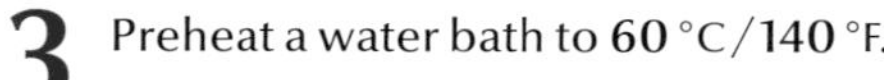

3 Preheat a water bath to **60** °C / **140** °F.

4 Sauté the onion in oil over medium heat until it becomes dry but not brown, about 12 minutes. Allow the onion to cool completely.

5 Combine the cooked onion with the ketchup, beaten egg, bread crumbs, fish sauce, mustard, Worcestershire sauce, Parmesan cheese, and black pepper.

6 Add the ground meat to the onions and seasonings, and mix them thoroughly.

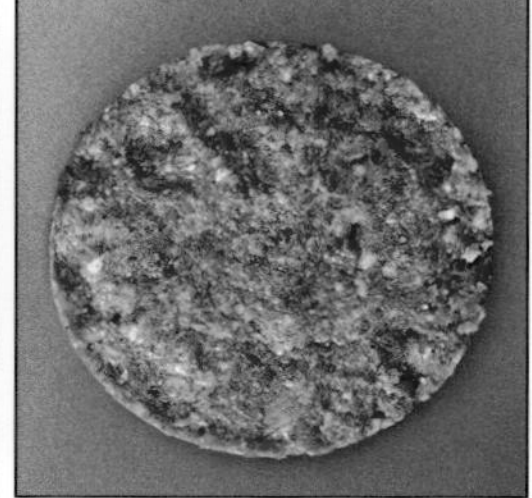

7 Form the meatloaf mix into four even patties (round or square) of about 160 g each. We find that patties no more than 2.5 cm / 1 in thick cook most evenly, and the sandwich is easiest to eat if the patties are about 2 cm / ¾ in thick.

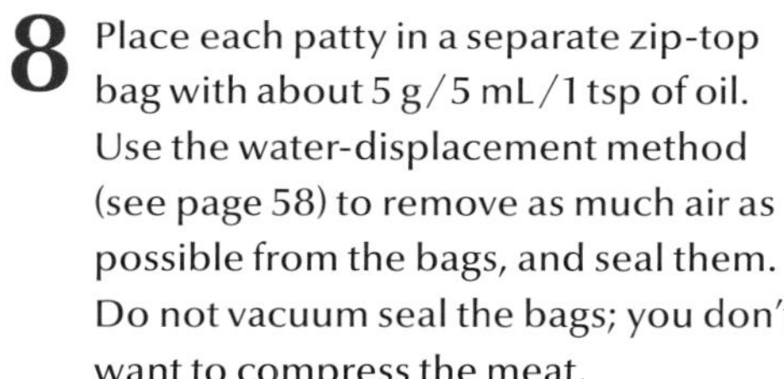

8 Place each patty in a separate zip-top bag with about 5 g / 5 mL / 1 tsp of oil. Use the water-displacement method (see page 58) to remove as much air as possible from the bags, and seal them. Do not vacuum seal the bags; you don't want to compress the meat.

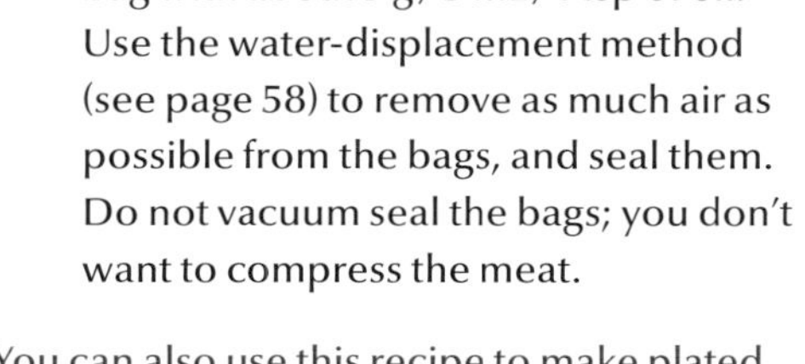

You can also use this recipe to make plated meatloaf. In that case, we still recommend cooking and searing the meatloaf in individual portions. Serve it with Pressure-Caramelized Ketchup (see page 110).

9 Cook the patties sous vide to a core temperature of **59** °C / **138** °F, about 35 minutes.

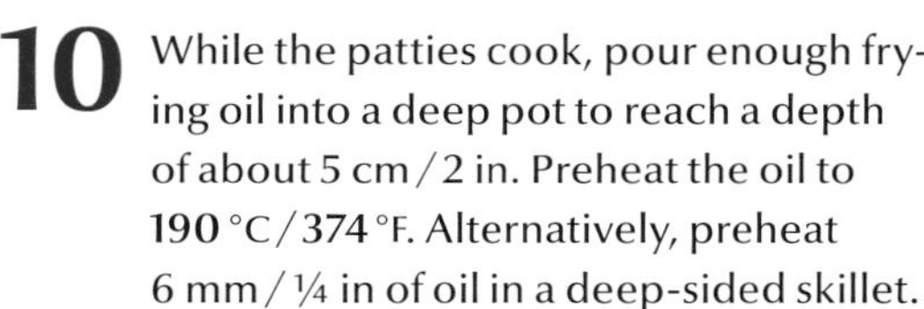

10 While the patties cook, pour enough frying oil into a deep pot to reach a depth of about 5 cm / 2 in. Preheat the oil to **190** °C / **374** °F. Alternatively, preheat 6 mm / ¼ in of oil in a deep-sided skillet.

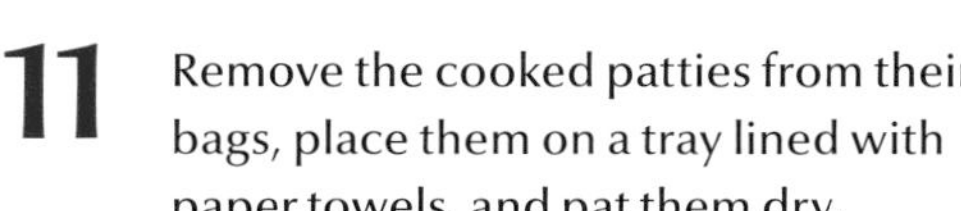

11 Remove the cooked patties from their bags, place them on a tray lined with paper towels, and pat them dry.

12 Coat the warm patties in dry bread crumbs.

13 Deep-fry the breaded patties, one at a time, until each becomes dark brown and crisp, about 30 seconds per patty (or 30 seconds per side if panfrying).

14 Drain the fried patties on paper towels.

15 Assemble the sandwiches by dividing the hot patties and onion slaw evenly among the bread slices. Serve them immediately.

CARNITAS

This chapter introduces the essentials of a Modernist Mexican feast: not only the carnitas but also a refried bean foam and *chicharrón*, a crispy treat made from pork skin. Together, these dishes highlight the traditional flavors and textures at the heart of Mexican cuisine.

The long, slow braise traditionally used to cook carnitas takes up to eight hours, and braising sous vide is even slower. We cut the cooking time to a mere 30 minutes by using a pressure cooker, which generates temperatures high enough to quickly melt the collagen that binds the tough fibers in active muscles, transforming it into gelatin. The beautiful result is tender, flaky meat that falls apart on the fork and in the mouth. Shredded carnitas are also a perfect filling for tamales (see page 340 for a recipe).

Pressure-cooking makes quick work of legumes as well. Refried beans usually get short shrift because they are too often poorly prepared and end up soupy and bland, crusty and dense, or undercooked and gritty. We cook them with care, puree them, and then aerate them by using a whipping siphon, which exploits the fact that kidney beans contain foam-stabilizing starches. The result is an intensely flavored yet ethereal bean puree.

THE SCIENCE OF HARD WATER AND SOFT BEANS

The mineral content of the water you use to cook beans has a huge effect on their texture. The harder the water, the harder the bean because hard water contains calcium and magnesium ions that interact with the protein in the beans. So if you want soft beans, cook them in soft water: either tap water that has passed through a water softener or bottled water. Deionized or distilled water are the best options. And if you want to make firmer beans—to use in a salad, for example—add a pinch of calcium chloride (also sold as Ball brand Pickle Crisp) to the water.

HIGHLIGHTS

Make succulent and tender carnitas in about an hour.

see page 218

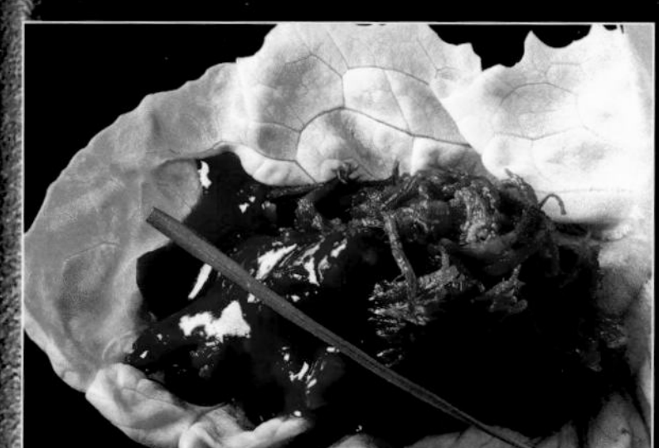

Use the same pressure-cooking technique to braise lamb, short ribs, and duck, as well as two other kinds of pork shoulder dishes.

see page 220

Drying and frying turns soft, flabby pork skin into a crispy puffed treat. You'll want to make extra.

see page 222

Pork belly adobo, a national dish of the Philippines, has a deceptively simple list of ingredients. The balance of sweet and sour flavors, though, is magical.

see page 224

FURTHER READING IN *MODERNIST CUISINE*

The science of traditional braising: see pages 2·93–99

How meat transforms when cooked: see pages 3·76–84

A plated-dish recipe for Cassoulet Toulousain with pressure-cooked tarbais beans: see pages 5·80–84

PRESSURE-COOKED CARNITAS

YIELD:	*six to eight servings (1 kg / 4 cups)*
TIME ESTIMATE:	*1¼ hours overall, including 15 minutes of preparation and 1 hour unattended*
STORAGE NOTES:	*keeps for 5 days when refrigerated or up to 6 months when frozen*
LEVEL OF DIFFICULTY:	*easy*
SPECIAL REQUIREMENTS:	*pressure cooker, achiote paste, Brown Pork Stock (see variation on page 86)*
GOES WELL WITH:	*Pressure-Cooked Fresh-Corn Tamales (see page 340), Salsa Verde (see page 111)*

Carnitas are traditionally made by slowly cooking big chunks of pork in vats of lard. Our recipe reduces both the fat and the cooking time—but not the flavor—by using a pressure cooker. We cut pork shoulder (commonly called pork butt or Boston butt) into bite-size pieces and use them as a filling for our Pressure-Cooked Fresh-Corn Tamales. Alternatively, shred the meat and use it to fill burritos or tacos. If you have a large pressure cooker, consider doubling the recipe; carnitas freeze very well.

INGREDIENT	WEIGHT	VOLUME	SCALING	PROCEDURE
Boneless, skinless pork shoulder, cut into 2.5–3 cm / 1–1¼ in cubes	1.3 kg / 2.9 lb		100%	① Combine in a pressure cooker. ② Pressure-cook at a gauge pressure of 1 bar / 15 psi for 30 minutes. Start timing when full pressure is reached.
Brown Pork Stock see variation on page 86	460 g	460 mL / 2 cups	35%	③ Depressurize the cooker. ④ Strain the cooking liquid into a large pot.
Achiote paste store-bought or see the next page	15 g	1 Tbsp	1.2%	⑤ Stir into the cooking liquid, and cook over high heat until syrupy, about 25 minutes.
Chipotle chili powder (optional)	2.5 g	1 tsp	0.19%	⑥ Add the pork to the reduced liquid, and simmer over medium-high heat, gently turning and basting the meat until it turns brown and the liquid reduces to a glaze, about 6 minutes.
Salt	to taste			⑦ Season the glazed pork, and serve it warm.
Lime juice	to taste			
Fresh cilantro	to taste			
Chili powder	to taste			

Safety tips for pressure-cooking: see page 33

1 Combine the pork shoulder and stock in a pressure cooker.

2 Pressure-cook the meat at a gauge pressure of 1 bar / 15 psi for 30 minutes. Start timing as soon as full pressure has been reached.

3 Let the cooker cool, or run tepid water over the rim, to depressurize it.

4 Strain the cooking liquid into a large pot. If you have time, you can refrigerate the meat and liquid together overnight for added flavor.

5 Stir the achiote paste and chili powder into the cooking liquid, and cook over high heat to reduce the liquid by at least two-thirds until it becomes syrupy, about 25 minutes.

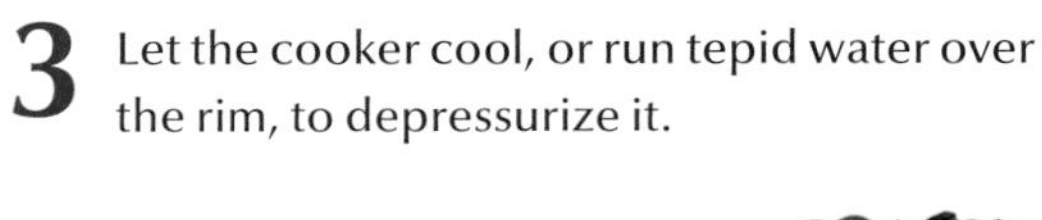

6 Add the pork to the reduced liquid. Simmer it over medium-high heat, gently turning and basting the meat until it browns and the liquid reduces to a glaze, about 6 minutes.

7 Season the glazed meat with the salt, lime juice, fresh cilantro, and chili powder to taste, and serve it warm.

To make shredded carnitas, use two forks to pull the glazed pork cubes apart into strands. Shredding is usually done only for carnitas destined to be a filling for a taco, burrito, or tamale. Garnish with chili powder and cilantro.

VARIATIONS

Sous Vide Carnitas

Vacuum seal cubes of pork shoulder with frozen cubes of Brown Pork Stock (see variation on page 86; you can freeze the stock in an ice cube tray), and cook sous vide at 65 °C / 149 °F for 36 hours. (To avoid off-flavors, do not use a zip-top bag.) Continue with step 4. Carnitas cooked sous vide are moister and less flaky than when pressure-cooked.

Whole Shoulder

Use bone-in, skin-on pork shoulder for added flavor. Combine 1.3 kg / 2.9 lb of pork shoulder with 460 g / 460 mL / 2 cups of Brown Pork Stock (see variation on page 86) in a pressure cooker, and pressure-cook at a gauge pressure of 1 bar / 15 psi for 2 hours. Depressurize the cooker, and then carefully remove the skin to make Pressure-Cooked Chicharrón (see page 222). Discard the bone. Break up the natural muscle groups of the meat, discarding any excess fat and cartilage. Continue with step 4.

WHILE YOU'RE AT IT: Achiote Paste

Ingredient	Weight	Volume
Annatto seeds	78 g	½ cup
Pressure-Cooked Garlic Confit see page 126	40 g	3 Tbsp
Habañero peppers, seeded and stemmed	25 g	2 peppers
Black peppercorns	7 g	1 Tbsp
Coriander seeds	2 g	½ Tbsp
Cumin seeds	2 g	1 tsp
Dried oregano	1 g	½ Tbsp
Allspice berries	1 g	8 berries
Whole cloves	0.7 g	8 cloves
Orange juice	124 g	125 mL / ½ cup
White wine vinegar	119 g	140 mL / ⅔ cup
Lemon juice	50 g	50 mL / ¼ cup
Tequila	4 g	5 mL / 1 tsp

Mix the first nine ingredients together, and grind in a coffee grinder. Combine the ground spices with the orange juice, vinegar, lemon juice, and tequila in a blender, and blend until smooth.

OTHER BRAISED MEAT AND POULTRY DISHES

Lamb Leg Tajine

Boneless lamb leg, cut into 2.5–3 cm / 1–1¼ in cubes	1.3 kg / 2.9 lb	
Brown lamb stock see page 86	460 g	46 mL / 2 cups
Neutral frying oil see page xxii	30 g	30 mL / 2 Tbsp
Yellow onion, minced	160 g	1⅛ cups
Dried apricot, small dice	40 g	¼ cup
Tomato paste	20 g	1 Tbsp
Honey	20 g	1 Tbsp
Ginger, minced	15 g	2 Tbsp
Cinnamon, ground	3 g	2 tsp
Cumin seed, ground	2 g	½ tsp
Lemon zest	0.3 g	¼ tsp
Salt	to taste	
Fresh mint	as needed	
Lemon wedges	as needed	

Follow steps 1–4 on page 218 to pressure-cook the lamb and lamb stock. (Alternatively, cook the lamb sous vide with lamb stock in a 62 °C / 144 °F water bath for 48 hours; see the Sous Vide Carnitas variation on the previous page for details.) Cook the strained liquid over medium-high heat until reduced to a syrup. In a large skillet, sweat the onion, apricot, tomato paste, honey, ginger, cinnamon, and cumin in the oil over medium heat until nearly dry. Add the reduced syrup, and finish with step 6. Season with lemon zest and salt. Garnish with mint and lemon wedges. Serve with rice or couscous.

Pork Shoulder Fricassee with Apples and Morels

Boneless, skinless pork shoulder, cut into 2.5–3 cm / 1–1¼ in cubes	1.3 kg / 2.9 lb	
Brown Pork Stock see variation on page 86	460 g	460 mL / 2 cups
Neutral frying oil see page xxii	30 g	30 mL / 2 Tbsp
Leeks, white parts only, minced	100 g	1½ cups
Dry morel or porcini mushrooms	14 g	⅔ cup
Garlic, minced	7 g	2¼ tsp
Thyme	1 g	1 sprig
Apple juice	150 g	150 mL / ⅔ cup
Applejack or apple brandy	100 g	125 mL / ½ cup
Heavy cream	100 g	110 mL / ½ cup
Black pepper	to taste	
Salt	to taste	
Baguette, toasted		1 whole
Green apple, thinly sliced	as needed	

Follow steps 1–4 on page 218 to pressure-cook the pork shoulder and pork stock. (Alternatively, cook the pork shoulder sous vide with pork stock in a 62 °C / 144 °F water bath for 48 hours; see the Sous Vide Carnitas variation on the previous page for details.) Cook the strained liquid over medium-high heat until reduced to a syrup. In a large skillet, sauté the leeks, dried mushrooms, garlic, and thyme in the oil over medium heat. Add the apple juice and applejack, and reduce the liquid to a second syrup. Combine the two syrups in the skillet, and finish with step 6. Stir in the cream, and season the mixture with salt and pepper. Serve on toasted slices of baguette with sliced green apple.

Pork Vindaloo with Naan

Boneless, skinless pork shoulder, cut into 2.5–3 cm / 1–1¼ in cubes	1.3 kg / 2.9 lb	
Brown Pork Stock see variation on page 86	460 g	460 mL / 2 cups
Neutral frying oil see page xxii	30 g	30 mL / 2 Tbsp
Yellow onion, minced	110 g	¾ cup
Vindaloo Spice Mix see variation on page 135	25 g	3 Tbsp
Ginger, minced	20 g	1 Tbsp
Garlic, minced	8 g	1 Tbsp
Tomato paste	40 g	2½ Tbsp
Rice vinegar	to taste	
Black pepper, ground	to taste	
Salt	to taste	
Naan	as needed	

Follow steps 1–4 on page 218 to pressure-cook the pork shoulder and pork stock. Cook the strained liquid over medium-high heat until reduced to a syrup. In a large skillet, sweat the onions, ginger, garlic, and Vindaloo Spice Mix in oil over medium heat until the onions and garlic are nearly translucent. Add the tomato paste, and cook over low heat until the mixture is nearly dry. Add the reduced syrup, and finish with step 6. Season the mixture with rice vinegar, salt, and pepper. Serve the pork and sauce with warm naan.

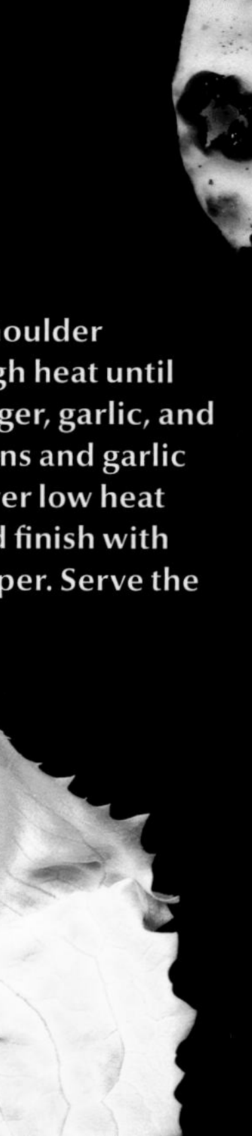

Korean Short-Rib Lettuce Wraps

Boneless short ribs, cut into 2.5 cm / 1 in cubes	900 g / 2 lb	
Brown beef stock see page 86	300 g	300 mL / 1¼ cups
Korean Wing Sauce see page 260	60 g	⅓ cup
Butter lettuce leaves	as needed	

Follow steps 1–4 on page 218 to pressure-cook the short ribs and beef stock. (Alternatively, cook them sous vide; see page 228.) Remove and discard the excess fat and cartilage. Shred the meat, or break it into chunks. At step 5, substitute the Korean Wing Sauce for the achiote paste and chili powder. Finish with step 6. Serve the beef and sauce in lettuce leaves.

Braised Duck with Steamed Buns

Duck legs, whole	900 g / 2 lb	
Duck stock see page 86	300 g	300 mL / 1¼ cups
Hoisin sauce (Lee Kum Kee brand)	35 g	3 Tbsp
Steamed buns (store-bought)	as needed	
Scallions, julienned	as needed	

Follow steps 1–4 on page 218 to pressure-cook the duck legs and duck stock. Remove and discard the duck skin, bones, and cartilage. Shred the meat, or break it into chunks. At step 5, substitute hoisin sauce for the achiote paste and chili powder. Finish with step 6. Serve the duck and sauce on warm, steamed buns (available at Asian markets) with julienned scallions.

PRESSURE-COOKED CHICHARRÓN

YIELD:	*200 g / two large sheets or 20 pieces*
TIME ESTIMATE:	*12½ hours overall, including 30 minutes of preparation and 12 hours unattended*
STORAGE NOTES:	*keeps in an airtight container for 1 day after dehydrating and for 2 days after frying*
LEVEL OF DIFFICULTY:	*moderate*
SPECIAL REQUIREMENTS:	*pressure cooker, food dehydrator (optional)*

Chicharrón is pork skin that has been dehydrated, fried, and puffed into crackling. It is an addictive snack or garnish: make plenty, or it may disappear before it gets to the table. You can buy pork skin from many butchers and at many Asian and Latin American markets.

The key to good *chicharrón* is drying the skin by just the right amount before frying it. The dried pieces should at that point flex slightly, and then snap in half. If they are too moist or too dry, they will not puff properly in the hot oil.

INGREDIENT	WEIGHT	VOLUME	SCALING	PROCEDURE
Water	460 g	460 mL / 2 cups	102%	① Combine in a pressure cooker.
Pork skin	450 g / 1 lb	2 large pieces	100%	② Pressure-cook at a gauge pressure of 1 bar / 15 psi for 2 hours. Start timing as soon as full pressure has been reached.
				③ Let the cooker cool, or run tepid water over the rim, to depressurize it.
				④ Strain the skin, and gently scrape any residual fat from it.
				⑤ Dehydrate the skin at **63 °C / 145 °F** (or as low a temperature as your oven allows) until the skin flexes slightly before snapping in half, about 10 hours.
Neutral frying oil see page xxii	as needed			⑥ Preheat the frying oil to **190 °C / 375 °F**.
				⑦ Snip or break the dehydrated skin into evenly sized pieces.
				⑧ Deep-fry the pieces until they puff and turn crispy, about 2 minutes.
				⑨ Drain on paper towels.
Salt	to taste			⑩ Season the skin, and serve it immediately, or store it in an airtight container.

Safety tips for pressure-cooking: see page 33
Safety tips for deep-frying: see page 26

Use a butter knife or other blunt utensil to gently scrape the fat from the cooked skin. Take care not to tear the skin.

A food dehydrator is the best tool for drying the skin, but if you don't have one, preheat the oven to its lowest temperature setting, arrange the pieces on a rack set over a baking sheet, and dry them until they become leathery and flexible like plastic, 8–10 hours.

Deep-fry the skin a few pieces at a time. Work in batches as needed.

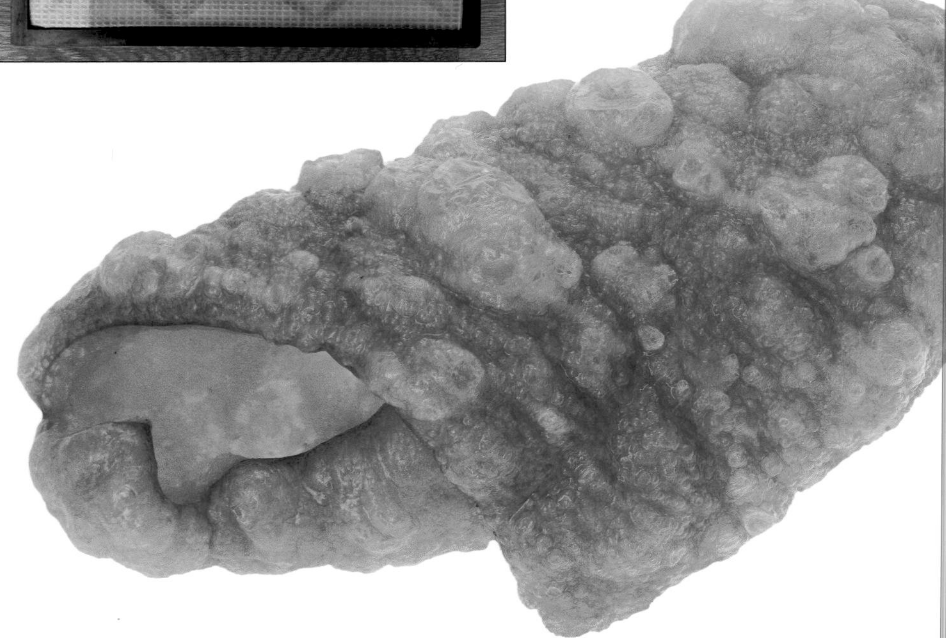

REFRIED BEAN FOAM

YIELD:	*four servings (665 g / 3¼ cups)*
TIME ESTIMATE:	*1½ hours overall, including 30 minutes of preparation and 1 hour unattended*
STORAGE NOTES:	*serve the foam immediately; the puree keeps for up to 1 day when refrigerated*
LEVEL OF DIFFICULTY:	*easy*
SPECIAL REQUIREMENTS:	*pressure cooker, 1 L whipping siphon, three cartridges of nitrous oxide*
GOES WELL WITH:	*Pressure-Cooked Carnitas (see page 218)*

This updated version of the classic Mexican dish combines two Modernist techniques. Pressure-cooking the beans directly from the dry state and in low-calcium water causes them to burst and become very tender. We then use a whipping siphon to aerate the perfectly smooth, pudding-like puree into a foam of unearthly lightness. To prevent splattering, dispense the foam into a container with high sides, and spoon the beans onto the serving plates. The foam remains stable for only about 10 minutes, so don't dispense the beans from the siphon until you are ready to serve them.

INGREDIENT	WEIGHT	VOLUME	SCALING	PROCEDURE
Brown Pork Stock or bottled water see variation on page 86	400 g	400 mL / 1⅔ cups	267%	① Combine in a pressure cooker, and pressure-cook at a gauge pressure of 1 bar / 15 psi for 1 hour. Start timing as soon as full pressure has been reached.
Dry pinto beans	150 g	¾ cup	100%	② Let the cooker cool, or run tepid water over the rim, to depressurize it.
Lard or neutral-tasting oil	10 g	10 mL / 2¼ tsp	7%	③ Allow the beans to cool slightly.
				④ Puree the beans and any remaining stock in a blender until smooth, and pour the puree into a pot.
Heavy cream	100 g	110 mL / ½ cup	67%	⑤ Whisk into the bean puree until it takes on a pudding-like consistency.
Salt	to taste			⑥ Heat the puree over medium heat to 55 °C / 131 °F, and season it generously; the flavor will become more delicate when the puree is foamed.
				⑦ Pour the hot puree into a 1 L whipping siphon, and charge the siphon with three cartridges of nitrous oxide.
				⑧ Dispense the foam into a deep container to minimize splattering.
				⑨ Spoon the warm foam onto plates.

Safety tips for pressure-cooking: see page 33

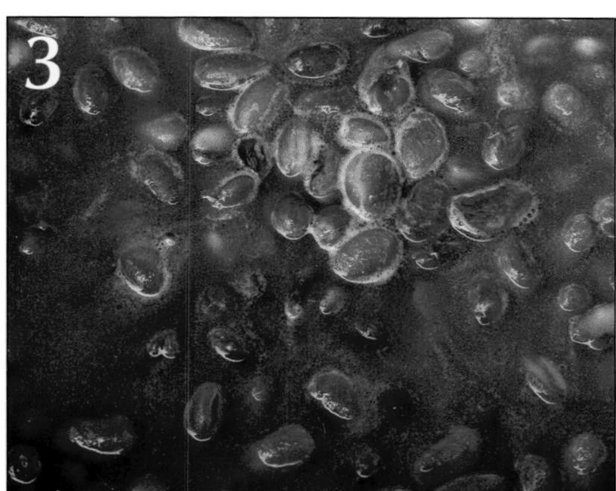
3

5

VARIATIONS

Refried Bean Puree

At step 5, add only as much heavy cream as is needed to create the texture you prefer, and then follow step 6 to season the puree to taste.

Other Bean Foams

You can substitute other fats for the lard or substitute other kinds of beans for the pinto beans; as long as the beans contain enough fat and natural starches, they will produce a stable foam. Try French flageolet beans with butter; gigante or lima beans with garlic and olive oil or butter; or chickpeas with tahini for a hummus-style foam. The puree should be perfectly smooth and have a texture similar to pudding before you pour it into the siphon.

TO MAKE AHEAD

You can refrigerate the pureed beans for up to 24 hours after step 5. Then continue with step 6.

After step 7, you can keep the siphon of warm puree in a 50 °C / 122 °F water bath for up to 1 hour before dispensing the foam.

Refried beans are traditionally made with lard, but you can easily make a vegetarian version of this recipe by cooking the beans in bottled water or vegetable stock and a neutral-tasting vegetable oil, such as coconut oil. The result has a slightly different consistency and flavor from the original.

PRESSURE-COOKED PORK BELLY ADOBO

YIELD:	*eight servings (1.2 kg / 6 cups)*
TIME ESTIMATE:	*1¾ hours overall, including 1 hour of preparation and 45 minutes unattended*
STORAGE NOTES:	*keeps for 3 days when refrigerated*
LEVEL OF DIFFICULTY:	*moderate*
SPECIAL REQUIREMENTS:	*pressure cooker*

Adobo, from the Old Spanish verb *adobar* meaning "to stew," can be found throughout the former Spanish colonial empire. But the dish varies from one region to another, reflecting local differences in both the spice mixtures and the stewed, braised, or roasted meats used. The version here is considered a national dish of the Philippines: a boldly seasoned stew of chicken or pork with soy sauce, vinegar, and plenty of black pepper. Here, we use fresh pork belly, available at specialty butchers, with the skin on to help thicken the cooking liquid and hold the pieces of meat together. You may remove the skin if you prefer the texture without it. Cubed pork shoulder also works as a leaner alternative. Serve the adobo with steamed rice, mashed sweet potatoes (see variation on page 230), or roasted sunchokes.

INGREDIENT	WEIGHT	VOLUME	SCALING	PROCEDURE
Neutral frying oil or lard see page xxii	50 g	55 mL / ¼ cup	3.3%	① Sauté over low heat until tender and lightly browned, 7–10 minutes.
Yellow onion, grated	550 g	2½ cups	37%	
Garlic cloves, crushed	10 g	1 Tbsp / 1½ cloves	0.7%	
Fresh pork belly, skin on, cut into 3.75 cm / 1½ in cubes	1.5 kg / 3.3 lb		100%	② Stir into the onion mixture. ③ Pressure-cook at a gauge pressure of 1 bar / 15 psi for 45 minutes. Start timing when full pressure is reached.
Rice vinegar	230 g	270 mL / 1⅛ cups	15%	④ Let the cooker cool, or run tepid water over the rim, to depressurize it.
Soy sauce	130 g	110 mL / ½ cup	8.7%	⑤ Lift the meat from the cooking liquid with a slotted spoon, and put it in a frying pan.
Asian fish sauce	85 g	70 mL / ⅓ cup	5.7%	
Sugar	62 g	5 Tbsp	4.1%	⑥ Strain the cooking liquid into a pot. Skim off as much fat as possible.
Star anise	3 g	1–2 pods	0.2%	⑦ Transfer 250 g / 250 mL / 1 cup of the cooking liquid to the pan with the pork belly, and simmer over medium-high heat, gently turning and basting the meat until it is glazed, 12–15 minutes.
Black peppercorns	0.7 g	¼ tsp	0.04%	
Fresh bay leaves, torn	0.7 g	3 leaves	0.04%	
Additional fresh bay leaves, torn	0.7 g	3 leaves	0.04%	⑧ Add to the pot of remaining cooking liquid, and bring to a boil. ⑨ Remove from the heat, and let the mixture infuse for 7–10 minutes.
Additional star anise	3 g	1–2 pods	0.2%	⑩ Strain.
Rice vinegar	to taste			⑪ Spoon the glazed pork belly into serving bowls, pour in the infused cooking liquid, and serve warm.
Cracked black pepper	to taste			

Safety tips for pressure-cooking: see page 33

TO MAKE AHEAD

After step 4, cool the pressure-cooked pork belly and cooking juices in the refrigerator overnight, or freeze them. Gently reheat, and continue with step 5.

VARIATION: Sous Vide Pork Belly Adobo

Cooking the pork belly sous vide yields a juicier, less flaky texture than pressure-cooking does. At step 3, vacuum seal the pieces of pork belly and sauce mixture. Cook sous vide at 62 °C / 144 °F for 48 hours. Continue with step 6.

1 Sauté the grated onion, crushed garlic, and oil or lard over low heat until the onion is tender and lightly browned, 7–10 minutes.

2 Combine the pork belly, rice vinegar, soy sauce, fish sauce, sugar, and aromatics with the onion mixture, and stir.

3 Pressure-cook at a gauge pressure of 1 bar / 15 psi for 45 minutes. Start timing as soon as full pressure has been reached.

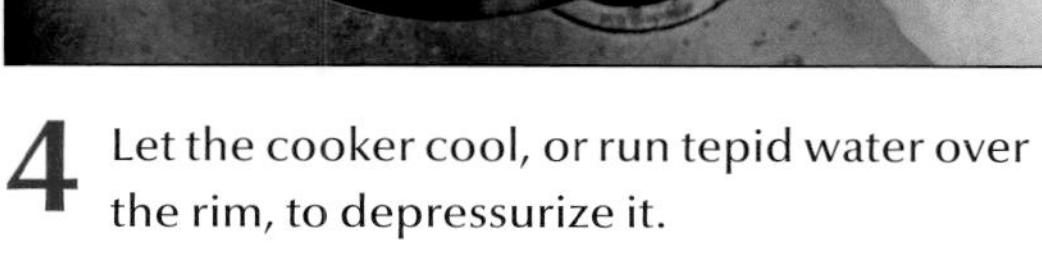

4 Let the cooker cool, or run tepid water over the rim, to depressurize it.

5 Lift the meat from the cooking liquid with a slotted spoon, and put it in a frying pan.

6 Strain the cooking liquid into a pot. Skim off as much fat as possible. Fat skimmers, sold at kitchen-supply stores, work well.

7 Transfer 250 g / 250 mL / 1 cup of cooking liquid to the pan with the pork belly. Simmer over medium-high heat, gently turning and basting until the meat is brown and the liquid forms a glaze, 12–15 minutes.

8 Add the additional bay leaves, star anise, vinegar, and pepper to the pot of cooking liquid. The flavor of the essential oils from the bay leaves weaken during cooking; adding more now enhances the fresh, spicy flavor. Bring the liquid to a boil.

9 Remove the pot from the heat, and let it sit for 7–10 minutes, or until ready to use, to infuse the flavors.

10 Strain the infused liquid.

11 Spoon the glazed pork belly into serving dishes. Pour the infused liquid over the top, and serve the adobo warm.

BRAISED SHORT RIBS

Seventy-two hours to make dinner? That sounds crazy, we know. But it's actually easy: vacuum seal the short ribs, set them in a water bath, and walk away. The result is so incredible, you won't want to go back to the stove-top version: flipping the meat, and relying on luck.

Short ribs are an ideal cut of meat for braising because they're readily available and very tasty, thanks to a nice marbling of fat and collagen throughout. We use them to showcase the range of textures you can achieve (see page 228) through the precision of cooking sous vide. But the technique works just as well with rib eye and tough cuts such as oxtail, beef shank, and tongue.

When slow-cooking meat, keep three things in mind. First, don't salt the meat before sealing it, or it will cure during the 72 hours, and you'll wind up with corned beef. (You can, however, seal the meat in unsalted beef jus or beef stock to intensify the beef flavor.) Second, trim off any gristle and silverskin; these don't get more tender with cooking. Third, if you want to sear the meat, do so after cooking to avoid producing off-flavors and unappetizing colors.

Our favorite finishing strategy for slow-cooked meat is the one described in the short-ribs recipe. We baste the warm meat for just a minute in a little pot of syrupy sauce (a red wine glaze, in this case) to add an extra touch of flavor and gloss. This warms it through without actually cooking it.

HIGHLIGHTS

Short ribs are just a start. Our table **Best Bets for Cooking Tough Cuts of Meat** provides cooking times and temperatures for all kinds of cuts, from brisket to oxtail to pork belly.

see page 228

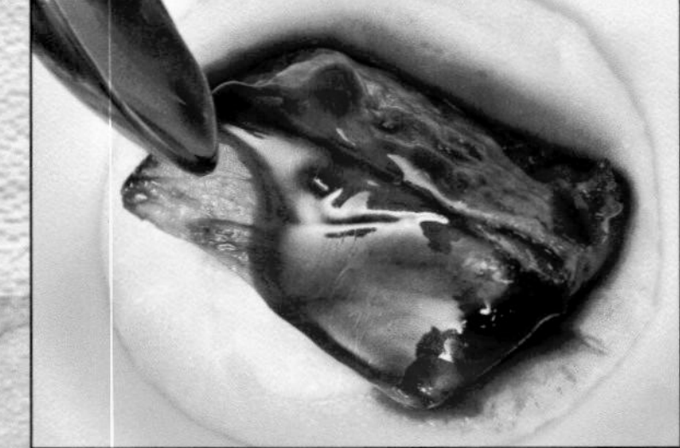

Enrich the meat flavor of a glaze by adding dark soy sauce and balsamic vinegar. This saves you from having to over-reduce the sauce to a sticky glaze.

see page 97

Ever made mashed potatoes that were gummy or a mound of grainy mush? A ricer is an essential tool for making **silky mashed potatoes without overworking them**.

see page 230

While you're at it, try brining and then slow-cooking a different meat to transform a classic sandwich. Our **B.L.T. made with a crispy yet tender pork belly** includes bacon mayonnaise for a bit of smokiness.

see page 232

FURTHER READING IN *MODERNIST CUISINE*

Braising meats: see pages 2·98–99

The role of collagen in cooking: see pages 3·80–81

Ideas for combining potatoes, liquids, and fats: see page 3·297

A plated-dish recipe for American Barbecue: see pages 5·66–79

THE SCIENCE OF COOKING TOUGH CUTS OF MEAT

Short ribs and other tough cuts of meat contain lots of tough collagen. To make such cuts tender and succulent, you must convert the collagen to gelatin through chemical reactions that occur only at temperatures of 50 °C / 122 °F and higher. The hotter the meat, the faster the conversion happens. But there is a trade-off: high heat also squeezes more juices out of muscle fibers and accelerates the unraveling of proteins. Cooking for long periods at 60 °C / 140 °F or lower strikes a good balance that preserves the color and juiciness of the meat while gelatinizing the collagen to create that silky texture typical of braised meats.

Pressure cookers produce temperatures much higher than this, so they can cook tough cuts faster, but they dry the meat as a result. You can compensate for some of that effect by allowing the meat to rest in its juices. While it cools, the muscle fibers will reabsorb some of this moisture, and the meat will recover some of its original juiciness.

We like to serve our Braised Short Ribs (see the next page) atop Potato Puree (see page 230)

Best Bets for Cooking Tough Cuts of Meat

To cook the tough cuts of meat listed below sous vide, select a texture, preheat a water bath to the temperature given, vacuum seal the meat, and then cook sous vide for the time indicated. Alternatively, pressure-cook the meat at a gauge pressure of 1 bar / 15 psi for the time indicated, and then allow it to cool in its juices to serving temperature. Tough meats require a lot of cooking, which means either high temperatures or very long cooking times at low temperatures. For more on cooking sous vide, see page 50. For more on pressure-cooking, see page 32.

	Cook sous vide											
	Tender, yielding			Tender, flaky			Very flaky			Pressure-cook		
Ingredient	(°C)	(°F)	(h)	(°C)	(°F)	(h)	(°C)	(°F)	(h)	(min)	Note	See page
beef short rib	58	136	72	62 65	144 149	72 24	88	190	7	50	use bone-in when available; texture is best when carved just before serving	229
beef brisket	60	140	72	63	145	72	70	158	72	40	use the fattier, thick end of the brisket, called the nose, especially when pressure-cooking	
oxtail, jointed	60	140	100	65	149	48	70	158	24	70	remove meat from the bone while warm	
lamb shank	62	144	48	85	185	5	88	190	5	60	remove silverskin before cooking	234
lamb shoulder, cut into large cubes	62	144	48	65	149	24	85	185	5	40	coat meat with 5% olive oil and 0.1% thyme to prevent strong lamb notes from developing	
pork belly	65	149	36	70	158	18	88	190	8	50	for firm texture, cure with the brine from step 1 on page 232 before cooking	232
pork shoulder or fresh ham, cut into 2.5 cm / 1 in cubes	60	140	72	65	149	36	84	183	4	30	use the more marbled, darker muscles when available	218
pork ribs	60	140	48	65	149	48	75	167	7	35	serve with our Grilling Spice Mix (see page 139)	

(temperatures in red are those that we prefer)

BRAISED SHORT RIBS

YIELD:	*four servings (600 g; one boneless rib per serving)*
TIME ESTIMATE:	*3 days overall, including 15 minutes of preparation and 72 hours unattended*
STORAGE NOTES:	*keeps for 3 days when refrigerated or up to 3 months when frozen*
LEVEL OF DIFFICULTY:	*easy*
SPECIAL REQUIREMENTS:	*sous vide setup, vacuum sealer, Red Wine Glaze (see page 97)*
GOES WELL WITH:	*Potato Puree (see next page)*

Short ribs cooked sous vide are, in a word, awesome. By varying the cooking time and temperature, you can produce dramatically different results in texture. If you want short ribs that have the color and texture of a medium-rare steak, cook them sous vide at 58 °C / 136 °F for 72 hours. If you want the ribs fork-tender but still pink, increase the temperature to 62 °C / 144 °F, and cook for 72 hours, as we do here. (Don't brown the meat before cooking it for such a long time, as that causes off-flavors.) The ribs take on a more traditional braised texture and color when cooked at temperatures higher than this. It is essential to vacuum seal the meat when cooking it for such a long time; see page 52 for more details. Both bone-in and boneless short ribs work in this recipe.

INGREDIENT	WEIGHT	VOLUME	SCALING	PROCEDURE
Beef short ribs, bone in or boneless	1.2 kg / 2.6 lb	4 ribs	100%	① Preheat a water bath to 62 °C / 144 °F. ② Vacuum seal, and cook sous vide for 72 hours. ③ Slice the meat from the bone.
Red Wine Glaze see page 97	200 g	½ cup	17%	④ Bring the glaze to a simmer in a pot. ⑤ Add the meat, and baste for 1 minute to glaze.
Salt	to taste			⑥ Season, and serve warm.

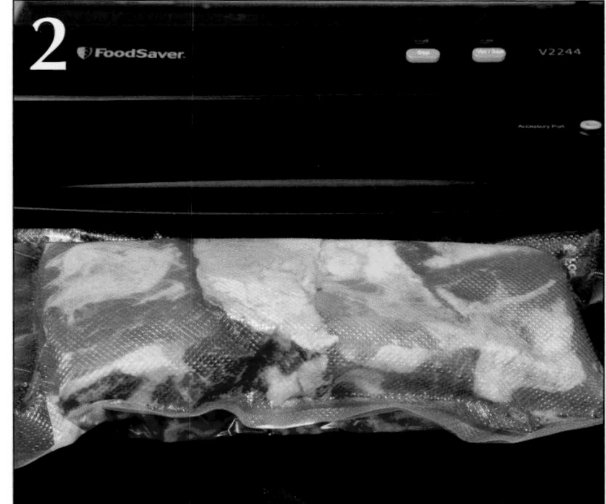

A zip-top bag is not recommended when cooking for long periods for both safety and reliability reasons. It's also important to vacuum seal the meat to avoid oxidation and off-flavors.

Take care not to undermine the benefits of cooking the meat sous vide by overheating it while basting with the glaze.

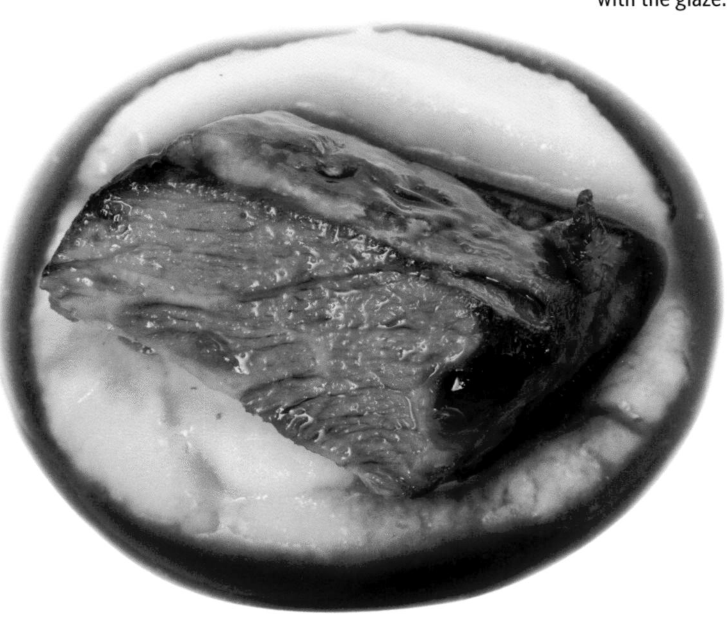

TO MAKE AHEAD

After cooking the ribs in step 2, plunge the bag into an ice bath to cool the meat completely, and then refrigerate it in the sealed bag. To reheat the ribs, remove them from the bag, and slice the meat from the bones. Vacuum seal the slices, and reheat them for 30 minutes in a water bath set to the same temperature used to cook the ribs. Then continue with step 4.

POTATO PUREE

YIELD:	*four to six servings (630 g / 2½ cups)*
TIME ESTIMATE:	*2 hours overall, including 30 minutes of preparation and 1½ hours unattended*
STORAGE NOTES:	*keeps for 2 days when refrigerated*
LEVEL OF DIFFICULTY:	*moderate*
SPECIAL REQUIREMENTS:	*sous vide setup, ricer*

Traditional fluffy mashed potatoes are best made with starchy varieties, such as the Russet or the Maris Piper. Adding just enough liquid and fat to moisten the mixture is all that is needed to finish the dish. To obtain a silky texture, in the style of the French *pommes puree*, choose waxy potatoes, such as Yukon Gold or fingerlings.

The real secret to a great potato puree, as revealed by food writer Jeffrey Steingarten and chef Heston Blumenthal, is a heat treatment prior to cooking that gelatinizes the starch and stabilizes the starch granules. It is also important to be gentle so as to rupture as few of the granules as possible when making the puree. Sieve the potatoes slowly—never use a food processor—and add lots of fat to prevent any freed starch from forming a sticky puree.

INGREDIENT	WEIGHT	VOLUME	SCALING	PROCEDURE
Yukon Gold potatoes, peeled	500 g	about 4 potatoes	100%	① Preheat a water bath to 70 °C / 158 °F. ② Cut the potatoes into 2.5 cm / 1 in pieces.
Water	1 kg	1 L / 4¼ cups	200%	③ Combine the potatoes and water in a zip-top bag, remove as much air as possible from the bag (see page 58), and seal it. ④ Cook sous vide for 35 minutes. ⑤ Drain the water from the bag, and refrigerate the potatoes, uncovered, until completely cooled, about 30 minutes.
Water	as needed			⑥ Transfer the potatoes to a pot, and cover with water. ⑦ Bring the water to a boil. Reduce the heat, and simmer until just tender, about 25 minutes. ⑧ Drain the potatoes, and pass them through a ricer.
Unsalted butter, cubed, room temperature	200 g	1¾ cups	40%	⑨ Stir into the potatoes. Optionally, for a finer texture, pass the potatoes through a fine sieve into a bowl holding the butter. Mix well.
Heavy cream or whole milk, brought to a simmer	125 g	140 mL / ½ cup	25%	⑩ Stir the hot cream or milk into the potatoes. ⑪ Warm the mixture in a saucepan over medium-low heat until hot, stirring often with a spatula to prevent sticking.
Salt	to taste			⑫ Season, and serve warm.

VARIATIONS

Infused-Cream Potato Puree

For a bolder potato flavor, reserve the potato peels, and add them to the heavy cream. Bring them to a simmer, and then remove from the heat and cover. Let them infuse for 30 minutes. Then strain the skins, and use the cream in step 10. Dried mushrooms (porcini, morel, or shiitake) can be steeped in this cream before step 10 to create a version of the classic French dish pommes forestières.

Garlic Mashed Potatoes

At step 11, fold in 200 g of pureed Pressure-Cooked Garlic Confit (see page 126).

Sweet Potato Puree

Substitute satsuma-imo or sweet potatoes for Yukon Golds.

TO MAKE AHEAD

After mixing the potatoes and butter in step 9, refrigerate until ready to serve. Then continue with step 10.

1 Preheat a water bath to 70 °C / 158 °F.

2 Cut the potatoes into pieces about 2.5 cm / 1 in thick and wide.

3 Place the potatoes and water into a zip-top bag, remove as much air as possible from the bag (see page 58), and seal it.

The ratio of potatoes to fat and liquid determines the texture of mashed potatoes. Classic recipes use up to half butter; this recipe calls for about a 2:5 ratio. If that is still too much butter for you, simply use less, or substitute olive oil or rendered chicken, pork, or veal fat for up to half of the butter added at step 9.

4 Cook sous vide for 35 minutes. This sets the starch to help prevent the potatoes from becoming sticky, but it does not fully cook them.

5 Open the bag, and drain out the water. Refrigerate the potatoes, uncovered, until they have cooled completely, about 30 minutes.

6 Transfer the potatoes to a pot. Pour in enough water to cover them.

7 Bring the water to a boil. Reduce the heat, and simmer until the potatoes are tender throughout, about 25 minutes. To ensure that the potatoes are tender enough to puree, insert a skewer through the thickest potato: there should be no resistance.

7

8 Drain the potatoes, and pass them through a ricer. A food mill works well, too.

9 Stir the butter into the potatoes. Optionally, for a finer texture, arrange a tamis or fine sieve over a bowl containing the cubed butter. Then use a thick rubber spatula or rubber bench scraper to pass the potatoes through the sieve and into the butter. Mix well.

9a

9b

This recipe is our homage to the chefs and passionate food writers who have spent a great deal of time refining the simple but incredible staple of creamy mashed potatoes. Joël Robuchon introduced the technique of fine sieving, and both Heston Blumenthal and Jeffrey Steingarten developed the step of cooking sous vide that pregelatinizes the potatoes.

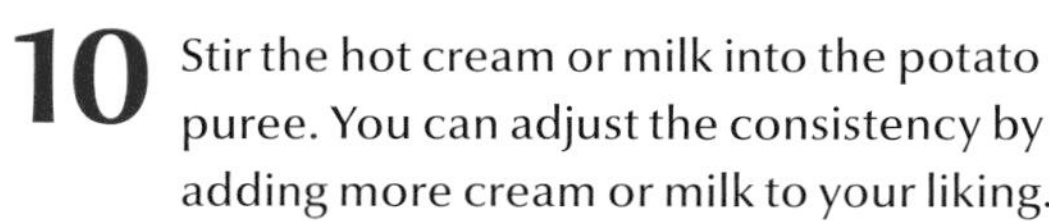

10 Stir the hot cream or milk into the potato puree. You can adjust the consistency by adding more cream or milk to your liking.

11 Warm the mixture in a saucepan over medium-low heat until it is hot, stirring often with a spatula to prevent sticking.

12 Season the puree with salt to taste, and serve it warm.

PORK BELLY B.L.T.

YIELD:	*four sandwiches (1.2 kg / 2.6 lb of cooked pork belly)*
TIME ESTIMATE:	*5½ days overall, including 30 minutes of preparation and 132 hours unattended*
STORAGE NOTES:	*cooked pork belly keeps for 3 days when refrigerated; serve assembled sandwich immediately*
LEVEL OF DIFFICULTY:	*moderate*
SPECIAL REQUIREMENTS:	*sous vide setup, vacuum sealer, Insta Cure #1 (optional), Bacon Mayonnaise (see variation on page 108)*

Our twist on a traditional B.L.T. substitutes a crispy yet tender pork belly for crunchy bacon. Brining the pork belly helps the meat retain its reddish color, firms its texture, and changes its flavor (think ham or corned beef). Even if you omit the brine, or buy prebrined belly from the store, the result is delicious, although different.

Bacon mayonnaise adds a bit of smokiness to the sandwich. If top-quality tomatoes are unavailable, use roasted onion, fresh apple or pear, or sautéed mushrooms instead. Or try our Tomato Confit (see page 128). Use leftover pork belly in stews or to enrich vegetable side dishes.

INGREDIENT	WEIGHT	VOLUME	SCALING	PROCEDURE
Water	1 kg	1 L / 4¼ cups	67%	① Mix until fully dissolved to make a brine.
Salt	70 g	½ cup	4.7%	
Sugar	30 g	3 Tbsp	2%	
Insta Cure #1 (optional)	30 g		2%	
Fresh pork belly, skin on	1.5 kg / 3.3 lb		100%	② Place the pork belly and brine in a zip-top bag, remove as much air as possible, and seal. Refrigerate for 72 hours, flipping the bag once a day. ③ Remove the belly from the brine, rinse it thoroughly, and pat it dry. ④ Vacuum seal the belly. Refrigerate it for 24 hours to let the brine now inside the belly equilibrate. ⑤ Preheat a water bath to 65 °C / 149 °F. ⑥ Cook the pork belly sous vide for 36 hours. ⑦ Plunge the bag in ice water to cool, and then refrigerate it until fully chilled, at least 4 hours.
Cooked pork belly, from above	as desired			⑧ Cut the pork belly into slices 1.5 cm / ⅝ in thick.
Neutral frying oil (see page xxii)	as needed			⑨ Heat a thin film of oil in a frying pan over high heat until very hot. Sear the pork on one side only until crispy, golden brown, and just warmed through, about 2 minutes.
White bread, toasted		8 slices		⑩ Spread the bacon mayonnaise on each slice of toast.
Bacon Mayonnaise (see variation on page 108)	60 g	¼ cup	4%	⑪ Top with the seared pork belly.
Cucumber, peeled and sliced		20 thin slices		⑫ Divide evenly among the sandwiches, and serve immediately.
Tomato, sliced		12–16 slices		
Avocado, sliced		12 thin slices		
Bibb or Boston lettuce		4–8 leaves		

VARIATIONS

Pressure-Cooked Pork Belly

If you're in a hurry, you can pressure-cook the meat, which produces a braised texture. Skip the curing step. The result is quite different from the sous vide version, but still very good. Pressure-cook the belly at a gauge pressure of 1 bar / 15 psi for 50 minutes. Cool the meat completely before slicing and searing it; otherwise, it will fall apart. Alternatively, make a sloppy-joe-style B.L.T. by shredding the meat and frying it.

Smoked Bacon B.L.T.

Begin at step 5, and use a slab of smoked bacon in step 6. Because of the strong cure used to create bacon, the texture will be less tender, but the flavor is tasty. Cook the bacon sous vide at 65 °C / 149 °F for 12 hours, and slice it as in step 8.

TO MAKE AHEAD

After cooling the pork belly in step 7, remove from the ice bath, keeping the pork sealed, and refrigerate it for up to 3 days. Then continue with step 8.

1 Mix the water, salt, sugar, and Insta Cure #1 until they have dissolved completely to make a brine. The Insta Cure is optional but helps preserve the color of the meat while it cooks. Do not substitute Insta Cure #2.

2 Place the pork belly in a large (4 L / 1 gal) zip-top bag, pour in the brine, remove as much air as possible from the bag, and seal it. Refrigerate for 72 hours, flipping the bag each day to ensure that the pork cures evenly.

3 Remove the pork belly from the brine, rinse it under running water, and pat it dry.

4 Vacuum seal the pork belly, and refrigerate it for 24 hours to allow the brine in the pork to diffuse evenly throughout the meat.

5 Preheat a water bath to **65** °C / **149** °F.

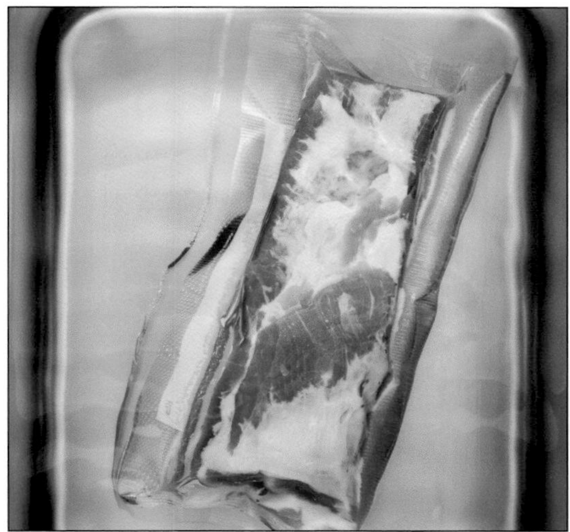

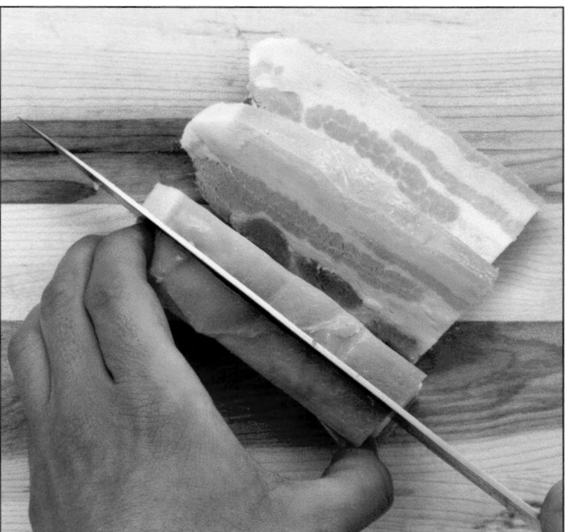

6 Cook the pork belly sous vide for 36 hours.

7 Plunge the bag in ice water to cool the meat, and then refrigerate the meat in the bag until it is thoroughly chilled.

8 Cut the pork belly into slices 1.5 cm / ⅝ in thick.

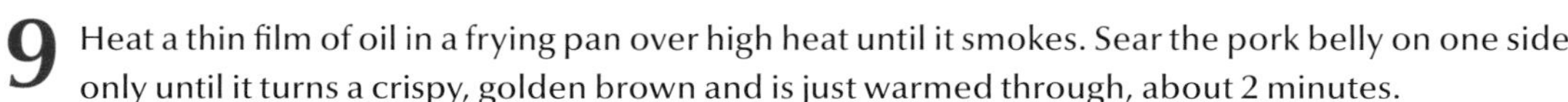

9 Heat a thin film of oil in a frying pan over high heat until it smokes. Sear the pork belly on one side only until it turns a crispy, golden brown and is just warmed through, about 2 minutes.

10 Spread bacon mayonnaise over the slices of toast. For added flavor, panfry the bread in bacon fat instead of toasting it.

11 Top the bread with the seared pork belly.

12 Divide the cucumber, tomato, avocado slices, and lettuce evenly among the sandwiches, and serve immediately.

You can make an entree of the pork belly by skipping step 8. Sear the pork on all sides as in step 9, and then slice it for serving.

LAMB CURRY

YIELD:	*four servings (850 g / 4 cups)*
TIME ESTIMATE:	*2 days overall, including 30 minutes of preparation and 48 hours unattended*
STORAGE NOTES:	*keeps for 2 days when refrigerated or up to 3 months when frozen*
LEVEL OF DIFFICULTY:	*easy*
SPECIAL REQUIREMENTS:	*sous vide setup, vacuum sealer, Mughal Curry Sauce (page 104)*

One frequent complaint voiced about lamb is that it has a strong gamey flavor. The reason this flavor develops is that lamb fat is fragile and tends to oxidize quickly—the same reason that reheated lamb can develop an unappealing, warmed-over flavor. To preserve the fresh flavor, you must vacuum seal the meat before cooking it sous vide. To make a delicious lamb stew, try replacing the curry with our Mushroom Jus (see page 91), thinly sliced onions, and fresh spinach.

INGREDIENT	WEIGHT	VOLUME	SCALING	PROCEDURE
Lamb shanks, bone in	1.4 kg / 3 lb	2 large or 4 small	100%	① Preheat a water bath to **62** °C / **144** °F. ② Trim the fat and silverskin from the lamb shanks. ③ Vacuum seal the lamb shanks individually with equal amounts of oil. ④ Cook sous vide for 48 hours. ⑤ Remove the meat from the bone, discarding any fat and gristle. Trim the meat into bite-size pieces.
Neutral-tasting oil	40 g	45 mL / 3 Tbsp	3%	
Mughal Curry Sauce see page 104	350 g	1¼ cups	25%	⑥ Warm the sauce in a large pot to the cooking temperature of the lamb. ⑦ Stir in the prepared lamb, and warm gently until heated through.
Salt	to taste			⑧ Season the curry.
Dates, thinly sliced	50 g	½ cup	4%	⑨ Garnish the curry, and serve it warm.
Mint leaves, julienned	2 g	12 small leaves	0.1%	

TO MAKE AHEAD

After breaking up the meat in step 5, refrigerate it until ready to use. Then continue with step 6.

VARIATIONS

Pressure-Cooked Lamb Shanks

Pressure-cooking the lamb yields a texture similar to traditional braising but is much faster. Combine the lamb shanks and 100 g / 100 mL / ⅜ cup of water in a pressure cooker, and pressure-cook at a gauge pressure of 1 bar / 15 psi for 1 hour. Strain, add the cooking liquid into the Mughal curry sauce, and simmer for 10 minutes. Follow step 5 to debone the shanks. Continue with step 7.

Whole Lamb Shank

To serve the lamb shank whole, cook as indicated through step 4, saving the cooking juices. Sear the cooked shanks until they turn deep brown by deep-frying them in very hot oil or by using a blowtorch (see page 15). Clean the bone for a nicer presentation. Strain the reserved cooking juices, and reduce them to add another layer of complexity to the sauce.

The Whole Lamb Shank variation can be made with any cut of lamb, including leg, shoulder, or neck.

2b

1 Preheat a water bath to 62 °C / 144 °F.

2 Trim the fat and silverskin from the lamb shanks. Even when cooked sous vide, silverskin—on any meat—never becomes tender.

3 Place each lamb shank in a separate bag with oil, and vacuum seal it.

4 Cook the shanks sous vide for 48 hours. Make sure the bags stay submerged.

5 Remove the meat from the bone. Discard any fat and gristle. While the lamb is still warm, separate the muscles by hand, and then cut the meat into bite-size pieces or break it up by using a fork.

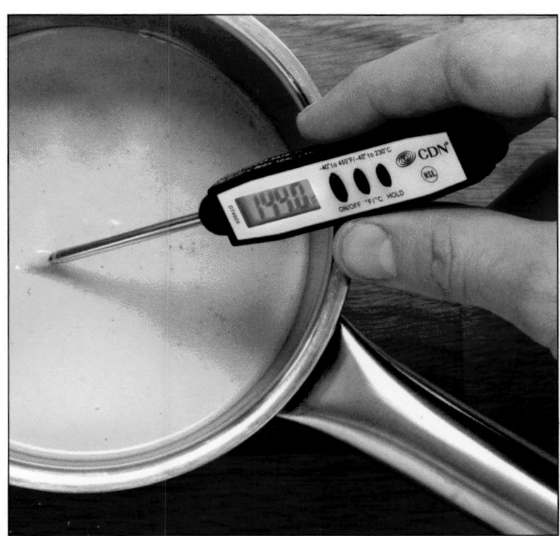

6 Warm the Mughal curry sauce in a large pot. Use a thermometer to ensure that the sauce does not get hotter than the cooking temperature of the lamb.

7 Stir the prepared lamb into the sauce. Warm it gently until it has heated through.

8 Season the curry with salt to taste.

9 Garnish the curry with dates and mint, and serve it warm.

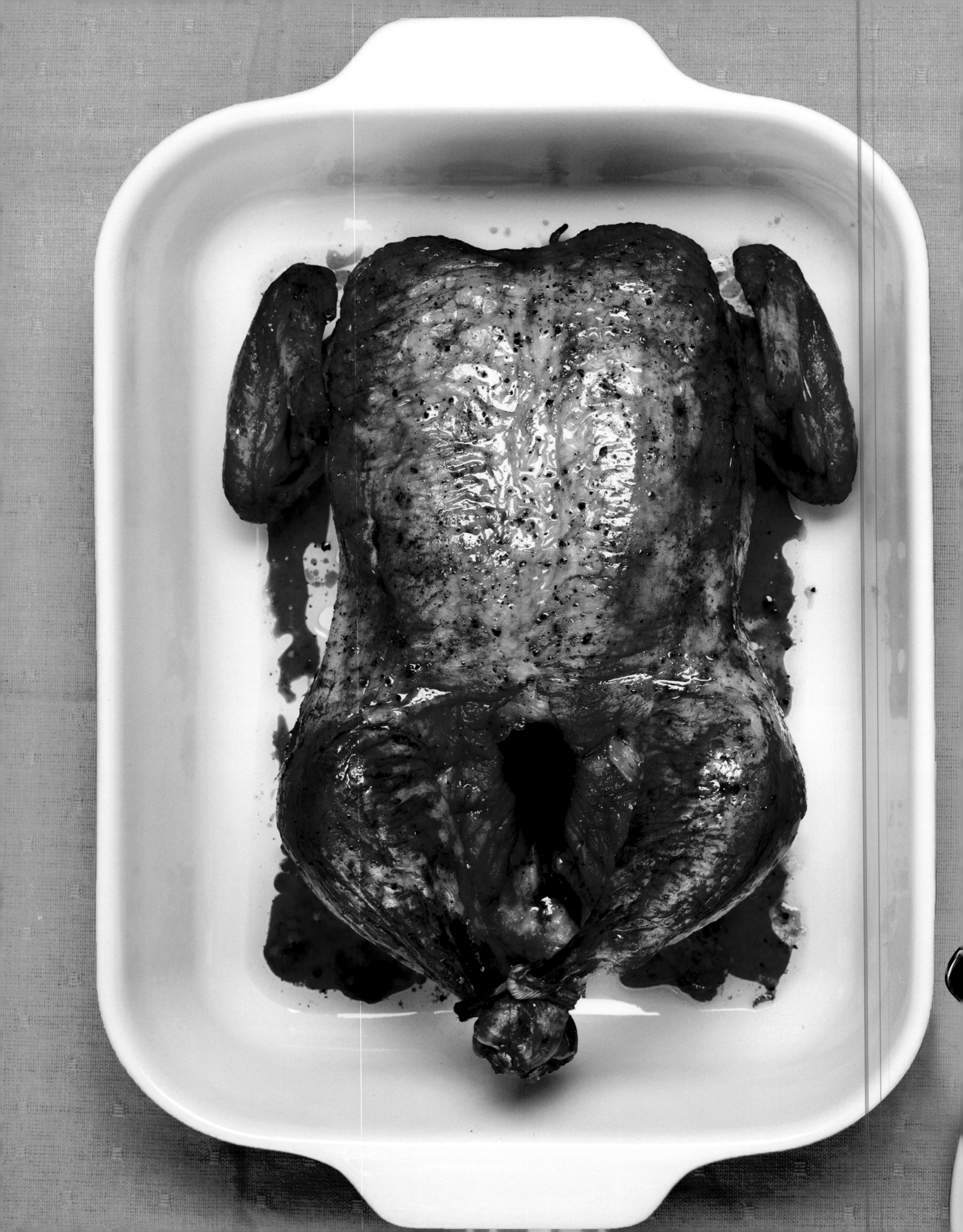

ROAST CHICKEN

At its best, roast chicken can be one of the world's greatest culinary achievements. Brown, crispy skin covers tender, juicy meat: the combination of flavors and textures is simply amazing. Yet the perfect roast chicken is nearly impossible to achieve in practice. The temperature required to brown and crisp the skin is so high that it leaves the meat underneath scorched and dry. The dark thigh and leg meat similarly need higher heat than is ideal for the white breast meat. Brining the chicken in salt water can help the delicate breast meat retain more juice at higher temperatures, but the brine has the same effect on the skin, which then ends up unpleasantly chewy.

The classical approach of roasting the bird whole thus inevitably trades perfect skin for dry, overcooked breasts, or else swaps perfect breast meat for yellow, rubbery skin. Those "perfect" roast chickens you see on magazine covers are often made by food-styling trickery and are either raw or so overcooked you wouldn't want to eat them.

A Modernist—and eminently practical—approach is to cook each part of the chicken separately to perfection. But that means cutting the bird up. Here, we present a technique for roasting a whole bird that produces the best roast chicken that we've ever made in a home oven. Admittedly, it isn't simple. The technique, which borrows some ideas from Peking Duck, involves blanching the skin repeatedly and then drying it; roasting the bird slowly; and browning the skin under a broiler or in a very hot oven or pan. The result is remarkable.

For a special dish such as this you should buy the best bird you can find. It should be plump and fresh: air-chilled and kosher chickens are usually excellent. Avoid birds that are sealed tightly with water. The quality of the meat reflects how the bird lived and was slaughtered, so buy from sources that treat the animals humanely.

THE SCIENCE OF DARK MEAT VS. WHITE MEAT

Why is chicken breast meat white while the leg meat is dark? The answer has to do with the different roles that these muscles—and the fibers that make them—play in a living bird. Look at breast meat under a microscope, and you'll see many light-colored, fast-twitch muscle fibers geared for intense bursts of activity, such as fluttering away from a hungry fox. These fibers do not burn fat, so this meat is lean. A chicken's legs and thighs, in contrast, are built for stamina. So they contain mostly dark fibers that are tuned for endurance. These muscles burn fat for fuel, so the meat is richer in flavor as well as color.

HIGHLIGHTS

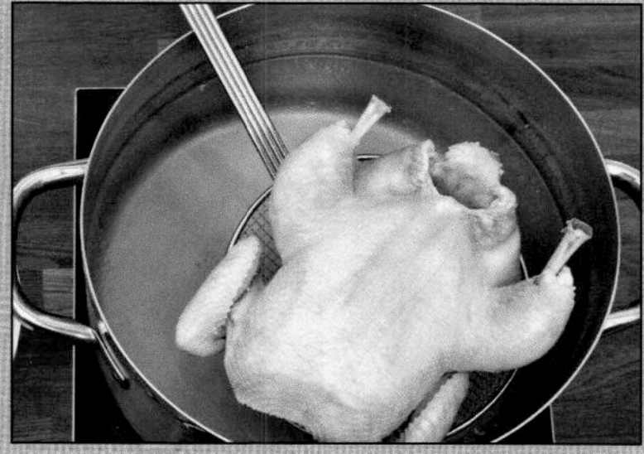

Blanching the chicken skin in boiling water before drying it overnight, a traditional technique for making Peking Duck, gelatinizes the protein in the skin and yields a much crisper texture.

see page 238

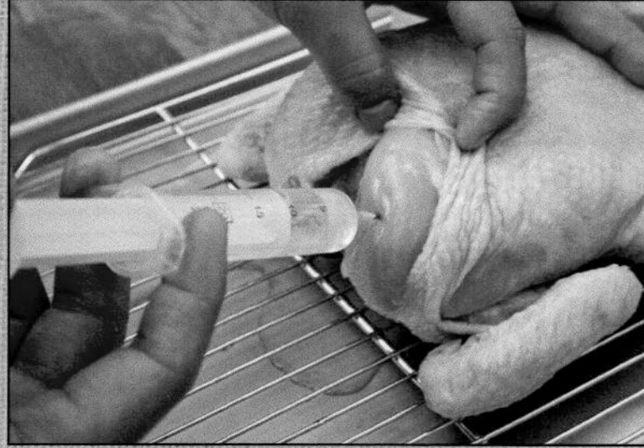

Protect the chicken breasts from overcooking by using an injector to brine them without piercing the skin.

see page 238

For perfectly crispy skin, cook the meat slowly at a low temperature, and then sear the skin briefly under the broiler or in a frying pan.

see page 238

Chicken cooked sous vide is fantastic, especially for soups and salads. Turkey legs and breasts are also best when cooked this way. In addition to recipes for common poultry, we give time-and-temperature suggestions for cooking duck, squab, and quail sous vide.

see pages 244–247

FURTHER READING IN *MODERNIST CUISINE*

What really goes on in the oven when you bake a turkey: see pages 2·104–105

How to roast a chicken in a combi oven: see pages 2·178–179

How muscle works, and the differences between red meat and white: see pages 3·6–18

A plated-dish recipe for Crispy Hay-Smoked Chicken: see pages 5·112–119

ROAST CHICKEN

YIELD:	*four to eight servings (1.5 kg)*
TIME ESTIMATE:	*about 29 hours overall, including 1 hour of preparation and 18–28 hours unattended*
STORAGE NOTES:	*serve immediately*
LEVEL OF DIFFICULTY:	*advanced (special handling and precise temperatures)*
SPECIAL REQUIREMENTS:	*brine injector or syringe, digital thermometer with oven-safe probe*
GOES WELL WITH:	*Home Jus Gras (see page 93), Pan Gravy (see page 95)*

This recipe requires advanced planning, patience, and a little practice; it is not something you would make every day. But for special occasions, this roast chicken is simply amazing. It's especially important to calibrate your oven (see page 35) to make this recipe properly. Soy sauce is not a traditional ingredient in roast chicken, but it acts as a drying and browning agent for the skin and also adds a great savory flavor. For an even deeper color, stir 5 g / ½ tsp of sweet paprika into the soy sauce before step 9.

INGREDIENT	WEIGHT	VOLUME	SCALING	PROCEDURE
Whole chicken	2 kg/4.4 lb	1 medium roaster	100%	① Cut away the wishbone. ② French the chicken legs by cutting the skin in a circle around the leg bone at the end of the leg, using the back of the knife to press the meaty parts toward the body to expose the bone, and then cutting the joints off the ends of the exposed leg bones.
Water Salt	200 g 12 g	200 mL/⅞ cup 1 Tbsp	10% 0.6%	③ Mix until completely dissolved to make a brine. ④ Inject 70 mL/¼ cup of the brine into each breast, and inject the rest of the brine into the thighs and legs. Try not to pierce the skin.
Soy sauce	20 g	15 mL/1 Tbsp	1%	⑤ Bring a large pot of water to a boil, and arrange an ice-water bath alongside. Both must be large enough to fully submerge the chicken. ⑥ Plunge the chicken into the boiling water, blanch it for 20 seconds, and then plunge it into the ice water for 20 seconds. ⑦ Repeat steps 5 and 6 two more times. ⑧ Pat the chicken dry with paper towels. ⑨ Brush it evenly with soy sauce. ⑩ Refrigerate it on a rack, uncovered, overnight or for up to 24 hours.
Cooking spray or neutral frying oil see page xxii	as needed			⑪ Preheat the oven to **95 °C/205 °F**. ⑫ Arrange a rack on a baking sheet, and spray both with cooking spray or brush them lightly with oil. Place the chicken on the rack, and insert the probe of a digital thermometer into the center of the thickest piece. ⑬ Wrap the exposed leg bones tightly in aluminum foil, and bake the chicken to a core temperature of **60 °C/140 °F**, 3–4 hours. ⑭ Allow the chicken to rest at room temperature for 45 minutes.
Neutral frying oil or clarified, unsalted butter see page 119	30 g	30 mL/2½ Tbsp	1.5%	⑮ Arrange an oven rack so that the top of the chicken will be 6 cm/2⅜ in from the upper heat source. ⑯ Preheat the broiler to high. ⑰ Brush the chicken with oil, and place it on the rack breast-side down. ⑱ Broil until the skin turns brown and crisp, 5–6 minutes. ⑲ Turn the chicken over, and broil it breast-side up until the skin turns brown and crisp, 4–5 minutes. ⑳ Serve the chicken hot.

Safety tips for lightly cooked food: see page xxv

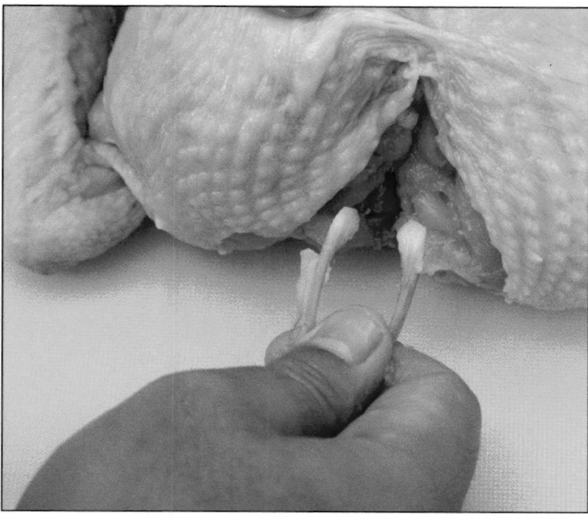

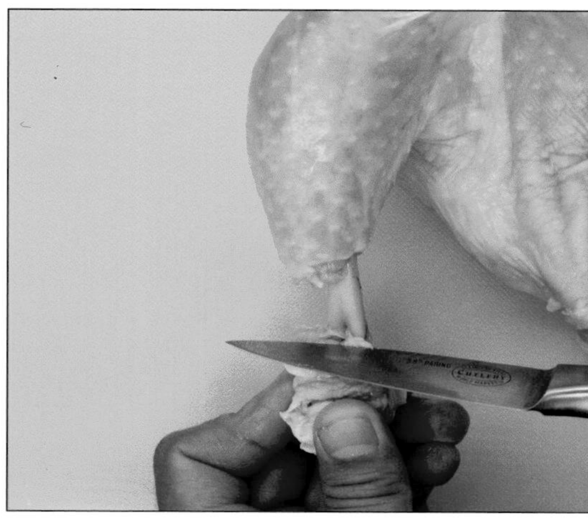

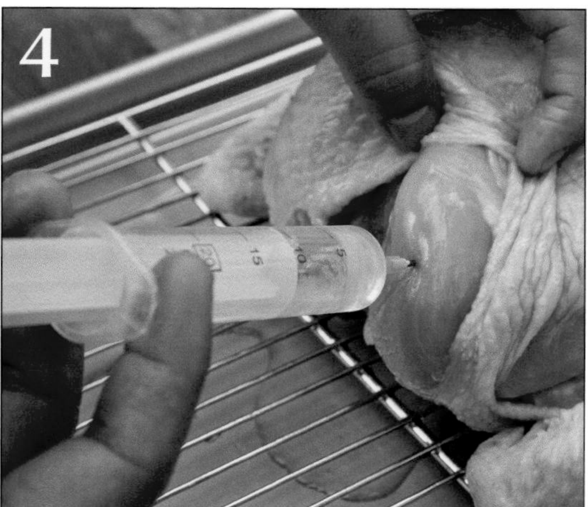

1 Cut away the wishbone by using a sharp boning knife. Avoid damaging the skin or cutting into the breast. This step helps heat flow evenly into the bird and makes it easier to carve the roast chicken.

2 French the leg bones. First, make a cut perpendicular to the bone and through the skin 2.5 cm / 1 in from the end of each leg. Continue the incision around the bone to release the skin. Next, use the back of the knife to push the skin up toward the body, exposing the bone. Cut off the joint at the end of each leg. Frenching the legs helps heat move into the thigh meat.

3 Mix the salt into the water, and stir until it has dissolved completely. This is the brine.

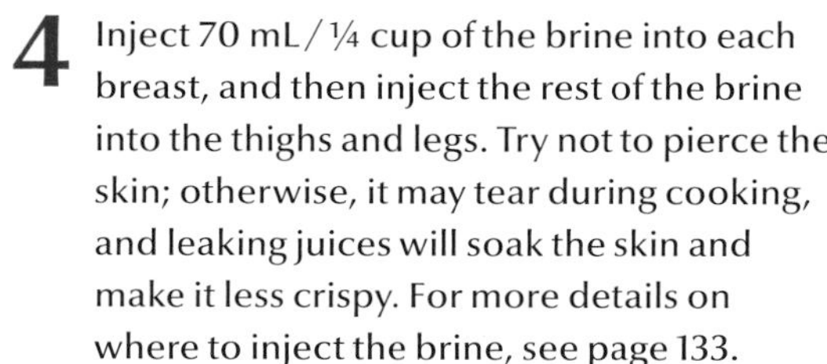

4 Inject 70 mL / ¼ cup of the brine into each breast, and then inject the rest of the brine into the thighs and legs. Try not to pierce the skin; otherwise, it may tear during cooking, and leaking juices will soak the skin and make it less crispy. For more details on where to inject the brine, see page 133.

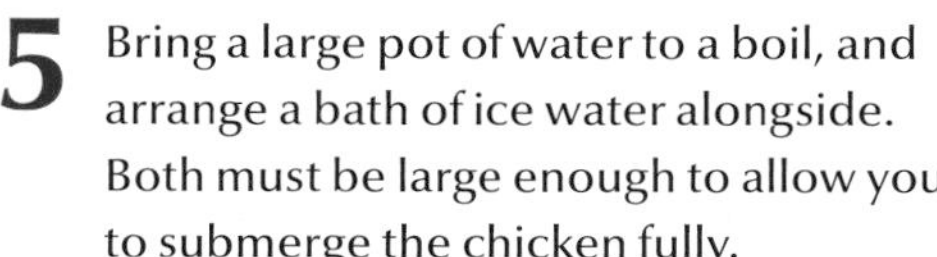

5 Bring a large pot of water to a boil, and arrange a bath of ice water alongside. Both must be large enough to allow you to submerge the chicken fully.

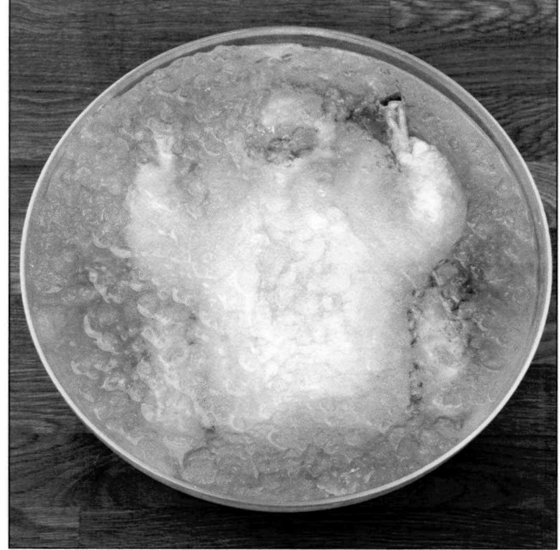

6 Fully submerge the chicken in boiling water for 20 seconds to blanch it, and then immediately plunge it into the ice water for 20 seconds. A large perforated skimmer or "spider" is the best tool for this step. The skin becomes very fragile after this step, so take care not to tear it.

7 Repeat the blanch-and-chill process in step 6 twice more. This technique renders some of the fat and tightens the skin, which yields a crispier roast chicken.

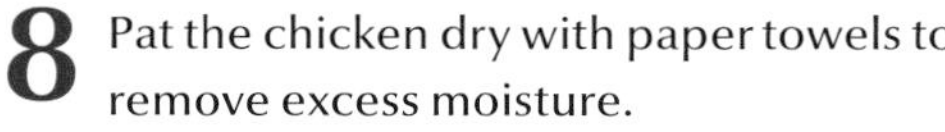

8 Pat the chicken dry with paper towels to remove excess moisture.

9 Brush soy sauce evenly over the chicken to improve the color and aid in crisping. You can add 5 g / ½ tsp of paprika to the soy sauce to give the bird a more amber color.

10 Put the chicken on a lightly oiled rack, and place it, uncovered, in the refrigerator for 12–24 hours.

During the refrigeration period, the brine equilibrates and the skin dries in the air—both of which help to produce a moist interior and a crispy exterior.

continued on the next page

11 Preheat the oven to **95** °C / **205** °F. Use the convection baking mode, if available on your oven.

12 Arrange a rack on a baking sheet, and coat both with cooking spray or brush them with oil. Place the chicken on the rack. Insert a digital probe thermometer into the center of the thickest piece.

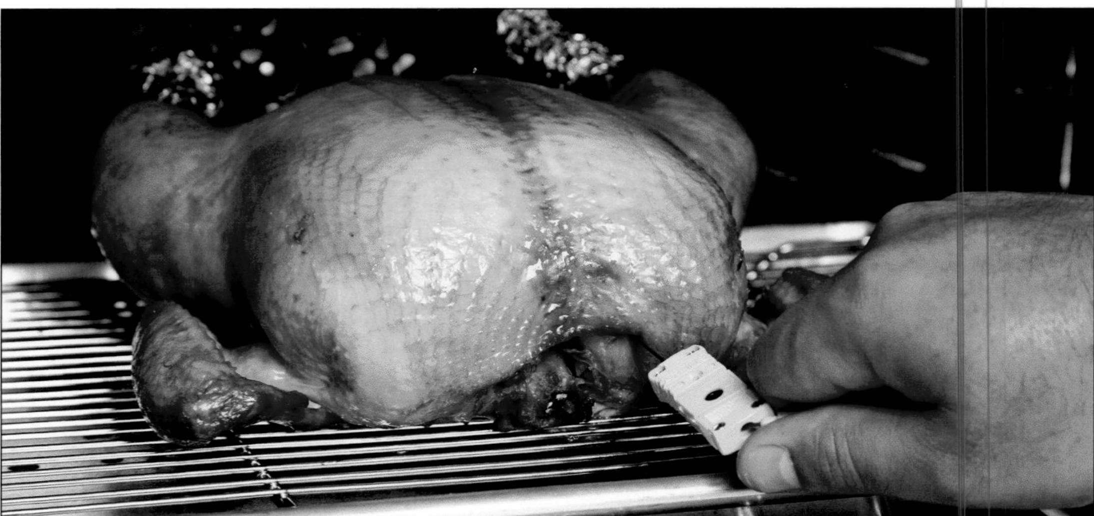

13 Wrap the exposed leg bones tightly in aluminum foil to enhance heat transfer and prevent burning. Bake the chicken in the oven until the core temperature reaches **60** °C / **140** °F, 3–4 hours.

14 Remove the chicken from the oven, and allow it to rest for 45 minutes at room temperature. Our experiments found that the juiciness of the carved chicken peaks after a 45-minute rest.

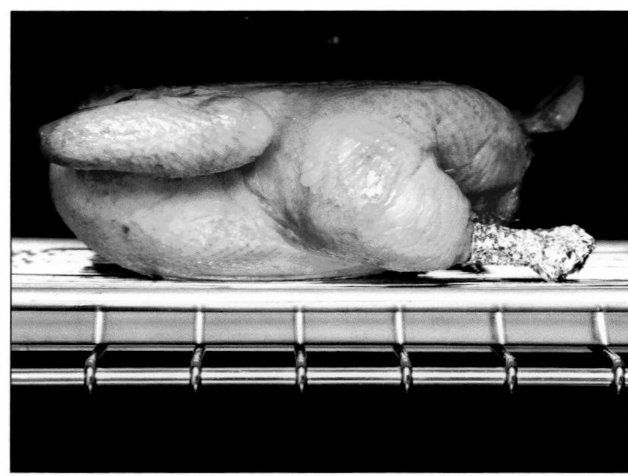

15 Arrange the oven rack at a height that will place the top of the chicken about 6 cm / 2⅜ in from the heat source at the top of the broiler.

16 Preheat the broiler to high.

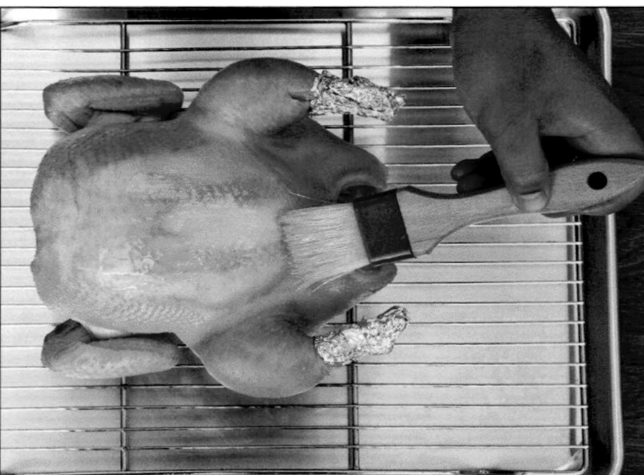

17 Brush oil or clarified butter evenly over the entire chicken, and arrange it on the rack, breast-side down.

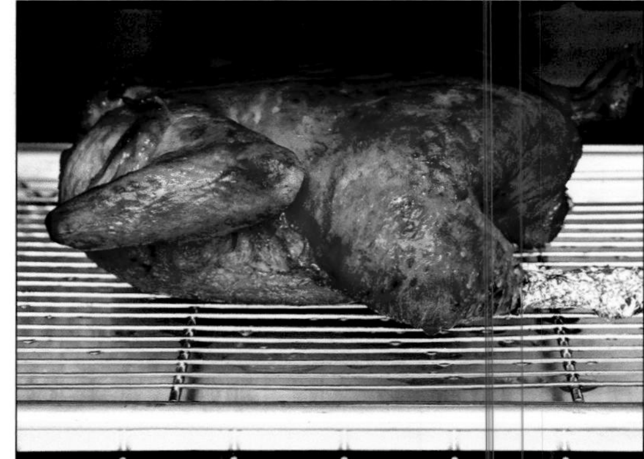

18 Broil the chicken until the skin on the back becomes brown and crisp, 5–6 minutes.

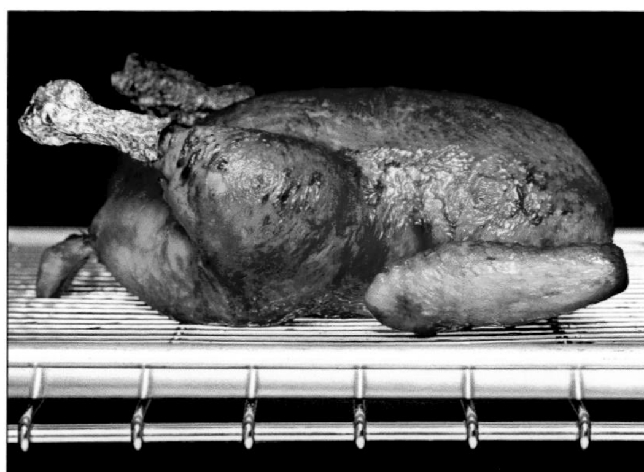

19 Turn the chicken over, and continue broiling, breast-side up, until the skin on the front turns brown and crisp, 4–5 minutes.

20 Carve the roast chicken, and serve it hot. The skin is crispiest when it emerges from the oven, so do not rest the bird again before serving.

VARIATIONS

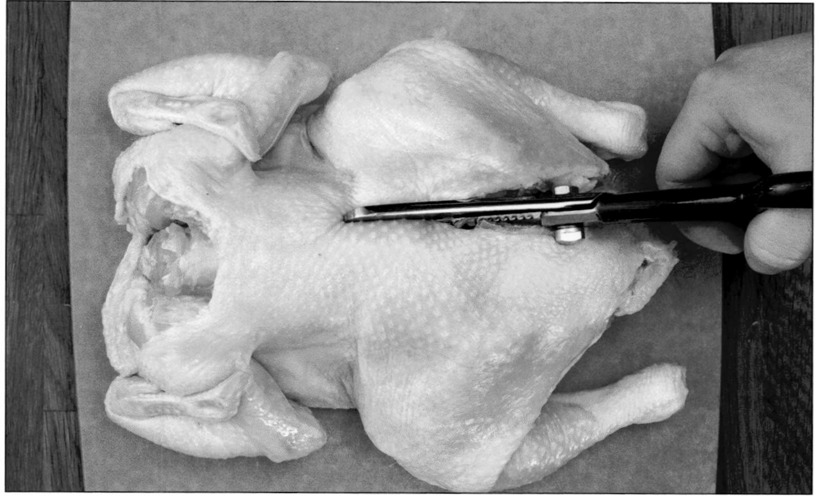

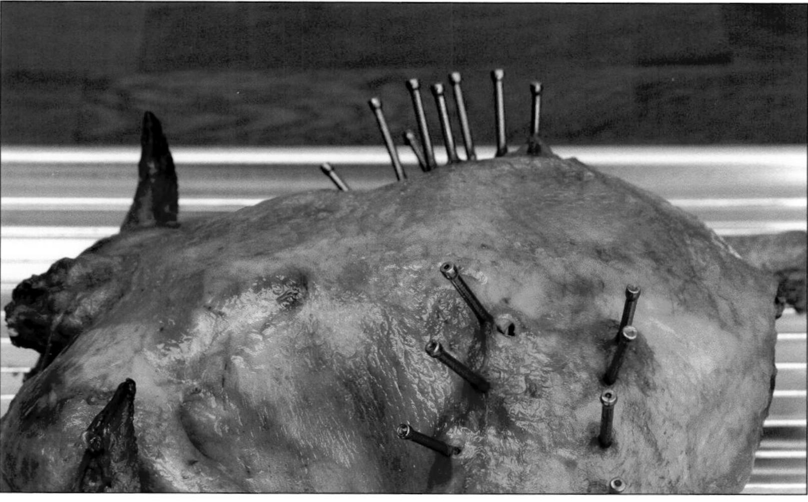

Pincushion Chicken

It may seem a tad brutal, but an effective way to conduct more heat toward the thighs of the chicken without overcooking its juicy breasts is to push 12 steel finishing nails into each thigh until they contact the bone. Do this at step 12; the nails should fit through the rack. The thigh meat can then be cooked more fully while the breast meat remains extremely juicy. Try this variation for your next Halloween dinner.

Extra-Juicy Chicken (not pictured)

Add 2.5 cm / 1 in of water in a separate pan at step 12, and place it in the bottom of the oven, below the baking sheet. Add an extra hour to the cooking time in step 13; your patience will be rewarded. Remove the pan of water at step 15.

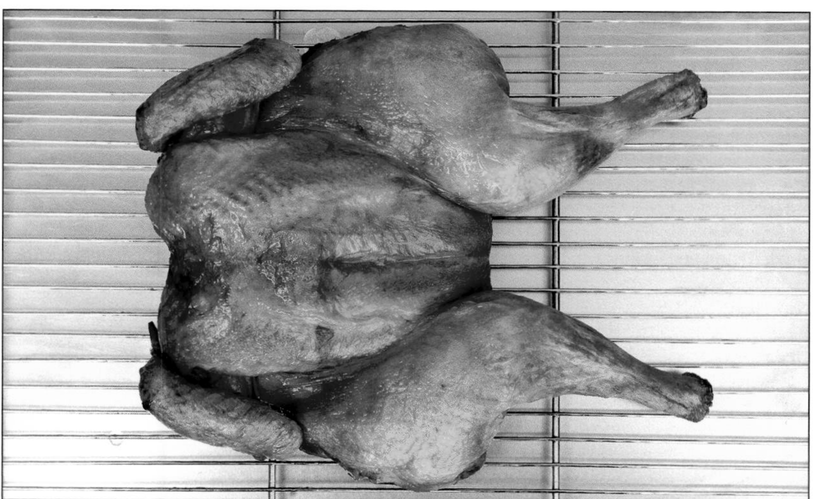

Spatchcock Chicken

After step 8, remove the backbone with kitchen shears, and then carefully flatten the chicken. Continue with the remaining steps, but broil skin-side up only. You do not need to french the bones.

Deep-Fried Chicken (below)

You can use a deep fryer rather than the broiler to brown and crisp the skin on the cooked chicken. Fill a deep stock pot no more than half full with neutral frying oil (see page xxii). Preheat the oil to **220 °C / 428 °F**. After step 14, lower the chicken carefully into the hot oil, breast-side down. Use caution to avoid splatters. Deep-fry the whole chicken until the skin browns, about 2 minutes. Drain it, and serve it hot. See page 26 for safety information about deep-frying.

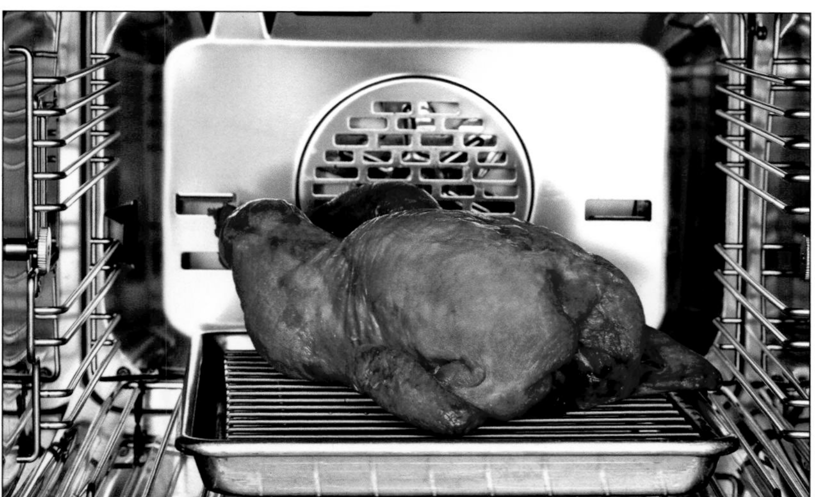

Combi Oven Roast Chicken

If you have a home combi oven that accurately holds low temperatures, then cook the chicken at step 13 in convection mode at **62 °C / 144 °F**. A medium-size roaster takes 3–3½ hours to cook at this temperature.

SLOW-BAKED CHICKEN WITH ONIONS

YIELD:	*four servings (900 g)*
TIME ESTIMATE:	*3½ hours overall, including 30 minutes of preparation and 3 hours unattended*
STORAGE NOTES:	*serve immediately*
LEVEL OF DIFFICULTY:	*moderate*
SPECIAL REQUIREMENTS:	*brine injector or syringe, digital thermometer with oven-safe probe*

One of the easiest ways to enjoy superjuicy meat with crisp golden skin is to brine chicken pieces, cook them smothered in shaved onions, and then panfry their skin. The onions not only add flavor but also prevent the poultry from drying out as you slow-cook the bird at low temperature. Although you can buy chicken breasts and thighs from your butcher, it's better to buy a high-quality whole chicken, and to cut it up yourself. You'll save money, and you can use the remaining parts in other recipes.

INGREDIENT	WEIGHT	VOLUME	SCALING	PROCEDURE
Water Salt	200 g 12 g	200 mL / ⅞ cup 1 Tbsp	13% 0.8%	① Preheat the oven to 75 °C / 170 °F; if your oven doesn't offer a setting this low, use the lowest setting available. ② Mix until fully dissolved to make the brine.
Whole chicken, or two bone-in thighs and two skin-on breasts	1.5 kg / 3.3 lb	1 small roaster	100%	③ Remove the thighs and breasts from the chicken. Try to keep the skin intact. ④ Inject the brine as evenly as possible into the chicken parts without piercing the skin.
Sweet onion, sliced paper thin on a mandoline Cooking spray or neutral-tasting oil	300 g as needed	3 cups (1½ medium onions)	20%	⑤ Pat the chicken skin dry, coat it lightly with cooking spray or oil, and then arrange the pieces, skin-side down, on a baking rack over a sheet pan. ⑥ Cover the chicken pieces evenly with a thick layer of shaved onions, and then insert the oven-safe probe of a digital thermometer into the center of the thickest breast piece. ⑦ Bake the breasts to a core temperature of **60** °C / **140** °F, about 3 hours, and then hold them at this temperature for 20 minutes more. Cook the thighs to a core temperature of **65** °C / **149** °F, about 15 minutes more. ⑧ Remove the onions, and set them aside for use in step 10.
Neutral frying oil (see page xxii) Salt	as needed as needed			⑨ Heat the oil in a large pan over medium-high heat, and then panfry the chicken, skin-side down only, until the skin turns brown and crisp, 2–3 minutes. ⑩ Remove the chicken, reduce the heat to medium, and cook the reserved onions in the oil until caramelized, about 2 minutes. ⑪ Slice the chicken, season it, and serve it hot with the caramelized onions.

Safety tips for lightly cooked food: see page xxv

1 Preheat the oven to 75 °C / 170 °F; use an oven-safe thermometer to check the temperature (see page 8). If your oven doesn't allow such low settings, use the lowest temperature available.

2 Make the brine by stirring the salt into the water until it dissolves fully.

3 Cut the thighs and breasts from the chicken while taking care to keep the skin intact. Save the legs, wings, and back for another use.

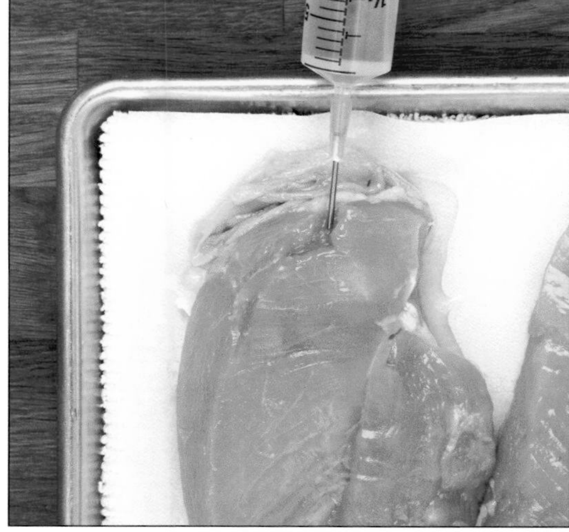

4 Fill a brine injector or syringe with the brine, and inject it into the thighs and breasts as evenly as you can without piercing the skin.

5 Pat the skin dry. Place a baking rack or a clean, dry towel in a sheet pan. Coat the skin lightly with oil, and then arrange the pieces, skin-side down, on the rack or towel.

6 Cover the chicken pieces with a thick, even layer of shaved onions. Insert the oven-safe probe of a digital thermometer into the center of the thickest piece.

7 Bake the breasts to a core temperature of 60 °C / 140 °F, about 3 hours, and then hold them at this temperature for another 20 minutes. Cook the thighs to a core temperature of 65 °C / 149 °F, about 15 minutes more. Increasing humidity in the oven may cause the core temperature to stop rising after 2–3 hours; if that happens, increase the oven temperature by 5 °C / 10 °F.

8 Remove the onions, and set them aside for use in step 10.

9 Heat the oil in a large pan over medium-high heat until hot, and then sear the chicken, skin-side down only, until the skin becomes brown and crispy, 2–3 minutes.

10 Remove the chicken from the pan, and reduce the heat to medium. Cook the reserved onions in the same cooking oil until they caramelize, about 2 minutes.

11 Slice the chicken, and serve it with the caramelized onions. Season the dish with additional salt to taste.

SOUS VIDE CHICKEN

YIELD:	*four servings (600 g)*
TIME ESTIMATE:	*2½ hours overall using one bath (or 1¾ hours using two baths), including 10 minutes of preparation and the remainder unattended*
STORAGE NOTES:	*keeps for 3 days when refrigerated*
LEVEL OF DIFFICULTY:	*easy*
SPECIAL REQUIREMENTS:	*sous vide setup (two baths are ideal)*

Chicken tastes fantastic when cooked sous vide; we almost always use this technique to cook chicken for soups and salads. To use this chicken in our Chicken Noodle Soup recipe on page 273, either add the slices immediately after step 7, or keep the skin on and pan-sear it in hot oil. We brown the meat when serving it in a robust, brown chicken stock (see variation on page 85).

INGREDIENT	WEIGHT	VOLUME	SCALING
Boneless chicken breast, skin on	400 g / 0.9 lb	1 breast	100%
Chicken thighs, whole, bone in, skin on	300 g / 0.7 lb	2 thighs	75%
Neutral-tasting oil	30 g	30 mL / 2 Tbsp	7.5%

PROCEDURE

① Preheat a water bath to **65 °C / 149 °F**.

② Place each piece of chicken in a separate zip-top bag with 10 g / 10 mL / 2 tsp of oil. Remove as much air as possible from the bag by using the water-displacement method (see page 58), and seal it.

③ Cook the thighs sous vide for 90 minutes, and then cool.

④ Reduce the temperature of the bath to **62 °C / 144 °F**.

⑤ Cook the breast meat sous vide to a core temperature of **60 °C / 140 °F**, about 40 minutes. Hold for another 20 minutes to pasteurize.

⑥ Return the thighs to the bath 10 minutes before the breast meat is done.

⑦ Remove the skin and bones from the chicken pieces, and cut the meat into slices 1 cm / ⅜ in thick. Serve warm or cold.

Safety tips for lightly cooked food: see page xxv

1 Preheat a water bath to **65 °C / 149 °F**. If you have a second bath, see the instruction on the next page.

2 Place each piece of chicken in a separate zip-top bag with 10 g / 10 mL / 2 tsp of oil. Use the water-displacement method (see page 58) to remove as much air as possible from the bag, and seal it.

3 Cook the thighs sous vide for 90 minutes. Alternatively, cook 3 hours for a stewed or braised texture. Cool in an ice-water bath. Do not open the bags.

4 Reduce the temperature of the water bath to **62 °C / 144 °F**, a couple degrees above the target temperature. Adding a few ice cubes lowers the water temperature quickly.

5 Cook the breast meat sous vide to a core temperature of **60 °C / 140 °F**, about 40 minutes. Hold it for another 20 minutes at that temperature to pasteurize it.

6 When the breast meat is 10 minutes from being done, add the bagged thighs back into the bath to gently reheat them. This ensures that all of the chicken is warm at the same time.

If you want to cook the drumsticks as well, seal them along with the thighs at step 2.

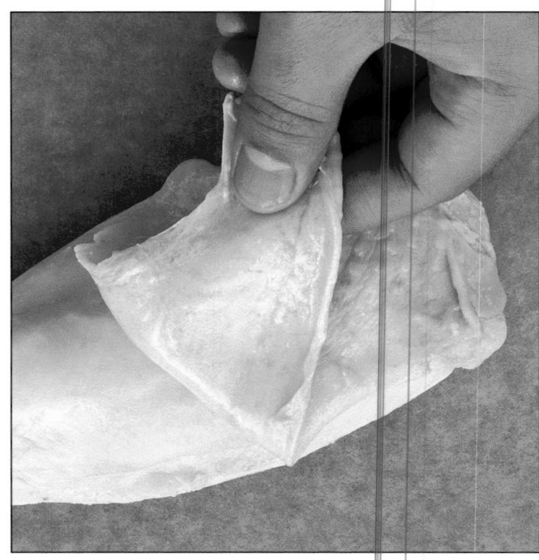

7 Remove the skin and bones, and cut the meat into slices 1 cm / ⅜ in thick. Alternatively, keep the skin on, and sear the chicken pieces skin-side down in a hot, oiled pan until the skin turns dark brown. Cut the meat from the thigh bone, and serve it warm or cold.

TO MAKE AHEAD

After cooking the chicken breast and thighs in steps 1–5, plunge the bags into an ice bath, and then refrigerate them. Reheat the meat in a 60 °C / 140 °F water bath for 10–15 minutes. Continue with step 7.

IF YOU HAVE TWO WATER BATHS

You can save 45 minutes by cooking the chicken breast and thighs in parallel. Preheat two water baths: one to 65 °C / 149 °F (for the thigh meat), and one to 62 °C / 144 °F (for the breast meat). Cook the thighs sous vide for 90 minutes. Cook the breast meat sous vide to a core temperature of 60 °C / 140 °F, about 40 minutes, and hold for another 20 minutes to pasteurize it. Continue with step 7.

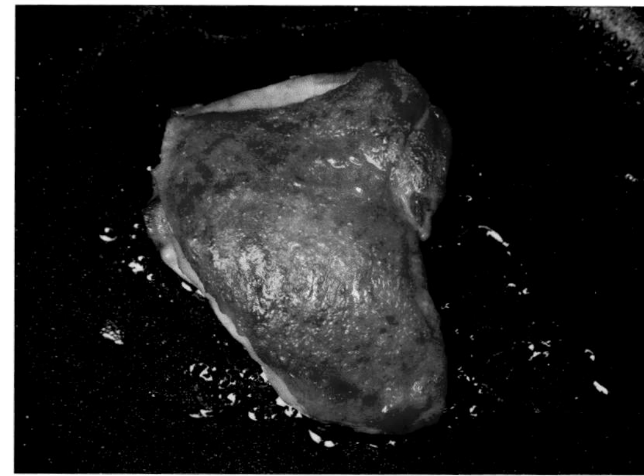

If you leave the skin on the breast when making Sous Vide Chicken, you can pan-sear it in hot oil to get the best of both worlds: perfectly cooked meat and beautifully browned skin.

SAFE COOKING OF POULTRY

The food safety of chicken and turkey has long been a subject of concern because poultry can harbor *Salmonella* and other pathogens. There is a big gap, however, between the best scientific information on safe cooking temperatures for poultry and official guidelines for cooking poultry published by the U.S. Food and Drug Administration. The tables on this page reflect the best scientific research as of 2010, which finds that poultry breast and thigh meat is safe to eat when cooked to 60 °C / 140 °F and held at that temperature for 20 minutes; shorter holding times are sufficient at higher temperatures. In contrast, the FDA recommends cooking poultry for 15 seconds at 74 °C / 165 °F, a ridiculously high temperature that is scientifically unsubstantiated.

If you are cooking for infants, the elderly, or anyone who has a compromised immune system, it is prudent to cook to a higher temperature standard. For more details, see page xxv.

Best Bets for Cooking Tender Poultry

To cook, follow the steps for chicken breast in the recipe on page 244. For more about the sous vide technique of cooking to a core temperature, see page 66. Once the meat reaches the target temperature, you can pasteurize it by keeping it in the water bath for the amount of time specified.

Ingredient	Medium rare (°C)	Medium rare (°F)	Hold at final temperature* (hours)	Medium (°C)	Medium (°F)	Hold at final temperature* (minutes)	Note	See page
chicken breast	n/a			60	140	20	we prefer to cook the breasts on the crown, although this takes at least twice as long; leaving the bone in helps the meat keep its shape and retain its juices	previous
				65	149	5		
duck breast	54	129	2 h 17 min	58	136	30	for a firmer texture, soak for a day before cooking in a brine of 5 g salt and 3.5 g sugar for every 100 g of water	133
quail breast	50	122	12	56	133	35	leave the skin on, and sear it over very high heat	
squab breast	54	129	2 h 17 min	58	136	30	remove the skin, and wrap it in thinly sliced bacon before cooking	
turkey breast	n/a			56	133	35	serve with a turkey variation of our Jus Gras	247
				62	144	8		

(times and temperatures in red are those that we prefer)
(required to pasteurize)

Best Bets for Cooking Tough Poultry

To cook legs, thighs, and wings sous vide, follow the steps for chicken thighs in the recipe on the previous page. In this sous vide technique, time and temperature indicate doneness rather than the core temperature of the food (see page 66).

Ingredient	Tender and juicy (°C)	Tender and juicy (°F)	Tender and juicy (hours)	Braised texture (°C)	Braised texture (°F)	Braised texture (hours)	Note	See page
chicken leg and thigh	65	149	1½	68	154	3	to make fried chicken, cook sous vide, coat with a mix of equal parts potato starch and Wondra flour, and deep-fry at 195 °C / 385 °F for 3 minutes	previous
chicken wing	65	149	1	62	144	12		249
duck leg	60	140	48	65	149	24	to make duck confit, brine the legs for 12 hours, and then cook each leg sealed in a plastic bag with 12 g / 1 Tbsp of duck fat	next
				82	180	5		
turkey leg	65	149	8	70	158	10	brush with barbecue sauce, and finish on the grill	next
turkey wing	62	144	18	80	176	8	in the U.S., turkey wings are more widely available near the end of the year	

(times and temperatures in red are those that we prefer)

TURKEY CONFIT

YIELD:	*four servings (450 g)*
TIME ESTIMATE:	*24½ hours, including 30 minutes of preparation and 24 hours unattended*
STORAGE NOTES:	*keeps for 5 days when refrigerated or up to 1 month when frozen*
LEVEL OF DIFFICULTY:	*easy*
SPECIAL REQUIREMENTS:	*sous vide setup, vacuum sealer, needle-nose pliers, duck fat, juniper berries*

Duck confit is a classic French preparation in which duck meat is cooked in an abundance of duck fat. In this Thanksgiving version, dark turkey meat is vacuum-cured with a complex mélange that blends the aroma of autumn herbs with the richness of duck fat.

If duck fat is unavailable, substitute butter or neutral-tasting oil. You can also substitute duck or chicken legs for the turkey. We serve the confit as an accompaniment to slices of juicy Sous Vide Turkey Breast (see the next page) and Home Jus Gras (see page 93).

INGREDIENT	WEIGHT	VOLUME	SCALING	PROCEDURE
Turkey legs	900 g / 2 lb	2 legs	100%	① Preheat a water bath to **60 °C / 140 °F**. ② Make a cut around the circumference of the ankle bone to sever the tendons. ③ Pull out the tendons, one at a time, by using needle-nose pliers. ④ Push the meat and skin up the leg from the ankle, and clean the bone.
Salt	40 g	3½ Tbsp	4.4%	⑤ Combine, and coat the turkey legs evenly in a thick layer. Set aside any salt and sugar that does not stick for use in the next step.
Sugar	4 g	1 tsp	0.4%	
Duck fat, cold	150 g	¾ cup	17%	⑥ Combine with the coated turkey legs and any remaining salt and sugar, and vacuum seal. ⑦ Cook sous vide for 24 hours. ⑧ Remove the legs from the bag, and brush off the aromatics. You can strain the cooking fat and use it for other recipes.
Rosemary	2 g	1 medium sprig	0.2%	
Thyme	2 g	5 sprigs	0.2%	
Juniper berries, crushed	2 g	½ Tbsp	0.2%	
Garlic, crushed	2 g	½ clove	0.2%	
Black peppercorns	0.5 g	⅛ tsp	0.05%	
Fresh bay leaf	0.2 g	1 leaf	0.01%	
Neutral frying oil see page xxii	as needed			⑨ Pour the oil into a pan to a depth of 6 mm / ¼ in, and heat to **220 °C / 428 °F**. ⑩ Panfry the legs until the skin turns brown and crispy, 2–4 minutes per side. Alternatively, broil them until brown, 3–5 minutes per side. ⑪ Serve immediately. You can also shred the meat.

Safety tips for deep-frying: see page 26

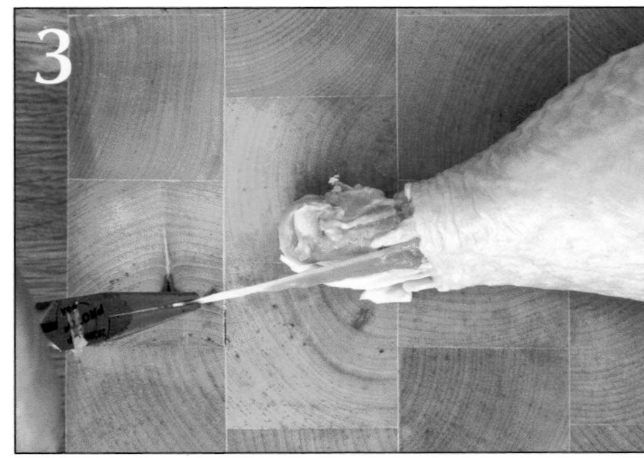
Once you have severed the tendons in the leg near the ankle bone, use needle-nose pliers to pull out the severed tendons one by one. Some will come out cleanly, but to remove the larger tendons, you may need to use a knife to separate them carefully from the meat.

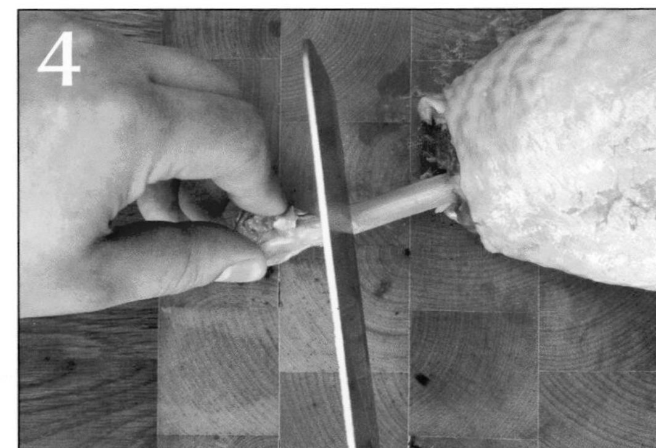
After you have removed all of the tendons, you can french the legs by using the flat of a knife to push the meat and skin toward the knee joint. This consolidates the meat on the bone. Scrape the exposed bone clean.

Not all of the sugar and salt will stick to the turkey legs, but gather up what is leftover and add it to the herbs and spices.

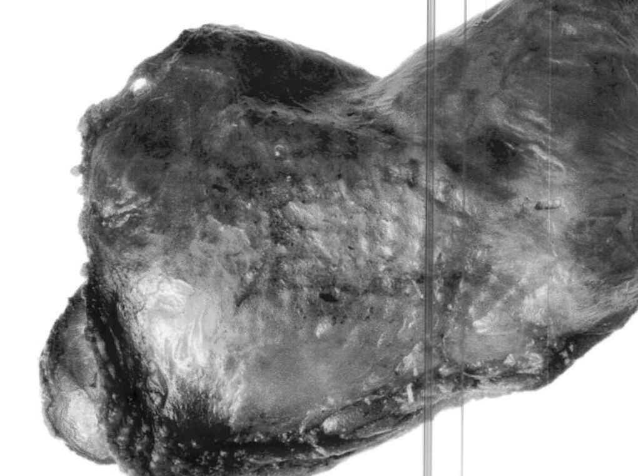

SOUS VIDE TURKEY BREAST

YIELD: *four to six servings (700 g)*
TIME ESTIMATE: *14 hours overall, including 15 minutes of preparation and 13¾ hours unattended*
STORAGE NOTES: *keeps for 3 days when refrigerated*
LEVEL OF DIFFICULTY: *moderate*
SPECIAL REQUIREMENTS: *sous vide setup, brine injector or syringe*

An injection of milk and apple juice into the turkey in this recipe infuses the meat with phosphates, which make it extremely tender when cooked. Apple juice is also effective alone, and an apple-juice brine gives the turkey a pleasantly sweet flavor.

Although turkey cooked to a core temperature of 56 °C / 133 °F will be surprisingly pink, don't worry; the long cooking time ensures that it is safely pasteurized. If you prefer your turkey to have a more traditional appearance, taste, and texture, simply set the water bath to 62 °C / 144 °F, and cook the turkey breast to a core temperature of 61 °C / 142 °F. It will still be quite juicy.

INGREDIENT	WEIGHT	VOLUME	SCALING	PROCEDURE
Apple juice	75 g	75 mL / ⅓ cup	10%	① Combine, and stir until dissolved to make a brine.
Whole milk	75 g	75 mL / ⅓ cup	10%	
Salt	10 g	2½ tsp	1.3%	
Sugar	9 g	2 tsp	1.2%	
Boneless, skinless turkey breast	750 g / 1.7 lb	1 medium or two small	100%	② Inject the brine into each part of the breast. Capture any that escapes. ③ Place the breast and all captured or leftover brine in a zip-top bag. Remove the air from the bag by using the water-displacement method (see page 58), and seal it. Refrigerate the sealed bag for 12 hours. ④ Preheat a water bath to 57 °C / 135 °F. ⑤ Remove the turkey from the bag, rinse it with cool water, and pat it dry. ⑥ Place the breast in a clean zip-top bag, remove as much air as possible from the bag (see page 58), and seal it. ⑦ Cook sous vide to a core temperature of 56 °C / 133 °F, about 1¾ hours, and then hold it at that temperature for 35 minutes more. ⑧ Serve the turkey warm or cold.

Safety tips for lightly cooked food: see page xxv

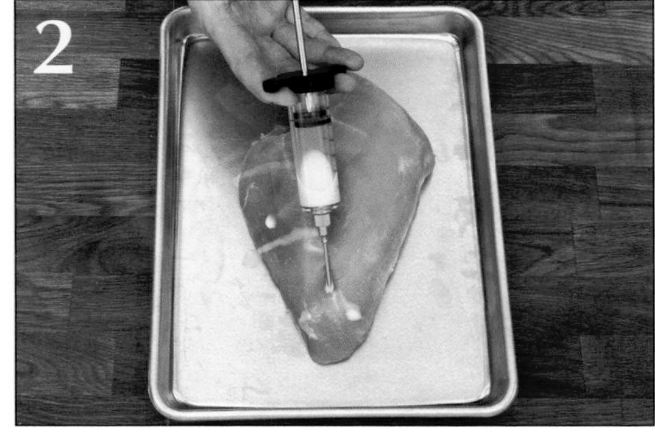

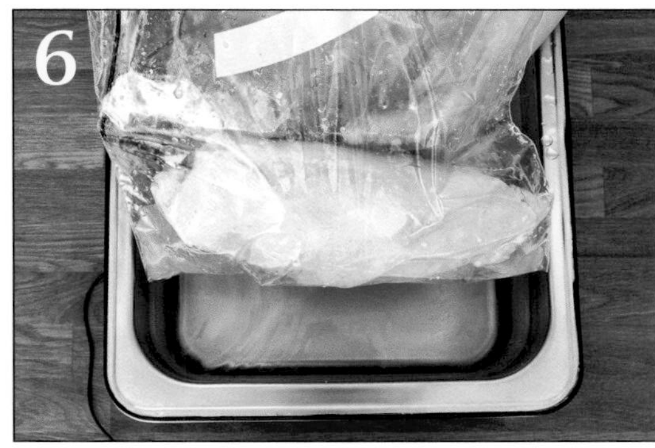

Serve the turkey with Pressure-Cooked Vegetables (see page 183) and Pressure-Cooked White Chicken Stock (see page 84).

For a restaurant-style presentation, roll the brined turkey breast into a tube shape at step 6, and wrap it with plastic wrap rather than sealing it in a zip-top bag. Tie the ends of the wrap closed, and then proceed with step 7.

CHICKEN WINGS

Buffalo wings—deep-fried and slathered in hot sauce, served with blue cheese dip and celery—combine hot and cold, crispy and juicy, spicy and savory. To Americans, they're as classic as chicken noodle soup (on which we also have a chapter—see page 264). But virtually every culture has snacks, bar food, or street food made of crispy chicken or other meat. Japan has yakitori, for example, Singapore and Malaysia have satay, and Turkey has kebabs.

One reason wings are so popular is that they have a high ratio of skin to meat. That translates into a lot of flavor, great mouthfeel, and enough richness to be satisfyingly filling. However you make them, chicken wings are the ultimate snack food.

Just as we did with roast chicken (see chapter 13 on page 237), we cooked and ate a lot of wings to find the best methods of cooking them. How do you simultaneously get the crispiest skin and the juiciest meat? How do you add sauce without sogginess? Batter is the usual way to add crunch, but it also insulates the skin and effectively creates a flabby layer between the juicy meat and the crispy batter. So we removed the skin—and found that this step makes a remarkable difference.

In search of a silky texture, we tried a Chinese technique called velveting, in which we marinated the wings, and then coated them in a starch slurry before frying them. In other experiments, we cured or brined the wings to add juiciness to the meat before cooking it sous vide until it was falling-off-the-bone tender. In this approach, a final plunge into hot oil turns the skin ultracrispy.

The right sauce can make a good wing great. A rich, low-moisture sauce keeps wings from going soggy. Although we suggest specific combinations in the recipes, each of the sauces here pairs well with all of the varieties of wings, as well as with other meats.

THE SCIENCE OF FRYING IN HOT OIL

The moment that food enters hot oil, a fast transformation begins. Swirling currents in the oil cause the temperature at the surface of the food to skyrocket within seconds. Once that temperature hits the boiling point of water, water in the food flashes to vapor and erupts as miniature steam volcanoes. As long as you see bubbles streaming from the food, you can be sure that the surface is still wet and thus no hotter than boiling water.

As the bubbles start to slow, pay close attention: a mere trickle indicates that the surface is drying and that a crust is forming. The food is approaching the final stage of deep-frying when it burns easily. Now the temperature of the crust rises quickly, and the boiling zone moves deeper into the food. This is the point at which the golden color and crispy or crunchy crust develop, the raisons d'être of deep-frying.

HIGHLIGHTS

The ultimate coating for a golden color and supercrispy texture is a light dusting of starches: equal parts Wondra and potato starch.

see page 252

Fried chicken with no skin? It's just as crispy when you **use a whipping siphon to aerate the batter** (healthier, too). Cooking the meat on the bone keeps it juicy.

see page 254

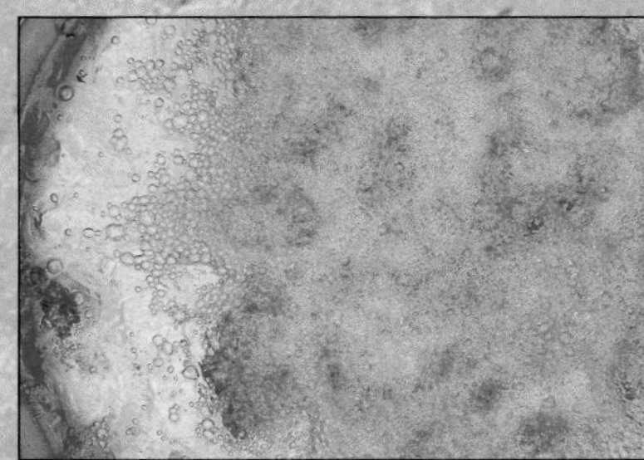

In some cases, we recommend **higher-than-usual frying temperatures** to create crunchy crusts. Working with oil is one of the riskier things cooks do in a kitchen, so heed the safety precautions on page 26.

see page 256

The trick to our Buffalo Sauce is the low water content, which ensures that **your chicken wings won't get soggy** as quickly.

see page 258

FURTHER READING IN *MODERNIST CUISINE*

FDA safe-cooking standards for chicken: see page 1·84–89
Deep-frying chicken at high pressure, KFC-style: see pages 2·120–121
The secret life of frying oil, illustrated: see pages 2·124–125
Brining chicken: see page 3·172
Batters and breadings for chicken: see pages 3·318–319

SOUS VIDE BUFFALO WINGS

YIELD:	*four servings (1 kg / 20–24 pieces)*
TIME ESTIMATE:	*4½ hours overall, including 4 hours unattended*
STORAGE NOTES:	*serve immediately*
LEVEL OF DIFFICULTY:	*moderate*
SPECIAL REQUIREMENTS:	*sous vide setup, vacuum sealer, Buffalo Sauce (see page 258)*
GOES WELL WITH:	*Aerated Blue Cheese Sauce (see variation on page 261)*

We brine these wings in an alkaline salt solution—a technique similar to that traditionally used in Chinese kung pao chicken—which tenderizes the meat and enhances the Maillard reactions that brown the wings. We then cook them sous vide and panfry them.

INGREDIENT	WEIGHT	VOLUME	SCALING	PROCEDURE
Water	500 g	500 mL / 2 cups	50%	① Stir together to make a brine.
Salt	35 g	3½ Tbsp	3.5%	
Baking soda	5 g	1 tsp	0.5%	
Chicken wings, jointed	1 kg / 2.2 lb	20–24 pieces	100%	② Cut apart at the joints; discard the tips or save them for making stock. ③ Combine with the brine in a zip-top bag, and refrigerate for 3 hours. ④ Preheat a water bath to 65 °C / 149 °F. ⑤ Drain the chicken wings, and pat them dry with paper towels. ⑥ Place the chicken pieces in a single layer in a new zip-top bag, remove as much air as possible from the bag by using the water-displacement method (see page 58), seal it. Cook sous vide for 1 hour. ⑦ Place the cooked chicken pieces on a tray, and pat them dry.
Neutral frying oil see page xxii	as needed			⑧ Preheat 1 cm / ⅜ in of frying oil in a deep skillet to 200 °C / 392 °F. ⑨ Fry a few wings at a time in the hot oil until the skin becomes crisp, about 3 minutes. ⑩ Drain the wings on paper towels.
Buffalo Sauce see page 258	as needed			⑪ Brush or toss the wings with sauce, and serve them hot.

Safety tips for deep-frying, see page 26

1 Stir together the water, salt, and baking soda to make a brine. Make sure that the salt dissolves completely.

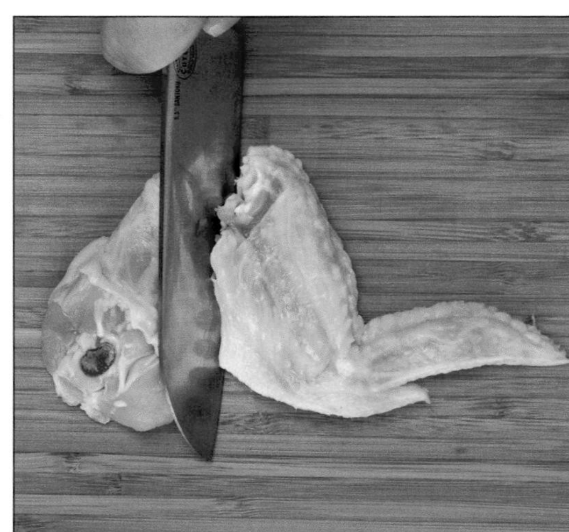

2 Cut each of the wings into three pieces at the joints. Don't use the wing tips in this recipe; you can use them to make stock (see page 84).

3 Seal the brine and chicken wing pieces together in a large (4 L / 1 gal) zip-top bag. Refrigerate for 3 hours.

4 Preheat a water bath to 65 °C / 149 °F.

For more on vacuum sealing and cooking sous vide, see chapter 3 on Cooking Sous Vide, page 48.

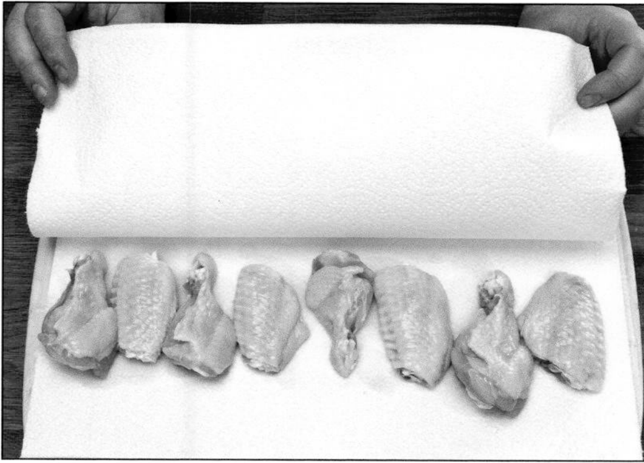

5 Drain the chicken wings, and pat them dry with paper towels.

6 Place the chicken pieces in a single layer in a large (4 L / 1 gal), new zip-top bag. Use multiple bags, if necessary. Use the water-displacement method (see page 58) to remove the air from the bag, and seal it. Cook sous vide for 1 hour.

7 Place the cooked wings on a tray, and pat them dry with paper towels. Excess moisture causes dangerous splattering when the wings are placed in the oil.

8 Pour frying oil into a deep skillet to a depth of 1 cm / ⅜ in, and preheat to **200 °C / 392 °F**. A traditional cast-iron skillet holds its temperature well during frying and browns the wings darkly and quickly.

9 Fry the wings, a few at a time, in the hot oil just long enough for the skin to crisp, about 3 minutes.

10 Drain the wings on paper towels.

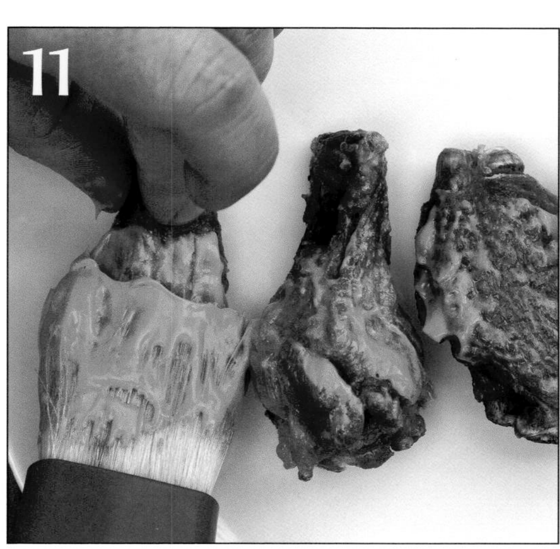

11 Brush or toss sauce over the wings, and serve them hot.

CRISPY CHICKEN WINGS, KOREAN-STYLE

YIELD:	*four servings (1 kg / 20–24 pieces)*
TIME ESTIMATE:	*1 hour overall, including 30 minutes of preparation and 30 minutes unattended*
STORAGE NOTES:	*marinate, refrigerated, for up to one day before cooking*
LEVEL OF DIFFICULTY:	*easy*
SPECIAL REQUIREMENTS:	*michiu rice wine, Wondra, potato starch, monosodium glutamate (MSG, optional), Korean Wing Sauce (see page 260)*

This adaptation pairs Chinese-style velveting with Korean-style marinade and sauce. During frying, the starchy coating forms a barrier against moisture that allows the wing meat to remain juicy while the skin browns to a crisp. After many tests, we found that this combination of potato starch and Wondra, a prehydrated flour, crisped and browned the best. We also got good, crunchy results when breading the wings with other starches, such as corn, tapioca, and water chestnut starches. The *michiu* rice wine has a low boiling point, so it evaporates very quickly during frying and produces a very delicate crust. If *michiu* wine is unavailable, use sake, dry white wine, or three parts water to one part vodka instead.

INGREDIENT	WEIGHT	VOLUME	SCALING	PROCEDURE
Peanut oil	100 g	110 mL / ½ cup	10%	① Combine, and stir until the salt and sugar are completely dissolved to make a marinade.
Michiu rice wine (light)	70 g	80 mL / ⅓ cup	7%	
Soy sauce	20 g	15 mL / 3½ tsp	2%	
Salt	5 g	1¼ tsp	0.5%	
Toasted-sesame oil	5 g	5 mL / 1 tsp	0.5%	
Monosodium glutamate (MSG), optional	3 g		0.3%	
Sugar	2 g	½ tsp	0.2%	
Chicken wings, cut up	1 kg / 2.2 lb	20–24 pieces	100%	② Toss with the marinade, cover, and refrigerate for 30 minutes.
Neutral frying oil see page xxii	as needed			③ Pour into a deep pot to no more than half full, and then preheat to 176 °C / 350 °F.
Wondra	40 g	¼ cup	4%	④ Combine.
Potato starch	38 g	¼ cup	3.8%	⑤ Dust over the marinade-soaked chicken wings, and stir until the wings are evenly coated with a thin batter. ⑥ Deep-fry five to seven wings at a time until cooked through and golden brown, about 7 minutes. ⑦ Drain the wings on paper towels.
Korean Wing Sauce see page 260	280 g	1½ cups	28%	⑧ Drizzle sauce generously over the wings, and toss to coat. Serve them hot.

Safety tips for deep-frying: see page 26

1 Combine the peanut oil, rice wine, soy sauce, salt, sesame oil, MSG (if using), and sugar, and mix thoroughly until the salt and sugar are completely dissolved. This mixture serves as the marinade.

2 Toss the chicken wings with the marinade, cover with plastic wrap, and refrigerate for 30 minutes.

3 Fill a deep pot or fryer no more than half full of frying oil, and preheat to 176 °C / 350 °F. The frying temperature for this recipe is slightly lower than in the other wing recipes because the Korean-style marinade is higher in sugar, and we want to avoid over-browning the batter.

4 Stir the Wondra and potato starch together until evenly mixed.

5 Dust the Wondra and starch mixture over the marinade-soaked chicken wings, and stir until the marinade and starch form a thin batter and the wings are evenly coated.

6 Deep-fry the wings in batches of five to seven until cooked through and golden brown, about 7 minutes per batch. The cooking time depends on the size of your pot or fryer. The more oil in the pot, the less it cools when the cold wings enter it.

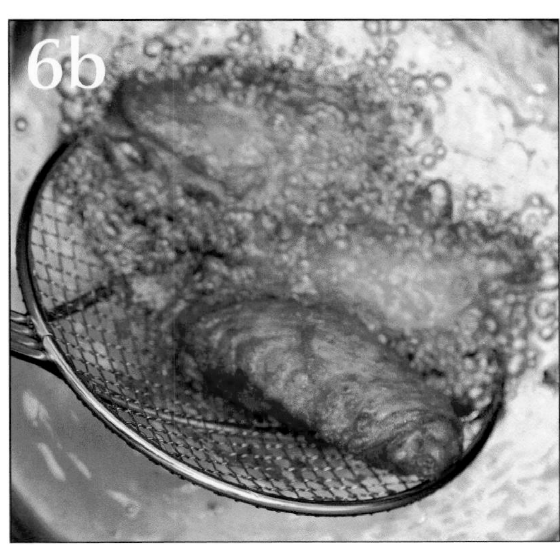

7 Drain the wings on paper towels.

8 Drizzle Korean wing sauce over the wings generously, and toss them until coated. Serve the wings hot.

CRISPY SKINLESS CHICKEN WINGS

YIELD:	*four servings (875 g / 20–24 pieces)*
TIME ESTIMATE:	*45 minutes overall*
STORAGE NOTES:	*serve immediately*
LEVEL OF DIFFICULTY:	*moderate*
SPECIAL REQUIREMENTS:	*500 mL whipping siphon, two cartridges of nitrous oxide, Chili Spice Mix (see page 138)*

This wing recipe captures everything we love about fried chicken. We remove the skin so that there is no barrier between the delightful crunch of the breading and the tender juiciness of the meat. The alcohol in the batter vaporizes very quickly and completely. As it does, it lowers the boiling point of the mixture, yielding a delicate crust that is crispier than skin ever could be. In effect, this is a tempura chicken wing. Be sure to bring the wings to room temperature before frying them; the frying oil will recover its temperature more quickly after you add the food. If the food goes in cold, it tends to turn out greasy and overcooked. The batter, on the other hand, should be kept cold.

INGREDIENT	WEIGHT	VOLUME	SCALING	PROCEDURE
All-purpose flour	57 g	⅓ cup	5.7%	① Combine all of the dry ingredients.
Cornstarch	45 g	⅓ cup	4.5%	
Salt	6 g	1½ tsp	0.6%	
Baking powder	1 g	¼ tsp	0.1%	
Water	200 g	200 mL / ⅞ cup	20%	② Whisk into the flour mixture to make a smooth batter.
Vodka	25 g	30 mL / 2 Tbsp	2.5%	③ Pour into a 500 mL siphon, charge with two cartridges of nitrous oxide, and refrigerate.
Chicken wings, cut up	1 kg / 2.2 lb	20–24 pieces	100%	④ Remove the skin from the wings.
Neutral frying oil see page xxii	as needed			⑤ Fill a deep pot to no more than half full of frying oil, and preheat to 190 °C / 374 °F.
Cornstarch	as needed for coating			⑥ Toss with the wings to coat evenly. Shake off excess starch. ⑦ Dispense the cold batter over the wings, and toss to coat thoroughly. ⑧ Deep-fry the wings, a few at a time, until cooked through and golden brown, 5–6 minutes. ⑨ Drain on paper towels.
Chili Spice Mix see page 138	20 g	2 Tbsp	2%	⑩ Season the wings generously, and serve them hot.
Salt	to taste			

Safety tips for deep-frying: see page 26

WHILE YOU'RE AT IT: **Puffed Chicken Skin**

The chicken skin you don't use here could become its own tasty snack. Seal it in a zip-top bag, and cook it sous vide at **88 °C / 190 °F** for 12 hours. Remove the skin from the bag, dust it with cornstarch, place it on a baking sheet, and allow it to dry in a dehydrator or low-temperature oven at **60–120 °C / 140–250 °F** for 4–8 hours. Then fry the skin pieces in 1 cm / ⅜ in of very hot oil until they puff up and turn brown and crispy. Dust them with salt or a spice mix, and serve.

For a recipe for puffed pork skin, see page 222.

1 Combine the flour, cornstarch, salt, and baking powder.

2 Whisk the water and vodka into the flour mixture until the batter becomes smooth.

3 Pour the batter into a 500 mL siphon, charge the siphon with two cartridges of nitrous oxide, and refrigerate it. The batter must be cold to form a crisp crust.

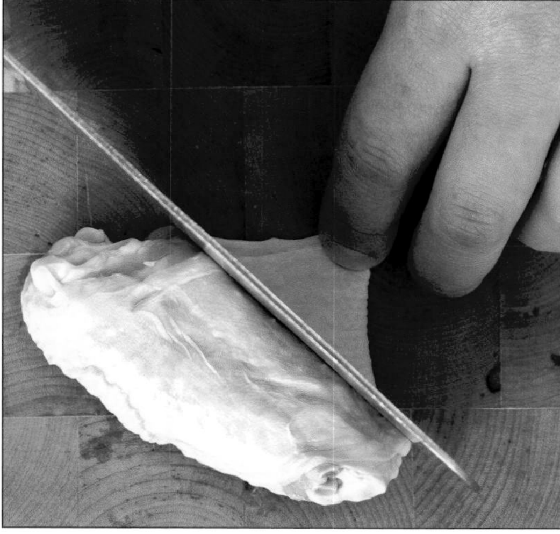

4 Remove the skin from the wings by trimming off the connective tissue, pulling sections of the skin away while holding the wing with the back of a knife, and then cutting off the pieces of skin. Alternatively, use scissors to make an incision, and then peel the skin away.

5 Fill a deep pot to no more than half full with frying oil, and preheat the oil to 190 °C / 374 °F.

6 Toss the wings with cornstarch until coated evenly, and shake off any extra. The starch helps the batter cling to the chicken.

7 Dispense the cold batter from the siphon over the wings, and then toss the wings until they are thoroughly coated with batter.

8 Deep-fry the wings in batches, a few at a time, until they are cooked through and golden brown, 5–6 minutes.

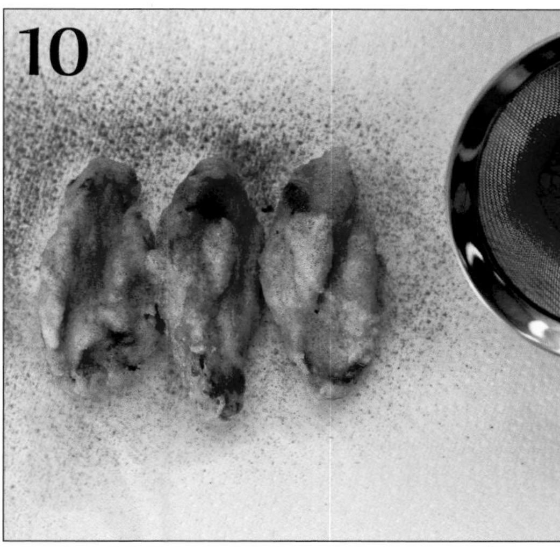

9 Drain the wings on paper towels.

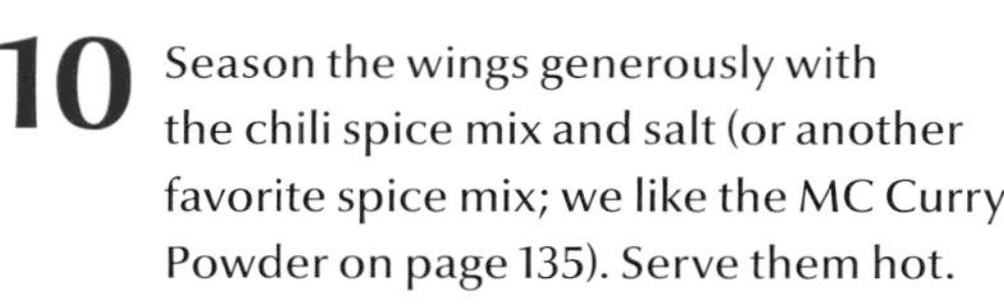

10 Season the wings generously with the chili spice mix and salt (or another favorite spice mix; we like the MC Curry Powder on page 135). Serve them hot.

BONELESS YAKITORI WINGS

YIELD:	*four servings (300 g / about 12 pieces)*
TIME ESTIMATE:	*25 hours overall, including 24 hours unattended*
STORAGE NOTES:	*keeps for up to 3 days when refrigerated before frying*
LEVEL OF DIFFICULTY:	*advanced (handling)*
SPECIAL REQUIREMENTS:	*sous vide setup, vacuum sealer, potato starch, Yakitori Sauce (see page 260)*

Boneless chicken wings are an unexpected treat. Use the center "forewing" portion. The trick is to cut off the bone ends, and then slide the bones out while the wings are warm.

Turkey wings make an excellent variation and offer a little reminder of Thanksgiving. Although turkey wings are larger than chicken wings, the cooking time is the same.

INGREDIENT	WEIGHT	VOLUME	SCALING	PROCEDURE
Chicken forewings	500 g / 1.1 lb	about 12	100%	① Trim the joint ends from the wings, cut away the connective tissues, and use the tip of a knife to loosen the meat around the exposed bones.
Water	500 g	500 mL / 2 cups	100%	② Combine, and stir until the salt and sugar are completely dissolved to make a brine.
Salt	30 g	3 Tbsp	6%	③ Cover the wings in the brine, and refrigerate them for 12 hours.
Sugar	25 g	2½ Tbsp	5%	④ Drain the brined wings, and pat them dry with paper towels.
Clarified, unsalted butter or neutral-tasting oil see page 119	15 g	5 tsp butter or 15 mL / 1 Tbsp oil	3%	⑤ Preheat a water bath to **62 °C / 144 °F**. ⑥ Vacuum seal the wings in a single layer with the butter or oil. ⑦ Cook the wings sous vide for 12 hours. ⑧ While the wings are still warm, carefully remove the bones without rupturing the skin. ⑨ Pat the skin dry with paper towels.
Neutral frying oil see page xxii	as needed			⑩ Heat 1 cm / ⅜ in of frying oil in a nonstick pan to **200 °C / 392 °F**. ⑪ Coat the wings with the starch, and shake off any excess.
Potato starch	25 g	2 Tbsp	5%	⑫ Fry the wings until brown and crisp, about 2 minutes on each side. ⑬ Drain the wings on paper towels.
Yakitori Sauce, warm see page 260	as needed			⑭ Spoon the sauce over the wings, and serve them hot.

Safety tips for frying: see page 26

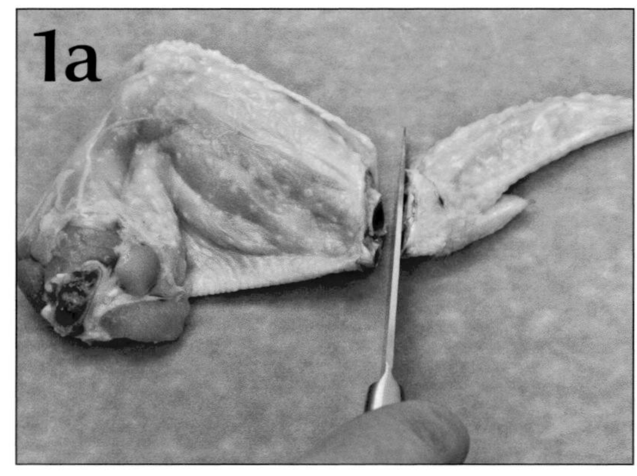

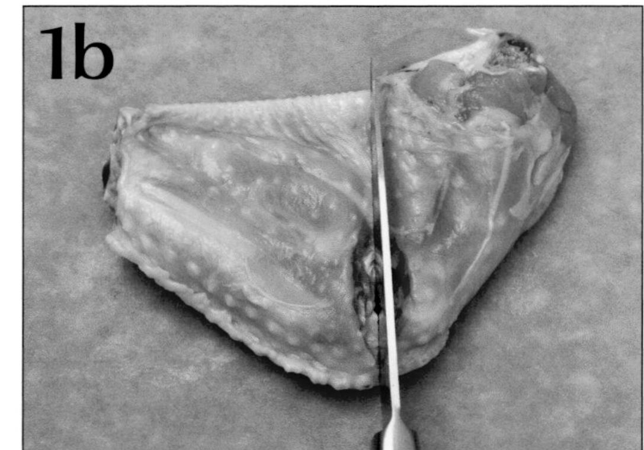

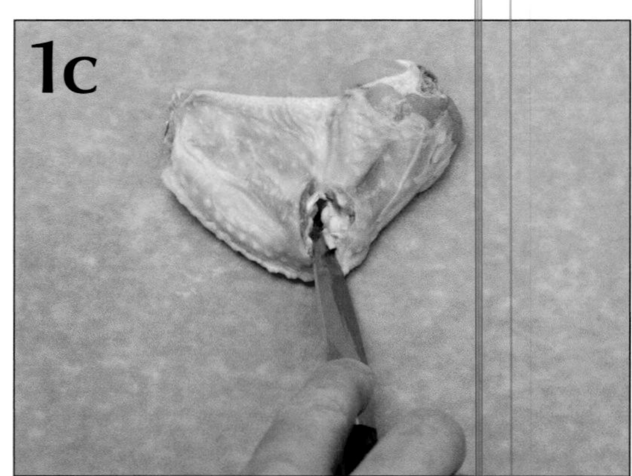

1 Trim the chicken wing pieces. Try to keep the skin intact. First, cut through both joints; keep the central forewing. Next, cut away the connective tissue. Finally, slide the tip of a knife around the exposed bones to loosen the meat. This step makes it much easier to remove the bones after cooking.

2 Stir the salt and sugar in the water until they are completely dissolved. This is the brine.

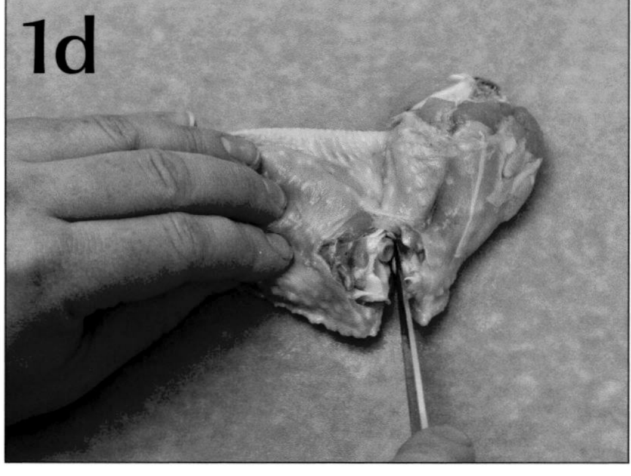

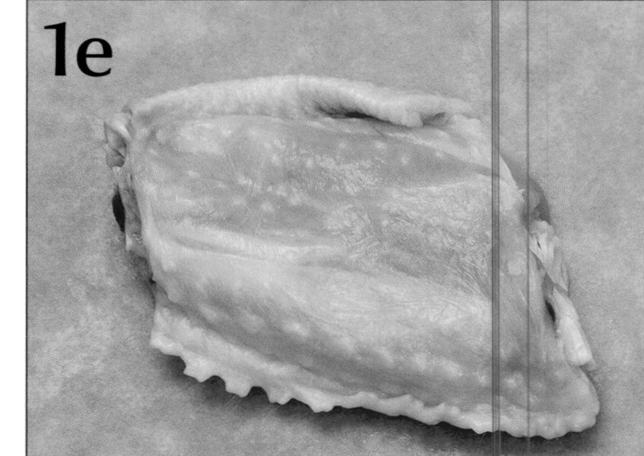

3 Cover the wings in the brine, and refrigerate them for 12 hours.

4 Drain the brined wings, and pat them dry with paper towels.

5 Preheat a water bath to **62** °C / **144** °F.

6 Vacuum seal the wings in a single layer with the butter or oil.

7 Cook the wings sous vide for 12 hours.

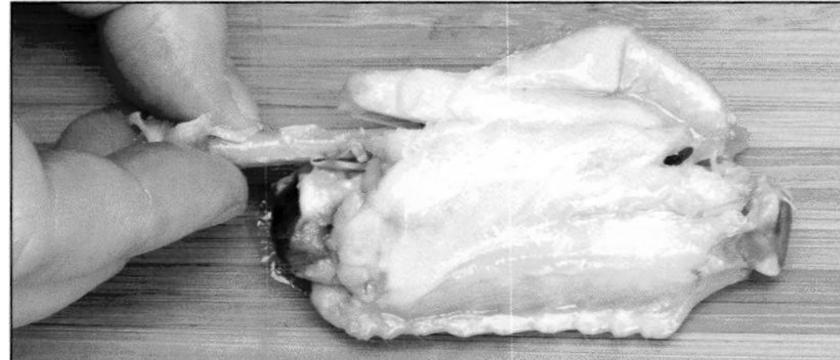

8 Remove the wings from the bag, and while they are still warm, carefully extract the bones. Avoid rupturing the skin.

9 Pat the wings dry with paper towels.

10 Heat 1 cm / 3/8 in of frying oil in a nonstick pan to **200** °C / **392** °F.

11 Coat the wings with the starch, and shake off any excess.

TO MAKE AHEAD

After you remove the bones and dry the cooked wings in step 9, refrigerate them for up to 3 days. To reheat, seal the wings in a bag, and place in a water bath at **62** °C / **144** °F for 30 minutes.Then continue with step 10.

12 Fry the wings until they turn brown and crispy, about 2 minutes on each side.

13 Drain the fried wings on paper towels.

14 Spoon yakitori sauce over the wings, and serve them hot.

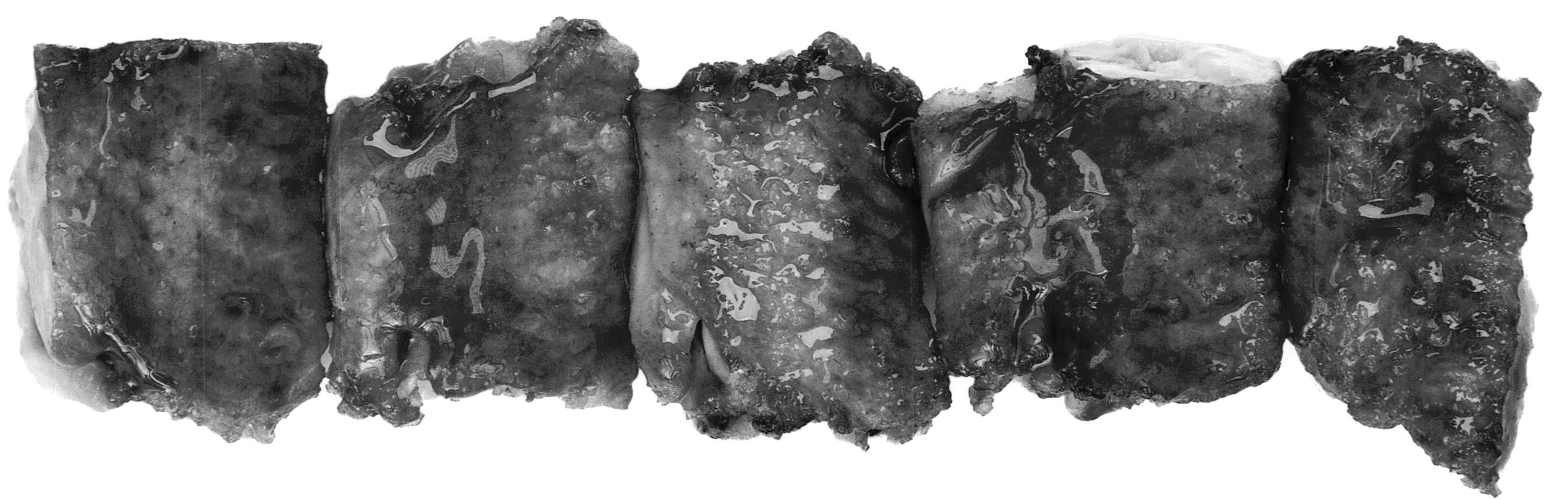

Buffalo Sauce

Korean Wing Sauce

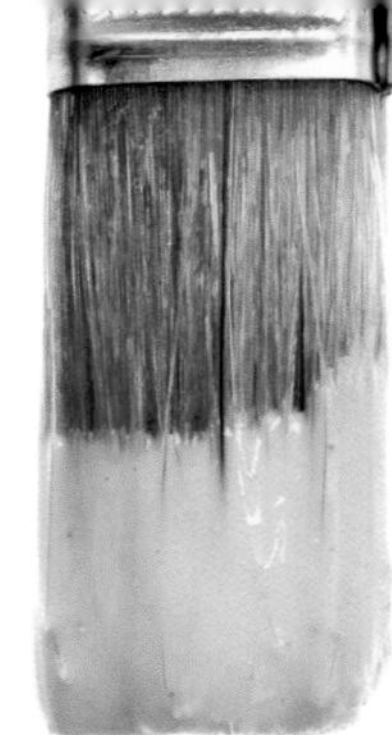

Blue Cheese Sauce

Chinese Garlic Chili Condiment

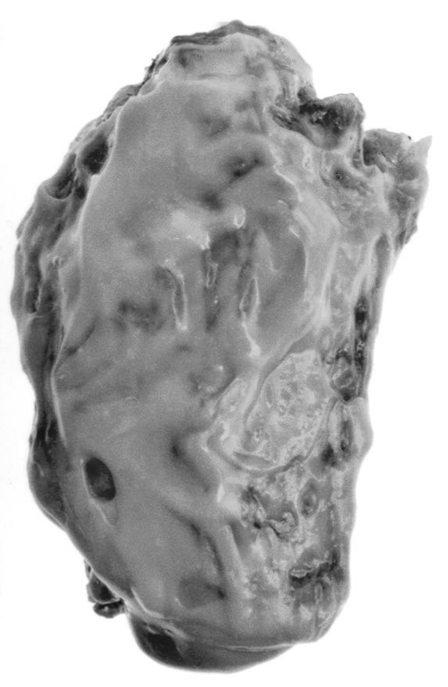

BUFFALO SAUCE

YIELD:	*235 g / 1 cup*
TIME ESTIMATE:	*1 hour overall, including 30 minutes of preparation and 30 minutes unattended*
STORAGE NOTES:	*keeps for 3 days when refrigerated*
LEVEL OF DIFFICULTY:	*moderate*

Our Buffalo wing sauce is essentially a spicy variation of mayonnaise made with a flavored oil (which, by the way, can be used by itself). Here we use raw egg yolks, but pasteurized eggs can be substituted (see page 142). You can use this spicy, creamy sauce on almost anything. Note that because this sauce contains very little water, it won't make your crispy chicken wings soggy. If at any point the sauce starts to separate and get oily, whisk it or puree it with an immersion blender until smooth.

INGREDIENT	WEIGHT	VOLUME	SCALING	PROCEDURE
Neutral-tasting oil	200 g	220 mL / 1 cup	100%	① Combine in a pot, and cook over low heat until the garlic and onions are completely soft, about 30 minutes. Alternatively, pressure-cook together in a canning jar for 10 minutes (see page 126).
Sweet onion, thinly sliced	80 g	¾ cup	40%	② Strain through a sieve lined with cheesecloth. Discard the solids, and cool the oil to room temperature.
Garlic, thinly sliced	80 g	⅝ cup	40%	③ Measure 150 g / ¾ cup of the flavored oil for use in the next step.
Jalapeño pepper, minced	30 g	3 Tbsp	15%	
Canned chipotle pepper in adobo, chopped	20 g	1 medium	10%	
Sweet paprika	10 g	1½ Tbsp	5%	
Cayenne	10 g	1½ Tbsp	5%	
Egg yolks (raw or pasteurized)	50 g	3–4 yolks	25%	④ Place the egg yolks in a bowl, and gradually blend in the flavored oil and lemon juice by using an immersion blender until fully emulsified.
Lemon juice	50 g	50 mL / 3½ Tbsp	25%	
Salt	8 g	2 tsp	4%	⑤ Season the sauce, and serve it at room temperature.

Yakitori Sauce

Pressure-Caramelized Peanut Sauce (see page 111)

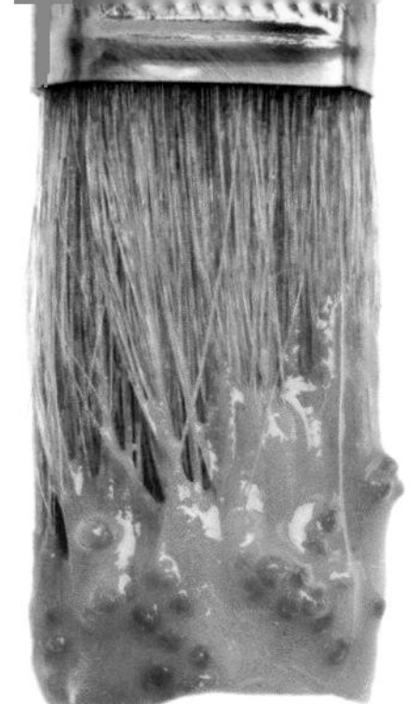

Honey Mustard Sauce

HONEY MUSTARD SAUCE

YIELD:	*200 g / 1 cup*
TIME ESTIMATE:	*5 minutes overall*
STORAGE NOTES:	*keeps for 7 days when refrigerated*
LEVEL OF DIFFICULTY:	*easy*

The flavor of this sauce depends greatly on the kind of honey and mustard you use; experiment with varieties you find intriguing. Maple syrup can be substituted for the honey. Sweet herbs or spices such as tarragon, cinnamon, or cloves provide a change of pace. Give the sauce more kick with dry mustard powder, chili powder, cayenne pepper, grated horseradish, or Japanese wasabi. Or add a few drops of liquid smoke for a smoky flavor. The pickled mustard seeds add a great popping texture, and you can add up to twice as many of them if you like.

INGREDIENT	WEIGHT	VOLUME	SCALING	PROCEDURE
Dijon mustard	100 g	⅜ cup	100%	① Stir together until thoroughly mixed.
Honey	50 g	3 Tbsp	50%	
Pressure-Cooked Pickled Mustard Seeds, drained see page 125	40 g	2½ Tbsp	40%	
Apple cider vinegar	12 g	15 mL / 1 Tbsp	12%	
Salt	to taste			② Season the sauce, and serve it warm or cold.

YAKITORI SAUCE

YIELD:	*500 g / 2 cups*
TIME ESTIMATE:	*12¼ hours overall, including 15 minutes of preparation and 12 hours unattended*
STORAGE NOTES:	*keeps for 3 days when refrigerated*
LEVEL OF DIFFICULTY:	*easy*
SPECIAL REQUIREMENTS:	*mirin, sake, bonito flakes*

Yakitori is Japanese for grilled (*yaki*) bird (*tori*); it is usually made with chicken. This popular bar food is somewhat akin to tapas in Spain. Yakitori comes in many forms, but in the most common style, small pieces of chicken are strung on bamboo skewers, grilled over a very hot charcoal fire, and then brushed with this delicious sauce. The pineapple in the sauce contains an enzyme, called bromelain, that tenderizes the surface of the meat. Teriyaki sauce can be substituted in a pinch.

INGREDIENT	WEIGHT	VOLUME	SCALING	PROCEDURE
Mirin	200 g	230 mL / 1 cup	89%	① Combine in a pot, and bring to a simmer.
Honey	110 g	⅓ cup	49%	
Light soy sauce	100 g	85 mL / ⅓ cup	44%	
Dry sake	100 g	120 mL / ½ cup	44%	
Bonito flakes	20 g	1 cup, packed	9%	
Ginger, finely grated	5 g	2 tsp	2%	
Pineapple rind and flesh, cubed	225 g	1½ cups	100%	② Pour the hot soy sauce mixture over the pineapple, and let it cool. ③ Refrigerate for 12 hours. ④ Strain through a sieve lined with cheesecloth, reserving the sauce. Discard the pineapple rind. The pineapple cubes can be used in stir-fry.
Rice vinegar	50 g	60 mL / ¼ cup	22%	⑤ Season the sauce, and serve it warm or cold.
Salt	15 g	5 tsp	6.7%	

KOREAN WING SAUCE

YIELD:	*280 g / 1 cup*
TIME ESTIMATE:	*15 minutes*
STORAGE NOTES:	*keeps for 5 days when refrigerated*
LEVEL OF DIFFICULTY:	*easy*
SPECIAL REQUIREMENTS:	*gochujang (Korean fermented chili paste), Shaoxing wine*

This sweet and spicy sauce is addictive. It is well worth the time to search your local Asian market for these specialty ingredients. Often sold in tubs, *gochujang* is a sweet, complex chili paste that you might find yourself slathering on almost everything. Look also for "thin mouth" (*usu kuchi*) soy sauce, the variety we prefer for this recipe. If you can't find Shaoxing wine (a Chinese rice wine), substitute medium-dry sherry.

INGREDIENT	WEIGHT	VOLUME	SCALING	PROCEDURE
Gochujang (Korean fermented chili paste)	135 g	½ cup	100%	① Combine, and whisk together until the sugar dissolves. ② Serve the sauce warm or cold.
Sugar	50 g	⅓ cup	37%	
Soy sauce	30 g	25 mL / 5 tsp	22%	
Shaoxing wine	27 g	30 mL / 2 Tbsp	20%	
Toasted-sesame oil	20 g	20 mL / 1½ Tbsp	15%	
Garlic, minced	10 g	1 Tbsp	7.4%	
Ginger, minced	8 g	1 Tbsp	6%	

BLUE CHEESE SAUCE

YIELD:	*600 g / 2¼ cups*
TIME ESTIMATE:	*15 minutes overall*
STORAGE NOTES:	*keeps for 3 days when refrigerated*
LEVEL OF DIFFICULTY:	*easy*
SPECIAL REQUIREMENTS:	*Wondra, sodium citrate*

Use a bold blue cheese, such as Maytag, Roquefort, Gorgonzola, or Stilton. Overheating cheese sauces usually is taboo, but to make a smooth sauce, the sodium citrate we use here as an emulsifier requires that the sauce simmers while you gradually blend in the cheese.

INGREDIENT	WEIGHT	VOLUME	SCALING	PROCEDURE
Wondra	12 g	5 tsp	3%	① Mix until thoroughly combined.
Sodium citrate	4 g		1%	
Whole milk, cold	200 g	210 mL / ⅞ cup	50%	② Whisk together with the Wondra mixture in a medium saucepan, and bring to a simmer. If the powders clump, the milk was not cold enough.
Blue cheese, crumbled	400 g	3⅓ cups	100%	③ Add gradually to the simmering milk mixture, and use an immersion blender to blend each addition until the cheese is melted and the sauce is completely smooth. ④ Cool the sauce completely, and serve it cold.

VARIATION: Aerated Blue Cheese Sauce
To make a light, airy version of the Blue Cheese Sauce, pour the warm sauce into a 1 L siphon, and charge the siphon with two cartridges of nitrous oxide. Dispense a cloud of blue cheese alongside chicken wings or on a raw vegetable platter.

CHINESE GARLIC CHILI CONDIMENT

YIELD:	*145 g / 1⅓ cups*
TIME ESTIMATE:	*30 minutes overall*
STORAGE NOTES:	*serve within 30 minutes*
LEVEL OF DIFFICULTY:	*moderate*

Variations of this condiment are often seen in Chinese "salt and pepper" dishes. Adjust the spiciness to suit your taste. For a more aromatic version, include minced ginger, cilantro, and lemongrass along with the jalapeño. This condiment tastes fabulous not only with chicken wings but also with fried frogs' legs, fried tofu, grilled pork chops (see page 202), and cold noodles dressed with sesame oil.

INGREDIENT	WEIGHT	VOLUME	SCALING	PROCEDURE
Neutral-tasting oil	432 g	470 mL / 2 cups	288%	① Set a strainer over a pot near the stove top.
Garlic, minced	150 g	1 cup	100%	② Combine the garlic and oil in another pot. Make sure the pot is no more than half full to allow space for bubbling and froth. ③ Cook over high heat, stirring constantly, until the garlic turns golden brown, about 6 minutes. Once the garlic darkens in color, it burns quickly, so watch it closely. ④ Pour through the strainer. ⑤ Spread the garlic on paper towels to drain.
Scallions, white parts only, minced	40 g	½ cup	27%	⑥ Add to the pot of hot, strained oil. Place the strainer over the empty pot. ⑦ Cook over high heat, stirring constantly, until the scallions turn golden brown, about 4 minutes. ⑧ Pour through the strainer. ⑨ Spread the scallions on paper towels to drain. ⑩ Measure 3 g / 3 mL / ½ tsp of the oil for use in the next step. You can use any remaining oil for flavoring steamed fish or pasta.
Jalapeño pepper, finely chopped	33 g	3 Tbsp	22%	⑪ Combine with the reserved oil, fried garlic, and fried scallions. Mix thoroughly.
Salt	8 g	2 tsp	5.3%	⑫ Serve within 30 minutes, while the garlic and scallions remain crisp.

SKEWERS

There's something inherently fun about food on a stick. Skewered foods pop up in food culture all over the world: in yakitori bars in Japan; in the astounding variety of satay sold by Thai and Malaysian street vendors; in cotton candy, deep-fried ice cream, and corn dogs at the Minnesota State Fair; and in candy apples and popsicles—even in "Spamsicles" and crispy crickets on a stick.

We give some of our favorites skewers a Modernist update by cooking the meat sous vide to the perfect temperature before skewering it. One benefit of this approach is that the skewers can be made in advance, vacuum sealed, and then refrigerated. When you are ready to serve them, simply place the bag in a 55 °C / 131 °F water bath for 15–20 minutes to reheat, and then sear them in a very hot pan, on a hot grill, under a blowtorch, or in hot oil (see page 193). The sauce is optional.

Safety tips for deep-frying: see page 26
Safety tips for blowtorching: see page 15

Pesto Chicken Thighs

Cut 300 g / 0.7 lb of boneless, skin-on chicken thigh into 2.5 cm / 1 in pieces. Vacuum seal the chicken in a single layer. Cook sous vide at **65 °C / 149 °F** for 1½ hours. Thread three to five pieces of cooked meat onto each skewer so that all of the skin faces the same direction. Finish by searing the chicken, skin-side down, in a hot dry pan. Brush with Pistachio Pesto (see page 102).

Korean Pork Belly

Cut 300 g / 0.7 lb of fresh pork belly, with its skin on, into 2.5 cm / 1 in cubes. Vacuum seal the pork in a single layer. Cook sous vide at **62 °C / 144 °F** for 48 hours. Remove the meat from the bag, and thread three to five pieces onto each skewer. Finish by using a blowtorch or by deep-frying the skewers in **190 °C / 375 °F** neutral frying oil, and then glazing with Korean Wing Sauce (see page 260).

Deep-Fried Tsukune

Prepare the skewers of chicken meatballs as described in the Tsukune recipe on the next page. Finish by deep-frying the meatballs in **190 °C / 375 °F** neutral frying oil until cooked through, about 3 minutes. Brush with Sous Vide Spiced Chili Oil (see page 118).

Chicken Skin Yakitori

Vacuum seal 200 g / 0.4 lb of chicken skin in a single layer. Cook sous vide at **88 °C / 190 °F** for 12 hours. Separate the pieces of skin while they are still warm, and thread them onto skewers. Cool completely, and then finish by deep-frying in **190 °C / 375 °F** neutral frying oil until crisp, 4–5 minutes. Glaze with Yakitori Sauce (see page 260).

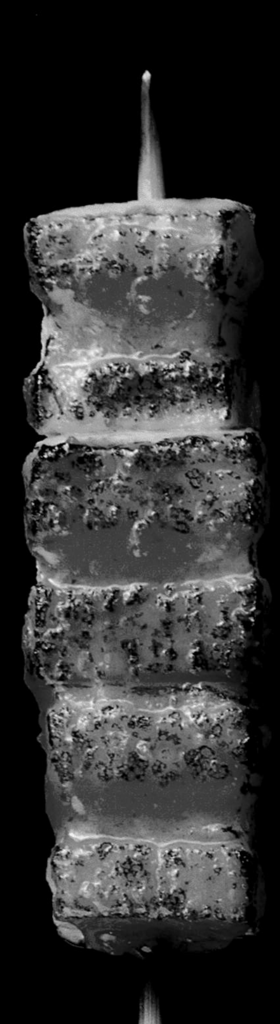

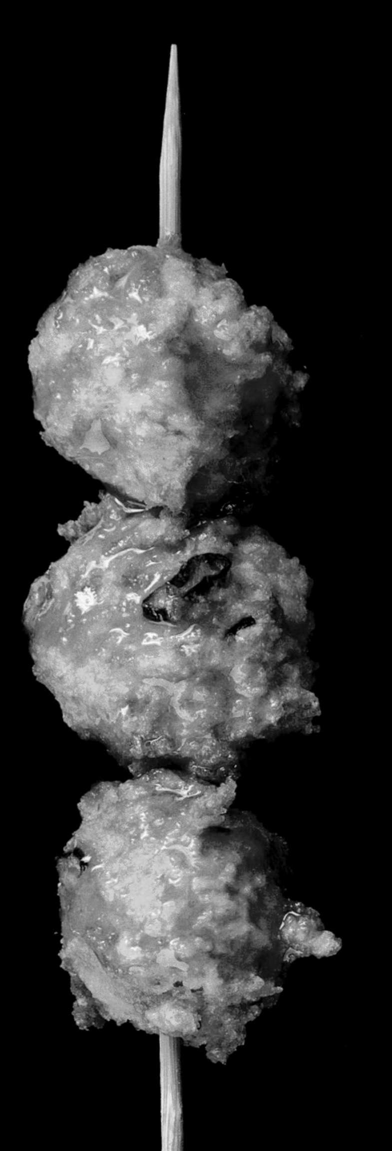

Tsukune

Boneless, skinless chicken thigh meat, finely ground	400 g / 0.9 lb	1⅝ cups from 3 thighs
Leeks, white parts only, minced	45 g	¾ cup
Egg white, beaten	35 g	3 Tbsp
Yakitori Sauce see page 220	20 g	1 Tbsp
Toasted-sesame oil	10 g	10 mL / 2¼ tsp
Ginger, minced	6 g	2 tsp
Wondra	5 g	1½ tsp
Salt	4 g	1 tsp

Chicken meatballs are called tsukune in Japanese. They are served on skewers and are delicious.

Combine all ingredients in the bowl of a stand mixer, and stir with the paddle attachment until the mix coheres, about 2 minutes. Refrigerate the mixture for 1 hour to firm and hydrate it. Adjust the oven rack so that the skewered meatballs will be about 5 cm / 2 in from the heat source, and then preheat the broiler to high.

Shape the mixture into 2.5 cm / 1 in meatballs by using a small scoop or your wet hands. Thread three meatballs onto each bamboo skewer. Place the meatballs on an oiled broiler rack, and broil until golden brown and cooked through, 3–4 minutes per side. Serve hot as is, or sweetened by brushing on additional yakitori sauce.

Lamb Skewers with Mint Yogurt

Cut 300 g / 0.7 lb of lamb leg into 2.5 cm / 1 in cubes. Vacuum seal the lamb in a single layer. Cook sous vide at **56 °C / 133 °F** for 3 hours. Remove the meat from the bag, and thread three to five pieces onto each skewer. Finish by searing the meat on all sides with a blowtorch. Serve with mint yogurt.

Mint Yogurt: Mix together 150 g / ⅝ cup of plain yogurt and 15 g / 5 Tbsp of chopped fresh mint. Season with salt to taste.

Chicken Breast Satay

Vacuum seal a whole, boneless, skinless chicken breast of about 300 g / 0.7 lb. Cook the chicken sous vide at 60 °C / 140 °F to a core temperature of 59 °C / 138 °F, and then hold at that temperature for 1 hour. Remove the meat from the bag, and cut it into 2.5 cm / 1 in pieces. Thread three to five pieces onto each skewer. Optionally, sear the cooked meat over a hot grill or under a blowtorch. Then brush with Pressure-Caramelized Peanut Sauce (see page 111).

Beef Short Ribs with Shiitake Marmalade

Trim 300 g / 0.7 lb of boneless beef short rib, and cut the meat into 2.5 cm / 1 in cubes. Vacuum seal the pieces in a single layer. Cook sous vide at **58 °C / 136 °F** for 72 hours. Remove the meat from the bag, and thread three to five pieces onto each skewer. Finish the meat by searing it or by deep-frying it in **190 °C / 375 °F** neutral frying oil until brown and crisp. Smother the skewers with Shiitake Marmalade (see page 151), and sprinkle grated Gruyère cheese over the top.

Filet Mignon with Montpellier Butter

Trim 300 g / 0.7 lb of filet mignon. Vacuum seal the filet whole. Cook sous vide at **54 °C / 129 °F** to a core temperature of **53 °C / 127 °F**, about 35 minutes. Remove the meat from the bag, and cut it into 2.5 cm / 1 in cubes. Thread three to five pieces onto each skewer. Finish by searing the meat on all sides with a blowtorch, topping with grated Montpellier Butter (see page 120), and blowtorching again briefly to melt the butter.

CHICKEN NOODLE SOUP

A quintessential comfort food, chicken soup has many renditions: matzo ball soup, *poule au pot*, Hainanese chicken rice, *phở gà*, and *tortellini en brodo*, to name just a few. But the idea of chicken noodle soup is usually more compelling than the soup itself. The broth is often so watery it tastes mainly of salt. And cooking the other ingredients together often leaves the chicken dry, the vegetables bland, and the noodles mushy.

This hearty classic really shines when you prepare each ingredient separately to highlight its best qualities. The chicken is succulent when cooked sous vide, the egg noodles are toothsome when fresh, and the vegetables are perfectly yielding when pressure-cooked. Boost the broth with an infusion of aromatics just before serving.

Try substituting other vegetables or replacing the meat with ground-chicken meatballs. For a heartier soup, crack in an egg poached at 65 °C / 149 °F (see page 142).

THE SCIENCE OF INFUSION

It's easy to turn a stock into an aromatic broth by infusing it with a fresh layer of flavors, but you must know which flavors are soluble in which liquids. The same ingredients release different flavors when soaked in water than they do when left to sit in vodka. And every ingredient has a particular temperature and time at which it is best extracted, as the perfume and essential-oil industries have cataloged extensively.

In *Modernist Cuisine,* we explored the science of infusion and extraction quite a bit and experimented with many different broths, infused extracts, and essential oils. Here we use a simple French press for our soup broth—treating the fresh herbs and toasted spices like you would tea leaves—to make a last-minute infusion before serving the soup. It's an easy concept to grasp for tea or coffee drinkers, who already understand the consequences of underextraction (a weak flavor from too few aromatics for the amount of water) and overextraction (a harsh, bitter flavor from letting the aromatics infuse for too long).

HIGHLIGHTS

Infusions with volatile ingredients such as thyme and tarragon are best done at the last second and off the heat. **A French press is a handy tool for infusing herbs and spices** into an aromatic chicken broth.

see page 266

Apply the infusion technique to make a wide range of aromatic noodle soups, including phở, goulash, tortilla, Thai, and Chinese noodle soups.

see page 267

The secret to making fantastic fresh pasta? Add gluten. Pasta is often missing that extra toothsome bite. To get it, add some vital wheat gluten. The gluten also adds some forgiveness to the noodles, so they are less likely to overcook.

see page 268

Present your soup like a pro. Our instructions guide you through the process of assembling the components of a soup just like a top chef would.

see page 273

FURTHER READING IN *MODERNIST CUISINE*

MODERNIST CUISINE 2

Food-safety misconceptions about chicken: see pages 1·180–181
How to extract flavors: see pages 2·288–317
How to infuse essences: see pages 2·318–331
Best bets for cooking poultry sous vide: see pages 3·99, 108
How to make pasta: see pages 3·378–381

AROMATIC CHICKEN BROTH

YIELD:	*four servings (1 kg / 4¼ cups)*
TIME ESTIMATE:	*10 minutes overall*
STORAGE NOTES:	*serve immediately*
LEVEL OF DIFFICULTY:	*easy*
SPECIAL REQUIREMENTS:	*blowtorch (optional), French press (optional), monosodium glutamate (optional)*

Use either a traditional white stock or a savory, roasted brown broth as the main ingredient in this recipe. For best results, prepare the ingredients but do not combine them until you are ready to plate the soup, as shown on page 273. The last-minute infusion gently draws out all of the aromatics from the herbs and spices just before you pour the broth at the table, creating a wonderfully fragrant experience. It's like making coffee or tea: although you can make and infuse the broth ahead of time, the natural perfume will fade as it sits. We like to infuse the broth in a French press and pour it at the table, but it can also be made in a saucepan and then strained.

INGREDIENT	WEIGHT	VOLUME	SCALING	PROCEDURE
Garlic	20 g	5 cloves	2%	① Cut each garlic clove lengthwise into thick slices. ② Char by using a blowtorch, or sear the slices on both sides.
Star anise	4 g	1 star anise	0.4%	③ Toast the spices in a dry frying pan over medium-high heat, stirring constantly, until fragrant, about 3 minutes.
Black peppercorns	4 g	½ tsp	0.4%	
Salt	15 g	5 tsp	1.5%	④ Combine with the charred garlic and toasted spices in the beaker of a large French press.
Chervil, bruised	14 g	12 branches	1.4%	
Thyme, bruised	2 g	4 sprigs	0.2%	
Tarragon, bruised	1 g	7 leaves	0.1%	
Bay leaves, sliced	0.4 g	2 leaves	0.04%	
Monosodium glutamate (MSG), optional	5 g		0.5%	
White or brown chicken stock see page 84	1 kg	1 L / 4¼ cups	100%	⑤ Bring to a boil. Pour over the ingredients in the French press, and stir. ⑥ Leave to infuse for 2 minutes. Then press, and serve hot.

Safety tips for blowtorching: see page 15

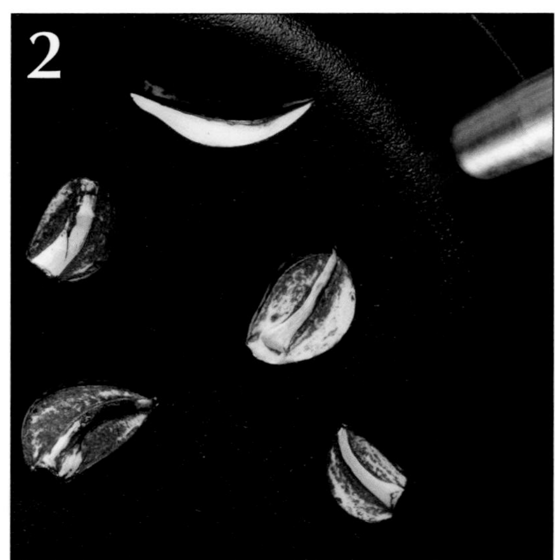

1 Cut each garlic clove lengthwise into thick slices.

2 Char both sides of each slice evenly with a blowtorch (use MAPP or propylene fuel), or sear them in a very hot, dry pan for 20 seconds. The surface should be dark and blistered, but the interior should remain moist. This step removes the raw garlic flavor and adds a complexity to the finished broth.

3 Toast the star anise and peppercorns in a dry frying pan over medium-high heat, stirring constantly, until fragrant, about 3 minutes. For a spicier flavor, crack the spices in a mortar and pestle.

4 Combine the herbs, salt, and MSG (optional) with the charred garlic and toasted spices in the beaker of a large French press.

5 Bring the chicken stock to a full boil. Pour over the ingredients in the French press, and stir. If you are not using a French press, simply remove the stock from the heat, stir in the aromatics, and cover.

6 Leave the stock to infuse for 2 minutes. Then press or strain it, and serve it hot.

OTHER AROMATIC BROTHS AND SOUPS

The infusion technique from our Aromatic Chicken Broth recipe on the previous page lends itself to a variety of flavorful soups and broths. Each of the recipes below uses the same simple procedure. First, combine all ingredients except the noodles. Then stir, cover, remove from the heat, and allow to infuse for 2–3 minutes. Finally, strain the broth, add the cooked noodles, and serve. Each of these recipes yields four servings (1 kg / 4¼ cups).

Pho Soup

Beef stock, very hot see page 86	1 kg	1 L / 4¼ cups
Onion, halved and charred	240 g	1 large
Ginger, sliced in half and charred	50 g	½ cup / 1 piece 6 cm / 2½ in long
Sugar	30 g	2 Tbsp
Asian fish sauce	10 g	9 mL / 1¾ tsp
Monosodium glutamate (MSG), optional	5 g	1 tsp
Black peppercorns	4 g	1⅓ tsp
Star anise	2 g	1–2 whole
Cinnamon stick, crumbled	2 g	1 large stick
Whole allspice	1 g	½ tsp
Rice Noodles see variation on page 271	as needed	

Thai Soup

Pressure-Cooked Crustacean Stock, very hot see page 88	1 kg	1 L / 4¼ cups
Coconut milk	100 g	100 mL / ⅞ cup
Palm sugar, grated	40 g	⅓ cup
Asian fish sauce	20 g	20 mL / 3½ tsp
Galangal, toasted and crushed	10 g	2 Tbsp / 3–4 slices
Lime juice	6 g	6 mL / 1¼ tsp
Lemongrass, thinly sliced	5 g	1 Tbsp
Lime leaf, crushed	1 g	1 leaf
Coconut Noodles see variation on page 271	as needed	

Goulash Broth

Pork stock, very hot see variation on page 86	1 kg	1 L / 4¼ cups
Canned tomatoes	150 g	1½ cups
Red bell pepper juice	150 g	150 mL / ⅔ cup
Fresh dill sprigs, bruised	30 g	2 cups
Sherry vinegar	20 g	25 mL / 1½ Tbsp
Caraway seeds	6 g	2¼ tsp
Hot paprika	2 g	1 tsp
Cumin seeds	1 g	½ tsp
Rye Noodles see variation on page 270	as needed	

Chinese Soup

Duck stock, very hot see page 84	1 kg	1 L / 4¼ cups
Ginger, sliced	15 g	2½ Tbsp
Shaoxing wine	10 g	10 mL / 2⅜ tsp
Scallion, sliced	8 g	2 Tbsp
Dry-cured ham, julienned	8 g	2 Tbsp
Monosodium glutamate (MSG), optional	5 g	1 tsp
Whole Wheat Noodles see variation on page 271	as needed	

Tortilla Soup

Chicken stock, very hot see page 84	1 kg	1 L / 4¼ cups
Canned tomatoes	100 g	⅜ cup
Onion, diced	50 g	⅜ cup
Tortilla chips, crumbled	10 g	¼ cup
Jalapeño chili, sliced	5 g	1 tsp
Cilantro sprigs	4 g	¼ cup
Lime juice	2 g	2 mL / ⅜ tsp
Cumin seeds	0.4 g	½ tsp
Masa Harina Noodles see variation on page 270	as needed	

FRESH EGG NOODLES

YIELD:	*four servings (640 g)*
TIME ESTIMATE:	*2½ hours overall, including 30 minutes of preparation and 2 hours unattended*
STORAGE NOTES:	*raw dough keeps for 2 days when vacuum sealed and refrigerated; noodles keep for 1 day when refrigerated*
LEVEL OF DIFFICULTY:	*moderate*
SPECIAL REQUIREMENTS:	*stand mixer with dough hook or food processor, vacuum sealer, pasta machine, vital wheat gluten*

The trick to making fresh noodles with extra chew is to add gluten. Try using whole wheat, buckwheat, and other flours for variety.

The time-consuming part of making fresh noodles is not cooking them—we cook ours for just 30 seconds—but resting the dough. If you're short on time, you can use 675 g of store-bought fresh noodles or dry noodles instead in the chicken soup; follow the directions on the package to cook them.

A linguine cutter will allow you to make wider noodles from the pasta sheets. And if you don't have a pasta machine, you can use a rolling pin, and then cut the pasta by hand using a knife.

INGREDIENT	WEIGHT	VOLUME	SCALING	PROCEDURE
All-purpose flour	420 g	3 cups	100%	① Combine in the bowl of a stand mixer, and mix with the dough hook for 8 minutes.
Water	125 g	125 mL / ½ cup	30%	② Vacuum seal the dough, or seal it in a zip-top bag, and refrigerate it for at least 1 hour.
Egg	50 g	1–2 eggs	12%	③ Divide the chilled dough into four even pieces.
Extra-virgin olive oil	25 g	30 mL / 2 Tbsp	6%	④ Dust the dough with flour, and press it flat. Line a tray with a lightly floured, dry cloth.
Vital wheat gluten (Bob's Red Mill brand)	16 g	2 Tbsp	4%	⑤ Roll the pieces of dough into sheets 2 mm / 1⁄16 in thick by using a pasta machine. Place the pasta sheets side by side on the prepared tray.
Salt	4 g	1 tsp	1%	⑥ Refrigerate the sheets, uncovered, for about 1 hour.
				⑦ Cut the pasta sheets into thin, spaghetti-like noodles.
				⑧ Dust the noodles with flour, and return them to the cloth-lined tray.
				⑨ Fill a large pot with a measured amount of water, add 0.5–0.75 g of salt for every 100 g of water, and bring to a boil.
				⑩ Boil the noodles for 30 seconds to make firm noodles or 60 seconds to make tender noodles.
Olive oil or Pressure-Rendered Chicken Fat see page 123	as needed			⑪ Drain the pasta, toss it with oil, rendered fat, or pasta sauce, and serve it immediately.

You can use a food processor in place of a stand mixer. Blend the wet ingredients in the processor. Dry-blend the flour, gluten, and salt. Combine them with the wet ingredients, and then pulse in the processor until the dough just starts to cohere. Transfer the dough to a clean surface, and knead it until it becomes elastic and smooth, about 3 minutes. Continue with step 2.

1 Combine the flour, water, egg, olive oil, gluten, and salt in the bowl of a stand mixer. Mix with the dough hook attachment for 8 minutes. The dough should gradually come together in dense, smooth, elastic balls that do not stick to the sides of the bowl.

2 Vacuum seal the dough, or seal it in a zip-top bag. Refrigerate it overnight, or for at least 1 hour. Sealing the dough keeps it from drying out and helps hydrate the starch.

3 Divide the chilled dough into four even pieces.

4 Dust a piece with flour, and use the palm of your hand to flatten it. Line a tray with a lightly floured, dry cloth.

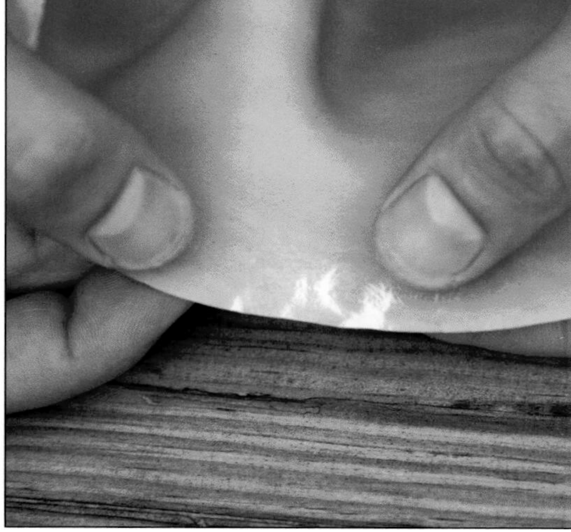

5 Roll the dough through a pasta roller into sheets 2 mm / 1⁄16 in thick. Place the pasta sheets side by side on the tray. The sheets of pasta should not overlap; use multiple trays if necessary.

6 Refrigerate the pasta sheets, uncovered, for about 1 hour. They should dry slightly and become slightly leathery.

7 Cut the sheets into spaghetti-like noodles. Any shape of pasta works in this dish, but thicker noodles require more time to cook.

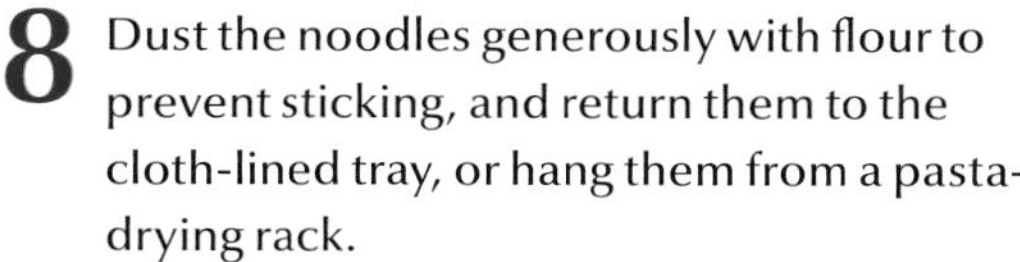

8 Dust the noodles generously with flour to prevent sticking, and return them to the cloth-lined tray, or hang them from a pasta-drying rack.

9 Pour a measured amount of water into a large pot, add 0.5–0.75 g of salt for every 100 g of water, and bring the water to a boil. This is less salt than is typically used in water when cooking pasta because we include a generous amount of salt in the pasta dough itself.

10 Boil the noodles for 30 seconds to make firm noodles or 60 seconds to make tender noodles. For thicker pasta, cook small test batches to find the optimal time.

11 Drain the pasta, toss it with oil, rendered fat, or pasta sauce, and serve it immediately.

Pasta sheets

This pasta dough, as well as the variations on the next two pages can also be rolled and cut to wide shapes for use in lasagna or cannelloni.

TO MAKE AHEAD

After dusting the noodles with flour in step 8, refrigerate them, covered, for up to 24 hours. To cook the noodles, continue with step 9.

DRESSED NOODLES

Each of the pasta dough variations below follows the same procedure as our Fresh Egg Noodles recipe on page 268 (and, like that recipe, incorporates vital wheat gluten). But each of the variations also includes a suggested sauce or other accompaniment. Quantities given here are for noodles made from 400 g of raw dough.

You can find most of the flours called for in these recipes at any good supermarket or specialty food store. Bob's Red Mill and King Arthur are two of our favorite producers of many less-common flour varieties—although "flour" is a misleading term for some of these products. Potato and coconut flours are obviously not milled grains; they are made by grinding dried potato or coconut very finely. Be aware, you may also find potato starch, coconut milk powder, and coconut cream powder at the store, but these do not work as substitutes for potato flour or coconut flour.

Potato Noodles

00 flour*	275 g	1½ cups
Water	120 g	120 mL / ½ cup
Eggs, blended	75 g	2 eggs
Potato flour	52.5 g	⅜ cup
Neutral-tasting oil	45 g	50 mL/3½ Tbsp
Vital wheat gluten (Bob's Red Mill brand)	20 g	2½ Tbsp
Salt	6 g	1¾ tsp

Serving suggestion: Cook 135 g of blended egg yolks (9–10 yolks) sous vide at 62 °C / 144 °F for 40 minutes. Sauté 115 g / 1½ cups of thinly sliced pancetta. Toss the cooked, drained noodles in the warm eggs, pancetta, 40 g / ½ cup of thinly sliced scallions, 60 g / 60 mL / ¼ cup of water from cooking the pasta, and black pepper.

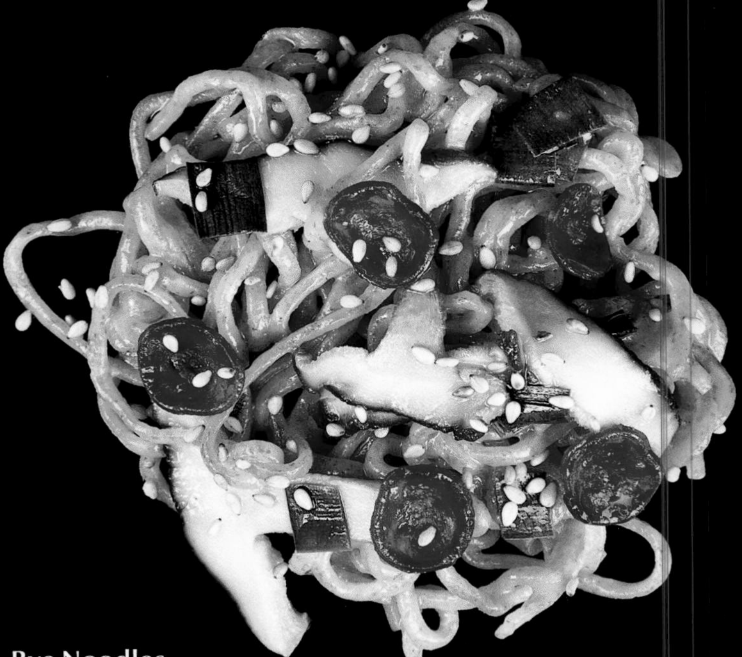

Rye Noodles

Water	125 g	125 mL / ½ cup
00 flour*	125 g	¾ cup
Rye flour	105 g	⅞ cup
Vital wheat gluten (Bob's Red Mill brand)	72 g	½ cup
Egg, blended	50 g	1 egg
Olive oil	12.5 g	15 mL / 1 Tbsp
Salt	2 g	½ tsp

Serving suggestion: Sauté 100 g / 1½ cups of sliced garlic chives and 200 g / 3 cups of thinly sliced shiitake mushrooms in 56 g / 60 mL / ¼ cup of neutral-tasting oil until just tender. Toss the cooked, drained noodles with 142 g / ¾ cup of Sesame Dressing (see variation on page 117). Garnish with toasted-sesame seeds and 43 g / ½ cup of thinly sliced Chinese sausage, fried crisp.

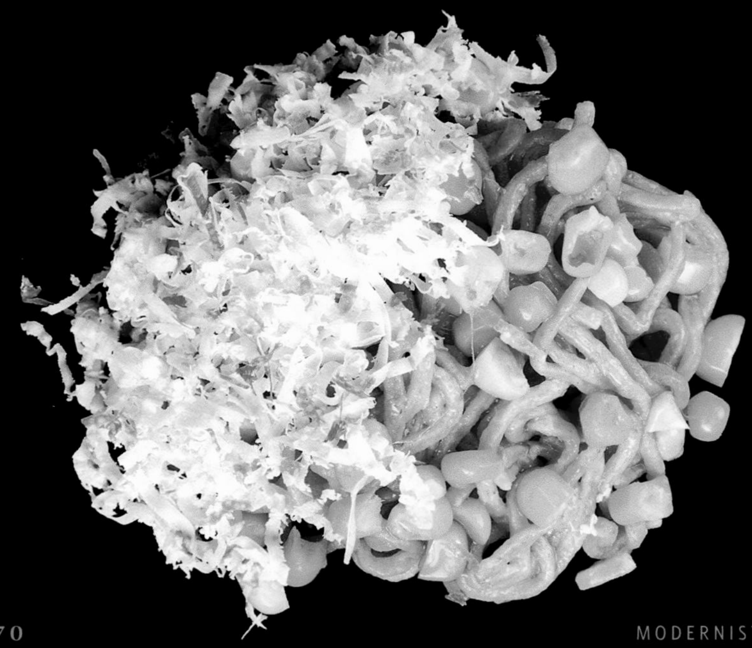

Masa Harina Noodles

Water	130 g	130 mL / ½ cup
00 flour*	125 g	¾ cup
Masa harina	105 g	¾ cup
Vital wheat gluten (Bob's Red Mill brand)	72 g	½ cup
Egg, blended	50 g	1 egg
Corn oil	12.5 g	15 mL / 1 Tbsp
Salt	2 g	½ tsp

Serving suggestion: Sauté 345 g / 2½ cups of freshly shucked sweet corn kernels in 56 g / 5 Tbsp of unsalted butter. Toss the cooked, drained noodles with corn and butter, and garnish with grated queso fresco or Cotija cheese and grated lime zest to taste.

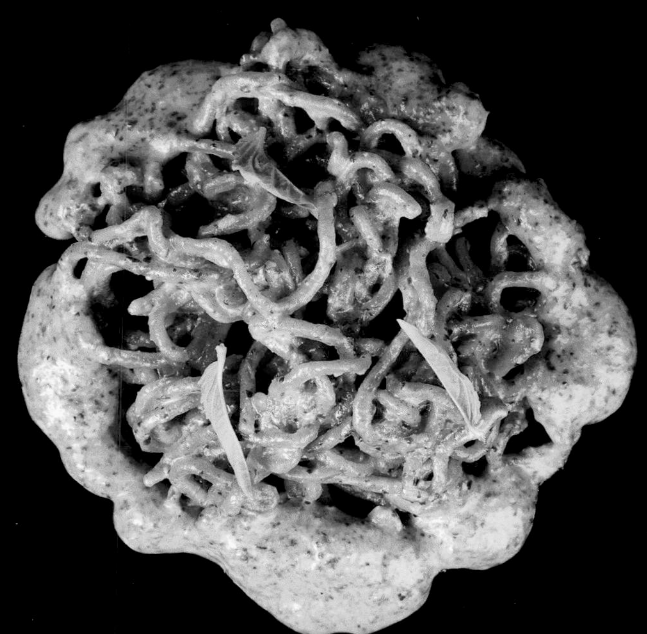

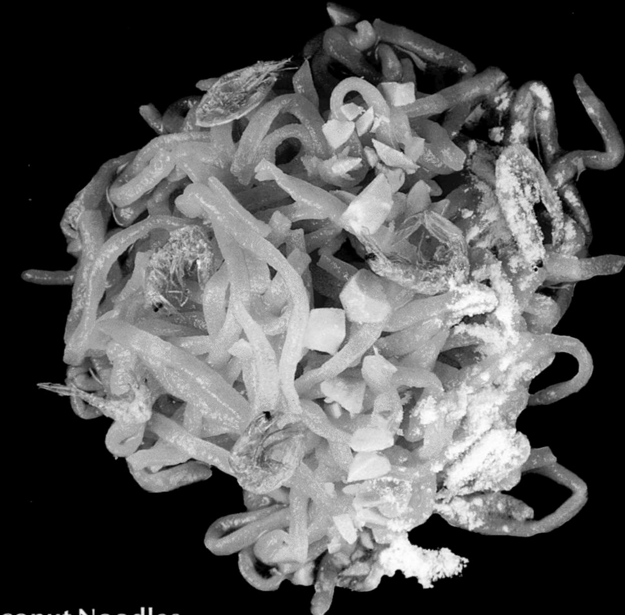

Barley Noodles

00 flour*	195 g	1⅓ cups
Egg yolks, blended	75 g	5 yolks
Water	60 g	60 mL / ¼ cup
Barley flour	53 g	½ cup
Olive oil	45 g	50 mL / 3½ Tbsp
Vital wheat gluten (Bob's Red Mill brand)	7.5 g	1 Tbsp
Salt	3 g	¾ tsp

Serving suggestion: Toss the cooked, drained noodles with 235 g / ¾ cup of Pistachio Pesto (see page 102).

Coconut Noodles

00 flour*	195 g	1¼ cups
Egg yolks, blended	75 g	5 yolks
Water	60 g	60 mL / ¼ cup
Coconut flour	53 g	⅜ cup
Neutral-tasting oil	53 g	55 mL / ¼ cup
Vital wheat gluten (Bob's Red Mill brand)	7.5 g	1 Tbsp
Salt	3 g	1 tsp

Serving suggestion: Toss the cooked, drained noodles with 160 g / ⅔ cup of Thai Sweet, Sour, and Savory Glaze (see page 115), and garnish with crushed, roasted peanuts, coconut cream powder, and tiny dried shrimp.

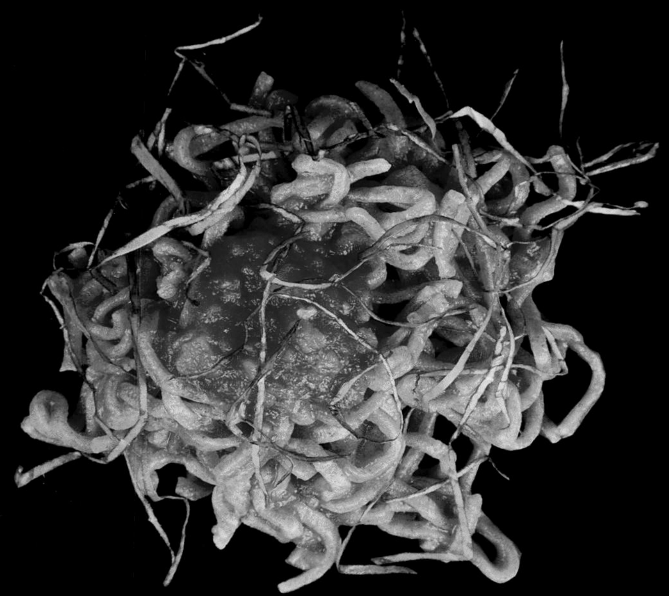

Whole Wheat Noodles

Whole wheat flour	260 g	1¾ cups
Water	90 g	60 mL / ⅜ cup
Egg, blended	50 g	1 egg
Olive oil	25 g	30 mL / 2 Tbsp
Vital wheat gluten (Bob's Red Mill brand)	5 g	2 tsp
Salt	2 g	½ tsp

Serving suggestion: Toss the cooked, drained noodles with 400 g / 1⅝ cups of Marinara (see page 112), and garnish with finely shredded basil.

*00 Flour is a very finely milled wheat flour from Italy that adds a certain texture to pasta. If it is unavailable, use all-purpose flour instead.

Rice Noodles

00 flour*	150 g	⅞ cup
Water	120 g	120 mL / ½ cup
Rice flour	100 g	⅞ cup
Egg, blended	50 g	1 egg
Vital wheat gluten (Bob's Red Mill brand)	40 g	5 Tbsp
Rice bran oil	20 g	20 mL / 1½ Tbsp
Salt	2 g	½ tsp

Serving suggestion: Toss the cooked, drained noodles with 145 g / ⅝ cup of Pressure-Caramelized Peanut Sauce (see page 111), and drizzle with 45 g / 50 mL / 3½ Tbsp of Pressure-Rendered Chicken Fat (see page 123), and a pinch of chili powder.

PRESSURE-COOKED CARROTS AND LEEKS

YIELD:	*four servings (250 g / 1 cup)*
TIME ESTIMATE:	*10 minutes overall*
STORAGE NOTES:	*keeps for 1 day when refrigerated*
LEVEL OF DIFFICULTY:	*easy*
SPECIAL REQUIREMENTS:	*pressure cooker*

This simple technique makes very tender vegetables in only a few minutes. The thickness of the vegetables determines the correct cooking time. If the vegetables are thicker or thinner than noted, increase or decrease the time accordingly.

INGREDIENT	WEIGHT	VOLUME	SCALING
Carrots, unpeeled, 2.5 cm / 1 in in diameter	200 g	2 carrots	100%
Leeks, 2.5 cm / 1 in in diameter, thoroughly washed	150 g	1–2 leeks	75%

PROCEDURE

① Place the vegetables on a rack or trivet in a pressure cooker, and add 1 cm / ⅜ in of water. The vegetables should cook above, not in, the water.

② Pressure-cook at a gauge pressure of 1 bar / 15 psi for 5 minutes. Start timing as soon as full pressure has been reached.

③ Depressurize the cooker quickly by running tepid water over the rim. If the vegetables are not yet tender enough for your liking, replace the lid, and continue to pressure-cook for 1–2 minutes more.

④ Rub the skins off the carrots, and peel and discard the outermost layer of the leeks.

⑤ Slice each on the bias into pieces 1 cm / ⅜ in thick.

⑥ Keep warm until ready to serve.

Safety tips for pressure-cooking: see page 33

1

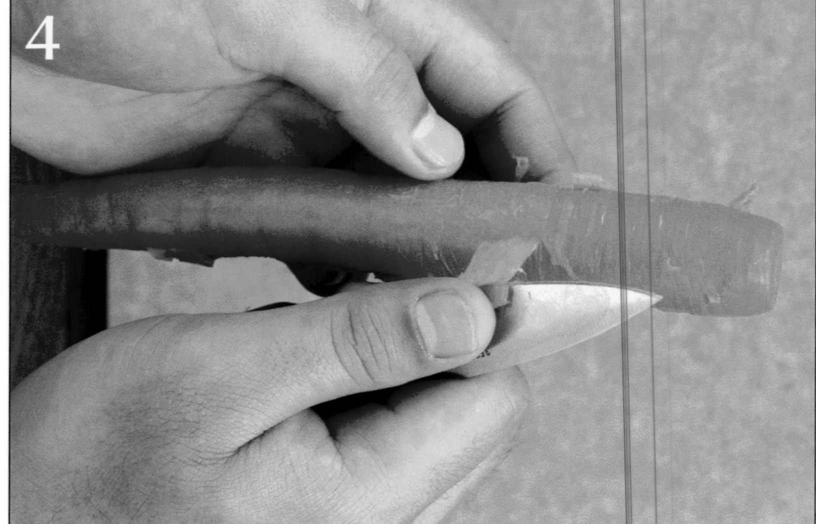
4

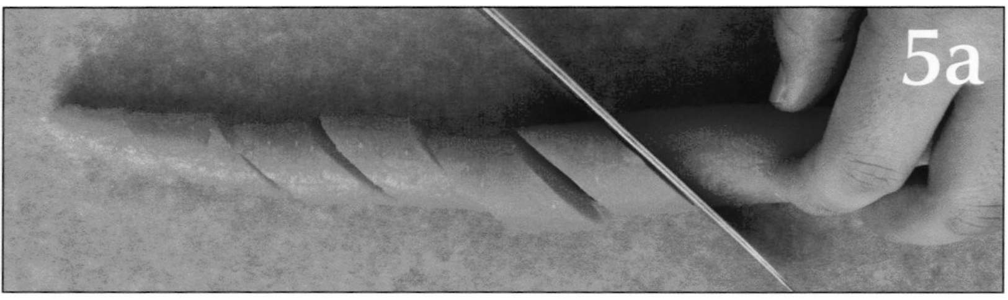
5a

5b

TO MAKE AHEAD

Refrigerate the cooked vegetables. Reheat them in a steamer for 2 minutes, or place them on a microwave-safe plate, cover with microwave-safe plastic wrap, and microwave at 500 watts until just warmed through, about 30 seconds.

VARIATIONS

This technique works well with other root vegetables such as beets, turnips, potatoes, celery root, and parsnips. Cut them into pieces of equal thickness when cooking them together. See Pressure-Cooked Vegetables on page 183.

CHICKEN NOODLE SOUP

YIELD:	*four servings (2.4 kg / 10 cups)*
TIME ESTIMATE:	*15 minutes*
STORAGE NOTES:	*serve immediately*
LEVEL OF DIFFICULTY:	*moderate*
SPECIAL REQUIREMENTS:	*Fresh Egg Noodles (see page 268), Pressure-Cooked Carrots and Leeks (see the previous page), Sous Vide Chicken (see page 244), Aromatic Chicken Broth (see page 266), Pressure-Rendered Chicken Fat (see page 123)*

The secret to perfecting this seemingly simple soup is ensuring that each component is cooked and seasoned to perfection. Make sure all of the ingredients are prepared and timed to be assembled quickly so that the soup is piping hot when it gets to the table.

INGREDIENT	WEIGHT	VOLUME	PROCEDURE
Fresh Egg Noodles, hot see page 268	400 g	4 cups	① Peel the mushrooms, and slice them on a mandoline to paper-thin slices. ② Divide evenly between four serving bowls.
Pressure-Cooked Carrots and Leeks, warm see the previous page	250 g	20 pieces of carrot 16 pieces of leek	
White button mushrooms	22 g	¾ cup	
Sous Vide Chicken, warm and sliced see page 244	700 g	2 cups	
Aromatic Chicken Broth, hot see page 266	1 kg	1 L / 4¼ cups	③ Pour into the prepared soup bowls.
Pressure-Rendered Chicken Fat, melted (optional) see page 123	40 g	45 mL / 3 Tbsp	④ Drizzle over the soup for added flavor.

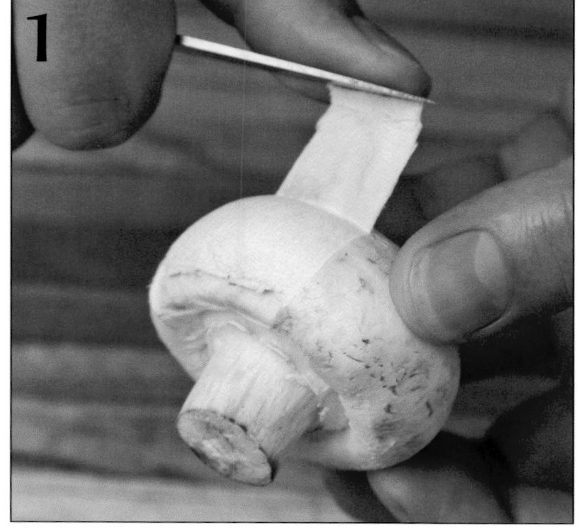
1

2a

2b

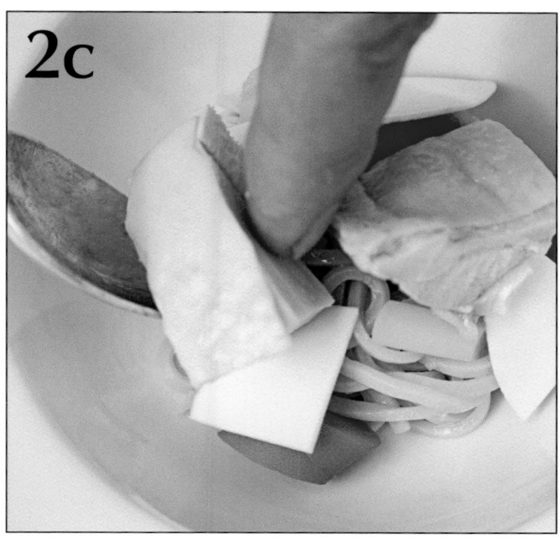
2c

3

4

SALMON

"Salmon" is almost as broad a designation as "poultry." The incredible diversity of salmon includes sockeyes harvested from the lakes; king and blackmouth Chinook caught in the sounds and rivers; cohos, pinks, and steelheads (which are technically trout) fished from the ocean; and salmon raised in fish farms.

In the Pacific Northwest, where we live, we are lucky to have a wide variety of salmon species that we eagerly await during the spring and summer months each year. Unfortunately, many wild populations are threatened. Organic tank-farmed salmon have appeared in markets in recent years as a sustainable alternative.

Home cooks and professional chefs alike frequently overcook salmon, which is easy to do because the flesh starts changing at such low temperatures. But the precision of cooking sous vide allows you to prepare salmon that is as silky as custard while preserving its sweet taste of the ocean. So if you think you don't like salmon, we encourage you to try it again.

THE SCIENCE OF WHY FISH IS BEST COOKED AT LOW TEMPERATURE

The ideal cooking temperatures for meats and seafood depend in part on the normal body temperature of the animal from which the food came. Most mammals have a body temperature near 37 °C / 99 °F. Fish, living as they do in the comparatively cool comfort of water, have much lower body temperatures, which range from below 5 °C / 41 °F near the poles to 30 °C / 86 °F in tropical waters. When cooked to temperatures that would leave most meats rare, fish proteins become entirely coagulated, and the flesh turns dry and mealy. To our taste, most kinds of fish are best cooked at 42–50 °C / 108–122 °F.

Note, however, that these temperatures will not pasteurize the fish. Then again, neither will the cooking temperatures recommended by the U.S. Food and Drug Administration. Following the agency's guidelines ensures that you overcook the fish, but doesn't make it appreciably safer. The small risk of eating fish that is unpasteurized but properly cooked is, in our view, one that is worth taking for most people. For more information about food safety, see page xxv.

HIGHLIGHTS

Brining the salmon before cooking it nicely seasons and firms the fish. It also prevents albumin from leaching to the surface and masking the beautiful orange-red pigment with an opaque whitish color.

see page 276

Baste the fish in hot butter or oil for a few seconds after cooking it sous vide: this firms the surface slightly, warms it, and adds a layer of flavor.

see page 276

Each type of fish has an **ideal range of cooking temperatures.** We give our favorites for cod, halibut, mackerel, salmon, snapper, sole, and tuna.

see page 280

Make a crispy fish skin **as delicious as bacon** by cooking it sous vide and then frying it.

see page 279

FURTHER READING IN *MODERNIST CUISINE*

Best bets for brining and curing fish: see page 3·172
An illustrated guide to the muscle structure of fish: see pages 3·20–23
Cooking additional kinds of fish sous vide: see page 3·102
Why slime is the key to crispy fish skin: see page 3·129

FRAGRANT SOUS VIDE SALMON

YIELD:	*four servings (600 g)*
TIME ESTIMATE:	*5¼ hours overall, including 15 minutes of preparation and 5 hours unattended*
STORAGE NOTES:	*serve immediately; brined fish keeps for up to 1 day when refrigerated*
LEVEL OF DIFFICULTY:	*easy*
SPECIAL REQUIREMENTS:	*sous vide setup, Fish Spice Mix (optional, see page 137)*

Use the highest-quality salmon you can find. We like to brine the fish before cooking to season it, firm it, and protect its delicate color. If you have time, decrease the salt to 20 g and the sugar to 15 g, and brine the fish for 24 hours—the effect is even gentler.

The cooked fish is delicious served hot or cold; if you're serving it cold, cook it sous vide in oil rather than butter so that the fat won't congeal. For firmer salmon, cook it sous vide to a core temperature of 51 °C / 124 °F.

INGREDIENT	WEIGHT	VOLUME	SCALING	PROCEDURE
Water	1 kg	1 L / 4¼ cups	100%	① Stir together until completely dissolved to make a brine.
Salt	50 g	4½ Tbsp	5%	
Sugar	40 g	2½ Tbsp	4%	
Salmon fillets, skin and pin bones removed	600 g / 1.3 lb	4 fillets	60%	② Submerge the salmon in the brine, and refrigerate for 3–5 hours. ③ Drain the brine from the salmon.
Neutral-tasting oil, olive oil, or melted butter	120 g	130 mL / ½ cup	12%	④ Preheat a water bath to **46 °C / 115 °F**. ⑤ Place each fillet with 30 g / 30 mL / 2 Tbsp of oil or butter in a separate zip-top bag. Remove as much air as possible from the bags by using the water-displacement method (see page 58), and seal them. ⑥ Cook sous vide to a core temperature of **45 °C / 113 °F**, about 25 minutes for fillets 2.5 cm / 1 in thick. ⑦ Transfer the cooked fillets gently from the bags to a plate.
Unsalted butter	80 g	⅜ cup	8%	⑧ Melt the butter in a nonstick frying pan over medium-low heat.
Fish Spice Mix (optional) see page 137	15 g	2 Tbsp	1.5%	⑨ Add the fish spice, if you are using it, and increase the heat until the butter just starts to bubble. ⑩ Add the fillets, and cook while basting with the hot butter for about 30 seconds per side. Serve immediately.

Safety tips for lightly cooked food: see page xxv

We love to serve this salmon with simple sautéed asparagus and peas during spring. Serve with cabbage, shiitake mushrooms, and thyme in the colder months.

TO MAKE AHEAD

After draining the brine in step 3, you may refrigerate the salmon for up to 24 hours.

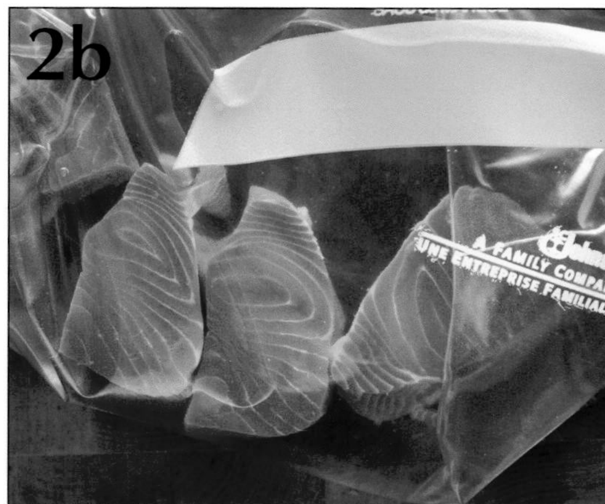

1 Make the brine by stirring the salt and sugar into the water until completely dissolved. If you use warm water (which dissolves the salt and sugar more quickly), cool the brine completely before adding the salmon.

2 Submerge the salmon in the brine, or seal salmon portions with the brine in a zip-top bag, and then refrigerate it for 3–5 hours. Brining the fish firms its surface and makes it both tastier and easier to handle.

3 Drain the brine from the salmon.

4 Preheat a water bath to 46 °C / 115 °F.

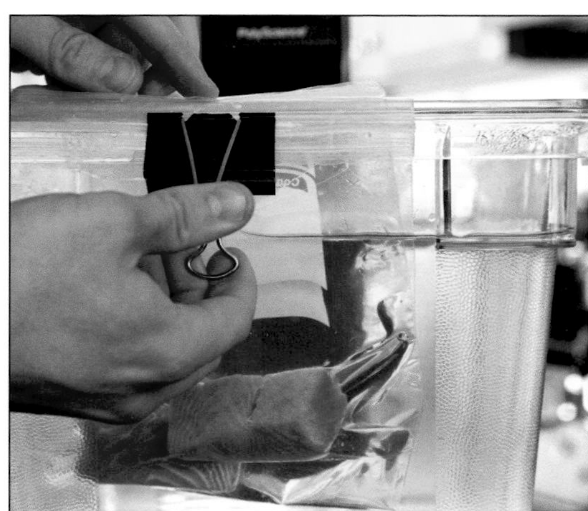

5 Place each fillet in a separate zip-top bag along with 30 g / 30 mL / 2 Tbsp of oil or butter. Arrange the fillets so that the longer, thicker sides are at the bottom of the bag; this prevents them from bending while cooking. Use the water-displacement method (see page 58) to remove as much air as possible from each bag, and seal it.

6 Cook the salmon sous vide to a core temperature of 45 °C / 113 °F. Fillets that are 2.5 cm / 1 in thick will require about 25 minutes to reach the target temperature at their thickest part. Thinner pieces may need just 12–15 minutes to cook; thicker pieces may take 30 minutes or more. Clip the bags to the side of the bath.

7 Transfer the cooked fillets gently from their bags to a plate so that they are easier to handle.

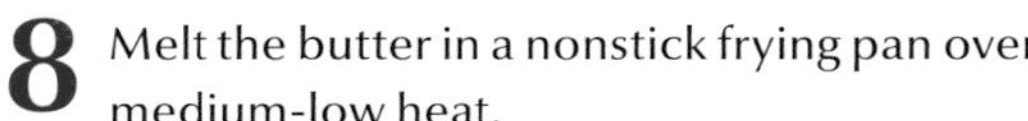

8 Melt the butter in a nonstick frying pan over medium-low heat.

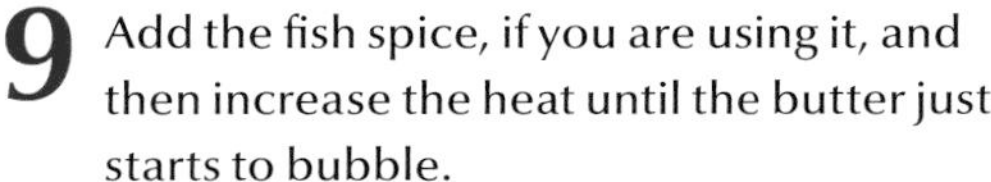

9 Add the fish spice, if you are using it, and then increase the heat until the butter just starts to bubble.

10 Add the fillets, and baste them in the pan with the hot butter for about 30 seconds per side. Serve the fish immediately; it is not very hot, so cools rapidly. The fish pairs well with seasonal vegetables.

HOW TO Poach Salmon in a Kitchen Sink

This is a fun and simple way to begin enjoying the virtues of low-temperature cooking without investing in sous vide equipment. A pot of water preserves a constant temperature for up to 1 hour, far more time than is necessary to cook fish—and even enough time to cook some steaks. (A picnic cooler keeps the water temperature stable for up to 5 hours; see page 198 for an example of this technique.) The more food you put in the water bath, and the colder that food is, the more the water temperature drops. To help hold the heat, bring the food to room temperature before cooking it, and use your largest pot and an abundant amount of water.

1 Brine the salmon by following steps 1–3 on the previous page (optional).

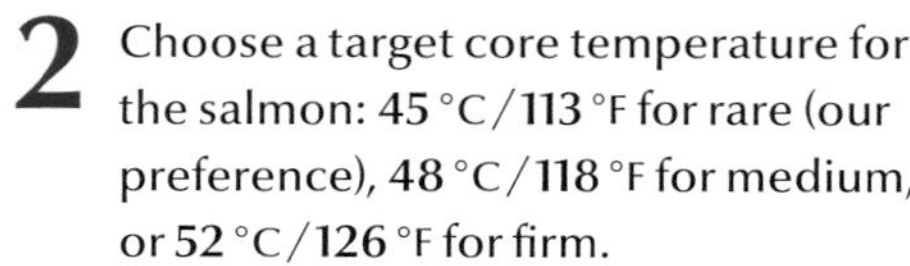

2 Choose a target core temperature for the salmon: 45 °C / 113 °F for rare (our preference), 48 °C / 118 °F for medium, or 52 °C / 126 °F for firm.

3 Adjust the temperature of the tap water until it is 2–5 °C / 5–9 °F higher than the target temperature, as measured with a digital thermometer.

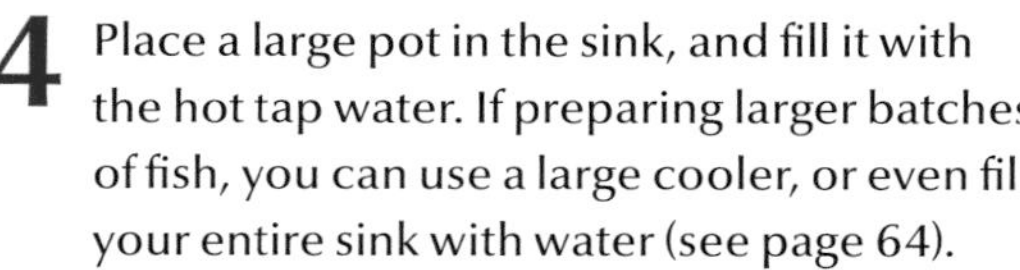

4 Place a large pot in the sink, and fill it with the hot tap water. If preparing larger batches of fish, you can use a large cooler, or even fill your entire sink with water (see page 64).

5 Place each fillet, along with 30 g / 30 mL / 2 Tbsp of oil or butter, in a separate zip-top bag. Use the water-displacement method (see page 58) to remove as much air as possible from the bags, and seal them.

6 Cook sous vide to the desired core temperature, about 25 minutes for fillets that are 2.5 cm / 1 in thick. Continue with step 7 of the recipe on the previous page to finish the salmon.

HOW TO Bake Salmon in a Toaster Oven

Your toaster oven can approximate cooking sous vide, and you won't need an additional finishing step. The texture of the salmon will be slightly more dense because of the higher cooking temperature and drier cooking environment. Cooking takes longer than in a water bath because dry heat is not as efficient at conducting heat, but the result is still excellent.

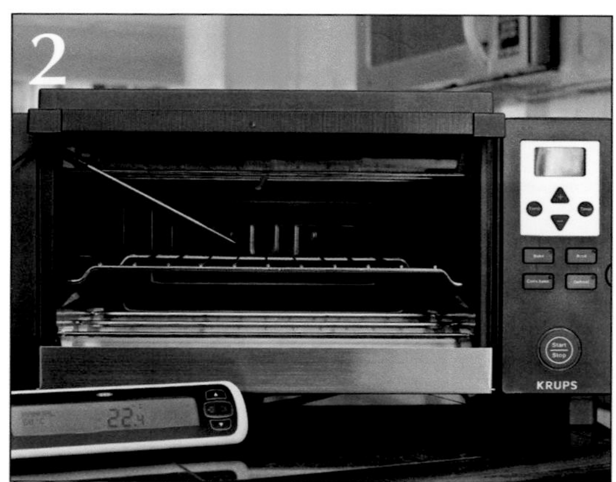

1 Brine the salmon by following steps 1–3 on the previous page (optional).

2 Calibrate your toaster oven (see page 35), and set it to 90–110 °C / 200–225 °F.

3 Place the salmon on a small baking sheet, and cook it until the core temperature reaches 45 °C / 113 °F, 38–40 minutes. Use a digital thermometer to monitor the core temperature. About halfway through the cooking, baste the fish with a neutral-tasting oil or clarified butter, and dust with the Fish Spice Mix on page 137, if desired.

CRISPY FISH SKIN

YIELD:	*four pieces (each 5 cm by 7.5 cm / 2 in by 3 in)*
TIME ESTIMATE:	*5¼ hours overall, including 15 minutes of preparation and 5 hours unattended*
STORAGE NOTES:	*serve immediately after frying; keeps for up to 1 day when refrigerated after cooking sous vide*
LEVEL OF DIFFICULTY:	*advanced (handling)*
SPECIAL REQUIREMENTS:	*sous vide setup, vacuum sealer*

Any flavorful fish skin works well in this recipe. Softer skins, such as those of cod and snapper, should be cooked sous vide for 3 hours rather than 5 hours. The ice-bath cooling in step 5 is crucial for handling and frying the skin properly.

INGREDIENT	WEIGHT	PROCEDURE
Salmon skin	2 pieces (10 cm by 15 cm / 4 in by 6 in)	① Preheat a water bath to 88 °C / 190 °F. ② Scale the fish skin. ③ Remove all of the meat, fat, and sinew from the inside of the skin to prevent it from curling. ④ Vacuum seal the pieces, and cook sous vide for 5 hours. ⑤ Plunge the bags into an ice bath to cool completely.
Neutral frying oil see page xxii	as needed	⑥ Cut open the bags, and carefully peel the cooked fish skin from the plastic. Pat the skin dry. ⑦ Cut the skin into pieces 5 cm by 7.5 cm / 2 in by 3 in square. ⑧ Preheat the frying oil to 185 °C / 365 °F in a pot no more than half full. ⑨ Put a few pieces of the fish skin, one at a time, into the oil. Use long tongs, and be very careful, as the moist skin reacts violently with the hot oil. ⑩ Deep-fry until very crispy, 1–3 minutes. ⑪ Drain on paper towels.
Salt	to taste	⑫ Season, and serve immediately.

Safety tips for deep-frying: see page 26

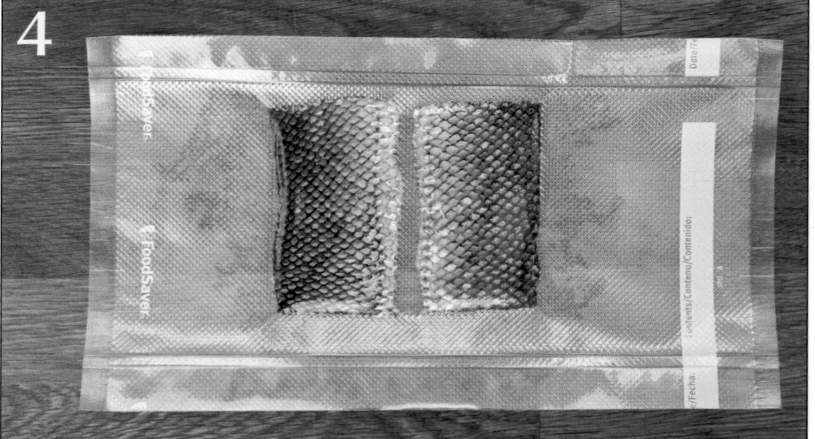

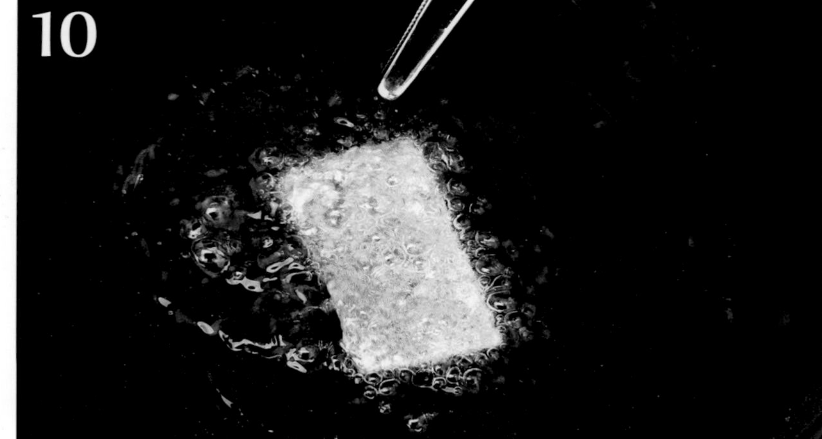

TO MAKE AHEAD

After cooling the fish skins in step 5, refrigerate the sealed bags for up to 24 hours. Continue with step 6.

VARIATIONS

Baked Fish Skin Chips

To make baked chips, brush or spray the cooked skin with oil, season it, and then sandwich it between two silicone mats and two baking sheets. Bake it in a 165 °C / 330 °F oven until crisp, 20–45 minutes.

Crispy Chicken or Pork Skin

Substitute chicken skin or pork skin for the salmon skin. At step 4, cook sous vide for 12 hours if making chicken skin or for 18 hours if making pork skin. Continue with step 5. For a recipe for Pressure-Cooked Chicharrón, see page 222.

SELECTING SALMON

Salmon is a fascinating group of seven fish species that includes a dizzying number of varieties. Born in freshwater, most species of salmon migrate to the oceans. When it's time to spawn, they return—literally following their noses—to the exact spots where they were born. This anadromous cycle determines the seasonality of the wild salmon populations. Six of the seven salmon species are native to the Pacific Ocean.

The salmon varieties shown here are some of the kinds you may find at your fishmonger. Check the Seafood Watch page of the Monterey Bay Aquarium website for recommendations on sustainable choices. Aquaculture has made great strides recently, and some salmon is farmed organically in fully sustainable ways.

Traditional methods of cooking fish require perfect timing that is challenging even for experienced cooks, as illustrated by this composite of salmon cooked to a range of core temperatures.

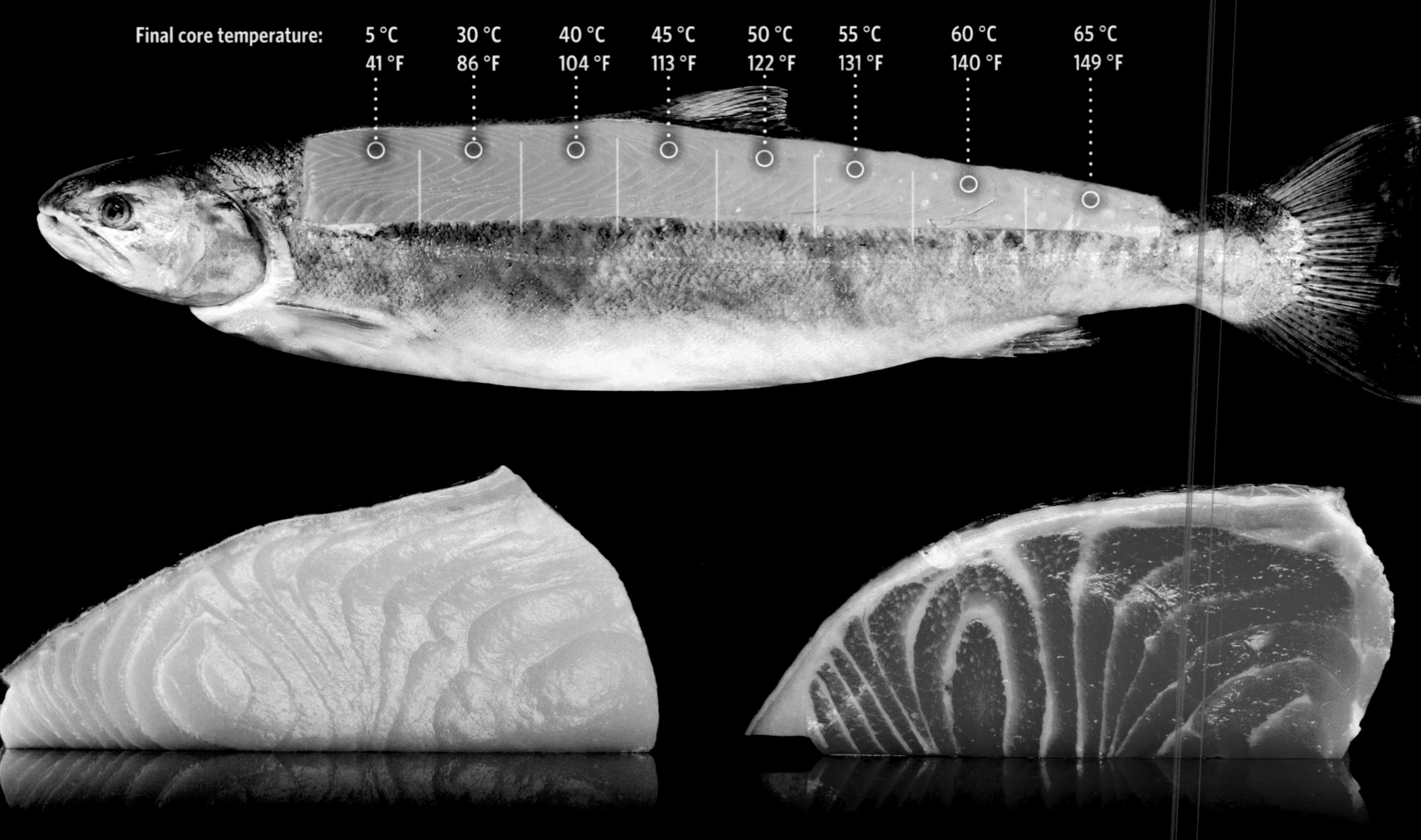

White King Salmon

The Chinook or king salmon is one of the best-tasting salmon varieties. Its succulent, oily flesh is usually bright pink or red, but about one in 100 have white flesh. Marine biologists think that these white specimens are missing a protein that absorbs the pink pigment of the krill that are a mainstay of the salmon diet.
Also known as: ivory king
Average weight: 7.25–9 kg / 16–20 lb
Average length: 90–100 cm / 35–40 in
In season: April–September

Steelhead Salmon

Steelhead are a variety of rainbow trout that leave freshwater rivers in which they are born to live in the ocean, as salmon do. They are related to salmon and may be cooked similarly.
Average weight: 1.8–2.7 kg / 4–6 lb
Average length: 50 cm / 20 in
In season: November–August

Best Bets for Cooking Fish Sous Vide

The steps for cooking salmon sous vide are described on page 276. The target core temperatures listed below are our favorites, but tastes vary, so feel free to experiment with others. We've found that about 25 minutes is usually sufficient to bring a 2.5 cm / 1 in thick piece of fish from refrigerator temperature to the target temperature. But times depend greatly on the thickness of the fish, so check for doneness by using a digital probe thermometer (see page 8). Be sure to set the water bath to 1 °C / 2 °F higher than the target core temperature given in the table. Fish cooked sous vide often benefits from a finishing step, such as searing in butter or a quick grilling, which both heats and firms the surface.

	Just cooked		Just flaking			
Ingredient	(°C)	(°F)	(°C)	(°F)	Note	See page
black cod or true cod	45	113	48	118	benefits from dry curing for 3 hours with 7 g of salt and 5 g of sugar for every 100 g of fish	133
halibut	42	108	46	115	great when seared over banked coals on the grill	193
mackerel or sardine	42	108	46	115	benefits from dry curing for 3 hours with 7 g of salt and 5 g of sugar for every 100 g of fish	132
salmon	40	104	45	113	brine with a solution of salt and sugar	276
snapper	46	115	50	122	delicious when drizzled with spiced oil after cooking	118
sole or fluke	48	118	52	126	with thin fillets, stack two and vacuum seal them together—the natural gelatin will bind them gently; with thicker fillets, fold the thin ends under so that the thickness is even from end to end; cook small fish on the bone, and sear them in butter	
tuna	42	108	55	131	give tuna a quick sear in brown butter after cooking sous vide; for cooking at 55 °C / 131 °F, we brine the fish first, and then finish it with an aromatic oil	133 (brine) 118 (oil)

(temperatures in red are those that we prefer)

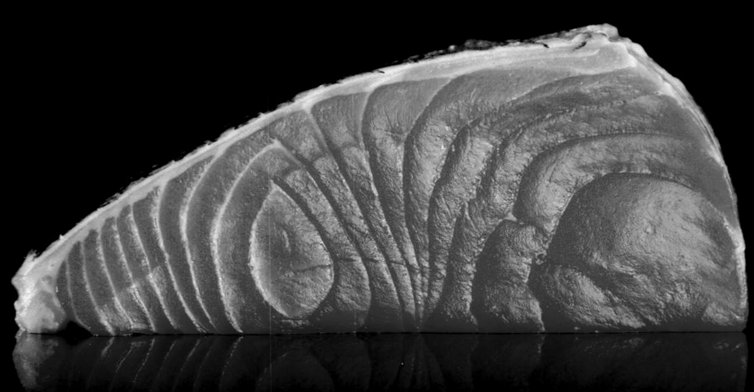

Copper River Salmon

Salmon that spawn in the Copper River in Alaska must swim upstream as far as 200 miles. They do not eat during that journey, so their bodies must store lots of energy as fat. This makes them delicious to eat! Both King salmon and the smaller sockeye and coho salmon are harvested from the Copper River during a short catch season each year.

Average weight: 2.25–2.7 kg / 5–6 lb
Average length: 60 cm / 24 in
In season: May–October

Farmed Atlantic Salmon

Atlantic salmon is the most common type sold at retail. More than 95% of farmed salmon are of the Atlantic variety. Salmon are often farmed in ocean pens, and their feeding regimen and waste tend to decimate their local ecosystems; consider your options. The natural color of farmed salmon is a lighter pink than that of wild salmon; some farmed species are injected with dye to enhance their color. Tank-raised fish are the most sustainable kind of farmed salmon.

Average weight: 3.5–4.5 kg / 8–10 lb
Average length: 50–65 cm / 20–25 in
In season: year-round (farmed)

SHELLFISH

We're lucky to be based in the Pacific Northwest, where we have abundant access to fresh seafood. So we would be remiss not to include a variety of shellfish—lobster, clams, mussels, snails—in this book. That is especially true because our favorite cooking technique, sous vide, provides the perfect antidote to overcooked shellfish, which is all too common. Take mussels marinière: the mussels are usually a rubbery afterthought to the creamy sauce.

The recipes in this chapter bring out the best in shellfish. The Lobster Roll, for example, is a study in contrasts: a warm, toasted roll filled with a refreshingly cool, savory, and tangy mixture of lobster and mayonnaise. We perfect this classic New England sandwich by ensuring that the lobster is perfectly cooked: succulent, juicy, and sweet.

Mussels Marinière uses sous vide cooking to improve on the French dish of mussels steamed in a delicate white-wine broth. Clams in Chowder Sauce is the Modernist essence of chowder: it dresses juicy clams in foamy sauce. And tender Sous Vide Braised Snails are great in paella or as classically prepared escargot.

THE SCIENCE OF SHOCKINGLY ORANGE BUTTER

The pigment in lobster shells that turns them crimson when cooked is fat-soluble, as is a lot of the lobster flavor. That means that when you cook the shells in butter, the color dissolves into the butter right along with the flavors. If you cook the shells in water, you get none of the color and only a slightly sweet and briny flavor, like that of shellfish stock. Making lobster butter is a great way to use the lobster shell and any meat left in it that you couldn't get out. For a recipe, see page 122.

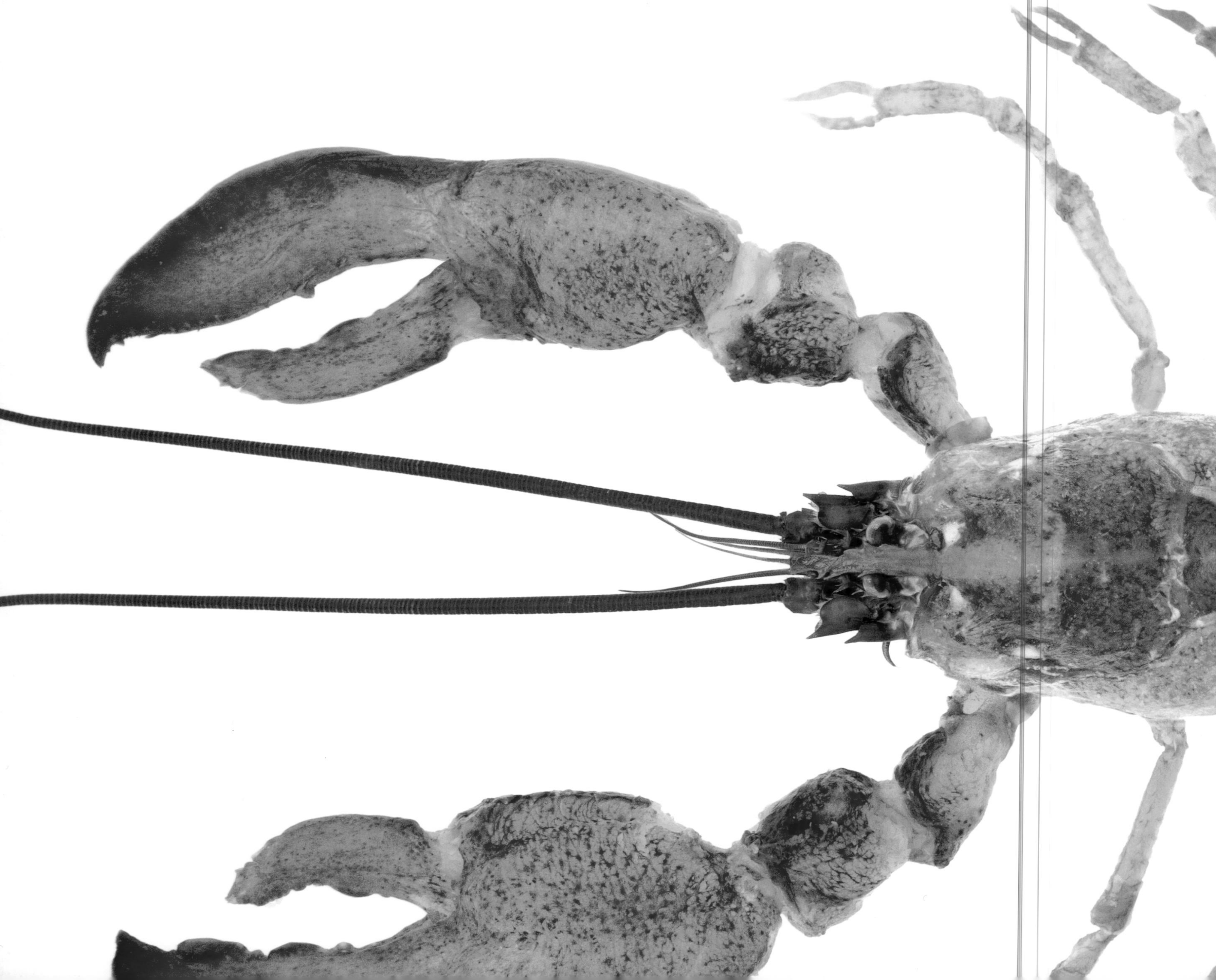

HIGHLIGHTS

It's a mistake to cook a lobster whole. One way we perfect our lobster is to cook the tail and claw meat separately, at different temperatures.

see page 288

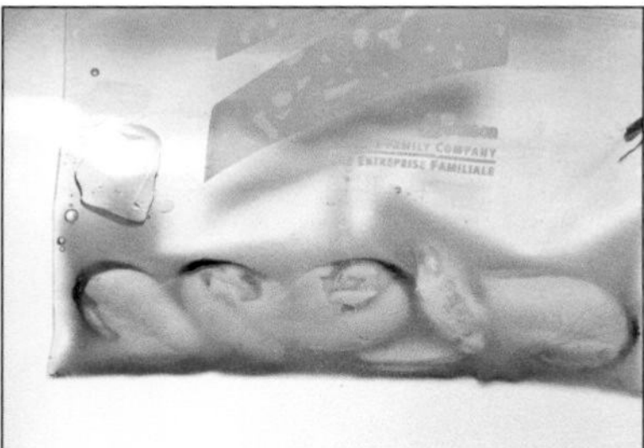

Mussels and clams typically are boiled or steamed until they open, but by then they're overdone. For **juicy mussels with an intense taste**, steam them briefly in white wine, and then shuck them and cook them sous vide in their own juices.

see page 290

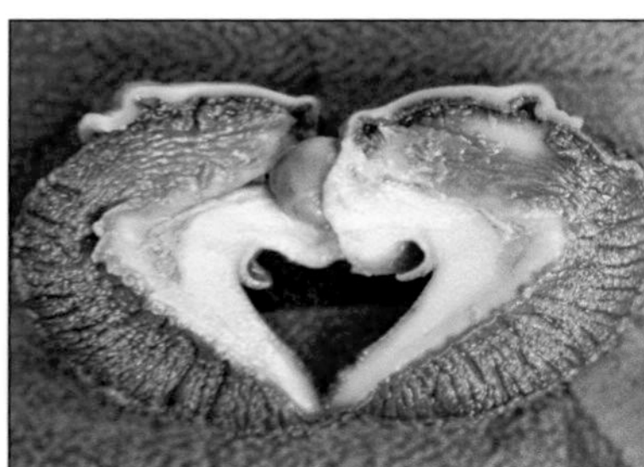

Forget rubbery snails floating in butter: **snails cooked sous vide make tender escargot** that you'll want to eat.

see page 293

Shucking mussels or clams and shelling lobster is easy when you follow our illustrated, step-by-step guides.

see pages 284–287

FURTHER READING IN *MODERNIST CUISINE*

Spineless meat in a shell—an overview of shellfish: see pages 3·26–27
How to select a lobster at its peak for cooking: see pages 3·28–30
The essentials of prawns, shrimp, and sea urchins: see pages 3·30–31
A plated-dish recipe for Lobster Américaine: see pages 5·184–187
A plated-dish recipe for Oyster Stew: see pages 5·205–207

We carefully removed the shell from a cooked lobster and then reassembled the parts to show the meat by itself.

HOW TO Kill and Shell a Lobster

With seafood, freshness is everything. The best way to get great shellfish is to identify a reputable fishmonger or fish market. Shellfish should smell like the sea—briny but not overpowering. Buy clams, mussels, and lobsters straight off the boat, or from tanks filled with clean water. Look for foods that move fast at the market; it helps to eat what the locals eat because uncommon foods tend to sit around.

Once you buy live shellfish, you have to kill it, clean it, and shell it. A lobster tastes better if you kill it just before you cook it. Research suggests that lobsters can feel pain, so it is worth taking the effort to dispatch the animals gently. Some claim that the technique shown below is the most humane method, while others put the lobsters to sleep in a freezer before boiling them (see the next page).

1 Place the tip of a large, sharp knife at the cross on the shell, about 2.5 cm / 1 in behind the eyes, pointing the blade away from the tail. In one quick movement, cut deep into the head, toward the front of the lobster.

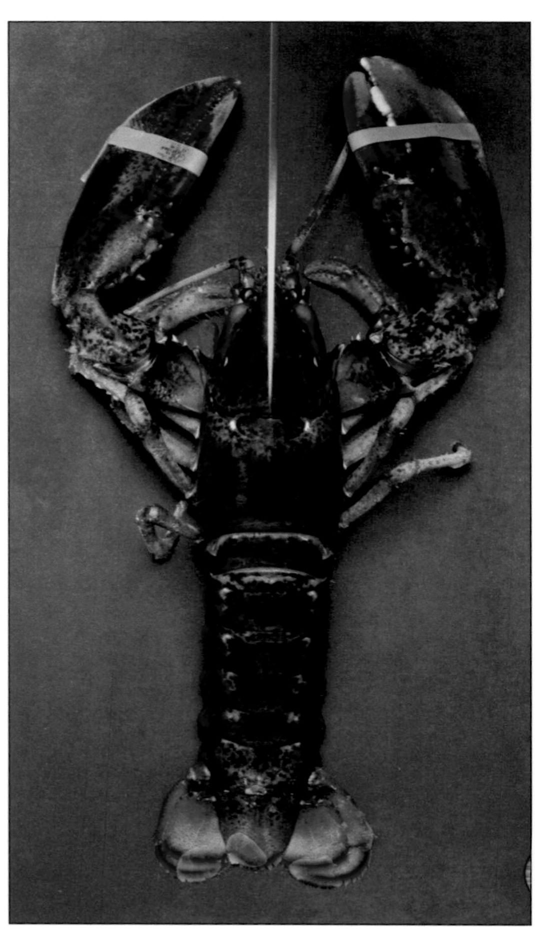

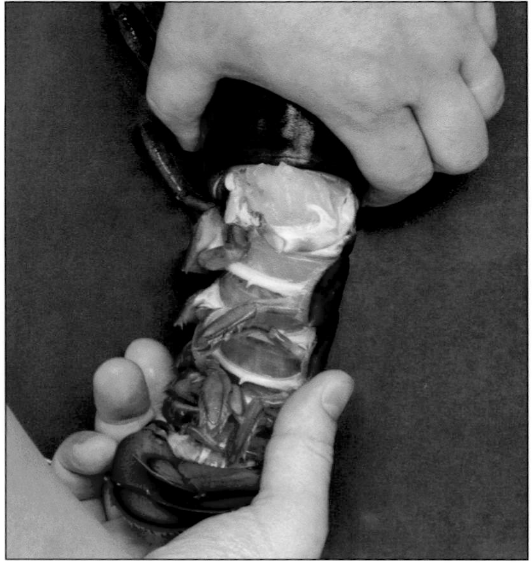

2 Twist the head from the body, and break off the claws. The lobster is dead as soon as step 1 is complete, but nervous reflexes may still be active, so expect the extremities to twitch briefly.

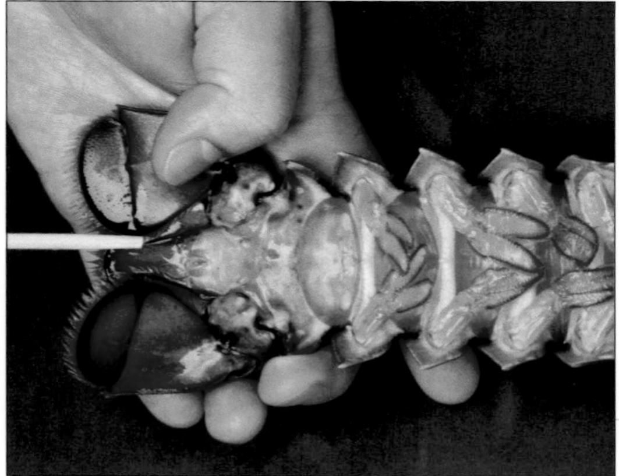

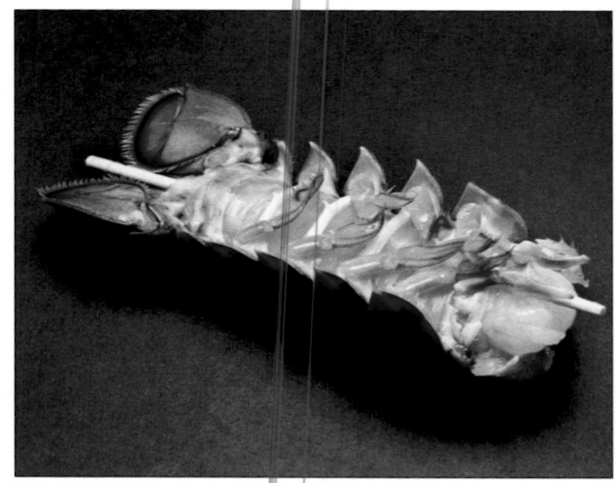

3 Thread a chopstick or skewer between the tail meat and the bottom shell to straighten it for aesthetic purposes (optional). Be sure to save the body, legs, and any dark green roe for making crustacean butter or stock (see page 122).

4 Bring a large pot of water to a rolling boil. Arrange an ice bath alongside.

5 Blanch the lobster tails in the boiling water for 90 seconds, and then plunge them in the ice water. Blanch the claws for 4 minutes, and then submerge them in ice water. This step loosens the meat from the shell so that it is easier to remove.

5a

5b

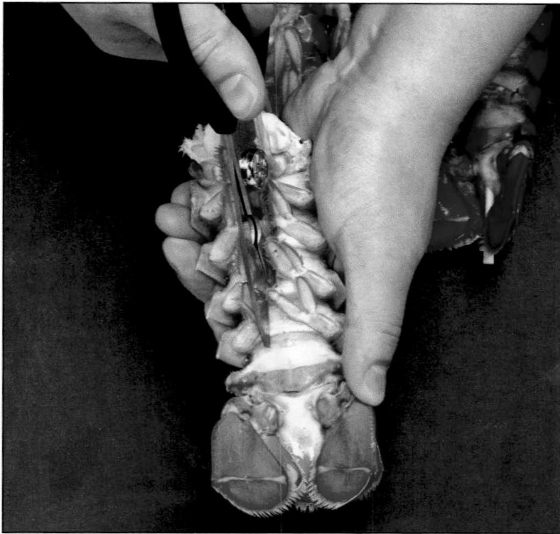

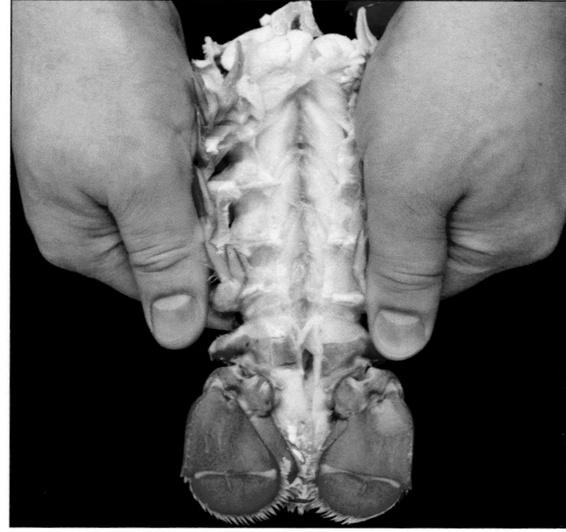

6 Clean the meat from the tails by cutting the shell with good kitchen shears and carefully peeling it off. Wear gloves to protect your hands from the sharp edges. Wash off any curd-like albumin that may have exuded during the blanching.

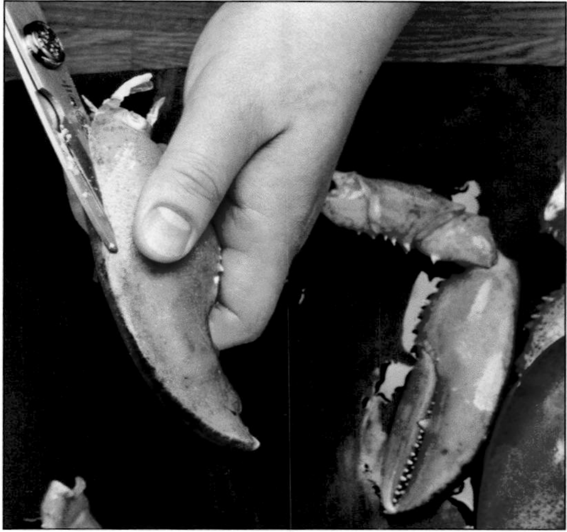

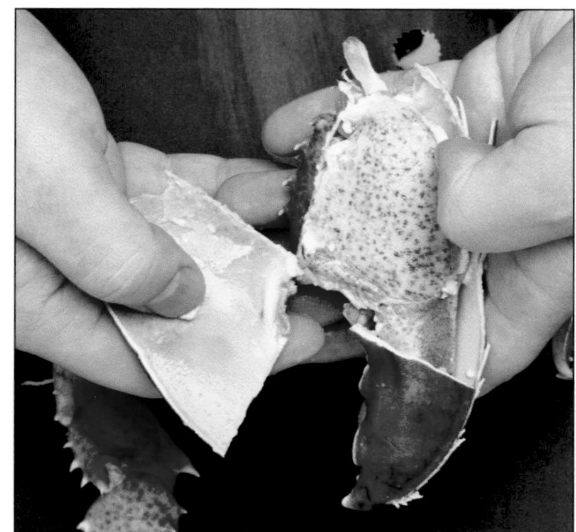

7 Clean the meat from the claws and knuckles (the pieces that connect the claws to the body) in the same manner.

8 Cook the meat immediately, or vacuum seal the lobster tails and lobster claws separately, and store refrigerated for up to 24 hours.

VARIATION: **Freezing the Lobster**

Place the live lobsters in the freezer for about 30 minutes to put them to sleep, but do not let the meat freeze. This reduces the shock of boiling. Bring a large pot of water to a boil. Arrange an ice bath alongside. Blanch the whole lobster in the boiling water for 2 minutes to kill it. Working quickly, separate the tail and claws from the body. Plunge the tails in ice water. Return the claws to the boiling water for an additional 2 minutes, and then plunge them in ice water. Finish with steps 6–8 above.

HOW TO Shuck Mussels

A quick steam, followed by a plunge into ice water, relaxes the adductor muscles that hold mussels and clams shut. The treatment makes it easier to shuck the mollusks, but don't assume that if the shell doesn't open, the meat inside is bad. The shell could simply be full of mud.

You must pay attention to how each mussel or clam looks and smells as you shuck it. If the meat smells terrible, that's a sure sign that it has spoiled. If it looks wrinkled and dry rather than plump and moist, throw it out.

1 Debeard the mussels. Use the flat of a knife or needle-nose pliers to pull out the entire beard. Just severing the visible portion will leave part of the beard inside.

2 Scrub the debearded mussels with a stiff brush. Smell each mussel, and discard any that do not close or are strong-smelling.

3 Place the mussels in a zip-top bag. Steam for 2 minutes over boiling water in a covered pot, and then plunge the bag into ice water.

4 Place a bowl under a strainer, and empty the contents of the bag into the strainer. Collect the juices—they give a flavorful boost to sauces and broths. Transfer the mussels to a clean bowl.

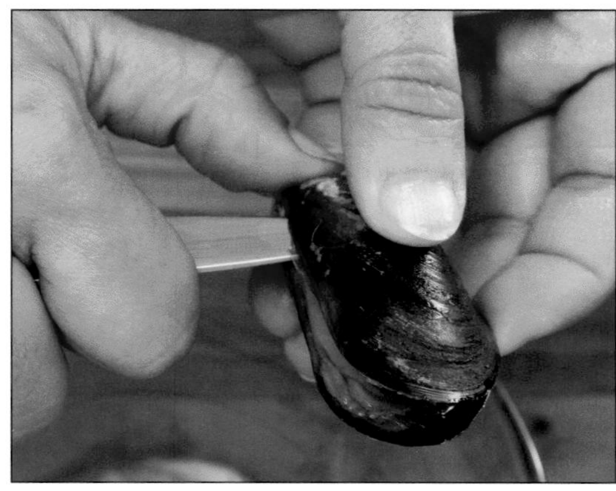

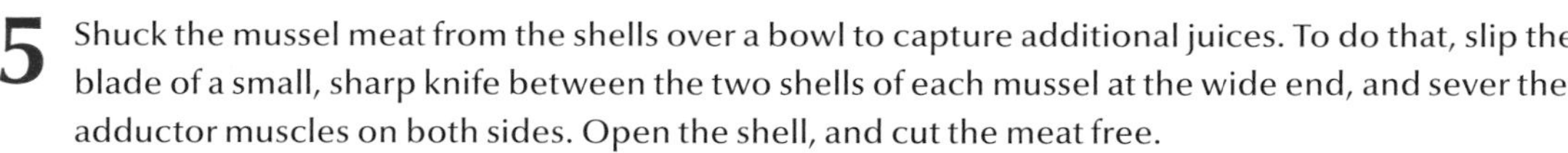

5 Shuck the mussel meat from the shells over a bowl to capture additional juices. To do that, slip the blade of a small, sharp knife between the two shells of each mussel at the wide end, and sever the adductor muscles on both sides. Open the shell, and cut the meat free.

6 Allow any grit to settle to the bottom of the reserved broth, and decant the collected juices through a fine strainer lined with cheesecloth or a coffee filter.

Best Bets for Cooking Shellfish Sous Vide

Blanch and shuck mussels and clams, as described above and on the next page, before cooking them sous vide. To cook these and other shellfish sous vide, seal the shucked meat along with any flavorings, fats, or liquids in a zip-top bag. Next, select a target core temperature from the table below to match the degree of doneness you prefer. Preheat a water bath to 1 °C / 2 °F higher than the target temperature, and then cook for the time indicated or until the core temperature of the food reaches the target. Shellfish is best lightly cooked; for food-safety information, see page xxv. Shellfish can be served immediately, or chilled and served cold. For dishes having multiple kinds of shellfish, cook each separately, and then combine.

		Barely cooked			Tender			Firm				
Ingredient	**Preparation**	(°C)	(°F)	(min)	(°C)	(°F)	(min)	(°C)	(°F)	(min)	Note	See page
clams	blanched and shucked	48	118	10	56	133	8	65	149	5	cook in its own juice	287
lobster claws	shelled	54	129	to core	60	140	to core	65	149	to core	best cooked in butter	288
lobster tails	shelled	49	120	to core	54	129	to core	59	138	to core	best cooked in butter	288
mussels	blanched and shucked	62	144	10	65	149	10	68	154	7	cook in its own juice	290
oysters	shucked	45	113	10	48	118	10	52	126	7	cook in its own juice	
scallops	shelled, with or without roe	42	108	to core	50	122	to core	54	129	4	sear in a very hot pan for 10 seconds on each side	
shrimp, prawns	peeled	48	118	to core	60	140	7	80	176	4	may look translucent	288

(times and temperatures in red are those that we prefer)

HOW TO Shuck Clams

There's nothing worse than a gritty clam. Deep-burrowing clams, such as the softshell (long-neck) varieties can accumulate a lot of grit. Hardshell clams, such as littlenecks, stay closed for most of their lives, so they tend to be cleaner. You can eliminate grit from particularly sandy clams by soaking them in a non-iodized salt brine, and by cutting away the small sack of innards that is attached to the bottom of each clam belly.

1 Soak the clams in cold, salted water in the refrigerator for at least 4 hours to purge the sand. Use 15 g of non-iodized salt for every 1 kg of water. (Iodine is lethal to clams.)

2 Pull the clams from the brine gently; do not disturb the sand on the bottom of the bowl. Scrub each shell with a dish sponge or nailbrush reserved for this purpose.

3 Place the clams in a zip-top bag. Steam them for 2 minutes above boiling water in a covered pot to relax the adductor muscles, and then plunge the bag into ice water.

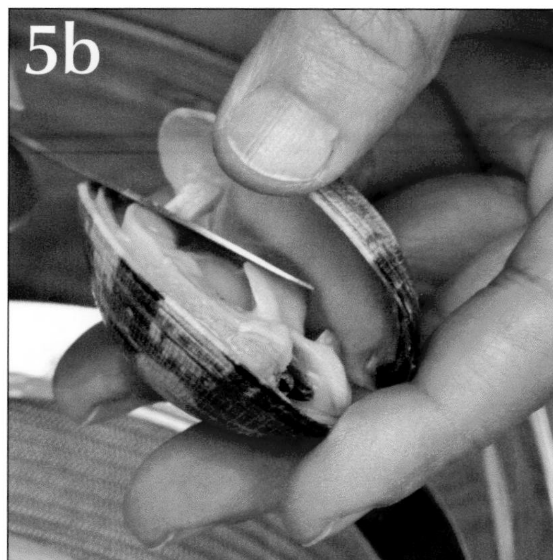

4 Place a bowl under a strainer, and empty the contents of the bag into the strainer. Collect the juices—they give a flavorful boost to sauces and broths. Transfer the clams to a clean bowl.

5 Shuck the clam meat from the shells over the strainer to capture additional juices. To do so, slip the blade of a small, sharp knife in between the two shells of each clam (5a), and sever the adductor muscle near the hinge (5b). Open the shell, and cut the meat free.

6 Allow any grit to settle to the bottom of the reserved broth, and decant the collected juices through a fine strainer lined with cheesecloth.

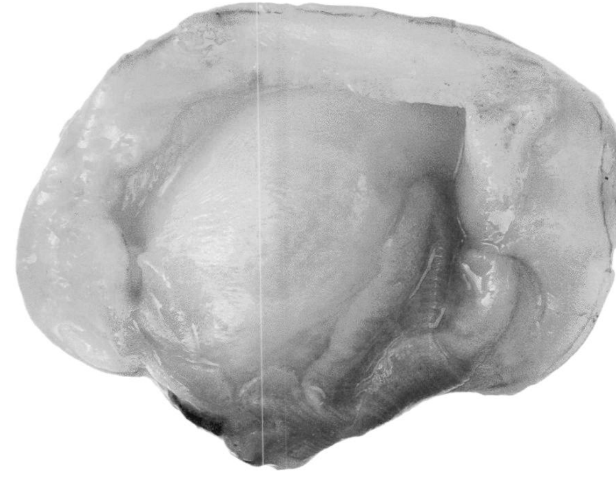

Clams cooked traditionally (right) lose so much of their juice that they often become wrinkled and chewy. Only the sauce that remains is any good. But clams cooked sous vide (left) are plump and juicy every time. In this photo, the innards have been cut away.

LOBSTER ROLL

YIELD:	*four servings (750 g / 3 cups of lobster salad)*
TIME ESTIMATE:	*2 hours overall, including 1½ hours of preparation and 30 minutes unattended*
STORAGE NOTES:	*cooked lobster and dressed lobster salad keep for up to 1 day when refrigerated*
LEVEL OF DIFFICULTY:	*moderate*
SPECIAL REQUIREMENTS:	*sous vide setup, Vacuum-Infused Celery (see page 131), Tomato Leather (optional, see page 129)*

You might think it's hard to improve on an old-fashioned lobster roll—until you taste one made with lobster cooked with precision to attain ideal sweetness and tenderness. Butter infused with lobster shells (see page 122) adds extra flavor and color to the toasted bun. Green apples and herbs freshen the lobster salad, and infused celery and tomato leather add a Modernist twist. Don't bother messing with a boutique hot dog bun in this New England classic—go with the usual supermarket variety. Fancier rolls detract from the lobster.

INGREDIENT	WEIGHT	VOLUME	SCALING	PROCEDURE
Live lobsters	1.5 kg / 3.3 lb	2 large lobsters	300%	① Preheat a water bath to 50 °C / 122 °F, and arrange an ice bath alongside. ② Kill, blanch, and clean the lobsters; see page 284 for instructions.
Neutral-tasting oil	10 g	10 mL / 2 tsp	2%	③ Place the tail meat pieces and half of the oil in a zip-top bag. Place the claw and knuckle meat with the rest of the oil in a separate zip-top bag. Remove as much air as possible from the bags, and seal them. ④ Cook the tail meat sous vide to a core temperature of 49 °C / 120 °F, about 15 minutes, and then plunge the bag in ice water. ⑤ Increase the water bath temperature to 55 °C / 131 °F. Cook the claw and knuckle meat sous vide to a core temperature of 54 °C / 129 °F, about 15 minutes, and then plunge the bag in ice water. ⑥ Cut all of the lobster meat into chunks no larger than 1 cm / ⅜ in.
Cooked lobster meat, from above	500 g / 1.1 lb	1½ cups	100%	⑦ Combine, and mix thoroughly.
Mayonnaise see page 108	200 g	1 cup	40%	
Granny Smith apple, finely diced	40 g	⅜ cup	8%	
Chives, thinly sliced	4 g	2 Tbsp	0.8%	
Tarragon, minced	4 g	1 Tbsp	0.8%	
Black pepper, ground	to taste			
Salt	to taste			⑧ Season the dressed lobster meat.
Hot dog buns (store-bought)		4 buns		⑨ Warm the crustacean butter to room temperature, and spread it generously on the inside of the buns. Place the buns facedown in a dry frying pan, and toast them over medium heat until golden brown, about 2 minutes.
Pressure-Cooked Crustacean Butter or clarified, unsalted butter see pages 122 or 119	30 g	2 Tbsp	6%	
Vacuum-Infused Celery see page 131	20 g	2½ Tbsp	4%	⑩ Divide the dressed lobster meat evenly among the toasted buns. Garnish with celery and tomato leather, and serve immediately.
Tomato Leather, strips (optional) see page 129	16 strips			

Safety tips for lightly cooked food: see page xxv

VARIATIONS

Shrimp or Crab Roll
Skip step 1–6. At step 7, substitute cooked shrimp or store-bought cooked crab for the lobster.

Sous Vide Lobster Tail
To make a main course of lobster, preheat a water bath to 55 °C / 131 °F. Seal the shelled lobster tail meat with 20 g of butter in a zip-top bag, remove the air, and seal. Cook sous vide to a core temperature of 54 °C / 129 °F, about 12 minutes. Serve with melted butter and fresh herbs, or with Caramelized Carrot Puree (see page 178) and a dusting of Chaat Masala (see page 136).

1 Preheat a water bath to 50 °C / 122 °F, and arrange an ice-water bath alongside.

2 Kill, blanch, and clean the lobsters; see the step-by-step procedure on page 284.

3 Place the tail meat pieces and half of the oil in a zip-top bag. Place the claw and knuckle meat with the rest of the oil in a separate zip-top bag. Remove as much air as possible from the bags, and seal them.

4 Cook the tail meat sous vide to a core temperature of 49 °C / 120 °F, about 15 minutes. Immediately plunge the bag in ice water.

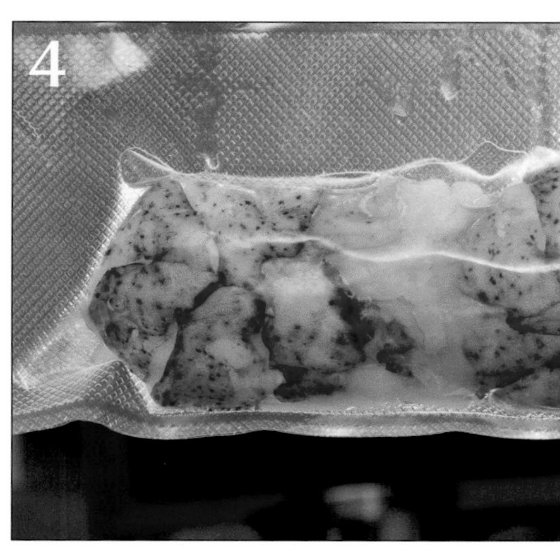

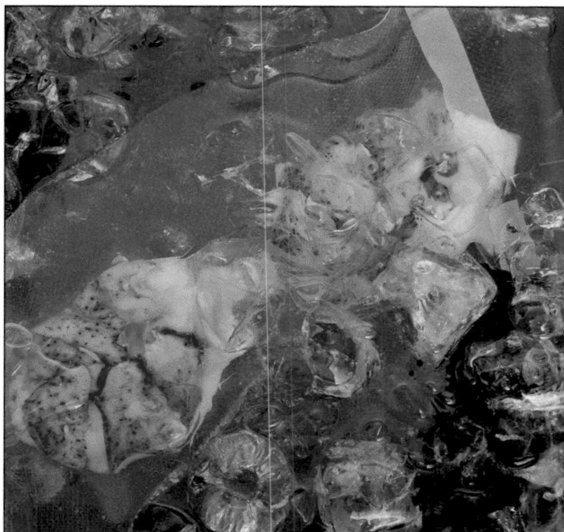

5 Increase the temperature of the water bath to 55 °C / 131 °F. Cook the claw and knuckle meat sous vide to a core temperature of 54 °C / 129 °F, about 15 minutes, and then submerge the bag in ice water.

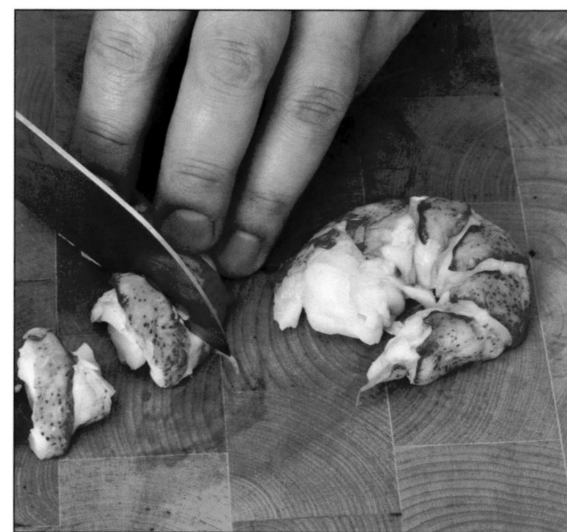

6 Cut all of the lobster meat into chunks no larger than 1 cm / ⅜ in. Discard any bits of shell you come across.

7 Combine the diced lobster, mayonnaise, apple, chives, tarragon, and pepper, and stir until thoroughly mixed.

8 Season the dressed lobster meat with salt to taste.

9 Spread crustacean butter generously on the inside of the buns. Place the buns, buttered-side down, in a frying pan over medium heat, and toast them until golden, about 2 minutes.

10 Divide the dressed lobster meat evenly among the toasted buns. Garnish the sandwiches with infused celery and tomato leather, and serve them immediately.

MUSSELS MARINIÈRE

YIELD:	*four servings (500 g / about 35 mussels)*
TIME ESTIMATE:	*45 minutes overall, including 35 minutes of preparation and 10 minutes unattended*
STORAGE NOTES:	*serve immediately*
LEVEL OF DIFFICULTY:	*moderate*
SPECIAL REQUIREMENTS:	*sous vide setup*

Throughout France, you see people sitting in bistros and brasseries feasting on bowls of sweet, tender mussels that have been cooked in wine, savory brine juices, and garlic. This classic dish is easy to overcook, however; all too often the mussels end up tough, dry, and disappointing. Cooking the mussels sous vide solves that problem.

Forget the old rule that any mussel that doesn't open when cooked is bad. By the time mussels pop all the way open, many of them are probably overcooked. A bad mussel either smells very strongly or looks dry and shriveled, so inspect them as you shuck them before cooking.

INGREDIENT	WEIGHT	VOLUME	SCALING	PROCEDURE
Live mussels Dry white wine Shallots, thinly sliced	500 g / 1.1 lb 150 g 100 g	about 35 mussels 150 mL / ⅝ cup 1 cup	100% 30% 20%	① Preheat a water bath to **62 °C / 144 °F**. Bring a pot of water to a boil, and set a large steamer rack above the water. Arrange an ice bath alongside. ② Debeard and scrub the mussels (see steps 1–2 on page 286). ③ Place the mussels, shallots, and wine in a heat-safe plastic bag. ④ Steam for 2 minutes, plunge the mussels into the ice bath, and then shuck them. Collect and strain the juices (see steps 3–6 on page 286). ⑤ Seal the strained juices with the mussel meats in a zip-top bag (see page 58), and cook them sous vide for 10 minutes. ⑥ Strain the mussels, and measure 70 g / 70 mL / ⅓ cup of the mussel juices for use in step 10.
Extra-virgin olive oil Shallots, minced Garlic, minced	10 g 10 g 8 g	10 mL / 2 tsp 1 Tbsp 2½ tsp	2% 2% 1.6%	⑦ Sauté over medium heat until the shallots and garlic are lightly browned and aromatic, about 5 minutes.
Chili flakes	0.5 g	¼ tsp	0.1%	⑧ Add to the pan, and cook for a few seconds.
Dry white wine	45 g	45 mL / 3 Tbsp	9%	⑨ Add, and reduce until syrupy, about 4 minutes.
Mussel juice, from above	70 g	70 mL / ⅓ cup	14%	⑩ Add, bring to a simmer, and then remove the pan from the heat.
Italian parsley, thinly sliced Tarragon, thinly sliced Thyme leaves	2 g 1 g 1 g	1 Tbsp 1 tsp 1 tsp	0.4% 0.2% 0.2%	⑪ Stir into the sauce, add the mussel meats, stir gently to coat, and then remove the mussel meats from the pan so as not to overcook them.
Salt Lemon juice	to taste to taste			⑫ Season, and serve immediately.

Safety tips for lightly cooked food: see page xxv

Mussel juices

The natural juices that come out of mussels when they open are very flavorful. Chefs use mussel juice to add depth to butter sauces for fish and soups. Be sure to save any extra juices—or at least have some good bread and olive oil handy so that you don't waste any of this precious liquid.

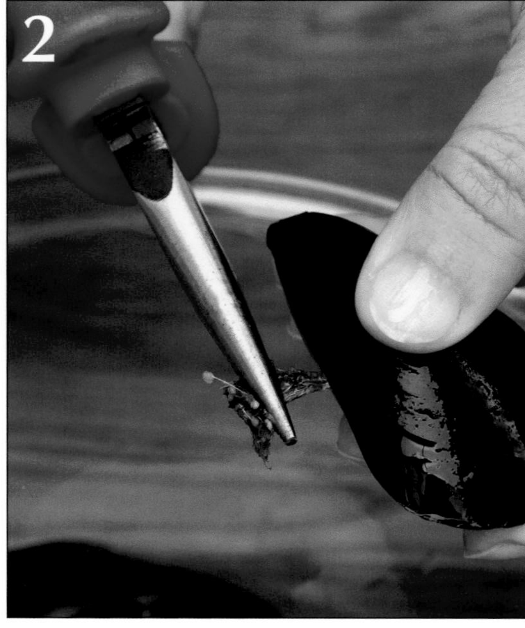

1 Preheat a water bath to **62 °C / 144 °F**. Bring a pot of water to a boil. Set a large steamer rack above the water, and arrange an ice bath alongside the pot.

2 Debeard and scrub the mussels by following steps 1–2 on page 286.

3 Place the mussels with the shallots and wine in a heat-safe plastic bag such as a roasting, freezer, or sous vide bag. The purpose of the bag is to capture the juice; it doesn't need to be sealed.

4 Steam the mussels for 2 minutes, plunge them immediately into the ice water, and then shuck them. Collect and strain the shucking juices (see steps 3–6 on page 286). The mussels should not be cooked through; this step simply makes them easier to shuck.

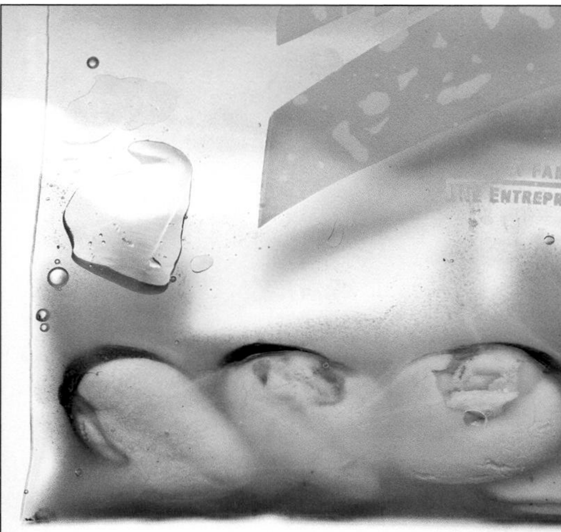

5 Place the strained juices and mussel meats in a zip-top bag. Remove as much air as possible (see page 58), and seal the bag. Cook the mussel meats sous vide for 10 minutes.

6 Strain the mussels, and measure 70 g / 70 mL / ⅓ cup of the juices for use in step 10.

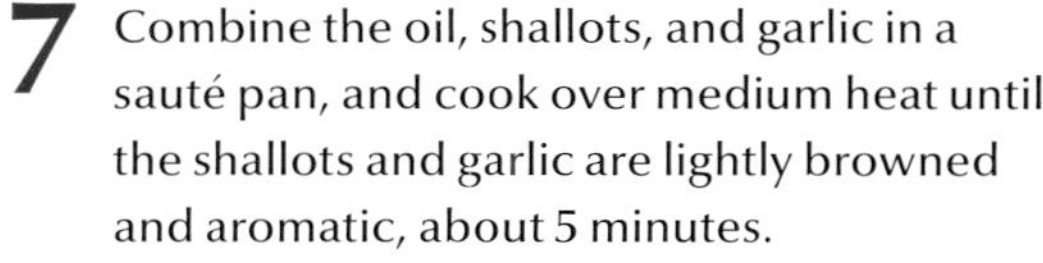

7 Combine the oil, shallots, and garlic in a sauté pan, and cook over medium heat until the shallots and garlic are lightly browned and aromatic, about 5 minutes.

8 Add the chili flakes, and cook for a few seconds.

9 Add the white wine, and continue cooking until the mixture turns syrupy, about 4 minutes.

10 Add the reserved mussel juice. Return the mixture to a simmer, and then remove the pan from the heat.

11 Stir in the Italian parsley, tarragon, and thyme, add the mussel meats, stir gently to coat, and then remove them from the pan to avoid overcooking them.

12 Season the dish with salt and lemon juice, and serve it immediately. Don't let the mussels sit in the hot juices for more than a few seconds, or else they will get too firm.

CLAMS IN CHOWDER SAUCE

YIELD:	*four servings (360 g / 30–40 clams)*
TIME ESTIMATE:	*1 hour overall, including 45 minutes of preparation and 15 minutes unattended*
STORAGE NOTES:	*keeps for 1 day when refrigerated*
LEVEL OF DIFFICULTY:	*moderate*
SPECIAL REQUIREMENTS:	*pressure cooker, aerolatte, whey protein isolate (optional)*

In this lighter take on the classic soup, clams are dressed in a warm, foamy sauce. For a more substantial dish that is closer to a typical chowder, add extra chowder broth, and stir in some caramelized onions (see page 127) and some microwave-steamed fingerling potatoes cut into bite-size pieces (see variation on page 126).

Whey protein isolate, which we add to make the broth foamy, is a protein derived from milk. You can find it at health-food stores, but do not confuse it with sweet or flavored whey powders sold for protein shake mixes. If you prefer more fully cooked clam meats, see the table on page 286 for sous vide time-and-temperature combinations.

INGREDIENT	WEIGHT	VOLUME	SCALING	PROCEDURE
Littleneck clams	750 g / 1.7 lb	30–40 clams	100%	① Soak and scrub the clams as shown in steps 1–2 on page 287.
Dry white wine	150 g	150 mL / ⅝ cup	20%	② Bring a pot of water to a boil, and set a large steamer rack above the water. Arrange an ice bath alongside.
Shallots, thinly sliced	100 g	1 cup	13%	③ Place the clams, wine, and shallots in a heat-safe plastic bag.
				④ Steam for 2 minutes, plunge the bag into the ice bath, and then shuck the clams. Collect and strain the juices (see steps 3–6 on page 287).
				⑤ Measure 240 g / 245 mL / 1 cup of clam juice for use in step 9.
				⑥ Rinse the clam meats in cold water.
Bacon, diced	36 g	¼ cup	4.8%	⑦ Sweat in the base of a pressure cooker over medium heat until lightly rendered but not brown, about 2 minutes.
Yellow onion, diced	65 g	½ cup	9%	⑧ Add to the bacon, and sweat until translucent, about 2 minutes.
Celery, diced	65 g	½ cup	9%	⑨ Add the reserved clam juice, and pressure-cook at a gauge pressure of 1 bar / 15 psi for 15 minutes. Start timing when full pressure is reached.
				⑩ Let the cooker cool, or run tepid water over the rim, to depressurize it.
				⑪ Strain, and measure 200 g / 200 mL / ⅞ cup of the clam chowder broth for use in the next step.
Heavy cream	300 g	330 mL / 1⅜ cups	40%	⑫ Combine in a saucepan with the reserved clam chowder broth, and simmer over low heat until reduced by about one third.
Whey protein isolate (optional)	6 g	1½ Tbsp	0.8%	⑬ Whisk into the simmering broth.
				⑭ Blend the broth until smooth and foamy by using an immersion blender or aerolatte.
Worcestershire sauce	0.5 g	1 drop	0.07%	⑮ Season the sauce.
Cayenne pepper	0.1 g	pinch	0.01%	⑯ Stir the clam meats into the sauce, and remove it from the heat. Allow to sit 20 seconds to just warm the clams through, and serve immediately.
Salt	to taste			

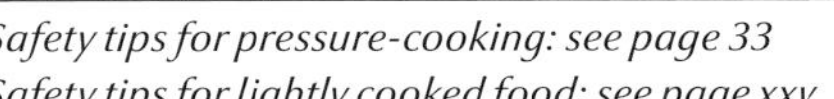
Safety tips for pressure-cooking: see page 33
Safety tips for lightly cooked food: see page xxv

TO MAKE AHEAD

After rinsing the clam meats in step 6, seal them in a zip-top bag with the remaining juices, and refrigerate for no more than 24 hours. When ready to make the chowder, continue with step 7. In step 16, let the clams sit for 1 minute in the hot sauce to warm through.

VARIATIONS

Oyster Stew

Substitute diced leeks for the bacon, and substitute oyster meats and juice for the clams.

Pistachio Clam Chowder

At step 13, stir in 36 g / 3 Tbsp of Pistachio Pesto (see page 102).

South of France Chowder

Add 39 g / 3 Tbsp of Rouille (see variation on page 108) at the last second before serving.

SOUS VIDE BRAISED SNAILS

YIELD:	*four servings (200 g / 24 snails)*
TIME ESTIMATE:	*5¼ hours overall, including 15 minutes of preparation and 5 hours unattended*
STORAGE NOTES:	*keeps for up to 5 days when refrigerated or up to 3 months when frozen*
LEVEL OF DIFFICULTY:	*easy*
SPECIAL REQUIREMENTS:	*sous vide setup, canned French Helix snails*
GOES WELL WITH:	*Pressure-Cooked Paella del Bosco (see page 326)*

Although canned snails are already cooked, the sous vide treatment described here infuses them with flavor and makes them wonderfully tender. Use braised snails in paella, or serve them solo as classic escargot by stirring them into melted butter with minced garlic and parsley, or into Montpellier Butter (see page 120).

INGREDIENT	WEIGHT	VOLUME	SCALING	PROCEDURE
Canned French Helix snails	200 g	24 large snails	100%	① Preheat a water bath to 68 °C / 154 °F. ② Clean the snails. Drain the liquid, and peel away and discard the stomach and intestines of the snails.
White chicken stock, frozen, or ice see page 84	300 g	300 mL / 1¼ cups	150%	③ Combine with the cleaned snails in a bag, and vacuum seal. ④ Cook sous vide for 5 hours. ⑤ Drain, reserving the juices. ⑥ Pick out the snail meat, and discard the vegetables and aromatics. ⑦ Serve warm, or store, refrigerated, in the reserved juices.
Carrots, thinly sliced	100 g	1 cup	50%	
Sweet onion, thinly sliced	90 g	⅞ cup	45%	
Salt	7.5 g	2 tsp	3.8%	
Thyme	0.7 g	1 large sprig	0.4%	
Fresh bay leaf	0.2 g	1 leaf	0.1%	

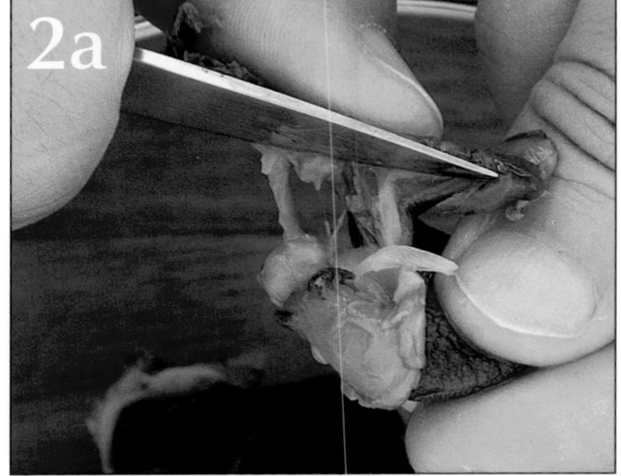

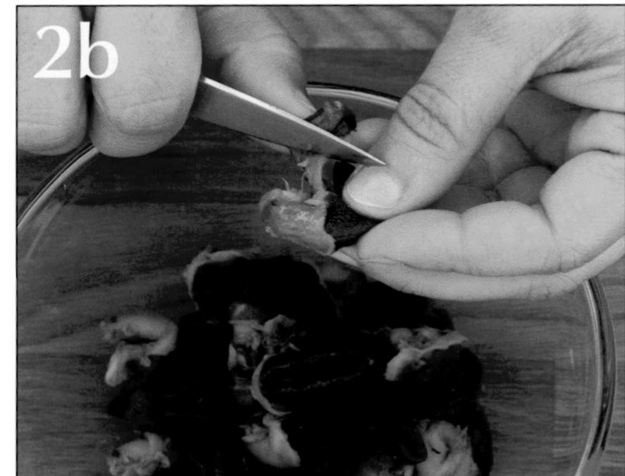

The stomach and intestines of the snails can be very gritty. Use the flat of a knife to pull them off.

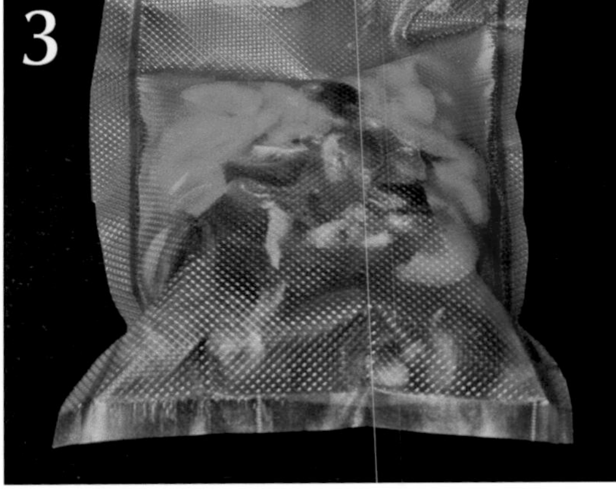

It doesn't take much to start a snail farm, and anthropologists think that snails were one of the first mollusks to have been farmed by humans. Only oysters have been cultivated longer.

Snails braised sous vide (left) and then stirred with melted Montpellier butter and minced Italian parsley (right) make a terrific snack or appetizer when spooned onto a toasted baguette.

PIZZA

The first pizza may have been born in Italy, but its descendants now cover the world and have evolved into diverse forms. New Yorkers love their large, thin-crust pizzas, served by the slice. In Chicago, the deep-dish pies are at least an inch thick. Traditionalists believe pizza crust must be slightly scorched on the bottom, preferably in a wood-fired oven. We say there's no point in arguing: they're all really good! The pizza recipes here are as close to the crispy yet tender Neapolitan style as a home oven can deliver. But the doughs work for other styles of pizza as well.

We've included our six favorite dough recipes: a classic traditional dough; a no-knead dough that creates a fluffy crust with little effort; two chewy, bread-like doughs that gets their complex flavors from the fermentation of a starter; and two nontraditional doughs—one made with quinoa, and the other made with buckwheat flour. Our simple tomato-and-garlic sauce yields enough to freeze for later—or turn some into a marinara sauce that goes perfectly with pasta or polenta. We also show you how to build a pizza, including how to avoid a soggy crust.

It is in the baking of the pizza, however, that we got a little obsessed. We figured there must be a way to approximate the performance of a wood-fired brick oven by inserting a metal plate of some kind into an ordinary home oven. After dozens of trials, we finally found a winning combination of material and temperature: a steel plate 12 mm / ½ in thick, preheated at 260 °C / 500 °F for an hour. Now you can get a light, crispy, blistered crust, cooked in mere minutes, without a trip to the pizzeria.

THE SCIENCE OF PERFECTLY CHEWY PIZZA CRUST

Gluten—the protein complex in wheat that becomes tangled into a sticky, stretchy dough when you knead flour with water—is crucial to a great crust. Bread flours need a large fraction of high-quality gluten to act as a binder. The more gluten in the flour, the more elastic a dough it will form, and the firmer the baked crust will be. Kneading the dough liberates starches that are attached to the proteins and allows the gluten to form networks that make the dough strong and stretchy. When you let the dough rest, the networks relax.

All yeast-leavened doughs—but pizza dough in particular—benefit from higher levels of gluten. So we tried adding more gluten, in its purified form. We found that the addition of as little as 0.5% vital wheat gluten produces a dough that requires less kneading and yields just the right amount of chewiness when baked.

HIGHLIGHTS

Stretching the dough into a smooth ball develops a network of gluten that traps gasses and bubbles inside the dough. These are essential to an ideal crust.

see page 296

Fried pizza is a new concept for most of us. It's fast and easy to make, and the crust, surprisingly, is not greasy.

see page 305

Root vegetables and ricotta; capicola and arugula: we provide **nine ideas for topping** our basic Pizza Margherita that will, we hope, inspire your own.

see page 306

Use a steel plate in your home oven to make it perform like a brick oven. We also give times and temperatures for baking on a pizza stone or cast-iron griddle.

see page 301

FURTHER READING IN *MODERNIST CUISINE*

Why a pizza can go from brown to burned in just a minute or two: see pages 1·285 and 2·25

How oven baking is mostly about drying the food: see pages 2·102–106

NEAPOLITAN PIZZA DOUGH

YIELD:	*800 g (enough for four 30–35 cm / 12–14 in pizzas)*
TIME ESTIMATE:	*1½ hours overall, including 30 minutes of preparation and 1 hour unattended*
STORAGE NOTES:	*keeps for 3 days when refrigerated in plastic wrap or up to 3 months when frozen*
LEVEL OF DIFFICULTY:	*moderate*
SPECIAL REQUIREMENTS:	*stand mixer with dough hook, Antico Caputo 00 wheat flour, vital wheat gluten*

This is a classic Neapolitan pizza dough. It's best when rolled thin and cooked quickly at a very high temperature. Antico Caputo 00 is an extremely fine wheat flour used by most pizzerias in Naples to create an elastic dough; buy it online or at specialty food markets. You can substitute all-purpose flour, but you may need to add up to 10% more water.

INGREDIENT	WEIGHT	VOLUME	SCALING	PROCEDURE
00 wheat flour (Antico Caputo brand)	500 g	3¾ cups	100%	① Mix in the bowl of a stand mixer with a dough hook until fully incorporated.
Water	310 g	310 mL / 1⅓ cups	62%	② Mix on medium speed for 5 minutes.
Honey or agave syrup	10 g	2 tsp	2%	③ Let the dough rest in the bowl for 10 minutes at room temperature, and then mix again for 5 minutes on medium speed.
Salt	10 g	2½ tsp	2%	
Vital wheat gluten (Bob's Red Mill brand)	2.5 g	1½ tsp	0.5%	④ Transfer the dough to a well-floured surface, and cut it into four 200 g chunks. Stretch and roll it into smooth, even balls.
Active dry yeast	2.5 g	¾ tsp	0.5%	
Neutral frying oil see page xxii	as needed			⑤ Coat the balls lightly with oil, cover them with plastic wrap, and let them rest at room temperature for 1 hour before using.

Pizza doughs (left to right): No-Knead (see page 300), Quinoa (see variation below), Rustic (see page 298), and Whole Wheat (see variation on page 298)

VARIATIONS

Quinoa Pizza Dough

Quinoa flour, available at health-food stores and gourmet supermarkets, makes a nutritious pizza dough that has a dense, chewy texture and a nutty taste. Quinoa dough is less stretchy than dough made only from wheat flour, so use care when forming it.

Substitute 250 g / 1⅞ cups of all-purpose flour and 250 g / 1⅜ cups of quinoa flour for the 00 wheat flour. Increase the amount of vital wheat gluten to 5 g / 2½ tsp.

Buckwheat Pizza Dough

Buckwheat is the grain used to make Japanese soba. It has a hearty flavor and a coarse mouthfeel.

Substitute fine, sifted buckwheat flour for 150 g / 1⅓ cups of Antico Caputo 00 wheat flour, and increase the amount of gluten to 5 g / 2½ tsp.

Breadsticks

Divide the rested dough into 55 g pieces, and shape the pieces into batons. Arrange the batons on a lightly greased baking sheet. Brush them lightly with beaten egg, and sprinkle about 1 g / ½ tsp of grated Parmesan cheese over each. Bake at 220 °C / 430 °F until golden brown, 12–15 minutes.

1

2

1 Mix the flour, water, honey, salt, gluten, and yeast in the bowl of a stand mixer with a dough hook until fully incorporated.

2 Mix on medium speed for 5 minutes.

3 Let the dough rest in the bowl for 10 minutes at room temperature, and then mix again for another 5 minutes on medium speed. Allowing the gluten to relax between kneadings creates an especially smooth, stretchy dough.

TROUBLESHOOTING TIP:
The finished dough should pull away from the sides (as shown above), not the bottom, of the mixing bowl. If it does not pull away from the sides, sprinkle in a teaspoon of flour, and let it fully mix, repeating until the sides of the bowl are clean.

4a

4b

4c

4 Transfer the dough to a well-floured surface, and cut it into four chunks of 200 g each. Stretch and roll the dough into smooth, even balls. Stretching the surface layer develops a network of gluten that traps air inside the ball, resulting in a lighter, more blistered crust.

5 Coat the balls lightly with oil, cover them with plastic wrap, and allow them to rise at room temperature for 1 hour before using. For a more complex flavor, refrigerate the dough balls overnight, and then let them rest at room temperature for 1 hour before using.

OTHER USES FOR DOUGH

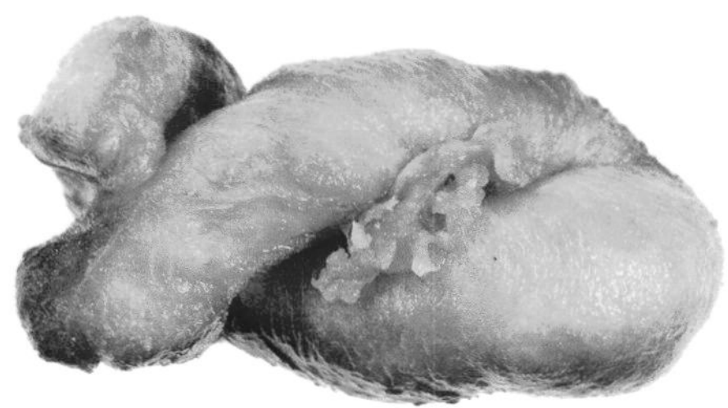

Garlic Knots
Shape 15 g (walnut-size) pieces of dough into ropes, and tie them loosely into knots. Deep-fry the knots in 175 °C / 350 °F neutral frying oil until golden brown, about 90 seconds, and drain. Alternatively, bake at 220 °C / 430 °F until golden brown, 3–4 minutes. Brush the cooked knots with Garlic Oil (see variation on page 118), sprinkle with salt, and serve hot.

"Everything" Pretzels
Divide the dough into 45 g portions, roll into long ropes, and shape into pretzels. Place the pretzels on a lightly greased baking sheet. Brush them lightly with beaten egg, and sprinkle them with a mixture of 20 g / 3 Tbsp of onion flakes, 10 g / 1¼ tsp of black sesame seeds, 7 g / 2 tsp of salt, 5 g / 2 tsp of poppy seeds, and 5 g / 1 Tbsp of garlic powder. Bake at 220 °C / 425 °F until golden brown, about 12 minutes.

Cinnamon-Sugar Doughnut Holes
Shape 10 g (grape-size) pieces of dough into balls. Deep-fry the balls in 175 °C / 350 °F neutral frying oil until golden brown, about 90 seconds. Drain, and toss in cinnamon sugar made by mixing 100 g / ½ cup of sugar with 2 g / 1 tsp of ground cinnamon. Serve hot.

RUSTIC PIZZA DOUGH

YIELD:	*1 kg (enough for five 30–35 cm / 12–14 in pizzas)*
TIME ESTIMATE:	*24½ hours overall, including 30 minutes of preparation and 24 hours unattended*
STORAGE NOTES:	*keeps for 3 days when refrigerated or up to 3 months when frozen*
LEVEL OF DIFFICULTY:	*advanced (handling)*
SPECIAL REQUIREMENTS:	*stand mixer with dough hook or dough scraper; Poolish (see the next page); vital wheat gluten*

The fermentation of the poolish, described on the next page, adds a complex flavor to this dough and the enzymatic activity enhances the browning of the crust by creating simple sugars. This country-style dough is softer and stickier than most pizza and bread doughs, so it's best to use a stand mixer. If you must knead it by hand, lightly flour your hands while handling it rather than stirring in more flour. Shape the pizzas gently so as not to tear them.

INGREDIENT	WEIGHT	VOLUME	SCALING	PROCEDURE
All-purpose flour	500 g	3⅓ cups	100%	① Mix in the bowl of a stand mixer with a dough hook until fully incorporated. For instructions on hand-kneading, see below.
Poolish see the next page	312 g	1½ cups	62%	② Continue mixing on medium speed for another 5 minutes. The dough will stick to the bowl; do not add extra flour.
Water	200 g	200 mL / ⅞ cup	40%	③ Let the dough rest in the bowl for 10 minutes at room temperature, and then mix again for 5 minutes on medium speed. If the dough does not pull away from the sides of the bowl, sprinkle in 1 tsp of flour, and resume mixing. Repeat as needed until the sides of the bowl are clean.
Honey or agave syrup	48 g	2½ Tbsp	10%	④ Transfer the dough to a well-floured surface, and cut it into five chunks of 200 g each.
Salt	15 g	5 tsp	3%	⑤ Stretch and roll the chunks into smooth, round balls.
Vital wheat gluten (Bob's Red Mill brand)	10 g	2 Tbsp	2%	
Active dry yeast	1 g	¼ tsp	0.2%	
Neutral frying oil see page xxii	as needed			⑥ Lightly coat the balls with oil, cover them with plastic wrap, and refrigerate them for 24 hours so that the flavor continues to develop.
				⑦ To make a pizza crust, remove the dough from the refrigerator, and let it rest at room temperature for 1 hour before forming the crust.

VARIATION: **Whole Wheat Pizza Dough**
Substitute whole wheat flour for all-purpose flour to make a dense, chewy, and wholesome variation.

Rustic Pizza Dough can be made with many different flours. Other flours may yield a slightly more complex flavor and a more elastic texture.

HOW TO Knead Dough by Hand

If you don't own a stand mixer, you can still make pizza! Here are simple instructions for properly kneading dough by hand, which can be used when making any of our recipes for pizza dough.

1 Mix the ingredients in a bowl until fully incorporated. Use a wooden spoon.

If you find the dough is sticking to your hands and becomes unworkable, fold the dough with one hand, and use a dough scraper in the other.

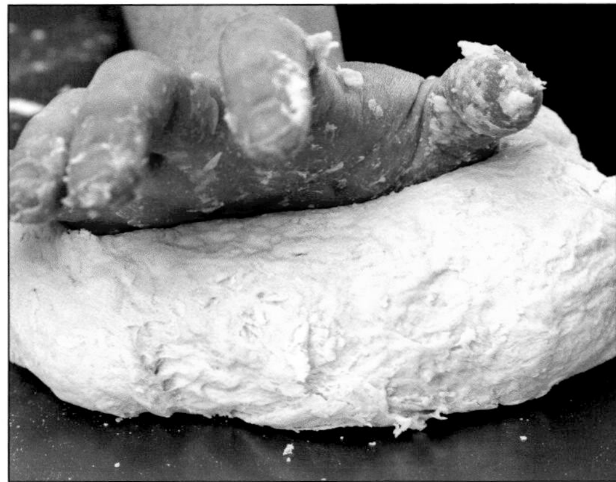

2 Knead the dough by hand for 7–8 minutes. Work on a cool steel or marble surface, if possible. The dough will stick to your hands, but try not to add extra flour. To release dough from your hands when you have finished kneading, rub your hands with flour.

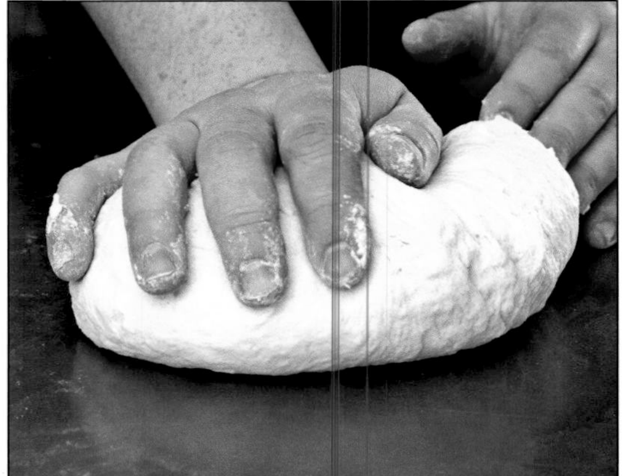

3 Let the dough rest for 10 minutes, and knead it again for 7–8 minutes. It should feel springy and smooth. If it is still sticky, sprinkle in a teaspoon of flour, and incorporate fully. Continue with steps 4–7.

POOLISH

YIELD:	*1.4 kg*
TIME ESTIMATE:	*24 hours overall, including 5 minutes of preparation and 24 hours unattended*
STORAGE NOTES:	*keeps indefinitely with regular care and feeding*
LEVEL OF DIFFICULTY:	*easy*

Poolish is not a misspelling of polish or Polish. It is the French term for "prefermented dough sponge." Similar in concept to a sourdough starter, poolish is a living organism, sometimes known as a "mother dough" or "pre-ferment." Temperature and humidity determine the rate at which poolish develops its flavor and aroma. This recipe will make a little more than you need for our Rustic Pizza Dough recipe on the previous page, but with regular care and feeding, the poolish can be kept alive for years. You can use it to make breads and pastries as well as pizza crusts. Don't omit the whole wheat flour; its nutrients help the poolish thrive.

INGREDIENT	WEIGHT	VOLUME	SCALING
Water	875 g	875 mL / 3¾ cups	350%
Bread flour	250 g	1¾ cups	100%
Whole wheat flour	250 g	1¾ cups	100%
Active dry yeast	1 g	¼ tsp	0.4%

PROCEDURE

① Mix all thoroughly.

② Place in a deep container, filling to no more than one-quarter full to allow for rising, and cover it.

③ Store the covered container in a dark place at 15–21 °C / 60–70 °F.

④ Check the next day for flavor and aroma. It should be bubbly and smell sweet and yeasty, with light sour notes. Stir before using.

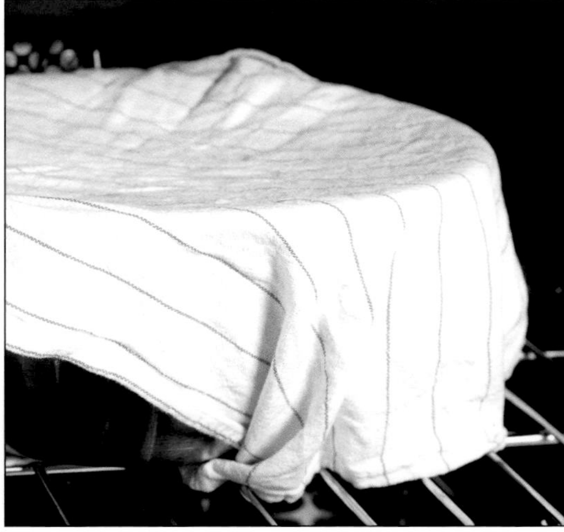

1 Mix the flours, water, and yeast thoroughly.

2 Place in a container large enough to allow the mixture to expand to four or five times its starting size as it rises, and cover it.

3 Store the container in a dark area, such as a kitchen cabinet, where the temperature will remain within the range 15–21 °C / 60–70 °F. Cooler temperatures slow fermentation; warmer temperatures can accelerate fermentation so much that the yeast dies.

4 Check the appearance, flavor, and aroma of the poolish after 24 hours. It should look bubbly, taste slightly sour, and smell sweet and yeasty, slightly like alcohol. Stir before using, and see the note below for instructions on how to care for the poolish.

Care and feeding of poolish

To keep the poolish alive, you must feed it every other day for the first two weeks after you build it. Do not refrigerate it during this period. To feed the poolish, remove half of it, weigh that portion, and then either discard it or use it for baking. Next, whisk equal weights of water and flour into the poolish remaining in the container; the total weight of the water and flour should equal the weight of the poolish you removed. Cover it until the next feeding.

After two weeks, refrigerate the poolish, which will cause the yeast to go dormant. Now you need to feed it only once a week. After each feeding, let the poolish sit out for a few hours before covering it and returning it to the refrigerator.

Starters

Sourdough starters are a form of poolish that are inoculated with both yeast and bacteria (usually lactobacilli) that produce lactic acid and, with it, the characteristic sour taste of sourdough. Sourdough poolish must be started from a culture. You can order many kinds of starter cultures from Sourdough International (www.sourdo.com).

NO-KNEAD PIZZA DOUGH

YIELD:	*850 g (enough for four 30–35 cm / 12–14 in pizzas)*
TIME ESTIMATE:	*17½ hours overall, including 30 minutes of preparation and 17 hours unattended*
STORAGE NOTES:	*keeps for 3 days when refrigerated or up to 3 months when frozen*
LEVEL OF DIFFICULTY:	*moderate*
SPECIAL REQUIREMENTS:	*vital wheat gluten*

This pizza crust is light and fluffy, flavorful, and easy to make. The dough is based on Jim Lahey's recipe for No-Knead Country Bread. Folding the dough may at first seem like a variation on kneading, but it is much gentler. Never press or work the dough, or you will squeeze out the bubbles; just fold, let rest, and repeat.

INGREDIENT	WEIGHT	VOLUME	SCALING	PROCEDURE
All-purpose flour	500 g	3⅓ cups	100%	① Mix in a large bowl.
Salt	10 g	2½ tsp	2%	
Vital wheat gluten (Bob's Red Mill brand)	5 g	1 Tbsp	1%	
Active dry yeast	1.5 g	½ tsp	0.3%	
Water	375 g	375 mL / 1⅝ cups	75%	② Add to the dry ingredients, and stir to combine. ③ Cover the bowl with a clean, dry dish towel, and let the dough rest in a warm place (**21–27** °C / **70–80** °F) for 16–48 hours. ④ Scrape the dough onto a well-floured work surface. ⑤ Fold the dough in half gently several times, without pressing or squeezing, and continue folding until it becomes so springy and elastic that it no longer folds easily. Let the dough rest for 1 minute. Repeat for a total of eight folds in 5 minutes. ⑥ Cut the dough into four chunks of 200 g each. Stretch and roll each piece into a smooth, round ball.
Neutral-tasting oil	as needed			⑦ Coat the balls lightly with oil, cover them with plastic wrap, and let them rest at room temperature for 1 hour before using.

Stir the water and other dough ingredients together just until they are combined and thoroughly moistened. The mixture does not need to be smooth.

As you fold the dough, be gentle: do not squeeze or knead it. At first, you may be able to fold it in half three or four times before it becomes too springy to fold easily. Pause for 1 minute to let the dough rest when that happens, and then begin folding again. Because the dough becomes progressively more resistant to handling, after the first resting period it will require further rest after only one or two folds. Stop once you have completed eight folds in 5 minutes. The goal is to maintain the natural bubbles that formed during the fermentation process while you develop new air bubbles and gluten threads in the dough.

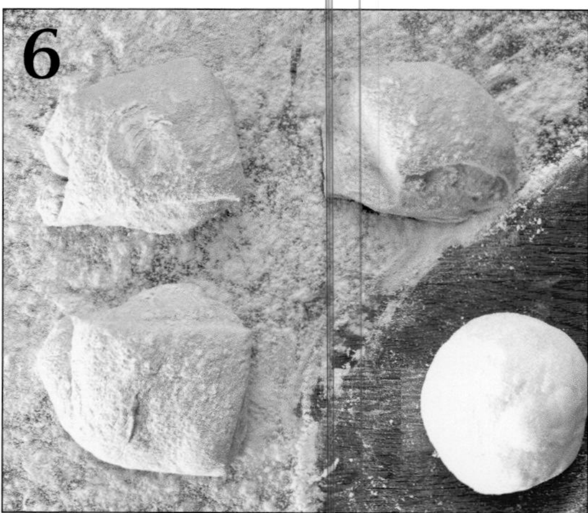

As you roll the chunks of dough into balls, the surface layer stretches, and a network of gluten traps air inside the ball. The result after baking is a lighter and nicely blistered crust.

Developing flavors

If you allow the dough to ferment for 48 hours or longer, more complex yeast and sourdough flavors will develop, similar to what you would get with a poolish (see previous page).

PIZZA STONES, PLATES, AND PANS

Some like it hot, but pizzas like it *really* hot. A traditional, wood-burning pizza oven can easily reach and hold a uniform temperature of 430–540 °C / 800–1,000 °F—the ideal range for making a crisp, blistered pizza. Higher temperatures risk burning the pizza before it is cooked all the way through. Too cool an oven can yield a flaccid, chewy crust.

A cold pizza immediately absorbs heat from the oven, so it's crucial to preheat the oven fully. It also helps to add mass to the oven that serves as a reservoir of heat and prevents the temperature from dipping too much. We have experimented in our research kitchen with a variety of metal plates, pizza stones, and pans to find the best options, which are shown below. Avoid aluminum plates, and steel plates thicker than about 2.5 cm / 1 in, as they tend to burn the bottom of the pizza.

Steel plate

Iron griddle

Steel plate, 6–12 mm / ¼–½ in thick

Preheating time: at least 1 hour
Pros: high thermal capacity cooks the crust evenly and produces lots of charred blisters
Cons: expensive; heavy; may require custom fabrication

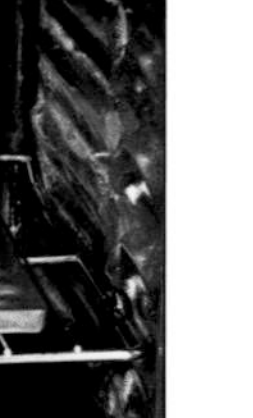

Pizza stone

Preheating time: at least 30 minutes
Pros: even heat distribution, develops a good crust color, with some blistering
Cons: lower thermal capacity and less temperature stability

Cast-iron griddle or pan

Preheating time: at least 30 minutes; coat lightly with oil before preheating
Pros: inexpensive; widely available; high thermal capacity
Cons: can dry pizzas slightly and produces few blisters; oil slightly alters the flavor of the crust

Stone

Iron frying pan

HOW WE FIGURED OUT

The Best Setup for Baking Pizza in a Home Oven

In dozens of experiments involving more than 100 pizzas, we explored a wide range of materials and methods for cooking a pizza at home. Computerized temperature-logging gear allowed us to track eight separate temperatures, from the oven wall to the baking surface to the dough, as the cooking progressed.

Our main goal was to find the cooking surface that best transfers heat to the raw pizza dough. Every surface will cool to some degree when the pizza goes in, but the dip in temperature should be as shallow and brief as possible.

As we expected, thick metal plates hold their preheated temperature better than thin ones, but they also take longer to preheat and to recover from a drop in temperature. Our bottom-line conclusion: a dark (not shiny) steel plate 12 mm / ½ in thick is the best option. A steel plate half that thick also works quite well.

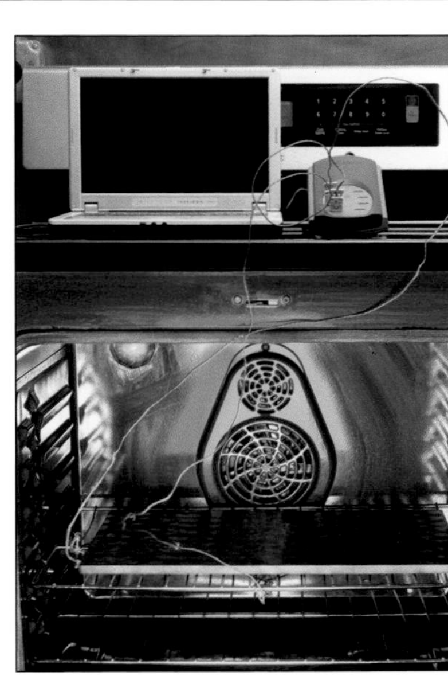

HOW TO Make a Pizza

You can build a great pizza if you master three crucial elements: the dough, the toppings, and the baking. Stretching out pizza dough is a delicate art that rewards patience and practice. Topping a pizza is all about balance: finding that ideal ratio of dough to toppings that allows the pizza to cook through quickly and evenly, producing a combination of crisp and chewy textures. Baking a pizza well requires the right tools—a very hot and stable oven and baking surface, a pizza peel of the right size—and a keen sense of timing.

1 Remove the pizza dough from the refrigerator, cover it, and let it warm for an hour to room temperature. If the dough was frozen, first defrost it in the refrigerator overnight. Covering the dough keeps the surface from drying out and forming a crust.

2 While the dough is warming, prepare a baking surface (see the previous page for options). Set the oven temperature as high as it will go; 260 °C / 500 °F is a minimum.

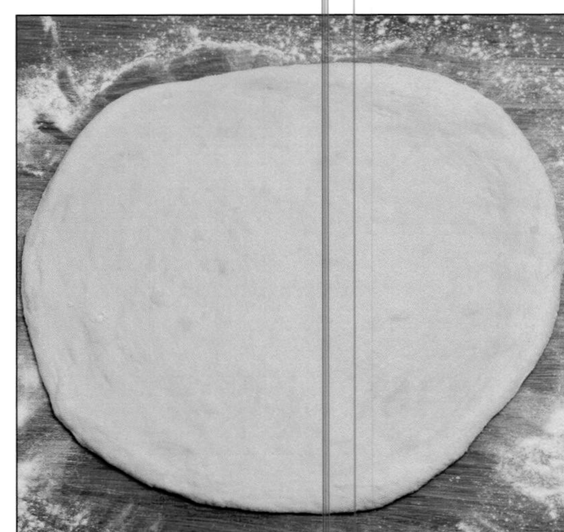

3 Stretch and flatten the dough on a floured work surface by using your fingers to press the middle of the dough flat, and then work the dough outward. Leave a narrow ridge at the perimeter.

4 Dust a pizza peel (or a baking sheet) with a light, even dusting of flour. Tap the side of the peel on the countertop to knock off any excess flour. If the cooked pizza crust tastes like burnt flour, the peel was overfloured. If the pizza crust sticks, you probably used too little flour.

5 Drape the dough over the back of your hand, and then rotate it slowly. The weight of the dough should gently stretch it to a circular shape and even thickness, 30–35 cm / 12–14 in. in diameter. Small blisters and bubbles should form in the dough. These are good!

4

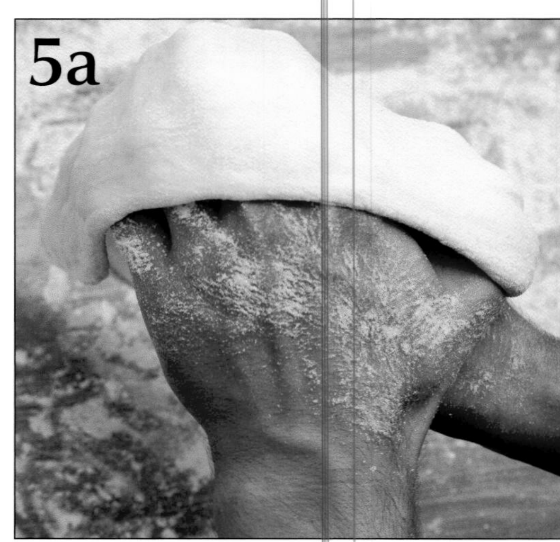
5a

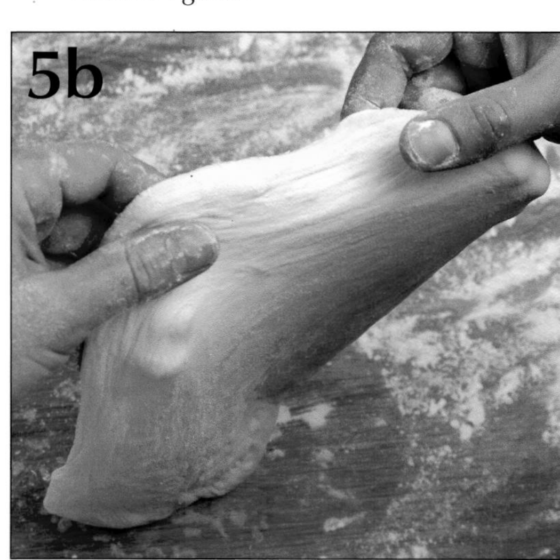
5b

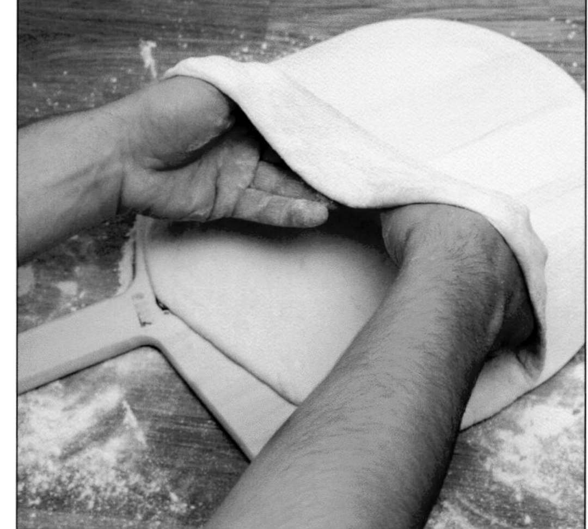

6 Place the dough onto a pizza peel. Jerk the peel sharply back and forth; this prevents the dough from sticking to the peel.

7 Spread the sauce evenly over the dough, but leave the outermost 2.5 cm / 1 in of the perimeter dry.

8 Sprinkle grated cheese evenly over the sauce.

9 To avoid losing heat from the oven, slide the pizza from the peel onto the baking surface as quickly as possible.

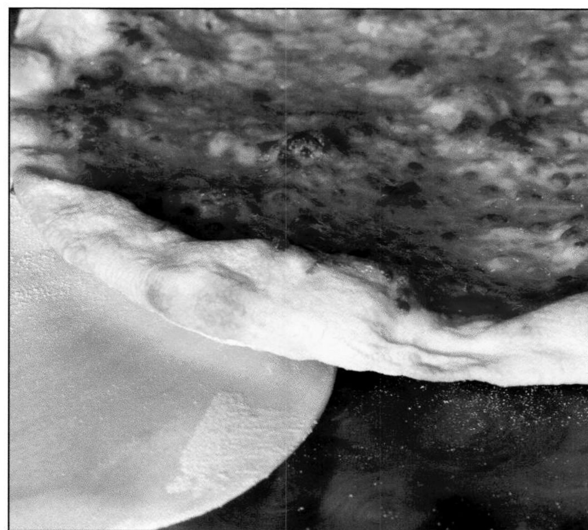

10 Cook the pizza until the crust turns brown and blisters, 3–5 minutes. Some of the larger bubbles should look almost burnt.

11 Remove the pizza from the oven by using the pizza peel or baking sheet, and slide it on a cooling rack. This keeps the crust crisp.

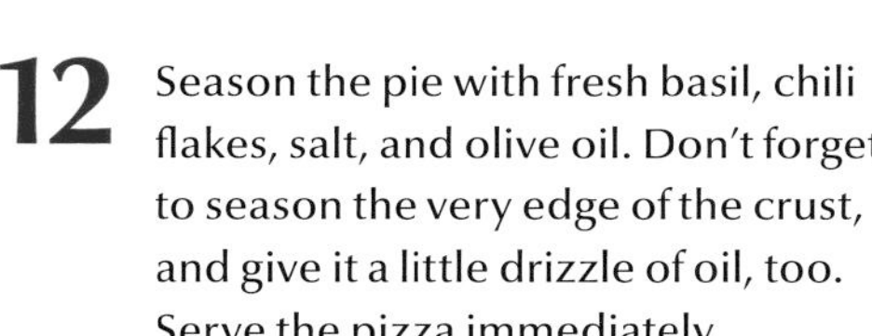

12 Season the pie with fresh basil, chili flakes, salt, and olive oil. Don't forget to season the very edge of the crust, and give it a little drizzle of oil, too. Serve the pizza immediately.

A well-cooked pizza has scorched blisters on the bottom of the crust—although pizza can also be delicious without a blistered crust. If you don't see any blisters, your cooking surface is not hot enough. You can try using a metal plate, as described on page 301. Also see page 34 for a guide to ovens and baking equipment.

CLASSIC PIZZA VARIATIONS

Napolitana Pizza

Pizza Sauce see variation on page 112	65 g	¼ cup
Mozzarella cheese, grated	125 g	1⅝ cups
Roasted red pepper, sliced	30 g	⅛ cup
Olives, sliced	25 g	2 Tbsp
White anchovy fillets	20 g	7–9 fillets
Pecorino Romano, shaved	15 g	¼ cup
Mint leaves	3 g	1 Tbsp

Follow steps 1–8. Add the peppers and olives, and continue with step 9. Garnish the baked pizza with the anchovies, Pecorino Romano, and torn mint leaves, and serve it immediately.

Funghi Pizza

Pizza Sauce see variation on page 112	65 g	¼ cup
Mozzarella cheese, grated	125 g	1⅝ cups
Wild mushrooms (such as chanterelles, yellow foot, maitake, or porcinis), sautéed	125 g	¾ cup

Follow steps 1–8. Add the sautéed wild mushrooms. (If using black trumpet mushrooms, add them raw rather than sautéed.) Continue with step 9.

Hawaiian Pizza

Pineapple Marinara Sauce see variation on page 112	100 g	⅝ cup
Mozzarella cheese, grated	125 g	1⅝ cups
Culatello or prosciutto, thinly sliced	50 g	3–5 slices

Follow steps 1–11. Garnish the baked pizza with the culatello or prosciutto, and serve it immediately.

PIZZA MARGHERITA

YIELD:	*one 30–35 cm / 12–14 in pizza*
TIME ESTIMATE:	*15 minutes overall (not including preheating time)*
STORAGE NOTES:	*serve immediately*
LEVEL OF DIFFICULTY:	*advanced (equipment)*
SPECIAL REQUIREMENTS:	*steel plate 12 mm / ½ in thick, pizza peel*

This is a great basic pizza. The variations you can create are endless, but don't go overboard with your toppings: more than 150–200 g of toppings can render the crust wet and doughy. Many people put too much sauce or cheese on a margherita pizza, so it quickly gets soggy. You can vacuum-dry buffalo mozzarella (see photos below) or use packaged, shredded mozzarella instead. Another approach is to add *burrata* or another wet mozzarella cheese to the pizza after you take it out of the oven. For an illustrated guide to making pizzas, see the previous pages.

INGREDIENT	WEIGHT	VOLUME	SCALING	PROCEDURE
Pizza dough see pages 296, 298, and 300	200 g	1 ball	100%	① Rest the dough until it has warmed to room temperature, about 1 hour if previously refrigerated. ② While the dough is warming, place a 12 mm / ½ in thick steel plate on the middle rack of the oven. Set the oven to its highest setting, a minimum of **260** °C / **500** °F, and preheat for 1 hour. ③ Stretch and flatten the dough on a floured work surface. Press the middle of the dough flat with your fingertips, and work the dough outward, leaving a narrow ridge at the perimeter. Stretch it over the back of your hand into a circle 30–35 cm / 12–14 in. in diameter. ④ Place the round onto a lightly floured pizza peel, and then give the peel a sharp jerk to prevent sticking.
Pizza Sauce see variation on page 112	80 g	5½ Tbsp	40%	⑤ Spread the sauce evenly over the dough, leaving a dry perimeter 2.5 cm / 1 in wide.
Vacuum-dried buffalo mozzarella cheese, torn into pieces, or shredded mozzarella	80 g	1¼ cups	40%	⑥ Sprinkle the cheese evenly over the sauce. ⑦ Slide the pizza onto the steel plate as quickly as possible. ⑧ Cook until the pizza crust has browned and blistered and some of the larger bubbles look almost burnt, 3–5 minutes. ⑨ Remove the pizza from the oven using the pizza peel, and place it on a cooling rack.
Fresh basil leaves, torn	3 g	7–8 leaves	4%	⑩ Season the pizza, drizzle olive oil around the perimeter of the crust, and serve it immediately.
Chili flakes	to taste			
Salt	to taste			
Extra-virgin olive oil	to taste			

Buffalo mozzarella is a very moist cheese that tends to make the pizza go soggy very quickly. You can avoid this problem by using packaged, shredded mozzarella, which is a much drier cheese. But we avoid this problem by vacuum-drying the buffalo mozzarella. Tear the cheese into small pieces, and place them between two paper towels. Slide the towels into a sous vide bag, and vacuum seal it. This technique uses air pressure to squeeze much of the moisture out of the mozzarella; it is then wicked up by the paper towels.

For pizza topping ideas, see Classic Pizza Variations on the previous page and Pizza Toppings on page 306. A Napolitana pizza is shown here.

OVEN-FRIED PIZZA

YIELD:	*one 30–35 cm / 12–14 in pizza*
TIME ESTIMATE:	*15 minutes overall (not including preheating time)*
STORAGE NOTES:	*serve immediately*
LEVEL OF DIFFICULTY:	*advanced (handling)*
SPECIAL REQUIREMENTS:	*large cast-iron skillet, pizza peel*

Old Forge, Pennsylvania, is a coal-mining town known for its unusual style of pizza, which is rectangular and fried in oil for a crispy crust. Our oven-fried pizza is not the true Old Forge style created by the Ghigiarelli family, but it is inspired by the original. Frying the pizza creates a crust with a completely different flavor than you find on a baked pizza. When done properly, most of the oil stays in the pan and does not make the pizza greasy. Don't overload the pizzas with toppings, or they won't cook evenly.

INGREDIENT	WEIGHT	VOLUME	SCALING	PROCEDURE
Pizza dough see pages 296, 298, and 300	200 g	1 ball of dough	100%	① Bring the pizza dough to room temperature. ② Preheat the oven to its highest setting, a minimum of **260** °C / **500** °F for at least 1 hour. ③ Stretch and flatten the pizza dough on a floured work surface. Press the middle of the dough flat with your fingertips, and work the dough outward, leaving a narrow ridge at the perimeter (see page 302). Stretch the dough over the back of your hand until it is the diameter of your cast-iron skillet. ④ Place the dough onto a lightly floured pizza peel. Top evenly with sauce, cheese, and desired toppings. When finished, give the peel a quick jerk to make sure it is not sticking to the crust. If it is, blow air underneath the crust, and add flour to the peel. ⑤ Cut a small X into the center.
Sauce, cheese, and toppings see the next page	no more than 175 g total			
Neutral frying oil see page xxii	80 g	85 mL / ⅜ cup	40%	⑥ Preheat a cast-iron skillet over high heat until very hot, 3–5 minutes. ⑦ Add the oil to the pan, and continue to heat until just smoking. ⑧ Slide the pizza carefully into the hot oil. Transfer the pan immediately into the hot oven, and cook until brown and bubbly, 3–4 minutes. ⑨ Remove the pan from the oven. Lift the pizza onto a baking sheet lined with paper towels, let it drain, and then serve it immediately. To make additional pizzas, scoop out any bits from the oil or add fresh oil, and reheat the skillet until the oil starts to smoke.

A vent cut into the center of the crust allows pressure from the steam to escape while the pizza cooks.

The bottom of the pizza should turn brown and bubbly after 3–4 minutes in the preheated skillet. You may need to experiment a bit to find the optimal baking time and preheating temperature for the skillet. If the bottom of the pizza overcooks, reduce the temperature of the pan slightly. If the top comes out undercooked, leave the pizza in the oven for a minute or two longer.

VARIATION: Deep-Dish Fried Pizza

For a thicker, chewier pie that is closer to a crispy focaccia, double the quantity of dough, and increase the cooking time at step 8 to 7–8 minutes.

PIZZA TOPPINGS

When adding toppings to a pizza, be judicious. Overdressing the pie can knock its flavors out of balance and make the dough soggy. Also take care to precook any ingredients that won't cook fully during the short time the pizza bakes. You can use fresh ingredients as a garnish after the baking is done to add contrast in texture and temperature. Season the finished pie just before serving with a drizzle of your best extra-virgin olive oil and a sprinkling of red pepper flakes and salt. The quantities listed here are scaled for a 30–35 cm / 12–14 in pizza. Steps and substitutions refer to the recipe for Pizza Margherita on page 304.

Broccoli Raab Pizza

Broccoli raab (rapini)	50 g	½ cup
Pressure-Cooked Garlic Confit, pureed see page 126	50 g	3 Tbsp
Ricotta cheese (goat's or cow's milk)	80 g	⅜ Tbsp
Chanterelle mushrooms, sautéed	65 g	⅜ cup
Lemon zest, grated	1 g	1 tsp

Roast the broccoli raab at 190 °C / 375 °F until it is lightly browned. Follow steps 1–4. In steps 5 and 6, substitute garlic confit puree for the pizza sauce and ricotta for the mozzarella. Top with sautéed chanterelles and roasted broccoli raab. Continue with step 7. Garnish the baked pizza with lemon zest, and serve it immediately.

Capicola Pizza

Pizza Sauce see variation on page 112	80 g	5½ Tbsp
Vacuum-dried buffalo mozzarella cheese see photos on page 304	100 g	⅜ cup
Capicola (Coppa), thinly sliced	25 g	4–5 slices
Arugula	35 g	1 cup
Green chilies, thinly sliced	10 g	1½ Tbsp

Follow steps 1–4. Add the pizza sauce and mozzarella, and then top with the capicola, and continue with step 7. Garnish the baked pizza with the arugula and green chilies, and serve it immediately.

Genovese Pizza

Pistachio Pesto see page 102	75 g	¼ cup
Vacuum-dried buffalo mozzarella cheese see photos on page 304	100 g	⅜ cup
Brussels sprouts, shaved	65 g	1¼ cups
Fresh basil leaves, torn	3 g	8 leaves
Cracked black pepper	to taste	

Follow steps 1–4. In step 5, substitute pistachio pesto for the pizza sauce. In step 6, use 100 g / ⅜ cup of vacuum-dried buffalo mozzarella. Top with the shaved Brussels sprouts, and continue with step 7. Garnish the baked pizza with the basil leaves and cracked black pepper, and serve it immediately.

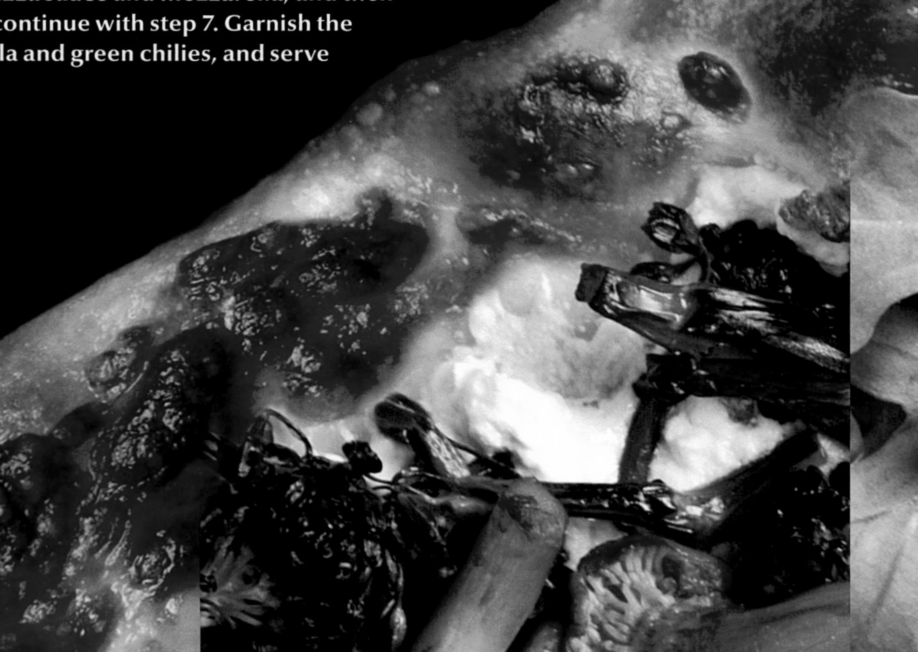

Uovo Pizza

Brown butter see page 119	20 g	20 mL / 1½ Tbsp
Pecorino Romano cheese, grated	35 g	⅜ cup
Sage leaves, julienned	1 g	4–5 leaves
Ground black pepper	to taste	
Quail eggs		5–7 eggs

Follow steps 1–4. Substitute brown butter for the pizza sauce in step 5 and Pecorino Romano for the mozzarella in step 6. Top with sage and black pepper, and continue with step 7. When the crust is just set but not brown, remove the pizza from the oven, and top it with the raw quail eggs. Return the pie to the oven, and continue with step 8.

Finocchiona Pizza (not shown)

Italian sausage with fennel seed, cooked	100 g	½ cup / 1–2 links
Heavy cream	50 g	55 mL / ¼ cup
Mozzarella cheese, grated	80 g	1¼ cups
Fennel, sliced and sautéed	33 g	⅜ cup
Leeks, sliced and sautéed	32 g	⅜ cup

Follow steps 1–4. Crumble the cooked sausage into the cream, mix well, and substitute for the pizza sauce in step 5. Top with the cheese, fennel, and leeks, and continue with step 7.

Pizza Cruda

Cherry tomatoes	50 g	⅓ cup
Prosciutto, thinly sliced and cut into ribbons	35 g	3 slices
Arugula	35 g	1 cup
Parmesan cheese, shaved	30 g	½ cup

Follow steps 1–9. Garnish the baked pizza with the cherry tomatoes, prosciutto, arugula, and shaved Parmesan cheese, and serve it immediately.

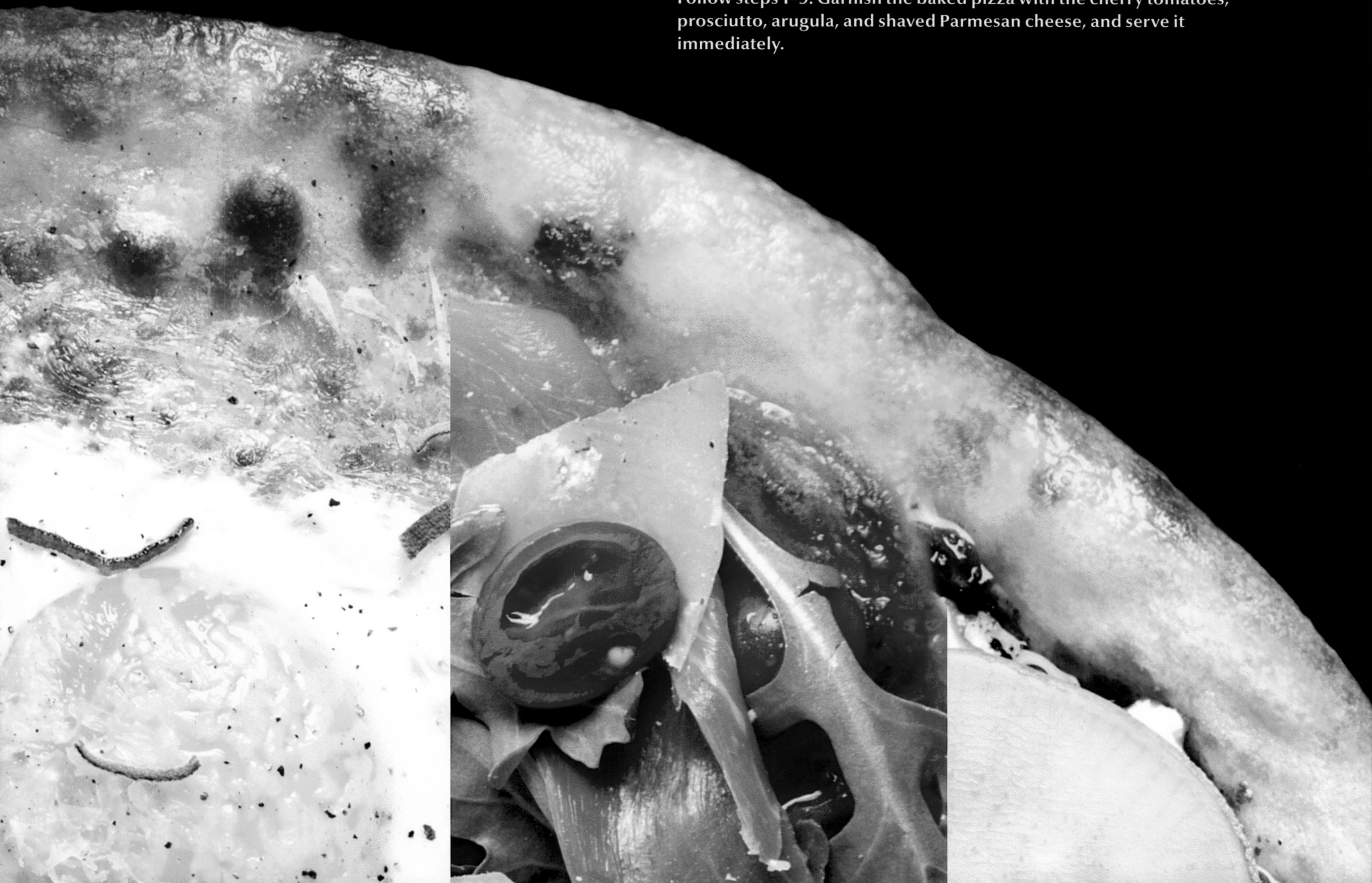

MAC AND CHEESE

All of the virtues of using good cheese are lost when you make a cheese sauce with flour, which is a standard ingredient in nearly all traditional macaroni and cheese recipes. Why dilute the rich flavor of the key ingredient by adding a starch that has poor flavor release and an unappealing texture? Frankly, you'd be better off using Velveeta and saving the good stuff to pair with a glass of wine (and that's no knock on Velveeta—we love it).

Our Modernist versions of mac and cheese allow you to use the good stuff without compromising its flavor. By employing a bit of basic emulsion science, you can produce an incredibly smooth cheese sauce that actually tastes like the cheese that went into it. Cheese is itself an emulsion of dairy fat and water, but that emulsion tends to break when it gets hot. We add an emulsifier called sodium citrate—a sodium salt of the citric acid found naturally in citrus fruits—to our cheese sauce to stabilize the emulsion so that it doesn't turn greasy when cooked. The resulting texture is as smooth as melted American cheese, but as complex and intense in flavor as any of your favorite cheeses.

In this chapter, we provide recipes for classic stove-top macaroni and cheese, as well as baked and fat-free versions. We also reveal the secret to making Velveeta-like sliceable cheeses from some of our favorite varieties of cheese. These slices are perfect for cheeseburgers and grilled cheese sandwiches.

THE SCIENCE OF HOT EMULSIONS

Melted cheese separates easily into its components (fat and water). Classic mac and cheese recipes use béchamel—a sauce of flour, butter, and milk—to prevent the cheese sauce from turning into a greasy slick. The starch particles and the milk proteins in the béchamel do act as emulsifiers, but they aren't very good at this job. So either you sacrifice the flavor of the cheese by adding far too much béchamel, or you dilute the cheese less at the cost of slight greasiness, which becomes more pronounced when the mac and cheese is baked.

We owe a wonderful piece of chemistry to James L. Kraft, who in 1916 patented the first American cheese slice. He showed that sodium phosphate keeps the fat droplets mixed within the water when the cheese is melted. Sodium citrate has the same effect and is easier to find.

HIGHLIGHTS

The cheese sauce is smooth with an intense cheese flavor, but it contains no starch. Instead, we use sodium citrate, an emulsifying salt, to produce that creamy result.

see pages 310 and 312

You don't have to sacrifice the taste to make a **low-calorie, nearly fat-free mac and cheese.** The secret is to **put the cheese flavor into the water** that you use to cook the pasta.

see page 314

A slight variation on the cheese sauce recipe allows you to **make sandwich slices from your favorite cheeses.**

see page 317

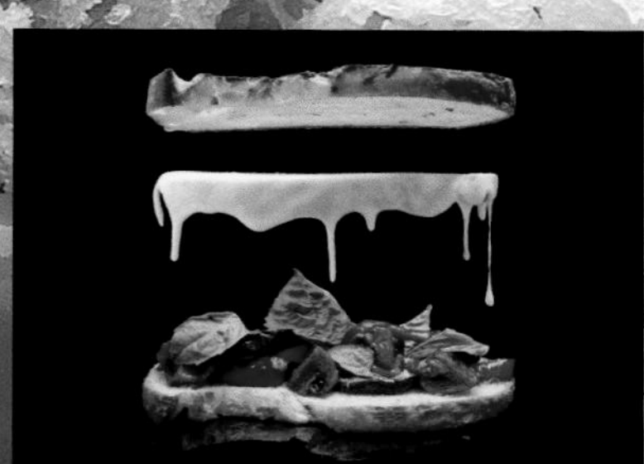

When you know how to make perfect slices of any cheese you want, the door is open to **fantastic grilled cheese sandwiches.** We provide recipes for five different kinds.

see page 318

FURTHER READING IN *MODERNIST CUISINE*

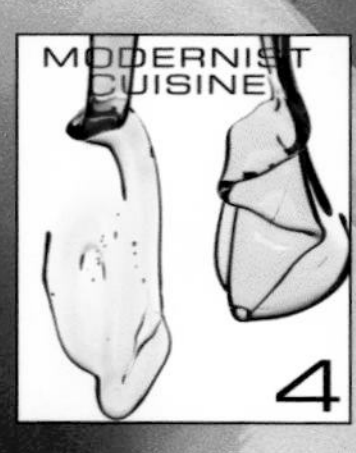

How to make your own pasta: see page 3·378
How to make superstable emulsions: see pages 4·206–213
Selecting and using Modernist emulsifiers: see pages 4·214–217
Constructing cheeses for fondue, raclette, and other uses: see pages 4·222–225

MAC AND CHEESE

YIELD:	*five servings (800 g / 5 cups)*
TIME ESTIMATE:	*30 minutes overall*
STORAGE NOTES:	*serve pasta immediately; cheese sauce keeps for 1 week when refrigerated or up to 2 months when frozen*
LEVEL OF DIFFICULTY:	*moderate*
SPECIAL REQUIREMENTS:	*sodium citrate*

This recipe has been one of the most popular in *Modernist Cuisine* since that book appeared. Use it as a template to create your own version of a refined mac and cheese. There are so many potentially great cheese mixes and accompaniments that it was hard to pick just the six that we have space for here.

Elbow macaroni is the classic pasta for mac and cheese, but any kind of pasta works. Those varieties having a rough surface hold the sauce better. Although cheese lovers might be tempted to boost the sauce-to-pasta ratio, keep in mind that the sauce is very rich. A little goes a long way.

INGREDIENT	WEIGHT	VOLUME	SCALING	PROCEDURE
Water or milk	265 g	265 mL / 1⅛ cups	93%	① Combine in a pot, whisk to dissolve, and bring to a simmer over medium heat.
Sodium citrate	11 g		4%	
White cheddar cheese, finely grated	285 g	4 cups	100%	② Add into the simmering liquid gradually, blending each addition with an immersion blender until melted and completely smooth.
Water	as needed for cooking the pasta			③ Bring a large pot of water to a boil.
Dry macaroni	240 g	2 cups	84%	④ Boil until al dente according to the package directions, 5–6 minutes. ⑤ Drain. Do not rinse the pasta. ⑥ Stir in the warm cheese sauce, and fold in any accompaniments you wish to add (see the variations below).
Salt	to taste			⑦ Season the mac and cheese, and serve it immediately.

(adapted from Harold McGee)

VARIATIONS

In the variations below, substitute the cheeses listed for the white cheddar cheese at step 2, and fold in the additions listed at step 6.

Mac with Jack and Stilton
Cheeses: 200 g / 3 cups of Jack and 50 g / ⅓ cup of Stilton
Fold in: roasted bell peppers and wilted baby spinach

Mac with Sharp Cheddar and Swiss
Cheeses: 200 g / 3 cups of sharp cheddar and 85 g / 1 cup of Swiss
Fold in: chunks of roasted apple and crispy bacon bits

Mac with Gorgonzola and Fontina
Cheeses: 50 g / ⅓ cup of Gorgonzola and 235 g / 3 cups of young Fontina
Fold in: walnuts and sautéed mushrooms

Mac and Gruyère
Cheeses: 285 g / 4 cups of Gruyère
Fold in: roasted cauliflower and roasted tomatoes

Mac with Goat Gouda and Cheddar
Cheeses: 142 g / 2 cups of goat Gouda and 142 g / 2 cups of goat cheddar
Fold in: Pressure-Caramelized Onions (see page 127) and black olives

WHILE YOU'RE AT IT

Broccoli with Cheese Sauce
Make a delicious side dish by substituting steamed broccoli for the pasta. We cut the broccoli into bite-size pieces so that the florets are enveloped by the cheese sauce, just as pasta would be. Also try substituting cauliflower, steamed fingerling potatoes, green beans, shelled edamame, sautéed button mushrooms, baby bok choy, or Brussels sprouts.

Fondue
At step 1, substitute 200 g / 200 mL / ⅞ cup of water and 118 g / 120 mL / ½ cup of dry white wine for the water. At step 2, whisk in the cheese rather than using a blender so that the fondue is appropriately stringy. For a classic Swiss interpretation, use Emmental cheese, and add a dash of kirsch.

1 Whisk the sodium citrate into the water or milk in a pot until fully dissolved, and then bring to a simmer.

2 Add the finely grated cheese, one spoonful at a time, to the simmering liquid on the stove top. Use an immersion blender to blend in each spoonful of cheese until the cheese has melted and becomes completely smooth. Set the cheese sauce aside while you cook the macaroni, or refrigerate it until you are ready to reheat it.

3 Bring a large pot of water to a boil.

TROUBLESHOOTING TIP:

If You See This, Stop

If the fat and liquid start to separate (in other words, the emulsion breaks), bring the mixture to a full boil, and then continue processing with the immersion blender. The mixture should pull together. If this fails, add a spoonful of heavy cream, and try again.

4 Boil the macaroni until it is al dente, as instructed by the package directions, or for 5–6 minutes.

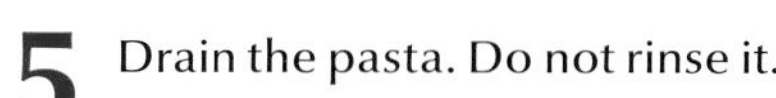

5 Drain the pasta. Do not rinse it.

6 Stir the warm cheese sauce into the pasta. Fold in any flavor accompaniments (see the variations on the previous page for ideas).

7 Season the mac and cheese with salt to taste. Serve it immediately.

BAKED MAC AND CHEESE

YIELD:	*five servings (900 g / 5 cups)*
TIME ESTIMATE:	*45 minutes overall, including 30 minutes of preparation and 15 minutes unattended*
STORAGE NOTES:	*keeps for 3 days when refrigerated before baking*
LEVEL OF DIFFICULTY:	*moderate*
SPECIAL REQUIREMENTS:	*sodium citrate, Cheese Crumble (see page 316)*

The key to excellent baked mac and cheese is to parcook (partially cook) the macaroni just long enough to ensure that it becomes tender rather than mushy during baking. The threshold between undercooking and overcooking is incredibly fine. You can substitute any of the cheese combinations from the variations on page 310 for the cheese mixture here.

INGREDIENT	WEIGHT	VOLUME	SCALING	PROCEDURE
Water	as needed for cooking the pasta			① Place a metal baking sheet in the freezer for at least 30 minutes. ② Preheat the oven to 260 °C / 500 °F. ③ Bring a large pot of water to a boil.
Dry macaroni	200 g	1½ cups	44%	④ Parcook for 2½ minutes. ⑤ Drain. Do not rinse the pasta. ⑥ Spread the macaroni immediately into a single layer on the cold baking sheet. Cool for 5 minutes, uncovered, and then measure 450 g / 3½ cups for use in step 11.
Water or milk	185 g	185 mL / ¾ cup	41%	⑦ Combine in a pot, whisk until dissolved, and then bring to a simmer over medium heat.
Sodium citrate	13 g		3%	
Gruyère cheese, grated	200 g	3⅓ cups	44%	⑧ Gradually add to the simmering liquid, using an immersion blender to blend each addition until it has melted and is completely smooth.
Cream cheese	85 g	⅓ cup	19%	
Sharp cheddar cheese, grated	65 g	½ cup	14%	⑨ Cool slightly; the cheese should remain fluid. Measure 450 g / 2 cups of the cheese mixture for use in the next step.
Cheese mixture, from above	450 g	2 cups	100%	⑩ Combine.
Dry mustard powder	0.5 g	pinch	0.1%	
Cayenne pepper (optional)	to taste			
Parcooked macaroni, from above	450 g	3½ cups	100%	⑪ Fold the reserved macaroni into the warm cheese mixture, and season it to taste.
Salt	to taste			⑫ Divide the mixture evenly into five ramekins, or pour it into one large baking dish.
Cheese Crumble see page 316	100 g	1½ cups	22%	⑬ Sprinkle generously over the mac and cheese. ⑭ Bake until golden brown and bubbly, 13–15 minutes. Serve hot.

TO MAKE AHEAD

After cooling the macaroni in step 6, toss it in enough neutral-tasting oil to lightly coat the pasta, and refrigerate it until ready to use.

The cheese sauce will keep for 1 week when refrigerated and for up to 2 months when frozen.

The mac and cheese can be prepared through step 11, and then refrigerated for up to 3 days. Keep in mind that the pasta will continue to absorb moisture, so it will soften over time. Do not top with the cheese crumble until just before baking. Baking the mac and cheese from the refrigerator will require an additional 10–12 minutes.

1 Place a metal baking sheet in the freezer to chill for at least 30 minutes.

2 Preheat the oven to 260 °C / 500 °F.

3 Bring a large pot of water to a boil.

4 Parboil the macaroni for 2½ minutes. Although the surface of the pasta will be cooked, the interior will still be raw and crunchy. The macaroni will finish cooking in the oven.

5 Drain the cooked pasta, but do not rinse it. Proceed immediately to the next step.

6 Spread the pasta into a single layer on the chilled baking sheet, and allow it to cool, uncovered, for 5 minutes. This technique efficiently cools the macaroni, but doesn't rinse any of the starch from its surface. When it has cooled, measure 450 g / 3½ cups of the pasta for use in step 11.

7 Whisk the sodium citrate into the water or milk in a pot until it has dissolved, and then bring the liquid to a simmer over medium heat.

8 Add the cheeses into the liquid, one spoonful at a time, while the mixture simmers on the stove. Use an immersion blender to blend each spoonful until it has melted and becomes completely smooth.

9 Cool the cheese slightly—it should remain fluid—and then measure 450 g / 2 cups for use in the next step.

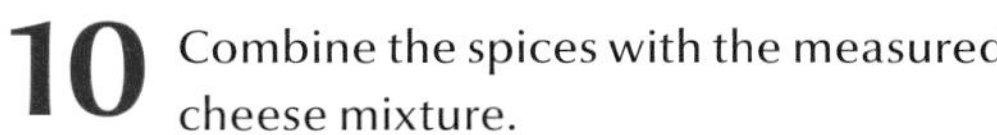

10 Combine the spices with the measured cheese mixture.

11 Fold the measured macaroni into the warm cheese mixture, and season it with salt to taste.

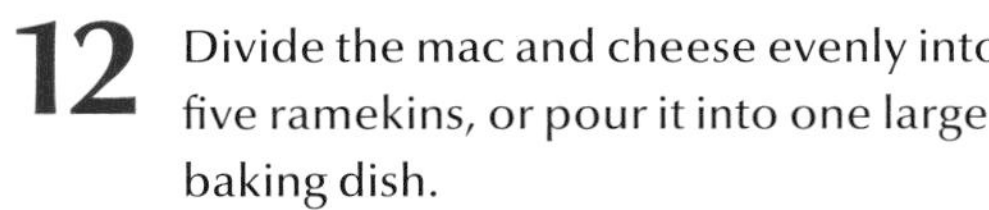

12 Divide the mac and cheese evenly into five ramekins, or pour it into one large baking dish.

13 Sprinkle the cheese crumble generously over the top of each serving.

14 Bake until the cheese turns golden brown and bubbly, 13–15 minutes. Place the dish in a baking pan to catch any bubbling sauce and prevent burning. Serve hot.

"FAT-FREE" MAC AND CHEESE

YIELD:	*five servings (750 g / 4 cups)*
TIME ESTIMATE:	*1¾ hours overall, including 30 minutes of preparation and 1¼ hours unattended*
STORAGE NOTES:	*serve immediately; cheese water keeps for 5 days when refrigerated or for up to 6 months when frozen*
LEVEL OF DIFFICULTY:	*moderate*
SPECIAL REQUIREMENTS:	*sous vide setup*

The flavor compounds in cheese, much like those in tea leaves and coffee beans, dissolve in water. We take advantage of that fact by cooking pasta in cheese water, a technique that transfers flavor to the macaroni and allows us to make a delicate, refined dish that contains little fat yet retains much of the robust flavor of traditional mac and cheese.

We also add pureed cauliflower, which mimics the rich mouth-feel and color of cheese sauce but doesn't weigh it down. It is easy to make cheese water, and once you've tasted it, you will probably want to make extra to keep on hand. It freezes well and makes a wonderful soup base. You can also use it as a broth for glazed spring vegetables or braised winter greens.

INGREDIENT	WEIGHT	VOLUME	SCALING	PROCEDURE
Water Cauliflower, thinly sliced	150 g 100 g	150 mL / ⅝ cup 1½ cups	30% 20%	① Combine the cauliflower and water in a pot, and simmer until very tender, about 30 minutes. ② Drain. ③ Puree until smooth. ④ Sieve, and measure 75 g / ¼ cup of the cauliflower puree for use in step 12.
Water Jack cheese, finely grated Gruyère cheese, finely grated	500 g 275 g 275 g	500 mL / 2⅛ cups 4 cups 4 cups	100% 55% 55%	⑤ Preheat a water bath to 80 °C / 176 °F. ⑥ Combine together in a large (4 L / 1 gal) zip-top bag, remove as much air as possible from the bag (see page 58), and seal it. ⑦ Cook sous vide for 30 minutes. ⑧ Cool for 15 minutes at room temperature. ⑨ Strain through a fine sieve lined with cheesecloth to collect the liquid. Measure 500 g / 500 mL / 2⅛ cups of the cheese water for use in the next step. (See note on the next page on uses for cheese solids.)
Sugar	2 g	½ tsp	0.4%	⑩ Combine with the cheese water in a medium pot, stir to dissolve, and bring to a boil over high heat.
Dry macaroni	180 g	1¼ cups	36%	⑪ Stir into the boiling cheese water, and reduce the heat to medium. ⑫ Cook until most of the cheese water has been absorbed and the macaroni is just al dente, about 7 minutes. Fold the reserved cauliflower puree into the mac and cheese.
Salt	to taste			⑬ Season the mac and cheese, and serve it warm.

VARIATIONS

Mac and Fontina
Cheese: 550 g / 6 cups of young Fontina, finely grated
Fold in: Pressure-Caramelized Onions (see page 127) or 75 g of Mushroom Puree (see page 150)

Mac and Parmesan
Cheese: 550 g / 9 cups of Parmesan, finely grated
Fold in: Creamed Spinach (see page 199) or thinly sliced sun-dried tomatoes

Mac and Cheddar
Cheese: 550 g / 8 cups of sharp cheddar, finely grated
Fold in: broccoli puree or cubes of roasted apples

1 Combine the cauliflower and water in a pot, and simmer until the cauliflower becomes very tender, about 30 minutes.

2 Drain the cauliflower.

3 Blend the cauliflower into a smooth puree.

4 Pass the puree through a sieve, and measure 75 g / ¼ cup of it for use in step 12.

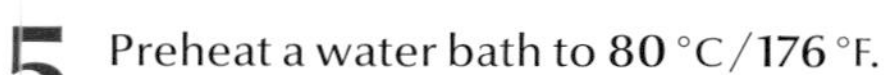

5 Preheat a water bath to 80 °C / 176 °F.

6 Combine the cheeses and the water in a large (4 L / 1 gal) zip-top bag. Use the water-displacement method (see page 58) to remove as much air as possible from the bag, and seal it.

7 Cook the cheeses sous vide for 30 minutes. The end result should look a bit like curdled milk.

8 Remove the bag from the bath, and let it cool for 15 minutes at room temperature.

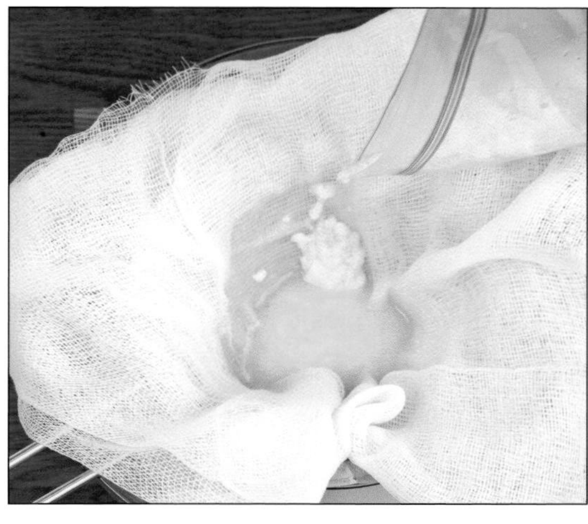

9 Place a fine sieve lined with cheesecloth over a bowl, and strain the cheese-water mixture, collecting the cheese water in the bowl. Reserve 500 g / 500 mL / 2⅛ cups of the cheese water for use in the next step. Store the remaining cheese water in the refrigerator or freezer for another use, and see the note below for suggested ways to use the remaining cheese solids.

10 Combine the reserved cheese water and the sugar in a medium pot. Stir until the sugar dissolves, and then bring the mixture to a boil over high heat. A lot of the natural sweetness of the cheese was left behind in the cheese solids, so the pinch of sugar helps to round out the flavor.

11 Stir the dry macaroni into the cheese water, and reduce the heat to medium.

12 Cook the pasta until it has absorbed most of the cheese water and is just al dente, about 7 minutes. Fold the reserved cauliflower puree into the mac and cheese.

13 Season the mac and cheese with salt to taste, and serve it warm.

WHILE YOU'RE AT IT: **Cheese Crisps**
The cheese solids left over after straining the cheese water in step 9 have lost some of their flavor, but they are very tasty when dried. Spread them on a baking sheet, and bake them at 175 °C / 350 °F until they turn golden, about 45 minutes. Then break them up, and use them as a garnish for baked potatoes or green salads, as part of a savory cracker, or as a substitute for the cheese crumbs in step 9 of our recipe for Cheese Crumble (see next page).

CHEESE CRUMBLE

YIELD:	*250 g / 2½ cups*
TIME ESTIMATE:	*1¼ hours overall, including 25 minutes of preparation and 50 minutes unattended*
STORAGE NOTES:	*keeps for 2–3 days when refrigerated*
LEVEL OF DIFFICULTY:	*moderate*
SPECIAL REQUIREMENTS:	*food processor (optional), sodium citrate, tapioca starch*
USED IN:	*Baked Mac and Cheese (see page 312)*

INGREDIENT	WEIGHT	VOLUME	SCALING	PROCEDURE
Water	60 g	60 mL / ¼ cup	30%	① Preheat the oven to 175 °C / 350 °F.
Sodium citrate	2.5 g		1.25%	② Combine in a pot, whisk until dissolved, and bring to a simmer.
Gruyère cheese, finely grated	200 g	3 cups	100%	③ Add gradually to the simmering liquid. Use an immersion blender to blend each addition until it is melted and completely smooth.
Tapioca starch	100 g	⅞ cup	50%	④ Add, one-third at a time. Stir well between additions to keep the mixture smooth and moist throughout. The mixture turns thick very quickly and resembles a dough when it is finished. ⑤ While the cheese mixture is still warm, scoop it onto a silicone mat, and use a rolling pin to roll it into a thin, even sheet. ⑥ Place the mat on a baking sheet, and bake until the cheese cracker is completely dry and golden brown, 45–50 minutes. ⑦ Cool the cheese cracker, and break it into pieces. ⑧ Grind the cheese cracker in a food processor to make fine crumbs. Alternatively, place pieces in a zip-top bag, and crush them with a rolling pin or mallet.
Gruyère cheese, finely grated	40 g	⅝ cup	20%	⑨ Combine with the ground or crushed cheese crumbs. ⑩ Store refrigerated.
Panko bread crumbs	20 g	2 Tbsp	10%	

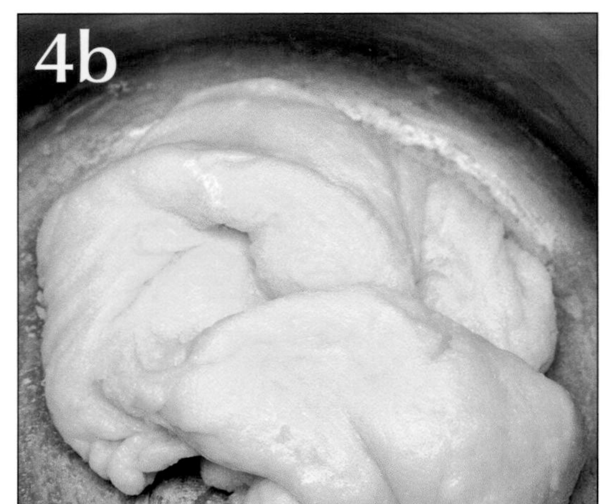

Top any au gratin dish with this cheese crumble: it goes well on scalloped potatoes, green bean casserole, and Apple Betty. You can substitute other firm or hard cheeses, such as cheddar or Parmesan, for the Gruyère.

TO MAKE AHEAD

For extended storage, keep the ground cheese crumbles from step 8 in an airtight container. Mix them with the grated Gruyère and panko bread crumbs just before you use them.

WHILE YOU'RE AT IT

PERFECTLY MELTING CHEESE SLICE

YIELD:	*500 g / 12–14 slices*
TIME ESTIMATE:	*2¼ hours overall, including 15 minutes of preparation and 2 hours unattended*
STORAGE NOTES:	*keeps for 10 days when refrigerated or up to 2 months when frozen*
LEVEL OF DIFFICULTY:	*moderate*
SPECIAL REQUIREMENTS:	*sodium citrate*
USED IN:	*Modernist Cheeseburger (see page 212), Grilled Cheese Sandwiches (see the next page)*

By using sodium citrate, an emulsifying salt, you can make any cheese into slices that melt as perfectly as American-style sandwich cheese does. These slices are perfect for cheeseburgers, grilled cheese sandwiches, vegetables, apple pie, or any other dish needing a melted cheese that doesn't separate. You can either form the cheese into a thin sheet, or mold it into a cylinder or block for slicing later.

INGREDIENT	WEIGHT	VOLUME	SCALING	PROCEDURE
Cold wheat beer (or water)	115 g	115 mL / ½ cup	57.5%	① Preheat the oven to its lowest temperature. ② Line a baking sheet with a silicone mat, or lightly oil the sheet, and place it in the oven to warm while you prepare the cheese. ③ Combine in a pot, stir until dissolved, and then bring to a simmer over medium heat.
Sodium citrate see page 71	14 g		7%	
Gruyère cheese, grated	200 g	3 cups	100%	④ Add gradually to the simmering liquid. Use an immersion blender to blend in each addition until it has melted and is completely smooth. ⑤ Pour the liquid cheese mixture onto the warm baking sheet. Tip the sheet as needed to form an even layer. Alternatively, pour the cheese into a mold coated with cooking spray. ⑥ Cover with plastic wrap, and refrigerate until fully set, at least 2 hours. ⑦ Cut into rounds or squares 7.5 cm / 3 in across. Place plastic wrap or parchment paper between the slices to prevent them from sticking together, and store refrigerated or frozen.
Sharp cheddar cheese, grated	180 g	3 cups	90%	

We developed this cheese slice technique for the Mushroom Swiss Burger recipe in *Modernist Cuisine*. In that version, we added a lot of additional liquid (beer!). We wanted the cheese to flow well, so we also added carrageenan, a thickener extracted from seaweed, to adjust the viscosity of the cold cheese. Since then, however, we have discovered that the carrageenan isn't necessary if you add less liquid, as we do here. The sodium citrate, on the other hand, is indispensable for preventing the cheese from separating when it melts.

SPECIAL SCALING FOR THE SODIUM CITRATE

If you are scaling the yield of this recipe up or down, you can calculate how much sodium citrate to use by weighing the liquid and the grated cheeses together, and multiplying by 2.8% of the total weight. For example, when making 750 g of cheese slices, use 21 g of sodium citrate.

GRILLED CHEESE SANDWICHES

To make a great grilled cheese sandwich, generously spread butter on the exterior of the bread, assemble the sandwich, and panfry it over medium heat until the bread is golden brown and the cheese is fully melted, 2–3 minutes per side. We use a cast-iron skillet, but a countertop sandwich grill (or panini press) works well, too. The bread should not be so thick that it detracts from the filling, but it also needs to hold the sandwich together; we slice ours 1–1.5 cm / ⅜–⅝ in thick. To make the cheese slice recipes here, use the instructions for the Perfectly Melting Cheese Slice on the previous page with the ingredients and quantities given below. You'll notice that some combinations call for less than half the water of others; it may seem counterintuitive, but crumbly cheeses tend to bind better with less water. If you need to finish many sandwiches in one batch, toast the slices, assemble the sandwiches, and then bake them in the oven at 190 °C / 375 °F until the cheese melts. These recipes make four sandwiches.

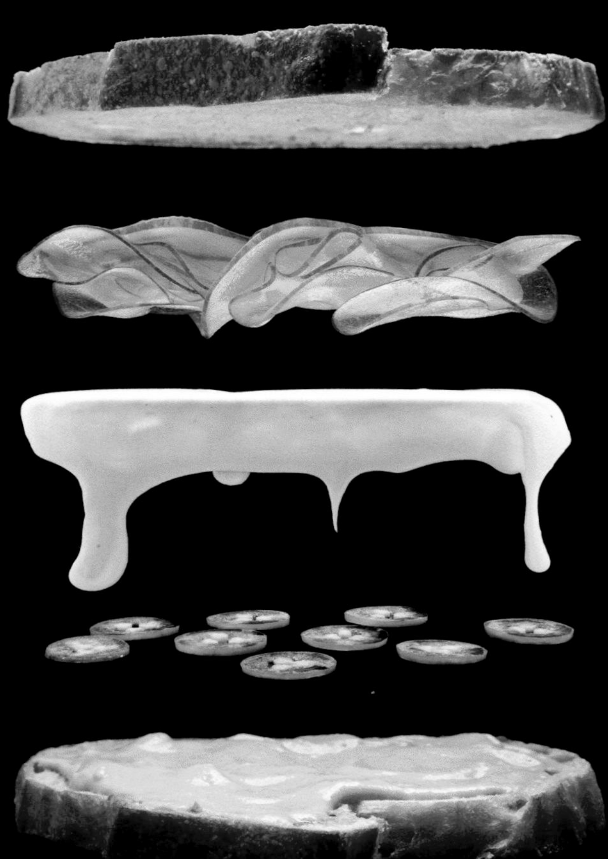

Aged White Cheddar on Sourdough with Apples

Sourdough bread		8 slices
Aged White Cheddar Cheese Slice		8 slices
Honeycrisp apple, thinly sliced		8 slices
or Grilled Applesauce without mustard see page 124	120 g	½ cup
Jalapeños, thinly sliced	30 g	3 Tbsp
Aged White Cheddar Cheese Slice:		
Water	115 g	115 mL / ½ cup
Sodium citrate	14 g	
Aged white cheddar cheese, grated	380 g	6 cups

Camembert and Gruyère on Brioche with Ham and Mushrooms

Brioche		8 slices
Camembert and Gruyère Cheese Slice		8 slices
Black Forest ham		8 slices
Button mushrooms, sliced and sautéed	100 g	⅓ cup
Dijon mustard	40 g	¼ cup
Fried eggs		4 eggs
Camembert and Gruyère Cheese Slice:		
Water	115 g	115 mL / ½ cup
Sodium citrate	14 g	
Camembert cheese, rind cut off	190 g	1½ cups
Gruyère cheese, grated	190 g	3½ cups

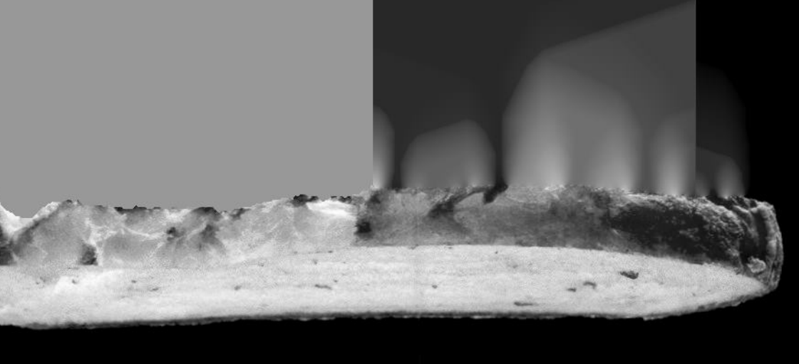

Feta on Potato Bread with Vegetable Confit

Potato bread		8 slices
Feta Cheese Slice		8 slices
Mediterranean Vegetable Confit see variation on page 126	120 g	½ cup
Basil		8–12 leaves

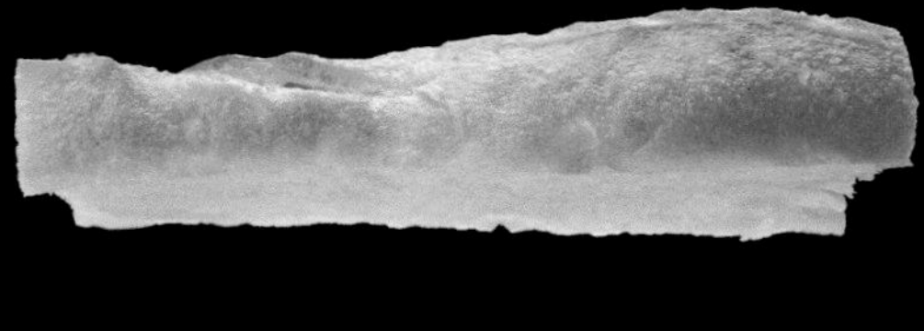

Feta Cheese Slice:

Water	38 g	38 mL / 2½ Tbsp
Sodium citrate	11 g	
Feta cheese, crumbled	380 g	3 cups

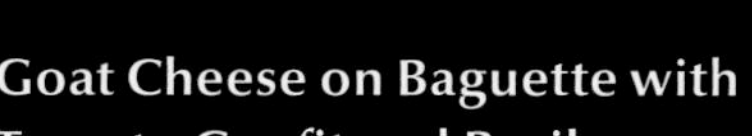

Goat Cheese on Baguette with Tomato Confit and Basil

Baguette, split in half and cut into segments 10 cm / 4 in long		4 segments
Goat Cheese Slice		8 slices
Tomato Confit see page 128	120 g	½ cup
Pistachio Pesto see page 102	80 g	¼ cup
Basil leaves		8–12 leaves

Goat Cheese Slice:

Water	38 g	38 mL / 2½ Tbsp
Sodium citrate	11 g	
Bûcheron goat cheese, rind cut off, crumbled	380 g	3 cups

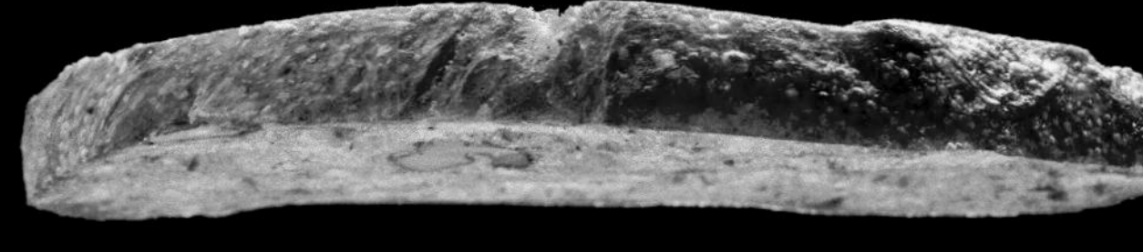

Stilton on Walnut Bread with Shallot Marmalade

Walnut bread		8 slices
Stilton Cheese Slice		8 slices
Shallot and Port Wine Marmalade	120 g	½ cup
Pear, thinly sliced		8 slices
Celery, peeled and thinly sliced	40 g	⅓ cup

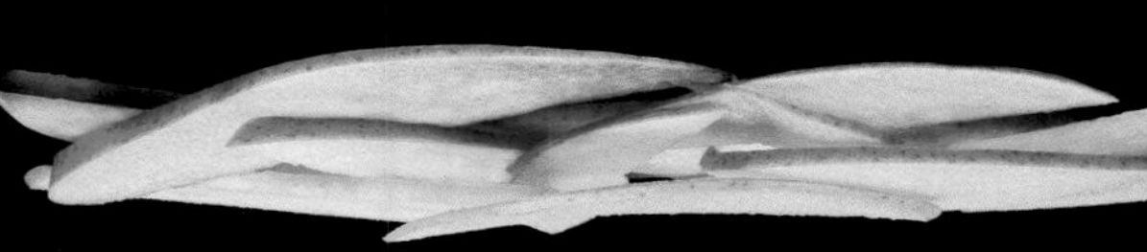

Stilton Cheese Slice:

Water	38 g	38 mL / 2½ Tbsp
Wondra	26 g	3½ Tbsp
Sodium citrate	11 g	
Stilton cheese, crumbled	380 g	3 cups

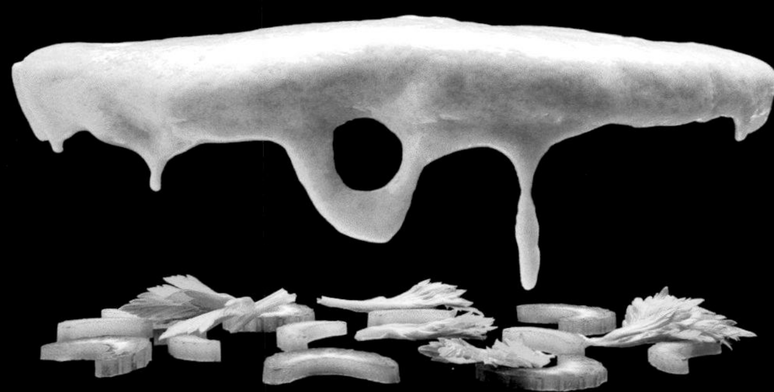

Shallot and Port Wine Marmalade:

Shallots, minced	200 g	1⅔ cups
Olive oil	30 g	35 mL / 2 Tbsp
Red port wine	130 g	130 mL / ½ cup
Thyme		1 sprig

Sweat the shallots in olive oil. Add the port and thyme, and then simmer over medium-low heat until tender and jam-like, about

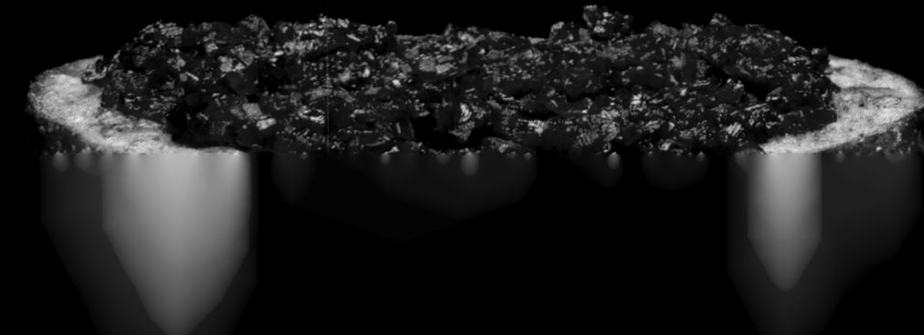

RISOTTO AND PAELLA

The time and attention necessary to make a good traditional paella or risotto can sometimes seem prohibitive. These are certainly not dishes that home cooks whip up any night for dinner. But what if we told you that you can cook paella or risotto from scratch in seven minutes flat? Or that you can parcook either one of these dishes up to three days in advance, and then finish the dish in four minutes? If you have a pressure cooker, there's no reason not to enjoy these wonderful one-pot meals more often.

Both risotto and paella get their body from short-grain rice, which releases starch during cooking to produce a thick and creamy texture. And both can be made using a variety of grains and flavors, from the classic Milanese version of risotto with white wine and saffron to more exotic concoctions, such as sea urchin, cocoa, and grapefruit. Our favorite grain and flavor combinations appear on pages 330–333.

Risotto and paella grains are best cooked until just al dente, not completely soft. Traditionally, you add liquid a little at a time, and then you stir constantly to create the starch slurry and keep it evenly dispersed. We discovered, however, that it works just as well to use a pressure cooker and to add all the water at once; the pressure cooker eliminates the need to stir.

The biggest disadvantage of the pressure cooker is that you can't just lift the lid and taste for doneness. So we aim to undercook the rice slightly, and then we put it on the stove top for a couple of minutes to perfect the texture.

THE SCIENCE OF WHY COOKS STIR RISOTTO

Starch, released by short-grain rice during cooking, is what thickens dishes like paella and risotto. Natural starches are composed of two types of polymers, amylose (which is better at gelling) and amylopectin (which thickens by binding up water). Plants contain differing ratios of each, which is why short-grain rice works for these dishes, but long-grain rice doesn't.

Inside a plant cell, starch is typically stored inside granules, which have a layered structure like an onion. During cooking, the starch granules absorb water, swell, and become sticky. But the rice doesn't thicken until the cells burst open and release the sticky granules.

That is why we stir the rice as it cooks: to break open the cells and release the starch into the cooking liquid, thereby thickening it. Continued gentle stirring then prevents lumps from forming. To see the gelling power of starch in action, allow a risotto to cool—it gels into a solid mass.

There is no need to stir rice when you cook it in a pressure cooker because the process forces so much water into the starch granules and plant cells that many more of the cells burst on their own.

Bomba Rice with Chorizo and Broccoli-Gruyère Puree, see variation on page 333

HIGHLIGHTS

Parcooking, a trick we learned from The French Laundry chef Thomas Keller, is a great time-saver. Use a freezing-cold baking sheet to **cool the rice quickly without washing away the starch**.

see page 328

These recipes work with **several kinds of short-grain rice:** carnaroli, Arborio, or Vialone Nano for risotto; bomba and Calasparra for paella; and other grains, as well.

see pages 324–325

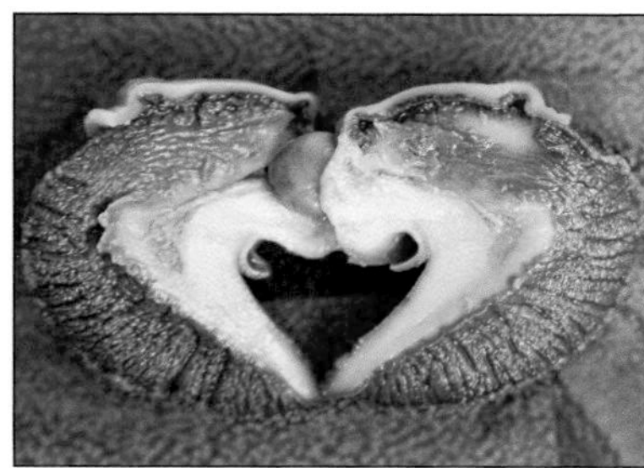

The original paella from Valencia was a humble rice stew cooked with rabbits and snails harvested from the field. Ours is garnished with snails, but less exotic toppings are good, too.

see page 326

Try our Bomba Rice with Chorizo and Broccoli-Gruyèe Puree or our **Forbidden Rice with Squid Ink and Sous Vide Clams**.

see pages 333 and 330

FURTHER READING IN *MODERNIST CUISINE*

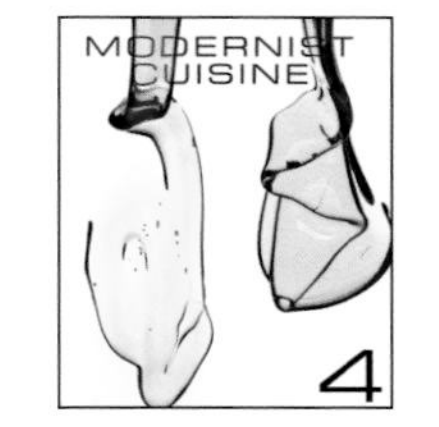

The science of starches: see pages 3·280–282, 4·20–22

Recipes for Sous Vide Clam and Oat Risotto, Root Vegetable Risotto: see pages 3·308–309

How thickening works: see pages 4·12–13

A plated-dish recipe for Paella Valenciana: see pages 5·239–245

As dry Arborio rice (far left) cooks to make a perfect al dente risotto (far right), it undergoes a remarkable transformation. See "The Science of Why Cooks Stir Risotto" on page 320 for details.

COOKING GRAINS

Great risotto and paella is traditionally a time- and labor-intensive process that requires a chef's undivided attention. Modern methods make these wonderful dishes much more practical for the home cook. Our favorite method is to pressure-cook the rice from start to finish, which can take as little as seven minutes.

If you want to prepare your grain dish in advance, parcooking followed by a quick chilling and resting step works great, as it allows you to finish the risotto for dinner in just a few minutes. We recommend this technique particularly if you are making larger quantities. Both techniques require less than a half hour of hands-on cooking time.

Below are all of the options for preparation, cooking, and finishing risotto and paella that we recommend for a variety of grains. Go with what fits the results you want and the time and equipment you have available.

HOW TO Pressure-Cook Risotto and Paella

1 Sauté the aromatic ingredients in oil or butter. Risotto and paella rices are typically cooked in a base of sautéed aromatics. In the case of risotto, classic partners are minced onion, fennel, and celery; for paella, the usual aromatic base is sofrito, a combination of minced bell pepper, seeded tomato, and onion.

2 Add the rice to the sautéing aromatics, and toast it over medium-high heat for 1–2 minutes. The grains should become shiny, golden, and slightly translucent.

3 Add a cooking liquid—typically stock for paella and a combination of wine and stock for risotto. You can instead cook the rice in water, or get creative and try combinations of vegetable juices, fruit juices, and wine or other kinds of alcohol. Whole grains require more liquid than hulled and polished grains do.

4 Pressure-cook the rice in liquid at a gauge pressure of 1 bar/15 psi until it is just al dente; see the table below for cooking times. Begin timing as soon as the cooker reaches full pressure.

5 Depressurize the cooker quickly by running tepid water over the rim.

6 Check the rice for doneness. It should be nearly cooked to a perfect al dente. You may need to add more liquid, as directed in the recipes, or to simmer it for 1–3 minutes more.

7 Season the rice with salt. Finish risotto dishes with butter and freshly grated cheese, or fold in cooked vegetables, vegetable purees, or fresh herbs. For paellas, chefs usually focus on the broth and garnishes. In traditional Valencia-style paella, for example, rabbit and snails are added. Modern versions often emphasize various kinds of fresh shellfish.

Cooking Times

If you don't have a pressure cooker, you can cook the risotto, paella, or other grain stew the traditional way. Use the times in the table below and the flavor ideas on pages 330–333 as guidelines. Batches that are larger than those in our recipes will take longer to cook.

	Pressure-cook (min)	Cook on the stove top (min)
bomba rice	7	22
forbidden rice	12	25
risotto rices (Arborio, Vialone Nano, carnaroli)	6	18–20
short-grain Japanese rice	4	13–15
farro	15	22–25
pearl barley	20	28–30
quinoa	4	15–18
steel-cut oats, rinsed	7	12–15

Safety tips for pressure-cooking: see page 33

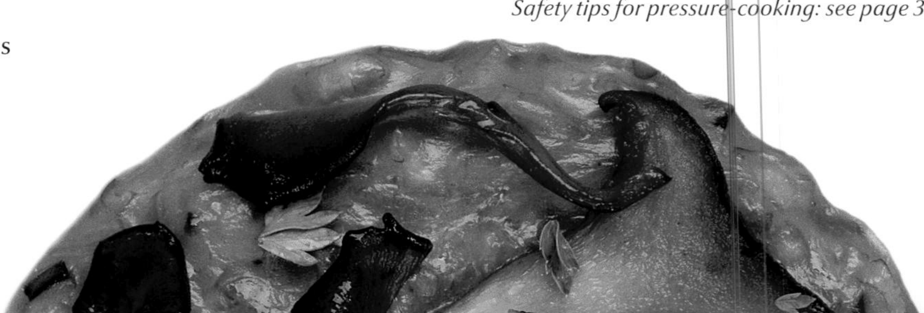

HOW TO Parcook and Finish Risotto and Paella

1 While sautéing the aromatic ingredients as described in step 1 on the previous page, freeze a metal baking sheet (or several, if you are making a large batch) for use in step 5.

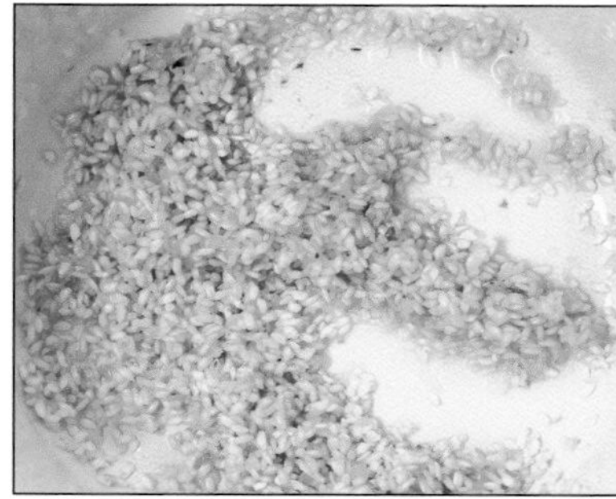

2 Add the rice, and toast it with the sautéed aromatics until it turns shiny, golden, and nearly translucent.

3 Add liquid, and parcook for the time indicated in the table below, stirring frequently. Alternatively, parcook in a pressure cooker at a gauge pressure of 1 bar / 15 psi, for the time indicated in the table, and then quickly depressurize the cooker by running tepid water over the rim.

4 Working quickly, strain the liquid from the parcooked grain, and reserve it for use in step 6.

5 Transfer the drained rice to the frozen baking sheet, and spread it into a thin layer to cool. Cover, and refrigerate the rice until you are ready to serve it.

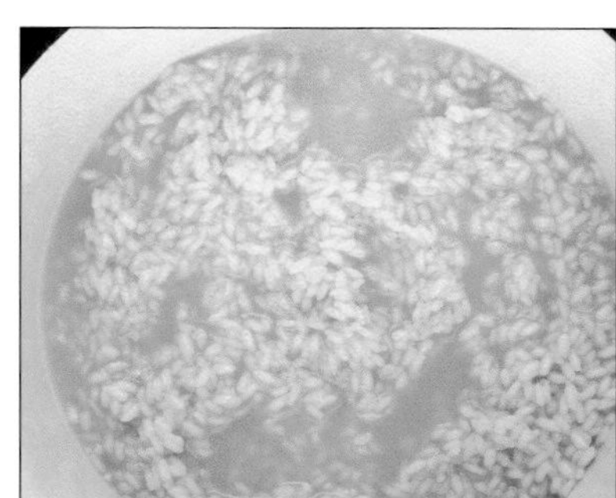

6 Just before serving, finish cooking the grain by stirring in the reserved liquid and simmering it in a pot until it becomes al dente. You may need to add a little more liquid.

7 Fold in any additional flavorings, season, and serve. The additions can be as simple as a bit of grated cheese and butter or as complex as vegetable purees and braised meats.

Parcooking Times

You can parcook rice and grains, and then refrigerate them for up to 3 days before finishing and serving. Use the times in the table below for parcooking in a pressure cooker or on the stove stop. When you are ready to finish the dish, simmer it as described in step 6 above for 2–5 minutes as a rule of thumb.

	In a pressure cooker (min)	On the stove top (min)
bomba rice	4	8
forbidden rice	7	17
risotto rices (Arborio, Vialone Nano, carnaroli)	3	6
short-grain Japanese rice	2½	4
farro	10	20–22
pearl barley	12	25
quinoa	2	7
steel-cut oats, rinsed	5	7

Safety tips for pressure-cooking: see page 33

PRESSURE-COOKED PAELLA DEL BOSCO

YIELD:	*four servings (400 g / 2 cups, excluding snails)*
TIME ESTIMATE:	*25 minutes overall*
STORAGE NOTES:	*serve immediately; cooked rice keeps for up to 3 days when refrigerated*
LEVEL OF DIFFICULTY:	*easy*
SPECIAL REQUIREMENTS:	*pressure cooker, bomba rice, pimentón dulce, piquillo peppers, Brown Chicken Stock (see variation on page 85), Sous Vide Braised Snails (optional, see page 293)*

Paella has gained a reputation as a dish for special occasions because it is so time-consuming to make. But it doesn't have to be: with little more than 25 minutes of total labor, you can use this recipe to make incredibly flavorful and creamy Valencia-style paella. We chose to add snails because they are historically an original garnish for paella.

Cooked chicken, shrimp, crabmeat, or duck breast can all be folded into the rice instead of, or along with, the snails. For an elegant touch, finely shave some fresh porcini mushrooms, when they are in season, over the finished dish.

INGREDIENT	WEIGHT	VOLUME	SCALING	PROCEDURE
Olive oil	40 g	45 mL / 3 Tbsp	27%	① Sweat the vegetables in oil in the base of a pressure cooker over medium heat until tender and translucent, about 3 minutes.
Piquillo peppers (store-bought), minced	50 g	⅓ cup	33%	
Fennel, minced	25 g	¼ cup	17%	
Sweet onion, minced	25 g	3 Tbsp	17%	
Carrot, minced	20 g	2 Tbsp	13%	
Garlic, minced	7.5 g	1 Tbsp	5%	
Bomba rice (or other short-grain paella rice)	150 g	¾ cup	100%	② Stir into the vegetable mixture, and cook until the rice turns shiny and translucent, about 2 minutes.
Brown Chicken Stock see variation on page 85	300 g	300 mL / 1¼ cups	200%	③ Stir into the rice mixture. ④ Pressure-cook at a gauge pressure of 1 bar / 15 psi for 7 minutes. Start timing when full pressure is reached. ⑤ Depressurize the cooker. ⑥ Check the rice for tenderness. It should be al dente. If necessary, simmer uncovered for a minute or two longer.
Dry sherry	70 g	70 mL / ⅓ cup	47%	
Pimentón dulce (smoked, sweet paprika)	7 g	1 Tbsp	5%	⑦ Stir into the rice, and let rest for 1 minute.
Thyme leaves	2 g	1 Tbsp	1%	
Saffron threads (optional)		5 threads		
Salt	to taste			⑧ Season.
Sous Vide Braised Snails (optional), cut in half and warmed see page 293	200 g	24 snails	133%	⑨ Fold into the paella, and serve it immediately.
Lemon zest, finely grated	to taste			

Safety tips for pressure-cooking: see page 33

TO MAKE AHEAD

Freeze a baking sheet for at least 30 minutes. Follow steps 1–5, but pressure-cook for just 4 minutes in step 4. Drain the rice, reserving the broth. Quickly cool the rice mixture by spreading it in a thin layer on the frozen baking sheet. Refrigerate the rice and cooking liquid in separate containers for up to 3 days. To finish, combine the rice mixture and broth in a pot, and simmer until al dente, about 4 minutes. Then continue with step 7.

1 Sweat the vegetables in olive oil in the base of a pressure cooker over medium heat until they become tender and translucent but not brown, about 3 minutes.

2 Stir the rice into the vegetable mixture, and cook until the rice turns shiny and slightly translucent, about 2 minutes.

3 Stir the chicken stock and sherry into the rice mixture.

4 Pressure-cook the mixture at a gauge pressure of 1 bar / 15 psi for 7 minutes. Start timing as soon as full pressure has been reached. Larger amounts of rice will need more time.

5 Run tepid water over the rim of the cooker to depressurize it quickly.

6 Check the rice for doneness. The grains should be al dente: firm to the bite but not hard or crunchy. If the rice is not quite done, simmer it for 1–2 minutes more, uncovered. Stir it constantly.

7 Stir the pimentón, thyme, and saffron into the rice. Let the paella rest for 1 minute so that the flavors infuse and the starch slightly cools and thickens.

8 Season the paella with salt to taste.

9 Fold the snails and lemon zest into the paella. Garnish with additional snails, and serve it immediately.

VEGETABLE RISOTTO

YIELD:	*four servings (500 g / 2 cups)*
TIME ESTIMATE:	*40 minutes overall, including 30 minutes unattended*
STORAGE NOTES:	*serve immediately; parcooked rice and cooking liquid keep for up to 3 days when refrigerated*
LEVEL OF DIFFICULTY:	*easy*
SPECIAL REQUIREMENTS:	*juicer*

For traditional risotto, chefs insist that the rice requires constant stirring and fussing until the very last minute. We agree that good risotto should be al dente and is best served immediately, but we prefer a quicker method that requires much less of the cook's attention: parcook the grains, and then chill them on a frozen baking sheet, which stops the cooking without rinsing away the valuable starches. Finishing, which can be done days later, then takes just a few minutes before serving.

The results are just as good as the old-fashioned method. Good stock, fresh vegetable juices, and aged Gouda cheese give this version a bold vegetable flavor. Risotto is a wonderful base for a variety of flavors; see pages 330–333 for suggestions.

INGREDIENT	WEIGHT	VOLUME	SCALING	PROCEDURE
Shallots, minced	40 g	6 Tbsp	20%	① Place a baking sheet in the freezer for at least 30 minutes.
Neutral frying oil see page xxii	20 g	20 mL / 1½ Tbsp	10%	② Sweat the shallots in oil in a medium pot until tender and translucent, about 2 minutes.
Carnaroli rice (or other short-grain rice for risotto, such as Arborio or Vialone Nano)	200 g	1 cup	100%	③ Stir into the shallot mixture, and cook until shiny and slightly toasted, about 2 minutes.
Vegetable stock see page 89	180 g	180 mL / ¾ cup	90%	④ Stir into the rice mixture, and simmer for 6 minutes to parcook the rice. ⑤ Drain, reserving the cooking liquid. ⑥ Spread the rice in a single layer on the frozen baking sheet to cool. ⑦ When you are ready to complete the risotto, combine the cooled rice and cooking liquid in a pot, and simmer the mixture over medium-high heat, stirring constantly, until the liquid has thickened and the rice is al dente, 3–5 minutes.
Fresh carrot juice	110 g	110 mL / ½ cup from 2–3 carrots	55%	
Fresh celery juice (or additional stock)	110 g	110 mL / ½ cup from 3–4 stalks	55%	
Dry vermouth or white wine	50 g	50 mL / 3½ Tbsp	25%	
Aged Gouda cheese, finely grated	100 g	1⅓ cups	50%	⑧ Stir into the warm risotto.
Unsalted butter, cubed	12 g	1 Tbsp	6%	
Salt	to taste			⑨ Season the risotto, and serve it immediately.

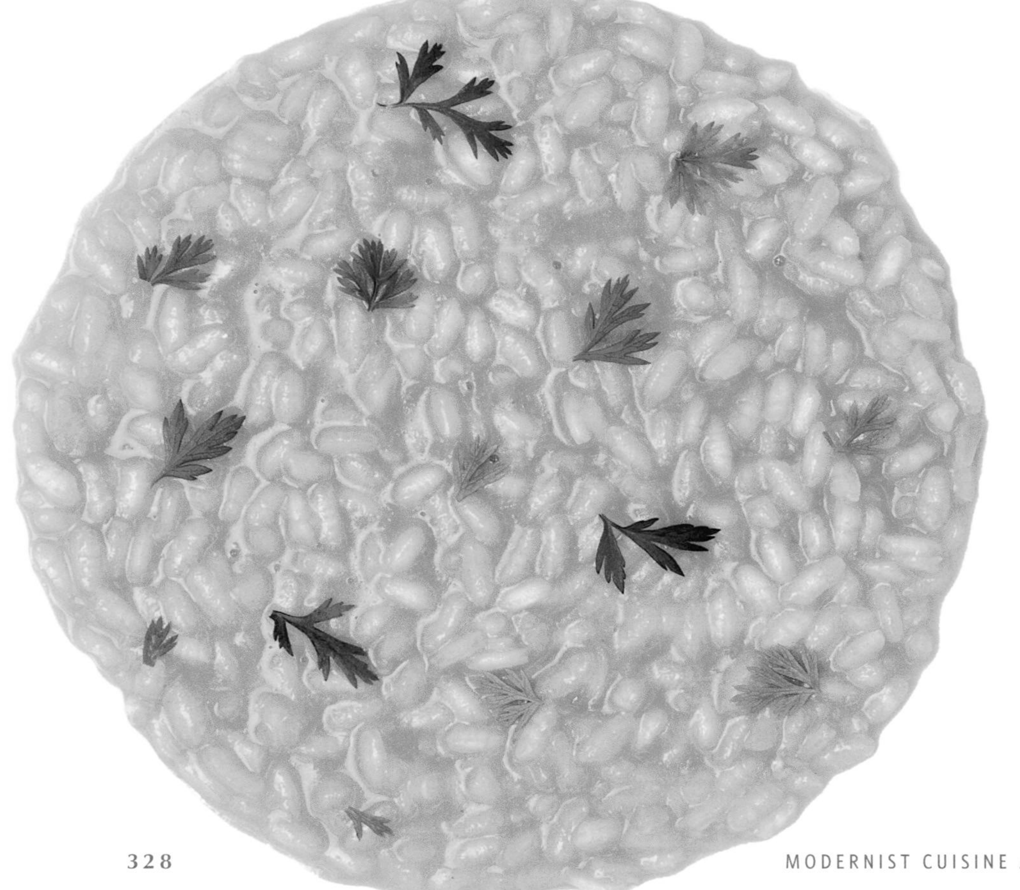

1 Place a baking sheet in the freezer, and allow it to chill for at least 30 minutes.

2 Place the shallots and oil together in a medium pot, and sweat until the shallots are tender and translucent but not brown, about 2 minutes.

3 Stir the rice into the shallot mixture, and cook until the rice turns shiny and slightly toasted, about 2 minutes.

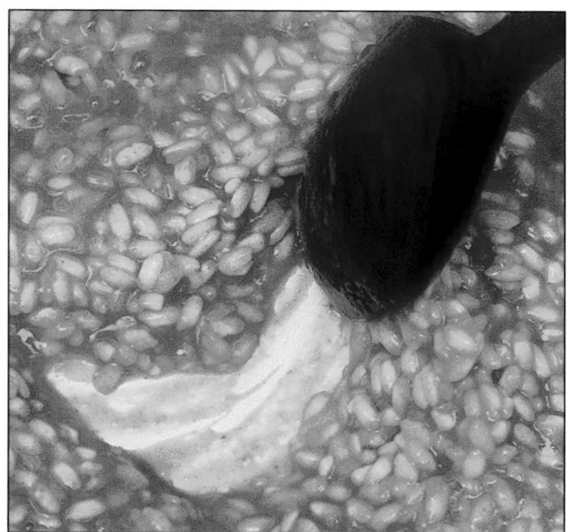

4 Stir the vegetable stock, vegetable juices, and vermouth or wine into the rice mixture, and simmer it for 6 minutes. This parcooks the grains, but they should remain firm on the inside.

5 Drain the rice, reserving the cooking liquid.

6 Quickly spread the rice in a single layer on the frozen baking sheet to stop the cooking. You can speed the chilling process by putting the baking sheet back in the freezer for 5 minutes.

7 When you are ready to finish the cooking, combine the cooled rice and cooking liquid, and simmer over medium-high heat, stirring constantly, until the liquid has thickened and the rice is al dente, 3–5 minutes. Add liquid as needed.

8 Stir the grated cheese and butter into the warm risotto.

9 Season the risotto with salt to taste, and serve it immediately.

VARIATION: **Pressure-Cooked Risotto**

To make risotto even faster than this recipe does, cook it in a pressure cooker. Follow steps 1–6 in the recipe for Pressure-Cooked Paella del Bosco (see page 326), but use the ingredients and quantities given for the Vegetable Risotto recipe. Then continue at step 8.

RISOTTO AND PAELLA VARIATIONS

Each of the variations below includes complete cooking instructions, but follows the general method for making Pressure-Cooked Paella del Bosco on page 326. In each case, use a gauge pressure of 1 bar / 15 psi, start timing as soon as full pressure has been reached, and depressurize the cooker quickly by running tepid water over the rim before opening it; see the safety tips for pressure-cooking on page 324. If the rice or grain is not quite done after pressure-cooking, simmer it for 1–2 minutes more. To make a dish having a drier consistency, simmer the mixture after pressure-cooking; for a soupy, creamier dish, add more liquid. If parcooking the grain, as described in the recipe on page 328, you may need to increase the quantity of liquid by up to 25% to allow for increased evaporation.

You can substitute finely minced sweet onions for the shallots in these recipes, and use additional butter or olive oil to add richness.

Forbidden Rice with Squid Ink and Sous Vide Clams

Shallots, minced	30 g	¼ cup
Neutral frying oil	20 g	20 mL / 1½ Tbsp
Forbidden rice	150 g	¾ cup
Pressure-Cooked Crustacean Stock see page 88	150 g	150 mL / ⅝ cup
Fino sherry	75 g	75 mL / 5 Tbsp
Squid ink	7.6 g	1½ tsp
Clam meat, cooked sous vide* see page 286		12 clams
Extra-virgin olive oil	50 g	55 mL / ¼ cup
Salt	to taste	
Meyer lemon zest, grated	as needed	

Sauté the shallots in oil over medium heat in the base of a pressure cooker until translucent, about 3 minutes. Add the rice, and cook over medium heat for 1 minute more. Stir in the crustacean stock, sherry, and squid ink, and pressure-cook for 12 minutes. While the rice is cooking, remove the bellies from the clams, and chop the remaining pieces. Fold the chopped clams and olive oil into the cooked rice. Season with salt, and garnish with the clam bellies and grated lemon zest.

**Safety tips for lightly cooked food: see page xxv*

Arborio Rice with Caramelized Squash and Saffron

Shallots, minced	20 g	2 Tbsp
Neutral frying oil	20 g	20 mL / 1½ Tbsp
Arborio or similar short-grain risotto rice	150 g	¾ cup
Fresh carrot juice	200 g	200 mL / ⅞ cup
Chardonnay or other fruity white wine	100 g	100 mL / ⅜ cup
Butternut squash puree see variation on page 180	100 g	⅜ cup
Saffron		4–5 threads
Grana Padano cheese, grated	90 g	1¾ cups
Salt	to taste	
Marcona almonds	as needed	

Sauté the shallots in oil over medium heat in the base of a pressure cooker until translucent, about 3 minutes. Stir in the rice, and cook for 1 minute more. Add the carrot juice and Chardonnay, and pressure-cook for 6 minutes. Stir in the squash puree, saffron threads, and cheese. Season with salt, and garnish with a fine shaving of Microplaned almonds.

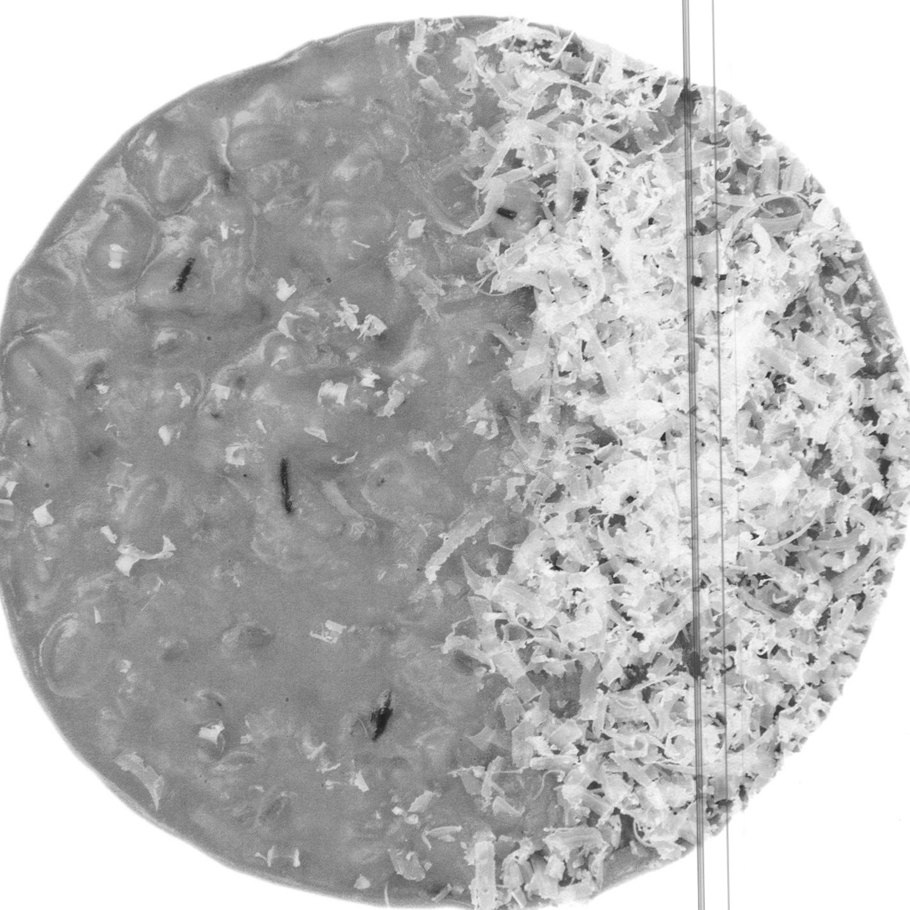

Barley with Wild Mushrooms and Red Wine

Wild mushrooms (maitake, oyster, shiitake), minced	140 g	1¾ cups
Shallots, minced	40 g	⅓ cup
Unsalted butter	35 g	3 Tbsp
Neutral frying oil see page xxii	20 g	20 mL / 1½ Tbsp
Pearl barley	150 g	¾ cup
Mushroom Stock, enhanced with crumbled dry porcinis see page 91	180 g	180 mL / ¾ cup
Red wine (Syrah)	100 g	100 mL / ⅜ cup
Gruyère cheese, grated	65 g	½ cup
Salt	to taste	
Black pepper	to taste	

Sauté the wild mushrooms and shallots in the butter and oil over medium heat in the base of a pressure cooker until translucent, about 3 minutes. Stir in the barley, and cook for 1 minute more. Add the mushroom stock and wine, and pressure-cook for 20 minutes. Stir in the grated cheese until melted. Season with salt and pepper. Garnish with additional cheese and sautéed mushrooms, if desired.

Steel-Cut Oats with Sous Vide Braised Snails

Steel-cut oats	150 g	⅞ cup
Chicken stock see page 84	230 g	230 mL / 1 cup
Pastis or ouzo	50 g	65 mL / ¼ cup
Pressure-Cooked Garlic Confit, sieved see page 126	60 g	⅜ cup
Unsalted butter	50 g	¼ cup
Parmigiano-Reggiano	40 g	½ cup
Sous Vide Braised Snails see page 293	65 g	about 8 snails
Salt	to taste	
Green apple, diced	25 g	¼ cup
Italian parsley, minced	8 g	2½ Tbsp

Combine the oats with the chicken stock and pastis or ouzo in a pressure cooker, and pressure-cook for 7 minutes. Stir in the garlic confit, butter, and Parmigiano-Reggiano. Fold in the snails gently. Season with salt, and garnish with the apple and Italian parsley. Garnish with additional snails and grated cheese, if desired.

This recipe was inspired by Heston Blumenthal's famous Snails with Porridge dish.

Farro with Chicken, Artichokes, and Black Olives

Shallots, minced	30 g	¼ cup
Neutral frying oil see page xxii	28 g	30 mL / 2 Tbsp
Farro	150 g	¾ cup
Vegetable stock see page 89	200 g	200 mL / ⅞ cup
Dry white wine	80 g	80 mL / ⅓ cup
Sous Vide Chicken, diced see page 244	120 g	¾ cup
Microwave-cooked artichoke hearts, sliced see table on page 347	100 g	2–3 hearts
Olive oil	40 g	45 mL / 3 Tbsp
Black olives, slivered	18 g	2 Tbsp
Salt	to taste	

Sauté the shallots in oil over medium heat in the base of a pressure cooker until translucent, about 3 minutes. Add the farro, and cook for 1 minute more. Stir in the vegetable stock and wine, and pressure-cook for 15 minutes. Fold in the chicken, artichoke hearts, olive oil, and olives. Season with salt.

Quinoa with Pistachio Pesto and Asparagus

Quinoa, rinsed and drained	150 g	⅞ cup
Neutral frying oil see page xxii	10 g	10 mL / 2 tsp
Vegetable stock see page 89	275 g	275 mL / 1⅛ cups
Dry vermouth	75 g	75 mL / 5 Tbsp
Asparagus, very thinly sliced	70 g	1 cup
Pistachio Pesto see page 102	200 g	¾ cup
Unsalted butter, cubed	20 g	2 Tbsp
Salt	to taste	
Ricotta salata, finely grated	40 g	¾ cup

Sauté the quinoa for 1 minute in oil over medium heat in the base of a pressure cooker. Add the vegetable stock and vermouth, and pressure-cook for 4 minutes. Stir in the sliced asparagus, pistachio pesto, and butter, and then season with salt. Garnish with grated ricotta salata and some sautéed asparagus tips.

Bomba Rice with Chorizo and Broccoli-Gruyère Puree

Shallots, minced	50 g	6 Tbsp
Neutral frying oil see page xxii	40 g	45 mL / 3 Tbsp
Spanish chorizo, casing removed	150 g	¾ cup
Bomba or similar short-grain paella rice	150 g	¾ cup
Water	230 g	230 mL / 1 cup
Wheat beer	80 g	80 mL / ⅓ cup
Broccoli-Gruyère Puree see variation on page 181	150 g	¾ cup
Extra-virgin olive oil	70 g	80 mL / ⅓ cup
Salt	to taste	
Garlic, thinly sliced and fried until crisp	as needed	

Sauté the shallots in oil over medium heat in the base of a pressure cooker until translucent, about 3 minutes. Add the chorizo and rice, and cook over medium heat for 1 minute more. Stir in the water and beer, and pressure-cook for 7 minutes. Stir in the broccoli puree and extra-virgin olive oil. Season with salt, and garnish with fried garlic, and a few blanched broccoli florets.

Arborio Rice with Sea Urchin and Cocoa

Shallots, minced	35 g	¼ cup
Neutral frying oil see page xxii	20 g	20 mL / 1½ Tbsp
Arborio or similar short-grain risotto rice	150 g	¾ cup
Sous Vide Fish Stock see page 87	200 g	200 mL / ⅞ cup
Dry sake	60 g	60 mL / ¼ cup
Freshly squeezed grapefruit juice	40 g	40 mL / ¼ cup
Sea urchin, pressed through a sieve*	30 g	3 Tbsp
Grapefruit zest, finely grated	4 g	1 Tbsp
Cocoa powder	as needed	
Tarragon leaves	as needed	

Sauté the shallots in oil over medium heat in the base of a pressure cooker until translucent, about 3 minutes. Add the rice, and cook over medium heat for 1 minute more. Add the fish stock, sake, and grapefruit juice, and pressure-cook for 6 minutes. Stir in the sea urchin and grapefruit zest. Season with salt, and garnish with tarragon leaves, a dusting of cocoa powder, and sea urchin tongue.

**Safety tips for lightly cooked food: see page xxv*

CORNMEAL

Corn, or maize, was domesticated in the New World, but it has become one of the most important foods across the globe. One of its most common forms is cornmeal: corn that has been dried and then ground. Cornmeal comes in various degrees of coarseness. It's generally cooked in liquid until tender and then either eaten immediately or set and fried.

Variations on cornmeal porridge are widely eaten as staple foods: it is known as polenta in Italy, and grits or mush in the American South. Firmer variations that use cornmeal as the base of a dough include johnnycakes and hush puppies. Tamales and tortillas are made throughout Latin America from nixtamalized maize (see "The Science of Nixtamalization" at right).

Coarser grinds of cornmeal are hearty, having an intense corn flavor. But traditional methods of making them require stirring over a hot flame for up to an hour. Cornmeal now comes in a more practical "instant" version, but that is finely ground, precooked, and thus stripped of both flavor and nutrients. Pressure-cooking the cornmeal in canning jars, as we do here, offers the best of both approaches. It's a hands-off, fast way to cook any grind of cornmeal.

THE SCIENCE OF NIXTAMALIZATION

In Mexico, coarse-ground corn flour called masa harina is used to make fresh corn tortillas and tamales. The corn is treated with limewater in a process called nixtamalization (for the Aztec word *nixtamal*, meaning cornmeal). The process makes it easier for humans to digest corn and to extract more of its nutrients, particularly the vitamin niacin.

When corn became a staple of diets in Europe and the United States, nixtamalization was not used, and the germ of the corn was also often removed during milling. The result was an outbreak of a disfiguring skin disease called pellagra among poorer people whose diets were largely limited to foods made from corn. For many years, the epidemic was blamed on germs or toxins carried by corn. But eventually scientific studies in the United States discovered the true cause: niacin deficiency. Dietary improvements have now all but eliminated pellagra from developed regions.

Nixtamalization gives masa harina a distinctive toasted, mineral flavor. You can substitute it in our grits or polenta recipes.

HIGHLIGHTS

Canning jars insulate the corn from the direct heat of the bottom of the pan, so you don't have to constantly stir to avoid sticking and burning.

see page 336

The focus of tamales is often the filling, not the corn. These fresh-corn tamales are more like a delicate steamed cornbread, good enough to eat alone.

see page 340

Use leftover tamale batter and a few egg whites to make hush puppies.

see page 340

Pressure-cook grits with shrimp stock to get the authentic texture and a taste of the Gulf without constant stirring.

see page 338

FURTHER READING IN *MODERNIST CUISINE*

The history of how corn went global: see page 3·268

Recipes for Corn Pebbles, Corn Foam, Corn Bread, and Crispy Corn Pudding: see pages 4·36, 4·273, 5·76, and 5·104

PRESSURE-COOKED POLENTA

YIELD:	*four servings (450 g / 2 cups)*
TIME ESTIMATE:	*20 minutes overall, including 8 minutes of preparation and 12 minutes unattended*
STORAGE NOTES:	*keeps for 3 days when refrigerated*
LEVEL OF DIFFICULTY:	*moderate*
SPECIAL REQUIREMENTS:	*pressure cooker, two 500 mL / 16 oz canning jars, ricotta salata or Cotija cheese*
GOES WELL WITH:	*Strawberry Marinara (see page 114)*

For generations, Italian cooks have adopted foreign ingredients and made them their own. Amazingly enough, tomatoes were not originally part of Italian cuisine—nor were basil, eggplant, garlic, or pasta. Once corn was introduced to Italy in the 16th century, it was grown widely in the Po Valley, and northeastern Italians developed polenta as we know it today. The traditional version can take more than an hour to cook; a pressure cooker greatly reduces the time and effort required. We cook the polenta in corn stock for an incredibly intense corn taste. Most dry polenta is made from plain field corn, so a stock made from sweet corn adds depth to the flavor profile.

INGREDIENT	WEIGHT	VOLUME	SCALING	PROCEDURE
Clarified, unsalted butter or neutral-tasting oil see page 119	15 g	15 mL / 1 Tbsp	15%	① Heat in a pan over low heat.
Dry polenta (ground cornmeal, not instant)	100 g	⅝ cup	100%	② Add to the pan, and toast, stirring constantly, until golden brown, about 4 minutes.
Toasted Corn Stock, vegetable stock, meat stock, or water see page 90	300 g	300 mL / 1¼ cups	300%	③ Divide the toasted cornmeal evenly into two 500 mL / 16 oz canning jars. ④ Stir half of the corn stock or water into each jar. Tighten the lids fully, and then unscrew one-quarter turn. ⑤ Place a metal rack or trivet on the base of a pressure cooker, add 2.5 cm / 1 in of water, and place the filled jars on the trivet. ⑥ Pressure-cook at a gauge pressure of 1 bar / 15 psi for 12 minutes. Start timing when full pressure is reached. ⑦ Depressurize the cooker, and let the jars cool slightly before opening. ⑧ Spoon the cooked polenta into a small pot.
Mascarpone or cream cheese	20 g	4 tsp	20%	⑨ Stir into the cooked polenta, over low heat, until fully incorporated.
Ricotta salata or Cotija cheese, finely grated	15 g	3 Tbsp	15%	
Basil, julienned	1 g	3 leaves	1%	⑩ Season the polenta, and garnish it with basil and grated cheese. It goes well with marinara sauce (see pages 112 and 114).
Ricotta salata	as needed			
Salt	to taste			

Safety tips for pressure-cooking: see page 33

1 Heat the clarified butter or oil in a pan over low heat. Using clarified butter avoids any specks of browned butter in the finished polenta.

2 Add the cornmeal to the pan, and toast it, stirring constantly, until it turns golden brown, about 4 minutes. This adds a nice, nutty flavor to the polenta.

3 Divide the toasted cornmeal evenly into two 500 mL / 16 oz canning jars.

4 Stir half (150 g / 150 mL / ⅝ cup) of the corn stock or water into each jar. Tighten the lids fully, and then unscrew them one-quarter turn so that the jars don't explode.

5 Place a metal rack or trivet on the base of the pressure cooker, pour in water to a depth of 2.5 cm / 1 in, and then place the filled jars on the trivet.

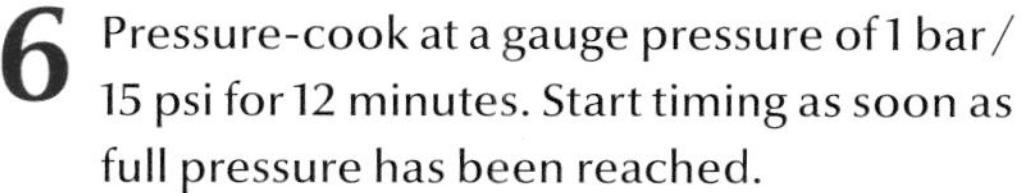

6 Pressure-cook at a gauge pressure of 1 bar / 15 psi for 12 minutes. Start timing as soon as full pressure has been reached.

7 Depressurize the cooker quickly by running tepid water over the rim. Let the jars cool slightly before opening them. This helps to avoid splattering.

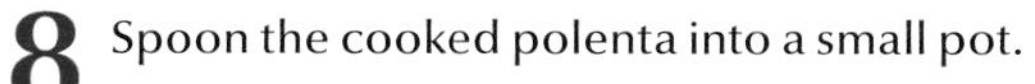

8 Spoon the cooked polenta into a small pot.

9 Stir the mascarpone and the ricotta salata into the polenta over low heat until the cheeses are fully incorporated. For special dinners, we add even more mascarpone for a richer mouthfeel.

10 Season the polenta, and garnish it with marinara sauce (see page 112), grated ricotta salata, and julienned basil.

TO MAKE AHEAD

After step 7, you can refrigerate the polenta until you are ready to use it. To reheat the polenta, warm it in a saucepan over low heat, and stir in a few additional tablespoons of water or cream.

VARIATION: **Corn Juice Grits**

For an even more intense corn flavor, substitute corn juice for the corn stock. Juice 1.5 kg / 10 cups of fresh or frozen corn kernels, and allow the juice to sit undisturbed until the natural starch settles to the bottom, about 2 hours. Use the juice in the recipe; discard the starch.

SHRIMP AND GRITS

YIELD:	*four servings (950 g / 4 cups)*
TIME ESTIMATE:	*50 minutes overall, including 30 minutes of preparation and 20 minutes unattended*
STORAGE NOTES:	*serve immediately*
LEVEL OF DIFFICULTY:	*easy*
SPECIAL REQUIREMENTS:	*sous vide setup, pressure cooker, two 500 mL / 16 oz canning jars, Pressure-Cooked Crustacean Stock (see page 88), Redeye Gravy (see page 96)*

You can make grits from course-ground cornmeal of nearly any variety: white, yellow, or blue. The kind of corn and size of the grind affect the cooking time and the amount of water needed, however. Avoid instant grits, which offer shorter cooking times but only at the cost of a much blander flavor. Instead, use a pressure cooker and enjoy the real dish, quickly and without constant stirring. For a slightly more traditional take, top a bowl of grits with prawns, either seared or poached sous vide (see the table on page 286).

INGREDIENT	WEIGHT	VOLUME	SCALING	PROCEDURE
Eggs		4 large		① Preheat a water bath to **65** °C / **149** °F. ② Cook the eggs in their shells sous vide for 45 minutes.
Pressure-Cooked Crustacean Stock (shrimp) see page 88	500 g	500 mL / 2 cups	400%	③ Stir well to combine, and then divide evenly between two 500 mL / 16 oz canning jars. Tighten the lids fully, and then unscrew one-quarter turn. ④ Place a rack or trivet in the base of a pressure cooker, add 2.5 cm / 1 in of water, and place the filled jars on the trivet. ⑤ Pressure-cook at a gauge pressure of 1 bar / 15 psi for 20 minutes. Start timing when full pressure is reached. ⑥ Depressurize the cooker quickly by running tepid water over the rim. Let the jar contents cool slightly before opening to avoid splattering. ⑦ Spoon the cooked grits into a small pot, and stir them well.
Corn grits (coarse-ground cornmeal)	125 g	¾ cup	100%	
Unsalted butter, cubed	50 g	3 Tbsp	40%	⑧ Stir into the grits over low heat.
Salt	to taste			⑨ Season the grits, and divide them evenly into serving bowls. ⑩ Top each bowl with a peeled, soft-cooked egg.
Redeye Gravy, warm see page 96	80 g	½ cup	64%	⑪ Pour over the grits and eggs, and serve immediately.

Safety tips for pressure-cooking: see page 33

VARIATION: **Cheese Grits**
Substitute milk, water, chicken stock, or vegetable stock for the crustacean stock. At step 8, stir in 100 g / ½ cup each of heavy cream and grated cheddar cheese when you add the butter. Top with sliced scallions and green chilies instead of gravy.

1 Preheat a water bath to **65** °C / **149** °F.

2 Cook the eggs sous vide in their shells for 45 minutes. This yields poached eggs with a delicate, creamy texture. You can proceed with steps 3–9 while the eggs cook.

3 Stir the crustacean stock and grits to combine them. Divide the mixture evenly between two 500 mL / 16 oz canning jars. Tighten the lids fully, and then unscrew them one-quarter turn; this prevents them from exploding. Alternatively, freeze the stock, and then vacuum seal it with the grits in a bag rated for the higher temperature of a pressure cooker (shown below).

4 Place a metal rack or trivet in the base of a pressure cooker, add water to a depth of 2.5 cm / 1 in, and then place the filled jars on the trivet.

5 Pressure-cook the grits at a gauge pressure of 1 bar / 15 psi for 20 minutes. Start timing as soon as full pressure has been reached. The grits cook slightly faster, in about 15 minutes, when vacuum sealed in a bag rather than placed in canning jars.

6 Depressurize the cooker quickly by running tepid water over the rim. Allow the jar contents to cool slightly before opening them so that they don't splatter.

7 Spoon the cooked grits into a small pot, and stir them well.

8 Stir the butter into the grits over low heat.

9 Season the grits with salt. Divide them evenly into four serving bowls.

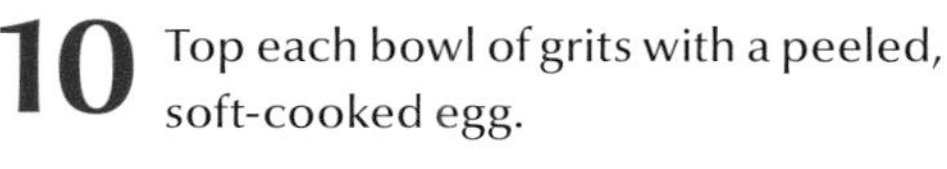

10 Top each bowl of grits with a peeled, soft-cooked egg.

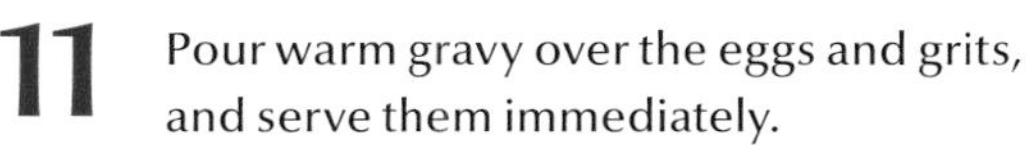

11 Pour warm gravy over the eggs and grits, and serve them immediately.

PRESSURE-COOKED FRESH-CORN TAMALES

YIELD:	*six to 10 servings (1.5 kg / about 20 tamales)*
TIME ESTIMATE:	*3½ hours overall, including 1 hour of preparation and 2½ hours unattended*
STORAGE NOTES:	*keeps for 3 days when refrigerated or up to 6 months when frozen*
LEVEL OF DIFFICULTY:	*moderate*
SPECIAL REQUIREMENTS:	*stand mixer, food processor, pressure cooker, masa harina, dried corn husks*
GOES WELL WITH:	*Pressure-Cooked Carnitas (see page 218), Salsa Verde (see page 111)*

Tamales, made of steamed corn batter, are the Latin American version of a set cornmeal mush popular in the American South or the set polenta popular in Italy. These tamales are intensely flavored of corn. They are a marvelous side dish. If you prefer more of an entree, fill them with shredded meat such as carnitas (see page 218), short ribs (see variation on page 221), or adobo (see page 224). Or experiment with nontraditional fillings: vegetables or grated Cotija, ricotta, or white cheddar cheese. Instead of lard, substitute rendered pork, chicken, or bacon fat (see page 123) to add considerably more flavor. Garnish with pickled chilies and Mexican salsa, either store-bought or Salsa Verde (see page 111).

INGREDIENT	WEIGHT	VOLUME	SCALING	PROCEDURE
Dried corn husks		20 husks		① Soak in warm water until the husks are pliable, at least 30 minutes. Shake them dry.
Lard or unsalted butter	225 g	1 cup	50%	② Whip in a stand mixer, scraping the sides often, until light and airy, about 5 minutes.
Masa harina (Maseca brand)	450 g	3½ cups	100%	③ Gradually add to the mixer, alternating between the two ingredients, until fully blended to make masa batter.
Toasted Corn Stock or water, lukewarm see page 90	300 g	300 mL / 1¼ cups	67%	
Fresh corn kernels, cut from the cob	525 g	3½ cups / 4 cobs	117%	④ Combine in a food processor, and blend to make corn puree. ⑤ Fold the corn puree and masa batter together to make the tamale batter. ⑥ Place a dollop of tamale batter, about 70 g / 5 Tbsp, in each corn husk, and wrap firmly. ⑦ Arrange the tamales, seam-side down, on a metal rack or trivet in a pressure cooker, and then add 2.5 cm / 1 in of water. ⑧ Pressure-cook at a gauge pressure of 1 bar / 15 psi for 20 minutes. Start timing when full pressure is reached. ⑨ Depressurize the cooker. ⑩ Allow the tamales to cool until set, about 2 hours. ⑪ Steam over boiling water for 15–20 minutes to reheat, and serve hot.
Unsalted butter, melted	22 g	25 mL / 2 Tbsp	4.9%	
Sour cream, crème fraîche, or crema	22 g	1½ Tbsp	4.9%	
Sugar	15 g	1 Tbsp	3.3%	
Salt	14 g	1 Tbsp	3.1%	

Safety tips for pressure-cooking: see page 33

VARIATION: Corn Juice Tamales

For a more intense corn flavor, substitute Corn Juice (see variation on page 337) for the water or corn stock in the tamale batter.

WHILE YOU'RE AT IT: Hush Puppies

Follow steps 2–5 above to make tamale batter. Deep-fry small (15 g / 1 Tbsp) balls of the tamale batter in 175 °C / 350 °F neutral frying oil (see page xxii) until they turn brown and crispy, 3–4 minutes. You might try a southern Ohio trick we learned from the family of one of our research chefs: substitute lemon-lime soda for one quarter of the stock or water. Another alternative we love is to lighten the batter by whipping 108 g / ½ cup of egg whites (from about 3 eggs), and then stirring them in after step 5. Yet another option is to grind freeze-dried corn to a powder, and then roll the batter in it to yield an extremely crunchy crust and an extra burst of corn flavor. For deep-frying safety tips, see page 26.

1 Soak the dried corn husks in warm water until they become pliable, at least 30 minutes. Shake them dry.

2 Whip the lard or butter in a stand mixer, scraping the sides of the bowl frequently, until it turns light and airy.

3 Add the masa harina and corn stock or water to the mixer gradually, alternating additions of the two ingredients. Mix until fully blended to make the masa batter. When the batter is properly whipped, a dollop will float in a glass of water.

4 Combine the fresh corn kernels, melted butter, sour cream, sugar, and salt in a food processor, and blend until evenly combined into a corn puree. The puree doesn't have to be perfectly smooth; the chopped corn kernels lend a nice texture to the tamales.

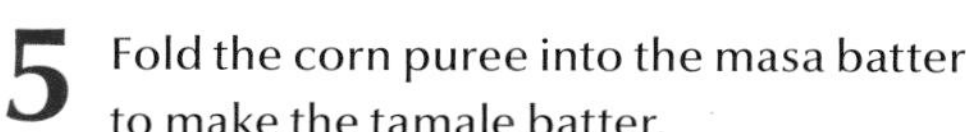

5 Fold the corn puree into the masa batter to make the tamale batter.

6 Place a dollop (about 70 g / 5 Tbsp) of the tamale batter in each corn husk, and wrap each one firmly. One side of each corn husk naturally forms a cup shape. Place the batter in this cup, use the natural curl of the corn husk to enclose the batter, and then fold the top of the husk down to seal the package. Tie it closed with a narrow strip of corn husk or a piece of string, if necessary.

7 Stack the tamales, seam-side down, on a trivet or rack in a pressure cooker. Pour in water to a depth of 2.5 cm / 1 in.

8 Pressure-cook the tamales at a gauge pressure of 1 bar / 15 psi for 20 minutes. Start timing as soon as full pressure has been reached.

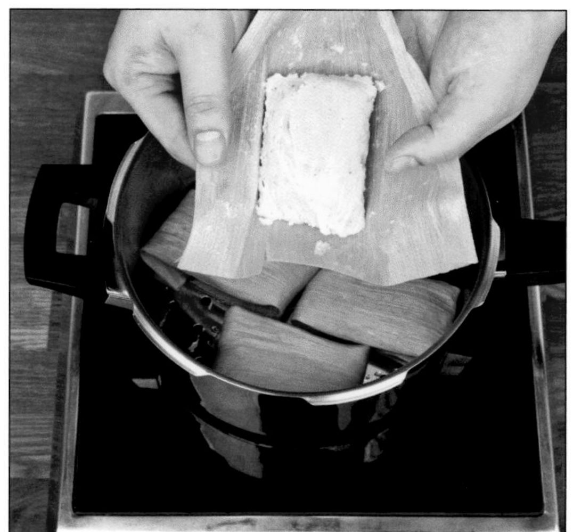

9 Let the cooker cool, or run tepid water over the rim, to depressurize it.

10 Cool the tamales completely, about 2 hours, to give the starches time to gel.

11 Reheat the tamales by steaming them over boiling water for 15–20 minutes. Alternatively, microwave them, a few at a time, on full power for 1–2 minutes. Serve them hot.

DISHES FOR THE MICROWAVE

The microwave oven is simultaneously one of the most used and most underappreciated tools in the home kitchen. People criticize it for cooking unevenly. But that problem has a straightforward solution: don't cook in open containers. Instead, enclose the food in a sous vide bag or put it on a plate and cover it loosely in microwave-safe plastic wrap. An envelope of hot, moist air and steam then forms around the food and cooks it evenly as well as quickly.

Speed is not the only reason to use a microwave oven. Some of the recipes in this chapter take almost as much time to prepare as when made conventionally because cooking time is a small fraction of the overall effort. But they all highlight the power of the microwave oven as a precision tool for steaming and drying.

Our recipe for Microwaved Eggplant Parmesan, for example, exploits both aspects to guarantee a creamy, rather than rubbery, texture to the water-laden vegetable. We use the classic technique of salting the eggplant slices to draw out excess moisture, but then steam them in the microwave between paper towels to make them very tender while continuing to draw out excess moisture. This is a simpler way to make a healthier dish that traditionally relies on deep-frying to boil off moisture.

THE SCIENCE OF COOKING WITH MICROWAVES

Why does frozen food cooked in a microwave oven become piping hot in some places yet remain frozen in others? The microwaves have a wavelength of 122 mm / 4.8 in long, so although they bounce around the cooking chamber, they heat some spots more than others (see page 42). And the waves penetrate only a couple of centimeters into moist food. Heat does diffuse within the food, evening out temperature differences, but this takes time. So cooking well with a microwave oven often means adjusting the power level. We tested all our recipes on an oven that outputs 1,100 watts. If you have a 1,350 W oven and the recipe says to cook at 1,100 W, set the power level to 80% (or level 8 if it has 10 levels) because 1,100 is about 80% of 1,350. You can find the power output in the oven manual or marked somewhere on the oven itself.

HIGHLIGHTS

Dense leafy greens contain a lot of moisture, so they lend themselves well to microwave cooking. You can use your microwave oven to make **Sichuan bok choy that is perfect—and fast.**

see page 346

The microwave is such an efficient dehydrator that you can **dry beef jerky in four minutes** rather than 12–24 hours.

see page 350

Fancy up your fried fish and other crispy dishes with **perfectly flat, fried herbs.**

see page 354

No need to heat the whole oven to **bake a sponge cake.** Just aerate the batter with a whipping siphon, and then dispense it into a paper cup.

see page 356

FURTHER READING IN *MODERNIST CUISINE*

The physics of cooking with microwaves: see pages 2·182–184

Myths about microwave cooking, and how not to do irresponsible things with a microwave: see page 2·190

How to use a microwave oven to make puffed snacks: see page 4·302

MICROWAVED EGGPLANT PARMESAN

YIELD:	*four servings (850 g)*
TIME ESTIMATE:	*45 minutes overall*
STORAGE NOTES:	*keeps for up to 3 days when refrigerated or up to 6 months when frozen*
LEVEL OF DIFFICULTY:	*moderate*

INGREDIENT	WEIGHT	VOLUME	SCALING	PROCEDURE
Panko bread crumbs	50 g	⅞ cup	15%	① Preheat the oven to 175 °C / 350 °F.
Parmigiano-Reggiano, grated	50 g	¾ cup	15%	② Toss together, spread evenly on a baking sheet, and toast until the cheese and bread crumbs turn golden, about 10 minutes. Reserve the crumbs for use in step 12.
Italian eggplant, peeled and sliced 6 mm / ¼ in thick	330 g	12 slices (from 1 eggplant)	100%	③ Arrange the eggplant slices in a single layer on a microwave-safe plate lined with paper towels, sprinkle with the salt, and cover with additional paper towels.
Salt	2 g	½ tsp	0.6%	④ Microwave at 1,100 W for 3 minutes. Work in batches if necessary.
Olive oil	50 g	55 mL / ¼ cup	15%	⑤ Brush the eggplant slices with olive oil on both sides, place them on a clean plate, and seal them with microwave-safe plastic wrap.
				⑥ Microwave at 1,100 W until fully tender, about 4 minutes.
Marinara sauce see page 112	400 g	1⅝ cups	121%	⑦ Spread a generous spoonful of marinara sauce across the bottom of a microwave-safe dish that is 12.7 cm / 5 in square.
Full-fat ricotta cheese	150 g	⅝ cup	45%	⑧ Lay four slices of the cooked eggplant over the sauce.
Fresh mozzarella, thinly sliced	150 g	1 cup	45%	⑨ Top the eggplant with one-third of the basil and cheeses. Lightly salt if desired.
Basil leaves, torn	10 g	½ cup	3%	⑩ Top with another generous spoonful of marinara sauce.
Salt	to taste			⑪ Repeat steps 8–10 twice more, and top with remaining marinara sauce.
				⑫ Sprinkle the toasted bread and cheese crumbs over the assembled dish.
				⑬ Microwave at 1,100 W until hot in the center and bubbly on the sides, 5–6 minutes. Serve immediately.

1 Preheat the oven to 175 °C / 350 °F.

2 Toss the bread crumbs and cheese together, spread them on a baking sheet, and toast them until they turn golden, about 10 minutes. Set the cheesy bread crumbs aside for use in step 12.

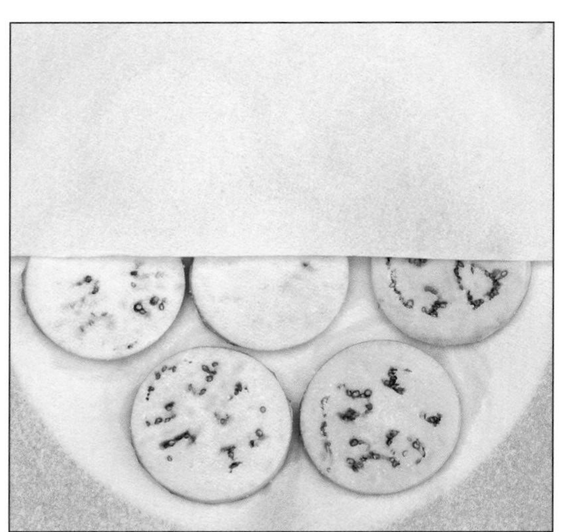

3 Arrange the slices of eggplant in a single layer on a microwave-safe plate lined with paper towels. Sprinkle them with the salt, and then cover them with additional paper towels.

4 Microwave the eggplant at 1,100 W for 3 minutes; add more time if your oven is less powerful than this. The paper towels absorb steam, so the eggplant doesn't get soggy. Work in batches if necessary; do not stack slices on top of one another.

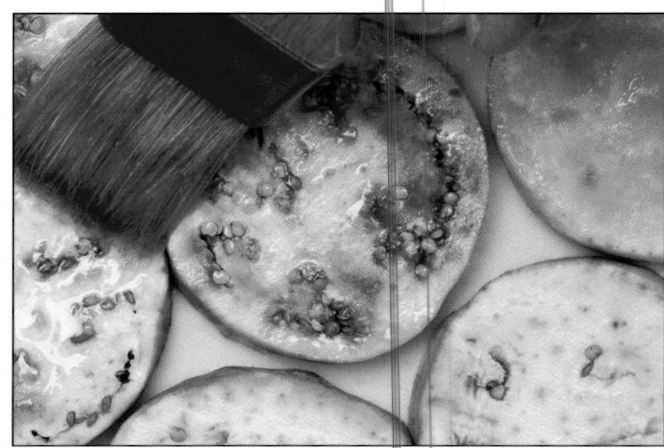

5 Brush the cooked slices with olive oil on both sides, place them on a clean microwave-safe plate, and seal them tightly with plastic wrap, which traps the steam produced during cooking. Use only plastic wrap specifically rated for microwaving.

6 Microwave the slices at 1,100 W until they are tender all the way through, about 4 minutes. If they are still slightly rubbery, cook for up to 2 minutes more.

7 Spread a generous spoonful of marinara sauce evenly across the bottom of a microwave-safe dish that is 12.7 cm / 5 in square and 5 cm / 2 in deep.

8 Arrange four slices of cooked eggplant on the sauce in a single layer.

9 Top the eggplant with one-third of the ricotta, sliced mozzarella, and basil. Add a little salt to taste, but it may already be quite salty. You can use scissors to snip the basil.

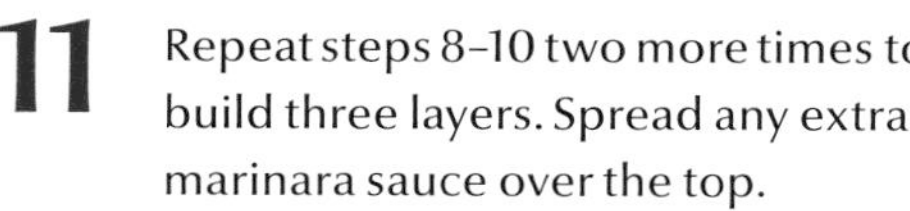

10 Spread another generous spoonful of marinara sauce over the top.

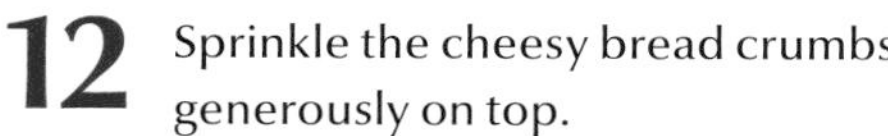

11 Repeat steps 8–10 two more times to build three layers. Spread any extra marinara sauce over the top.

12 Sprinkle the cheesy bread crumbs generously on top.

13 Microwave again at 1,100 W until the food is hot in the center and bubbly on the sides, 5–6 minutes. The sauce may bubble over, so it's a good idea to place a plate underneath the dish.

SICHUAN BOK CHOY

YIELD:	*four servings (350 g / four heads of bok choy)*
TIME ESTIMATE:	*10 minutes overall*
STORAGE NOTES:	*serve immediately*
LEVEL OF DIFFICULTY:	*easy*
SPECIAL REQUIREMENTS:	*black bean and chili paste, Shaoxing wine, Sous Vide Spiced Chili Oil (see page 118)*

This is such a practical and fast way to cook vegetables perfectly. Sealing the produce in a plastic bag captures steam to help the microwave do the cooking. If you can't find black bean and chili paste, replace it with a combination of garlic black bean sauce and *sambal ulek*, a salt-cured chili sauce (use a 2:1 ratio by weight). Alternatively, use our Korean Wing Sauce (see page 260) or 100 g of our Pressure-Caramelized Peanut Sauce with some extra minced lemongrass (see page 111) to obtain a different set of flavors.

INGREDIENT	WEIGHT	VOLUME	SCALING	PROCEDURE
Hoisin sauce (Lee Kum Kee brand)	20 g	20 mL / 4 tsp	7%	① Combine in a pot, and bring to a simmer. ② Set aside to cool slightly.
Fermented black bean and chili paste (Lee Kum Kee brand)	15 g	1 Tbsp	5%	
Shaoxing wine	8 g	9 mL / 2 tsp	2.6%	
Soy sauce	5 g	4 mL / ⅞ tsp	1.7%	
Toasted-sesame oil	1 g	1 mL / ¼ tsp	0.3%	
Baby bok choy, cleaned and halved	300 g	4 medium heads	100%	③ Place in a zip-top bag, remove as much air as possible from the bag, and seal it. ④ Microwave it at 1,100 W for 2 minutes, and then let it rest for 2 minutes in the bag. ⑤ Remove the bok choy from the bag, shake off any excess water, and arrange it on plates.
Water	50 g	50 mL / ¼ cup	17%	
Sous Vide Spiced Chili Oil see page 118	10 g	10 mL / 2¼ tsp	3.3%	⑥ Season the bok choy with the spicy sauce, chili oil, and salt. Serve it hot.
Salt	to taste			

VARIATIONS

Bok Choy Medley

Baby bok choy, halved	300 g	4 medium heads
Pressure-Cooked Barley, warmed see page 184	60 g	4 Tbsp
Ibérico ham, sliced paper thin	40 g	8 pieces
Cauliflower florets	32 g	8 florets
Romanesco cauliflower florets	32 g	8 florets
Brussels sprout leaves	12 g	12–16 leaves
Spinach Butter, warm see variation on page 121	12 g	1 Tbsp
Meyer lemon zest, grated	1 g	1 tsp

Deep-fry both kinds of cauliflower florets in 175 °C / 350 °F neutral frying oil until golden, about 10 minutes. Blanch the Brussels sprout leaves for 60 seconds in boiling water, and then immediately plunge them into an ice-water bath. Follow steps 3–5 above to cook the bok choy. Take apart the cooked bok choy leaves. Arrange the bok choy leaves, ham, barley, and vegetables artfully on plates. Drizzle the spinach butter over the top, garnish with the lemon zest, and season with salt.

Autumn Flavors Bok Choy

Baby bok choy, halved	300 g	4 medium heads
Broccoli-Gruyère Puree see variation on page 181	60 g	¼ cup
Pickled Honeycrisp apple, finely diced see page 130	24 g	3 Tbsp
Comté cheese, grated	8 g	4 tsp
Hazelnut oil	4 g	4 mL / 1 tsp

Follow steps 3–5 above to cook the bok choy. Spoon the warm broccoli puree onto the plate, and garnish with the pickled apple. Sprinkle the grated cheese and hazelnut oil over the top.

Microwaved Potato Salad

Small fingerling potatoes	400 g	3 cups
Water	15 g	1 Tbsp
Red onion, minced	55 g	⅓ cup
Bacon Mayonnaise see variation on page 108	55 g	¼ cup
Dijon mustard	15 g	1½ Tbsp
Salt	to taste	

Place the potatoes and water in a zip-top bag, and microwave at 1,100 watts until tender, about 4 minutes. Allow to cool, and slice into coins 1 in thick. Combine with the onion, mayonnaise, and mustard. Season with salt to taste. Garnish with Pressure-Cooked Pickled Mustard Seeds (see page 125) and crispy bacon bits.

1 Combine the hoisin sauce, black bean and chili paste, wine, soy sauce, and sesame oil in a pot, and bring the mixture to a simmer.

2 Remove the sauce from the heat, and allow it to cool slightly.

3 Place the cleaned bok choy halves and the water in a zip-top bag. Remove as much air as possible from the bag, and seal it. Alternatively, arrange the bok choy on a microwave-safe plate, add water, and then tightly cover the plate with microwave-safe plastic wrap.

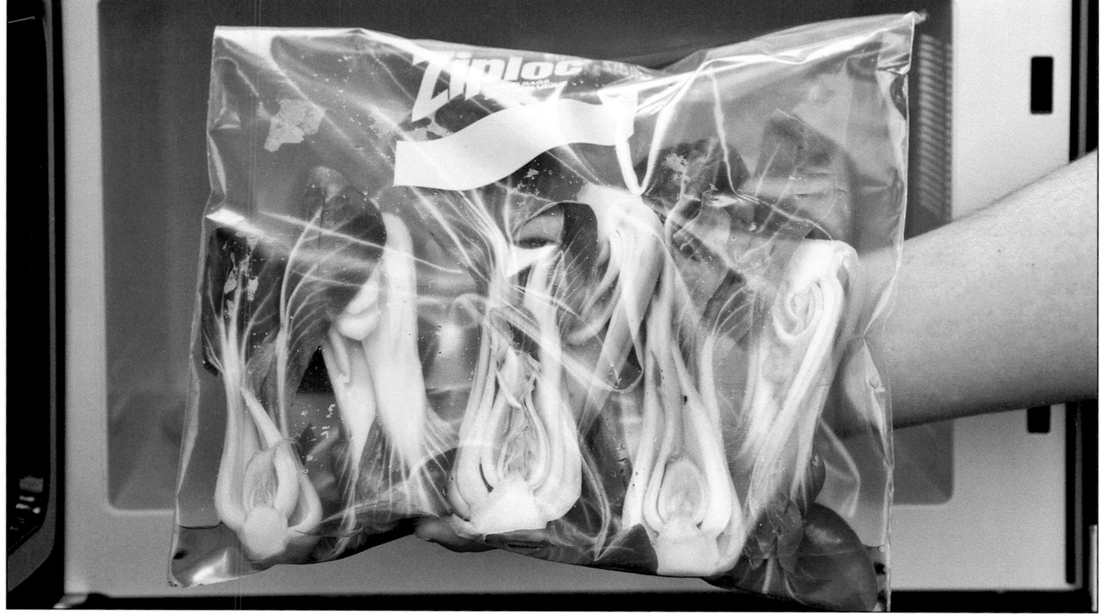

4 Microwave the bok choy at 1,100 W for 2 minutes (or at full power for a bit longer, if your oven is less powerful than this), and then let it rest for 2 minutes in the bag or plastic wrap. If you're using a microwave-safe dish, cooking may take an extra minute. Microwave ovens vary widely in their power output, so check the power of yours before cooking, and adjust the power level or cooking time accordingly.

5 Remove the bok choy from the bag, shake off any excess water from it, and arrange it on plates.

6 Season the bok choy with the spicy sauce, chili oil, and salt. Serve it hot.

Best Bets for Cooking Vegetables in the Microwave Oven

All of the recipes in this chapter were tested by using a 1,100 watt microwave oven at full power, unless indicated otherwise. The time required to cook vegetables in a microwave depends on the thickness to which you cut them, as well as on their density and water content. Drier vegetables cook more evenly if you seal the vegetables in a bag or under microwave-safe plastic wrap on a plate with a little water.

Technique	Ingredients	Preparation	Procedure	Time (min)
cooking root vegetables	beets, carrots, celery root, potatoes, turnips	whole	vacuum seal, or arrange on a plate and seal with microwave-safe plastic wrap; cook medium beets for 6 minutes, and rub off the skin	3–7
cooking leafy greens	bok choy, broccoli, cabbage	whole	place in a zip-top bag with 50 mL / ¼ cup of water; alternatively, arrange in a microwave-safe dish with 2 mm / 1⁄16 in of water, and cover with microwave-safe plastic wrap	2–5
cooking bulbs and fibrous vegetables	artichokes, cardoon, celery, fennel, leeks, onions	whole	vacuum seal	2–5

MICROWAVED BLACK COD WITH SCALLIONS AND GINGER

YIELD:	*two servings (450 g)*
TIME ESTIMATE:	*15 minutes overall*
STORAGE NOTES:	*serve immediately*
LEVEL OF DIFFICULTY:	*easy*

This recipe was adapted from Margaret Lu, the mother of Johnny Zhu, one of the development chefs at The Cooking Lab. Mrs. Lu originally made the dish with tilapia. Johnny adapted it to cod, but you can substitute halibut fillets or small whole snapper, rockfish, trout, black sea bass, pomfret, or sole for the black cod. Fishes differ a bit in their densities, so you may need to adjust the cooking time.

INGREDIENT	WEIGHT	VOLUME	SCALING	PROCEDURE
Black cod, skin on	450 g/1 lb	2 fillets	100%	① Place each fillet in a separate, microwave-safe zip-top bag, and then place each one, skin-side down, on a microwave-safe plate.
Scallion, white parts only, julienned	25 g	5–6 scallions	5.6%	② Combine, and mound half on top of each fillet in the bag.
Ginger, peeled and cut into coins	10 g	2–3 coins	2.2%	③ Pour half of the wine into each bag.
Shaoxing wine	5 g	5 mL/1¼ tsp	1%	④ Microwave each fillet at 800 W until the fish becomes opaque and flakes easily, 3½–5 minutes, and then remove it from the bag, and scrape off the scallion and ginger. If your microwave oven is more powerful than 800 W, lower the power level accordingly.
Soy sauce	25 g	20 mL/4¼ tsp	5.6%	⑤ Combine, and pour half of the mixture evenly over each fish fillet.
Toasted-sesame oil	2 g	2 mL/⅜ tsp	0.4%	
Scallion, green parts only, finely julienned	10 g	¾ cup	2.2%	⑥ Garnish each cooked fillet.
Ginger, peeled and finely julienned	3 g	1 Tbsp	0.7%	
Peanut oil	50 g	55 mL/3½ Tbsp	11%	⑦ Heat in a small pan to **190 °C/374 °F**.
				⑧ Drizzle the hot peanut oil over the garnished fish. Serve immediately.

VARIATIONS

Microwaved Sea Bass, Tilapia, Halibut, or Sole

To make this recipe with other kinds of fish, use the cooking times given below.

Aromatic Microwaved Cod

For a more intensely aromatic dish, combine the Shaoxing wine with 10 g/4 tsp of minced ginger and 25 g/4 tsp of minced scallion, white parts only. Rub the mixture gently and evenly all over the surface of each fillet, and then place the fillets in bags as directed in step 1. Continue at step 3.

Whole black sea bass (450 g): 6½ minutes

Whole tilapia (800 g): 6 minutes

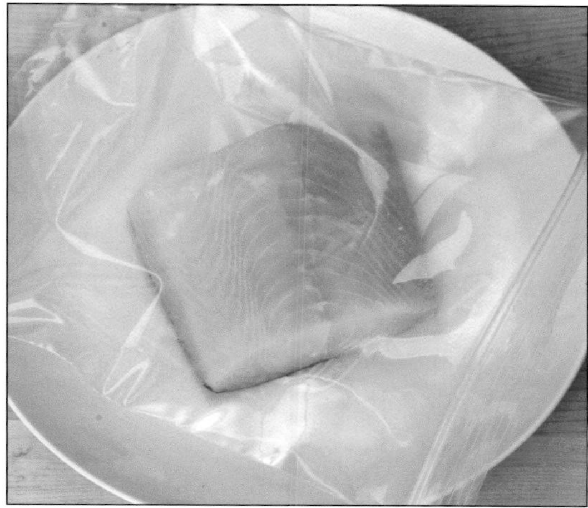

1 Place each fillet in a separate, microwave-safe zip-top bag, and then place each one, skin-side down, on a microwave-safe plate. The plate makes it easier to handle the fish.

2 Combine the scallion whites and ginger coins, and mound them on each fillet in its bag.

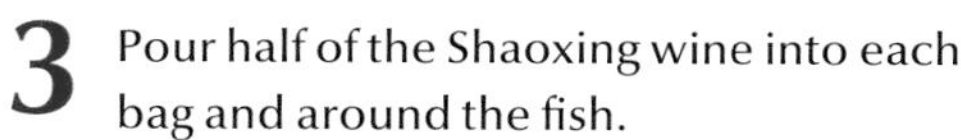

3 Pour half of the Shaoxing wine into each bag and around the fish.

4 Microwave each fillet at 800 W until the fish becomes opaque and flakes easily, 3½–5 minutes, and then remove it from its bag, and scrape off the scallion and ginger. Use caution: the bags contain very hot steam. If your microwave oven is more powerful than 800 W, lower the power level accordingly. Set the power level of an 1,100 W oven, for example, to 75% or level 7.

5 Combine the soy sauce and toasted-sesame oil, and pour half of the mixture evenly over each of the two cooked fillets.

6 Garnish each fillet with the julienned ginger and scallion greens.

7 Heat the peanut oil in a small pan to 190 °C / 374 °F.

8 Drizzle one half of the hot peanut oil slowly and evenly over the top of each fillet. The oil should sizzle and pop as it releases the aromas of the scallions. Serve the fish immediately.

Halibut fillet (170 g): 2¼ minutes

Dover sole fillet (170 g): 1½ minutes

MICROWAVED BEEF JERKY

YIELD:	*310 g / about 32 strips*
TIME ESTIMATE:	*5–25 hours overall, including 1 hour of preparation and 4–24 hours unattended*
STORAGE NOTES:	*keeps for 5 days when stored in an airtight container*
LEVEL OF DIFFICULTY:	*moderate*
SPECIAL REQUIREMENTS:	*1 L whipping siphon and two cartridges of nitrous oxide (optional)*

Making beef jerky involves two time-consuming steps: marinating and drying, each of which can take a day or more when done the traditional way. Modernist techniques can cut the time to just 5 hours. You can use a whipping siphon to pressure-marinate the beef, and then dry it in mere minutes in a microwave oven.

Jerky should be made of lean meat because beef fat quickly turns rancid at room temperature. Flank steak is ideal, but any lean cut of red meat will do, including venison or lamb. We prefer thick jerky, but if you are using a tougher cut, such as a flatiron steak, cut the strips as thinly as possible. This recipe uses soy sauce and fish sauce to impart a mild Asian flavor; see below for spicy, smoky, and South African variations.

INGREDIENT	WEIGHT	VOLUME	SCALING	PROCEDURE
Beef flank steak, trimmed	715 g / 1.5 lb		100%	① Slice, against the grain, into strips that are 10 cm / 4 in long and 12 mm / ½ in thick.
Soy sauce	60 g	50 mL / 3½ Tbsp	8.3%	② Combine, and stir until the sugar dissolves to make a marinade.
Asian fish sauce	30 g	25 mL / 1½ Tbsp	4.2%	③ Stir the beef strips in the marinade until coated.
Sugar	40 g	3 Tbsp	5.6%	④ Transfer the meat and marinade to a 1 L siphon, charge with two cartridges of nitrous oxide, and refrigerate it for 4 hours. Alternatively, combine the meat and marinade in a zip-top bag, remove as much air as possible from the bag, seal it, and refrigerate it for 15–24 hours.
Maple syrup (grade B)	15 g	1 Tbsp	2.1%	⑤ Drain the beef strips, and pat them dry with paper towels.
Worcestershire sauce	4 g	3 mL / ½ tsp	0.6%	⑥ Place the strips on a microwave-safe plate, leaving ample space between the pieces for proper air circulation.
Black pepper	0.2 g	⅛ tsp	0.03%	⑦ Cover with plastic wrap, and microwave at 500 W for 2½ minutes.
Cayenne pepper	0.2 g	⅛ tsp	0.03%	⑧ Let the strips rest for 1–2 minutes.
				⑨ Remove the plastic wrap, drain off the liquid, and blot the pieces dry. Flip and rotate the pieces to place the rarer parts facing up and near the outside of the plate.
				⑩ Microwave the strips, uncovered, at 500 W for 30 seconds. Blot and flip the pieces.
				⑪ Continue cooking in short bursts at 500 W, blotting any liquid that forms and rotating as needed until the pieces are dark brown and dry, 2–3 minutes more.
				⑫ Transfer the cooked jerky to a clean plate, and cover it with plastic wrap.
				⑬ Repeat steps 7–12 with all of the remaining beef strips.
				⑭ Serve the jerky at room temperature.

VARIATIONS

Spicy Jerky
In step 2, add 4 g / 2 tsp of red chili flakes to the marinade.

Smoky Jerky
In step 2, add 1.7 g / ½ tsp of liquid hickory smoke to the marinade.

Biltong Jerky
In step 2, add 7.5 g / 1½ Tbsp of ground coriander to the marinade, and increase the quantity of black pepper to 7.5 g / 1½ Tbsp.

A brief history of drying meat
The technique of salt curing and drying meat was developed millennia ago as one of the earliest methods of preserving food, and it is still widely used in parts of the world where refrigeration is unavailable. Many cultures have versions of lean dried meat. In the United States, it's called beef jerky. In South Africa, it's called biltong and is often made of eland or other game. Switzerland has *Bündnerfleisch*, and Italy has *bresaola*. Although necessity drove the invention of cured and dried meats, they live on because people have come to like their unique combination of flavor and texture.

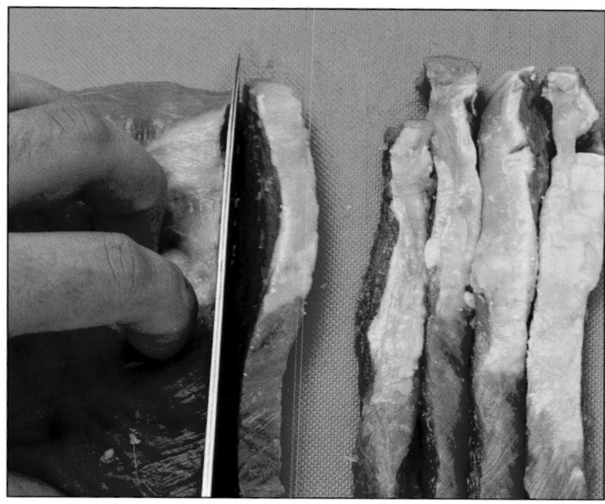

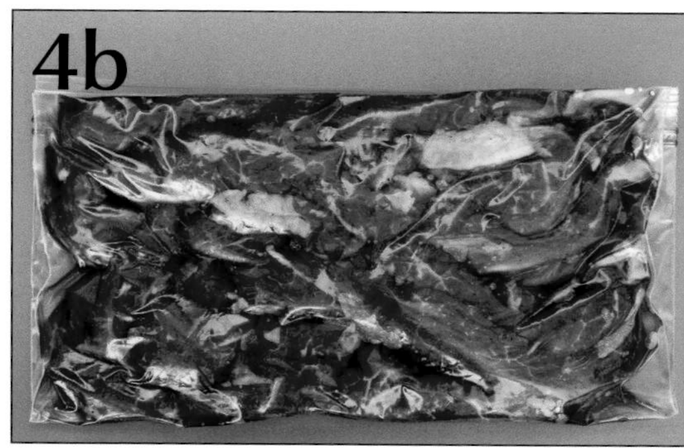

1 Slice the flank steak, cutting against the grain, into strips that are 10 cm / 4 in long and 12 mm / ½ in thick. We like our jerky quite thick, but make the strips thinner if using a tougher cut, such as flatiron steak.

2 Combine the soy sauce, fish sauce, sugar, maple syrup, Worcestershire sauce, and peppers, and stir until dissolved to make a marinade.

3 Stir the strips of meat into the marinade until they are well coated.

4 Transfer the meat and marinade to a 1 L siphon, charge the siphon with two cartridges of nitrous oxide, and refrigerate it for 4 hours (4a). The high pressure accelerates marination. Alternatively, combine the meat and marinade in a zip-top bag, remove as much air as possible from the bag, and seal it (4b). Then refrigerate the sealed bag for 15–24 hours. Lay the bag flat, if possible, and flip it periodically so that the strips brine evenly.

5 Drain the marinade from the beef strips, and use paper towels to pat them dry.

6 Arrange as many of the beef strips as will fit on a microwave-safe plate while spacing them well apart. Proper drying requires air circulation, so don't crowd the strips; work in batches as needed.

7 Cover the plate with microwave-safe plastic wrap, and microwave at 500 W for 2½ minutes to cook the meat.

Beef strips raw (left), marinated (middle), and cooked.

8 Let the strips rest for a minute or two. Cooking and resting the meat helps keep it tender and reduces the drying time.

9 Remove the plastic wrap, drain off the liquid, and blot the pieces dry with paper towels. Flip and rotate the pieces to place the rarer parts facing up and near the outside of the plate.

10 Microwave the strips, uncovered, at 500 W for 30 seconds. Blot and flip the pieces.

11 Continue cooking in short bursts at 500 W, blotting any liquid that forms and rotating as needed until the pieces are dark brown and dry, 2–3 minutes more.

12 Transfer the cooked jerky to a clean plate, and cover it with plastic wrap. This helps to equalize the remaining moisture among the strips.

13 Repeat steps 7–12 as needed to cook the remaining beef strips.

14 Serve the jerky at room temperature.

CRISPY BEEF STRANDS

YIELD:	*80 g / 2 cups*
TIME ESTIMATE:	*49½ hours overall, including 1½ hours of preparation and 48 hours unattended*
STORAGE NOTES:	*keeps for 5 days when stored in an airtight container*
LEVEL OF DIFFICULTY:	*moderate*

This recipe, which uses a cooking and drying technique very similar to that used to make Microwaved Beef Jerky, produces delicate, crispy strands of fried beef. We use them in a Thai-inspired beef and shallot salad (see next page), but you can also use them to garnish steak (see page 194), braised short ribs (see page 229), or any other meat dish that benefits from a crisp texture and an intense burst of umami flavor.

INGREDIENT	WEIGHT	VOLUME	SCALING	PROCEDURE
Beef flank steak, trimmed	500 g / 1.1 lb		100%	① Slice with the grain into strips that are 10 cm / 4 in long and 12 mm / ½ in thick. Long, uncut threads of beef make better strands.
Soy sauce	125 g	110 mL / ½ cup	25%	② Combine, and stir to dissolve.
Asian fish sauce	85 g	70 mL / 4½ Tbsp	17%	③ Stir the meat and brine together to coat.
Sugar	14 g	1 Tbsp	2.8%	④ Transfer to a zip-top bag, remove as much air as possible from the bag, and seal it.
Salt	5 g	1¼ tsp	1%	⑤ Refrigerate for 48 hours.
				⑥ Drain off the brine, and pat the beef strips dry with paper towels.
				⑦ Place the strips of beef on a microwave-safe plate, leaving at least 2 cm / ¾ in between the pieces for proper air circulation.
				⑧ Microwave the strips, a few at a time, at 800 W for 3–5 minutes, flipping them every minute or two, and patting them dry. Cook the strips until they become brown and dry; they should still be slightly flexible.
Neutral frying oil see page xxii	as needed			⑨ Fill a deep pot with oil to a depth of 2.5 cm / 1 in, and preheat the oil to **180 °C / 356 °F**.
				⑩ Pull the strips of dried beef apart into long, very thin strands.
				⑪ Fry the beef strands in the hot oil until dry and crispy, about 1 minute.
				⑫ Drain on paper towels.
				⑬ Serve hot.

Safety tips for deep-frying: see page 26

A few minutes in a microwave oven is sufficient to cook and dry marinated beef (left) into jerky-like meat.

CRISPY BEEF AND SHALLOT SALAD

YIELD:	*four servings (200 g / 3 cups)*
TIME ESTIMATE:	*20 minutes overall*
STORAGE NOTES:	*serve immediately; fried shallots keep for up to 5 days in an airtight container*
LEVEL OF DIFFICULTY:	*moderate*
SPECIAL REQUIREMENTS:	*Crispy Beef Strands (see the previous page); Thai Sweet, Sour, and Savory Glaze (see page 115)*

We developed this salad as a garnish to our recipe in *Modernist Cuisine* for short ribs cooked sous vide. It was inspired by the Australian chef David Thompson. The crispy beef strands are delicious and set up a wonderful contrast with the Asian flavors of the salad.

To make the salad more substantial, try adding shredded pineapple and green papaya (available at Asian or Latin American markets), or julienned jicama and cucumber. For a Western version, try baby arugula, shredded fennel, and red onion.

INGREDIENT	WEIGHT	VOLUME	SCALING	PROCEDURE
Neutral frying oil see page xxii	as needed			① Preheat 1 cm / ⅜ in of frying oil to 170 °C / 338 °F in a deep-sided skillet.
Shallot, sliced 1 mm / 1⁄32 in thick	50 g	½ cup	63%	② Deep-fry until dry and golden, about 2 minutes. ③ Drain on paper towels.
Salt	to taste			④ Season the fried shallots, and set them aside.
Crispy Beef Strands see the previous page	80 g	2 cups	100%	⑤ Toss together with the fried shallots.
Cilantro stems, cut to 1 cm / ⅜ in lengths	3 g	1 Tbsp	3.8%	
Scallion, finely julienned	2 g	1 Tbsp	2.5%	
Small cilantro leaves	2 g	1 Tbsp	2.5%	
Small mint leaves	2 g	1 Tbsp	2.5%	
Small Thai basil leaves	2 g	1 Tbsp	2.5%	
Lime zest, finely julienned	1.5 g	1½ Tbsp	1.8%	
Thai chili, seeded and sliced paper thin	1 g	1–2 chilies	1.3%	
Thai Sweet, Sour, and Savory Glaze see page 115	100 g	½ cup	125%	⑥ Warm the glaze, and drizzle it into the salad.
Lime juice	to taste			⑦ Season the salad, and serve it immediately.
Salt	to taste			

Safety tips for deep-frying: see page 26

Dress the salad lightly for a savory crunch or heavily for an intensely tangy and chewier version.

VARIATION: Crispy Shallots

After step 4, store the crispy, salted shallots in an airtight container. Use them on steaks, in salads, or in Savory Cheese Pie (see variation on page 379).

MICROWAVE-FRIED PARSLEY

YIELD:	*about 50 leaves*
TIME ESTIMATE:	*15 minutes overall*
STORAGE NOTES:	*best served immediately, but keeps for 1 day when stored in an airtight container*
LEVEL OF DIFFICULTY:	*easy*

The microwave oven is the secret to making an impressive herb garnish quickly, without the mess of frying in oil. After microwaving, the Italian parsley remains a brilliant emerald green, the texture becomes intriguingly crisp, and the leaves lie perfectly flat. We find that sage, basil, dill, carrot tops, baby spinach, and lovage work equally well. Verbena and lemon balm, however, tend to brown and wilt too quickly. Inexpensive PVC-based plastic wrap is not recommended; use plastic specifically designed for use in microwave ovens.

INGREDIENT	WEIGHT	VOLUME	PROCEDURE
Neutral-tasting oil or cooking spray	as needed		① Stretch a piece of microwave-safe plastic wrap taut over a microwave-safe plate. The plastic should seal tightly to the edge of the plate. ② Brush the plastic wrap with a thin film of oil, or coat it with cooking spray.
Italian parsley	about 50 leaves	½ cup	③ Lay the parsley leaves on the prepared plastic wrap, leaving about 2 cm / ¾ in between the leaves. Work in batches as needed. ④ Brush the tops of the leaves lightly with oil, or use cooking spray or your fingers to dab on the oil. ⑤ Microwave at 800 W until crisp, about 4 minutes. Check the leaves every 90 seconds; do not let them burn.
Salt	to taste		⑥ Transfer the fried leaves to a tray lined with paper towels, and season them. ⑦ Repeat with the remaining oil and parsley leaves. Change the plastic wrap on every other batch to prevent overheating. ⑧ Serve the fried herbs at room temperature.

(adapted from Heston Blumenthal)

1 Stretch a piece of microwave-safe plastic wrap taut over a microwave-safe plate. The plastic should seal tightly to the edge of the plate.

2 Brush the plastic wrap with a thin film of oil, or coat it with cooking spray.

3 Lay the parsley leaves on the prepared plastic wrap. Space the leaves about 2 cm / ¾ in apart. Work in batches as needed.

Italian parsley

Dill

Chervil

Carrot green

4 Brush the tops of the leaves lightly with oil, or use cooking spray or your fingers to dab on the oil.

5 Microwave at 800 W until crisp, about 4 minutes. Check the leaves every 90 seconds to make certain that they don't burn.

6 Transfer the crisp, fried parsley leaves to a tray lined with paper towels, and season them.

7 Repeat with the remaining oil and parsley leaves. Change the plastic wrap on every other batch to keep it from overheating.

8 Serve the fried herbs at room temperature.

Check that your cling wraps or plastic bags are rated microwave-safe before using them in the microwave oven. Bags and wraps made from polyethylene generally are microwave-safe, whereas those that contain polyvinyl chloride (PVC) plastics generally are not.

INSTANT CHOCOLATE SPONGE

YIELD:	*six to eight servings (650 g)*
TIME ESTIMATE:	*40 minutes overall, including 20 minutes unattended*
STORAGE NOTES:	*batter keeps for 24 hours when refrigerated*
LEVEL OF DIFFICULTY:	*easy*
SPECIAL REQUIREMENTS:	*1 L whipping siphon, three cartridges of nitrous oxide, six to eight heavy-duty paper cups, Wondra, xanthan gum (optional)*

With a whipping siphon, you can prepare and cook a fluffy, warm cake in just minutes. It will have a rough, rustic texture unlike a conventional cake—more like a coarse, steamed sponge. Serve it alone or with fruit, ice cream, or Sous Vide Lemon Curd (see page 365).

If heavy-duty paper cups are not available, use pairs of stacked regular cups. Never use waxed cups; they will melt. The xanthan gum in this recipe helps bind the batter so that it stays lighter when it sets. But the recipe works fine without it.

INGREDIENT	WEIGHT	VOLUME	SCALING	PROCEDURE
Whole milk	150 g	150 mL / ⅔ cup	120%	① Cut four slits spaced equally around the bottom edge of a heavy-duty paper cup; repeat for the remaining five to seven cups.
Semisweet chocolate, chopped	115 g	¾ cup	92%	② Combine the milk, chocolate, and butter in a microwave-safe bowl, and microwave at 1,100 W until melted, about 1 minute.
Unsalted butter, cubed	75 g	⅜ cup	60%	③ Whisk until smooth. Cool slightly.
Eggs, blended	100 g	½ cup / about 2 eggs	80%	④ Whisk into the cooled chocolate mixture.
Wondra	125 g	1 cup	100%	⑤ Sift together.
Powdered sugar	125 g	1¼ cups	100%	⑥ Fold a third of the chocolate mixture into the dry ingredients, and then stir in the remainder to form a smooth batter.
Dutch-processed cocoa powder	6 g	2 tsp	4.8%	⑦ Pour the batter into a 1 L siphon, and charge it with three cartridges of nitrous oxide.
Salt	5.5 g	1½ tsp	4.4%	⑧ Allow the siphon to sit at room temperature for 20 minutes.
Baking soda	0.6 g	⅛ tsp	0.48%	
Xanthan gum (Bob's Red Mill brand), optional	0.3 g		0.24%	
Cooking spray	as needed			⑨ Spray the inside of each paper cup with cooking spray, wiping away any excess oil.
				⑩ Dispense enough batter to fill a quarter of one paper cup.
				⑪ Microwave the cake at 1,100 W for 50 seconds to cook through.
				⑫ Let the cake rest for a few seconds, and then upend it onto a plate.
				⑬ Repeat steps 10–12 with the remaining batter and cups. Serve warm.

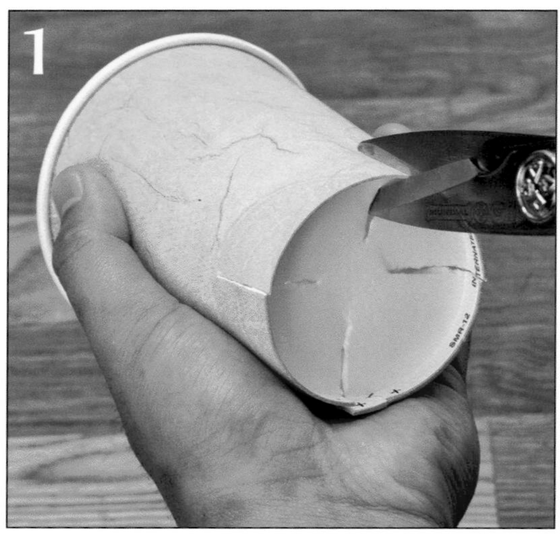

Use scissors or a razor blade to cut four slits on the bottom of six to eight heavy-duty paper cups. Space the slits evenly to provide ventilation. The thick cake batter won't ooze out.

After whisking the chocolate mixture, allow it to cool slightly so that the eggs do not cook when they are added.

You can avoid overbeating the batter by adding only a third of the chocolate mixture to the dry ingredients at first, and then stirring in the remainder.

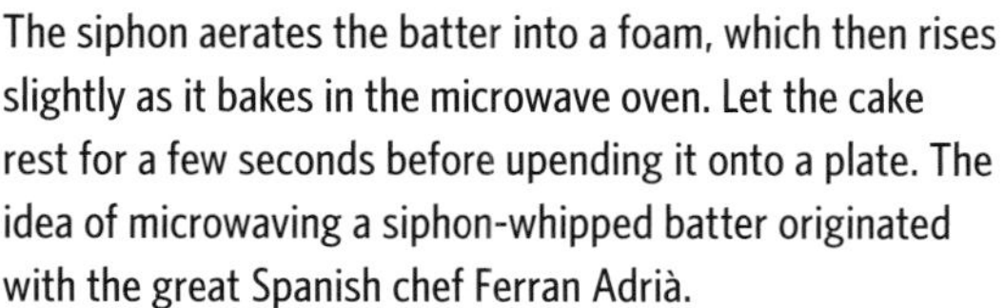
The siphon aerates the batter into a foam, which then rises slightly as it bakes in the microwave oven. Let the cake rest for a few seconds before upending it onto a plate. The idea of microwaving a siphon-whipped batter originated with the great Spanish chef Ferran Adrià.

VARIATIONS

In each of the variations below, first follow step 1 to prepare the cups. Then whisk together the first group of ingredients listed for the variation. Next, sift together the dry ingredients listed in the second group. Then continue with steps 6–13.

Peanut Butter Sponge

Whole milk	150 g	150 mL / ⅔ cup
Natural peanut butter, smooth	115 g	½ cup
Eggs, beaten	100 g	2 eggs
Hazelnut oil	76 g	80 mL / ⅜ cup
Powdered sugar	187 g	1⅝ cups
Wondra	125 g	1 cup
Salt	9 g	2¼ tsp
Baking soda	0.6 g	⅛ tsp

Sesame Sponge

Whole milk	150 g	150 mL / ⅔ cup
Tahini	115 g	½ cup
Eggs, beaten	100 g	2 eggs
Toasted-sesame oil	50 g	55 mL / ¼ cup
Powdered sugar	187 g	1⅝ cups
Wondra	125 g	1 cup
Salt	9 g	2¼ tsp
Baking soda	0.6 g	⅛ tsp

Raspberry Macadamia Nut Sponge

Raspberry juice	150 g	150 mL / ⅔ cup
Macadamia butter	115 g	⅜ cup
Eggs, beaten	100 g	2 eggs
Macadamia oil	76 g	80 mL / ⅜ cup
Egg white, beaten	40 g	3 Tbsp
Powdered sugar	187 g	1⅝ cups
Wondra	125 g	1 cup
Freeze-Dried Raspberry Powder see page 377	15 g	2 Tbsp
Salt	9 g	2¼ tsp
Powdered milk	5 g	2 tsp
Baking soda	0.6 g	⅛ tsp

CUSTARDS AND PIES

Modernist techniques and ingredients apply just as well to desserts as they do to savory foods—indeed, one could easily fill an entire book exploring the applications of Modernist concepts to crafting sweets. That is not our focus in this book, but we felt it important to include recipes for all the elements that go into a great meal. So this final chapter focuses on two particularly versatile forms of dessert: custards and pies.

From these recipes, you can learn how to make impressive custards that span the range from the liquid form (crème anglaise) to firm (panna cotta), and from desserts that are finished on top with burnt sugar (crème brûlée), jam, or lemon curd (posset) to those that are frozen and vegan (an eggless, dairy-free ice cream).

The chapter concludes with a healthy handful of examples that illustrate how you can compose custards of various kinds to make classic pies that combine contrasting flavors and textures. Use these as inspiration for whatever satisfies your sweet tooth.

HIGHLIGHTS

Raspberry panna cotta, coffee crème brûlée, chocolate cream pie—the possibilities are endless. **Mix and match from our favorite flavor combinations and techniques** to create your own heavenly dessert.

see page 361

Gelatin is not just for Jell-O. We show you how to use this amazing ingredient with precision and confidence in panna cottas and other desserts.

see page 366

A dairy-free, egg-free pistachio gelato is possible, thanks to the thickening powers of tapioca starch and xanthan gum. And it tastes so delicious and smooth, it's not just for vegans—everyone loves this gelato.

see page 370

The **pressure-caramelizing technique** we use for carrot soup (see page 178) also works wonders with bananas, lending them a deep golden color and intense flavor that we include in our Banana Cream Pie.

see page 379

FURTHER READING IN *MODERNIST CUISINE*

A complete guide to making egg custards from thin crème anglaise to firm omelets: see page 4·84

The science of how emulsions work: see pages 4·199–205

Recipes for Smoked Egg Crème Caramel, Salmon Custard, and Deep-Fried Custard: see pages 4·101, 119, and 120

MAKING CUSTARD

The term "custard" spans so many possible ingredients and techniques that it is most useful to think of custard as simply a particular texture and mouthfeel. Custards have been made for centuries by lightly cooking a blend of eggs and heavy cream, but Modernist chefs have invented myriad new ways to make them. These techniques offer greater consistency and more control over the texture, which can range from airy and fluid to dense and firm. Many of the lighter varieties of custard can be aerated in a whipping siphon into smooth, creamy foams. The one constant among custards is the use of plenty of fat, which not only provides that distinctive mouthfeel but also makes custard an excellent carrier of fat-soluble flavors and aromas.

Recipe	Thickening or gelling process	Texture	Application or garnish	Note	See page
crème anglaise	egg yolks and heat	light, pourable	sauce for fruit salads or warm cakes; base for ice cream or milk shakes	cook sous vide for a smoother texture	368
crème brûlée, pot de crème	egg yolks and heat	very rich, smooth	stand-alone, single-portion desserts	avoid overcooking, weeping, or bubbling by cooking in a water bath; vary the ratio of egg yolk to white to explore a range of appealing textures	362
flan	whole eggs and heat	bouncy, brittle			
gelato	nut milk, dairy or thickening gum, and cold	rich, silky	ice-cream sandwiches; composed desserts	fat content should be 30%–50%; the finer the ice crystals, the better; use hydrocolloid thickeners to make vegan gelato	370
panna cotta	dairy, gelatin or agar, and heat	firm, springy, and very smooth; can be rubbery	molded and cut desserts	firms over time when made with gelatin; use agar to make a vegetarian version	366
pastry cream	egg yolks and heat	pudding-like	pie fillings; napoleons; cream puff fillings; puddings	make as a fluid gel to avoid using starch as a thickener; blend the yolks with liquid while still warm	374
posset	dairy, acid, and heat	very rich, dense	sweet accompaniment to acidic fruits and sauces	measure weights and temperatures accurately for consistent results	364
sabayon	egg yolks and heat	foamy, airy	pie topping; in savory form, an accompaniment to steamed vegetables	use a whipping siphon to foam the custard instantly	369

Crème anglaise

Flan

Gelato

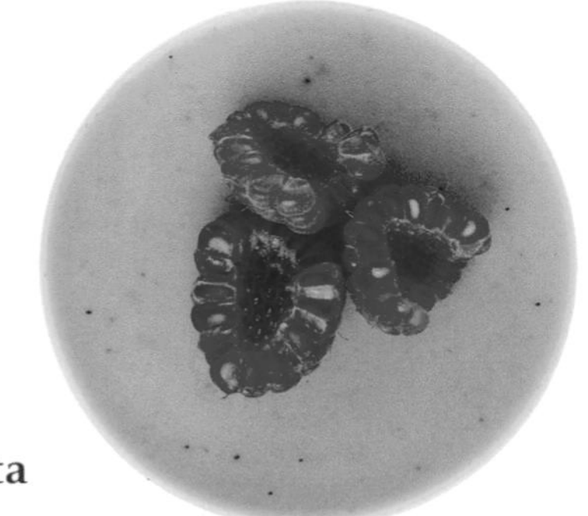

Panna cotta

Pastry cream

Posset

HOW TO Make a Milk or Cream Infusion

Many of our dessert recipes use a flavored liquid. Often the dominant flavor is infused into cream or milk. You can use the information below to create variations of many of the recipes on pages 362–369. You may need to adjust the yield to fit the recipe you are adapting.

INFUSIONS

1 Measure 300 g / 300 mL / 1¼ cups of milk, cream, sugar syrup, or equal parts of cream and milk.

2 Mix the ingredients into the liquid.

3 If the instructions say to seal the ingredients together, place them in a zip-top bag, remove as much air from the bag as possible by using the water-displacement method (see page 58), and seal it.

4 Infuse as instructed; typically this requires overnight refrigeration or cooking sous vide in a preheated water bath.

5 Strain the infusion, and substitute it in the custard recipe for the flavored syrup, milk, or cream.

Bacon Brown Sugar Infusion
Replace the sugar in the recipe with brown sugar. Seal the liquid with 60 g / ⅜ cup of thinly sliced bacon in a zip-top bag, and cook sous vide at 85 °C / 185 °F for 2 hours. Cool the infused liquid, and then strain it.

Cinnamon Vanilla Infusion
Seal the liquid with 10 g / 2 sticks of cinnamon and 1 g / ¼ tsp of vanilla seeds (scraped from 1 pod) in a zip-top bag. Infuse the mixture overnight, refrigerated. Strain. (Alternatively, if time is limited, simply add 2 g / 1 tsp of freshly grated cinnamon and the vanilla seeds to the cream and milk mixture, and skip the overnight infusion.)

Citrus Infusion
Seal the liquid with 3 g / 1 Tbsp of grated lemon zest, 3 g / 1 Tbsp of grated lime zest, and 3 g / 1 Tbsp of grated orange zest in a zip-top bag. Infuse the mixture overnight, refrigerated. Strain.

Coconut Infusion
Replace the heavy cream with coconut cream, and the milk with coconut milk. Seal the liquid with 25 g / ⅓ cup of toasted coconut in a zip-top bag. Infuse the mixture overnight, refrigerated. Strain.

Fruity Pebbles Infusion
Seal the liquid with 50 g / 1¼ cups of Fruity Pebbles brand cereal in a zip-top bag. Infuse the mixture overnight, refrigerated. Strain.

Middle Eastern Infusion
Seal the liquid with 8 g / 1½ Tbsp of cardamom seeds and 4–5 threads of saffron in a zip-top bag. Infuse the mixture overnight, refrigerated. Strain. Add 3 g / ⅝ tsp of orange blossom water and 3 g / ⅝ tsp of rose flower water.

Mint Infusion
Seal the liquid with 32 g / 1 cup of mint leaves in a zip-top bag, and cook sous vide at 80 °C / 176 °F for 1 hour. Cool the infused liquid, and then strain it.

Lemongrass Ginger Infusion
Seal the liquid with 100 g / 1¼ cup of thinly sliced lemongrass and 15 g / 1 Tbsp of thinly sliced ginger in a zip-top bag. Infuse the mixture overnight, refrigerated. Strain.

Popcorn Infusion
Combine the liquid with 45 g / 2½ cups of popped, butter-flavored microwave popcorn. Blend the mixture coarsely; an immersion blender works well. Seal the coarse puree in a zip-top bag, and infuse the mixture overnight, refrigerated. Strain. Use a ladle to press all of the liquid from the swollen popcorn.

Earl Grey Tea Infusion
Seal the liquid with 15 g / 3 Tbsp of loose-leaf Earl Grey tea in a zip-top bag. Infuse the mixture overnight, refrigerated. Strain. Add 3–5 drops of bergamot essential oil (optional).

FLAVORINGS

The flavorings below are adaptations of the Coffee Crème Brûlée recipe on the next page. You can use the techniques illustrated here to create a widge range of creamy desserts.

Honey Flavoring
Replace the sugar in the recipe with 50 g / 2½ Tbsp of honey.

Green Tea Flavoring
Add 4 g / 2 tsp of matcha green tea powder to the blended custard mixture.

Mandarin Flavoring
Add 15 drops of mandarin essential oil to the blended custard mixture.

Pistachio Flavoring
Use 160 g / ⅞ cup of egg yolks and 80 g / ⅜ cup of sugar. Add 80 g / ¼ cup of smooth pistachio butter to the blended custard.

Almond Flavoring
When making the custard, use 80 g / ⅜ cup of sugar and 160 g / ⅞ cup of egg yolks. Add 80 g / ¼ cup of roasted, smooth almond butter and 1 drop of high-quality bitter almond extract to the blended custard mixture.

Caramel Flavoring
Cook the sugar in a saucepan to a dark amber. Add the cream and milk; take care to protect your face and hands from the steam. Whisk to combine. Chill the mixture before using it.

Chocolate Flavoring
Melt 100 g / ⅝ cup of finely chopped, dark chocolate into the liquid. Cool it to room temperature before using it in the recipe.

Raspberry Flavoring
Replace the milk with 125 g / ½ cup of fresh raspberry syrup or sieved raspberry puree. Use 175 g / 190 mL / ¾ cup of heavy cream and 42 g / 3 Tbsp of sugar in the custard.

COFFEE CRÈME BRÛLÉE

YIELD:	*four servings (330 g / 1½ cups)*
TIME ESTIMATE:	*15¾ hours overall, including 15 minutes of preparation and 15½ hours unattended*
STORAGE NOTES:	*keeps for up to 2 days when refrigerated*
LEVEL OF DIFFICULTY:	*easy*
SPECIAL REQUIREMENTS:	*sous vide setup, blowtorch, four 100 mL / 3 oz ramekins*

The flavor of coffee custard is much brighter and more intense when the coffee is infused cold than it is in the traditional, hot-infused version. Cold-infusing retains many volatile aromas that would dissipate quickly if the coffee were heated. And the technique could hardly be easier: simply soak whole coffee beans in cream overnight.

As with most egg dishes, accurate temperature control is crucial for making a custard with just the right texture. Use a thermometer to check that your water bath or combi oven hits and holds the set temperature. (If using a combi oven, set the oven to full steam at 82 °C / 180 °F in step 3.)

INGREDIENT	WEIGHT	VOLUME	SCALING	PROCEDURE
Heavy cream	150 g	165 mL / ¾ cup	100%	① Combine, and refrigerate for 12 hours to infuse.
Whole milk	150 g	150 mL / ⅔ cup	100%	② Strain, and measure 200 g / ⅞ cup of the infused cream for use in step 4.
Whole, dark-roast coffee beans	80 g	¾ cup	53%	③ Place four 100 mL / 3 oz ramekins on a rack in a water bath, and fill with water to 1 cm / ⅜ in below the tops of the ramekins. Preheat the bath to 82 °C / 180 °F.
Egg yolks	80 g	4–5 yolks	53%	④ Blend together with 200 g / ⅞ cup of the infused cream until fully blended.
Sugar	50 g	¼ cup	33%	⑤ Sieve and let settle.
Salt	0.3 g	pinch	0.2%	⑥ Divide evenly among four ramekins.
				⑦ Seal the ramekins tightly with plastic wrap.
				⑧ Cook to a core temperature of 80 °C / 176 °F, about 1 hour.
				⑨ Remove the ramekins carefully from the water bath by using tongs.
				⑩ Refrigerate the custards until they are fully chilled, about 2 hours, and then remove the plastic wrap.
Sugar	as needed			⑪ Sprinkle onto the tops of the custards.
				⑫ Melt and caramelize the sugar by using a blowtorch.
				⑬ Let cool to a crisp crust, and serve.

Safety tips for blowtorching: see page 15

VARIATIONS

Pot de Crème

Skip steps 10–12, and serve the custard chilled.

Bain-Marie Crème Brûlée

To cook the custard traditionally, preheat the oven to 162 °C / 325 °F at step 3. Place a kitchen towel in the bottom of a baking dish, fill it with water to the level specified in step 3, and then proceed with step 4. At step 7, cook for 25–30 minutes. Continue with step 8.

Flan

Flan has a more elastic texture than crème brûlée does, but it is made similarly. Simply substitute whole milk for the heavy cream, and 100 g / 7 Tbsp of blended whole eggs (5–6 eggs) for the egg yolks. You can make caramel (see the Finishing Variation, next page) and pour it into the ramekin before you fill it with custard.

To reduce the cooking time, temper the yolks by heating the infused cream before step 4. At step 4, whisk the warmed cream gently into the yolks.

1 Combine the cream, milk, and coffee beans. Refrigerate the mixture for 12 hours to infuse.

2 Strain the mixture, and measure 200 g / ⅞ cup of the infused cream to use in step 4.

3 Place four 100 mL / 3 oz ramekins (or small cups or bowls) into an empty water bath, and fill with enough water to reach 1 cm / ⅜ in below the tops of the vessels. Use a rack or shelf to allow water to circulate beneath the vessels. Preheat the water bath to 82 °C / 180 °F.

4 Blend the 200 g / ⅞ cup of infused cream with the egg yolks, sugar, and salt. An immersion blender works well. This is the custard base.

5 Sieve the mixture, and let it settle. Fewer air bubbles translates into a richer, denser texture.

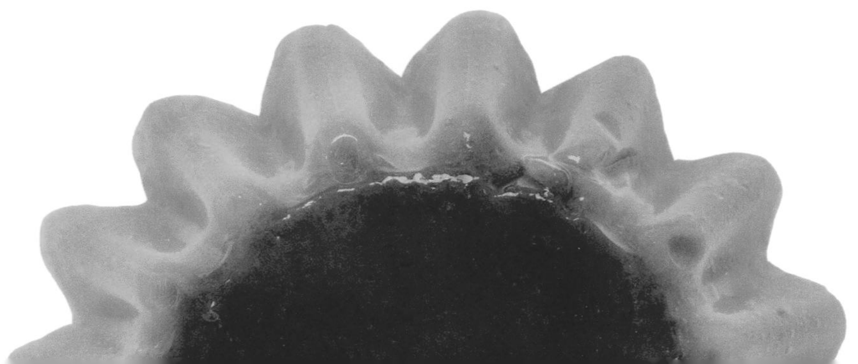

6 Divide the custard base evenly among the ramekins.

7 Seal the ramekins tightly with plastic wrap.

8 Cook the custard base in the water bath to a core temperature of 80 °C/176 °F, about 1 hour. Use a thermometer to check the temperature. The cooking time depends on the size of the ramekins, the starting temperature of the cream, and the bath design. The custards cook faster in a bath heated from the bottom.

9 Lift the ramekins carefully from the water bath. Use tongs.

10 Refrigerate the custards until they are fully chilled, about 2 hours, and then remove the plastic wrap.

11 Sprinkle sugar over the tops of the cold custards.

12 Melt and caramelize the sugar by sweeping the flame of a blowtorch over it.

13 Let the sugar cool to a crisp crust before serving it.

FINISHING VARIATION

Instead of blowtorching the custards, you can make caramel by carefully heating sugar in a shallow pan over medium heat until it turns dark brown; remove it from the heat before it burns. After step 10, pour the caramel over each custard, and allow it to cool to a crisp crust before serving it. If you are making many servings, this method is faster than using a blowtorch.

LEMON POSSET

YIELD:	*six servings (415 g)*
TIME ESTIMATE:	*12½ hours overall, including 30 minutes of preparation and 12 hours unattended*
STORAGE NOTES:	*keeps for 4 days when refrigerated*
LEVEL OF DIFFICULTY:	*easy*
SPECIAL REQUIREMENTS:	*citric acid, Sous Vide Lemon Curd (optional, see the next page)*

Perhaps the oldest way to make a dairy gel is to add an acid, such as citrus juice (which contains citric acid). The acid causes the proteins in the milk to coagulate into curds. Fresh cheeses such as ricotta and *paneer* are made this way, and so is posset, a creamy delicacy so old that Shakespeare refers to it in *Macbeth*. Our Modernist version uses citric acid, which is more consistent than lemon juice, but you can substitute 57 g / 57 mL / ¼ cup of lemon juice. Garnish the posset with seasonal berries or a citrus salad, according to the season.

INGREDIENT	WEIGHT	VOLUME	SCALING	PROCEDURE
Heavy cream	300 g	330 mL / 1⅜ cups	100%	① Combine in a pot, and stir to dissolve the sugar.
Sugar	51 g	¼ cup	17%	② Heat to 88 °C / 190 °F while stirring constantly.
Citric acid	2.1 g		0.7%	③ Remove the pot from the heat, and stir in until the citric acid crystals are completely dissolved and the mixture thickens to a thin custard. ④ Cool at room temperature for 10 minutes so that condensation does not build up in steps 5 or 7 and make the curd runny. ⑤ Divide evenly into six ramekins or other small dishes. ⑥ Cover the ramekins with plastic wrap, and place them in the refrigerator for 12 hours.
Sous Vide Lemon Curd (optional) see the next page	120 g	¾ cup	40%	⑦ Pipe or spoon a thin layer onto each portion of posset while the custard is still soft; it firms as it cools. ⑧ Stir the posset to soften it, and serve it chilled.

2

3a

3b

7

SOUS VIDE LEMON CURD

YIELD:	*six to eight servings (850 g / 3 cups)*
TIME ESTIMATE:	*4¾ hours overall, including 15 minutes of preparation and 4½ hours unattended*
STORAGE NOTES:	*keeps for 3–4 days when refrigerated*
LEVEL OF DIFFICULTY:	*easy*
SPECIAL REQUIREMENTS:	*sous vide setup, citric acid, 1 L whipping siphon and two cartridges of nitrous oxide (optional), lemon essential oil (optional)*

By cooking the eggs in basic lemon curd sous vide, you can make large amounts without the hassle of a double boiler or the risk of overcurdling. If you have a whipping siphon, you can also foam the curd by pouring it into the siphon before it has fully set; bring the curd to room temperature first to make a more fluid foam. You can adjust the acidity of the curd without altering the texture by tailoring the amount of citric acid. You can substitute freshly grated lemon zest for the lemon essential oil.

INGREDIENT	WEIGHT	VOLUME	SCALING	PROCEDURE
Egg yolks, blended	120 g	½ cup / 8–10 yolks	30%	① Preheat a water bath to 65 °C / 149 °F. ② Place in a zip-top bag, remove as much air as possible from the bag by using the water-displacement method (see page 58), and seal it. ③ Cook sous vide for 35 minutes. ④ Plunge the bag into ice water.
Sugar	300 g	1½ cups	75%	⑤ Combine in a medium saucepan, and boil until the sugar and citric acid dissolve completely, about 2 minutes. ⑥ Cool the syrup to room temperature. ⑦ Pour the cooked egg yolks into a blender. Add the syrup gradually while blending.
Water	40 g	40 mL / 2½ Tbsp	10%	
Citric acid	8 g		2%	
Unsalted butter, room temperature, cubed	400 g	1¾ cups	100%	⑧ Continue blending, and drop cubes of butter into the mixture until all of the butter is completely incorporated.
Lemon essential oil (optional)	1 g	1 mL / ¼ tsp	0.3%	⑨ Stir in. ⑩ Cover and refrigerate until thickened, about 4 hours. ⑪ Serve cold.
Salt	0.5 g	⅛ tsp	0.1%	

Temperature is key to combining the ingredients smoothly: if the butter is too cold, it will not blend in evenly. If the butter is too warm, the curds will separate or seem greasy.

VARIATIONS

Fruit Curds

Substitute fresh citrus juice, such as grapefruit, mandarin, orange, Meyer lemon, or lime juice, for the water and citric acid in step 5. At step 9, add the grated zest of the fruit. Alternatively, use fresh pineapple juice that has been simmered until reduced by half, fresh passion fruit puree, or cranberry juice in place of the citrus juice.

Foamed Lemon Curd

After step 9, pour half of the curd into a 1 L siphon while it is still runny, charge the siphon with two cartridges of nitrous oxide, and then dispense the foam. If you are substituting lemon zest for the essential oil, strain the curd before putting it into the siphon.

RASPBERRY PANNA COTTA

YIELD:	*six servings (350 g)*
TIME ESTIMATE:	*5½ hours overall, including 30 minutes of preparation and 5 hours unattended*
STORAGE NOTES:	*keeps for up to 2 days when refrigerated*
LEVEL OF DIFFICULTY:	*easy*
SPECIAL REQUIREMENTS:	*gelatin (or agar and xanthan gum, or iota and kappa carrageenan, for vegetarian versions)*

This panna cotta recipe illustrates how even a very simple dish can be enhanced by one fundamental Modernist step—weighing the gelatin! Don't dump in a whole envelope or teaspoonful; use a scale to measure just enough gelatin to set the custard. If you scale the recipe, use 0.8 g of Knox brand powdered gelatin for every 100 g of liquid.

Gels made with gelatin strengthen as they age, so the panna cotta will be firmer if you make it a day or two in advance. Although panna cotta is usually served cold, you can soften it slightly by warming it to room temperature before serving. Gelatin melts at 37 °C / 100 °F, so don't warm it too much.

INGREDIENT	WEIGHT	VOLUME	SCALING	PROCEDURE
Whole milk, cold	30 g	30 mL / 2 Tbsp	10%	① Sprinkle the gelatin over the cold milk.
Powdered gelatin (Knox brand)	4.3 g		1.4%	② Let stand for 5–10 minutes to soften the gelatin.
Heavy cream	300 g	330 mL / 1⅜ cups	100%	③ Blend together, and then mix with the softened gelatin and milk in a pot.
Fresh raspberry puree	200 g	⅞ cup	67%	④ Bring to a simmer over medium-low heat until the gelatin dissolves.
Sugar	75 g	⅜ cup	25%	⑤ Strain through a fine sieve.
Salt	0.3 g	pinch	0.1%	⑥ Cool to room temperature, and then divide it evenly into six small bowls.
				⑦ Cover and refrigerate until fully set, at least 5 hours.

WORKING WITH GELATIN

Gelatin is the gelling agent used in many traditional dishes, from French pâtés to British aspics to American Jell-O. It is sold in sheet, granule, and powder form, all of which come in a variety of gelling strengths, or Bloom ratings. The higher the Bloom rating, the stronger the gel that forms when a given amount of gelatin is dissolved in a fixed amount of water.

The recipe above calls for Knox brand powdered gelatin, which has a Bloom strength of 225. You can use sheet gelatin instead as long as the Bloom rating is comparable. Gelatins are sometimes labeled as bronze, silver, gold, and platinum rather than with a Bloom rating; the table at right connects the two rating systems. Gold or platinum gelatin can be substituted directly for Knox powdered gelatin. Alternatively, substitute 1.3 g of bronze gelatin or 1.1 g of silver gelatin for every 100 g of liquid.

Sheet gelatin is sold at some specialty food markets. To use the sheets, soak them in water until they soften, and then drain and squeeze them gently to remove excess moisture. The softened sheets can then be dissolved in hot liquid as in steps 3 and 4.

Kinds of Gelatin

Name	Bloom strength	Grams per sheet
bronze	125–155	3.3
silver	160	2.5
gold	190–220	2.0
Knox brand	225	n/a
platinum	235–265	1.7

Converting Bloom strengths

If you know both the weight MA and the Bloom strength BA of gelatin A, you can calculate the equivalent weight MB of gelatin B having a Bloom strength of BB by using the formula MB = MA × BA ÷ BB.

For example, if a recipe calls for 2.6 g of Knox gelatin, you can instead use 2.6 × 225 ÷ 160 = 3.7 g of silver gelatin.

VARIATIONS

Fruit Jellies

Use 0.8 g of Knox brand powdered gelatin with any fruit juice to make a fun, colorful dessert.

Vegetarian Panna Cotta

Substitute a mixture of 0.8 g agar and 0.65 g xanthan gum for the gelatin. Alternatively, use a mixture of 0.65 g of iota carrageenan and 0.5 g of kappa carrageenan. These gelling agents are derived from seaweed or bacterial fermentation; whereas gelatin is made from animal sources, such as pig or fish skin. For more details on making gels, see page 98.

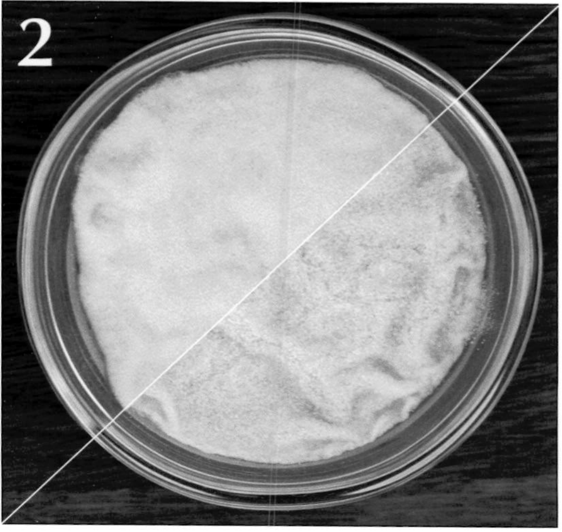

1 Sprinkle the gelatin over the cold milk.

2 Let stand for 5–10 minutes to soften the gelatin.

3 Blend together the cream, raspberry puree, sugar, and salt, and then mix with the softened gelatin and milk in a pot.

4 Bring the mixture to a simmer over medium-low heat until the gelatin dissolves completely.

5 Strain the mixture through a fine sieve.

6 Cool the panna cotta to room temperature, and then divide it evenly into six small bowls, about 60 g per serving.

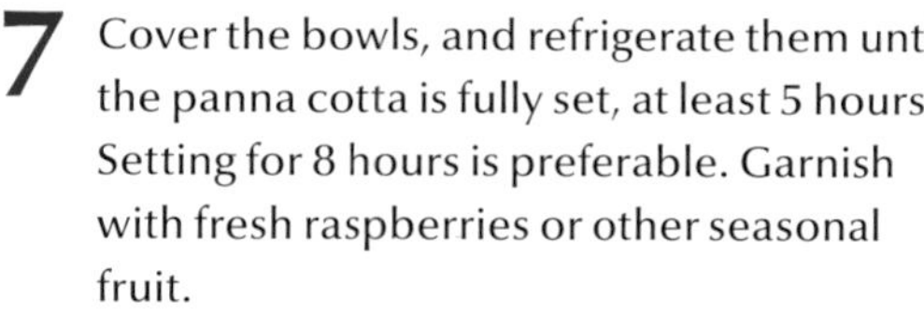

7 Cover the bowls, and refrigerate them until the panna cotta is fully set, at least 5 hours. Setting for 8 hours is preferable. Garnish with fresh raspberries or other seasonal fruit.

SOUS VIDE VANILLA CRÈME ANGLAISE

YIELD:	*six to eight servings (775 g / 3 cups)*
TIME ESTIMATE:	*1 hour overall, including 15 minutes of preparation and 45 minutes unattended*
STORAGE NOTES:	*keeps for 3 days when refrigerated*
LEVEL OF DIFFICULTY:	*easy*
SPECIAL REQUIREMENTS:	*sous vide setup*

Crème anglaise is a thin custard that has myriad uses: transform it into a rich milk shake, pour it over fresh berries, or churn it into unctuous ice cream. The classic stove-top method for making it is laborious; cook it sous vide instead, and you can do other things while it cooks. The custard turns out just as smooth.

We chose vanilla seeds to use in this recipe because of the intense flavor they lend to the custard. Vanilla lovers may even want to double the amount of seeds used. But you can substitute many other kinds of flavorings for the vanilla. Try foaming crème anglaise in a whipping siphon to make an ethereal garnish to fresh fruit or apple pie.

INGREDIENT	WEIGHT	VOLUME	SCALING
Whole milk	500 g	520 mL / 2⅛ cups	100%
Egg yolks, blended	150 g	⅝ cup / 8–10 yolks	30%
Heavy cream	63 g	70 mL / 5 Tbsp	13%
Sugar	63 g	5 Tbsp	13%
Vanilla seeds	1.8 g	from 1–2 pods	0.36%

PROCEDURE

1. Preheat a water bath to 83 °C / 181 °F.
2. Whisk together, and spoon off any foam.
3. Pour into a zip-top bag, remove as much air as possible from the bag by using the water-displacement method (see page 58), and seal it.
4. Cook sous vide for 45 minutes.
5. Remove the bag from the water bath, and immerse it in ice water until the mixture has cooled completely.
6. Puree the mixture until smooth by using an immersion blender.
7. Pass the crème through a fine sieve, and serve it warm or cold.

Vanilla and its extract

Vanilla is the oily residue that coats the tiny seeds of a tropical orchid grown in Tahiti, Madagascar, the Seychelles, and Mexico. For the best flavor, the seedpods should be plump and a bit moist inside. Vanilla extract is made by infusing the seedpods in alcohol. You can substitute vanilla extract for the vanilla seeds in this recipe, but we find that the flavor is not as good as when using the seeds.

1 Preheat a water bath to 83 °C / 181 °F.

2 Whisk the milk, egg yolks, cream, sugar, and vanilla seeds together. Try not to create bubbles; if foam appears on the surface, spoon it off.

3 Pour the custard into a zip-top bag. Remove as much air as possible from the bag by using the water-displacement method (see page 58), and seal it.

4 Cook sous vide for 45 minutes.

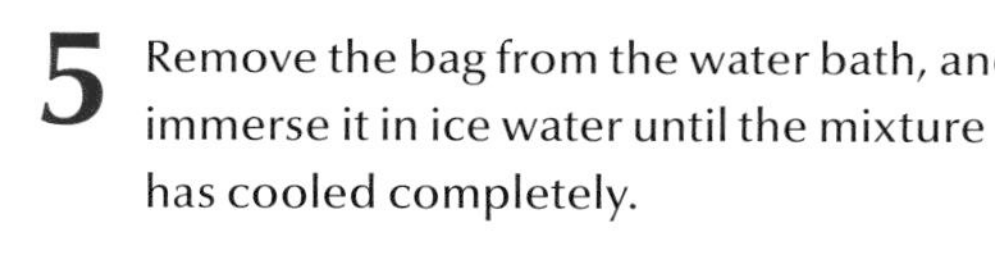

5 Remove the bag from the water bath, and immerse it in ice water until the mixture has cooled completely.

6 Puree the mixture until smooth by using an immersion blender.

7 Pass the crème through a fine sieve, and serve it warm or cold. The vanilla seeds tend to settle over time, so stir or blend as needed before serving.

VARIATION: Sabayon

In Italian cuisine, a light foam stabilized by an egg yolk custard is called a zabaglione and often contains marsala wine or another alcohol. In France, it is called sabayon and is made without alcohol. To make it, pour 150 g / ⅝ cup of blended egg yolks (about 10 yolks) into a zip-top bag, remove as much air as possible from the bag, and seal it. Cook sous vide in a 70 °C / 158 °F water bath for 35 minutes. Blend the cooked yolks while they are still warm with 50 g / ¼ cup of sugar and 175 g / 180 mL / ¾ cup of milk, water, or fruit juice. Cool, and then pour into a whipping siphon. Charge with three cartridges of nitrous oxide, and shake. Dispense the foam immediately, or refrigerate it in the siphon.

PISTACHIO GELATO

YIELD:	*eight servings (1 kg / 4 cups)*
TIME ESTIMATE:	*5 hours overall, including 30 minutes of preparation and 4½ hours unattended*
STORAGE NOTES:	*best when served within 24 hours; keeps for up to 1 week when frozen*
LEVEL OF DIFFICULTY:	*moderate*
SPECIAL REQUIREMENTS:	*ice-cream machine, tapioca starch, xanthan gum, pistachio butter, pistachio oil*

This gelato has become a signature dish from *Modernist Cuisine*; we serve it at most of our events. Vegans particularly enjoy it because it is as smooth and intense as the best gelato, but contains no eggs or dairy. A side benefit of that feature is that the gelato can be melted and safely rechurned if it freezes too hard. You may find that you need to warm the gelato for 10 minutes before serving it if it has been in the freezer for 24 hours or more.

The recipe works with any kind of nut butter, whether you buy it commercially or make your own by using a powerful blender, such as a Vitamix. The variations listed below are just a starting point; cashew and almond butters also make delicious gelati. Use the highest-quality nut butter you can find. For pistachio gelato, it is crucial to use 100% pistachio butter that has no coloring or other additives.

INGREDIENT	WEIGHT	VOLUME	SCALING	PROCEDURE
Cold water	680 g	680 mL / 2⅞ cups	100%	① Measure into a pot.
Sugar	155 g	¾ cup	23%	② Combine.
Tapioca starch	25 g	¼ cup	3.7%	③ Blend into the cold water gradually by using an immersion blender.
Salt	7 g	1¾ tsp	1%	④ Bring to a boil while blending constantly.
Xanthan gum (Bob's Red Mill brand)	0.3 g		0.04%	⑤ Remove the pot from the heat.
Pistachio butter, pure (Bronte Sicilian, PreGel brand)	210 g	¾ cup	31%	⑥ Blend into the mixture until thoroughly combined. ⑦ Chill the mixture over an ice bath. ⑧ Churn the mixture in an ice-cream machine until it freezes and thickens, about 30 minutes.
Pistachio oil (Castelmuro brand)	102 g	110 mL / ½ cup	15%	⑨ Cover the top of the gelato with plastic wrap, and freeze it in a sealed container until firm, at least 4 hours.

VARIATIONS

Hazelnut Gelato

Substitute hazelnut butter and hazelnut oil for the pistachio butter and pistachio oil. Because of its high fat content, hazelnut gelato does not look as smooth as pistachio gelato does, but its mouthfeel is just as creamy.

Strawberry Macadamia Gelato

Substitute fresh strawberry juice for the water, and substitute raw macadamia butter and raw macadamia oil for the pistachio butter and pistachio oil. It is important to use raw nut butter in this case because the flavor of roasted nut butter clashes with that of the strawberry juice.

P. B. & J. Gelato

Substitute peanut butter and roasted peanut oil for the pistachio butter and pistachio oil, and substitute either fresh strawberry juice or fresh Concord grape juice for the water. Reduce the amount of sugar used to 125 g / ⅝ cup.

1 Measure the water into a pot.

2 Combine the sugar, tapioca starch, salt, and xanthan gum. Dry-blending the thickening agents helps to ensure that they are distributed evenly in the next step.

3 Blend the dry ingredients into the water by using an immersion blender.

4 Bring the mixture to a boil while blending constantly.

5 Remove the pot from the heat.

2

3

6 Blend the pistachio butter and pistachio oil gradually into the pot until thoroughly combined. Use an immersion blender.

7 Chill the mixture over an ice bath. Whisk the mixture occasionally to help it cool evenly.

8 Transfer the mixture to an ice-cream machine, and churn it until it thickens and freezes.

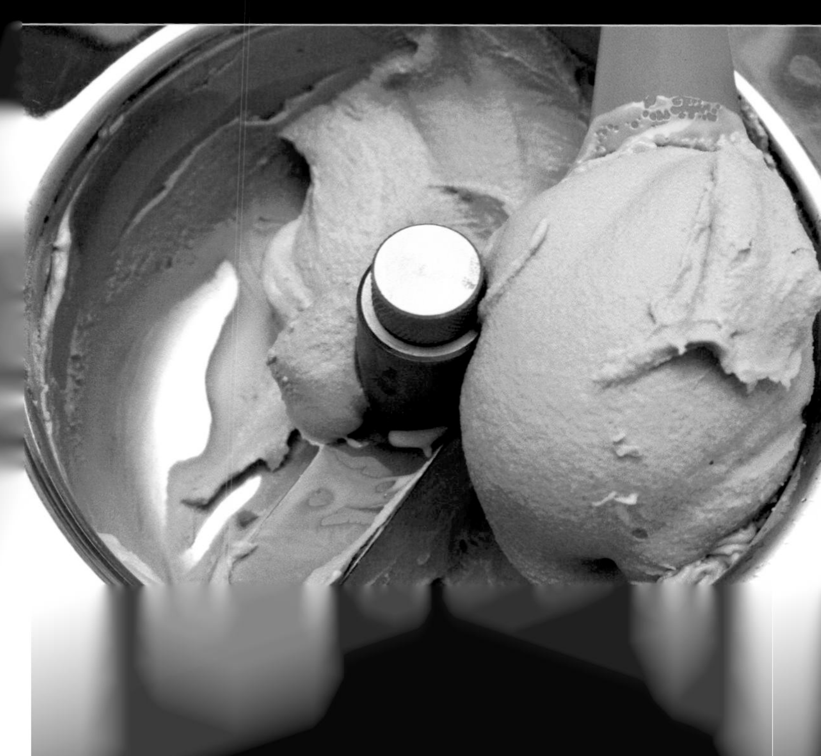

9 Transfer the gelato to a container, press plastic wrap onto the surface of the gelato, and seal the container. Then place it in the freezer until the gelato is firm, at least 4 hours. The plastic wrap prevents a skin from forming on the gelato. You may need to temper the gelato at room temperature slightly before serving it.

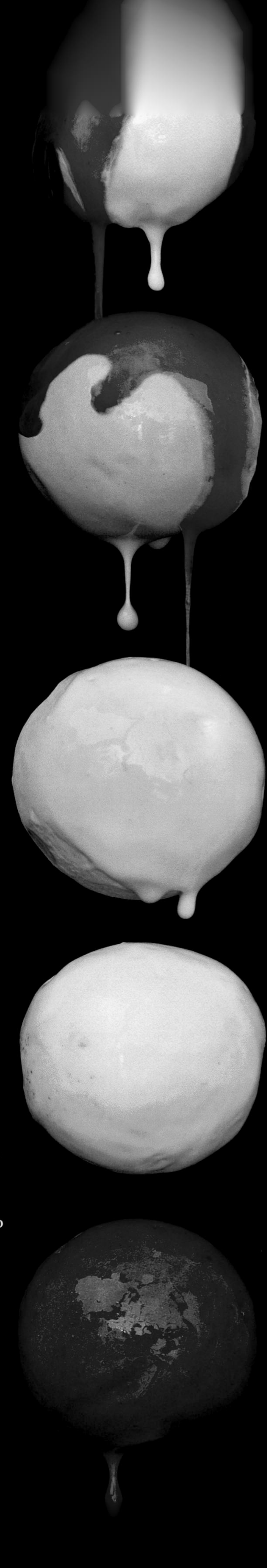

FLAKY PIE CRUST

YIELD:	*475 g of crust (enough for one 30 cm / 12 in pie or four 11 cm / 4½ in tarts)*
TIME ESTIMATE:	*2½ hours overall, including 30 minutes of preparation and 2 hours unattended*
STORAGE NOTES:	*keeps for up to 3 days when refrigerated and 3 months when vacuum sealed and frozen*
LEVEL OF DIFFICULTY:	*moderate*
SPECIAL REQUIREMENTS:	*sous vide setup, food processor, almond flour*

We tested more than 40 versions of sweet pastry crust (*pâte sucrée*) and tart crust (*pâte sablée*). This recipe combines the advantages of both kinds of dough and was the best by far. It includes a little almond flour and yields a sweet, delicate, and buttery crust that goes well with any tart or pie—although it pairs especially well with velvety custard fillings (see page 375). The recipe is easily adapted to create exciting flavor variations; we've included some of our favorites below.

INGREDIENT	WEIGHT	VOLUME	SCALING	PROCEDURE
Egg yolks, blended	50 g	3½ Tbsp / 3–4 yolks	25%	① Preheat a water bath to **67 °C / 153 °F**. ② Place the yolks in a zip-top bag, remove as much air as possible from the bag by using the water-displacement method (see page 58), and seal it. ③ Cook the yolks sous vide for 45 minutes.
All-purpose flour	200 g	1½ cups	100%	④ Combine in a food processor, and pulse until blended to the texture of cornmeal. ⑤ Add the cooked egg yolks gradually while processing. ⑥ Continue processing in pulses until the dough begins to cohere. ⑦ Shape the dough into a thick disk, wrap it with plastic, and refrigerate it for at least 1 hour. ⑧ Preheat the oven to **190 °C / 375 °F**. ⑨ Roll the dough into a circle about 5 cm / 2 in wider than the diameter of the pie pan. If making smaller tarts, divide the dough into four equal pieces, and roll out each one separately. ⑩ Line the pan with the dough; allow excess dough to hang over the edges. ⑪ Prick the dough all over with a fork, and then cover it with parchment paper, and fill it with baking beads or dried beans. ⑫ Bake until golden brown, about 12 minutes for a single piecrust or 8–9 minutes for four smaller tart crusts. ⑬ Remove the beans and parchment. Bake 2–3 minutes more if needed. ⑭ Cool to room temperature, and then trim excess crust from the edges.
Unsalted butter, very cold, diced	165 g	¾ cup	83%	
Powdered sugar	80 g	¾ cup	40%	
Almond flour (Bob's Red Mill brand)	30 g	⅜ cup	15%	
Salt	4 g	1 tsp	2%	
Baking powder	2 g	½ tsp	1%	

VARIATIONS

Double Almond Crust
At step 5, add 2.5 g / ¾ tsp of almond extract.

Brown Butter Crust
At step 4, substitute frozen chunks of brown butter (see page 119) for half of the unsalted butter.

Gingerbread Crust
At step 4, add 53 g / 6½ Tbsp of Autumn Spice Mix (see page 138).

Peanut Crust
At step 4, substitute finely ground, roasted peanuts for the almond flour, and add 40 g / 3 Tbsp of smooth peanut butter.

Carrot Crust
Increase the amount of egg yolks to 63 g / ¼ cup (about 4 yolks). Add 70 g / ⅞ cup of freeze-dried carrot powder at step 4.

Cheese Crust
At step 4, add 60 g / ⅞ cup of shredded Parmesan cheese, and reduce the amount of powdered sugar to 20 g / 3 Tbsp.

Coconut Crust
Increase the amount of blended egg yolks to 63 g / ¼ cup, and add 70 g / ⅞ cup of coconut cream powder at step 4.

Raspberry Crust
Increase the amount of blended egg yolks to 63 g / ¼ cup (about 4 yolks). Add 70 g / ⅞ cup of Freeze-Dried Raspberry Powder (see page 377) at step 4.

Chocolate Crust
Increase the amount of blended egg yolks to 68 g / 4½ Tbsp (4–5 yolks). At step 4, add 186 g / 1⅛ cups of finely chopped dark chocolate, 80 g / 8 Tbsp of granulated sugar, 34 g / ⅜ cup of Dutch-processed cocoa powder, and 2 g / ¼ tsp of vanilla extract. Substitute baking soda for the baking powder. At step 12, add 1–2 minutes to the baking time. Take extra care when removing the parchment paper in step 13.

To keep a pie shell crisp, brush a thin coat of melted cocoa butter onto the interior of the piecrust, and allow the fat to solidify at room temperature before you fill the shell with pastry cream. The layer of cocoa fat forms a moisture barrier that prevents the piecrust from getting soggy.

1 Preheat a water bath to 67 °C / 153 °F.

2 Place the egg yolks in a zip-top bag. Remove as much air as possible from the bag by using the water-displacement method (see page 58), and seal it. You can skip this step and the next, but using raw yolks will cause the crust to shrink and tighten more as it bakes.

3 Cook the egg yolks sous vide for 45 minutes.

4 Combine the flours, diced butter, powdered sugar, salt, and baking powder in a food processor, and pulse until the mixture takes on the texture of cornmeal.

5 Drizzle in the egg yolks while pulsing the food processor.

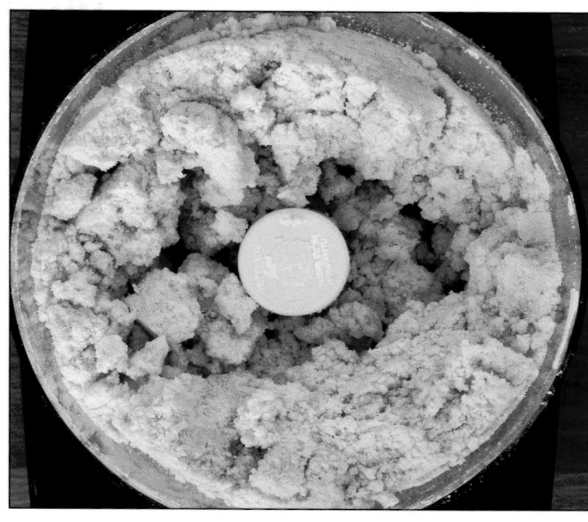

6 Continue processing in pulses until the dough starts to bind. Although it looks very dry, it will eventually cohere.

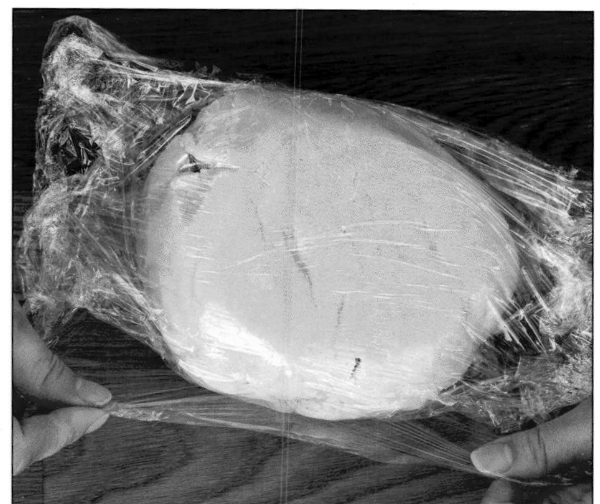

7 Form the dough into a ball, flatten it to a thick disk, and wrap it tightly with plastic wrap. Refrigerate it for at least 1 hour to allow the gluten to rest and the butter to harden.

8 Preheat the oven to 190 °C / 375 °F.

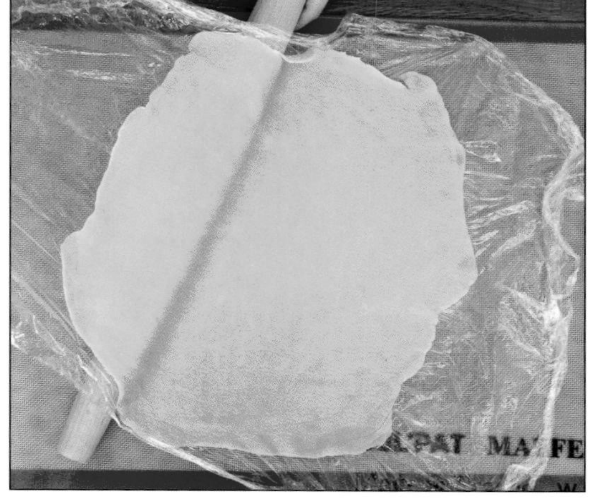

9 Roll the dough into a circle 3 mm / ⅛ in thick and about 5 cm / 2 in larger than the pie pan. If making smaller tart crusts, divide the dough into four equal parts, and roll out each one separately. If the dough sticks, roll it out between two sheets of plastic or parchment, or chill briefly in the refrigerator.

10 Line the pan with the dough. Do not trim any excess dough; let it drape over the edges of the pan. Press the dough firmly into the interior edges of the pan. If you will not be baking the crust immediately, store it in the refrigerator.

11 Prick the dough all over with a fork. Press a protective layer of parchment paper over it. Fill the pan with baking beads or dry beans, and press them against the walls so that the dough doesn't droop while baking.

12 Place the tart pan on a baking sheet, and bake the crust until it turns golden brown, about 12 minutes for a single piecrust or 8–9 minutes for four smaller tart crusts. Rotate the pie a half-turn midway through baking.

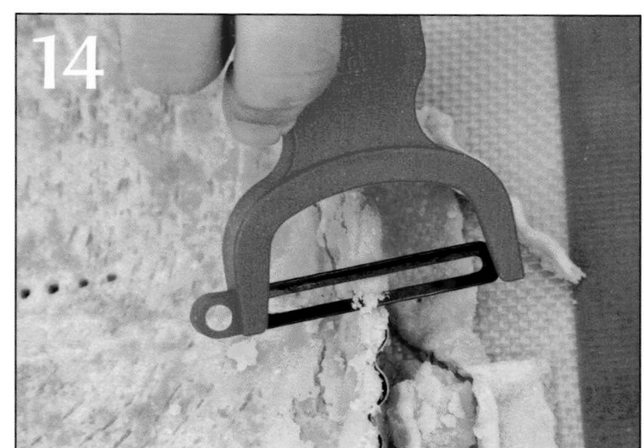

13 Remove the beans and parchment carefully. If the crust still looks slightly wet, bake it for an additional 2–3 minutes.

14 Cool the crust to room temperature, and then trim any excess crust from the margins of the pan.

SOUS VIDE VANILLA-CINNAMON PASTRY CREAM

YIELD:	*500 g / 2 cups; fills one 23 cm / 9 in piecrust or four 11 cm / 4½ in tart shells; half-fills one 30 cm / 12 in piecrust*
TIME ESTIMATE:	*2¾ hours overall, including 15 minutes of preparation and 2½ hours unattended*
STORAGE NOTES:	*keeps for up to 2 days when refrigerated*
LEVEL OF DIFFICULTY:	*easy*
SPECIAL REQUIREMENTS:	*sous vide setup*

Pastry cream, or *crème pâtissière*, is the workhorse of custards. Traditional recipes for it are heavy on starch, which stabilizes the egg yolk emulsion but dilutes the taste and coarsens the texture.

This recipe dodges those problems by cooking the egg yolks sous vide before they are blended into a cream infused with cinnamon and vanilla. Our approach eliminates the risk of curdling the custard and also opens up a virtually endless variety of flavor and texture combinations, some of which are presented on the next page.

INGREDIENT	WEIGHT	VOLUME	SCALING	PROCEDURE
Heavy cream	100 g	110 mL / ½ cup	100%	① Preheat a water bath to **80** °C / **176** °F.
Whole milk	100 g	100 mL / ⅜ cup	100%	② Combine in a pot, and whisk over medium-low heat until the sugar and salt dissolve completely.
Sugar	64 g	5 Tbsp	64%	③ Refrigerate for 2 hours.
Cinnamon stick	3 g	1 stick	3%	④ Remove and discard the cinnamon stick.
Vanilla seeds, scraped from the bean	1 g	¼ tsp / from 1 bean	1%	
Salt	0.3 g	pinch	0.3%	
Egg yolks, blended and strained	200 g	¾ cup / 11–12 yolks	200%	⑤ Place in a zip-top bag, remove as much air as possible from the bag by using the water-displacement method (see page 58), and seal it. ⑥ Cook sous vide for 35 minutes. ⑦ Puree immediately in a blender. ⑧ Add the infused milk and cream gradually while blending.
Unsalted butter, softened	50 g	¼ cup	50%	⑨ Increase the blender speed to high, add the softened butter, and blend until smooth and creamy. ⑩ Serve the custard warm or cold.

1 Preheat a water bath to **80** °C / **176** °F.

2 Combine the cream, milk, sugar, cinnamon stick, vanilla seeds, and salt in a pot, and whisk over medium-low heat until the sugar and salt dissolve completely.

3 Refrigerate the mixture for 2 hours to infuse it with the cinnamon and vanilla.

4 Remove and discard the cinnamon stick. Optionally, sieve the liquid to remove the vanilla seeds.

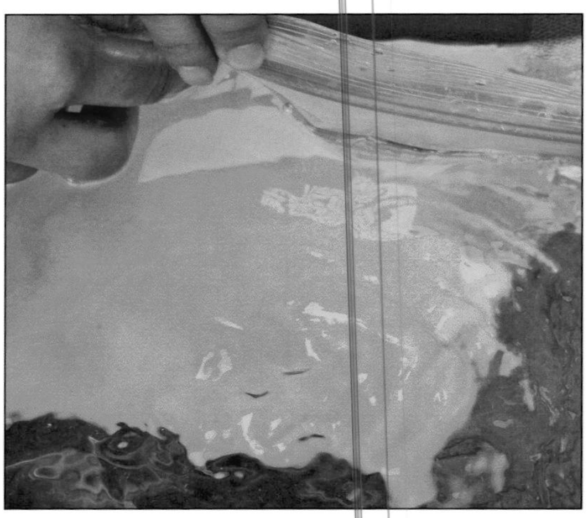

5 Place the blended and strained egg yolks into a zip-top bag, remove as much air as possible from the bag by using the water-displacement method (see page 58), and seal it.

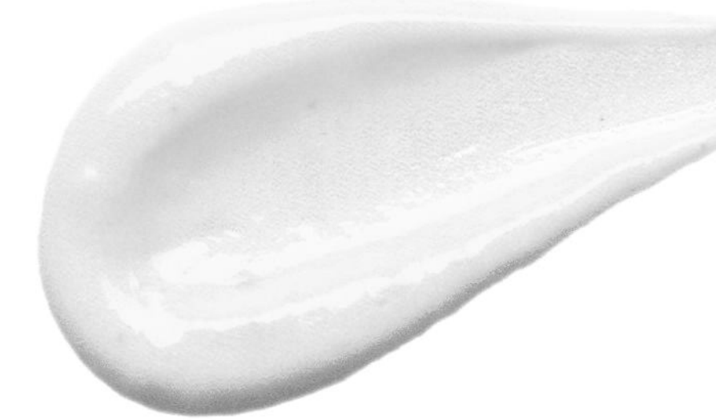

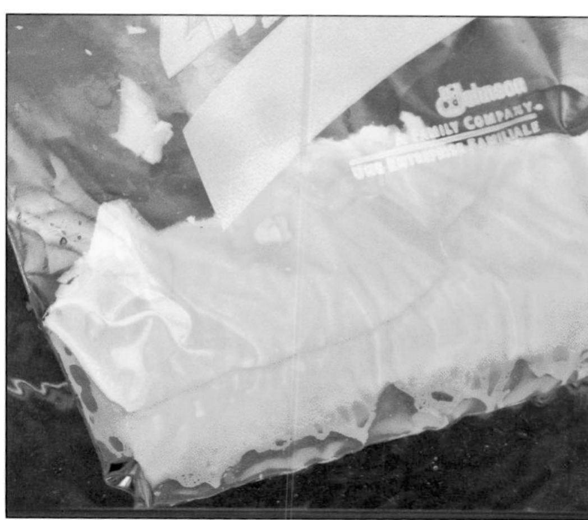

6 Cook the egg yolks sous vide for 35 minutes. The yolks will be firm and fully set after cooking.

7 Puree the yolks immediately at low speed in a blender. If you cannot puree the yolks immediately, be sure to keep them warm, or else the pastry cream will become slightly grainy.

8 Add the mixture of infused milk and cream to the blender gradually as it continues to run at low speed.

9 Increase the blender speed to high, and add the softened butter. Scrape down the sides of the blender if necessary. Continue blending until the mixture becomes smooth and creamy. You can optionally sieve the custard after blending it.

10 The custard can be served warm or cold. It will thicken as it cools. To prevent a skin from forming, press plastic wrap directly onto the custard before storing it.

VARIATIONS

Amaretto Pastry Cream

Omit the cinnamon stick and vanilla seeds. At step 8, add 5 g / 6 mL / ¼ tsp of amaretto liqueur.

Lemon Pastry Cream

Substitute 7.5 g / 2½ Tbsp of grated lemon zest (from 2 lemons) for the cinnamon stick and vanilla seeds. At step 8, add 4 g of citric acid.

Coconut Pastry Cream

Substitute unsweetened coconut cream or coconut milk for the heavy cream and milk, increase the amount of sugar to 80 g / ½ cup, and omit the cinnamon stick and vanilla seeds. At step 9, use just 20 g / 2 Tbsp of soft, unsalted butter.

Ginger Pastry Cream

At step 2, omit the cinnamon stick and vanilla seeds, reduce the amount of sugar to 57 g / 5½ Tbsp, and add 100 g / ⅔ cup of minced candied ginger, 0.5 g / ½ tsp of ground ginger powder, and 0.1 g / ⅛ tsp of freshly ground black pepper. At step 4, sieve the infused milk and cream mixture before adding it to the blender.

Cheese Pastry Cream

This savory variation makes an excellent cheese dip or unsweetened filling for cream puffs. At step 2, omit the sugar, cinnamon stick, and vanilla seeds, and use an immersion blender to gradually blend 200 g / 2 cups of shredded Gruyère cheese into the hot milk and cream until it is smooth and completely melted. Cool the cheese mixture just to room temperature; it will solidify if refrigerated. Continue at step 5.

Pressure-Infused Coffee Pastry Cream

Pour 150 g / 165 mL / ¾ cup of heavy cream and 150 g / 150 mL / ⅔ cup of whole milk into a whipping siphon, and add 120 g / 1⅛ cups of whole, dark-roast coffee beans. Charge the siphon with two cartridges of nitrous oxide, and then refrigerate it for 4 hours. Release the pressure on the siphon slowly; do not dispense the cream. Strain the coffee-infused cream into a saucepan, and then continue with step 1, omitting the cinnamon stick and vanilla seeds. If you do not have a siphon, simply refrigerate the coffee beans in the cold liquid for 12 hours, strain, and then continue at step 1.

Chocolate Pastry Cream

Omit the cinnamon stick, vanilla seeds, and butter. At step 2, combine the milk, sugar, and salt (but not the cream) with 100 g / ⅝ cup of finely chopped dark chocolate and 24 g / ⅓ cup of Dutch-processed cocoa powder in the top of a double boiler. Whisk the mixture over medium heat until smooth and completely melted. Cool the mixture to room temperature. Continue at step 5. At step 8, blend the chocolate mixture gradually into the cooked egg yolks, and then gradually add the heavy cream. Add additional cream as needed to adjust the consistency of the custard.

Firm Pastry Cream

You can make a firmer custard by adding gelatin. Use 1 g of Knox brand powdered gelatin for every 500 g of pastry cream; the recipe above, for example, yields 500 g, so would require 0.9 g of gelatin. To soften the gelatin, mix it into an additional 20 g / 20 mL / 1½ Tbsp of cold cream or milk, and then warm the mixture over low heat until the gelatin melts completely. At step 9, add the melted gelatin mixture along with the butter. If using as a pie filling, pour the custard into the crust immediately after step 9, and then refrigerate the pie until fully set, at least 3 hours.

Add the gelatin to the milk or cream while the liquid is cold, and then melt it over medium heat. For more information, see Working with Gelatin, page 366.

PIE TOPPINGS

Our approach to making pies is simple but powerful: we mix and match different bases and toppings to create myriad delicious combinations. The sweet garnishes described below can be used to accentuate the pies on pages 378–379 or any of the other desserts in this chapter.

Coconut Cream Pie

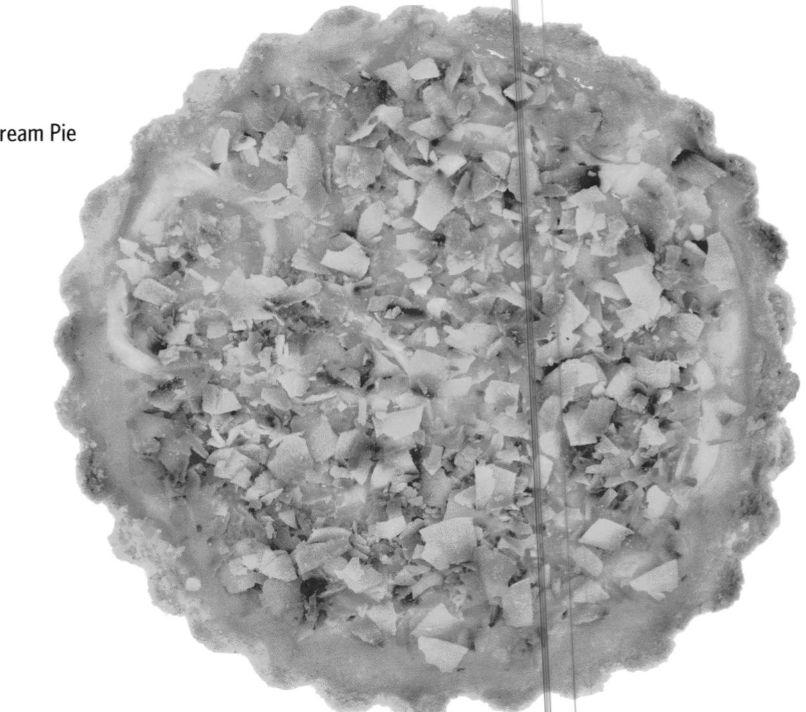

Apple Foam

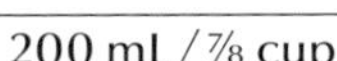

Granny Smith apple juice	200 g	200 mL / ⅞ cup
Powdered gelatin (Knox brand)	2.4 g	
Fresh lime juice	to taste	
Sugar	to taste	
Salt	to taste	

Measure 20 g / 20 mL / 4 tsp of the cold apple juice in a small dish, and sprinkle the gelatin into it. Wait several minutes for the gelatin to soften, and then warm the mixture over low heat until the gelatin melts. Add the remaining apple juice (see photo), and season with fresh lime juice, sugar, and salt. The mixture should be intensely flavored. Pour it into a whipping siphon, and charge the siphon with two cartridges of nitrous oxide. For best results, refrigerate the mixture in the siphon for 4 hours before dispensing the foam. This recipe can be easily adapted to make a foam from virtually any flavorful fruit juice or other liquid.

Passion Fruit Glaze

Passion fruit puree (Perfect Purée of Napa Valley brand)	20 g	4 tsp
Xanthan gum	1.5 g	

Blend together until thickened. You can also make the puree from scratch by passing fresh passion fruit pulp through a sieve.

Cocoa Nib and Cardamom Dust

Pulse 20 g / ¼ cup of cardamom seeds in a coffee grinder until the mixture resembles coarse cornmeal. Add 20 g / 2½ Tbsp of cocoa nibs, and continue pulsing until they are finely ground. Sift the mixture to remove any hulls or large pieces. This topping also makes a nice garnish for lattes and cappuccinos.

Apple Cream Pie

Chocolate Cream Pie

Banana Cream Pie

Almond and Cherry Cream Pie

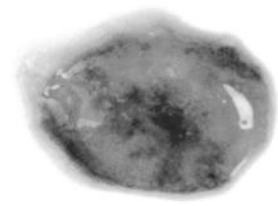

Blowtorch-Caramelized Bananas

Banana, sliced on the bias 5 mm / ¼ in thick	120 g	1 large
Sugar	30 g	3 Tbsp

Arrange banana slices on a baking sheet, and freeze them until firm, about 20 minutes. Sprinkle with one quarter of the sugar. Melt and caramelize the sugar by using a blowtorch (see page 15). Repeat three times to coat the banana in a layer of dark caramel, returning the bananas to the freezer as needed to prevent them from softening and starting to cook. Store frozen.

Caramelized Almonds

Sliced almonds	50 g	½ cup
Sugar	25 g	2½ Tbsp
Egg white, blended	10 g	2½ tsp
Salt	pinch	

Preheat the oven to 175 °C / 350 °F. Line a baking sheet with parchment paper. Thoroughly combine all of the ingredients, and spread them in an even layer on the parchment. Bake until golden brown, about 6 minutes. Cool to room temperature, and then break into pieces. Store in an airtight container.

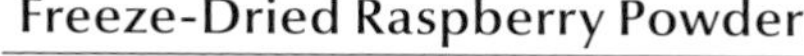

Freeze-Dried Raspberry Powder

Pulse freeze-dried raspberries to a powder in a coffee grinder, food processor, or blender. Sift to remove any seeds or large pieces.

Raspberry Lemon Cream Pie

Ginger Cream Pie

CREAM PIES

The pie recipes here combine crust, filling, and topping variations from the preceding pages of this chapter, and then add a few extra flourishes to create stunning desserts that are suitable for virtually any menu. First, make the crust indicated; the recipes are on page 372. Next, prepare the filling, using the instructions on page 374. (Note that you'll need to double the quantities given there if you're making a large, 30 cm / 12 in, pie.) Pour the pastry cream into the baked crust, and refrigerate the pie until it becomes firm, at least 1 hour. Top the pie with the topping indicated (instructions are on pages 376–377) or with whipped cream or fresh fruit. The topping instructions here assume that you are making four 11 cm / 4½ in tarts, but they are easily adapted to make larger pies.

Almond and Cherry Cream Pie

Crust: Double Almond Crust
Filling: Amaretto Pastry Cream
Topping: Top each tart with six fresh cherries, halved, and 15 g / 1 Tbsp of crumbled Caramelized Almonds.

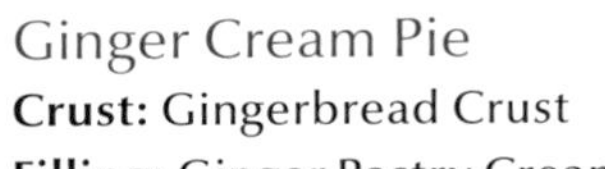

Ginger Cream Pie

Crust: Gingerbread Crust
Filling: Ginger Pastry Cream
Topping: Top each tart with 15 g / 1 Tbsp of candied ginger (store-bought), finely minced.

Coconut Cream Pie

Crust: Coconut Crust
Filling: Coconut Pastry Cream
Topping: Smooth the surface of the pastry cream, and then spread 5 g / 1 tsp of Passion Fruit Glaze in a thin layer over each tart. Scatter julienned young coconut over the glaze. For extra crunch, crumble toasted, shredded coconut over the tarts just before serving.

Chocolate Cream Pie

Crust: Chocolate Crust
Filling: Chocolate Pastry Cream
Topping: Combine 200 g / 220 mL / 1 cup of whipping cream and 53 g / ½ cup of whole, dark-roast coffee beans, and refrigerate for 12 hours to infuse. Strain, and pour the cream into a whipping siphon. Charge the siphon with two cartridges of nitrous oxide, and dispense the coffee whipped cream onto the tarts. Garnish with Cocoa Nib and Cardamom Dust.

Banana Cream Pie

Crust: Peanut Crust
Filling: 65 g / ¼ cup of Pressure-Caramelized Banana Puree (see page 181), smoothed and then covered with Pressure-Infused Coffee Pastry Cream
Topping: Top with frozen Blowtorch-Caramelized Bananas just before serving.

Apple Cream Pie

Crust: Brown Butter Crust
Filling: Sous Vide Vanilla-Cinnamon Pastry Cream
Topping: Top with Apple Foam just before serving.

Savory Cheese Pie

Crust: Cheese Crust
Filling: 50 g / ¼ cup of Pressure-Caramelized Onions (see page 127), smoothed and then covered with Cheese Pastry Cream
Topping: Top each tart with 10 g / 2½ Tbsp of cheese bread crumbs (see page 316), Crispy Shallots (see variation on page 353), and chopped fresh thyme just before serving.

Raspberry Lemon Cream Pie

Crust: Raspberry Crust
Filling: Lemon Pastry Cream or Sous Vide Lemon Curd (see page 365)
Topping: Dust with Freeze-Dried Raspberry Powder.

FURTHER READING

Achatz, G. *Alinea*. Achatz, 2008.

Adrià, F. *The Family Meal: Home Cooking with Ferran Adrià*. Phaidon, 2011.

Adrià, F., Soler, J., and Adrià, A. *elBulli 1983–1993*. RBA Practica, 2004.

Adrià, F., Soler, J., and Adrià, A. *elBulli 1994–1997*. Ecco, 2006.

Adrià, F., Soler, J., and Adrià, A. *elBulli 1998–2002*. Ecco, 2005.

Adrià, F., Soler, J., and Adrià, A. *elBulli 2003–2004*. Ecco, 2006.

Adrià, F., Soler, J., and Adrià, A. *A Day at elBulli: An Insight into the Ideas, Methods and Creativity of Ferran Adrià*. Phaidon, 2008.

Aduriz, A. L. *Mugaritz: A Natural Science of Cooking*. Phaidon, 2012.

Aftel, M. and Patterson, D. *Aroma: The Magic of Essential Oils in Food & Fragrance*. Artisan, 2004.

Alford, J. and Duguid, N. *Mangoes & Curry Leaves: Culinary Travels Through the Great Subcontinent*. Artisan, 2005.

Andrés, J. and Wolffe, R. *Made in Spain: Spanish Dishes for the American Kitchen*. Clarkson Potter, 2008.

Angier, B. *Field Guide to Edible Wild Plants*. Stackpole Books, 2008.

Baldwin, D. E. *Sous Vide for the Home Cook*. Paradox, 2010.

Beranbaum, R. L. *The Cake Bible*. William Morrow Cookbooks, 1988.

Barham, P. *The Science of Cooking*. Springer, 2001.

Batali, M. *The Babbo Cookbook*. Clarkson Potter, 2002.

Blumenthal, H. *Family Food: A New Approach to Cooking*. Michael Joseph, 2002.

Blumenthal, H. *In Search of Perfection: Reinventing Kitchen Classics*. Bloomsbury USA, 2006.

Blumenthal, H. *The Big Fat Duck Cookbook*. Bloomsbury USA, 2008.

Blumenthal, H. *Heston Blumenthal at Home*. Bloomsbury USA, 2011.

Bouley, D., Lohninger, M., and Clark, M. *East of Paris: The New Cuisines of Austria and the Danube*. Ecco, 2003.

Boulud, D. and Kaminsky, P. *Chef Daniel Boulud: Cooking in New York City*. Assouline, 2002.

Bras, M. *Essential Cuisine*. Ici La Press, 2002.

Brown, A. *Good Eats: The Early Years*. Stewart, Tabori & Chang, 2009.

Chang, D. and Meehan, P. *Momofuku*. Clarkson Potter, 2009.

Child, J., Bertholle, L., and Beck, S. *Mastering the Art of French Cooking*. Knopf, 2001.

Clark, M. *Cook This Now: 120 Easy and Delectable Dishes You Can't Wait to Make*. Hyperion, 2011.

Cook's Illustrated, the editors of. *The New Best Recipe*. America's Test Kitchen, 2004.

Corriher, S. O. *BakeWise: The Hows and Whys of Successful Baking with Over 200 Magnificent Recipes*. Scribner, 2008.

Corriher, S. O. *CookWise: The Secrets of Cooking Revealed: The Hows and Whys of Successful Cooking with Over 230 Great-Tasting Recipes*. William Morrow Cookbooks, 1997.

The Culinary Institute of America. *The Professional Chef*, Ninth Edition. Wiley, 2011.

Curious Cook. curiouscook.com

Davidson, A. *Mediterranean Seafood: A Comprehensive Guide with Recipes*. Ten Speed Press, 2002.

Davidson, A. *Seafood: A Connoisseur's Guide and Cookbook*. Simon & Schuster, 1989.

Davidson, A. *The Oxford Companion to Food*, Second Edition. Oxford University Press, 2006.

Ducasse, A. and Piège, J.-F. *Grand Livre de Cuisine: Alain Ducasse's Culinary Encyclopedia*. Ducasse Books, 2005.

Escoffier, A. *The Escoffier Cookbook and Guide to the Fine Art of Cookery: For Connoisseurs, Chefs, Epicures*. Crown Publishers, 2000.

Gayler, P. *The Sauce Book: 300 World Sauces Made Simple*. Kyle Books, 2009.

Girardet, F. *The Cuisine of Fredy Girardet: The Incomparable Recipes of the Greatest Chef in Europe*. William Morrow and Company, 1987.

Green, C. and Scott, S. *The Wild Table: Seasonal Foraged Food and Recipes*. Studio, 2010.

Henderson, F. *The Whole Beast: Nose to Tail Eating*. Ecco, 2004.

Herbst, S. T. and Herbst, R. *The Deluxe Food Lover's Companion*. Barron's, 2009.

Humm, D. and Guidara, W. *Eleven Madison Park: The Cookbook*. Little, Brown and Company, 2011.

Ideas in Food. blog.ideasinfood.com

Iuzzini, J. and Finamore, R. *Dessert FourPlay: Sweet Quartets from a Four-Star Pastry Chef*. Clarkson Potter, 2008.

Joachim, D., Schloss, A., and Handel, A. P. *The Science of Good Food: The Ultimate Reference on How Cooking Works*. Robert Rose, 2008.

Kamozawa, A. and Talbot, H. A. *Ideas in Food: Great Recipes and Why They Work*. Clarkson Potter, 2010.

Katz, S. E. *Wild Fermentation: The Flavor, Nutrition, and Craft of Live-Culture Foods*. Chelsea Green Publishing, 2003.

Keller, T. *The French Laundry Cookbook*. Artisan, 1999.

Keller, T. *Bouchon*. Artisan, 2004.

Keller, T. *Ad Hoc at Home: Family-Style Recipes*. Artisan, 2009.

Kunz, G. and Kaminsky, P. *The Elements of Taste*. Little, Brown and Company, 2001.

Kurlansky, M. *Salt: A World History*. Penguin, 2003.

Lahey, J. *My Pizza: The Easy No-Knead Way to Make Spectacular Pizza at Home*. Clarkson Potter, 2012.

Librairie Larousse's Gastronomic Committee. *Larousse Gastronomique: The World's Greatest Culinary Encyclopedia*. Clarkson Potter, 2009.

Lo, E. Y.-F. *The Chinese Kitchen: Recipes, Techniques, Ingredients, History, and Memories from America's Leading Authority on Chinese Cooking*. William Morrow Cookbooks, 1999.

Logsdon, J. *Cooking Sous Vide: A Guide for the Home Cook*. CreateSpace, 2009.

McGee, H. *Keys to Good Cooking: A Guide to Making the Best of Foods and Recipes*. Penguin Press, 2010.

McGee, H. *On Food and Cooking: The Science and Lore of the Kitchen*. Scribner, 2004.

McLagan, J. *Bones: Recipes, History, & Lore*. William Morrow Cookbooks, 2005.

Migoya, F. J., The Culinary Institute of America. *The Modern Café*. Wiley, 2009.

Mikanowski, L. and Mikanowski, P. *Egg*. Flammarion, 2007.

Myhrvold, N., Young, C., and Bilet, M. *Modernist Cuisine: The Art and Science of Cooking*. The Cooking Lab, 2011.

North, J. *French Lessons: Recipes and Techniques for a New Generation of Cooks*. Hardie Grant Books, 2007.

Oliver, J. *Jamie's Food Revolution: Rediscover How to Cook Simple, Delicious, Affordable Meals*. Hyperion, 2009.

Passard, A. *The Art of Cooking with Vegetables*. Frances Lincoln, 2012.

Pelaccio, Z. *Eat with Your Hands*. Ecco, 2012.

Pépin, J. *Jacques Pépin's Complete Techniques*. Black Dog & Leventhal, 2001.

Peterson, J. *Vegetables: The Most Authoritative Guide to Buying, Preparing, and Cooking, with More than 300 Recipes*. William Morrow Cookbooks, 1998.

Peterson, J. *Sauces: Classical and Contemporary Sauce Making*, Third Edition. Wiley, 2008.

Peterson, J. *Kitchen Simple: Essential Recipes for Everyday Cooking*. Ten Speed Press, 2011.

Pollan, M. *The Omnivore's Dilemma: A Natural History of Four Meals*. Penguin Press, 2006.

Pollan, M. *In Defense of Food: An Eater's Manifesto*. Penguin, 2008.

Potter, J. *Cooking for Geeks: Real Science, Great Hacks, and Good Food*. O'Reilly Media, 2010.

Psilakis, M. *How to Roast a Lamb: New Greek Classic Cooking*. Little, Brown and Company, 2009.

Redzepi, R. *Noma: Time and Place in Nordic Cuisine*. Phaidon, 2010.

Reinhart, P. *American Pie: My Search for the Perfect Pizza*. Ten Speed Press, 2003.

Richard, M. and Heller, S. *Happy in the Kitchen: The Craft of Cooking, the Art of Eating*. Artisan, 2006.

Ripert, E. and Le Coze, M. *Le Bernardin Cookbook: Four-Star Simplicity*. Clarkson Potter, 1998.

Ripert, E. and Muhlke, C. *On the Line: Inside the World of Le Bernardin*. Artisan, 2008.

Robuchon, J. *Cooking Through the Seasons*. Rizzoli, 1995.

Robuchon, J. *The Complete Robuchon*. Knopf, 2008.

Roca, J. and Brugués, S. *Sous Vide Cuisine*. Montagud Editores, 2005.

Roden, C. *Arabesque: A Taste of Morocco, Turkey, & Lebanon*. Knopf, 2005.

Ruhlman, M. *The Elements of Cooking: Translating the Chef's Craft for Every Kitchen*. Scribner, 2007.

Ruhlman, M. *Ratio: The Simple Codes Behind the Craft of Everyday Cooking*. Scribner, 2010.

Ruhlman, M. *Ratio: Ruhlman's Twenty: 20 Techniques, 100 Recipes, A Cook's Manifesto*. Chronicle Books, 2011.

Sass, L. *Pressure Perfect: Two Hour Taste in Twenty Minutes Using Your Pressure Cooker*. William Morrow Cookbooks, 2004.

Silverton, N., Molina, M., and Carreño, C. *The Mozza Cookbook: Recipes from Los Angeles's Favorite Italian Restaurant and Pizzeria*. Knopf, 2011.

Sokolov, R. *Why We Eat What We Eat: How Columbus Changed the Way the World Eats*. Touchstone, 1993.

Stampfer, V. *Sous-vide: Cooking in a Vacuum*. Matthaes, 2008.

Standage, T. *An Edible History of Humanity*. Walker & Company, 2009.

Steingarten, J. *The Man Who Ate Everything*. Vintage, 1998.

Steingarten, J. *It Must've Been Something I Ate: The Return of the Man Who Ate Everything*. Knopf, 2002.

Stewart, M. *Martha Stewart's Cooking School: Lessons and Recipes for the Home Cook*. Clarkson Potter, 2008.

This, H. *Kitchen Mysteries: Revealing the Science of Cooking*. Columbia University Press, 2007.

This, H. *The Science of the Oven*. Columbia University Press, 2009.

Thompson, D. *Thai Food*. Ten Speed Press, 2002.

Thompson, D. *Thai Street Food: Authentic Recipes, Vibrant Traditions*. Ten Speed Press, 2010.

Thompson, R. B. *Illustrated Guide to Home Chemistry Experiments*. O'Reilly Media, 2008.

Tierno, P. M., Jr. *The Secret Life of Germs: What They Are, Why We Need Them, and How We Can Protect Ourselves Against Them*. Atria Books, 2004.

Tosi, C. *Momofuku Milk Bar*. Clarkson Potter, 2011.

Trotter, C. *Charlie Trotter's Vegetables*. Ten Speed Press, 1996.

Tsuji, S. *Japanese Cooking: A Simple Art*. Kodansha International, 2007.

van Wyk, B.-E. *Food Plants of the World: An Illustrated Guide*. Timber Press, 2005.

de La Varenne, F.-P. *La Varenne's Cookery: The French Cook, The French Pastry Chef, The French Confectioner*. Prospect Books, 2006.

Vega, C., Ubbink, J., and van der Linden, E., editors. *The Kitchen as Laboratory: Reflections on the Science of Food and Cooking*. Columbia University Press, 2012.

Vetri, M. *Rustic Italian Food*. Ten Speed Press, 2011.

Vetri, M. and Joachim, D. *Il Viaggio di Vetri: A Culinary Journey*. Ten Speed Press, 2008.

Voltaggio, B. and Voltaggio, M. *VOLT ink.: Recipes, Stories, Brothers*. Olive Press, 2011.

Vongerichten, J.-G. *Asian Flavors of Jean-Georges*. Clarkson Potter, 2007.

Vongerichten, J.-G. and Ko, G. *Home Cooking with Jean-Georges: My Favorite Simple Recipes*. Clarkson Potter, 2011.

Vongerichten, M. and Turshen, J. *The Kimchi Chronicles: Korean Cooking for an American Kitchen*. Rodale, 2011.

Wolfert, P. *The Cooking of Southwest France: Recipes from France's Magnificent Rustic Cuisine*. Wiley, 2005.

Wolke, R. L. and Parrish, M. *What Einstein Told His Cook: Kitchen Science Explained*. W. W. Norton & Company, 2002.

Wolke, R. L. and Parrish, M. *What Einstein Told His Cook 2: The Sequel: Further Adventures in Kitchen Science*. W. W. Norton & Company, 2005.

Wrangham, R. *Catching Fire: How Cooking Made Us Human*. Basic Books, 2009.

GLOSSARY OF COOKING TERMS

00 wheat flour—Italian wheat flour milled from only the core of the wheat grain, yielding a flour with high-quality protein that makes it excellent for forming noodles and breads such as pizza and ciabatta.

accuracy—how close an instrument's reading is to the true value of what is being measured. Note that accuracy is different from precision.

achiote paste—red paste made from the pulp surrounding the seed of the achiote tree. It adds both color and a slight peppery flavor to food.

active dry yeast—dry yeast granules available at most supermarkets. Dehydrating keeps the yeast alive but dormant.

adductor muscle—muscle that pulls tissue closer to the middle of the body. The muscle that pulls the two sides of a bivalve closed.

adobo—stewed meat with a vinegar-rich glaze. Considered the national dish of the Philippines.

aerolatte—brand name of a battery-powered, handheld whipping tool often used to froth milk.

agar—(agar agar) clear, tasteless gelling agent derived from seaweed. Can also be used as a thickener or stabilizer. Available from Asian markets or food ingredient companies. The latter sell agar powders, graded by gelling strength, that have more consistent performance.

agave syrup—(agave nectar) sweetener made from agave, a desert shrub-like succulent with sword-shaped leaves.

aioli—French term for a mayonnaise-like sauce boldly flavored with garlic. Traditional versions often contain potato or bread.

ajowan—(ajwain) tiny, seed-like fruits of a variety of lovage with a flavor similar to thyme and caraway. Used in Indian foods.

albumin powder—(albumen) dehydrated egg-white protein.

alkaline—having a pH value greater than 7.

amchoor—(amchur) dried green mango powder; used as a seasoning to add a tangy flavor.

amino acid—one of the chemical building blocks from which proteins are composed. Virtually all proteins are made from a repertoire of just 22 kinds of amino acids.

amylopectin—type of polymer composed of glucose that makes natural starches. Binds up water and thickeners better than amylose.

amylose—type of polymer composed of glucose that makes natural starches. Better for forming gels than amylopectin.

anaerobic—living or occurring without oxygen.

anaerobic bacterium—bacterium that does not require oxygen to survive.

anardana—(dried pomegranate seeds) Indian spice of air-dried pomegranate seeds, or arils, often used as an acidic agent for chutneys and curries. Chiefly from tart, wild pomegranates.

annatto seeds—red seeds from a tropical tree that are used as a food coloring and a mild, peppery spice. Used to make achiote powder and paste.

antioxidant—any compound that inhibits oxidation reactions. Lemon juice or citric acid work as antioxidants on cut apple slices.

aquaculture—cultivation of aquatic animals or plants.

Arborio rice—starchy, short-grain rice; most often used in risotto and rice pudding.

ascorbic acid—a form of vitamin C.

Ashkenazi—one of the major groups of Jews. Ashkenazis generally speak Yiddish and live mainly in Eastern Europe.

Asian fish sauce—(garum, nam pla, nuoc mam, muria) clear, salty condiment or seasoning made from salted, fermented fish. Used widely in Southeast Asian cuisine.

bacteria (singular bacterium)—large group of single-celled microorganisms that lack a nucleus or chlorophyll.

bar—metric unit of measurement of barometric pressure. Standard atmospheric pressure at sea level is 1.013 bar (1,013 millibar). A gauge pressure of 1 bar, as in a pressure cooker, means that the interior pressure is 1 bar higher than the ambient air pressure of the surrounding atmosphere.

béchamel—white sauce. A classic French "mother sauce" of roux-thickened, mildly flavored milk.

beurre blanc—French term for "white butter," a white wine and shallot-flavored, emulsified butter sauce.

beurre noir—French term for "black butter" made by heating butter to the point where the milk solids become very dark brown but not burnt.

beurre noisette—French term for "nut butter," or brown butter, made by heating butter to the point where the milk solids become brown with a nutty aroma.

biltong—South African term for dried, spiced meat similar to jerky.

bird's eye chili—(Thai chili) fresh, tiny, very hot red and green chilies. Often used in Thai cooking but similar varieties are used internationally.

bisque—thick, rich soup often made with crustacean stock that is thickened slightly with rice or pureed vegetables and finished with cream.

black salt (kala namak)—Indian spice made from impure sodium chloride crystals. The salt is dark in color and flavor from other minerals such as iron sulfide and other sulfur compounds.

blanch—to whiten or draw out, to briefly cook the exterior. To submerge food in boiling liquid briefly to loosen a peel, sanitize its surface, or to remove undesirable tastes or aromas.

Bloom—measurement of the strength of a gelatin gel with a device created by Oscar Bloom.

bomba rice—Spanish, short-grain white rice traditionally used for paella.

bonito flakes—(katsuo bushi) shavings of cured and dried bonito, a variety of fish from the mackerel family. A principal ingredient in dashi, and also used as a seasoning or garnish.

braise—to slow-cook food (usually meat) in liquid or humid air in a closed vessel.

brine—salt solution. Also, to imbue food with a salt solution, either by soaking or injection, in order to change its flavor and texture.

broccoli raab—(rabe, rapini) Italian, leafy green vegetable with tender flower buds.

bromelain—naturally forming enzyme found in pineapple that breaks down protein and is used as a meat tenderizer.

Bronte Sicilian pistachio—very green pistachio with an intense, sharp flavor grown in and around Bronte, Sicily, in the shadow of Mount Etna.

brûlée—French term for burn or brown, often used in reference to caramelized sugar in dishes such as crème brûlée.

calcium chloride—mineral salt of calcium, used to firm up the skin of beans. Also used in making Modernist gels.
calcium lactate—salt created by the interaction of lactic acid and calcium carbonate, used in baking powder. Also used as an alternative to calcium chloride to toughen the skins on beans and to add a crispness to pickles. Used commonly by Modernist chefs in making spherical gels.
calibrate—to check the performance of a piece of equipment, such as a thermometer or oven, against a known standard so that it may be adjusted to conform to the standard or so that recipe steps may be altered to compensate for its inaccuracies.
canning jar—heat-tolerant jar made of thick glass and having an airtight, resealable screw lid.
capicola—(capicollo, coppa) Italian cured and rolled pork shoulder often served as salami.
carbonation—the process of dissolving carbon dioxide gas into a substance. It is common in beverages and soft drinks, but solid foods can also be carbonated.
carbonize—to char or burn.
cardoon—European vegetable in the artichoke family with edible, fibrous stalks.
Carnaroli rice—starchy Italian rice often used to make risotto.
carnitas—Mexican dish of slow-cooked pork that is shredded and browned.
carotene—fat-soluble pigments found in plants like carrots and squash that can transform into vitamin A. Beta-carotene is the most abundant of the carotenes.
carrageenan—vegetarian gelling alternative to gelatin, extracted from a variety of red seaweed sometimes called Irish moss. Iota type makes soft, elastic gels. Kappa type makes firm, brittle gels. Lambda type thickens but does not gel.
centrifugal force—the outward force exerted by a body as it revolves around an external axis.
chaat—term used in India to refer to snacks, which are often savory dishes sold by street vendors.
chaat masala—combination of spices used as a sprinkle on everyday foods and fruits in India. Blends vary by region and producer.
chamber sealer—device used for vacuum sealing food in plastic bags. It includes a pump for evacuating air from the chamber, as well as one or more sealing bars that melt the open end of the bags closed once nearly all of the air has been removed.
chanterelles—(girolle) wild, funnel-shaped mushrooms, valued for their golden color and nutty, buttery flavor. Black, white, and gray varieties are less common.
chawanmushi—(chawan mushi) Japanese term for savory egg custard steamed in a bowl or cup, often made with seafood.
chervil—tender, parsley-like herb with a faint licorice taste; a traditional ingredient in the French fines herbes mix.
chicharrón—crispy fried pork skin.
chicken forewing—segment of chicken wing that contains the ulna and radius bones, located between the pinion and the drummette.
chickpeas—(garbanzo, ceci bean, Bengal gram) high-protein legume. Available dried, canned, and occasionally fresh.
chiffonade—thinly sliced, leafy greens or vegetables often used as a base or garnish.
chimichurri—Argentinian condiment made of chopped herbs and aromatics in oil. Often used with grilled meats.
Chinese sausage—(lap cheong, lop chong) slightly sweet, fatty pork sausage that is traditionally cured and air-dried. Also available flavored with liver.
chorizo—highly spiced pork sausage. Spanish chorizo is often smoked or cured. Mexican chorizo is commonly sold fresh.
clarified—made clear. Clarified fats are melted, skimmed, and decanted to make clarified fat.
coagulate—to thicken or gel.
coconut cream—thick creamy liquid made by grinding fresh coconut meat in water and then skimming the fatty "cream" from the top.
coconut cream powder—dehydrated, powdered coconut cream available at Asian markets and specialty stores.
coconut milk—liquid, usually clear or nearly clear, drained from the interior of a whole coconut.
coddle—to cook gently in warm water; often referring to eggs.
cohere—to stick together or bind as part of the same mass.
collagen—fibrous proteins found in the skin, flesh, bones, and connective tissues that yield gelatin when cooked.
combi oven—oven capable of cooking both by heated air distributed with a fan (as convection ovens do) and by steam injected into the cooking chamber.
compound butter—butter that has been softened, blended with flavorings, and then chilled again. Often used as a sauce or condiment.
Comté—aged French cow's milk cheese with a buttery, nutty flavor. Comté that does not meet the regional standard in flavor and production is often sold as French Gruyère.
conduction—heat transfer that occurs through energy exchanged between particles, such as by the direct contact of surfaces.
confit—French term meaning "preserved." Meat confit has historically meant a preparation of salt-cured meat cooked and kept in fat to provide an airtight seal that helps preserve the food. For fruits, confit or confiture means preserves—as in jams and jellies. Confit has come to mean almost any food cooked slowly in oil or fat until tender.
consommé—thin, flavorful, and very clear liquid. Traditionally made from meat broths; today, it's often prepared from vegetable and fruit juices as well.
convection—heat transfer that occurs within a fluid because of the movement of particles within the fluid, such by hot air or water.
convection current—moving stream of fluid created by convection.
convection oven—oven that includes a fan to distribute heated air.
cooking spray—neutral-tasting cooking oil in aerosol form. Some commercially available cooking sprays also contain lecithin.
cook to a core temperature—phrase used to describe the technique of cooking an ingredient until the temperature in the center of the thickest part reaches a target value.
core temperature—temperature at the very center of the food. Usually monitored by using a probe attached to a digital thermometer.
Cotija—(queso añejo) dry, salty Mexican cow's milk cheese.
crème fraîche—French term for thick and tangy cream; traditionally prepared by wild fermentation, but now prepared with a commercial culture.
crown—cut of poultry that includes the breasts, rib cage, and wings.
crustacean—class of aquatic invertebrate, such as lobster, crab, or shrimp, having a segmented, protective shell.
curd—thickened milk gel that has been treated with a coagulant to make cheese.
cure—to preserve food with salt. Often combined with smoking. Confusingly, a curing brine is sometimes called a "pickle," and sometimes foods pickled in an acidic solution are referred to as cured, although the underlying processes are different.
curing—soaking meat in a chemical solution (or rubbing dry chemicals on it) to induce changes in texture, flavor, and color.
curry leaves—(kari leaves) fresh, shiny, aromatic leaves used frequently in Indian and Sri Lankan cooking. In South India, the leaves are often fried in oil and used as a condiment or garnish.
decant—to pour a liquid from one vessel to another, often in order to separate liquid from sediment.
deglaze—to add liquid to a pan to dissolve the flavorful brown film and bits formed from dehydrated juices when many foods are cooked at a high temperature.

deionized water—water that has been purified by a process in which its mineral ions are entirely removed.
Demerara—coarse, flavorful brown sugar crystals. The sugar originally came from the colony of Demerara, which is now part of Guyana.
denaturing—the unfolding of a protein, which makes it nonfunctional. High and low temperatures, changing pH, high salt levels, and the addition of solvents such as alcohol can all denature proteins.
desiccant—substance, such as silica gel, that readily absorbs moisture. Desiccants are used to keep dry food dry.
desiccate—to dry out completely.
diastatic malt powder—powder containing the enzyme diastase that converts starches into sugars. Made from malted grains.
diffusion—natural process by which heat or a substance (such as a brine) moves from a region of high concentration to adjacent regions of lower concentration, until all areas in contact are at equilibrium.
disperse—to distribute evenly, an important step when working with hydrocolloid thickeners and gelling agents, such as agar and xanthan gum.
dosa—South Indian pancake made from a lightly fermented batter of beans (urad dal) and rice.
dry-blend—to evenly combine dry ingredients before adding them to a recipe, an important step when combining various hydrocolloid thickeners or gelling agents.
dry-bulb temperature—temperature measurement of air. Unlike the wet-bulb temperature, humidity in the atmosphere is not a factor in the measurement.
dry rub—sugar or seasonings rubbed into meat to improve flavor and retain water.
edamame—Japanese name for green soybeans, often sold in the pod.
efficiency—the amount of useful work a device produces during a time period, usually expressed as a fraction of the amount of energy required to operate it during that period.
emulsifier—any compound, such as sodium citrate, that helps to stabilize a mixture of two otherwise immiscible liquids.
emulsion—mixture of two normally immiscible liquids, such as oil and water.
energy—in physics, the capacity for doing work.
enzyme—protein molecule that catalyzes chemical reactions of other substances but isn't destroyed or altered in the process.
equilibrate—to gradually attain the same level as something else, such as when food equilibrates to the temperature of its environment.
equilibrium—state in which no change occurs because of the balance between opposing forces or rates of reaction.
equilibrium cooking—cooking with a heat source (such as a water bath for sous vide) that is at or very close to the final desired food temperature. The food is allowed to equilibrate with that temperature.
essential oil—concentration of volatile aromatic compounds in spices, herbs, flowers, and other botanicals. Collected oils are used widely in perfumery and are often of a grade suitable for food and cooking.
evaporation—the change from the liquid state to the vapor (gaseous) state.
extraction—the removal of material from a substance that contains it, such as by means of a solvent.
farro—(emmer) ancient grain related to wheat with a dense, chewy texture.
fat-soluble—molecules that dissolve in fat.
fenugreek leaves—fresh greens from a plant in the pea family. Fenugreek seeds are used as a spice. The taste is bitter when raw but becomes sweeter when cooked.
fermentation—the modification of a food by the deliberate growth of microorganisms in it, such as using yeast to make wine or bread.
fermented black bean and chili paste—commercially available.
fiddlehead ferns—tender, edible coiled sprouts of the fiddlehead fern. Collected in early spring.
fines herbes—traditional French mix of herbs, including fresh parsley, chervil, chives, and tarragon; ubiquitous in French cuisine. Marjoram, cress, and lemon balm may be added.
fingerling potatoes—varieties of waxy, thin-skinned, slightly sweet potatoes that grow in long, narrow oblongs resembling fingers.
fino sherry—pale, dry Spanish fortified wine.
fish eye—lumps formed from incomplete dispersion of a starch or hydrocolloid gum in water.
fish sauce—see Asian fish sauce.
flageolet beans—French legume with a pale green color and a size similar to that of cannellini or Great Northern beans. Prized for its nutty, buttery flavor and meaty texture.
flaky salt—salt crystals that grow as broad, flat flakes. Maldon brand sea salt is a well-known example.
flash—to expose food to extreme hot or cold temperatures, such as flash-freezing with liquid nitrogen or flash-frying with hot oil or in a hot pan.
fluid gel—gel in which the gel structure has been broken, enabling it to flow like a liquid.
foam—the bubbles that compose a frothy mass. They are formed on a liquid's surface by agitating it or by subjecting it to a chemical process.
foam stabilizer—substance used to prevent foam from dissipating.
fond—French term for a dish's base or foundation, such as a stock or broth.
forbidden rice—especially nutritious strain of Chinese black rice once reserved for royalty. Consists of small, smooth grains that, when cooked, do not have the glutinous quality of many Asian rice varieties.
forced convection—heat transfer that occurs when a fan or pump is used to move a hot fluid (such as air or water) across a food.
french—butcher's technique of cleaning and scraping away meat to expose the bone for a more elegant presentation. Lamb chops are commonly frenched.
frequency—how often a periodic event repeats within a given interval of time. For electromagnetic waves, the number of wave crests that pass a point in a second.
fresh turmeric—small, bright orange rhizome of the turmeric plant available at Indian and some Asian markets. Peel, grate, and use in place of dried turmeric for a more vibrant color and peppery flavor. A 2.5 cm / 1 in piece of fresh turmeric is equivalent to 10 g / 1 tsp of dried.
friable—easily crumbled.
fricassee—(fricassée) a white meat preparation, traditionally chicken, that is stewed in a white gravy. Various vegetables are often incorporated, and the gravy sometimes includes white wine.
friction—the force resisting relative motion between two bodies in contact.
fructose—sugar that is about 50% sweeter than sucrose (table sugar). Fructose is found in honey and many fruits. Granulated fructose is commercially available.
galangal—variety of ginger rhizome (root). It tastes like ginger with a little more pepper and a light camphor aroma. Often used in Thai cooking.
gauge pressure—the amount of pressure inside a pressure vessel that exceeds the ambient air pressure. This is the pressure reading indicated on the gauge of the vessel.
gelatinize—to convert starch or collagen into gelatin or a jelly-like consistency.
genus—species that are closely related, and thus considered a group.
geoduck—(king clam) a large bivalve mollusk having a very long siphon, native to the Northwest coast of North America.
ghee—slowly clarified unsalted butter. Used prominently in Indian cooking.
gigahertz —unit of frequency indicating billion cycles per second.
gigante beans—very large, flat, white dried beans. Often served as a salad or starter in Greece.
gluten—combination of proteins found in cereals, notably wheat, that gives dough its characteristic cohesiveness.
gochujang—(kochujang) salty Korean paste of fermented soybeans and chilies used as a condiment and flavoring.

granita—flavored ice similar to sorbet but with large ice crystals that form as a result of low sugar and dissolved solids content.
green mango—tart, firm mango picked before it has ripened. Can be pickled or added fresh to South Asian dishes; dried, it makes the Indian seasoning amchoor.
green papaya—unripe papaya, a popular salad ingredient in Southeast Asian cuisine. Sold whole or shredded.
guar gum—thickener from the endosperm of guar seeds. Similar to locust bean gum.
gum—polysaccharide derived from plants that swells when wet and can thicken or gel depending on various factors.
Hainanese chicken rice—simple chicken preparation originating in Hainan, China, that is especially popular in Singapore and Malaysia. Poached chicken is served with savory rice, a spicy dipping sauce, and a bowl of the flavorful poaching broth used to cook the chicken. Often accompanied with sliced cucumbers and tomatoes.
hard water—water containing particular dissolved ions, such as magnesium or calcium salts.
heat—transfer of energy due to a difference in temperature.
Helix snails—(Helix pomatia, Burgundy snail, vineyard snail) genus of large, edible land snail. Available canned. Often baked with garlic herb butter and served as escargot.
hoisin sauce—(Peking sauce) sweet, spicy reddish-brown Chinese sauce made from soybeans, garlic, chili peppers, and spices.
homogenized—mixed with sufficient shearing force to break droplets into very small sizes. Homogenizing produces a smooth mixture of two or more kinds of liquid.
honey powder—granules of spray-dried honey, available at health-food stores and Asian markets.
hydrate—to treat a powder so that it absorbs water fully; an important step when using hydrocolloids that renders them functional. To be fully hydrated, most thickening and gelling agents must be dispersed evenly in a liquid and then heated above a certain temperature, which depends on the specific hydrocolloid and nature of the liquid it is dispersed in.
hydrocolloid—any substance that thickens or gels water or a liquid containing a significant fraction of water.
Ibérico ham—(jamón ibérico, Iberian ham) Spanish dry-cured ham made from black Iberian pigs. The most prized hams come from pigs that roam and feed naturally, often on a diet rich in olives or acorns.
immersion blender—(stick blender) a handheld electric device that chops, blends, and purees food in the container in which it is being prepared.
immersion circulator—device that, when attached to a vessel that contains water, heats and circulates the water to create a circulating bath.
immiscible—resistant to mixing and tending to separate after stirring halts. Oil and water are immiscible, for example.
induction —physical phenomena in which an alternating current in a coil of wire sets up an oscillating magnetic field, which in turn induces corresponding electric currents in nearby conductive material. Used by induction cooktops to heat pots and pans having bases made of certain kinds of metals, such as steel and iron.
infuse—to steep or soak so that the flavors or particulates dissolve into the liquid.
infusion—a liquid flavored or colored by steeping a substance in it, such as brewed tea or vanilla extract.
Insta Cure #1—curing salt blend of 93.75% salt, 6.25% sodium nitrite, and safety coloring. Insta Cure #2 is different and should not be used as a substitute.
insulator—substance that is a poor medium for conduction.
Jaccard—brand name of a handheld meat tenderizer containing several slender, sharp blades used to cut through tissues.
julienned—cut into thin sticks.
jus—French term for juice. The liquid that seeps out of meat during cooking.
jus gras—French for "fat juice," jus gras refers to meat juice thickened or emulsified into a sauce by using fat rather than starch.
kabocha squash—(Japanese pumpkin) round, sweet winter squash with green skin and bright orange interior.
kala namak—see black salt.
kalbi—(galbi) Korean word for "rib." Usually refers to sliced short ribs. Also describes a soy sauce marinade used in Korean barbecue.
Kashmiri chili—long, bright red, dried chili popular in South India. Adds color and complex chili flavor without much heat.
Kewpie mayonnaise—popular brand of Japanese mayonnaise made with rice vinegar that includes a small amount of monosodium glutamate for an enhanced umami taste.
kinome—young leaves of the prickly ash or sansho plant, best in the spring when the leaves are tender, with a citrus-like, bright pepper bite. Dried, ground leaves are also called sansho.
kombu—Japanese term for dried kelp, an important ingredient in the flavor and seasoning of Japanese food. Many varieties and grades are commercially available. Kombu powder is ground dried kelp.
knucklebones—the joints that connect the knee bones, usually referring to beef.
lactic acid—the acid found in sour milk, yogurt, cheese, and many other dairy foods. Can be used to give a preparation a dairy-like tartness. Also can be used as a coagulant for protein gels.
lardon—narrow strips of fat or bacon, fried crisp.
lecithin—the principal emulsifier in egg yolks, also found in soybeans. Most commercially available lecithin products are derived from soy.
lemon balm—an herb in the mint family having large, pale green leaves and a light, lemony aroma.
lemon thyme—variety of fresh thyme having variegated leaves and a bright, lemony aroma.
lobster mushroom—large reddish-orange fungus having a firm, dense texture. Not a true mushroom, but a fungus that colonizes and alters a mushroom host; thus, they must come from a trusted source.
lotus root—immature root from the lotus plant. More tender than a mature lotus.
lovage—green, leafy plant similar to celery; long used in southern Europe as an herb or a green, often in savory pies.
mace—frond of the dried formations that cling to the nutmeg seed.
magnetron—electronic device that generates microwaves.
Maillard reaction—complex set of reactions among amino acids and sugars that creates the deep brown color and many of the essential aromas and flavors of baked, roasted, and fried foods. In cooking, the Maillard reaction usually occurs well above the boiling point of water and is therefore associated with cooking methods that use high heat. Browning due to the Maillard reaction is often confused with caramelizing sugar, which is unrelated.
maitake—(hen of the woods) wild mushroom prized for an excellent savory flavor.
Makrud lime leaves—(kaffir) aromatic leaves of a thorny bush. Often used in Thai cookery.
malic acid—acid derived from apples and many other fruits.
mandoline—metal or plastic manual slicer on a thin plane with an adjustable blade.
MAPP gas—relatively clean- and hot-burning fuel gas made from methylacetylene and propadiene and used in kitchen blowtorches. MAPP gas is no longer available in North America, but propylene-based substitutes work as well. Propane and butane fuels are different and are not as effective for some culinary uses.
Marcona almond—short, round, slightly sweet almond from Spain that is often sold fried in oil and salted.
marmalade—citrus jelly with visible pieces of suspended fruit and rind.
marrons glacés—French term for candied chestnuts.

masa harina—dried, powdered dough made from a paste of lye-cured corn kernels (masa). Used to make tortillas and tamales.
mascarpone—fresh, very mild, thick cream cheese originally from the Lombardy region of Italy.
matcha—Japanese green tea powder made from very high-grade tea.
matzo ball soup—Jewish soup made of chicken broth and dumplings made from unleavened dough (matzo). Traditionally served during Passover.
Meyer lemon—citrus cultivar thought to be a cross between a lemon and a mandarin orange. It has a thin yellow skin with a pungent citrus aroma, a slightly sweet taste, and mild acidity.
michiu—(mijiu) Chinese fermented rice wine similar to sake. Bottles labeled as "cooking wine" have salt added to make them unpalatable so that they can be sold as an ingredient rather than a beverage in stores not licensed to sell alcoholic beverages.
Microplane—brand of kitchen rasp, used for fine grating or shaving.
microwave—an electromagnetic wave with a wavelength ranging from about 0.3–30 cm / 0.1–11.8 in and a frequency of 1–100 GHz.
mirin—sweet Japanese rice wine similar to sake but with a lower alcohol content. Brands such as Kikkoman Aji-Mirin are meant for cooking and not drinking and can contain 40%–50% sugar as well as corn syrup and salt.
miso—Japanese fermented soybean paste used for seasoning. Available in many varieties: shiro miso is pale and mild; aka miso is a more mature red miso with a more pronounced flavor and salty taste.
monosodium glutamate—(MSG) salt of an amino acid that adds savory umami taste. Naturally found in many foods, but also sold in retail markets in a form resembling table salt.
mother dough—see preferment.
mounting—from the French "monter" or "beurre monté." To enrich a sauce by stirring in cold pieces of butter just before serving.
muscle fiber—cell that is capable of contracting and that forms muscle.
mushroom gills—dark, papery ribs that hold the spores on the underside of mushroom caps; used to color sauces.
myosin—muscle protein that combines with actin to form actomyosin (a complex involved in muscle contraction). Myosin constitutes half of all the protein in muscle.
naan—teardrop-shaped, leavened flat bread from Northern India. Traditionally cooked in a tandoor, or clay oven.
natural convection—heat transfer that occurs within a substance such as a fluid, due only to fluid movement caused by density changes arising from heat.
neutral frying oil—any variety of cooking oil that can withstand high temperatures and adds no strong or specific flavor of its own.
neutral-tasting oil—any variety of cooking oil that adds no strong or specific flavor of its own.
N-Zorbit—brand name that National Starch uses for tapioca maltodextrin.
oefs en cocotte—eggs baked or cooked in a small casserole or dish.
offal—organ meats.
oxidation—a chemical reaction in which oxygen is chemically bound to a compound. Can cause color changes in foods.
Pacojet—device that grinds frozen food while also blowing high-pressure air jets at it to reduce the food to extremely fine particles in order to puree, blend, or emulsify it.
palm sugar—(jaggery) unrefined, coarse sugar made from boiled, crystallized palm sap.
pancetta—Italian cured, unsmoked pork belly. Similar to bacon but often sold as thin slices from a tight roll.
Panko—Japanese-style large, flaky bread crumbs.
pasteurize—to heat a substance to a certain temperature for a certain amount of time to kill a prescribed fraction of any harmful organisms that may be in it.
pastis—French, anise-scented aperitif.
pastry comb—tool with teeth; used to create even ridges and lines in pastry work.
pathogen—disease-causing agent, typically a bacteria, protist, or virus.
phở—Vietnamese beef and rice noodle soup.
phosphate—salt of a phosphoric acid; used as tenderizers, preservatives, and to activate gelling agents.
phospholipid—phosphorus-bearing fat; a principal component of animal cell walls.
Piave vecchio—aged Italian cow's milk cheese. Piave is a younger, fresher cheese. Piave vecchio is aged and dry, similar to Parmesan.
pimentón—Spanish smoked paprika, available in sweet (dulce) and hot (picante) varieties.
pin bones—intermuscular or "floating" bones that are not attached to the main skeleton of certain fish, such as salmon. They should be removed from fish fillets before cooking.
pinion—tip segment of poultry wings.
piquillo pepper—firm, cone-shaped red pepper from Spain. Commonly sold in jars, packed in oil.
polyethylene—lightweight thermoplastics that are resistant to chemicals and moisture, having good insulating properties and used especially in packaging and insulation.
polyvinyl chloride—see PVC.
pomegranate seeds—see anardana.
pomelo—(pommelo) giant, semisweet citrus fruit thought to be the ancestor of the grapefruit. Native to Malaysia.
poolish—fairly wet preferment of water, flour, and active yeast cultures used as a "mother dough" in French bread making. Similar to Italian biga and American sourdough.
posset—delicate dessert of sweet cream thickened by coagulation. Historically, a warm, spiced, and sweetened drink of fresh milk mixed with wine or ale.
potato flour—flour made from finely ground, dehydrated potatoes.
potato starch—fine powder of the starch extracted from potatoes. Used as a thickener.
poule au pot—French term for "chicken in a pot" a traditional Sunday family meal of a stuffed whole chicken poached with vegetables in a flavorful chicken broth.
precision—the fineness with which an instrument can discriminate in its measurements among slightly different values. Note that this is not the same as accuracy.
preferment—(pre-ferment) living mixture of yeast, flour, and water used to create fermented bread doughs. Italian biga, French poolish, and American sourdough are all types of preferment.
pressure-infuse—to use pressure to hasten the infusion process. Whipping siphons can be used to pressure-infuse herbs and spices into a marinade or coffee flavors into cream.
pressure-render—to render fats using a pressure cooker to give them a more roasted, savory flavor.
primal cut—butcher's term for large sections of the whole animal. Primal cuts are then commonly cut into more familiar steaks and portions.
proportional-integral-derivative (PID) controller—automated digital controller for accurate control of temperature, used in water baths, modern ovens, and high-end espresso machines.
protein—any of a large class of complex molecules containing amino acids. Proteins are essential parts of all livings cells and of the diets of all animals. Proteins are a primary constituent of animal tissue but are also found in plants.
psi—abbreviation of pounds per square inch, a measurement of barometric pressure. Standard atmospheric pressure at sea level is 14.7 psi. A gauge pressure of 15 psi, as in a pressure cooker, means that the interior pressure is 15 psi higher than the ambient air pressure of the surrounding atmosphere.
purslane—low, trailing succulent often used as a salad green. Has a fresh, slightly tart flavor.
PVC—the most widely produced plastic, polyvinyl chloride.

queso fresco—(queso blanco) Latin American soft, mild white cheese. Describes a number of different varieties.
quinoa—ancient, tiny, round grain originally cultivated by the Incas. Higher in protein and lower in carbohydrates than many grains.
radiant heat—see radiative heating.
radiation—energy that flows through a medium or space via electromagnetic waves. In cooking, the radiation is typically infrared light.
radiative heating—heating by means of energy that flows through a medium or space via electromagnetic waves.
ramps—wild leeks, gathered in the spring; served whole or pureed.
ras el hanout—North African spice blend that can include as many as 50 different ingredients.
reduce—concentrate a liquid through evaporation by simmering or boiling.
relative humidity—the ratio of the mass of water vapor in air to the maximum mass of water vapor that the air could hold at that temperature.
render—to separate out the fat from meat by heating it slowly.
resting—cooking technique in which food that has been heated is allowed to sit for a period of time. Resting allows temperature and distribution of water (juices) to equilibrate.
rice bran oil—oil extracted from the germ and inner husk of rice. Has a nutty flavor. Heat-tolerant enough to be used as a frying oil.
ricotta salata—Italian white, salty cheese with a crumbly texture similar to feta. Made by salting, pressing, and aging fresh ricotta. Often made with sheep's milk.
Romanesco—a pale green vegetable related to broccoli and cauliflower. It has slightly cone-shaped florets and a delicate flavor.
rouille—French term for rust, usually referring to a reddish mayonnaise-like sauce flavored boldly with garlic and red peppers.
sake—Japanese, mildly alcoholic beverage made from polished rice. Often called rice wine, but as the drink is brewed, it is technically more similar to beer.
salinity—salt concentration.
San Marzano tomatoes—cultivar or type of Italian pear or plum tomato prized for its robust flavor. Most commonly available canned.
saturated—condition in which a substance (such as a molecule or a liquid) has combined with or dissolved into another substance as much as possible.
sauce soubise—a traditional French creamy onion sauce.
schmaltz—Yiddish term for chicken fat.
seasoning—material added to food to add a desirable taste and/or odor.
Shaoxing wine—one of the most famous Chinese rice wines, originating from the eastern province of Shaoxing; similar to dry sherry.
shear—to blend or mix by stirring.
shirred—baked in a small casserole or dish; often referring to eggs.
shiso—Japanese term for perilla, an intensely flavored annual with jagged edges in the mint family. Widely used in Japanese sushi, sashimi, tempura, and salads.
shrimp paste—(belacan, gapi, kapi) fermented ground shrimp sold in blocks. An important seasoning in many South Asian dishes. Available in many varieties and names.
Sicilian pistachios—bright green and revered for their flavor. The Italian pistachio nut is often sold shelled.
Silpat—name brand of a fiberglass-filled silicone sheet.
silverskin—tough, inedible kind of connective tissue in meat. It has a silvery color.
siphon—see whipping siphon.
sodium citrate—the salt of citric acid. Often used as an emulsifier in reconstructed cheese products. Used to impart a tart taste to many beverages. Also functions as a preservative.
sofrito—fried mixture of oil, onions, peppers, and garlic that is considered the backbone of Latin cooking.
solution—mixture of at least two components that are distributed in a uniform fashion to form a homogeneous whole.
sorrel—herb with large flat leaves and a bright lemony flavor used as a flavoring or salad green.
sous vide—cooking technique in which food is usually (but not necessarily) vacuum sealed, and is then cooked at accurately controlled temperatures.
soy lecithin—see lecithin.
spatchcock—to remove the backbone of poultry so that the bird can be flattened for easy grilling, roasting, or broiling.
species—structurally similar organisms that form an interbreeding population.
spider—a term used by many professional chefs for a long-handled flat-bowled strainer, often made with a "web" of interconnected wire.
stage—internship completed by prospective chefs.
star anise—small, brown, star-shaped pungent fruit of a Chinese and Vietnamese tree that has a flavor similar to but stronger than anise and is dried and used whole or ground as a spice, especially in Chinese cooking.
steam—invisible vapor or gas phase of water. Steam is often confused with the visible fog of condensed moisture droplets.
suet—very pure fat gathered from around the kidneys of lamb, cows, and other animals.
sumac—dried fruit of the sumac shrub. Ground and used as a tangy, slightly astringent spice, popular in the Middle East and Native American cuisine. Often seen sprinkled on hummus.
sweat—to cook vegetables slowly in a minimal amount of fat at low temperatures so that they will soften without browning.
tahini—oily paste of toasted, ground sesame seeds.
tajine—(tagine) spiced Moroccan stew often served with couscous.
tamarind concentrate—tangy, dark syrup made by infusing tamarind pulp with water and reducing the liquid until it resembles molasses.
tamis—(drum sieve) very fine mesh cloth used as a sieve.
tapioca maltodextrin—a modified starch derived from tapioca. Unique in its ability to transform oils into powders that melt back into oils when wetted.
tapioca starch—purified starch taken from the root known as manioc, cassava, or yuca.
tare—to reset a scale to zero by subtracting the current weight. Also means the weight of an empty container.
tartaric acid—powdered acid most often derived from grapes. Used as an acidifier and antioxidant, and sometimes to prevent crystallization in sugar syrup by converting some sucrose to noncrystallizing glucose.
temper—various culinary meanings include heating slowly and gently, and progressively warming a mixture by adding a hot liquid.
temperature—the value of "heat" or "coldness" that determines the direction in which heat flows between contacting objects as measured on a relative scale, such as Celsius or Fahrenheit.
Thai basil—aromatic form of basil popular in Southeast Asian cuisine with small, purplish leaves and an intense, slightly peppery flavor. More heat-tolerant than European or large-leaf basil.
Thai chili—see bird's eye chili.
tortellini en brodo—northern Italian dish of tortellini served in a rich chicken broth.
tsukune—Japanese term for a kneaded, round ball of ground meat, often chicken. Commonly skewered and grilled like yakitori.
turbot—large North Atlantic flatfish prized for the quality of its flesh.
umami—the savory taste of the amino acid glutamic acid, or its salt monosodium glutamate. Naturally occurring at high concentrations in a wide variety of foods, including milk, cheese, tomatoes, mushrooms, and especially seaweed.
vacuole—in plant cells, a cavity filled with air and water.

vacuum-infused—(vacuum-impregnated) to saturate the vacuoles of a food with a flavored liquid or water with vacuum pressure.
velveting—Chinese term for cooking technique of battering in a thin starch mixture and then flash-frying before cooking through.
vindaloo—Indian term for a spicy curry dish originally from the Portuguese region of Goa. The sauce most often includes plenty of pepper and the added tang of vinegar and/or dried mango skins. Often made with pork.
viscosity—the ability of a gas or liquid to resist flowing when shear force is applied to it.
vital wheat gluten—(gluten flour, gluten powder) extracted, dried gluten containing two proteins, glutenin and gliadin, that together give a dough its strength and elasticity. As a commercial product, vital gluten can be used to add strength, or "bite," to noodles or to improve the texture of bread.
Wagyu beef—(Wagyū) several cattle breeds of Japanese origin that yield highly marbled meat. Wagyu beef has become synonymous with prized Japanese Kobe beef.
watercress—edible, slightly bitter green that has been collected from a safe water source.
water-displacement method—technique for removing air from a zip-top bag by slowly immersing the partially open bag in a water bath. The water pressure squeezes the bag around the contents, and it may then be sealed with very little air inside.
water-vapor oven—oven that uses heated water vapor as well as hot air to cook. CVap, made by Winston Industries, is the best-known brand.
wavelength—the distance between two points in a wave along the line of the direction in which the wave is advancing.
weather-stripping tape—sticky-backed ribbons of foam often used to insulate doors and windows, available at most hardware stores.
wet-bulb temperature—temperature of a wet object in equilibrium with the surrounding air. If the relative humidity of the air is less than 100%, then the wet-bulb temperature will be lower than the dry-bulb temperature because of evaporative cooling. Food exposed to air typically cooks at the wet-bulb temperature for much of its cooking time. Wet-bulb temperature is measured using a thermometer that is kept wet with a wick.
whey protein isolate—concentrated whey protein that has the lactose sugar removed. Can be used as an emulsifier, foaming agent, thickener, and gelling compound. Not to be confused with flavored whey powder.
whipping siphon—device used to create foam in which particles of pressurized gas inserted into a liquid-filled metal tube expand into bubbles in the liquid as they leave the tube.
white poppy seeds—hard, off-white seeds used in Indian, Middle Eastern, and Asian cuisine to add thickness, texture, and flavor to sauces. A flavorful oil similar to olive oil can be pressed from them.
white port—variety of fortified wine from Portugal made from white grapes. Varies in flavor from dry to sweet and often with a fruitier flavor than a similar vermouth or sherry.
Wondra—brand of pregelatinized wheat flour made by General Mills. Thickens without clumping or adding the "raw" taste of uncooked wheat flour.
xanthan gum—thickener made from fermented carbohydrates. Works over a wide temperature and pH range, making it a versatile hydrocolloid. Xanthan-thickened sauces become thinner when stirred, and set again when allowed to settle.
yakitori—Japanese term for grilled chicken, most often served as small pieces threaded on skewers.
yeast—single-cell fungus used in fermenting wine and in creating the gas bubbles that cause bread to rise.
yuzu—aromatic, tart, Japanese citrus fruit. Often used to make the dipping sauce ponzu. Salted yuzu juice is called yuzu kosho.

REFERENCE TABLES

Converting Temperature

To convert temperatures from Celsius to Fahrenheit, multiply by 1.8, and then add 32 to the product.

To convert from Fahrenheit to Celsius, subtract 32, and then multiply the result by 5⁄9 (0.56).

Celsius to Fahrenheit		Fahrenheit to Celsius	
(°C)	(°F)	(°F)	(°C)
-196.0	-320.8	-200.0	-128.9
-78.5	-109.3	-80.0	-62.2
-60.0	-76.0	-60.0	-51.1
-40.0	-40.0	-40.0	-40.0
-20.0	-4.0	-20.0	-28.9
0	32.0	0	-17.8
1	33.8	1	-17.2
2	35.6	2	-16.7
3	37.4	3	-16.1
4	39.2	4	-15.6
5	41.0	5	-15.0
6	42.8	6	-14.4
7	44.6	7	-13.9
8	46.4	8	-13.3
9	48.2	9	-12.8
10	50.0	10	-12.2
11	51.8	11	-11.7
12	53.6	12	-11.1
13	55.4	13	-10.6
14	57.2	14	-10.0
15	59.0	15	-9.4
16	60.8	16	-8.9
17	62.6	17	-8.3
18	64.4	18	-7.8
19	66.2	19	-7.2
20	68.0	20	-6.7
21	69.8	21	-6.1
22	71.6	22	-5.6
23	73.4	23	-5.0
24	75.2	24	-4.4
25	77.0	25	-3.9
26	78.8	26	-3.3
27	80.6	27	-2.8

Converting Temperature

Celsius to Fahrenheit		Fahrenheit to Celsius	
(°C)	(°F)	(°F)	(°C)
28	82.4	28	-2.2
29	84.2	29	-1.7
30	86.0	30	-1.1
31	87.8	31	-0.6
32	89.6	32	0.0
33	91.4	33	0.6
34	93.2	34	1.1
35	95.0	35	1.7
36	96.8	36	2.2
37	98.6	37	2.8
38	100.4	38	3.3
39	102.2	39	3.9
40	104.0	40	4.4
41	105.8	41	5.0
42	107.6	42	5.6
43	109.4	43	6.1
44	111.2	44	6.7
45	113.0	45	7.2
46	114.8	46	7.8
47	116.6	47	8.3
48	118.4	48	8.9
49	120.2	49	9.4
50	122.0	50	10.0
51	123.8	51	10.6
52	125.6	52	11.1
53	127.4	53	11.7
54	129.2	54	12.2
55	131.0	55	12.8
56	132.8	56	13.3
57	134.6	57	13.9
58	136.4	58	14.4
59	138.2	59	15.0
60	140.0	60	15.6
61	141.8	61	16.1
62	143.6	62	16.7
63	145.4	63	17.2
64	147.2	64	17.8
65	149.0	65	18.3
66	150.8	66	18.9
67	152.6	67	19.4
68	154.4	68	20.0

Converting Temperature

Celsius to Fahrenheit		Fahrenheit to Celsius	
(°C)	(°F)	(°F)	(°C)
69	156.2	69	20.6
70	158.0	70	21.1
71	159.8	71	21.7
72	161.6	72	22.2
73	163.4	73	22.8
74	165.2	74	23.3
75	167.0	75	23.9
76	168.8	76	24.4
77	170.6	77	25.0
78	172.4	78	25.6
79	174.2	79	26.1
80	176.0	80	26.7
81	177.8	81	27.2
82	179.6	82	27.8
83	181.4	83	28.3
84	183.2	84	28.9
85	185.0	85	29.4
86	186.8	86	30.0
87	188.6	87	30.6
88	190.4	88	31.1
89	192.2	89	31.7
90	194.0	90	32.2
91	195.8	91	32.8
92	197.6	92	33.3
93	199.4	93	33.9
94	201.2	94	34.4
95	203.0	95	35.0
96	204.8	96	35.6
97	206.6	97	36.1
98	208.4	98	36.7
99	210.2	99	37.2
100	212	100	37.8
105	221	105	40.6
110	230	110	43.3
115	239	115	46.1
120	248	120	48.9

Converting Temperature

Celsius to Fahrenheit		Fahrenheit to Celsius	
(°C)	(°F)	(°F)	(°C)
125	257	125	51.7
130	266	130	54.4
135	275	135	57.2
140	284	140	60.0
145	293	145	62.8
150	302	150	65.6
155	311	155	68.3
160	320	160	71.1
165	329	165	73.9
170	338	170	76.7
175	347	175	79.4
180	356	180	82.2
185	365	185	85.0
190	374	190	87.8
195	383	195	90.6
200	392	200	93.3
205	401	205	96.1
210	410	210	98.9
215	419	215	101.7
220	428	220	104.4
225	437	225	107.2
230	446	230	110.0
235	455	235	112.8
240	464	240	115.6
245	473	245	118.3
250	482	250	121.1
255	491	255	123.9
260	500	260	126.7
265	509	265	129.4
270	518	270	132.2
275	527	275	135.0
280	536	280	137.8
285	545	285	140.6
290	554	290	143.3
295	563	295	146.1
300	572	300	148.9

Converting Weights

To convert weights from grams to ounces, divide by 28.35. To convert from ounces to grams, multiply by 28.35.

Grams to ounces		Ounces to grams	
(g)	(oz)	(oz)	(g)
0.1	0.004	0.1	2.8
0.2	0.007	0.2	5.7
0.3	0.011	0.3	8.5
0.4	0.014	0.4	11.3
0.5	0.018	0.5	14.2
0.6	0.021	0.6	17.0
0.7	0.025	0.7	19.8
0.8	0.028	0.8	22.7
0.9	0.032	0.9	25.5
1	0.035	1	28.4
2	0.071	2	56.7
3	0.106	3	85.1
4	0.141	4	113.4
5	0.176	5	141.8
6	0.212	6	170.1
7	0.247	7	198.5
8	0.282	8	226.8
9	0.317	9	255.2
10	0.353	10	283.5
11	0.388	11	311.9
12	0.423	12	340.2
13	0.459	13	368.6
14	0.494	14	396.9
15	0.529	15	425.3
16	0.564	16	453.6
17	0.600	17	482.0
18	0.635	18	510.3
19	0.670	19	538.7
20	0.705	20	567.0
21	0.741	21	595.4
22	0.776	22	623.7
23	0.811	23	652.1
24	0.847	24	680.4
25	0.882	25	708.8
30	1.058	30	850.5
35	1.235	35	992.3
40	1.411	40	1,134.0

Converting Weights

Grams to ounces		Ounces to grams	
(g)	(oz)	(oz)	(g)
45	1.587	45	1,275.8
50	1.764	50	1,417.5
55	1.940	55	1,559.3
60	2.116	60	1,701.0
65	2.293	65	1,842.8
70	2.469	70	1,984.5
75	2.646	75	2,126.3
80	2.822	80	2,268.0
85	2.998	85	2,409.8
90	3.175	90	2,551.5
95	3.351	95	2,693.3
100	3.527	100	2,835.0
110	3.880	110	3,118.5
120	4.233	120	3,402.0
130	4.586	130	3,685.5
140	4.938	140	3,969.0
150	5.291	150	4,252.5
160	5.644	160	4,536.0
170	5.996	170	4,819.5
180	6.349	180	5,103.0
190	6.702	190	5,386.5
200	7.055	200	5,670.0
250	8.818	250	7,087.5
300	10.582	300	8,505.0
350	12.346	350	9,922.5
400	14.109	400	11,340.0
450	15.873	450	12,757.5
500	17.637	500	14,175.0
550	19.400	550	15,592.5
600	21.164	600	17,010.0
650	22.928	650	18,427.5
700	24.691	700	19,845.0
750	26.455	750	21,262.5
800	28.219	800	22,680.0
850	29.982	850	24,097.5
900	31.746	900	25,515.0
950	33.510	950	26,932.5
1,000	35.273	1,000	28,350.0

1 pound = 453.59 g / 16 oz; 1 kg = 2.2 lb

Common Conversion Factors

To convert from:	To:	Multiply by:
mL	tsp	0.203
tsp	mL	4.93
mL	Tbsp	0.068
Tbsp	mL	14.787
mL	cup	0.004
cup	mL	236.59
tsp	cup	0.021
cup	tsp	48
Tbsp	cup	0.063
cup	Tbsp	16
mL	oz	0.034
oz	mL	29.574
pint	qt	0.5
qt	pint	2
qt	gal	0.25
gal	qt	4
qt	L	0.946
L	qt	1.057
L	gal	0.264
gal	L	3.785
oz	lb	0.063
lb	oz	16
g	oz	0.035
oz	g	28.35
g	lb	0.002
lb	g	453.592
oz	kg	0.028
kg	oz	35.274
lb	kg	0.454
kg	lb	2.2
mm	in	0.394
in	mm	25.4
cm	in	0.394
in	cm	2.54
m	ft	3.3
ft	m	0.305
s	min	0.017
J	BTU	0.001
BTU	J	1,055.10
kcal	BTU	3.966
BTU	kcal	0.252

Common Conversion Factors

To convert from:	To:	Multiply by:
kcal	J	4,184
J	kcal	0.000
W	BTU/h	0.001
BTU/h	W	1,055.04
W	hp	0.001
hp	W	745.7
g/cm^3	oz/in^3	0.578
oz/in^3	g/cm^3	1.73
N	lb force	0.225
lb force	N	4.482
mbar	torr	0.75
torr	mbar	1.333
mbar	psi	0.015
psi	mbar	68.95
bar	psi	14.5
psi	bar	0.069
Pa	mbar	0.01
mbar	Pa	100
bar	atm	0.987
atm	bar	1.013

Converting Volume Measures

Metric	U.S.	Imperial	
(mL)		(pint)	(fl oz)
5	1 tsp		¼
10	2 tsp		⅓
15	1 Tbsp		½
20	4 tsp		⅔
30	2 Tbsp		1
60	¼ cup		2⅛
90	⅓ cup	⅛	3⅛
120	½ cup	¼	4¼
150	⅝ cup	¼	5¼
180	¾ cup	⅓	6⅓
240	1 cup	⅜	8½
300	1¼ cups	½	10½
480	2 cups	⅞	17
600	2½ cups	1	21
1,000	4¼ cups	1¾	35

Converting Grams to Volume for Common Ingredients

You can use the table below to calculate the approximate volume equivalent of a certain weight of an ingredient. For thin liquids, multiply the number of mL in the rightmost column by the number of grams to obtain the number of milliliters (mL). For example, 75 g of vinegar is about 75 × 1.16 = 87 mL.

It is important to understand, however, that all of the recipes in this book were developed and tested by weighing the ingredients. We did not use volume measurements, for good reason: even when using calibrated spoon and cup measures, it is nearly impossible to measure volumes with precision and accuracy. How finely the food is chopped, how firmly it is packed, how rounding was done to get to the nearest common fraction—these factors and others routinely throw off volume measurements by up to 15%, enough to diminish the quality of some recipes. So we urge you to do as we do, and weigh your ingredients when cooking from this book.

That said, we recognize that measuring volumes is often faster and is in any case common practice, so we converted our weights to volumes—except for certain ingredients, such as emulsifiers or gelling agents, where the inherent imprecision of volume measurement can ruin a recipe. To make these volumes as precise as possible, we calculated the volumes of thin liquids from their densities. For thick liquids and dry ingredients, we scooped the ingredient and then leveled it with a straight edge. All volumes have been rounded to the nearest measures that are available from kitchen-supply stores, including half tablespoons, thirds or eighths of cups, and eighths of teaspoons. Metric volumes were rounded to the nearest 1 mL for volumes up to 10 mL, to 5 mL for volumes up to 100 mL, and to the nearest 10 mL or 25 mL above that.

Due to the effects of rounding, you may notice that, say, 20 mL is paired with 3½ tsp in one recipe, but in another the volume given is 20 mL / 1½ Tbsp. That can happen if the conversion from the weight resulted in 17.7 mL (rounded to 20 mL) in the first case but produced 22.2 mL (also rounded to 20 mL) in the second. When converted to spoon measures, 17.7 mL and 22.2 mL yield different equivalents.

If you see 4 Tbsp given for a dry ingredient and wonder why we did not simply write ¼ cup, it is because the two are not actually the same for ingredients, such as flours, that become packed down at greater volumes. Try it yourself: measure ¼ cup of flour, and then remove four level tablespoons, one at a time. You'll find that there is still flour left in the cup measure when you are done. To avoid such complexity, weigh the ingredients.

COMMON LIQUIDS	1 g	5 g	25 g	100 g	450 g	Equivalents
Water, stock, broth, and jus	1 mL / ¼ tsp	5 mL / 1 tsp	25 mL / 5 tsp	100 mL / ⅜ cup	450 mL / 2 cups	1 g = 1.0 mL
Wine, vermouth, sake, and beer	1 mL / ¼ tsp	5 mL / 1 tsp	25 mL / 5 tsp	100 mL / ⅜ cup	450 mL / 2 cups	1 g = 1.0 mL
Thin fruit and vegetable juices, such as apple, lemon, and carrot	1 mL / ¼ tsp	5 mL / 1 tsp	25 mL / 5 tsp	100 mL / ⅜ cup	450 mL / 2 cups	1 g = 1.0 mL
Vinegars	1 mL / ¼ tsp	6 mL / 1 tsp	30 mL / 2 Tbsp	120 mL / ½ cup	525 mL / 2¼ cups	1 g = 1.16 mL
Liquor, such as bourbon or vodka	1 mL / ¼ tsp	6 mL / 1½ tsp	30 mL / 2 Tbsp	125 mL / ½ cup	560 mL / 2⅜ cups	1 g = 1.25 mL
Soy sauce, fish sauce	1 mL / ¼ tsp	4 mL / ¾ tsp	20 mL / 4¼ tsp	85 mL / ⅓ cup	380 mL / 1⅝ cups	1 g = 0.84 mL
Purees and thick vegetable juices	1 mL / ¼ tsp	5 mL / 1 tsp	30 mL / 5 tsp	110 mL / ½ cup	490 mL / 2 cups	
OILS AND FATS						
Refined oils, such canola, soy, vegetable, and corn oil	1 mL / ¼ tsp	5 mL / 1 tsp	25 mL / 2 Tbsp	110 mL / ½ cup	490 mL / 2 cups	1 g = 1.08 mL
Cold-pressed oils, such as olive, grapeseed, nut, and sesame oil	1 mL / ¼ tsp	6 mL / 1¼ tsp	30 mL / 2 Tbsp	110 mL / ½ cup	500 mL / 2⅛ cups	1 g = 1.11 mL
Melted fats and butters	1 mL / ¼ tsp	6 mL / 1¼ tsp	30 mL / 2 Tbsp	110 mL / ½ cup	500 mL / 2⅛ cups	1 g = 1.11 mL
Solid fats and butters	¼ tsp	1½ tsp	2½ Tbsp	½ cup	2 cups	1 Tbsp = 15 g

DAIRY PRODUCTS	1 g	5 g	25 g	100 g	450 g	Equivalents
Whole milk	1 mL / ¼ tsp	5 mL / 1 tsp	25 mL / 2 Tbsp	100 mL / ⅜ cup	460 mL / 2 cups	1 g = 1.03 mL
Heavy cream	1 mL / ¼ tsp	6 mL / 1¼ tsp	30 mL / 2 Tbsp	110 mL / ½ cup	495 mL / 2 cups	1 g = 1.1 mL
Crème frâiche, sour cream		1¼ tsp	2 Tbsp	⅜ cup	1½ cups	
Dry cheeses, such as Parmesan and Romano, finely grated and packed		5 tsp	6 Tbsp	2 cups	7 cups	1 cup = 60 g
Semisoft cheeses, such as Gruyère, cheddar, and Gouda, shredded		1 Tbsp	⅓ cup	1⅓ cup	6½ cups	1 cup = 67 g
Soft cheeses, such as cream cheese, mascarpone, and chevre		1 tsp	5 tsp	½ cup	1½ cups	1 cup = 230 g
Dry cheeses, such as blue cheese and feta, finely crumbled		½ Tbsp	2½ Tbsp	¾ cup	3¾ cups	1 cup = 115 g
EGGS (chicken, U.S. size large)						
Whole eggs, blended		1¼ tsp	1½ Tbsp	7 Tbsp		45 g each
Egg whites, blended		1¼ tsp	1½ Tbsp	7 Tbsp		30 g each
Egg yolks, blended		1¼ tsp	1½ Tbsp	6½ Tbsp		15 g each
PANTRY ITEMS (scoop to fill the measure, and then level it by using a straightedge)						
Salt, kosher ("salt" in our recipes)	¼ tsp	1¼ tsp	2½ Tbsp			1 tsp = 4 g
Salt, fine sea salt	¼ tsp	¾ tsp	5 tsp			1 tsp = 5.5 g
Sugar, granulated white	¼ tsp	½ Tbsp	2½ Tbsp	½ cup	2⅜ cups	1 cup = 202 g
Sugar, powdered	½ tsp	2½ tsp	4 Tbsp	1 cup		
Sugar, grated palm		2 tsp	3 Tbsp	¾ cup		
Finely ground spices, such as cinnamon, coriander, and paprika	½ tsp	2½ tsp	3 Tbsp			1 tsp = 2 g
Chili flakes	½ tsp	1 Tbsp	5 Tbsp			1 tsp = 2.25 g
Vanilla seeds, scraped from 1 large, moist bean						1 g
All-purpose flour		1 Tbsp	4 Tbsp	¾ cup	3⅛ cups	1 cup = 115 g
00 wheat flour		2 tsp	3 Tbsp	¾ cup	3½ cups	
Whole wheat flour		2½ tsp	3 Tbsp	¾ cup	3⅛ cups	
Masa harina		2 tsp	3 Tbsp	¾ cup	3½ cups	1 cup = 130 g
Wondra		1½ tsp	3½ Tbsp	¾ cup		1 Tbsp = 10 g
Vital wheat gluten		1 Tbsp	4 Tbsp	¾ cup		1 Tbsp = 5 g
Baking soda	¼ tsp	1 tsp	1½ Tbsp			1 tsp = 5 g
Gelatin, Knox's powdered	¼ tsp	1¼ tsp				1 envelope = 7 g
Gelatin sheets, silver (160 Bloom)						1 sheet = 2.5 g
Yeast, instant dry	¼ tsp	1¼ tsp	5 tsp			1 envelope = 7 g
Whole coffee beans	9–12 beans	1 Tbsp	⅓ cup	1½ cups		1 cup = 67 g
Dry macaroni, small elbow				¾ cup	3¾ cups	1 cup = 125 g
Coarse-ground cornmeal, polenta, and corn grits			2½ Tbsp	⅝ cup	3 cups	1 cup = 164 g

PANTRY ITEMS, continued	1 g	5 g	25 g	100 g	450 g	Equivalents
Panko bread crumbs		1½ Tbsp	½ cup	2 cups		1 cup = 76 g
Short grain rice, such as Arborio, bomba, brown rice				½ cup	2⅜ cups	1 cup = 200 g
Whole grains, such as barley and farro				½ cup	2⅓ cups	1 cup = 200 g
Small grains, such as quinoa and steel-cut oats				½ cup	2⅝ cups	
Whole dried beans, such as garbanzo, pinto, and black beans				½ cup	2½ cups	1 cup = 200 g
Dried lentils				½ cup	2¼ cups	
Chopped nuts			2½ Tbsp	¾ cup		
Nut butters, such as pistachio, almond, and macadamia		1 tsp	5 tsp	⅓ cup		1 cup = 240 g
Tomato paste		1 tsp	5 tsp	⅓ cup		
Honey		1 tsp	4 tsp	⅓ cup		
Syrup, such as maple or agave		1 tsp	1½ Tbsp	⅓ cup		1 cup = 310 g
Dijon mustard		1¼ tsp	2 Tbsp	⅜ cup		
Ketchup		1 tsp	2 Tbsp	⅓ cup		
Mayonnaise		1½ tsp	2 Tbsp	½ cup		
FRUITS AND VEGETABLES						
Parsley leaves		½ cup	2 cups			1 sprig = 3 g
Basil leaves		¼ cup	1½ cups			1 sprig = 2 g
Chives, minced		2 Tbsp	¾ cup			1 chive = 0.3 g
Large-leaf herbs, such as parsley, basil, cilantro, and tarragon, minced	1 tsp	5 tsp	6 Tbsp			1 sprig = 2.5 g
Small-leaved herbs, such as thyme and rosemary, minced	1 tsp	5 tsp	½ cup			1 sprig = 1 g
Fresh bay leaf						1 leaf = 0.2 g
Citrus zest, finely grated with a Microplane	1 tsp		¼ cup			1 lemon = 2.5 g
Fresh jalapeño			2½ Tbsp			1 pepper = 30 g
Onion, small dice		2 tsp	3 Tbsp	¾ cup	3½ cups	
Onion, thinly sliced (2 mm)			¼ cup	1 cup	4 cups	
Onion, grated		1 tsp	1½ Tbsp	½ cup	2⅔ cups	
Shallots, finely minced		2 tsp	3 Tbsp	⅞ cup		
Shallots, thinly sliced (1 mm)			¼ cup	1 cup		
Leeks, thinly sliced (2 mm)			⅜ cup	1½ cups		
Leeks, diced (6 mm)		1 Tbsp	5 Tbsp	1 cup		
Garlic clove, peeled, average size						1 clove = 3 g
Garlic, thinly sliced (1 mm)		1 Tbsp	5 Tbsp	1 cup		
Garlic, minced	¼ tsp	2 tsp	3 Tbsp			

FRUITS AND VEGETABLES, continued	1 g	5 g	25 g	100 g	450 g	Equivalents
Ginger, sliced into coins (4 mm)						1 coin = 3 g
Ginger, peeled and minced	¼ tsp	2 tsp	3 Tbsp			
Carrots, thinly sliced (2 mm)			¼ cup	1 cup	4¼ cups	
Cauliflower or broccoli, small florets			¼ cup	1 cup	4½ cups	1 head = 500 g
Celery, thinly sliced (2 mm)			¼ cup	1 cup		
Corn kernels			2½ Tbsp	⅝ cup	3 cups	1 ear = 140 g of kernels
Mushrooms, fresh button, minced			¼ cup	1 cup	4½ cups	1 mushroom = 20 g
Mushrooms, fresh shiitake caps, sliced (6 mm)			½ cup	2 cups	10 cups	
Scallions, whole trimmed						1 scallion = 15 g
Scallions, green parts only, thinly sliced (1 mm)		1½ Tbsp	½ cup			
Scallions, white parts only, thinly sliced (1 mm)		2½ tsp	¼ cup			
Fresh tomatoes, peeled, seeded, and diced			5 tsp	½ cup	1½ cups	
Canned tomatoes, crushed			5 tsp	⅓ cup	1⅞ cups	

SOURCES

Where to Buy Meat

Purveyor	Address	Phone	Website	Products
Heritage Meats	18241 Pendleton St. SW Rochester, WA 98579	360-273-2202	heritagemeatswa.com	beef, veal
Kapowsin Meats, Inc.	29401 118th Ave. E Graham, WA 98338	253-847-1777		pork
Mad Hatcher Farms	1437 D St. SW Ephrata, WA 98823	509-237-1351		poularde, pigeon, rabbit
Stokesberry Sustainable Farm	7429 85th Lane SE Olympia, WA 98513	360-485-2558	stokesberrysustainablefarm.com	chickens, roosters
Zoe's Meats	Petaluma, CA 94952	707-763-9637	zoesmeats.com	meats

Where to Buy Seafood

Purveyor	Address	Phone	Website	Products
Browne Trading Company	Merrill's Wharf 260 Commercial St. Portland, ME 04101	800-944-7848	brownetrading.com	caviar, other seafood
Taylor Shellfish Farms, Inc.	130 SE Lynch Rd. Shelton, WA 98584	360-426-6178	taylorshellfishfarms.com	shellfish, geoduck
True World Foods	24 Link Dr. Rockeleigh, NJ 07647	201-750-0024	trueworldfoods.com	shellfish, sashimi-grade fish, other seafood

Where to Buy Produce

Purveyor	Address	Phone	Website	Products
The Chef's Garden	9009 Huron-Avery Rd. Huron, OH 44839	800-289-4644	chefs-garden.com	microgreens
Foraged & Found Edibles		866-951-1031	foragedandfoundedibles.com	foraged mushrooms, other produce
Full Circle Farm	31904 NE Eighth St. Carnation, WA 98014	425-333-4677	fullcircle.com	organic produce
Mikuni Wild Harvest		866-862-9866	mikuniwildharvest.com	foraged mushrooms, other produce, fish and seafood, oils and vinegars, truffles
Sun Grown Organic Distributors	San Diego, CA	800-995-7776	sungrownorganics.com	microgreens

Where to Buy Spices and Seasonings

Purveyor	Address	Phone	Website	Products
L'Epicerie	106 Ferris St. Brooklyn, NY 11231	866-350-7575	lepicerie.com	salts, vinegars, essential oils
H Mart	various locations	800-648-0980	hmart.com	Korean and international ingredients and specialty foods
My Spice Sage	5774 Mosholu Ave. Bronx, NY 10471	877-890-5244	myspicesage.com	herbs, spices, and tea
Penzeys	12001 W. Capitol Drive Wauwatusa, WI 53222	800-741-7787	penzeys.com	herbs, spices, and spice mixes

Where to Buy Equipment

Purveyor	Address	Phone	Website	Products
A & D Weighing	1756 Automation Pkwy. San Jose, CA 95131	408-263-5333	andweighing.com	scales
AccuTemp Products, Inc.	8415 N. Clinton Park Fort Wayne, IN 46825	800-210-5907	accutemp.net	Accu-Steam griddle
Aerolatte	2 Codicote Rd. Welwyn AL6 9NB United Kingdom	(+44) 845 872 4954	aerolatte.com	aerolatte
Berkel, Co.	701 S. Ridge Ave. Troy, OH 45374	800-348-0251	berkelequipment.com	slicer
Biro Manufacturing, Co.	1114 W. Main St. Marblehead, OH 43440	419-798-4451	birosaw.com	meat grinder
Cambro	5801 Skylab Rd. Huntington Beach, CA 92647	800-833-3003	cambro.com	food storage
Carpigiani Corp. of North America	3760 Industrial Dr. Winston-Salem, NC 27107	336-661-9893	carpigiani.com	ice-cream machine
Champion Juicer / Plastaket Mfg. Co.	6220 E. Highway 12 Lodi, CA 95240	866-935-8423	championjuicer.com	juicer
Corning	Tower 2, Fourth Floor 900 Chelmsford St. Lowell, MA 01851	800-492-1110	corning.com	hot plates; Pyrex beakers
Cuisinart	150 Milford Rd. East Windsor, NJ 08520	800-726-0190	cuisinart.com	food processor
Drummond Scientific Co.	500 Pkwy., Box 700 Broomall, PA 19008	800-523-7480	drummondsci.com	calibrated pipettes
Fisher Scientific	300 Industry Dr. Pittsburgh, PA 15275	800-766-7000	fishersci.com	water bath
Fluke Corp.	6920 Seaway Blvd. Everett, WA 98203	425-347-6100	us.fluke.com	thermometers
Hamilton Beach Brands, Inc.	261 Yadkin Rd. Southern Pines, NC 28387	800-851-8900	hamiltonbeach.com	milk shake blender
Hanna Instruments, Inc.	270 George Washington Hwy. Smithfield, RI 02917	800-426-6287	hannainst.com	pH meter
Henkelman BV	PO Box 2117 5202 CC's-Hertogenbosch Netherlands	(+31) 73 621 36 71	henkelman.com	vacuum sealer
Hi-Tech Vacuum, Inc.	1445A, RR5 Saint-Cyrille-de Wendover Quebec J1Z 1S5 Canada	819-397-4888	hitechvacuum.com	vacuum sealer
Hualian Packaging Machines; dist. by Sealer Sales	18327 Sherman Way Reseda, CA 91335	818-705-0203	sealersales.com	strip sealer
iSi North America, Inc.	175 Route 46 W. Fairfield, NJ 07004	973-227-2426	isinorthamerica.com	siphons
Iwatani Group	2050 Center Ave., Suite 425 Fort Lee, NJ 07024	201-585-2442	iwatani.com	induction burner
JB Prince	36 E. 31st St. New York, NY 10016	800-473-0577	jbprince.com	books; kitchen utensils
Julabo USA	884 Marcon Blvd. Allentown, PA 18109	610-231-0250	julabo.de	cooling bath
Kuhn Rikon	Neschwilerstrasse 4 CH-8486 Rikon Switzerland	(+41) 52 396 01 01	kuhnrikon.ch	pressure cookers

Purveyor	Address	Phone	Website	Products
Labline Scientific Instruments	C/108 Maruti Darshan Hanuman Chowk L.T. Road, Mulund (East) Mumbai 400 081 Maharashtra, India	(+91) 22 216 33671	labline.in	water bath
Lenox	301 Chestnut St. E. Longmeadow, MA 01028	413-525-3961	lenoxtools.com	MAPP gas torches
LISS America	106 Skyline Dr. S. Plainfield, NJ 07080	908-222-1015	liss-america.com	nitrous and carbon dioxide chargers
Mettler Toledo, Inc.	1900 Polaris Parkway Columbus, OH 43240	800-METTLER	mt.com	scales
Microplane	614 SR 247 Russelville, AR 72802	800-555-2767	microplane.com	microplanes
Moschetti, Inc.	11 Sixth St. Vallejo, CA 94590	800-556-4414	moschetti.com	pasta machine
Pacojet AG	Bundesstrasse 7 CH-6300 Zug Switzerland	(+41) 41 710 2522	pacojet.com	Pacojet
PolyScience	6600 W Touhy Ave. Niles, IL 60714	800-229-7569	cuisinetechnology.com	circulators
Rational / Akro Ltd.	85 Gregory Rd. Mildenhall, Suffolk IP287DF United Kingdom	(+44) 1638 712 522	rational-ovens.co.uk	combi oven
Sartorius AG	Weender Landstrasse 94-108 D-37075 Goettingen Germany	(+49) 551 3080	sartorius.com	scales
Sunpentown	14625 Clark Ave. City of Industry, CA 91745	800-330-0388	sunpentown.com	induction burner
Taylor Company	750 N. Blackhawk Blvd. Rockton, IL 61072	800-255-0626	taylor-company.com	ice-cream machine
Thermo Fisher Scientific	81 Wyman St. Waltham, MA 02454	781-622-1000	thermofisher.com	water bath
Thermo Sensors Corp.	PO Box 461947 Garland, TX 75046	800-889-5478	thermosensors.com	thermocouples
UK Thermomix	Thorp Building Whitmore Lane Sunningdale Berkshire SL5 0NS United Kingdom	(+44) 1344 622 344	ukthermomix.com	Thermomix blender
Viking Range Corp.	111 Front St. Greenwood, MS 38930	662-455-1200	vikingrange.com	mixer
Vita-Mix Corp.	8615 Usher Rd. Cleveland, OH 44138	800-437-4654	vitamix.com	Vita-Prep blender
The Vollrath Co.	1236 N. 18th St. Sheboygan, WI 53081	800-624-2051	vollrathco.com	cookware
VWR International	Radnor Corporate Center Building One, Ste. 200 100 Matsonford Rd, PO Box 6660 Radnor, PA 19087	610-386-1700	vwrsp.com	water bath
Waring Commercial	314 Ella T. Grasso Ave. Torrington, CT 06790	800-492-7464	waringproducts.com	deep fryer
Winston Industries	2345 Carton Dr. Louisville, KY 40299	800-234-5286	winstonind.com	CVap; pressure fryer

Scientific Ingredients

Ingredient	Local Sourcing	North America	Europe	Notes
agar (agar agar)	widely available at Asian and specialty food markets, health-food stores, gourmet supermarkets	chefrubber.com le-sanctuaire.com iherb.com	msk-ingredients.com infusions4chefs.co.uk solegraells.com	Powder or granules are preferred. Flakes or strips can be ground into powder. Avoid colored sticks and sweetened agar dessert powders.
albumin powder (powdered egg whites, egg white powder, meringue powder)	widely available at supermarkets, health-food stores, cake decorating and craft shops	kingarthurflour.com chefrubber.com lepicerie.com modernistpantry.com	sosa.cat infusions4chefs.co.uk solegraells.com	Pure albumin is preferred.
calcium chloride (Pickle Crisp: Ball brand; Calcic: Texturas brand)	often available where pickling or cheese-making supplies are sold; ask local cheese makers	chefrubber.com cheesemaking.com bulkfoods.com	solegraells.com infusions4chefs.co.uk msk-ingredients.com	Powder or granules are preferred. Liquid is available from cheese-making suppliers. Calcium lactate and calcium lactate gluconate work similarly.
carrageenan		modernistpantry.com chefrubber.com le-sanctuaire.com	solegraells.com infusions4chefs.co.uk	Iota type creates soft, elastic gels. Kappa type creates firm, brittle gels. Lambda type thickens without gelling.
citric acid (sour salt)	widely available at gourmet/specialty food stores, health-food and supplement stores, and where kosher foods and canning/preserving supplies are sold	chefrubber.com lepicerie.com le-sanctuaire.com iherb.com	infusions4chefs.co.uk msk-ingredients.com solegraells.com	
diastatic malt powder (diastatic malt enzyme, diastatic malt flour)	widely available; ask at bakeries and brewing-supply stores	kingarthurflour.com chefrubber.com		Products labeled nondiastatic have no active enzymes and are used for flavoring only. Brewers measure enzyme strength in degrees Lintner (°L).
essential oils	widely available at herbal and natural medicine shops; ask at pastry shops, spas, aromatherapists, and soap makers	essentialoil.com iherb.com lepicerie.com	solegraells.com sosa.cat	Organic, 100% pure, and food-grade oils are preferred.
freeze-dried fruits and vegetables	widely available at supermarkets, health-food stores, and outlets selling survival goods; check at camping and outdoor stores	chefrubber.com justtomatoes.com lepicerie.com	infusions4chefs.co.uk lyofood.com sosa.cat	Buy whole fruits and vegetables and grind into powders as needed for best results. Spray-dried juice powders are also useful, but often contain additional ingredients and may not be as flavorful.
gelatin	Knox's instant gelatin is available at supermarkets. Sheet gelatin can be found at specialty food markets and import stores; ask at pastry shops and bakeries, and confirm the Bloom strength before using	chefrubber.com modernistpantry.com pastrychef.com	infusions4chefs.co.uk msk-ingredients.com sosa.cat	Strengths vary greatly. Knox's instant gelatin and silver sheets (160 Bloom) are most common. Industrial strength gelatins and gelatins made specifically for fish, beef, or pork are sold by chefrubber.com.
honey powder (powdered honey, honey granules)	widely available at Asian markets and health-food stores	chefrubber.com modernistpantry.com		Honey powders may include cane juice, agave syrup, and stabilizers. Check the label if you have a preference.

Ingredient	Local Sourcing	North America	Europe	Notes
Insta Cure #1 (Prague powder #1)	widely available where sausage-making supplies are sold; also try sporting goods/outdoor stores that cater to hunters, or ask your butcher	sausagemaker.com		Insta Cure #2 contains additional sodium nitrate and should not be used as a substitution.
liquid soy lecithin	available at health-food stores and some soap- and candle-making suppliers	iherb.com lepicerie.com modernistpantry.com		Do not confuse with powdered soy lecithin or lecithin powders used for making light foams.
malic acid	ask at brewing- and wine-making supply stores; also try health-food and supplement stores.	lepicerie.com modernistpantry.com chefrubber.com	infusions4chefs.co.uk	Avoid capsules and tablets, as they often include additional, unnecessary ingredients.
sodium citrate (Citras: Texturas brand)		le-sanctuaire.com modernistpantry.com chefrubber.com	infusions4chefs.co.uk	
specialty flours and starches	widely available at gourmet supermarkets, international markets, and natural foods stores	bobsredmill.com kingarthurflour.com	toutelabio.com	The terms flour and starch are often used interchangeably, but the products can differ greatly. Review ingredients listed on the packaging for clarification.
tapioca maltodextrin (N-Zorbit: National Starch brand)		modernistpantry.com lepicerie.com le-sanctuaire.com	msk-ingredients.com	Sold as fine, very light flakes or powder. Tapioca maltodextrin is different from tapioca starch and maltodextrin.
Ultra-Sperse 3		modernistpantry.com willpowder.com le-sanctuaire.com		
vital wheat gluten	available at supermarkets and health-food stores; ask at bakeries and vegetarian restaurants	bobsredmill.com kingarthurflour.com	toutelabio.com	
whey protein isolate	available at health-food and supplement stores, and at stores specializing in sports nutrition	iherb.com bulkfoods.com		Most commonly sold in large tubs. Avoid flavored or sweetened whey protein powders or pure powdered whey.
Wondra (Robin Hood Easy Blend flour)	widely available at supermarkets			Avoid instant thickening flours or "gravy granules" made of potato starch; they are not interchangeable.
xanthan gum (Xantana: Texturas brand; Bob's Red Mill brand)	widely available at natural foods markets and health-food stores	bobsredmill.com chefrubber.com iherb.com	infusions4chefs.co.uk msk-ingredients.com	Always measure carefully to avoid gumminess.

CONTRIBUTORS

Nathan Myhrvold

Maxime Bilet

Culinary Team

Grant Lee Crilly
Developmental chef

Anjana Shanker
Developmental chef

Johnny Zhu
Developmental chef

Sam Fahey-Burke
Developmental chef

Chris Love
Cutaway machinist

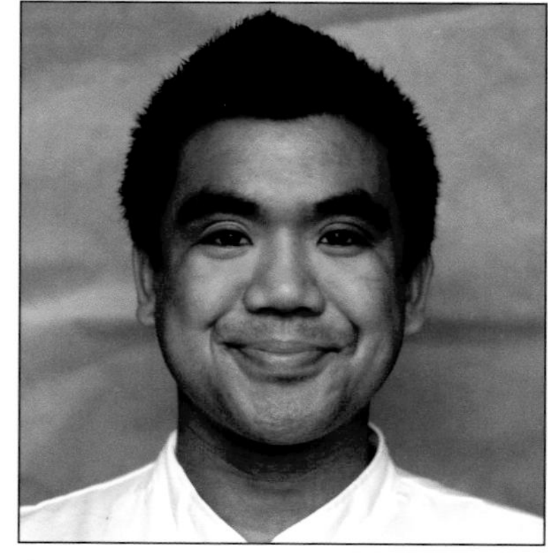

Aaron Verzosa
Developmental chef

Kimberly Schaub
Developmental chef

Jonathan Biderman
Culinary reviewer

Other contributors:
Ryan Matthew Smith, Alexandra Nickerson, Krystanne Casey, Larry Lofthouse, Aaron Shattuck, Richard Sherman, Ted Ellis, Mike Vinton, Amy Hatch

Editorial Team

Wayt Gibbs
Editor in chief

Tracy Cutchlow
Managing editor

Mark Clemens
Art director

Jennifer Sugden
Production manager

Carrie Wicks
Copy editor

Susan Volland
Recipe tester and editor

Daniel McCoy
Editorial assistant

Judy Oldfield-Wilson
Online writer

Photo Team

Melissa Lehuta
Lead photographer

Chris Hoover
Photo editor

Stephanie Billmayer
Assistant photo editor

Tyson Stole
Photographer

Publishing Team

Bruce Harris
Publishing consultant

Mark Pearson
Publishing consultant

Carrie Bachman
Publicist

Scott Heimendinger
Business development manager

ACKNOWLEDGMENTS

The authors would like to acknowledge the generous contributions of the many companies and individuals who supported the effort to create this book. In addition to those mentioned in the contributors section above, we benefited from the expertise, advice, material support, and valuable assistance of the people and companies listed here. Of course, any errors that remain in the final product are the responsibility of the authors alone.

Individuals Providing Expertise and Advice

John Bailey, Shelby Barnes, Kim Christiansen, Lee Dicks Guice, Gary Hawkey, Claudia Leschuck

Companies Providing Equipment

Chef Rubber, CookTek, Electrolux, Fresh Meals Solutions, Gaggenau, iSi, Kuhn Rikon, Mikuni Wild Harvest, Omni, Pacojet, Polyscience, Rationale, Robinson Laser, SousVide Supreme, Taylor Shellfish, Terra Spice, Viking, Vitamix, Vollrath, Winston Industries

Photo Credits

Position indicators: t = top, m = middle, b = bottom, l = left, c = center, r = right, u = upper, L = lower

Covers and Endpapers

Melissa Lehuta: front cover, front endpaper, back inside endpaper
Nathan Myhrvold: back cover
Ryan Smith: front inside endpaper, back endpaper

Front Matter

Scott Duncan/Martha Stewart Living Omnimedia, Inc.: xii
Deborah Jones: xiii
Melissa Lehuta: xiv–xvi; xxii
Ryan Smith: xxiv–xxv

Chapter 1: Countertop Tools

Melissa Lehuta: 02–03; 06: l; 07: ur; 08–10; 11: ul, uc, ur, Lr; 12; 14: Lr; 15: Lc; 16–17; 18: l, lc, rc, r; 20: l, ur; 21
Nathan Myhrvold: 04–05; 06: r
Ryan Smith: 05: b; 11: Ll; 13; 14: ur, Ll; 15: ul, Ll, Lr; 18: b; 19; 20: Lr
Tyson Stole: 07: ul, Ll, Lc, Lr

Chapter 2: Conventional Cooking Gear

Chris Hoover: 45; 46
Melissa Lehuta: 22–23; 24: r; 25; 27: ul, uc, Ll, Lc, Lr; 29; 32: ul, ur, ml, mc, mr; 33–34; 35: r; 36–38; 39: ul, ur, Ll, Lr; 41: ul, Ll, Lc; 44
Ryan Smith: 22: b; 24: l; 28; 32: Ll, Lr; 39: b; 40; 41: Lr; 42–43; 45–46
Tyson Stole: 27: ur; 30–31; 35: l, c; 41: uc, ur; 42–43; 47

Chapter 3: Cooking Sous Vide

Chris Hoover: 51: uc; 64: l
Melissa Lehuta: 48–49; 51: ul, ur, Ll, Lr; 53: ur; 59: ml, mr, Ll, Lr; 60; 63: t; 64: r; 66; 67: Ll
Nathan Myhrvold: 54–55
Ryan Smith: 49: t, b; 53: ul, uc, Ll, Lc, Lr; 54: ur, Ll; 57: ul, ml, Lr; 61–62; 64: b; 65: ur, b
Tyson Stole: 50; 52; 56; 57: uc, ur, mc, mr, Ll, Lc; 58; 59: ul, uc, ur; 63: m, b; 65: Ll; 67: ul, ur, m, Lr

Chapter 4: Ingredients

Melissa Lehuta: 70–71; 72: ul, Lr; 73: ul, Ll; 74; 75: ul, ur, Ll; 76–77; 79
Nathan Myhrvold: 68–69
Ryan Smith: 69: b; 72: ur; 73: ur, Lr, b
Tyson Stole: 69: r; 72: Ll; 75: Lr; 78
Chef Rubber: 72: b

Chapter 5: Basics

Chris Hoover: 91: r; 102; 103: t; 112: t; 116: t; 121: Lr; 135; 139: t
Melissa Lehuta: 82–83; 85; 87: ul, ur, Ll, Lc; 90: uc, ur, Ll; 91: ul, um, Ll, Lm; 92–93; 96; 98: Lc, Lr, b; 99: t, Ll; 100–101; 103: l, c, r; 104–107; 109; 111; 112: l, c, r; 113: ul, uc, ur, Lr; 118; 120; 121: ul, ur, Ll, Lc; 122; 123: l; 124–127; 128: ul, uc, ur; 130–134; 136: l, uc, Lc; 137: ul, uc, Ll, Lc; 139: b
Ryan Smith: 84; 86; 87: Lr; 88–89; 90: ul; 94; 97; 114–115; 116: b; 119: Ll; 123: c, r; 128: Ll, Lr; 129; 137: r
Tyson Stole: 95; 98: ul, uc, ur, Ll; 99: ul, uml, Loml; 108; 110; 113: ml, mc, mr, Ll; 117; 119: ul, uc, ur, ml, mr; 136: r

Chapter 6: Breakfast Eggs

Chris Hoover: 140–141; 145; 151: b
Melissa Lehuta: 144: uc, ur, Ll; 147: ur, Ll, Lr; 149–150; 151: r; 152–153
Nathan Myhrvold: 149: Ll
Ryan Smith: 141: b; 142–143; 144: ul, Lr; 146; 147: ul, uc
Tyson Stole: 151: l, c

Chapter 7: Salads and Cold Soups

Chris Hoover: 154–155; 166–167
Melissa Lehuta: 156–160; 162: b; 163–164; 165: l, c, r; 167: t, ur; 168: r; 169: ul; 170–175
Ryan Smith: 155: b; 162: t; 166: b
Tyson Stole: 161; 165: b; 167: Lr; 168: l; 169: uc, ur, b

Chapter 8: Pressure-Cooked Vegetable Soups

Melissa Lehuta: 180–181
Nathan Myhrvold: 176–177; 179: b
Ryan Smith: 176: b; 178; 179: ul, uc, ur, Lm; 182–183; 184: l, c, r; 185
Tyson Stole: 184: b

Chapter 9: Steak

Chris Hoover: 189: Lr; 202: r
Melissa Lehuta: 188: ul, Ll; 189: ul, buc, ml, Ll, Lc; 191: ur, b; 192; 193: ul, ur, ml, mlc, mrc, Ll, Llc, Lrc; 194; 195: ul, uc, ur, b; 196–200; 201: ul, ml, b; 203
Nathan Myhrvold: 186–187; 190: b; 191: ul
Ryan Smith: 187: b; 188: uc, ur; 189: tuc, ur, mr; 190: ul, uc, ur
Tyson Stole: 193: mr, Lr; 195: m; 201: uc, ur, mr; 202: l
Carol Zuber-Mallison: 188: Lr (diagram)

Chapter 10: Cheeseburger

Melissa Lehuta: 207–210; 211: ul, uc, ur, ml, mc, mr, Ll; 212: ur, Lr; 213–214; 215: mc, mr
Ryan Smith: 204–205; 205: b; 206
Tyson Stole: 211: Lr; 212: ul, uc, ml, Ll; Lr; 215: ul, ur, ml, Lr, b

Chapter 11: Carnitas

Melissa Lehuta: 218: l, c, r; 219: ul, uc, ur, Lc; 220–221; 222: ul, ur, Lr; 223–225
Ryan Smith: 217: b
Tyson Stole: 216–217; 218: b; 219: Lr, b; 222: Ll

Chapter 12: Braised Short Ribs

Melissa Lehuta: 230; 231: ul, ur, ml, mr, Ll, Lr; 232–233; 235
Nathan Myhrvold: 226–227
Ryan Smith: 228–229; 231: b; 234

Chapter 13: Roast Chicken

Melissa Lehuta: 236–237; 238–240; 241: Ll, Lr; 242–243; 246: Lr, b; 247
Ryan Smith: 237: b
Tyson Stole: 241: ul, ur, m; 243: Lc; 244-245; 246: ul, uc, ur

Chapter 14: Chicken Wings

Melissa Lehuta: 250: l, r; 251–257; 262–263
Nathan Myhrvold: 248–249; 258–261
Ryan Smith: 249: b
Tyson Stole: 250: c

Chapter 15: Chicken Noodle Soup

Chris Hoover: 264–265
Melissa Lehuta: 267; 269: ur, Lr, Ll; 270–271
Ryan Smith: 265: b; 268: r; 269: ul, uc; 273
Tyson Stole: 266; 268: l, c; 272

Chapter 16: Salmon
Melissa Lehuta: 279; 280: Ll, Lr; 281
Nathan Myhrvold: 274-275
Ryan Smith: 275: b; 276; 277: ur, ml, mc, mr, Ll, Lr; 278: ul, uc, ur, Ll; 280: t
Tyson Stole: 277: ul, uc; 278: Lc, Lr

Chapter 17: Shellfish
Chris Hoover: 284; 285: ul, uc, ur, ml, mc, mr, Ll
Melissa Lehuta: 285: Lr; 286; 287: ul, uc, ur, ml, mc, Ll; 290-292
Ryan Smith: 282-283; 283: c; 288; 289: ul, ur, ml, mr, Ll; 293: Ll
Tyson Stole: 287: Lr; 289: mc, Lr; 293: ul, uc, ur, Lr

Chapter 18: Pizza
Chris Hoover: 294-295; 306-307
Melissa Lehuta: 296-303; 304: l; 305
Ryan Smith: 295: b
Tyson Stole: 304: c, r

Chapter 19: Mac and Cheese
Chris Hoover: 308-309; 309: r; 318-319
Melissa Lehuta: 311: b; 312; 315-319
Nathan Myhrvold: 308-309
Ryan Smith: 309: b; 311: ul, uc, ur, Ll, Lc, Lr; 313
Tyson Stole: 310; 314

Chapter 20: Risotto and Paella
Melissa Lehuta: 320-323; 324-325; 328-333
Ryan Smith: 321: b; 326-327

Chapter 21: Cornmeal
Melissa Lehuta: 334-335; 336; 337: ul, uc, ur; 338: l; 339: ul, uc, ur, ml, mr; 340-341
Nathan Myhrvold: 334-335
Ryan Smith: 335: b; 337: ml, Ll, Lr
Tyson Stole: 338: r; 339: Ll, Lr

Chapter 22: Dishes for the Microwave
Melissa Lehuta: 344: c, r; 345: ul, uc, ur, ml, mr, Ll; 347-348; 349: Ll, Lr; 351; 354-355; 357: m, b
Ryan Smith: 342-343
Tyson Stole: 344: l; 345: Lr, b; 346; 349: ul, uc; ur, m; 350; 352-353; 356; 357: ul, uc, ur

Chapter 23: Custards and Pies
Melissa Lehuta: 358-359; 360: ul, uc, ur, Lc; 361-363; 364: uc; 365: Lr, b; 366: b; 367: ul; 368-370; 371: ul, uc, ml, Ll; 372-375; 376: ur, mr, Lr; 377; 378: ul, Ll, Lr; 379: ul, Ll
Nathan Myhrvold: 358-359
Ryan Smith: 359: b
Tyson Stole: 360: Ll, Lr; 364: ul, ur, Ll, Lr; 365: ul, ur, Ll; 366: t; 367: uc, ur, ml, mc, mr, b; 371: r; 376: ml, Ll; 378: ur; 379: ur, Lr

Contributors
Stephanie Billmayer: ulc
Melissa Lehuta: XXIV: ul, ur, mrc, Ll, Lrc, Lr; XXV: ul, urc, ur, uml, umrc, umr, Lml, Lmlc, Lmrc, Lmr, Llc, Lr
Lou Manna: XXV: Lrc
Ryan Smith: XXIV: ml, mlc, mr; XXV: umlc
Aaron Verzosa: XXIV: Llc
Rosemary Harris: XXV: Ll

Kitchen Manual
Nathan Myhrvold: back cover
Tyson Stole: back inside cover
Melissa Lehuta: front cover, front inside cover

STEP BY STEP PROCEDURES AND TABLES OF BEST BETS

How To

Best Bets

INDEX

B

C

D

E

F

G

H

I

J

K

L

M

N

O

P

Q

R

S

T

U

V

W

X

Y

Z

Colophon

This first edition, second printing of *Modernist Cuisine at Home*
was printed by Shenzhen Artron Color Printing Co., Ltd., of Shenzhen, China.
Print management by iocolor, LLC, of Seattle, Washington.
Design by Modernist Cuisine, LLC, of Bellevue, Washington.
Published by The Cooking Lab, LLC, of Bellevue, Washington.
http://modernistcuisine.com

Printed using stochastic color separation and Chroma Centric inks
on Stora Enso 128 gsm matte art paper. Typefaces used include Arno Pro,
Optima Nova, Whitney, and Square 721.

Purple kale

Blood orange